The
AMERICAN
CENSUS
HANDBOOK

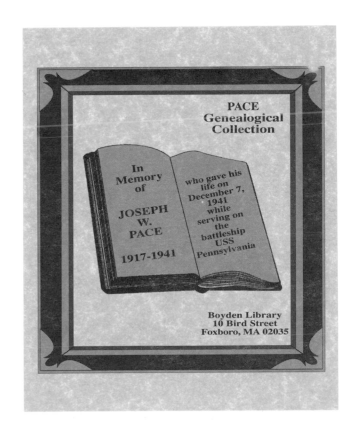

The
AMERICAN
CENSUS
HANDBOOK

THOMAS JAY KEMP

SR *Scholarly Resources Inc.*
Wilmington, Delaware

© 2001 by Scholarly Resources Inc.
All rights reserved
First published 2001
Printed and bound in the United States of America

Scholarly Resources Inc.
104 Greenhill Avenue
Wilmington, DE 19805-1897
www.scholarly.com

Library of Congress Cataloging-in-Publication Data

Kemp, Thomas Jay.
  The American census handbook / Thomas Jay Kemp.
    p. cm.
  Includes bibliographical references.
  ISBN 0-8420-2924-9 (alk. paper) — ISBN 0-8420-2925-7 (pbk. : alk. paper)
1. United States—Genealogy—Handbooks, manuals, etc. 2. United States—Census—
Handbooks, manuals, etc. I. Title.

CS49 .K4 2000
016.929'1'072073—dc21   00-059500

To the hundreds of indexers

who made it their life's work to index our American census records—

their efforts have made our research so much easier

About the Author

THOMAS JAY KEMP, a well-known librarian and genealogist, is the chair of the Genealogy Committee of the American Library Association and serves as a member on the board of directors of the Federation of Genealogical Societies. He also has served as chair of the Council of National Library and Information Associations and president of the American Society of Indexers. He is a life member of the Association for the Bibliography of History, the New England Archivists, the New Hampshire Library Association, and the New York Genealogical and Biographical Society.

He is the author of numerous books and articles including *The Genealogist's Virtual Library: Full-Text Books on the World Wide Web* (2000); *Virtual Roots: A Guide to Genealogy and Local History on the World Wide Web* (1997), and the *Connecticut Researcher's Handbook* (1981). His articles have appeared in *Library Journal, New York G&B Newsletter, School Library Journal, Connecticut Libraries, Illinois Library Reporter, Archival Outlook, NAGARA Clearinghouse, College and Research Libraries,* and *Today's Librarian.*

Contents

Introduction, *xi*

For Further Reading, *xiii*

CENSUS RECORDS BY STATE, *1*

Alabama, *1*
Alaska, *13*
Arizona, *13*
Arkansas, *16*
California, *35*
Colorado, *41*
Connecticut, *44*
Delaware, *48*
District of Columbia, *51*
Florida, *54*
Georgia, *63*
Hawaii, *92*
Idaho, *93*
Illinois, *95*
Indiana, *135*
Iowa, *157*
Kansas, *171*
Kentucky, *181*
Louisiana, *228*
Maine, *241*
Maryland, *244*
Massachusetts, *255*
Michigan, *261*
Minnesota, *273*
Mississippi, *278*
Missouri, *290*

Montana, *313*
Nebraska, *315*
Nevada, *319*
New Hampshire, *321*
New Jersey, *324*
New Mexico, *328*
New York, *331*
North Carolina, *344*
North Dakota, *361*
Ohio, *366*
Oklahoma, *388*
Oregon, *391*
Pennsylvania, *396*
Rhode Island, *406*
South Carolina, *409*
South Dakota, *417*
Tennessee, *419*
Texas, *436*
Utah, *454*
Vermont, *456*
Virginia, *459*
Washington, *474*
West Virginia, *477*
Wisconsin, *486*
Wyoming, *492*

GENERAL TOPICS, *495*

African Americans, *495*
General, *495*
Alabama, *495*
Arkansas, *495*

California, *496*
Delaware, *496*
District of Columbia, *496*
Florida, *496*
Georgia, *497*
Kentucky, *498*
Louisiana, *498*
Maryland, *499*
Mississippi, *499*
Missouri, *500*
New Jersey, *500*
New York, *500*
North Carolina, *500*
North Dakota, *501*
Ohio, *501*
South Carolina, *501*
South Dakota, *501*
Tennessee, *502*
Texas, *502*
Virginia, *503*

Chinese Americans, *503*
Dutch Americans, *503*
Franco-Americans, *503*
Immigration, *503*
Irish Americans, *504*
Italian Americans, *504*
Jewish Americans, *504*
Mexican Americans, *504*

Military—General, *504*
1793, *504*
1900, *504*
1905, *504*
1910, *504*
1920, *504*

Military—Revolutionary War, *505*
General, *505*
Kentucky, *505*
New Jersey, *505*
New York, *505*
Tennessee, *505*

Military—Civil War, *505*
General, *505*

Alabama, *506*
Arkansas, *506*
District of Columbia, *506*
Georgia, *506*
Illinois, *506*
Kansas, *507*
Kentucky, *507*
Louisiana, *507*
Maine, *507*
Maryland, *508*
Massachusetts, *508*
Michigan, *508*
Minnesota, *508*
Mississippi, *508*
Missouri, *509*
Montana, *509*
Nebraska, *509*
Nevada, *509*
New Hampshire, *509*
New Jersey, *509*
New Mexico, *510*
New York, *510*
North Carolina, *510*
North Dakota, *510*
Ohio, *510*
Oklahoma, *511*
Oregon, *511*
Rhode Island, *511*
South Carolina, *511*
South Dakota, *511*
Tennessee, *512*
Texas, *512*
Utah, *512*
Vermont, *512*
Virginia, *512*
Washington, *512*
West Virginia, *513*
Wisconsin, *513*
Wyoming, *513*

Native Americans, *513*
General, *513*
Arkansas, *513*
Bannock, *514*
California, *514*
Cherokee, *514*

Chickasaw, *514*
Choctaw, *514*
Colorado, *515*
Comanche, *515*
Creek, *515*
Kiowa, *515*
Michigan, *515*
North Dakota, *516*

Oklahoma, *516*
Shawnee, *516*
Shoshone, *516*
Utes, *516*

Polish Americans, *516*
Russian Americans, *517*
Swedish Americans, *517*

Introduction

AMERICAN GENEALOGISTS have long been constructing their family histories using information gathered from census records. Researchers must sift through thousands of pages of these records looking for individuals arranged by the random routes taken by census enumerators every ten years since 1790. While the federal government made several efforts to index these census records, most were not indexed.

Fortunately over the past twenty-five years there has been an outpouring of dedicated volunteers and commercial enterprises that have produced census indexes. *The American Census Handbook* is a guide to the thousands of published census indexes currently available to researchers. Indexes published in journals are not included but can be readily identified in the *Genealogical Periodical Annual Index*, the *PERSIndex*, and similar indexes to genealogical and historical periodicals. *The American Census Handbook* includes indexes up to and including the 1920 census, the last publicly released Federal Census.

This guide to census indexes is arranged geographically and by general topics. The geographic section is listed alphabetically by state and county and then chronologically within that local area. The general topics section includes those indexes that focus on specific ethnic groups such as Chinese Americans and Dutch Americans as well as indexes to current and former military personnel and other subjects.

Creating an index, particularly to handwritten documents, is difficult and painstaking work, and it is impressive to see the quality and quantity of the hundreds of individual indexers who have compiled these indexes. Some specialized in only one county or state; others worked on a national scale. Their contributions have been the foundation of assisting genealogists at a time when family history research has grown to dominate the public research in archives and public libraries across the country. The current and rising generations of genealogists owe them a real debt of gratitude.

Are there errors among the millions of entries in these indexes? Yes. There are a number of books and articles that discuss the problems with some census indexes. But, with improved computers and electronic tools, these records are being re-indexed and made even more accessible to genealogists.

In looking back at this great effort there are two important developments that changed the work and pace of census research. The work of the late Ronald Vern Jackson, who created indexes for every state and most territories under the imprint of his company, Accelerated Indexing Systems, transformed our access to census records. A handful of indexes quickly grew to hundreds of indexes, which are still marketed today by several different companies in print, microfiche, CD-ROM, and online editions.

The second significant development in census indexing has been the work of Brad and Raeone Steuart and their company, Heritage Quest. Their efforts over the past two decades to improve the quality of commercially available census indexes have set a high standard that has made it more convenient for genealogists to find individuals in census records. The inclusion of additional information as place of origin, occupation, or age has made it much easier to differentiate between the many families with the same or similar sounding surname. Their work in indexing in itself is an important achievement. But perhaps their most significant contribution is the landmark digitization of the entire Federal Census schedules, which have been made available on thousands of CD-ROMs and online. The efforts of the Steuarts and the late Ron Jackson have made it much easier to use census records and changed the pace of genealogical research across the country.

The census is generally the first resource that genealogists use to document a family. Having each page of the census from 1790 to 1920 on call, seven days a week, twenty-four hours a day is an incredible step forward. Having *The American Census Handbook* to guide genealogists to the thousands of published census indexes currently available will make researching these records much easier, whether in the original, microfilm, or digital versions.

For Further Reading

Bibliography and Reel Index, a Guide to the Microfilm Edition of the United States Decennial Census Publications, 1790-1970. Woodbridge, CT: Research Publications, 1975. 276p.

Brewer, Mary Marie. *Index to Census Schedules in Printed Forms, Those Available and Where to Obtain Them*. Huntsville, AR: Century Enterprises, Genealogical Services, 1969. 63p.

Cross Index to Selected City Streets and Enumeration Districts, 1910 Census. Washington, DC: National Archives, 1993. 51 fiche.

Dilts, G. David. "Census and Tax Lists," in *Printed Sources: A Guide to Genealogical Records*. Edited by Kory L. Meyerink, pp. 300–52. Salt Lake City, UT: Ancestry, 1998. 840 p.

Dollarhide, William. *The Census Book*. Bountiful, UT: Heritage Quest, 1999. 183p. CD-ROM.

A Key to the United States 1880 Federal Census, Identifying Enumeration District Numbers and Microfilm Numbers of the National Archives and the Family History Library. 3rd ed. Bountiful, UT: AGLL Publishing, 1995. 86p.

Lainhart, Ann. *State Census Records*. Baltimore, MD: Genealogical Publishing Co., 1992, 1997. 116p.

The 1900 Federal Population Census, a Catalog of National Archives Microfilm. Rev. ed. Washington, DC: National Archives, 1996. 57p.

Parker, J. Carlyle. *City, County, Town and Township Index to the 1850 Federal Census Schedules*. Detroit, MI: Gale Research, 1979. 215p.

_____. _____. Turlock, CA: Marietta Pub. Co., 1994. 215p.

Saldana, Richard H. *A Practical Guide to the "Misteaks" Made in Census Indexes*. Bountiful, UT: Heritage Quest, 1987, 1998. 63p.

U.S. Bureau of the Census. *1920 Federal Census of Cities and Towns of the United States, with Key Index Showing Location on Maps. Arranged in Alphabetical Order by States. Also Population of All the States and the United States for the Years 1900, 1910 and 1920 and the Percentage of Increase or Decrease to 1921*. Cleveland, OH: Barnum Co. 63p.

Watkins, Susan Cotts. *After Ellis Island, Newcomers and Natives in the 1910 Census*. New York, NY: Russell Sage Foundation, 1994. 451p.

CENSUS RECORDS BY STATE

Alabama

Feldman, Lawrence H. *Anglo Americans in Spanish Archives, Lists of Anglo American Settlers in the Spanish Colonies of America*. Baltimore, MD: Genealogical Publishing Co., 1991. 349p.

Jackson, Ronald Vern. *Early Alabama*. Bountiful, UT: Accelerated Indexing, 1981. Unpgd.

1810

Jackson, Ronald Vern. *Alabama Census Index, Online Edition*. Orem, UT: Ancestry.com, Inc., 1999. **http://www.ancestry.com**

_____. *Alabama 1810*. North Salt Lake City, UT: Accelerated Indexing Systems, 1981. 55; 24p.

1811-1819

Jackson, Ronald Vern. *Alabama 1811-1819 Decennary Census Index*. North Salt Lake City, UT: Accelerated Indexing Systems, 1983. 16; 77p.

1820

Alabama Census Returns, 1820 and an Abstract of Federal Census of Alabama. Wetumpka, AL: State Department of Archives and History, 1945. 41p.

Index to Alabama Census Returns, 1820. Bosie, ID: Idaho Genealogical Society, 1974. 80p.

Jackson, Ronald Vern. *Alabama Census Index, Online Edition*. Orem, UT: Ancestry.com, Inc., 1999. **http://www.ancestry.com**

_____. *Alabama 1820 Census Index*. Salt Lake City, UT: Accelerated Indexing Systems, 1981. 55; 80p.

_____. *Early Records, Alabama 1820-1829*. North Salt Lake City, UT: Accelerated Indexing Systems, 1983. 61; 85p.

1821-1829

Jackson, Ronald Vern. *Alabama 1821-1829 Decennary Census Index*. Salt Lake City, UT: Accelerated Indexing Systems, 1983. 85p.

1830

Census Index: U.S. Selected States/Counties, 1830. Family Archive CD 315. Novato, CA: Broderbund Software. CD-ROM.

1830-1839 U.S. Census Indexes, Mid-Atlantic, South, Mid-West. Orem, UT: Automated Archives, 1993. CD-ROM.

Gandrud, Pauline Myra Jones. *Alabama, an Index to the 1830 United States Census*. Hot Springs National Park, AR: B. Jones McLane, 1973. 392p.

Jackson, Ronald Vern. *Alabama Census Index, Online Edition*. Orem, UT: Ancestry.com, Inc., 1999. **http://www.ancestry.com**

_____, and Gary Ronald Teeples. *Alabama 1830 Census Index*. Bountiful, UT: Accelerated Indexing, 1976. 79p.

U.S. Federal Population Census Schedules. 1830, M19, Microfilm Reel Nos. 1-4.

1831-1839

Jackson, Ronald Vern. *Alabama Decennary Census Index, 1831-1839*. North Salt Lake City, UT: Accelerated Indexing Systems, 1983. 166p.

1832

1832 Census of the Creek Nation, East. Mobile, AL: South Eastern Native American Exchange, 1996. 198p.

Watson, Larry S. *Creek Census 1832, Abbott & Parsons Roll*. Yuma, AZ: Histree, 1987. 223p.

1840

Census Index: U.S. Selected States/Counties, 1840. Family Archive CD 316. Novato, CA: Broderbund Software. CD-ROM.

Jackson, Ronald Vern. *Alabama Census Index, Online Edition*. Orem, UT: Ancestry.com, Inc., 1999. **http://www.ancestry.com**

_____, and Gary Ronald Teeples. *Alabama 1840 Census Index*. Bountiful, UT: Accelerated Indexing, 1977. 137p.

Posey, Betty Sue Drake, and Seth A.R. Posey. *Alabama 1840 Census Index*. Easley, SC: Southern Historical Press, 1983.

U.S. Federal Population Census Schedules. 1840, M704, Microfilm Reel Nos. 1-16.

1850

Barefield, Marilyn Davis. *Alabama Mortality Schedule 1850, Seventh Census of the United States, Original Returns of the Assistant Marshals, Third Series, Persons Who Died during the Year Ending June 30, 1850*. Easley, SC: Southern Historical Press, 1983. 279p.

Census Index: U.S. Selected States/Counties, 1850. Family Archive CD 317. Novato, CA: Broderbund Software. CD-ROM.

Census Microfilm Records: Alabama, Arkansas, Louisiana and Mississippi, 1850. Family Archive CD 453. Novato, CA: Broderbund Software. CD-ROM.

Corley, Betty J. *Index, Yeoman(s), Yeaman(s), Youman(s), U.S. Census Index, 1850, 1860, 1880, Alabama, Florida, Kentucky, Louisiana, Maryland, Mississippi, Tennessee, Texas, Virginia, Includes Various Other Spellings*. Hyrum, UT: Author, 1988. 5p.

Hahn, Marilyn Davis. *Alabama Mortality Schedule. 1850 Seventh Census of the United States, Original Returns of the Assistant Marshals, Third Series, Persons Who Died during the Year Ending June 30, 1850*. Easley, SC: Southern Historical Press, 1983. 279p.

Jackson, Ronald Vern. *Alabama Census Index, Online Edition*. Orem, UT: Ancestry.com, Inc., 1999. **http://www.ancestry.com**

_____, and Gary Ronald Teeples. *Alabama 1850 Census Index*. Bountiful, UT: Accelerated Indexing, 1976. 242p.

_____. *Alabama 1850 Slave Schedule Census Index*. Salt Lake City, UT: Accelerated Indexing Systems International, 1988. 160p.

_____. *Mortality Schedules Index, Online Edition*. Orem, UT: Ancestry.com, Inc., 1999. **http://www.ancestry.com**

U.S. Census Index Series, Alabama, Arkansas, Georgia, Florida, Louisiana, Mississippi, South Carolina, 1850. Orem, UT: Automated Archives, 1991. CD-ROM.

U.S. Federal Population Census Schedules. 1850, M432, Microfilm Reel Nos. 1-16.

U.S. Federal Population Census Schedules. 1850, M432, Slave Schedules, Microfilm Reel Nos. 17-24.

1855

Jackson, Ronald Vern, W. David Samuelson, and Scott D. Rosenkilde. *Alabama 1855 State Census Index.* North Salt Lake City, UT: Accelerated Indexing Systems, 1981. 47; 288p.

1860

Barefield, Marilyn Davis. *Alabama Mortality Schedule 1860, Eighth Census of the United States, Original Returns of the Assistant Marshals, Third Series, Persons Who Died during the Year Ending June 30, 1860.* Easley, SC: Southern Historical Press, 1987. 188p.

Census Index: U.S. Selected States/Counties, 1860. Family Archive CD 318. Novato, CA: Broderbund Software. CD-ROM.

Corley, Betty J. *Index, Yeoman(s), Yeaman(s), Youman(s), U.S. Census Index, 1850, 1860, 1880, Alabama, Florida, Kentucky, Louisiana, Maryland, Mississippi, Tennessee, Texas, Virginia, Includes Various Other Spellings.* Hyrum, UT: Author, 1988. 5p.

Jackson, Ronald Vern. *Alabama Census Index, Online Edition.* Orem, UT: Ancestry.com, Inc., 1999. **http://www.ancestry.com**

_____. *Alabama 1860 Census Index.* North Salt Lake City, UT: Accelerated Indexing Systems, 1985. 550p.

_____. *Alabama 1860 Slave Schedule.* North Salt Lake City, UT: Accelerated Indexing Systems, 1990. 645p.

_____. *Mortality Schedules Index, Online Edition.* Orem, UT: Ancestry.com, Inc., 1999. **http://www.ancestry.com**

U.S. Census Index, 1860, Alabama, Arkansas, Florida, Louisiana, Mississippi, South Carolina. Orem, UT: Automated Archives, 1992. 1 CD-ROM.

U.S. Federal Population Census Schedules. 1860, M653, Microfilm Reel Nos. 1-26.

U.S. Federal Population Census Schedules. 1860, M653, Slave Schedules, Microfilm Reel Nos. 27-36.

1870

Census Index: U.S. Selected States/Counties, 1870. Family Archive CD 319. Novato, CA: Broderbund Software. CD-ROM.

Jackson, Ronald Vern. *Alabama Census Index, Online Edition.* Orem, UT: Ancestry.com, Inc., 1999. **http://www.ancestry.com**

_____. *Alabama 1870 Federal Census Index.* Salt Lake City, UT: Accelerated Indexing Systems International, 1989. 1,100p.

_____. *U.S. Federal Census Index Alabama, 1870.* West Jordan, UT: Genealogical Services, 1998. 1,512p.

U.S. Federal Population Census Schedules. 1870, M593, Microfilm Reel Nos. 1-45.

1880

Census Index: U.S. Selected States/Counties, 1880. Family Archive CD 320. Novato, CA: Broderbund Software. CD-ROM.

Corley, Betty J. *Index, Yeoman(s), Yeaman(s), Youman(s), U.S. Census Index, 1850, 1860, 1880, Alabama, Florida, Kentucky, Louisiana, Maryland, Mississippi, Tennessee, Texas, Virginia, Includes Various Other Spellings.* Hyrum, UT: Author, 1988. 5p.

U.S. Federal Population Census Schedules. 1880, T9, Microfilm Reel Nos. 1-35.

U.S. Federal Population Census Schedules. 1880, Soundex. T734, 74 Microfilm Reels.

1890

Jackson, Ronald Vern. *Alabama Census Index, Online Edition.* Orem, UT: Ancestry.com, Inc., 1999. **http://www.ancestry.com**

U.S. Federal Population Census Schedules. 1890, M407, Microfilm Reel No. 1.
U.S. Federal Population Census Schedules. 1890, Index. M496, 2 Microfilm Reels.
Veterans' Schedules: U.S. Selected States, 1890. Family Archive CD 131. Novato, CA: Broderbund Software. CD-ROM.

1900

U.S. Federal Population Census Schedules. 1900, T623, Microfilm Reel Nos. 1-44.
U.S. Federal Population Census Schedules. 1900, Soundex. T1030, 180 Microfilm Reels.
U.S. Federal Population Census Schedules. 1900, Military & Naval Bases. T1081, Microfilm Reel Nos. 1838-1842.
U.S. Federal Population Census Schedules. 1900, Military & Naval Bases, Soundex. T1081, 32 Microfilm Reels.

1907

Jones, Homer T. *Census of Confederate Veterans Residing in Southeast Alabama in 1907.* Carollton, MS: Pioneer Publishing, 1998. 261p.
Master Index to 1907 Census of Alabama Confederate Soldiers, Indexed and Compiled from Alabama State Archives Microfilm. Cullman, AL: Gregath Pub. Co. 100p.

1910

U.S. Federal Population Census Schedules. 1910, T624, Microfilm Reel Nos. 1-37.
U.S. Federal Population Census Schedules. 1910, Soundex. T1259, 118 Microfilm Reels.
U.S. Federal Population Census Schedules. 1910, Separate Soundex for Cities of Birmingham, Mobile and Montgomery, 1910, T1259, Microfilm Reel Nos. 118-140.

1920

U.S. Federal Population Census Schedules. 1920, T625, Microfilm Reel Nos. 1-45.
U.S. Federal Population Census Schedules. 1920, Soundex. M1548, 159 Microfilm Reels.

Baker County
1870

Thomas, Sue Hardy, and Elizabeth Jones Collins. *1870 Federal Census, Baker County, (Now Chilton County), Alabama.* Birmingham, AL: Authors, 1985. 217p.

Baldwin County
1850

Brooks, Mary McCoulskey. *1850 Census Records, Alabama, Baldwin County.* San Angelo, TX: Author, 1996. 79p.
USGenWeb Census Project. Alabama, 1850 Baldwin County.
ftp://ftp.rootsweb.com/pub/census/al/baldwin/1850/
1907
Hageness, MariLee Beatty. *1907 Confederate Soldiers Census, Baldwin County, Alabama.* Author, 1995. 8p.

Barbour County
1833
Foley, Helen S. *1833 State Census for Barbour County, Alabama.* Eufaula, AL: Author, 1976. 66p.
1840
Foley, Helen Sylvester. *U.S. Census of 1840, Barbour County, Alabama.* Fort Worth, TX: American Reference Pub. Co., 1971. 75p.

1850

Seventh Census of the United States, 1850 Census, Barbour County, Alabama. Lewis Chapter, DAR, 1974-1975. 267p.

Benton County
1850

Daniell, Anne C. *Benton County, Alabama Index to Heads of Households 1850 Census Plus Mortality Schedule (Abstract)*. Anniston, AL: Annie Calhoun Book Shop, Anniston-County Public Library, 1996. 33p.

Bibb County
1850

Adams, Terri Jean. *1850 Bibb County Alabama Census*. Weaverville, NC: Author, 1996. 88p.

McIlvain, R. *1850 Federal Census of Bibb County, Alabama from September 17, 1850-December 23, 1850*. Author, 1973. 126p.

1907

Hageness, MariLee Beatty. *1907 Confederate Soldiers Census, Bibb County, Alabama*. Author, 1995. 13p.

Birmingham (Jefferson County)
1910

U.S. Federal Population Census Schedules. Separate Soundex for Cities of Birmingham, Mobile and Montgomery, T1259, Microfilm Reel Nos. 118-140.

Blount County
1850

USGenWeb Census Project. Alabama, 1850 Blount County.
ftp://ftp.rootsweb.com/pub/census/al/blount/1850/

Butler County
1830

1830 Census, Butler County, Alabama. Greenville, AL: Butler County Historical Society, 1967. 23p.

1850

1850 Census, Butler County, Alabama. Greenville, AL: Butler County Historical Society, 1970. 231p.

1850 U.S. Census, Butler County, Alabama. Wichita, KS: S-K Publications, 1991. Unpgd.

1860

McManus, Grace Kelly. *Butler County, Alabama 1860 Federal Census and Schedule of Deaths*. Montgomery, AL: Author, 1951. 251p.

Calhoun County
1860

Doss, Doris P. *Index to 1860 Census of Calhoun County, Alabama, with Mortality Schedule and Index*. Anniston, AL: Public Library of Anniston, 1983. 139p.

_____. Rev. ed. Anniston, AL: Public Library of Anniston, 1990. 70p.

1870

Daniell, Anne C. *Index to Heads of Households, 1870 Federal Census, Calhoun County, Alabama and 1870 Mortality Schedule, Calhoun County, Alabama*. Anniston, AL: AlaBenton Book Shop, 1986. 42p.

1880

Daniell, Anne C. *Index, Heads of Household, 1880 Federal Census, Calhoun County, Alabama and 1880 Mortality Schedule, Calhoun County, Alabama*. Anniston, AL: AlaBenton Book Shop, 1986. 82p.

Cherokee County

1840

Surname Index of 1840 Census, Cherokee County, Alabama. Gadsden, AL: Northeast Alabama Genealogical Society, 1972. 14p.

1860-1880

Daniell, Anne C. *Cherokee County, Alabama, Index, Heads of Households 1860, 1870, 1880 Federal Population Schedules, Plus Federal Mortality Schedules*. Anniston, AL: Annie Calhoun Book Shop, 1989. 71p.

Chilton County

1870

Thomas, Sue Hardy, and Elizabeth Jones Collins. *1870 Federal Census, Baker County, (Now Chilton County), Alabama*. Birmingham, AL: Authors, 1985. 217p.

1880

USGenWeb Census Project. Alabama, 1880 Chilton County. (Partial).
ftp://ftp.rootsweb.com/pub/census/al/chilton/1880/

Clay County

1870, 1880

Daniell, Anne C. *Clay County, Alabama, Index, 1870 and 1880 Federal Population Schedules, Plus Federal Mortality Schedules*. Anniston, AL: Annie Calhoun Book Shop, 1989. 28, 39p.

Cleburne County

1870

Crumpton, Barbara. *Cleburne County, Alabama 1870 Census*. Duncan, OK: Creative Copies, 1987. 143p.

Daniell, Anne C. *Cleburne County, Alabama Index to Heads of Households 1870 and 1880 Federal Population Schedules Plus Federal Mortality Schedules*. Anniston, AL: Annie Calhoun Book Shop, 1989. Unpgd.

1880

Daniell, Anne C. *Cleburne County, Alabama Index to Heads of Households 1870 and 1880 Federal Population Schedules Plus Federal Mortality Schedules*. Anniston, AL: Annie Calhoun Book Shop, 1989. Unpgd.

1907

Hageness, MariLee Beatty. *1907 Confederate Soldiers Census, Cleburne County, Alabama*. Author, 1994.

Colbert County

1907

Hageness, MariLee Beatty. *1907 Confederate Soldiers Census, Colbert County, Alabama*. Author, 1995. 10p.

Conecuh County

1850

Brooks, Mary McCoulskey. *1850 Census, Alabama, Conecuh County* San Angelo, TX: Author, 1995. Unpgd.

USGenWeb Census Project. Alabama, 1850 Conecuh County.
ftp://ftp.rootsweb.com/pub/census/al/conecuh/1850/

1870

Stephens, Gertrude Louise Johnson. *Conecuh County, Alabama, Census Returns, 1870*. Spanish Fort, AL: Author, 1978. 239p.

1880

Coker, Sarah R., and Willene J. Whatley. *Conecuh County, Alabama, Census Returns, 1880*. Evergreen, AL: Authors, 1991. 365p.

Coosa County
1850
Brooks, Mary McCoulskey. *1850 Census, Alabama, Coosa County*. San Angelo, TX: Author, 1995. Unpgd.

Covington County
1850
Brooks, Mary McCoulskey. *1850 Census Records, Alabama, Covington County*. San Angelo, TX: Author, 1996. Unpgd.

Cullman County
1880
Gregath, Anna May Cochrane Herman. *1880 Cullman County, Alabama Census Index*. Cullman, AL: Author, 1977. 76p.
1900
Cullman County, Alabama 1900 Census Index from Microfilm. Cullman, AL: Gregath. 17p.
Lott, Dewell C. *1900 Cullman County Alabama Census*. Cullman, AL: Blalock Pub., 1994. 2 vols.
1907
Drake, Camilla Livingston. *Cullman County, Alabama, 1907 Census of Confederate Soldiers*. Cullman, AL: Gregath Co., 1981. 17p.

Dale County
1850
Brooks, Mary McCoulskey. *1850 Census, Alabama, Dale County* San Angelo, TX: Author, 1995. Unpgd.

Dallas County
1850
Brooks, Mary McCoulskey. *1850 Census Records, Alabama, Dallas County*. San Angelo, TX: Author, 1996. Unpgd.
1860
Knight, Anne F. *Index to the 1860 Dallas County, Alabama Census*. Author, 1982. 52p.

DeKalb County
1850
Brooks, Mary McCoulskey. *1850 Census Records, Alabama, DeKalb County*. San Angelo, TX: Author, 1996. Unpgd.
1907
Hageness, MariLee Beatty. *1907 Confederate Soldiers Census, DeKalb County, Alabama*. Author, 1995. 12p.

Elmore County
1870
Riggs, Nell Bass. *Elmore County, Alabama, 1870, Federal Census Index*. Centre, AL: Stewart University Press of the Stewart University System, 1982. 108p.

Etowah County
1907
Hageness, MariLee Beatty. *1907 Confederate Soldiers Census, Etowah County, Alabama*. Author, 1995. 12p.

Fayette County
1850

Brooks, Mary McCoulskey. *1850 Census Records, Alabama, Fayette County*. San Angelo, TX: Author, 1996. Unpgd.

1860

Newell, Herbert Moses, and Jeanie P. Newell. *1860 Federal Census, Fayette County, Alabama*. Fayette, AL: Author, 1978. 225p.

Greene County
1850

USGenWeb Census Project. Alabama, 1850 Greene County.
ftp://ftp.rootsweb.com/pub/census/al/greene/1850/

Henry County
1850

USGenWeb Census Project. Alabama, 1850 Henry County.
ftp://ftp.rootsweb.com/pub/census/al/henry/1850/

1855

Franklin, Lisa R. *Tracking Your Henry County, Alabama Roots, 1855 State Census*. Montgomery, AL: 1993. Unpgd.

1907

Hageness, MariLee Beatty. *1907 Confederate Soldiers Census, Henry County, Alabama*. Author, 1995. 20p.

Jackson County
1840

Cooper, Rhonda G. Smith. *1840 Jackson County, Alabama, Federal Census*. Rossville, GA: Author, 1989. 72p.

1850

Cooper, Rhonda G. Smith. *1850, Jackson County, Alabama Federal Census, Transcribed from National Archives Microfilm Publications, Microcopy No. 432, Roll 7, Population Schedules of the Seventh Census of the United States, 1850*. Rossville, GA: Author, 1989. 140p.

USGenWeb Census Project. Alabama, 1850 Jackson County.
ftp://ftp.rootsweb.com/pub/census/al/jackson/1850/

1880

Black, Clifford D. *1880 Jackson County, Alabama Census Index*. Signal Mountain, TN: Author, 1992. 238p.

Jefferson County
1850

Brooks, Mary McCoulskey. *1850 Census Records, Alabama, Jefferson County*. San Angelo, TX: Author, 1996. Unpgd.

USGenWeb Census Project. Alabama, 1900 Jefferson County. (Partial).
ftp://ftp.rootsweb.com/pub/census/al/jefferson/1900/

Lauderdale County
1850

Brown, Albert. *The 1850 Census of Lauderdale County, Alabama*. Bethel Springs, TN: Author, 1998. 46p.

1860

Warren, Polly Colagross. *Lauderdale County, Alabama, Civil War Records, 1860 Census*. Columbia, TN: P-Vine Press, 1978. 234p.

Lawrence County

1820

1820 State Census of Lawrence County, Alabama. Huntsville, AL: The Society, 1977. 43p.

1860

USGenWeb Census Project. Alabama, 1860 Lawrence County.
ftp://ftp.rootsweb.com/pub/census/al/lawrence/1860/

Limestone County

1840

Wellden, Eulalia Yancey. *1840 Limestone County Census*. Athens, AL: Author, 1987. 195p.

1850

Bueckner, Flossie Dement. *Limestone County, Alabama, Surname Index, 1850 Census*. Cypress, TX: Author, 1980. 8p.

1907

Johnson, Dorothy Scott. *1907 Confederate Census, Limestone, Morgan & Madison Counties, Alabama*. Huntsville, AL: Johnson Historical Publications, 1981. 65p.

1920

Smith, Linda Hardiman. *The 1920 Limestone County, Alabama Census*. Athens, AL: Limestone County Dept. of History & Archives, 1996. 564p.

Lowndes County

1850

USGenWeb Census Project. Alabama, 1850 Lowndes County.
ftp://ftp.rootsweb.com/pub/census/al/lowndes/1850/

Macon County

1850

Brooks, Mary McCoulskey. *1850 Census Records, Alabama, Macon County*. San Angelo, TX: Author, 1996. Unpgd.

Madison County

1850

USGenWeb Census Project. Alabama, 1850 Madison County.
ftp://ftp.rootsweb.com/pub/census/al/madison/1850/

1907

Johnson, Dorothy Scott. *1907 Confederate Census, Limestone, Morgan & Madison Counties, Alabama*. Huntsville, AL: Johnson Historical Publications, 1981. 65p.

Marengo County

1907

Hageness, MariLee Beatty. *1907 Confederate Soldiers Census, Marengo County, Alabama*. Author, 1995. 17p.

Marshall County

1880

Taylor, Betty Jean, and Margene Hemrick Black. *Inhabitants of Marshall County, Alabama, 1880*. Cullman, AL: Gregath Pub. Co., 1989. 167p.

Mobile County

1910

U.S. Federal Population Census Schedules. Separate Soundex for Cities of Birmingham, Mobile and Montgomery, T1259, Microfilm Reel Nos. 118-140.

Monroe County
1850

USGenWeb Census Project. Alabama, 1850 Monroe County.
ftp://ftp.rootsweb.com/pub/census/al/monroe/1850/
1910
Hines, Jacqueline. *Thirteenth Census of the United States, 1910, Indian Population, Monroe County, Alabama*. Mobile, AL: South Eastern Native American Exchange, 1995. 13p.

Montgomery County
1830
Hailes, Frances. *Montgomery County, Alabama, 1830 Census Index*. Pass Christian, MS: Willo Institute of Genealogy, 1964. pp. 55-76.
1910
U.S. Federal Population Census Schedules. Separate Soundex for Cities of Birmingham, Mobile and Montgomery, T1259, Microfilm Reel Nos.118-140.

Morgan County
1850
Burks, Janet Baker. *Morgan County, Alabama 1850 Federal Census*. Hartsdale, AL: Marine Wells Historical Publications, 1984. 146p.
Marine, Marilyn Sue Short, and Ivydene Simpson Walls. *Morgan County, Alabama, 1850 Federal Census, Schedule 4 Agricultural Census, Schedule 5 Industrial Census, Schedule 6 Social Statistics*. Hartselle, AL: Marine/Walls Historical Publications, 1984. 53p.
1907
Johnson, Dorothy Scott. *1907 Confederate Census, Limestone, Morgan & Madison Counties, Alabama*. Huntsville, AL: Johnson Historical Publications, 1981. 65p.

Patrick Henry County
1830
The U.S. Census of Patrick Henry County, Alabama, 1830. Abbeville, AL: Henry County Historical Society, 1994. 9p.

Perry County
1850
Daws, Elia Griffin. *Perry County, Alabama 1850 Census*. Centreville, AL: Author, 1990. 77, 11p.
1860
Daws, Elia Griffin. *Perry County, Alabama 1860 Census*. Centreville, AL: Author, 1993. 88, 11p.
1890
U.S. Federal Population Census Schedules. 1890, M407, Microfilm Reel No. 1.
U.S. Federal Population Census Schedules. 1890, Index. M496, 2 Microfilm Reels.
1907
Hageness, MariLee Beatty. *1907 Confederate Soldiers Census, Perry County, Alabama*. Author, 1995. 13p.

Pickens County
1830
Carmichael, Lisa R. Franklin. *Tracking Your Pickens County, Alabama Roots, 1830 Federal Census*. Author. 56p.
1850
Sudduth, Maggie Hubbard. *1850 Federal Census of Pickens County, Alabama*. Tuscaloosa, AL: Author, 1996. 131p.
USGenWeb Census Project. Alabama, 1850 Pickens County.
ftp://ftp.rootsweb.com/pub/census/al/pickens/1850/

1880
USGenWeb Census Project. Alabama, 1880 Pickens County.
ftp://ftp.rootsweb.com/pub/census/al/pickens/1880/

Pike County
1860
Senn, Susie K. *The 1860 Federal Slave Schedule for Pike County, Alabama.* Brundige, AL: Author, 1995.
53p.

Randolph County
1860
Daniell, Anne C. *Randolph County, Alabama, an Index, to Heads of Households, 1860, 1870 and 1880 Federal Population Schedules, Plus Federal Mortality Schedules.* Anniston, AL: AlaBenton Book Shop, 1987. 61, 41, 52p.
Scarborough, Becky. *Index to the 1860 Census of Randolph County, Alabama.* Author, 1981. 35p.
1870
Arnette, Casey W. *1870 Alabama Census, Randolph County.* Decatur, GA: Author, 1991. 248p.
Daniell, Anne C. *Randolph County, Alabama, an Index, to Heads of Households, 1860, 1870 and 1880 Federal Population Schedules, Plus Federal Mortality Schedules.* Anniston, AL: AlaBenton Book Shop, 1987. 61, 41, 52p.
1880
Daniell, Anne C. *Randolph County, Alabama, an Index, to Heads of Households, 1860, 1870 and 1880 Federal Population Schedules, Plus Federal Mortality Schedules.* Anniston, AL: AlaBenton Book Shop, 1987. 61, 41, 52p.

Taladega County
1870, 1880
Daniell, Anne C. *Talladega County, Alabama, Index, Heads of Households, 1870 and 1880 Federal Population Schedules, Plus Federal Mortality Schedules.* Anniston, AL: Annie Calhoun Book Shop, 1989. 88, 78p.

Tallapoosa County
1850
Brooks, Mary McCoulskey. *1850 Census Records, Alabama, Tallapoosa County.* San Angelo, TX: Author, 1996. Unpgd.
1860
Iwanski, Steve. *Census Index, 1860, Tallapoosa County, Alabama.* Dadeville, AL: Genealogical Society of East Alabama, 1984. 80p.
1907
Hageness, MariLee Beatty. *1907 Confederate Soldiers Census, Tallapoosa County, Alabama.* Author, 1994. 21p.

Tuscaloosa County
1840
Lockard, Billie T. *Index 1840 Census Tuscaloosa County, Alabama, with Some Marriages Added.* Tuscaloosa, AL: Tuscaloosa Genealogical Society, 1988. 29p.
1850
Sudduth, Maggie Hubbard. *Tuscaloosa County, Alabama, 1850 State Census.* Author, 1994. 80p.
1855
Index, 1855 State Census of Tuscaloosa County, Alabama. 111p.

1860

Sudduth, Maggie Hubbard. *1860 Census of Tuscaloosa County, Alabama*. Tuscaloosa, AL: Author, 1986. 183p.

1870

Sudduth, Maggie Hubbard. *1870 Census of Tuscaloosa County, Alabama*. Tuscaloosa, AL: Author, 1988. 159p.

Walker County
1850

Brooks, Mary McCoulskey. *1850 Census Records, Alabama, Walker County*. San Angelo, TX: Author, 1996. 2 vols.

Washington County
1830

USGenWeb Census Project. Alabama, 1830 Washington County.
ftp://ftp.rootsweb.com/pub/census/al/washington/1830/

Waddell, Barbara, and Doris Brown. *Records of Washington County, Alabama, 1795-1797 Pioneers, 1808-1810 Census Index; 1816 Early Alabama Inhabitants; 1830-1840-1850-1860-1870-1880 Census Index, 1850 Census Abstracted*. Chatom, AL: Author, 1988. 72p.

1840

USGenWeb Census Project. Alabama, 1840 Washington County.
ftp://ftp.rootsweb.com/pub/census/al/washington/1840/

Waddell, Barbara, and Doris Brown. *Records of Washington County, Alabama, 1795-1797 Pioneers, 1808-1810 Census Index; 1816 Early Alabama Inhabitants; 1830-1840-1850-1860-1870-1880 Census Index, 1850 Census Abstracted*. Chatom, AL: Author, 1988. 72p.

1850

Brooks, Mary McCoulskey. *1850 Census Records, Alabama, Washington County*. San Angelo, TX: Author, 1996. 31p.

USGenWeb Census Project. Alabama, 1850 Washington County.
ftp://ftp.rootsweb.com/pub/census/al/washington/1850/

USGenWeb Census Project. Alabama, 1850 Washington County. Slave Schedule.
ftp://ftp.rootsweb.com/pub/census/al/washington/1850/

Waddell, Barbara, and Doris Brown. *Records of Washington County, Alabama, 1795-1797 Pioneers, 1808-1810 Census Index; 1816 Early Alabama Inhabitants; 1830-1840-1850-1860-1870-1880 Census Index, 1850 Census Abstracted*. Chatom, AL: Author, 1988. 72p.

1860

Felldin, Jeanne Robey. *1860 United States Census Surname Index, the Alabama Counties of Washington and Wilcox*. Tomball, TX: Genealogical Publications, 1976. 10p.

Waddell, Barbara, and Doris Brown. *Records of Washington County, Alabama, 1795-1797 Pioneers, 1808-1810 Census Index; 1816 Early Alabama Inhabitants; 1830-1840-1850-1860-1870-1880 Census Index, 1850 Census Abstracted*. Chatom, AL: Author, 1988. 72p.

1870, 1880

Waddell, Barbara, and Doris Brown. *Records of Washington County, Alabama, 1795-1797 Pioneers, 1808-1810 Census Index; 1816 Early Alabama Inhabitants; 1830-1840-1850-1860-1870-1880 Census Index, 1850 Census Abstracted*. Chatom, AL: Author, 1988. 72p.

Wilcox County
1850

USGenWeb Census Project. AL, 1850 Wilcox County.
ftp://ftp.rootsweb.com/pub/census/al/wilcox/1850/

1860

Felldin, Jeanne Robey. *1860 United States Census Surname Index, the Alabama Counties of Washington and Wilcox*. Tomball, TX: Genealogical Publications, 1976. 10p.

Alaska

1870

Census Index: U.S. Selected States/Counties, 1870. Family Archive CD 319. Novato, CA: Broderbund Software. CD-ROM.

Jackson, Ronald Vern. *Alaska Census Index, Online Edition (1870-1907).* Orem, UT: Ancestry.com, Inc., 1999.

http://www.ancestry.com

_____. *Alaska Census Records 1870-1907.* Bountiful, UT: Accelerated Indexing Systems, 1976. 68p.

1880

Census Index: U.S. Selected States/Counties, 1880. Family Archive CD 320. Novato, CA: Broderbund Software. CD-ROM.

1890

Jackson, Ronald Vern. *Alaska Census Index, Online Edition (Naval Veterans).* Orem, UT: Ancestry.com, Inc., 1999.

http://www.ancestry.com

United States. Census Office. *Report on Population and Resources of Alaska at the Eleventh Census, 1890.* Washington, DC: Government Printing Office, 1893. 282p.

1900

U.S. Federal Population Census Schedules. 1900, T623, Microfilm Reel Nos. 1828-1832.

U.S. Federal Population Census Schedules. 1900, Soundex. T1031, 15 Microfilm Reels.

U.S. Federal Population Census Schedules. 1900, Military & Naval Bases. T1081, Microfilm Reel Nos. 1838-1842.

U.S. Federal Population Census Schedules. 1900, Military & Naval Bases, Soundex. T1081, 32 Microfilm Reels.

1907

Jackson, Ronald Vern. *Alaskan Census Records, 1870-1907.* Bountiful, UT: Accelerated Indexing Systems, 1976. 68p.

1910

U.S. Federal Population Census Schedules. 1910, T624, Microfilm Reel Nos. 1,748-1,750. (No Soundex/Miracode Index was prepared by the Government for this State.)

1920

U.S. Federal Population Census Schedules. 1920, T625, Microfilm Reel Nos. 2030, 2031.

U.S. Federal Population Census Schedules. 1920, Soundex. M1597, 6 Microfilm Reels.

Arizona

De Leon, Arnoldo. *Tejanos and the Numbers Game, a Socio-historical Interpretation from the Federal Censuses, 1850-1900.* Albuquerque, NM: University of New Mexico Press, 1989. 119p.

Federal Census, Territory of Arizona, Territory of New Mexico. Washington, DC: Government Printing Office, 1965. 253p.

_____. *Online Database Edition.* Orem, UT: Ancestry.com, Inc., 1999.

http://www.ancestry.com

McCarty, Kiernan. *Mexican Census, Pre-territorial*. Tucson, AZ: Arizona State Genealogical Society, 1986. 3 vols.

1831

Jackson, Ronald Vern. *Territorial Census Index, Arizona 1831, Territory of Mexico*. West Jordan, UT: Genealogical Services, 1994. 19p.

1860

Census Index: U.S. Selected States/Counties, 1860. Family Archive CD 318. Novato, CA: Broderbund Software. CD-ROM.

Federal Census, Territory of New Mexico and Territory of Arizona. Washington, DC: Government Printing Office, 1965. 253p.

Jackson, Ronald Vern, and Gary Ronald Teeples. *Arizona 1860 Mortality Schedule*. Bountiful, UT: Accelerated Indexing Systems, 1984. 18p.

_____. *Arizona 1860 Territorial Census Index*. Bountiful, UT: Accelerated Indexing, 1978. 78, 36p.

Underhill, Lonnie E. *Index to the Federal Census of Arizona for 1860, 1864 and 1870*. Tucson, AZ: Roan Horse Press, 1981. 67p.

1862

Jackson, Ronald Vern. *Arizona Census Index, Online Edition*. Orem, UT: Ancestry.com, Inc., 1999.
http://www.ancestry.com

1864

Federal Census, Territory of New Mexico and Territory of Arizona. Washington, DC: Government Printing Office, 1965. 253p.

Historical Records Survey, Works Progress Administration. *Census of Arizona Territory, April 1864*. Phoenix, AZ: Author, 1938. 20p.

_____. *Online Database Edition*. Orem, UT: Ancestry.com, Inc., 1999.
http://www.ancestry.com

Jackson, Ronald Vern. *Arizona Census Index, Online Edition*. Orem, UT: Ancestry.com, Inc., 1999.
http://www.ancestry.com

_____, and Gary Ronald Teeples. *Arizona 1864 Territorial Census Index*. Bountiful, UT: Accelerated Indexing, 1978. 94; 54p.

Schreier, Jim, and Mary Schreier. *An Index to the Territorial Manuscript of the 1864 Census of Arizona, Correlated to the Historical Records Survey of 1938 and the U.S. Senate Document Number 13, 1965; Drawn from the Original Document in the Department of Library and Archives, Arizona*. Phoenix, AZ; Author, 1975. 37p.

Underhill, Lonnie E. *Index to the Federal Census of Arizona for 1860, 1864 and 1870*. Tucson, AZ: Roan Horse Press, 1981. 67p.

1866

Jackson, Ronald Vern. *Arizona Census Index, Online Edition*. Orem, UT: Ancestry.com, Inc., 1999.
http://www.ancestry.com

_____. *Arizona 1866 Territoral*. Salt Lake City, UT: Accelerated Indexing Systems International, 1982. 55, 64p.

Schreier, Jim, and Mary Schreier. *An Index to the 1866 Census of the Arizona Territory*. Phoenix, AZ; Arizona Territorial Genealogy, 1975. 37p.

_____. *Indexes to the Census of the Arizona Territory, 1866, 1867, Yavapai County, 1869*. Phoenix, AZ: Arizona Territorial Genealogy. 1976. 102p.

1867

Jackson, Ronald Vern. *Arizona Census Index, Online Edition*. Orem, UT: Ancestry.com, Inc., 1999.
http://www.ancestry.com

_____. *Arizona 1867 State Census Index*. West Jordan, UT: Genealogical Services, 1983; 1998. 113p.

_____. *Arizona 1867 Territorial Census Index*. Salt Lake City, UT: Accelerated Indexing Systems, 1983. 8, 54p.

Schreier, Jim, and Mary Schreier. *Indexes to the Census of the Arizona Territory, 1866, 1867, Yavapai County, 1869*. Phoenix, AZ: Arizona Territorial Genealogy. 1976. 102p.

Underhill, Lonnie E. *Index to the Federal Census of Arizona for 1860, 1864 and 1870*. Tucson, AZ: Roan Horse Press, 1981. 67p.

1869

Jackson, Ronald Vern. *Arizona 1869 Territorial Census Index*. Salt Lake City, UT: Accelerated Indexing Systems International, 1982. 55; 31p.

1870

Census Index: U.S. Selected States/Counties, 1870. Family Archive CD 319. Novato, CA: Broderbund Software. CD-ROM.

Federal Census, Territory of New Mexico and Territory of Arizona. Washington, DC: Government Printing Office, 1965. 253p.

Jackson, Ronald Vern. *Arizona Census Index, Online Edition*. Orem, UT: Ancestry.com, Inc., 1999.
http://www.ancestry.com

_____, and Gary Ronald Teeples. *Arizona 1870 Territorial Census Index*. Salt Lake City, UT: Accelerated Indexing Systems, 1978. 119, 111p.

_____, Wylma Winmill, Shirley P. Zachrison. *Arizona 1870 Mortality Schedule*. Bountiful, UT: Accelerated Indexing Systems, 1980. 19p.

U.S. Federal Population Census Schedules. 1870, M593, Microfilm Reel No. 46.

1880

Census Index: U.S. Selected States/Counties, 1880. Family Archive CD 320. Novato, CA: Broderbund Software. CD-ROM.

Jackson, Ronald Vern. *Arizona Census Index, Online Edition*. Orem, UT: Ancestry.com, Inc., 1999.
http://www.ancestry.com

_____. *Arizona 1880 Census Index*. Bountiful, UT: Accelerated Indexing Systems, 1980. 507p.

_____. *Mortality Schedules Index, Online Edition*. Orem, UT: Ancestry.com, Inc., 1999.
http://www.ancestry.com

Tenth Census, 1880 Arizona Territory. Southern Arizona Genealogical Society, Card File Index.

U.S. Federal Population Census Schedules. 1880, T9, Microfilm Reel Nos. 36-37.

U.S. Federal Population Census Schedules. 1880, Soundex. T735, 2 Microfilm Reels.

1900

U.S. Federal Population Census Schedules. 1900, T623, Microfilm Reel Nos. 45-48.

U.S. Federal Population Census Schedules. 1900, Soundex. T1032, 22 Microfilm Reels.

U.S. Federal Population Census Schedules. 1900, Military & Naval Bases. T1081, Microfilm Reel Nos. 1838-1842.

U.S. Federal Population Census Schedules. 1900, Military & Naval Bases, Soundex. T1081, 32 Microfilm Reels.

1910

U.S. Federal Population Census Schedules. 1910, T624, Microfilm Reel Nos. 38-42. (No Soundex/Miracode Index was prepared by the Government for this State.)

1920

U.S. Federal Population Census Schedules. 1920, T625, Microfilm Reel Nos. 46-52.

U.S. Federal Population Census Schedules. 1920, Soundex. M1549, 30 Microfilm Reels.

1932

Bowen, Jeff. *1932 Hopi and Navajo Native American Census, with Birth and Death Rolls.* Hixson, TN: Bowen Genealogy, Native American Research and Publications, 1997. Unpgd.

Federal Census, Territory of Arizona, Territory of New Mexico. Washington, DC: Government Printing Office, 1965. 253p.

Santa Cruz County
1831

Jackson, Ronald Vern. *Arizona Census Index, Online Edition (1831).* Orem, UT: Ancestry.com, Inc., 1999. **http://www.ancestry.com**

Sierras, Eugene L. *Mexican Census Pre-Territorial Tucson, Tubac and Santa Cruz, 1831.* Tucson, AZ: Arizona State Genealogical Society, 1986. 30p.

Tubac
1831

Sierras, Eugene L. *Mexican Census Pre-Territorial Tucson, Tubac and Santa Cruz, 1831.* Tucson, AZ: Arizona State Genealogical Society, 1986. 30p.

Tucson
1831

Sierras, Eugene L. *Mexican Census Pre-Territorial Tucson, Tubac and Santa Cruz, 1831.* Tucson, AZ: Arizona State Genealogical Society, 1986. 30p.

Yavapai County
1869

Schreier, Jim, and Mary Schreier. *Indexes to the Census of the Arizona Territory, 1866, 1867, Yavapai County, 1869.* Phoenix, AZ: Arizona Territorial Genealogy. 1976. 102p.

1900

Whiteside, Dora M. *1900 Census, Yavapai County, Arizona Surname Index.* Prescott, AZ: Author, 1990. 143p.

Arkansas

1820

Jackson, Ronald Vern. *Arkansas Census Index, Online Edition.* Orem, UT: Ancestry.com, Inc., 1999. **http://www.ancestry.com**

_____. *Arkansas 1820 Census Index.* Bountiful, UT: Accelerated Indexing Systems, 1982. 55, 11p.

1823

Jackson, Ronald Vern, and Gary Ronald Teeples. *Arkansas Sheriff's Censuses, 1823 & 1829.* Salt Lake City, UT: Accelerated Indexing Systems, 1976, 65p.

1829

Jackson, Ronald Vern, and Gary Ronald Teeples. *Arkansas Sheriff's Censuses, 1823 & 1829.* Salt Lake City, UT: Accelerated Indexing Systems, 1976, 65p.

1830

Census Index: U.S. Selected States/Counties, 1830. Family Archive CD 315. Novato, CA: Broderbund Software. CD-ROM.

1830-1839 U.S. Census Indexes, Mid-Atlantic, South, Mid-West. Orem, UT: Automated Archives, 1993. CD-ROM.

Jackson, Ronald Vern. *Arkansas Census Index, Online Edition.* Orem, UT: Ancestry.com, Inc., 1999. **http://www.ancestry.com**

_____. *Arkansas 1830 Census Index.* Bountiful, UT: Accelerated Indexing Systems, 1981. 54p.

McLane, Bobbie Lee Jones. *An Index to Fifth Census of the United States, 1830, Population Schedules, Territory of Arkansas.* Hot Springs, AR: Author, 1965. 45p.

U.S. Federal Population Census Schedules. 1830, M19, Microfilm Reel No. 5.

1840

Census Index: U.S. Selected States/Counties, 1840. Family Archive CD 316. Novato, CA: Broderbund Software. CD-ROM.

Coyle, Thomas E., and Berniece D. Coyle. *Arkansas 1840 Census.* Lewisville, TX: Authors, 1994. 2 vols.

Jackson, Ronald Vern. *Arkansas Census Index, Online Edition.* Orem, UT: Ancestry.com, Inc., 1999. **http://www.ancestry.com**

_____, Gary Ronald Teeples, and David Schaefermeyer. *Arkansas 1840 Census Index.* Bountiful, UT: Accelerated Indexing Systems, 1976. 18; 32p.

McLane, Bobbie Lee Jones, and Inez Halsell Cline. *An Index to 1840 United States Census of Arkansas.* Hot Springs, AR: Author, 1967. 127p.

_____. *An Index to Fifth (Sixth) United States Census of Arkansas.* Fort Worth, TX: Arrow Printing Co., 1963. 104p.

_____. *Online Database Edition.* Orem, UT: Ancestry.com, Inc., 1999. **http://www.ancestry.com**

U.S. Federal Population Census Schedules. 1840, M704, Microfilm Reel Nos. 17-20.

1850

Census Index: U.S. Selected States/Counties, 1850. Family Archive CD 317. Novato, CA: Broderbund Software. CD-ROM.

Census Microfilm Records: Alabama, Arkansas, Louisiana and Mississippi, 1850. Family Archive CD 453. Novato, CA: Broderbund Software. CD-ROM.

Jackson, Ronald Vern. *Arkansas Census Index, Online Edition.* Orem, UT: Ancestry.com, Inc., 1999. **http://www.ancestry.com**

_____, Gary Ronald Teeples, and David Schaefermeyer. *Arkansas 1850 Census Index.* Bountiful, UT: Accelerated Indexing Systems, 1976. 98p.

_____. *Arkansas 1850 Slave Schedule Census Index.* Salt Lake City, UT: Accelerated Indexing Systems International, 1988. 55; 112p.

_____. *Mortality Schedules Index, Online Edition.* Orem, UT: Ancestry.com, Inc., 1999. **http://www.ancestry.com**

McLane, Bobbie Lee Jones, and Desmond Walls Allen. *Arkansas 1850 Census Every-name Index.* Conway, AR: Arkansas Research, 1995. 456p.

McLane, Bobbie Lee Jones, and Capitola Hensley Glazer. *1850 Mortality Schedule of Arkansas.* Hot Springs, AR: Authors, 1974. 64p.

Presley, Mrs. Leister E. *Arkansas Census, 1850, Surname Index.* Searcy, AR: Author, 1974. 318p.

U.S. Census Index Series, Alabama, Arkansas, Georgia, Florida, Louisiana, Mississippi, South Carolina, 1850. Orem, UT: Automated Archives, 1991. CD-ROM.

U.S. Federal Population Census Schedules. 1850, M432, Microfilm Reel Nos. 25-31.

U.S. Federal Population Census Schedules. 1850, M432, Slave Schedules, Microfilm Reel No. 32.

1851

Hines, Richard. *Index to the 1851 Cherokee Old Settler Roll.* Mobile, AL: Sena Exchange, 1995. 35p.

1860

Bonner, Kathryn Marie Rose. *Arkansas 1860 U.S. Census Index.* Marianna, AR: Author, 1984. 239p.

Census Index: U.S. Selected States/Counties, 1860. Family Archive CD 318. Novato, CA: Broderbund Software. CD-ROM.

Federal Population Schedule of the United States Census, 1860. Indian Lands West of Arkansas. Tulsa, OK: Oklahoma Yesterday Publications. 79p.

Jackson, Ronald Vern. *Arkansas Census Index, Online Edition.* Orem, UT: Ancestry.com, Inc., 1999. **http://www.ancestry.com**

_____. *Arkansas 1860 Census Index.* Salt Lake City, UT: Accelerated Indexing Systems, 1985. 339p.

_____. *Arkansas 1860 Slave Schedule.* North Salt Lake City, UT: Accelerated Indexing Systems International, 1991. 237p.

_____. *Mortality Schedules Index, Online Edition.* Orem, UT: Ancestry.com, Inc., 1999. **http://www.ancestry.com**

McLane, Bobbie Lee Jones, and Capitola Hensley Glazer. *1860 Mortality Schedule of Arkansas.* Hot Springs, AR: Authors, 1974. 108p.

U.S. Census Index, 1860, Alabama, Arkansas, Florida, Louisiana, Mississippi, South Carolina. Orem, UT: Automated Archives, 1992. 1 CD-ROM.

U.S. Federal Population Census Schedules. 1860, M653, Microfilm Reel Nos. 37-52.

U.S. Federal Population Census Schedules. 1860, M653, Slave Schedules, Microfilm Reel Nos. 53-54.

USGenWeb Census Project. Arkansas, 1860 Indian Lands. **ftp://ftp.rootsweb.com/pub/census/ar/indianlands/1860/**

1870

Census Index: U.S. Selected States/Counties, 1870. Family Archive CD 319. Novato, CA: Broderbund Software. CD-ROM.

Jackson, Ronald Vern. *Arkansas Census Index, Online Edition.* Orem, UT: Ancestry.com, Inc., 1999. **http://www.ancestry.com**

_____. *Arkansas 1870.* North Salt Lake City, UT: Accelerated Indexing Systems, 1987. 562p.

U.S. Federal Population Census Schedules. 1870, M593, Microfilm Reel Nos. 47-67.

Vaughn. Martha. *Arkansas 1870 Census Index.* Conway, AR: Arkansas Research, 1999. 932p.

1880

McLane, Bobbie Lee Jones, and Capitola Hensley Glazer. *1880 Mortality Schedule of Arkansas.* Hot Springs, AR: Authors, 1975. 261p.

U.S. Federal Population Census Schedules. 1880, T9, Microfilm Reel Nos. 38-60.

U.S. Federal Population Census Schedules. 1880, Soundex. T736, 48 Microfilm Reels.

1900

U.S. Federal Population Census Schedules. 1900, T623, Microfilm Reel Nos. 49-80.

U.S. Federal Population Census Schedules. 1900, Soundex. T1033, 132 Microfilm Reels.

U.S. Federal Population Census Schedules. 1900, Military & Naval Bases. T1081, Microfilm Reel Nos. 1838-1842.

U.S. Federal Population Census Schedules. 1900, Military & Naval Bases, Soundex. T1081, 32 Microfilm Reels.

1910

Hart, James M., and Lillian Noles Hart. *Some Immigrants Settled in Arkansas, Compiled from 1910 Arkansas Census of 13 Counties.* Hot Springs, AR: Author, 1985. 37p.

U.S. Federal Population Census Schedules. 1910, T624, Microfilm Reel Nos. 43-68.

U.S. Federal Population Census Schedules. 1910, Miracode (Index) T1260, 139 Microfilm Reels.

1911

McLane, Bobbie Lee Jones. *An Index to the Three Volumes, Arkansas 1911 Census of Confederate Veterans.* Hot Springs, AR: Author, 1988. 245p.

1920

U.S. Federal Population Census Schedules. 1920, T625, Microfilm Reel Nos. 53-86.
U.S. Federal Population Census Schedules. Soundex. M1550, 131 Microfilm Reels.

Arkansas County
1850

Hook, Charlene. *1850 Arkansas County, Arkansas Census.* Tulsa, OK: Indian Nations Press, 1973. 46p.
1860

Dhonau, Robert Will Fred. *Federal Census 1860, Arkansas County, Arkansas.* Little Rock, AR: Author, 1977. 82p.
1870

Dhonau, Robert Will Fred. *Federal Census 1870, Arkansas County, Arkansas.* Little Rock, AR: Author, 1978. 173p.

Ashley County
1850

Hook, Charlene. *1850 Ashley County, Arkansas Census.* Tulsa, OK: Indian Nations Press, 1973. 26p.
McLane, Bobbie Lee Jones. *1850 Census of Southern Arkansas, Ashley, Bradley, Clark, Dallas, Drew, Hempstead, Lafayette, Ouachita, Pike, Polk, Sevier, and Union Counties.* Conway, AR: Arkansas Research, 1995. 158p.
1860

Mowlin, Faith White. *1860 Federal Census of Ashley County, Arkansas, Copied from Microfilm Roll #37 on File at the National Archives in Washington, DC and the Arkansas Historical Commission in Little Rock, Arkansas.* Crossett, AR: Southeast Arkansas Research, 1990. 89p.
1870

1870 Federal Census of Ashley County, Arkansas. Crossett, AR: Ashley County Genealogical Society, 1995. 160p.

Baxter County
1880

Garr, Marjorie Fay, and F. Gene Garr. *Baxter County, Arkansas 1880 Federal Census.* Author, 1992. 155p.
1890

1890 Census of Baxter County, Arkansas. Arkansas DAR Genealogical Records Committee Report, s2; v12. Arkansas: Prudence Hall Chapter, DAR, 1990. 72p.

Benton County
1850

McLane, Bobbie Lee Jones. *1850 Census of Northwest Arkansas, Benton, Carroll, Crawford, Franklin, Johnson, Madison, Newton, Pope and Washington Counties.* Conway, AR: Arkansas Research, 1995. 158p.
1860

The 1860 Benton County, Arkansas, United States Census. Siloam Springs, AR: Benton County Historical Society. 95p.
1870

Langley, Elizabeth B., and Lea Wilson. *Benton County, Arkansas 1870 United States Census.* Author, 1967. 3 vols.

Boone County
1870

Looney, Janice Soutee. *Boone County, Arkansas 1870 Federal Census.* Walnut Grove, MO: Author, 1990. 84p.

Bradley County
1850
McLane, Bobbie Lee Jones. *1850 Census of Southern Arkansas, Ashley, Bradley, Clark, Dallas, Drew, Hempstead, Lafayette, Ouachita, Pike, Polk, Sevier, and Union Counties*. Conway, AR: Arkansas Research, 1995. 158p.

Mowlin, Faith White. *1850 Federal Census of Bradley County, Arkansas, Copied from Microfilm Roll No. 25 on File at the National Archives in Washington, DC and the Arkansas Historical Commission in Little Rock, Arkansas*. Crossett, AR: Southeast Arkansas Research, 1990. 46p.

1860
Dhonau, Robert Will Fred. *Bradley County, Arkansas, Federal Census, 1860*. Little Rock, AR: Author, 1984. 131p.

1890
New, Billie W. *Bradley County, Arkansas, 1890*. Jacksonville, AR: Author, 1988. 68p.

Calhoun County
1860
1860 Census of Calhoun County, Arkansas. Camden, AR: Ouachita Calhoun Genealogical Society, 1983. 67p.

1880
1880 Federal Census, Calhoun County, Arkansas. Cumbly, TX: Skinner, 1988. 165p.

Carroll County
1830
Lair, James. *An Outlander's History of Carroll County, Arkansas, 1830-1983*. Marceline, MO: Walsworth Pub., 1983. 424p.

1840
Lair, James. *An Outlander's History of Carroll County, Arkansas, 1830-1983*. Marceline, MO: Walsworth Pub., 1983. 424p.

USGenWeb Census Project. Arkansas, 1840 Carroll County.

ftp://ftp.rootsweb.com/pub/census/ar/carroll/1840/

1850
McLane, Bobbie Lee Jones. *1850 Census of Northwest Arkansas, Benton, Carroll, Crawford, Franklin, Johnson, Madison, Newton, Pope and Washington Counties*. Conway, AR: Arkansas Research, 1995. 158p.

1860
Langley, Elizabeth B. *Carroll County, Arkansas 1860 United States Federal Census*. Billings, MT: Pioneer Enterprises, Genealogical Servcies, 1969. 105p.

Chicot County
1850
McLane, Bobbie Lee Jones. *1850 Census of Eastern Arkansas, Chicot, Crittenden, Desha, Greene, Mississippi, Monroe, Phillips, Poinsett and St. Francis Counties*. Conway, AR: Arkansas Research, 1995. 100p.

Mowlin, Faith White. *1850 Federal Census of Chicot County, Arkansas Copied from Microfilm Roll No. 25 on File at the National Archives in Washington, DC and the Arkansas Historical Commission in Little Rock, Arkansas*. Crossett, AR: Southeast Arkansas Research, 1990. 27p.

1860
Trigleth, Ken, and Elizabeth Trigleth. *1860 Census, Chicot County, Arkansas*. Duncan, OK: Genealogical Research Aids, 1986. 66p.

1870
Trigleth, Ken. *1870 Census, Chicot County, Arkansas*. Duncan, OK: Genealogical Research Aids, 1987. 262p.

Clark County
1840
USGenWeb Census Project. Arkansas, 1840 Clark County.
ftp://ftp.rootsweb.com/pub/census/ar/clark/1840/
1850
McLane, Bobbie Lee Jones. *Clark County, Arkansas Annotated Census of 1850*. Hot Springs, AR: Arkansas Ancestors, 1985. 50p.

_____. *1850 Census of Southern Arkansas, Ashley, Bradley, Clark, Dallas, Drew, Hempstead, Lafayette, Ouachita, Pike, Polk, Sevier, and Union Counties*. Conway, AR: Arkansas Research, 1995. 158p.

USGenWeb Census Project. Arkansas, 1850 Clark County.
ftp://ftp.rootsweb.com/pub/census/al/clark/1850/
1860
Felldin, Jeanne Robey. *1860 United States Census Surname Index, the Arkansas Counties of Clark, Columbia and Conway*. Tomball, TX: Genealogical Publications, 1976. 7p,

McLane, Bobbie Lee Jones, and Charlotte Magee Tucker. *Clark County 1860 United States Census*. Hot Springs, AR: Arkansas Ancestors, 1988. 107p.
1870
McLane, Bobbie Lee Jones. *Clark County, Arkansas 1870 United States Census*. Hot Springs, AR: Arkansas Ancestors, 1989. 393p.
1880
Dennis, Pamela, Lori Hoggard, and Angela Nation. *Clark County, Arkansas 1880 Census* index. Arkadelphia, AR: Clark County Historical Association, 1992. 81p.
1890
Newberry, William L. *1890 Census of Clark County, Arkansas*. Arkadelphia, AR: Clark County Historical Association, 1988. 123p.
1900
Dennis, Pamela, Lori Hoggard, and Angela Nation. *Clark County, Arkansas 1900 Census Index*. Arkadelphia, AR: Clark County Historical Association, 1992. 116p.
1910
Dennis, Pamela, Lori Hoggard, and Angela Nation. *Clark County, Arkansas 1910 Census Index*. Arkadelphia, AR: Clark County Historical Association, 1992. 134p.

Clay County
1880
Pollard, Una Lee Dover. *The Tenth Census of the United States 1880, Clay County, Arkansas*. Piggott, AR: Author, 1983. 156p.

Cleburne County
1900
Latch, Mildred J. Williamson. *Twelfth U.S. Census 1900 Cleburne County, Arkansas When You Search for Ancestors You Find Friends!* Heber Springs, AR: Author, 1997. Unpgd.

Columbia County
1860
Columbia County, Arkansas Free Population Schedules, 1860. Magnolia, AR: South West Arkansas Genealogical Society, 1980. 91p.

Felldin, Jeanne Robey. *1860 United States Census Surname Index, the Arkansas Counties of Clark, Columbia and Conway*. Tomball, TX: Genealogical Publications, 1976. 21p.
1870
Columbia County, Arkansas Ninth Census of the United States, 1870 and 1870 Mortality Schedule of Columbia County, Arkansas. Magnolia, AR: South West Arkansas Genealogical Society, 1983. 110p.

1880

Columbia County, Arkansas Tenth Federal Population Census 1880. Little Rock, AR: South Western Arkansas Genealogical Society, 1989. 289p.

Conway County
1830, 1840

Tindall, Emogene. *Index to Conway County, Arkansas Census, 1830, 1840, 1850*. North Little Rock, AR: Author, 1980. 27p.

1850

McLane, Bobbie Lee Jones. *1850 Census of North Central Arkansas, Conway, Fulton, Independence, Izard, Jackson, Lawrence, Marion, Randolph, Searcy, Van Buren and White Counties*. Conway, AR: Arkansas Research, 1995. 139p.

Tindall, Emogene. *Index to Conway County, Arkansas Census, 1830, 1840, 1850*. North Little Rock, AR: Author, 1980. 27p.

1860

Felldin, Jeanne Robey. *1860 United States Census Surname Index, the Arkansas Counties of Clark, Columbia and Conway*. Tomball, TX: Genealogical Publications, 1976. 21p.

Tindall, Emogene. *Conway County, Arkansas Index to 1860 Census*. North Little Rock, AR: Author, 1984. 28p.

1870

Tindall, Emogene. *Index to the 1870 Census of Conway County, Arkansas*. North Little Rock, AR: Author. 29p

Crawford County
1850

Brandenburg, Beth. *Crawford County, Arkansas 1850 Federal Census*. Van Buren, AR: Author. 190p.

McLane, Bobbie Lee Jones. *1850 Census of Northwest Arkansas, Benton, Carroll, Crawford, Franklin, Johnson, Madison, Newton, Pope and Washington Counties*. Conway, AR: Arkansas Research, 1995. 158p.

USGenWeb Census Project. Arkansas, 1850 Crawford County.
ftp://ftp.rootsweb.com/pub/census/ar/crawford/1850/

Crittenden County
1850

McLane, Bobbie Lee Jones. *1850 Census of Eastern Arkansas, Chicot, Crittenden, Desha, Greene, Mississippi, Monroe, Phillips, Poinsett and St. Francis Counties*. Conway, AR: Arkansas Research, 1995. 100p.

Dallas County
1850

Foster, Ardith G. *Dallas County, Arkansas Seventh Census Free Population Schedules, 1850*. Newport, AR: Arkansas Records Association, 1972. 41p.

McLane, Bobbie Lee Jones. *1850 Census of Southern Arkansas, Ashley, Bradley, Clark, Dallas, Drew, Hempstead, Lafayette, Ouachita, Pike, Polk, Sevier, and Union Counties*. Conway, AR: Arkansas Research, 1995. 158p.

1860

Tindall, Emogene. *1860 Census, Dallas County, Arkansas*. North Little Rock, AR: Author. 103p.

Desha County
1840

USGenWeb Census Project. Arkansas, 1840 Desha County.
ftp://ftp.rootsweb.com/pub/census/ar/desha/1840/

1850

Foster, Ardith G. *Desha County, Arkansas Seventh Census Free Population Schedules, 1850*. Newport, AR: Arkansas Records Association, 1972. 18p.

McLane, Bobbie Lee Jones. *1850 Census of Eastern Arkansas, Chicot, Crittenden, Desha, Greene, Mississippi, Monroe, Phillips, Poinsett and St. Francis Counties*. Conway, AR: Arkansas Research, 1995. 100p.

1860

Dhonau, Robert Will Fred. *Desha County, Arkansas, Federal Census, 1860, Marriage Record Books, A, 1852-1859, C, 1856-1860 (Part)*. Little Rock, AR: Author, 1980. 97p.

Drew County
1850

Foster, Ardith G. *Drew County, Arkansas Seventh Census Free Population Schedules, 1850*. Newport, AR: Arkansas Records Association, 1972. 23p.

McLane, Bobbie Lee Jones. *1850 Census of Southern Arkansas, Ashley, Bradley, Clark, Dallas, Drew, Hempstead, Lafayette, Ouachita, Pike, Polk, Sevier, and Union Counties*. Conway, AR: Arkansas Research, 1995. 158p.

1860

Dhonau, Robert Will Fred. *Drew County, Arkansas 1860 Federal Census*. Little Rock, AR: Author, 1983. 117p.

Franklin County
1850

McLane, Bobbie Lee Jones. *1850 Census of Northwest Arkansas, Benton, Carroll, Crawford, Franklin, Johnson, Madison, Newton, Pope and Washington Counties*. Conway, AR: Arkansas Research, 1995. 158p.

USGenWeb Census Project. Arkansas, 1850 Franklin County.
ftp://ftp.rootsweb.com/pub/census/ar/franklin/1850/

1860

McLane, Bobbie Lee Jones. *Franklin County, Arkansas 1860 Census*. Hot Springs, AR: Arkansas Ancestors, 1986. 82p.

1870

Hanks, Bill. *Franklin County, Arkansas 1870 United States Census*. Author, 1990. 139p.

Fulton County
1850

McLane, Bobbie Lee Jones. *1850 Census of North Central Arkansas, Conway, Fulton, Independence, Izard, Jackson, Lawrence, Marion, Randolph, Searcy, Van Buren and White Counties*. Conway, AR: Arkansas Research, 1995. 139p.

Morgan, James Logan. *Fulton County, Arkansas Seventh Census Free Population Schedules, 1850*. Newport, AR: Northeast Arkansas Genealogical Assn., 1971. 18p.

1860

McLane, Bobbie Lee Jones. *Fulton County, Arkansas 1860, United States Census*. Hot Springs, AR: Arkansas Ancestors, 1988. 61p.

Garland County
1880

Stephens, Lewis C. *1880 United States Census, Garland County, Arkansas*. Author. 135p.

1900

Hart, James M., and Lillian Noles Hart. *Index, 1900 Census, Garland County, Arkansas*. Hot Springs, AR: Author, 1979, 1980. 65p.

Greene County

1850

Foster, Ardith G. *Greene County, Arkansas Seventh Census Free Population Schedules, 1850.* Newport, AR: Arkansas Records Association, 1971. 24p.

McLane, Bobbie Lee Jones. *1850 Census of Eastern Arkansas, Chicot, Crittenden, Desha, Greene, Mississippi, Monroe, Phillips, Poinsett and St. Francis Counties.* Conway, AR: Arkansas Research, 1995. 100p.

1880

Greene County 1880 Federal Census, Arkansas. Paragould, AR: Greene County Historical and Genealogical Society, 1988. 134p.

1900

1900 Federal Census, Greene County, Arkansas. Paragould, AR: Greene County Historical and Genealogical Society, 1988. 316p.

1910

1910 Federal Census, Greene County, Arkansas. Paragould, AR: Greene County Historical and Genealogical Society, 1991. 463p.

1920

Greene County 1920 Federal Census, Arkansas. Paragould, AR: Greene County Historical and Genealogical Society, 1994. 505p.

Hempstead County

1830, 1840

Hempstead County, Arkansas, United States Census of 1830, 1840, 1850 and Alphabetical Listings of Head of Household Taxes for the Years of 1828, 1829, 1830, 1831, 1832, 1839, 1841, 1842, 1847, 1848, 1849. Hope, AR: Hempstead County Genealogical Society, 1995. 137p.

1850

Hempstead County, Arkansas, United States Census of 1830, 1840, 1850 and Alphabetical Listings of Head of Household Taxes for the Years of 1828, 1829, 1830, 1831, 1832, 1839, 1841, 1842, 1847, 1848, 1849. Hope, AR: Hempstead County Genealogical Society, 1995. 137p.

McLane, Bobbie Lee Jones. *1850 Census of Southern Arkansas, Ashley, Bradley, Clark, Dallas, Drew, Hempstead, Lafayette, Ouachita, Pike, Polk, Sevier, and Union Counties.* Conway, AR: Arkansas Research, 1995. 158p.

1860

Glazner, Capitola Hensley. *Hempstead County, Arkansas, United States Census of 1860.* Author, 1969. 129p.

1870

Hempstead County, Arkansas, United States Census of 1870. Hope, AR: Hempstead County Genealogical Society, 1984. 189p.

1900

Hempstead County, Arkansas, United States Census of 1900. Hope, AR: Hempstead County Genealogical Society, 1998. 320p.

Hot Spring County

1850

McLane, Bobbie Lee Jones. *1850 Census of Central Arkansas, Hot Spring, Jefferson, Montgomery, Perry, Prairie, Pulaski, Saline, Scott and Yell Counties.* Conway, AR: Arkansas Research, 1995. 107p.

_____. *Hot Spring County, Arkansas, United States Census of 1850 Including Heads of Families, 1830 and 1840 Hot Spring County, Arkansas and Marriage Book A.* Hot Springs National Park, AR: Author, 1965. 69p.

1860

McLane, Bobbie Lee Jones. *Hot Spring County, Arkansas 1860 Census.* Hot Springs, AR: Arkansas Ancestors, 1985. 76p.

Howard County
1880

Davis, Jackie Dossey, and Shelly Davis. *1880 Federal Census, Howard County, Arkansas*. Broken Bow, OK: Kiamichi Country Genealogy Society, 1992. 188p.

1890

Westbrook, Lucille. *1890 Census of Howard County, Arkansas*. 1985. 64p.

Independence County
1850

McLane, Bobbie Lee Jones. *1850 Census of North Central Arkansas, Conway, Fulton, Independence, Izard, Jackson, Lawrence, Marion, Randolph, Searcy, Van Buren and White Counties*. Conway, AR: Arkansas Research, 1995. 139p.

Morgan, James Logan. *Independence County, Arkansas Seventh Census Free Population Schedules, 1850*. Newport, AR: Northeast Arkansas Genealogical Assn., 1971. 69p.

USGenWeb Census Project. Arkansas, 1850 Independence County.

ftp://ftp.rootsweb.com/pub/census/ar/independence/1850/

1860

Foster, Ardith G. *1860 Census of Independence County, Arkansas*. Newport, AR: Arkansas Records Association, 1982. 125p.

1870

Tindall, Emogene, and Dana McCoy. *1870 Census, Independence County, Arkansas*. North Little Rock, AR: Author, 1983. 54p.

Izard County
1850

Allen, Desmond Walls. *1850 Federal Census Reports for Izard County, Arkansas, Actual Copies of the Census Book Pages Including Slave Schedules and a Surname Index*. Conway, AR: Arkansas Research, 1987. 162p.

Foster, Ardith G., and James Logan Morgan. *Izard County, Arkansas Seventh Census Free Population Schedules, 1850*. Newport, AR: Arkansas Records Association, 1971. 30p.

McLane, Bobbie Lee Jones. *1850 Census of North Central Arkansas, Conway, Fulton, Independence, Izard, Jackson, Lawrence, Marion, Randolph, Searcy, Van Buren and White Counties*. Conway, AR: Arkansas Research, 1995. 139p.

1860

Miller, Mary Cooper. *1860 Federal Census of Izard County, Arkansas*. Batesville, AR: M-F Publications, 1984. 89p.

1870

Foster, Ardith G. *1870 Census, Izard County, Arkansas*. Batesville, AR: M-F Publications. 68p.

1900

Miller, Mary Cooper. *The 1900 Federal Census of Izard County, Arkansas*. Batesville, AR: Batesville Genealogical Society, 1989. 315p.

1920

O'Neal, Patricia, and Clede O'Neal. *1920 Census Index Izard County, Arkansas*. Authors, 1994. 138p.

Jackson County
1830

USGenWeb Census Project. Arkansas, 1830 Jackson County.

ftp://ftp.rootsweb.com/pub/census/ar/jackson/1830/

1840

USGenWeb Census Project. Arkansas, 1840 Jackson County.

ftp://ftp.rootsweb.com/pub/census/ar/jackson/1840/

1850

Lyle, Jane Belle, James Logan Morgan, and Ardith G. Foster. *Jackson County, Arkansas Seventh Census Free Population Schedules, 1850*. Newport, AR: Northeast Arkansas Genealogical Assn., 1971. 40p.

McLane, Bobbie Lee Jones. *1850 Census of North Central Arkansas, Conway, Fulton, Independence, Izard, Jackson, Lawrence, Marion, Randolph, Searcy, Van Buren and White Counties*. Conway, AR: Arkansas Research, 1995. 139p.

Jefferson County
1830

Glazner, Capitola Hensley. *Jefferson County, Arkansas, United States Census of 1850 and Marriage Book A and B, February 1830 - August 1861*. Hot Springs National Park, AR: Author, 1967. 115p.

1850

McLane, Bobbie Lee Jones. *1850 Census of Central Arkansas, Hot Springs, Jefferson, Montgomery, Perry, Prairie, Pulaski, Saline, Scott and Yell Counties*. Conway, AR: Arkansas Research, 1995. 107p.

1860

Dhonau, Robert Will Fred. *Jefferson County, Arkansas, Federal Census 1860, Marriage Record Books, Volume V, 1861-1863, Volume VI, 1863-1871*. Little Rock, AR: Author, 1980. 222p.

Johnson County
1840

Mickel, Mrs. R. W. *Johnson County, Arkansas, Probate Court Records, Wills, Estate Settlements, Deeds, 1835 Tax List, 1840 Census*. Clarksville, AR: Author. 183p.

1850

Dewberry, Jimmie. *Johnson County, Arkansas Federal Census 1990*. Conway, AR: Arkansas Research, 1997. 434p.

McLane, Bobbie Lee Jones. *1850 Census of Northwest Arkansas, Benton, Carroll, Crawford, Franklin, Johnson, Madison, Newton, Pope and Washington Counties*. Conway, AR: Arkansas Research, 1995. 158p.

1860

Hanks, Bill. *Johnson County, Arkansas 1860 United States Census*. Hot Springs, AR: Arkansas Ancestors, 1989. 157p.

1880

Dewberry, Jimmie, and Doris Evans Dewberry. *Johnson County, Arkansas 1880 Federal Census*. Conway, AR: Arkansas Research, 1996. 305p.

Lafayette County
1850

Foster, Ardith G. *Lafayette County, Arkansas Seventh Census Free Population Schedules, 1850*. Newport, AR: Arkansas Records Association, 1972. 19p.

McLane, Bobbie Lee Jones. *1850 Census of Southern Arkansas, Ashley, Bradley, Clark, Dallas, Drew, Hempstead, Lafayette, Ouachita, Pike, Polk, Sevier, and Union Counties*. Conway, AR: Arkansas Research, 1995. 158p.

1860

McLane, Bobbie Lee Jones. *Lafayette County, Arkansas 1860 United States Census*. Hot Springs, AR: Arkansas Ancestors, 1985. 66p.

Lawrence County
1829

Craig, Marion Stark. *Lawrence County, Arkansas 1829 Sheriff's Census*. Author, 1994. 30p.

1850

McLane, Bobbie Lee Jones. *1850 Census of North Central Arkansas, Conway, Fulton, Independence, Izard, Jackson, Lawrence, Marion, Randolph, Searcy, Van Buren and White Counties*. Conway, AR: Arkansas Research, 1995. 139p.

Morgan, James Logan. *Lawrence County, Arkansas Seventh Census Free Population Schedules, 1850*. Newport, AR: Northeast Arkansas Genealogical Assn., 1971. 46p.

1860

USGenWeb Census Project. Arkansas, 1860 Lawrence County. (Partial).

ftp://ftp.rootsweb.com/pub/census/ar/lawrence/1860/

1870

Richey, Catherine S., and Susan Hilburn. *Census of Lawrence County, Arkansas, 1870*. Powhatan, AR: Authors, 1991. 177p.

Lonoke County

1860

Dhonau, Robert Will Fred. *Prairie County, Arkansas (and Lonoke before 1873) 1860 Federal Census*. Little Rock, AR: Author, 1982. 127p.

1870

Dhonau, Robert Will Fred. *Prairie County, Arkansas (and Lonoke before 1873) 1870 Federal Census*. Little Rock, AR: Author, 1982. 127p.; 1988. 138p.

Madison County

1850

Keeney, Wayne C. *Madison County, Arkansas Population Schedules of the United States Census of 1850*. 65p.

McLane, Bobbie Lee Jones. *1850 Census of Northwest Arkansas, Benton, Carroll, Crawford, Franklin, Johnson, Madison, Newton, Pope and Washington Counties*. Conway, AR: Arkansas Research, 1995. 158p.

1900

Madison County, Arkansas Census, 1900. Madison County Genealogical and Historical Society, 1984. 2 vols.

1920

The 1920 Madison County, Arkansas, Census. Huntsville, AR: Madison County Genealogical & Historical Society, 1994. 2 vols.

Marion County

1850

McLane, Bobbie Lee Jones. *1850 Census of North Central Arkansas, Conway, Fulton, Independence, Izard, Jackson, Lawrence, Marion, Randolph, Searcy, Van Buren and White Counties*. Conway, AR: Arkansas Research, 1995. 139p.

Marion County, Arkansas Census, 1850. San Jose, CA: York Genealogical Research, 1969. 56p.

1870

Looney, Janice Soutee. *Marion County, Arkansas 1870 Federal Census*. Walnut Grove, MO: Author, 1986. 57p.

1880

Brown, Gladys Horn. *Marion County, Arkansas, 1880 U.S. Census*. Pine Bluff, AR: Author, 1992. 184p.

Miller County

1880

Bird, Reba Frances. *1880 Census, Sulphur Township, Miller County, Arkansas*. Atlanta, TX: Bowman, 1980. 44p.

Mississippi County

1840

Wade, Ophelia Richardson. *Mississippi County, Arkansas Vital Records, Land Entry Book 1826-1889, Index to Wills 1862-1925, Post Office History 1836-1974; Complete 1840 Federal Census, 1850-1860 Slave Schedules, 1850-1860-1870 Mortality Records*. Bragg City, MO: Author, 1974. 87p.

1850

Foster, Ardith G. *Mississippi County, Arkansas Seventh Census Free Population Schedules, 1850.* Newport, AR: Arkansas Records Association, 1972. 15p.

McLane, Bobbie Lee Jones. *1850 Census of Eastern Arkansas, Chicot, Crittenden, Desha, Greene, Mississippi, Monroe, Phillips, Poinsett and St. Francis Counties.* Conway, AR: Arkansas Research, 1995. 100p.

Wade, Ophelia Richardson. *Mississippi County, Arkansas Vital Records, Land Entry Book 1826-1889, Index to Wills 1862-1925, Post Office History 1836-1974; Complete 1840 Federal Census, 1850-1860 Slave Schedules, 1850-1860-1870 Mortality Records.* Bragg City, MO: Author, 1974. 87p.

1860

Wade, Ophelia Richrdson. *1860 Mississippi County, Arkansas Census.* Bragg City, MO: Author, 1973. 49p.

_____. *Mississippi County, Arkansas Vital Records, Land Entry Book 1826-1889, Index to Wills 1862-1925, Post Office History 1836-1974; Complete 1840 Federal Census, 1850-1860 Slave Schedules, 1850-1860-1870 Mortality Records.* Bragg City, MO: Author, 1974. 87p.

1870

Looney, Janice Soutee. *1870 Mississippi County, Arkansas Federal Census.* Walnut Grove, MO: Author. 48p.

Wade, Ophelia Richardson. *Mississippi County, Arkansas Vital Records, Land Entry Book 1826-1889, Index to Wills 1862-1925, Post Office History 1836-1974; Complete 1840 Federal Census, 1850-1860 Slave Schedules, 1850-1860-1870 Mortality Records.* Bragg City, MO: Author, 1974. 87p.

Monroe County
1830, 1840

English, Jo Claire Knoll. *Pages from the Past, Revisited. Historical Notes on Clarendon, Monroe County and Early, Arkansas.* Clarendon, AR: Author, 1991. 121p.

1850

English, Jo Claire Knoll. *Pages from the Past, Revisited. Historical Notes on Clarendon, Monroe County and Early, Arkansas.* Clarendon, AR: Author, 1991. 121p.

Foster, Ardith G. *Monroe County, Arkansas Seventh Census Free Population Schedules, 1850.* Newport, AR: Arkansas Records Association, 1972. 17p.

McLane, Bobbie Lee Jones. *1850 Census of Eastern Arkansas, Chicot, Crittenden, Desha, Greene, Mississippi, Monroe, Phillips, Poinsett and St. Francis Counties.* Conway, AR: Arkansas Research, 1995. 100p.

1860

1860 Federal Population Census of Monroe County, Arkansas. Marvell, AR: Tri County Genealogical Society, 1988. 73p.

Montgomery County
1850

McLane, Bobbie Lee Jones. *1850 Census of Central Arkansas, Hot Springs, Jefferson, Montgomery, Perry, Prairie, Pulaski, Saline, Scott and Yell Counties.* Conway, AR: Arkansas Research, 1995. 107p.

1860

Hart, James M., and Lillian Noles Hart. *Abstract of 1860 Federal Census Montgomery County, Arkansas.* Hot Springs, AR: Authors, 1983. 76p.

1900

Hart, James M., and Lillian Noles Hart. *Index, 1900 Census, Montgomery County, Arkansas.* Hot Springs, AR: Authors, 1981. 25p.

Nevada County
1880

Nevada County, Arkansas United States Census of 1880. Hope, AR: Hempstead County Genealogical Society, 1995. 163p.

Newton County
1850
Boyd, Charles Lynn, and Lina J. Owens Boyd. *1850 Census, Newton County, Arkansas*. Dover, AR: Authors, 1992. 39p.

Dean Ross, Vera Leona. *Newton County, Arkansas Census Index, 1850-1900, from M-432, Roll 28*. Richmond, CA: Dean, 1980. 39p.

McLane, Bobbie Lee Jones. *1850 Census of Northwest Arkansas, Benton, Carroll, Crawford, Franklin, Johnson, Madison, Newton, Pope and Washington Counties*. Conway, AR: Arkansas Research, 1995. 158p.

1860
Boyd, Lina J. Owens. *1860 United States Census, Newton County, Arkansas, Will Books B and C, 1910*. Dover, AR: Author, 1993. 81p.

Dean Ross, Vera Leona. *Newton County, Arkansas Census Index, 1850-1900, from M-432, Roll 28*. Richmond, CA: Dean, 1980. 39p.

1870, 1880
Dean Ross, Vera Leona. *Newton County, Arkansas Census Index, 1850-1900, from M-432, Roll 28*. Richmond, CA: Dean, 1980. 39p.

1900
Dean Ross, Vera Leona. *Newton County, Arkansas Census Index, 1850-1900, from M-432, Roll 28*. Richmond, CA: Dean, 1980. 39p.

Merritt, Belinda. *1900 Newton County, Arkansas Census. Online Database Edition*. Orem, UT: Ancestry.com, Inc., 1999.

http://www.ancestry.com

Ouachita County
1850
Foster, Ardith G. *Ouachita County, Arkansas Seventh Census Free Population Schedules, 1850*. Newport, AR: Arkansas Records Association, 1972. 61p.

McLane, Bobbie Lee Jones. *1850 Census of Southern Arkansas, Ashley, Bradley, Clark, Dallas, Drew, Hempstead, Lafayette, Ouachita, Pike, Polk, Sevier, and Union Counties*. Conway, AR: Arkansas Research, 1995. 158p.

1860
McLane, Bobbie Lee Jones. *Annotated 1860 Census, Ouachita County, Arkansas*. Hot Springs, AR: Arkansas Ancestors, 1987. 130p.

Perry County
1850
McLane, Bobbie Lee Jones. *1850 Census of Central Arkansas, Hot Springs, Jefferson, Montgomery, Perry, Prairie, Pulaski, Saline, Scott and Yell Counties*. Conway, AR: Arkansas Research, 1995. 107p.

Perry County, Arkansas Census 1850. San Jose, CA: York Genealogical Research, 1969. 27p.

Phillips County
1850
McLane, Bobbie Lee Jones. *1850 Census of Eastern Arkansas, Chicot, Crittenden, Desha, Greene, Mississippi, Monroe, Phillips, Poinsett and St. Francis Counties*. Conway, AR: Arkansas Research, 1995. 100p.

1860
White, Rose Craig. *1860 Census, Phillips County, Arkansas*. Author, 1991. 122p.

1870
White, Rose Craig. *1870 Federal Population Census, Phillips County, Arkansas*. 101p.

Pike County
1850

McLane, Bobbie Lee Jones. *1850 Census of Southern Arkansas, Ashley, Bradley, Clark, Dallas, Drew, Hempstead, Lafayette, Ouachita, Pike, Polk, Sevier, and Union Counties*. Conway, AR: Arkansas Research, 1995. 158p.

Pike County, Arkansas Census, 1850. San Jose, CA: York Genealogical Research, 1969. 52p.

1860

McLane, Bobbie Lee Jones. *Pike County, Arkansas 1860 United States Census*. Hot Springs, AR: Arkansas Ancestors, 1985. 55p.

USGenWeb Census Project. Arkansas, 1860 Pike County.

ftp://ftp.rootsweb.com/pub/census/ar/pike/1860/

1870

Partain, Dorothy Kennedy. *1870 Federal Census, Pike County, Arkansas*. Ft. Smith, AR: Ancestor Shoppe, 1987. 123p.

USGenWeb Census Project. Arkansas, 1870 Pike County.

ftp://ftp.rootsweb.com/pub/census/ar/pike/1870/

1880

Partain, Dorothy Kennedy. *1880 Federal Census, Pike County, Arkansas*. Author-. 222p.

USGenWeb Census Project. Arkansas, 1880 Pike County.

ftp://ftp.rootsweb.com/pub/census/ar/pike/1880/

1900

Hill, J. Shane, and Dorothy Kennedy Partain. *1900 Pike County, Arkansas Federal Census*. Murfreesboro, AR: Pike County Archives & History Society, 1995. 303p.

Poinsett County
1850

McLane, Bobbie Lee Jones. *1850 Census of Eastern Arkansas, Chicot, Crittenden, Desha, Greene, Mississippi, Monroe, Phillips, Poinsett and St. Francis Counties*. Conway, AR: Arkansas Research, 1995. 100p.

Polk County
1850

McLane, Bobbie Lee Jones. *1850 Census of Southern Arkansas, Ashley, Bradley, Clark, Dallas, Drew, Hempstead, Lafayette, Ouachita, Pike, Polk, Sevier, and Union Counties*. Conway, AR: Arkansas Research, 1995. 158p.

1870

Helderlein, Georgia D. *Polk County, Arkansas, 1870 Census*. Grass Valley, CA: Author, 1985. 72p.

Pope County
1850

McLane, Bobbie Lee Jones. *1850 Census of Northwest Arkansas, Benton, Carroll, Crawford, Franklin, Johnson, Madison, Newton, Pope and Washington Counties*. Conway, AR: Arkansas Research, 1995. 158p.

_____, and Capitola Glazner. *Pope County, Arkansas United States Census of 1850 and Marriage Book A, April 1830 - Novemer 1849*. Hot Springs National Park, AR: Authors, 1966. 95p.

USGenWeb Census Project. Arkansas, 1850 Pope County.

ftp://ftp.rootsweb.com/pub/census/ar/pope/1850/

1860

Glazner, Capitola Hensley, and Bobbie Lee Jones McLane. *Pope County, Arkansas, United States Census of 1860 and Marriage Books B and C, December 1849 thru December 1859*. Hot Springs National Park, AR; Authors, 1967. 139p

1870

Pope County, Arkansas, United States Census of 1870. Russellville, AR: Pope County Genealogical Group, 1975. 2 vols.

1880

Lemley, J. B., and Elaine Weir Cia. *Pope County, Arkansas, United States Census of 1880*. Russellville, AR: Pope County Genealogical Group, 1976. 416p.

1900

Index to the 1900 Pope County Census. Russellville, AR: Author, 1980. 57p.

Prairie County

1850

McLane, Bobbie Lee Jones. *1850 Census of Central Arkansas, Hot Springs, Jefferson, Montgomery, Perry, Prairie, Pulaski, Saline, Scott and Yell Counties*. Conway, AR: Arkansas Research, 1995. 107p.

Prairie County, Arkansas Census, 1850. San Jose, CA: York Genealogical Research, 1969. 51p.

1860

Dhonau, Robert Will Fred. *Prairie County, Arkansas (and Lonoke before 1873) 1860 Federal Census*. Little Rock, AR: Author, 1982. 127p.

1870

Dhonau, Robert Will Fred. *Prairie County, Arkansas (and Lonoke before 1873) 1870 Federal Census*. Little Rock, AR: Author, 1982. 127p.

———. ———. 1988. 138p.

1880

Hubbard, Margaret Harrison. *Prairie County, Arkansas, 1880 Census*. Hot Springs, AR: Author, 1989. 231p.

Pulaski County

1850

Dhonau, Robert Will Fred. *Pulaski County, Arkansas 1850 Federal Census*. Little Rock, AR: Author, 1982. 102p.

McLane, Bobbie Lee Jones. *1850 Census of Central Arkansas, Hot Springs, Jefferson, Montgomery, Perry, Prairie, Pulaski, Saline, Scott and Yell Counties*. Conway, AR: Arkansas Research, 1995. 107p.

1860

Dhonau, Robert Will Fred. *Pulaski County, Arkansas 1860 Federal Census*. Little Rock, AR: Author, 1982. 184p.

Randolph County

1850

Barnhart, Margaret A. *Alphabetical Census of Randolph County, Arkansas 1850*. Warm Springs, AR: Pegasearch, 1990. 49p.

McLane, Bobbie Lee Jones. *1850 Census of North Central Arkansas, Conway, Fulton, Independence, Izard, Jackson, Lawrence, Marion, Randolph, Searcy, Van Buren and White Counties*. Conway, AR: Arkansas Research, 1995. 139p.

1860

Barnhart, Margaret A. *Alphabetical Census of Randolph County, Arkansas 1860*. Warm Springs, AR: Pegasearch, 1990. 99p.

Saint Francis County

1850

McLane, Bobbie Lee Jones. *1850 Census of Eastern Arkansas, Chicot, Crittenden, Desha, Greene, Mississippi, Monroe, Phillips, Poinsett and St. Francis Counties*. Conway, AR: Arkansas Research, 1995. 100p.

Saline County

1840

Billingsley, Carolyn Earle. *1840 Saline County, Arkansas Census*. Alexander, AR: Author, 1987. 24p.

1850

Billingsley, Carolyn Earle. *1850 Saline County, Arkansas Census*. Alexander, AR: Author, 1988. 260p.

McLane, Bobbie Lee Jones. *1850 Census of Central Arkansas, Hot Springs, Jefferson, Montgomery, Perry, Prairie, Pulaski, Saline, Scott and Yell Counties*. Conway, AR: Arkansas Research, 1995. 107p.

1860

Dhonau, Robert Will Fred. *Saline County, Arkansas Federal Census, 1860*. Little Rock, AR: Author, 1985. 129p.

McLane, Bobbie Lee Jones. *Saline County, Arkansas 1860 United States Census*. Hot Springs, AR: Arkansas Ancestors, 1985. 92p.

1870

Chilton, Shirlene, and Virginia Prothro. *Saline County, Arkansas 1870 United States Census*. 1990. 101p.

1880

Saline County, Arkansas 1880 Census. Bryant, AR: Saline County History and Heritage Society, 1989. 198p.

1890

Billingsley, Carolyn Earle. *1890 Saline County, Arkansas Census*. Alexander, AR: Author, 1986. 103p.

1910

Landreth, Eddie G. *1910 Saline County, Arkansas Federal Census Index*. Bryant, AR: Saline County History and Heritage Society, 1989. 132p.

Scott County

1850

McLane, Bobbie Lee Jones. *1850 Census of Central Arkansas, Hot Springs, Jefferson, Montgomery, Perry, Prairie, Pulaski, Saline, Scott and Yell Counties*. Conway, AR: Arkansas Research, 1995. 107p.

O'Nale, John Paul. *Scott County, Arkansas Federal Census 1850*. Waldron, AR: Author, 1994. 91p.

1860

Hanks, Bill, and Bobbie Lee Jones McLane. *Scott County, Arkansas 1860 United States Census*. Hot Springs, AR: Arkansas Ancestors, 1989. 150p.

1870

Ellsworth, Carole, and Sue Elmer. *1870 United States Census of Scott County, Arkansas*. Gore, OK: Authors, 1982. 87p.

Hanks, Bill, and Bobbie Lee Jones McLane. *Scott County, Arkansas 1870 United States Census*. Hot Springs, AR: Arkansas Ancestors, 1989. 225p.

1880

Dhonau, Robert Will Fred. *1880 Scott County, Arkansas Census*. Little Rock, AR: Author, 1985. 222p.

Edwards, Delaine, and Gloryann Young. *1880 Scott County, Arkansas Census*. Wister, OK: Author, 1985. 222p.

1900

1900 Scott County, Arkansas, United States Census. Waldron, AR: Scott County Historical and Genealogical Society, 1992. 4 vols.

1910

Edwards, Delaine. *Scott County, Arkansas 1910 United States Census*. Waldron, AR; Author, 1992. 4 vols.

1920

Scott County, Arkansas 1920 United States Census. Waldron, AR: Author, 1993. 4 vols.

Searcy County

1850

Lacy, Ruby Sullivan. *Arkansas, Searcy County, 1850 Census*. Ashland, OR: Author, 1977. 53p.

McLane, Bobbie Lee Jones. *1850 Census of North Central Arkansas, Conway, Fulton, Independence, Izard, Jackson, Lawrence, Marion, Randolph, Searcy, Van Buren and White Counties*. Conway, AR: Arkansas Research, 1995. 139p.

1860

Lacy, Ruby Sullivan. *Arkansas, Searcy County, 1860 Census*. Ashland, OR: Author, 1981. 63p.

1870
Lacy, Ruby Sullivan. *Arkansas, Searcy County, 1870 Census*. Ashland, OR: Author, 1984. 47p.
1880
Dean, Vera L. *1880 Census of Searcy County, Arkansas, (Except Beaver, Campbell, and Tomahawk Townships)*. Richmond, CA: Author, 1979. 140p.
Lacy, Ruby Sullivan. *Arkansas, Searcy County, 1880 Census*. Ashland, OR: Author, 1987. 71p.
1900
Lacy, Ruby Sullivan, Judith Keeler, and Larry Watts. *Arkansas, Searcy County, 1900 Census*. Ashland, OR: Author, 1990. 322p.
1910
Lacy, Ruby Sullivan, Judith Keeler, and Larry Watts. *Arkansas, Searcy County, 1910 Census*. Ashland, OR: Author, 1995. 409p.

Sebastian County
1860
Scott, Gail. *Federal Census 1860 Sebastian County, Arkansas Transcribed from Census Roll Number 50*. Rogers, AR: Northwest Arkansas Genealogical Society, 1979. 121p.

Sevier County
1850
Glazner, Capitola Hensley, and Bobbie Lee Jones McLane. *Seveier County, Arkansas United States Census of 1850, Including Heads of Families 1830 and 1840 Sevier County, Arkansas Census and Available Marriage Records to 1852*. Hot Springs National Park, AR: Authors, 1964. 72p.
McLane, Bobbie Lee Jones. *1850 Census of Southern Arkansas, Ashley, Bradley, Clark, Dallas, Drew, Hempstead, Lafayette, Ouachita, Pike, Polk, Sevier, and Union Counties*. Conway, AR: Arkansas Research, 1995. 158p.
1860
Glazner, Capitola Hensley, and Bobbie Lee Jones McLane. *Sevier County, Arkansas, United States Census of 1860 and Marriage Book 2, April 1853 - June 1865*. Authors, 1967. 145p.

Sharp County
1870
Whitten, Joyce Hambleton. *1870 Census of Sharp County, Arkansas*. Monettee, AR: Author, 1978. 76p.
1880
USGenWeb Census Project. Arkansas, 1880 Sharp County.
ftp://ftp.rootsweb.com/pub/census/ar/sharp/1880/
Whitten, Joyce Hambleton. *1880 Census of Sharp County, Arkansas*. Monettee, AR: Author, 1980. 164p.

Union County
1850
McLane, Bobbie Lee Jones. *1850 Census of Southern Arkansas, Ashley, Bradley, Clark, Dallas, Drew, Hempstead, Lafayette, Ouachita, Pike, Polk, Sevier, and Union Counties*. Conway, AR: Arkansas Research, 1995. 158p.
1860
1860 Federal Population Census, United States Census, Arkansas. Vol. 1. El Dorado, AR: Union County Genealogical Society, 1991. 100p.
1900
1900 Federal Population Census, United States Census, Arkansas. Vol. 1. El Dorado, AR: Union County Genealogical Society, 1985. 416p.

Van Buren County
1850
McLane, Bobbie Lee Jones. *1850 Census of North Central Arkansas, Conway, Fulton, Independence, Izard, Jackson, Lawrence, Marion, Randolph, Searcy, Van Buren and White Counties*. Conway, AR: Arkansas Research, 1995. 139p.

Washington County
1850
McLane, Bobbie Lee Jones. *1850 Census of Northwest Arkansas, Benton, Carroll, Crawford, Franklin, Johnson, Madison, Newton, Pope and Washington Counties*. Conway, AR: Arkansas Research, 1995. 158p.

USGenWeb Census Project. Arkansas, 1850 Washington County.
ftp://ftp.rootsweb.com/pub/census/ar/washington/1850/
Woods, Frances. *Washington County, Arkansas Population Census of the United States Census of 1850*. Austin, TX: Author, 1964. 143p.
1860
Sorensen, Willa Thomas. *Index to the 1860 Census of Washington County, Arkansas*. Tomball, TX: Genealogical Publications, 1977. 88p.
1865
Maxwell, Nancy. *Washington County Arkansas Sheriff's Census for 1865*. Bowie, MD: Heritage Books, Inc., 1993. 67p.
1880
Talbot, Virgil. *Index to 1880 Census, Illinois Township, Washington County, Arkansas*. Concord, OK: Author, 1993. 13p.

White County
1840
Presley, Cloie. *White County, Arkansas Census, 1840*. Searcy, AR: Author. 38p.
1850
McLane, Bobbie Lee Jones. *1850 Census of North Central Arkansas, Conway, Fulton, Independence, Izard, Jackson, Lawrence, Marion, Randolph, Searcy, Van Buren and White Counties*. Conway, AR: Arkansas Research, 1995. 139p.
Presley, Cloie. *White County, Arkansas Census, 1850*. Searcy, AR: Author. 38p.
1860
Sorensen, Willa Thomas. *Index to the 1860 Census of White County, Arkansas*. Tomball, TX: Genealogical Publications, 1977. 56p.

Yell County
1850
McLane, Bobbie Lee Jones. *1850 Census of Central Arkansas, Hot Springs, Jefferson, Montgomery, Perry, Prairie, Pulaski, Saline, Scott and Yell Counties*. Conway, AR: Arkansas Research, 1995. 107p.
Presley, Cloie. *Yell County, Arkansas Census of 1850*. Searcy, AR: Author. 45p.
1860
Dhonau, Robert Will Fred. *Yell County, Arkansas 1860 Federal Census*. Little Rock, AR: Author, 1982. 117p.
Sorensen, Willa Thomas. *Index to the 1860 Census of Yell County, Arkansas*. Tomball, TX: Genealogical Publications, 1977.
1870
Murdoch, Katie, Carlene Austin, and Mary V. Humphrey. *Yell County, Arkansas, 1870 Federal Census*. Russelville, AR: Authors, 1983. 126p.
1880
Daniels, Cornelia, and Mary Humphrey. *Yell County, Arkansas 1880 United States Census*. Dadanell, AR: Authors, 1984. 154p.

California

De Leon, Arnoldo. *Tejanos and the Numbers Game, a Socio-historical Interpretation from the Federal Censuses, 1850-1900*. Albuquerque, NM: University of New Mexico Press, 1989. 119p.

1850

Bowman, Alan P. *Index to the 1850 Census of the State of California*. Baltimore, MD: Clearfield, 1972, 1997. 605p.

Census Index: U.S. Selected States/Counties, 1850. Family Archive CD 317. Novato, CA: Broderbund Software. CD-ROM.

Jackson, Ronald Vern. *California Census Index, Online Edition*. Orem, UT: Ancestry.com, Inc., 1999.
http://www.ancestry.com

_____. *Mortality Schedules Index, Online Edition*. Orem, UT: Ancestry.com, Inc., 1999.
http://www.ancestry.com

_____, and Gary Ronald Teeples. *California 1850 Census Index*. Bountiful, UT: Accelerated Indexing Systems, 1978. 57; 144p.

Lloyd, Glenda Gardner. *California Mortality Schedules, 1850, 1860, 1870, 1880*. Citrus Heights, CA: Root Cellar, Sacramento Genealogical Society, 1995. 259p.

Ohioans in the California Census of 1850. Hillsboro, OH: Southern California Chapter, OGS, 1988. 88p.

U.S. Federal Population Census Schedules. 1850, M432, Microfilm Reel Nos. 33-36.

1852

Index to California Census of 1852. Piedmont, CA: DAR, California State Society, 1935. 3 vols.

1860

Census Index: U.S. Selected States/Counties, 1860. Family Archive CD 318. Novato, CA: Broderbund Software. CD-ROM.

Dilts, Bryan Lee. *1860 California Census Index, Heads of Households and other Surnames in Households Index*. Salt Lake City, UT: Index Pub., 1984. 960p.; 8 fiche.

Jackson, Ronald Vern. *California Census Index, Online Edition*. Orem, UT: Ancestry.com, Inc., 1999.
http://www.ancestry.com

_____. *California 1860*. Boutiful, UT: Accelerated Indexing Systems, 1981. 726p.

Lloyd, Glenda Gardner. *California Mortality Schedules, 1850, 1860, 1870, 1880*. Citrus Heights, CA: Root Cellar, Sacramento Genealogical Society, 1995. 259p.

Steuart, Raeone Christensen. *California 1860 Census Index*. Bountiful, UT: Heritage Quest, 1999. 2 vols.

U.S. Federal Population Census Schedules. 1860, M653, Microfilm Reel Nos. 55-72.

1870

California DAR, *U.S. Census, 1870 California Mortality List*. Genealogical Records Committee Report,, s1, v104, California, DAR, 1961. 185, 76p.

Census Index: U.S. Selected States/Counties, 1870. Family Archive CD 319. Novato, CA: Broderbund Software. CD-ROM.

Jackson, Ronald Vern. *California Census Index, Online Edition*. Orem, UT: Ancestry.com, Inc., 1999.
http://www.ancestry.com

_____. *California 1870 Federal Census Index, Except the City of San Francisco*. Salt Lake City, UT: Accelerated Indexing Systems, 1988. 786p.

Lloyd, Glenda Gardner. *California Mortality Schedules, 1850, 1860, 1870, 1880*. Citrus Heights, CA: Root Cellar, Sacramento Genealogical Society, 1995. 259p.

Pompey, Sherman Lee. *Missourians in the San Francisco, California Death Records 1848-1863; Missourians in the 1870 Mortality Census Records of California; Missourians in the Death Records of California; Missourians in the Death Records of Marysville, Yuma County, California, 1870-1900*.

U.S. Federal Population Census Schedules. 1870, M593, Microfilm Reel Nos. 68-93.

1880

Lloyd, Glenda Gardner. *California Mortality Schedules, 1850, 1860, 1870, 1880*. Citrus Heights, CA: Root Cellar, Sacramento Genealogical Society, 1995. 259p.

U.S. Federal Population Census Schedules. 1880, T9, Microfilm Reel Nos. 61-86.

U.S. Federal Population Census Schedules. 1880, Soundex. T737, 34 Microfilm Reels.

1890

Jackson, Ronald Vern. *California Census Index, Online Edition (Veterans Schedules; Naval Veterans Schedule)*. Orem, UT: Ancestry.com, Inc., 1999.

http://www.ancestry.com

1900

U.S. Federal Population Census Schedules. 1900, T623. Microfilm Reel Nos. 81-116.

U.S. Federal Population Census Schedules. 1900, Soundex. T1034, 193 Microfilm Reels.

U.S. Federal Population Census Schedules. 1900, Military & Naval Bases. T1081, Microfilm Reel Nos. 1838-1842.

U.S. Federal Population Census Schedules. 1900, Military & Naval Bases, Soundex. T1081, 32 Microfilm Reels.

1905, 1906

Kelsey, C. E. *Census of Non-reservation California Indians, 1905-1906*. Berkeley, CA: Archaeological Research Facility, Dept. of Anthropology, 1971. 118p.

1910

U.S. Federal Population Census Schedules. 1910, T624, Microfilm Reel Nos. 6-111.

U.S. Federal Population Census Schedules. 1910, Miracode (Index) T1261, 272 Microfilm Reels.

Watson, Larry. S. *California Special Indian Census, 1910*. Yuma, AZ: Histree, 1993. 211p.

1920

U.S. Federal Population Census Schedules. 1920, T625, Microfilm Reel Nos. 87-154.

U.S. Federal Population Census Schedules. 1920, Soundex. M1551, 327 Microfilm Reels.

Alameda County
1852

Coppage, A. Maxim, and F. A. Scott. *Contra Costa County, California State Census, 1852, (Including 2/3 Present Day Alameda County)*. Walnut Creek, CA: Authors, 1994. 209-256p.

Alpine County
1870

Thornburg, Nancy C. *Ninth Census of the United States, 1870, Alpine County, California*. Markleeville, CA: Alpine County Museum, 1991. 194p.

1880

Thornburg, Nancy C. *Tenth Census of the United States, 1880, Alpine County, California*. Markleeville, CA: Alpine County Museum, 1991. 119p.

1900

Thornburg, Nancy C. *Twelfth Census of the United States, Schedule No. 1, Population, 1900, Alpine County, California, Including Special Inquiries Relating to Indians*. Markleeville, CA: Alpine County Museum, 1994. 150p.

1910

Thornburg, Nancy C. *Thirteenth Census of the United States, 1910, Population, Alpine County, California, Including Special Inquiries Relating to Indians*. Markleeville, CA: Alpine County Museum, 1990. 125p.

Butte County
1860
Butte County, California 1860 Federal Census Index. Paradise, CA: Paradise Genealogical Society, 1993. 161p.
1880
Butte County, California 1880 Federal Census Index. Paradise, CA: Paradise Genealogical Society, 1996. 153p.

Contra Costa County
1852
Coppage, A. Maxim, and F. A. Scott. *Contra Costa County, California State Census, 1852, (Including 2/3 Present Day Alameda County).* Walnut Creek, CA: Authors, 1994. 209-256p.

Del Norte County
1900
Felkel, Mildred. *Del Norte County, California 1900 Census.* Medford, OR: Rogue Valley Genealogical Society, 1984. 60p.

Humboldt County
1860
1860 Census Index of Humboldt County, California. Fortuna, CA: Redwood Genealogical Society. 25p.
1870
Humboldt County, California 1870 Census. Fortuna, CA: Redwood Genealogical Society, 1992. 84p.

Klamath County
1870
Dunham, Pat, and Leona Mackley. *There Really Was a Klamath County! 1851-1874.* Fortuna, CA: Redwood Genealogical Society, 1985. 111p.

Lake County
1870
1870 Census and 1870 Mortality Schedule of Lake County, California (With Additions and Corrections). Lakeport, CA: Lake County Genealogical Society, 1990. 42p.

Lassen County
1870
USGenWeb Census Project. California, 1870 Lassen County.
ftp://ftp.rootsweb.com/pub/ca/lassen/1870/

Los Angeles County
African Americans in Los Angeles and Los Angeles Township, Extracts from United States Censuses. Los Angeles, CA: California African American Genealogical Society, 1995. Unpgd.
1836
1836 Mexican Census of Los Angeles and Orange County Area, Including the Rancho Santiago de Santa Ana after which the Rancho Santiago Community was Named. Santa Ana, CA: Santa Ana College, 1976. 104p.
1850
Alliot, Hector. *Census of City and County of Los Angeles, 1850.* Los Angeles, CA: Times Mirror Press, 1929.
_____. *Online Database Edition.* Orem, UT: Ancestry.com, Inc., 1999.
http://www.ancestry.com

Newmark, Maurice Harris, and Marco Ross, Newmark. *Census of the City and County of Los Angeles, California, for the Year 1850; Together with an Analysis and an Appendix*. Los Angeles, CA: Times-Mirror Press, 1929. 139p.

Mariposa County
1850
Chastain, Ila, Frances Parker, and L. Carter Fite. *Population Schedule of the United States Census for 1850 Mariposa County, California*. Merced, CA: Merced County Genealogical Society, 1992. 100p.

Mendocino County
1850
Pompey, Sherman Lee. *The 1850 Census Records of Mendocino County, California*. Independence, CA: Historical & Genealogical Pub. Co., 1965. 2p.
1852-1880
Mendocino County, California, 1852, 1860, 1870, 1880 Census. Mendocino, CA: Kelley Historical Museum, Typescript.

Napa County
1850
Ogle, Sandra K. Lyon. *1850 Napa County Census Index, Being a Transcription and an Every Name Index to the National Archives Microfilm M432, Roll 35*. Napa, CA: Ancestors Unlimited, 1985. 14p.
1860
McAlear, Robert. *1860 Census, Clear Lake Township, Napa County, California, with Additions and Corrections*. Decorah, IA: Anundsen, 1982. 16p.

Orange County
1836
1836 Mexican Census of Los Angeles and Orange County Area, Including the Rancho Santiago de Santa Ana after which the Rancho Santiago Community was Named. Santa Ana, CA: Santa Ana College, 1976. 104p.

Plumar County
1860
Styles, Florence. *Sierra County 1860 Census, Plumar County 1860, Yuba County 1880 Census Abstracts*. Paradise, CA: Paradise Genealogical Society.

Riverside County
1880
1880 Federal Census, Riverside, California. Riverside, CA: Riverside Genealogical Society, 1991. 55p.

Sacramento County
1870, 1880
Sacramento County, California Census 1870, and 1880. Citrus Heights, CA: Sacramento Genealogical Society, 1991. 272p.

San Diego County
1850, 1852
San Diego Census, 1850 Federal, 1852 California. San Diego, CA: San Diego Genealogical Society, 1984. 64p.
1860
San Diego Census, 1860 Federal. San Diego, CA: San Diego Genealogical Society, 1984. 64p.

1870

San Diego Census, 1870 Federal. San Diego, CA: San Diego Genealogical Society, 1984. Unpgd.

1900

White, Evelyn Jean. *San Diego County, California Census Index, 1900*. Carlsbad, CA: North San Diego County Genealogical Society, 1981. 136p.

San Francisco
1870

California 1870 San Francisco, California Federal Census Index. West Jordan, UT: Genealogical Services, 1996. Unpgd.

Jackson, Ronald Vern. *California Census Index, Online Edition*. Orem, UT: Ancestry.com, Inc., 1999. **http://www.ancestry.com**

_____. *California 1870 San Francisco County Federal Census Index*. Salt Lake City, UT: Accelerated Indexing Systems, 1988. Unpgd.

_____. _____. West Jordan, UT: Genealogical Services, 1989. Unpgd.

San Joaquin County
1850

1850 Census of San Joaquin County, California. Stockton, CA: San Joaquin Genealogical Society, 1959. 95p.

San Luis Obispo County
1870

San Luis Obispo County, 1870 United States Census, San Luis Obispo County, California. Morro Bay, CA: California Central Coast Genealogical Society, 1973. 152p.

San Mateo County
1870

San Mateo County, California, 1870 Federal Census Index. San Mateo, CA: San Mateo County Genealogical Society, 1985. 82p.

Santa Barbara County
1834

Jackson, Ronald Vern. *California Census Index, Online Edition*. Orem, UT: Ancestry.com, Inc., 1999. **http://www.ancestry.com**

1850

USGenWeb Census Project. California, 1850 Santa Barbara County. **ftp://ftp.rootsweb.com/pub/ca/santabarbara/1850/**

Shasta County
1850, 1860

Belden, Beryl Ramey. *Shasta County, California, 1850-1860 U.S. Census*. Anderson, CA: Shasta Genealogical Society, 1979. 101p.

1880

1880 Census of Shasta County, California. Redding, CA: Shasta Genealogical Society, 1983. 132p.

Sierra County
1860

Gould, Helen Weaver. *Sierra County 1860 Census Index*. Paradise, CA: Paradise County Genealogical Society. Unpgd.

Styles, Florence. *Sierra County 1860 Census, Plumar County 1860, Yuba County 1880 Census Abstracts.* Paradise, CA: Paradise Genealogical Society. Unpgd.

Siskiyou County
1867
Dye, John Andrew Rubidoux. *The 1867 Grand Register for Siskiyou County California.* Kent, WA: Author, 1988. 24p.
1892
Dye, John Andrew Rubidoux. *The 1892 Grand Register for Siskiyou County California.* Kent, WA: Author, 1986. 60p.

Solano County
1852
Cowat, Cordell. *Solano County, California, 1852 State Census Index.* Fairfield, CA: Solano County Genealogical Society, 1992. 60p.
1870
Ninth United States Census, 1870, Index of Solano County, California. Fairfield, CA: Solano County Genealogical Society, 1988. 164p.

Sonoma County
1850
Harris, Dennis E. *1850 United States Federal Census, Schedule 1, Population an Alphabetical Index and Reprint of the Schedules for the Residents of Sonoma County, California, October 20 — November 2, 1850.* Santa Rosa, CA: Sonoma County, 1983. 34p.
1852
Harris, Dennis E. *1852 California State Census, Schedule 1, Population and Schedules 2 & 3, Productions and Capital, an Alphabetical Index and Reprint of the Schedules for the Residents of Sonoma County, California, June 21 — October 21 1852.* Santa Rosa, CA: Sonoma County, 1983. 146p.
1860
Harris, Dennis E. *Sonoma County, 1860 Eighth Census of the United States.* Santa Rosa, CA: Sonoma County Historical Records Commission, 1992. 387-695p.

Stanislaus County
1860
Census Index 1860 Stanislaus County, California. Modesto, CA: Genealogical Society of Stanislaus County California, 1997. 246p.
1870, 1880
Starr, Mildred G. *Stanislaus County, California Census Extract, 1870 Census Index 1880.* Modesto, CA: Genealogical Society of Stanislaus County, California, 1999. 312p.
1900
Census Index 1900, Census Index 1910 Stanislaus County, California. Modesto, CA: Genealogical Society of Stanislaus County California, 1993. 353p.

Tulare County
1860
Benson, Donna D. *1860 Census, Tulare County, California, Alphabetized, Minimal Listing with an Enumeration of the Indian Population.* Visalia, CA: Sequoia Genealogical Society, 1974. 78p.
1870
Benson, Donna D. *1870 Census, Tulare County, California, Alphabetized, Minimal Listing with an Enumeration of the Chinese Population.* Visalia, CA: Sequoia Genealogical Society, 1982. 93p.

1880

Benson, Donna D. *1880 Census, Tulare County, California, Alphabetized by Enumeration Districts or Subdivisions*. Visalia, CA: Sequoia Genealogical Society, 1985. Unpgd.

1900

Benson, Donna D. *Tulare County, California 1900 Census*. Visalia, CA: Sequoia Genealogical Society, 1985. Unpgd.

Yolo County
1850

Pompey, Sherman Lee. *Missourians in the 1850 Census of Yolo County, California*. Bakersfield, California, Historical and Genealogical Pub. Co., 1965. 4p.

Yuba County
1850

Federal Census, 1850, Yuba County, California. Yuba City, CA: Sutter Yuba Genealogical Society, 1978. 91p.

1860

Styles, Florence. *Sierra County 1860 Census, Plumar County 1860, Yuba County 1880 Census Abstracts*. Paradise, CA: Paradise Genealogical Society. Unpgd.

Colorado

1860

Census Index: U.S. Selected States/Counties, 1860. Family Archive CD 318. Novato, CA: Broderbund Software. CD-ROM.

Jackson, Ronald Vern. *Colorado Census Index, Online Edition*. Orem, UT: Ancestry.com, Inc., 1999.
http://www.ancestry.com

_____. *Colorado 1860*. North Salt Lake City, UT: Accelerated Indexing Systems International, 1981. 55; 20p.

1870

Census Index: U.S. Selected States/Counties, 1870. Family Archive CD 319. Novato, CA: Broderbund Software. CD-ROM.

1870 Colorado Territory Census Index. Greeley, CO: Weld County Genealogical Society, 1977. 13, 377p.

Jackson, Ronald Vern. *Colorado Census Index, Online Edition*. Orem, UT: Ancestry.com, Inc., 1999.
http://www.ancestry.com

_____. *Colorado 1870 Census Index*. North Salt Lake City, UT: Accelerated Indexing Systems International, 1976. 512p.

_____. *Colorado 1870 Mortality Schedule*. Bountiful, UT: Accelerated Indexing Systems, 1981. 15p.

_____. *Mortality Schedules Index, Online Edition*. Orem, UT: Ancestry.com, Inc., 1999.
http://www.ancestry.com

U.S. Federal Population Census Schedules. 1870, M593, Microfilm Reel Nos. 94-95.

1880

Census Index: U.S. Selected States/Counties, 1880. Family Archive CD 320. Novato, CA: Broderbund Software. CD-ROM.

Jackson, Ronald Vern. *Colorado Census Index, Online Edition*. Orem, UT: Ancestry.com, Inc., 1999.
http://www.ancestry.com

_____. *Colorado 1880 Census Index*. Bountiful, UT: Accelerated Indexing Systems International, 1980. 48; 470p.

_____. *Colorado 1880 Mortality Schedule*. Bountiful, UT: Accelerated Indexing Systems, 1981. 34p.

_____. *Mortality Schedules Index, Online Edition*. Orem, UT: Ancestry.com, Inc., 1999.
http://www.ancestry.com
U.S. Federal Population Census Schedules. 1880, T9, Microfilm Reel Nos. 87-93.
U.S. Federal Population Census Schedules. 1880, Soundex. T738, 25 Microfilm Reels.

1900

U.S. Federal Population Census Schedules. 1900, T623, Microfilm Reel Nos. 117-130.
U.S. Federal Population Census Schedules. 1900, Soundex. T1035, 68 Microfilm Reels.
U.S. Federal Population Census Schedules. 1900, Military & Naval Bases. T1081, Microfilm Reel Nos. 1838-1842.
U.S. Federal Population Census Schedules. 1900, Military & Naval Bases, Soundex. T1081, 32 Microfilm Reels.

1910

U.S. Federal Population Census Schedules. 1910, T624, Microfilm Reel Nos. 112-126. (No Soundex/Miracode Index was prepared by the Government for this State.)

1920

U.S. Federal Population Census Schedules. 1920, T625, Microfilm Reel Nos. 155-173.
U.S. Federal Population Census Schedules. 1920, Soundex. M1552, 80 Microfilm Reels.

Arapahoe County
1880
USGenWeb Census Project. Colorado, 1880 Arapahoe County.
ftp://ftp.rootsweb.com/pub/census/co/araphahoe/1880/

Baca County
1910
Millican, Valorie. *United States Population Census, 1910 Index Baca County, Colorado*. Author. 45p.

Bent County
1885
Glavinick, Jacquelyn Gee. *Bent County, Colorado, 1885 State Census*. Pueblo, CO: Southeastern Colorado Genealogical Society, 1992. 51p.

Black Hawk (Gilpin County)
1870
Granruth, Alan. *Abstract of the 1870 United States Census for Black Hawk, Gilpin County, Colorado*, Author, 1995. 28p.

Boulder County
1860-1885
Gladden, Sanford Charles. *Alphabetized Listing of Census Returns and Mortality Schedules for Boulder County, Colorado 1860-1885*. Boulder, CO: University of Colorado Library, 1978. Unpgd.
1900
Boulder County, Colorado 1900 Census Index. Boulder, CO: Boulder Genealogical Society, 1986. 187p.

Central City (Gilpin County)
1870
Granruth, Alan. *Abstract of the 1870 United States Census for Central City Gilpin County, Colorado*: Author, 1995. 28p.

Clear Creek County
1880

Kyler, Dorothy, and Fae Tarrant. *Clear Creek County, Colorado Census of 1880*. Lakewood, CO: Foothills Genealogical Society of Colorado, 1987. 308p.

1885

Kyler, Dorothy, and Fae Tarrant. *Clear Creek County, Colorado Census of 1885*. Lakewood, CO: Foothills Genealogical Society of Colorado, 1994. 162p.

_____. *Combined 1885 Clear Creek County, Colorado and State Census*. Lakewood, CO: Foothills Genealogical Society of Colorado, 1994. 213p.

Custer County
1885-1910

Custer County, Colorado, Census Index, 1885 State Census, 1900 & 1910 Federal Census. Pueblo, CO: Southeastern Colorado Genealogy Society, 1987. 83p.

Delta County
1885

Lynn, John W. *The 1885 Census of Delta County, Colorado*. Grand Junction, CO: Lynn Research, 1987. 40p.

Dolores County
1885

Lynn, John W. *The 1885 Census of Dolores County, Colorado*. Grand Junction, CO: Lynn Research, 1987. 22p.

El Paso County
1885

Index for the Colorado, El Paso County 1885 Census. Pikes Peak Genealogical Society, 1992. 176p.

Garfield County
1900

Colorado DAR. *Index, 1900 Federal Census, Garfield County, Colorado*. Genealogical Records Committee Report, s2, v22. Colorado DAR, 1993. 55p.

Gilpin County
1860

Granruth, Alan. *Index to Gilpin County, Colorado 1860, United States Census*. Lakewood, CO: Foothills Genealogical Society of Colorado, 1995. 134p.

1870

Granruth, Alan. *Index to Gilpin County, Colorado 1870, United States Census*. Lakewood, CO: Foothills Genealogical Society of Colorado, 1995. 146p.

1885

McKeown, Julie. *Gilpin County, Colorado 1885 State Census*. Author, 1995. 332p.

Greenwood County
1870

USGenWeb Census Project. Colorado, 1870 Greenwood County. (Partial).
ftp://ftp.rootsweb.com/pub/census/co/greenwood/1870/

Gunnison County

McCollum, Oscar D., Jr. *Census Records Gunnison County, Colorado, Present Precinct 2*. Marble, CO: Marble Historical Society, 1983. 50p.

Huerfano County
1885
Riffe, Noreen I. *Huerfano County, Colorado, 1885 Census*. Pueblo, CO: Southeastern Colorado Genealogical Society, 1995. 135p.

Navajo Springs
Robinson, Doreen. *Census Records for Southern Utes of Navajo Springs, Colorado. Online Database Edition*. Orem, UT: Ancestry.com, Inc., 1998.
http://www.ancestry.com

Park County
1885
Longino, Opal Kendall. *Park County, Colorado 1885 State Census*. Lakewood, CO: Foothills Genealogical Society of Colorado, 1995. 91p.

Pueblo County
1885
Riffe, Noreen I., and Betty Polunci. *1885 Census, Pueblo County, Colorado*. Pueblo, CO: Southeastern Colorado Genealogical Society, 1995. 45p.

Weld County
1870
1870 Census of the Territory of Colorado. Greely, CO: Weld County Genealogical Society, 1977. 377p.
1885
Glavinick, Jacquelyn Gee. *1885 State Census of Weld County, Colorado*. Pueblo, CO: Weld County Genealogical Society, 1984. 408p.
1900
Glavinick, Jacquelyn Gee. *Index to Twelfth Census of the United States, 1900, Weld County Colorado*. Greeley, CO: Genealogical Society of Weld County, 1986. 163p.
1910
Glavinick, Jacquelyn Gee. *Weld County, Colorado Index to Thirteenth Census of the United States, 1910*. Pueblo, CO: Weld County Genealogical Society, 1993. 358p.

Connecticut

1670
Holbrook, Jay Mack. *Connecticut 1670 Census*. Oxford, MA: Holbrook Research Institute, 1977. 74p.

1790
Jackson, Ronald Vern. *Connecticut 1790, Rhode Island 1790 Federal Census Indexes*. North Salt Lake City, UT: Accelerated Indexing Systems International, 1990. 709, 197p.
_____. *Connecticut Census Index, Online Edition*. Orem, UT: Ancestry.com, Inc., 1999.
http://www.ancestry.com
U.S. Bureau of the Census. *Heads of Families at the First Census of the United States Taken in the Year 1790, Connecticut*. Washington, DC: Government Printing Office, 1908. 227p.
_____. _____. Bountiful, UT: Accelerated Indexing Systems, 1978. 227p.
_____. _____. *Online Database Edition*. Orem, UT: Ancestry.com, Inc., 1999.
http://www.ancestry.com
_____. *U.S. Federal Population Census Schedules*. 1790, T498, Microfilm Reel No. 1.
U.S. Federal Population Census Schedules. 1790, M637, Microfilm Reel No. 1.

1800

Jackson, Ronald Vern. *Connecticut Census Index, Online Edition*. Orem, UT: Ancestry.com, Inc., 1999.
http://www.ancestry.com
_____, and Gary Ronald Teeples. *Connecticut 1800 Census Index*. Bountiful, UT: Accelerated Indexing Systems, 1974. 157p.
Steuart, Raeone Christensen. *Connecticut 1800 Census Index*. Bountiful, UT: Heritage Quest, 2000. 260p.
_____. *United States 1800 Census Index*. Bountiful, UT: Heritage Quest, 2000. CD-ROM.
U.S. Federal Population Census Schedules, 1800. M32, Microfilm Reel Nos. 1-3.

1810

Jackson, Ronald Vern. *Connecticut Census Index, Online Edition*. Orem, UT: Ancestry.com, Inc., 1999.
http://www.ancestry.com
_____. *Connecticut 1810 Census Index*. Bountiful, UT: Accelerated Indexing Systems, 1976. 109p.
U.S. Census Index Series, New England, New York, 1810. Orem, UT: Automated Archives, 1992. CD-ROM.
U.S. Federal Population Census Schedules, 1810. M252, Microfilm Reel Nos. 1-3.

1820

Jackson, Ronald Vern. *Connecticut Census Index, Online Edition*. Orem, UT: Ancestry.com, Inc., 1999.
http://www.ancestry.com
_____, and Gary Ronald Teeples. *Connecticut 1820 Census Index*. Bountiful, UT: Accelerated Indexing Systems, 1977. 124p.
U.S. Federal Population Census Schedules. 1820, M33, Microfilm Reel Nos. 1-3.

1830

Census Index: U.S. Selected States/Counties, 1830. Family Archive CD 315. Novato, CA: Broderbund Software. CD-ROM.
Jackson, Ronald Vern. *Connecticut Census Index, Online Edition*. Orem, UT: Ancestry.com, Inc., 1999.
http://www.ancestry.com
_____, and Gary Ronald Teeples. *Connecticut 1830 Census Index*. Bountiful, UT: Accelerated Indexing Systems, 1977. 138p.
U.S. Census Index, 1830-1839, New England, New York, Pennsylvania. Orem, UT: Automated Archives, 1992. 1 CD-ROM.
U.S. Federal Population Census Schedules. 1830, M19, Microfilm Reel Nos. 6-11.

1840

Census Index: U.S. Selected States/Counties, 1840. Family Archive CD 316. Novato, CA: Broderbund Software. CD-ROM.
Jackson, Ronald Vern. *Connecticut Census Index, Online Edition*. Orem, UT: Ancestry.com, Inc., 1999.
http://www.ancestry.com
_____, and Gary Ronald Teeples. *Connecticut 1840 Census Index*. Bountiful, UT: Accelerated Indexing Systems, 1978. 150p.
U.S. Federal Population Census Schedules. 1840, M704, Microfilm Reel Nos. 21-32.

1850

Census Index: U.S. Selected States/Counties, 1850. Family Archive CD 317. Novato, CA: Broderbund Software. CD-ROM.
Census Microfilm Records: Connecticut and Rhode Island, 1850. Family Archive CD 308. Novato, CA: Broderbund Software. CD-ROM.
Jackson, Ronald Vern. *Connecticut Census Index, Online Edition*. Orem, UT: Ancestry.com, Inc., 1999.
http://www.ancestry.com
_____, and Gary Ronald Teeples. *Connecticut 1850 Census Index*. Bountiful, UT: Accelerated Indexing Systems, 1978. 339p.

_____. *Connecticut Mortality Schedule*. Bountiful, UT: Accelerated Indexing Systems, 1981. 107p.
_____. *Mortality Schedules Index, Online Edition*. Orem, UT: Ancestry.com, Inc., 1999.
http://www.ancestry.com
U.S. Census Index Series, New England, 1850. Orem, UT: Automated Archives, 1991. CD-ROM.
U.S. Federal Population Census Schedules. 1850, M432, Microfilm Reel Nos. 37-51.

1860

Census Index: U.S. Selected States/Counties, 1860. Family Archive CD 318. Novato, CA: Broderbund Software. CD-ROM.
Connecticut 1860 Census Index. Bountiful, UT: Heritage Quest, 1999.
Dilts, Bryan Lee. *1860 Connecticut Census Index, Heads of Households and other Surnames in Households Index*. Salt Lake City, UT: Index Pub., 1985. 707p.
Jackson, Ronald Vern. *Connecticut 1860*. Salt Lake City, UT: Accelerated Indexing Systems International, 1986. 687p.
_____. *Connecticut 1860 Mortality Census Index*. North Salt Lake City, UT: Accelerated Indexing Systems International, 1981. 150p.
_____. *Mortality Schedules Index, Online Edition*. Orem, UT: Ancestry.com, Inc., 1999.
http://www.ancestry.com
Steuart, Raeone Christensen. *Connecticut 1860 Census Index*. Bountiful, UT: Heritage Quest, 1999. 962p.
U.S. Census Index, 1860, Connecticut. Orem, UT: Automated Archives, 1994. CD-ROM.
U.S. Federal Population Census Schedules. 1860, M653, Microfilm Reel Nos. 73-93.

1870

Jackson, Ronald Vern, Wylma Winmill, and Shirley P. Zachrison. *Connecticut 1870 Mortality Census Index*. North Salt Lake City, UT: Accelerated Indexing Systems International, 1981. 112p.
_____. *Mortality Schedules Index, Online Edition*. Orem, UT: Ancestry.com, Inc., 1999.
http://www.ancestry.com
Steuart, Raeone Christensen. *Connecticut 1870 Census Index*. Bountiful, UT: Heritage Quest, 2000. 2 vols.
_____. *Connecticut and Rhode Island 1870 Census Index*. Bountiful, UT: Heritage Quest, 2000. CD-ROM.
U.S. Federal Population Census Schedules. 1870, M593, Microfilm Reel Nos. 96-117.

1880

Ledoux, Albert H. *The Franco-Americans of Connecticut, 1880*. Altoona, PA: Author, 1977. 257p.
U.S. Federal Population Census Schedules. 1880, T9, Microfilm Reel Nos. 94-110.
U.S. Federal Population Census Schedules. 1880, Soundex. T739, 25 Microfilm Reels.

1890

Jackson, Ronald Vern. *Connecticut Census Index, Online Edition (Veterans Schedule)*. Orem, UT: Ancestry.com, Inc., 1999.
http://www.ancestry.com

1900

U.S. Federal Population Census Schedules. 1900, T623, Microfilm Reel Nos. 131-152.
U.S. Federal Population Census Schedules. 1900, Soundex. T1033, 107 Microfilm Reels.
U.S. Federal Population Census Schedules. 1900, Military & Naval Bases. T1081, Microfilm Reel Nos. 1838-1842.
U.S. Federal Population Census Schedules. 1900, Military & Naval Bases, Soundex. T1081, 32 Microfilm Reels.

1910

U.S. Federal Population Census Schedules. 1910, T624, Microfilm Reel Nos. 127-144. (No Soundex/Miracode Index was prepared by the Government for this State.)

1917

Kemp, Thomas Jay. "The Connecticut State Military Preparedness Census of 1917." *Connecticut Ancestry*. Vol. 22 (February 1980) pp. 117-122.

State Military Preparedness Census. 1917. Originals at Connecticut State Library, RG 29.

1920

U.S. Federal Population Census Schedules. 1920, T625, Microfilm Reel Nos. 174-199.

U.S. Federal Population Census Schedules. 1920, Soundex. M1553, 111 Microfilm Reels.

Bridgewater (Litchfield County)
1860

Holt, Nellie Beardsley and Charles Ebenezer Holt. *The Hop Brook Section*. Bridgewater, CT: Author 1952. 131p.

Durham (Middlesex County)
1810

Original Return. Connecticut State Library. RG 62.

Fairfield County
1800

Volkel, Lowell M. *An Index to the 1800 Census of Fairfield and Hartford Counties, State of Connecticut*. Danville, IL: Author, 1968. 89p.

Hartford County
1800

Volkel, Lowell M. *An Index to the 1800 Census of Fairfield and Hartford Counties, State of Connecticut*. Danville, IL: Author, 1968. 89p.

Litchfield County
1800

Volkel, Lowell M. *An Index to the 1800 Census of Litchfield, New Haven, Tolland and Windham Counties, State of Connecticut*. Danville, IL: Author, 1969. Unpgd.

Middlesex County
1800

Volkel, Lowell M. *An Index to the 1800 Census of Middlesex and New London Counties, State of Connecticut*. Danville, IL: Author, 1969. 58p.

New Cannan (Fairfield County)
1790, 1800

Bayless, Lois B. *Town of New Canaan Census 1790-1800*. New Canaan, CT: Author, 1969.

1810

Bayless, Lois B. *Town of New Canaan Census 1810-1840*. New Canaan, CT: Author, 1968. 89p.

1820

Bayless, Lois B. *Town of New Canaan Census 1810-1840*. New Canaan, CT: Author, 1968. 89p.

Card, Lester. *1820 Census of New Canaan, Connecticut*. South Norwalk, CT: Author, 1941. 17p.

1830, 1840

Bayless, Lois B. *Town of New Canaan Census 1810-1840*. New Canaan, CT: Author, 1968. 89p.

1850

Bayless, Lois B. *Town of New Canaan Census 1850*. New Canaan, CT: Author, 1968. 71p.

1860
Bayless, Lois B. *Town of New Canaan Census 1860.* New Canaan, CT: Author, 1968. 83p.
1870
Bayless, Lois B. *Town of New Canaan Census 1870.* New Canaan, CT: Author. 74p.
1880
Bayless, Lois B. *Town of New Canaan Census 1880.* New Canaan, CT: Author, 1969. 81p.

New Haven (New Haven County)
1790
Connecticut, DAR. *New Haven County, Census 1790 Errata.* Genealogical Records Committee Report, s1, v013, pp21-26. Connecticut DAR, 1926.
1800
Volkel, Lowell M. *An Index to the 1800 Census of Litchfield, New Haven, Tolland and Windham Counties, State of Connecticut.* Danville, IL: Author, 1969. Unpgd.

New London County
1800
Volkel, Lowell M. *An Index to the 1800 Census of Middlesex and New London Counties, State of Connecticut.* Danville, IL: Author, 1969. 58p.

Newington (Hartford County)
1776
Welles, Edwin Stanley. *A Census of Newington, Connecticut Taken According to Households in 1776 by Josiah William Together with Some Documents Relating to the Early History of the Parish.* Hartford, CT: Frederic B. Hartranft, 1909. 41p.

Tolland County
1800
Volkel, Lowell M. *An Index to the 1800 Census of Litchfield, New Haven, Tolland and Windham Counties, State of Connecticut.* Danville, IL: Author, 1969. Unpgd.

Waterbury (New Haven County)
1876
Judd, Sturges M. *1876 Census of Waterbury.* Waterbury, CT: Author.

Windham County
1800
Volkel, Lowell M. *An Index to the 1800 Census of Litchfield, New Haven, Tolland and Windham Counties, State of Connecticut.* Danville, IL: Author, 1969. Unpgd.

Woodbury (Litchfield County)
1880
Woodbury's Census Containing a Complete List of the Names of the Inhabitants of Woodbury, as Taken from the Census Returns of June, 1880. Woodbury, CT: A.E. Knox Publisher, 1880. 21p.

Delaware

Jackson, Ronald Vern, and Gary Ronald Teeples. *Early Delaware Census Records, 1665-1697.* Bountiful, UT: Accelerated Indexing Systems, 1977. 32p.

1671

Delaware DAR. *Delaware Census 1671*, Genealogical Records Committee Report, s2, v018. Delaware DAR, 1991. 122p.

1693

Craig, Peter Stebbins. *The 1693 Census of the Swedes on the Delaware Family Histories of the Swedish Lutheran Church Members Residing in Pennsylvania, Delaware, West New Jersey and Cecil County, Maryland, 1638-1693*. Studies in Swedish American Genealogy No. 3. Winter Park, FL: SAG Publications, 1993. 213p.

1782

Nelson, Ralph D., Jr. *Delaware 1782 Tax Assessment and Census Lists*. Wilmington, DE: Delaware Genealogical Society, 1994. 380p.

1790

Jackson, Ronald Vern. *Early Delaware, 1790*. Bountiful, UT: Accelerated Indexing Systems, 1981. 114p.

1800

Jackson, Ronald Vern. *Delaware Census Index, Online Edition*. Orem, UT: Ancestry.com, Inc., 1999. **http://www.ancestry.com**
_____, and Gary Ronald Teeples. *Delaware 1800 Census Index*. Bountiful, UT: Accelerated Indexing Systems, 1972. 171p.
Maddux, Gerald, and Doris Ollar Maddux. *1800 Census, Delaware*. Montgomery, AL: Authors, 1964. 200p.
Steuart, Raeone Christensen. *Delaware 1800 Census Index*. Bountiful, UT: Heritage Quest, 2000. 66p.
_____. *United States 1800 Census Index*. Bountiful, UT: Heritage Quest, 2000. 4 vols. CD-ROM.
U.S. Federal Population Census Schedules, 1800. M32, Microfilm Reel No. 4.

1810

Jackson, Ronald Vern. *Delaware Census Index, Online Edition*. Orem, UT: Ancestry.com, Inc., 1999. **http://www.ancestry.com**
_____, and Gary Ronald Teeples. *Delaware 1810 Census Index*. Bountiful, UT: Accelerated Indexing Systems, 1972, 1976. 26p.
U.S. Federal Population Census Schedules, 1810. M252, Microfilm Reel Nos. 4.

1820

Jackson, Ronald Vern. *Delaware Census Index, Online Edition*. Orem, UT: Ancestry.com, Inc., 1999. **http://www.ancestry.com**
_____, and Gary Ronald Teeples. *Delaware 1820 Census Index*. Bountiful, UT: Accelerated Indexing Systems, 1974. 27p.
U.S. Federal Population Census Schedules. 1820, M33, Microfilm Reel Nos. 4.

1830

Census Index: U.S. Selected States/Counties, 1830. Family Archive CD 315. Novato, CA: Broderbund Software. CD-ROM.
Jackson, Ronald Vern. *Delaware Census Index, Online Edition*. Orem, UT: Ancestry.com, Inc., 1999. **http://www.ancestry.com**
_____, and Gary Ronald Teeples. *Delaware 1830 Census Index*. Bountiful, UT: Accelerated Indexing Systems, 1977. 32p.
U.S. Federal Population Census Schedules. 1830, M19, Microfilm Reel Nos. 12-13.

1840

Census Index: U.S. Selected States/Counties, 1840. Family Archive CD 316. Novato, CA: Broderbund Software. CD-ROM.

Jackson, Ronald Vern. *Delaware Census Index, Online Edition*. Orem, UT: Ancestry.com, Inc., 1999.
http://www.ancestry.com

_____, and Gary Ronald Teeples. *Delaware 1840 Census Index*. Bountiful, UT: Accelerated Indexing Systems, 1977. 32p.

U.S. Federal Population Census Schedules. 1840, M704, Microfilm Reel Nos. 33-34.

1850

Census Index: U.S. Selected States/Counties, 1850. Family Archive CD 317. Novato, CA: Broderbund Software. CD-ROM.

Jackson, Ronald Vern. *Delaware Census Index, Online Edition*. Orem, UT: Ancestry.com, Inc., 1999.
http://www.ancestry.com

_____. *Mortality Schedules Index, Online Edition*. Orem, UT: Ancestry.com, Inc., 1999.
http://www.ancestry.com

_____, and Gary Ronald Teeples. *Delaware 1850 Census Index*. Bountiful, UT: Accelerated Indexing Systems, 1977. 83p.

_____. *Delaware 1850, 1860 Slave Schedules*. North Salt Lake City, UT: Accelerated Indexing Systems International, 1986. 59, 18p.

Olmsted, Virginia Langham. *Index to the 1850 Census of Delaware*. Baltimore, MD: Genealogical Pub. Co., 1977. 370p.

U.S. Census Index Series, Pennsylvania, Delaware and New Jersey, 1850. Orem, UT: Automated Archives, 1991. CD-ROM.

U.S. Federal Population Census Schedules. 1850, M432, Microfilm Reel Nos. 52-55.

1860

Census Index: U.S. Selected States/Counties, 1860. Family Archive CD 318. Novato, CA: Broderbund Software. CD-ROM.

Delaware 1860 Census Index. Bountiful, UT: Heritage Quest, 1999. 216p.

Dilts, Bryan Lee. *1860 Delaware Census Index, Heads of Households and other Surnames in Households Index*. Salt Lake City, UT: Index Pub., 1984. 153p.

Jackson, Ronald Vern. *Delaware Census Index, Online Edition*. Orem, UT: Ancestry.com, Inc., 1999.
http://www.ancestry.com

_____. *Delaware 1850, 1860 Slave Schedules*. North Salt Lake City, UT: Accelerated Indexing Systems International, 1986. 59, 18p.

_____. *Mortality Schedules Index, Online Edition*. Orem, UT: Ancestry.com, Inc., 1999.
http://www.ancestry.com

_____, and Gary Ronald Teeples. *Delaware 1860 Census Index*. Salt Lake City, UT: Accelerated Indexing Systems, 1984. 377p.

U.S. Census Index, 1860, Delaware, New Jersey and Pennsylvania. Orem, UT: Automated Archives, 1992. CD-ROM.

U.S. Federal Population Census Schedules. 1860, M653, Microfilm Reel Nos. 95-99.

U.S. Federal Population Census Schedules. 1860, M653, Slave Schedules, Microfilm Reel No. 100.

1870

Census Index: U.S. Selected States/Counties, 1870. Family Archive CD 319. Novato, CA: Broderbund Software. CD-ROM.

Delaware and New Jersey 1870 Census Index. ACD 0033. Bountiful, UT: Heritage Quest, 1998. CD-ROM.

Dilts, Bryan Lee. *1870 Delaware Census Index, Heads of Households and Other Surnames in Households Index*. Salt Lake City, UT: Index Pub., 1985. 153p.

Jackson, Ronald Vern. *Delaware Census Index, Online Edition*. Orem, UT: Ancestry.com, Inc., 1999.
http://www.ancestry.com

_____. *Delaware 1870*. North Salt Lake City, UT: Accelerated Indexing Systems International, 1987. 171p.
_____. *Delaware 1870 Mortality Schedule*. Bountiful, UT: Accelerated Indexing Systems, 1981. 44p.
_____. *Mortality Schedules Index, Online Edition*. Orem, UT: Ancestry.com, Inc., 1999.
http://www.ancestry.com
Steuart, Raeone Christensen. *1870 Delaware Census Index, A-Z*. Bountiful, UT: Heritage Quest, 1998. 273p.
_____. *Delaware and New Jersey 1870 Census Index*. Bountiful, UT: Heritage Quest, 2000. CD-ROM.
U.S. Federal Population Census Schedules. 1870, M593, Microfilm Reel Nos. 119-122.

1880
Jackson, Ronald Vern. *Delaware 1880 Mortality Schedule*. Bountiful, UT: Accelerated Indexing Systems, 1981. 61p.

1890
Jackson, Ronald Vern. *Delaware Census Index, Online Edition (Veterans Schedule)*. Orem, UT: Ancestry.com, Inc., 1999.
http://www.ancestry.com
U.S. Federal Population Census Schedules. 1880, T9, Microfilm Reel Nos. 116-120.
U.S. Federal Population Census Schedules. 1880, Soundex. T741, 9 Microfilm Reels.

1900
U.S. Federal Population Census Schedules. 1900, T623, Microfilm Reel Nos. 153-157.
U.S. Federal Population Census Schedules. 1900, Soundex. T1037, 21 Microfilm Reels.
U.S. Federal Population Census Schedules. 1900, Military & Naval Bases. T1081, Microfilm Reel Nos. 1838-1842.
U.S. Federal Population Census Schedules. 1900, Military & Naval Bases, Soundex. T1081, 32 Microfilm Reels.

1910
U.S. Federal Population Census Schedules. 1910, T624, Microfilm Reel Nos. 145-148. (No Soundex/Miracode Index was prepared by the Government for this State.)

1920
U.S. Federal Population Census Schedules. 1920, T625, Microfilm Reel Nos. 200-204.
U.S. Federal Population Census Schedules. 1920, Soundex. M1554, 20 Microfilm Reels.

New Castle County
1800
Rogers, Ellen Stanley, and Louise E. Easter. *1800 Census of New Castle County, Delaware*. Bladensburg, MD: Genealogical Recorder, 1960. 112p.

Sussex County
1860
Leonard, Rosetta Bernice. *1860 Census of Sussex County, Delaware*. Silver Spring, Family Line Publications, 1982. 178p.

District of Columbia

1800
Jackson, Ronald Vern. *District of Columbia Census Index, Online Edition*. Orem, UT: Ancestry.com, Inc., 1999.
http://www.ancestry.com

_____, and Richard A. Moore. *District of Columbia 1800*. Salt Lake City, UT: Gen-Dex Worldwide, 1972. 21p.

Steuart, Raeone Christensen. *District of Columbia 1800 Census Index*. Bountiful, UT: Heritage Quest, 2000. 11p.

_____. *United States 1800 Census Index*. Bountiful, UT: Heritage Quest, 2000. 4 vols. CD-ROM.

U.S. Federal Population Census Schedules, 1800. M32, Microfilm Reel No. 5.

1810

Jackson, Ronald Vern. *District of Columbia, 1810 Census Index*. Salt Lake City, UT: Accelerated Indexing Systems, 1981. 42p.

1820

Jackson, Ronald Vern. *District of Columbia Census Index, Online Edition*. Orem, UT: Ancestry.com, Inc., 1999.

http://www.ancestry.com

_____, and Gary Ronald Teeples. *District of Columbia 1820 Census Index*. Bountiful, UT: Accelerated Indexing Systems, 1976. 86p.

Parks, Gary W. *Index to the 1820 Census of Maryland and Washington, D.C.* Baltimore, MD: Genealogical Publishing Co., 1986. 274p.

U.S. Federal Population Census Schedules. 1820, M33, Microfilm Reel Nos. 5.

1830

1830-1839 U.S. Census Indexes, Mid-Atlantic, South, Mid-West. Orem, UT: Automated Archives, 1993. CD-ROM.

Jackson, Ronald Vern. *District of Columbia Census Index, Online Edition*. Orem, UT: Ancestry.com, Inc., 1999.

http://www.ancestry.com

_____, and Gary Ronald Teeples. *District of Columbia 1830 Census Index*. Bountiful, UT: Accelerated Indexing Systems, 1976. 69p.

U.S. Federal Population Census Schedules. 1830, M19, Microfilm Reel No. 14.

1840

Census Index: U.S. Selected States/Counties, 1840. Family Archive CD 316. Novato, CA: Broderbund Software. CD-ROM.

Jackson, Ronald Vern. *District of Columbia Census Index, Online Edition*. Orem, UT: Ancestry.com, Inc., 1999.

http://www.ancestry.com

_____, and Gary Ronald Teeples. *District of Columbia 1840 Census Index*. Bountiful, UT: Accelerated Indexing Systems, 1977. 71p.

U.S. Federal Population Census Schedules. 1840, M704, Microfilm Reel No. 35.

1850

Bell, Mrs. Alexander H., Mrs. Joseph L. Anderson, and Mrs. William S. Kenyon. *Index to District of Columbia Mortality Records, 1850, 1860, 1870, 1880*. Authors, 1945-1946. 4 vols.

Census Index: U.S. Selected States/Counties, 1850. Family Archive CD 317. Novato, CA: Broderbund Software. CD-ROM.

Jackson, Ronald Vern. *District of Columbia Census Index, Online Edition*. Orem, UT: Ancestry.com, Inc., 1999.

http://www.ancestry.com

_____. *District of Columbia 1850 Mortality Schedule*. Bountiful, UT: Accelerated Indexing Systems, 1981. 35p.

_____. *District of Columbia 1850 Slave Schedule*. North Salt Lake City, UT: Accelerated Indexing Systems International, 1988. 52, 26p.

_____, and Gary Ronald Teeples. *District of Columbia 1850 Census Index*. Bountiful, UT: Accelerated Indexing Systems, 1977. 97p.

U.S. Census Index Series, Virginia, West Virginia, Maryland, North Carolina and the Distirct of Columbia, 1850. Orem, UT: Automated Archives, 1991. CD-ROM.

U.S. Federal Population Census Schedules. 1850, M432, Microfilm Reel Nos. 56-57.

1860

Bell, Mrs. Alexander H., Mrs. Joseph L. Anderson, and Mrs. William S. Kenyon. *Index to District of Columbia Mortality Records, 1850, 1860, 1870, 1880*. Authors, 1945-1946. 4 vols.

Census Index: U.S. Selected States/Counties, 1860. Family Archive CD 318. Novato, CA: Broderbund Software. CD-ROM.

Dilts, Bryan Lee. *1860 District of Columbia Census Index, Heads of Households and other Surnames in Households Index*. Salt Lake City, UT: Index Pub., 1983. 109p.; 1 Microfiche.

Jackson, Ronald Vern. *District of Columbia Census Index, Online Edition*. Orem, UT: Ancestry.com, Inc., 1999.

http://www.ancestry.com

_____. *District of Columbia 1860 Mortality Schedule*. Bountiful, UT: Accelerated Indexing Systems, 1981. 41p.

_____. *Mortality Schedules Index, Online Edition*. Orem, UT: Ancestry.com, Inc., 1999.

http://www.ancestry.com

Steuart, Raeone Christensen. *District of Columbia 1860 Census Index*. Bountiful, UT: Heritage Quest, 1999.

U.S. Census Index, 1860, District of Columbia, Maryland, North Carolina, Virginia, West Virginia. Orem, UT: Automated Archives, 1992. CD-ROM.

U.S. Federal Population Census Schedules. 1860, M653, Microfilm Reel Nos. 101-104.

U.S. Federal Population Census Schedules. 1860, M653, Slave Schedules, Microfilm Reel No. 105.

1870

Bell, Mrs. Alexander H., Mrs. Joseph L. Anderson, and Mrs. William S. Kenyon. *Index to District of Columbia Mortality Records, 1850, 1860, 1870, 1880*. Authors, 1945-1946. 4 vols.

Census Index: U.S. Selected States/Counties, 1870. Family Archive CD 319. Novato, CA: Broderbund Software. CD-ROM.

Dilts, Bryan Lee. *1870 District of Columbia Census Index, Heads of Households and Other Surnames in Households Index*. Salt Lake City, UT: Index Publications, 1985.

Jackson, Ronald Vern. *District of Columbia Census Index, Online Edition*. Orem, UT: Ancestry.com, Inc., 1999.

http://www.ancestry.com

_____. *District of Columbia 1870*. North Salt Lake City, UT: Accelerated Indexing Systems, 1986. 614p.

_____. *District of Columbia 1870 Mortality Schedule*. Bountiful, UT: Accelerated Indexing Systems, 1981. 51p.

_____. *Mortality Schedules Index, Online Edition*. Orem, UT: Ancestry.com, Inc., 1999.

http://www.ancestry.com

Maryland and District of Columbia, 1870 Census Index. ACD 0016. Bountiful, UT: Heritage Quest, 1998. CD-ROM.

Steuart, Raeone Christensen. *District of Columbia 1870 Census Index*. Bountiful, UT: Heritage Quest, 1998. 334p.

U.S. Federal Population Census Schedules. 1870, M593, Microfilm Reel Nos. 123-127.

1880

Bell, Mrs. Alexander H., Mrs. Joseph L. Anderson, and Mrs. William S. Kenyon. *Index to District of Columbia Mortality Records, 1850, 1860, 1870, 1880*. Authors, 1945-1946. 4 vols.

Jackson, Ronald Vern. *District of Columbia 1880 Mortality Schedule*. Salt Lake City,UT: Accelerated Indexing Systems, 1980. 69p.

_____. *Mortality Schedules Index, Online Edition*. Orem, UT: Ancestry.com, Inc., 1999.
http://www.ancestry.com

U.S. Federal Population Census Schedules. 1880, T9, Microfilm Reel Nos. 121-124.

U.S. Federal Population Census Schedules. 1880, Soundex. T742, 9 Microfilm Reels.

1890

Jackson, Ronald Vern. *District of Columbia Census Index, Online Edition (Veterans Schedule; Naval Veterans Schedule)*. Orem, UT: Ancestry.com, Inc., 1999.
http://www.ancestry.com

_____. *1890 District of Columbia Census Index, Special Schedule of the Eleventh Census (1890) Enumerating Union Veterans and of Union Veterans of the Civil War, this Index Includes Every Name Listed on the Census Record*. North salt lake city, UT: Accelerated Indexing Systems, 1983. 44p.

U.S. Federal Population Census Schedules. 1890, M407, Microfilm Reel No. 2.

U.S. Federal Population Census Schedules. 1890, Index. M496, 2 Microfilm Reels.

U.S. Federal Population Census Schedules, Special Schedule, Enumerating Union Veterans and Widows of Union Veterans of the Civil War. 1890, M123, 118 Microfilm Reels.

Veterans' Schedules: U.S. Selected States, 1890. Family Archive CD 131. Novato, CA: Broderbund Software. CD-ROM.

1900

U.S. Federal Population Census Schedules, 1900. T623, Microfilm Reel Nos. 158-164.

U.S. Federal Population Census Schedules. 1900, Soundex. T1038, 42 Microfilm Reels.

U.S. Federal Population Census Schedules. 1900, Military & Naval Bases. T1081, Microfilm Reel Nos. 1838-1842.

U.S. Federal Population Census Schedules. 1900, Military & Naval Bases, Soundex. T1081, 32 Microfilm Reels.

1910

Garlet, Charles B. *Washington, DC Enumeration Districts for the 1910 Census*. Rockville, MD: Author, 1983. 76p.

U.S. Federal Population Census Schedules. 1910, T624, Microfilm Reel Nos. 149-155.

1920

U.S. Federal Population Census Schedules. 1920, T625, Microfilm Reel Nos. 205-213.

U.S. Federal Population Census Schedules. 1920, Soundex. M1555, 49 Microfilm Reels.

Florida

Feldman, Lawrence H. *Anglo Americans in Spanish Archives, Lists of Anglo American Settlers in the Spanish Colonies of America*. Baltimore, MD: Genealogical Publishing Co., 1991. 349p.

Jackson, Ronald Vern. *Early Florida Censuses*. Bountiful, UT: Accelerated Indexing Systems, 1984. 2 vols.

1820

Jackson, Ronald Vern. *Florida Census Index, Online Edition*. Orem, UT: Ancestry.com, Inc., 1999.
http://www.ancestry.com

_____. *Florida 1820*. North Salt Lake City, UT: Accelerated Indexing Systems, 1985. 56p.

Pre-1821

Mills, Donna Rachal. *Florida's First Families, Translated Abstracts of Pre-1821 Spanish Censuses.* Tuscaloosa, AL: Mills Historical Press, 1992. 201p.

1830

Census Index: U.S. Selected States/Counties, 1830. Family Archive CD 315. Novato, CA: Broderbund Software. CD-ROM.

1830-1839 U.S. Census Indexes, Mid-Atlantic, South, Mid-West. Orem, UT: Automated Archives, 1993. CD-ROM.

Jackson, Ronald Vern. *Florida Census Index, Online Edition.* Orem, UT: Ancestry.com, Inc., 1999. **http://www.ancestry.com**

_____, and Gary Ronald Teeples. *Florida 1830 Census Index.* Bountiful, UT: Accelerated Indexing Systems, 1976. 62p.

Shaw, Aurora C. *1830 Florida U.S. Census.* Jacksonville, FL: Southern Genealogist's Exchange Quarterly, 1961. 38p.

U.S. Federal Population Census Schedules. 1830, M19, Microfilm Reel No.15 .

1840

Census Index: U.S. Selected States/Counties, 1840. Family Archive CD 316. Novato, CA: Broderbund Software. CD-ROM.

Coyle, Thomas E., and Berniece D. Coyle. *Florida 1840 Census.* Lewisville, TX: Authors, 1996. 2 vols.

Jackson, Ronald Vern. *Florida Census Index, Online Edition.* Orem, UT: Ancestry.com, Inc., 1999. **http://www.ancestry.com**

_____, and Gary Ronald Teeples. *Florida 1840 Census Index.* Bountiful, UT: Accelerated Indexing Systems, 1976. 28p.

Mallon, Lucille S. *1840 Index to Florida Census.* Mobile, AL: Author, 1975. 42p.

Shaw, Aurora C. *1840 Florida U.S. Census, a Statewide Index to All Heads of Households in all Twenty Counties Formed by 1840, Showing Counties in Which They Resided.* Jacksonville, FL: Southern Genealogist's Exchange Quarterly, 1968. 44p.

U.S. Federal Population Census Schedules. 1840, M704, Microfilm Reel No. 36.

1850

Census Index: U.S. Selected States/Counties, 1850. Family Archive CD 317. Novato, CA: Broderbund Software. CD-ROM.

Corley, Betty J. Index, *Yeoman(s), Yeaman(s), Youman(s), U.S. Census Index, 1850, 1860, 1880, Alabama, Florida, Kentucky, Louisiana, Maryland, Mississippi, Tennessee, Texas, Virginia, Includes Various Other Spellings.* Hyrum, UT: Author, 1988. 5p.

Index to 1850 Florida Census. Jacksonville, FL: Southern Genealogist's Exchange Society, 1976. 131p.

Jackson, Ronald Vern. *Florida Census Index, Online Edition.* Orem, UT: Ancestry.com, Inc., 1999. **http://www.ancestry.com**

_____, and Gary Ronald Teeples. *Florida 1850 Census Index.* Bountiful, UT: Accelerated Indexing Systems, 1976. 54p; 1978. 36p.

_____. *Florida 1850 Mortality Schedule.* Salt Lake City, UT: Accelerated Indexing Systems, 1982. 38p.

_____. *Florida 1850 Slave Schedule Census Index.* Salt Lake City, UT: Accelerated Indexing Systems International, 1988. 68p.

_____. *Mortality Schedules Index, Online Edition.* Orem, UT: Ancestry.com, Inc., 1999. **http://www.ancestry.com**

U.S. Census Index Series, Alabama, Arkansas, Georgia, Florida, Louisiana, Mississippi, South Carolina, 1850. Orem, UT: Automated Archives, 1991. CD-ROM.

U.S. Federal Population Census Schedules. 1850, M432, Microfilm Reel Nos. 58-59.

U.S. Federal Population Census Schedules. 1850, M432, Slave Schedules, Microfilm Reel No. 60.

1860

Census Index: U.S. Selected States/Counties, 1860. Family Archive CD 318. Novato, CA: Broderbund Software. CD-ROM.

Corley, Betty J. *Index, Yeoman(s), Yeaman(s), Youman(s), U.S. Census Index, 1850, 1860, 1880, Alabama, Florida, Kentucky, Louisiana, Maryland, Mississippi, Tennessee, Texas, Virginia, Includes Various Other Spellings.* Hyrum, UT: Author, 1988. 5p.

Dilts, Bryan Lee. *1860 Florida Census Index, Heads of Households and other Surnames in Households Index.* Salt Lake City, UT: Index Pub., 1984. 93p.; 1 Microfiche.

Florida 1860 Census Index. Bountiful, UT: Heritage Quest, 1999.

Jackson, Ronald Vern. *Florida Census Index, Online Edition.* Orem, UT: Ancestry.com, Inc., 1999. 138p. **http://www.ancestry.com**

_____. *Florida 1860 Census Index.* Salt Lake City, UT: Accelerated Indexing Systems, 1984. 283p.

_____. *Florida 1860 Slave Schedule Census Index.* Salt Lake City, UT: Accelerated Indexing Systems International, 1990. 55, 106p.

_____. *Mortality Schedules Index, Online Edition.* Orem, UT: Ancestry.com, Inc., 1999. **http://www.ancestry.com**

_____, Wylma Winmill, Shirley P. Zachrison. *Florida 1860 Mortality Schedule.* Bountiful, UT: Accelerated Indexing Systems, 1983. Unpgd.

U.S. Census Index, 1860, Alabama, Arkansas, Florida, Louisiana, Mississippi, South Carolina. Orem, UT: Automated Archives, 1992. 1 CD-ROM.

U.S. Federal Population Census Schedules. 1860, M653, Microfilm Reel Nos. 106-109.

U.S. Federal Population Census Schedules. 1860, M653, Slave Schedules, Microfilm Reel No. 110.

1870

Census Index: U.S. Selected States/Counties, 1870. Family Archive CD 319. Novato, CA: Broderbund Software. CD-ROM.

Dilts, Bryan Lee. *1870 Florida Census Index, an Every-name Index.* Salt Lake City, UT: Index Pub., 1984; 1997. 662p.

Jackson, Ronald Vern. *Florida Census Index, Online Edition.* Orem, UT: Ancestry.com, Inc., 1999. **http://www.ancestry.com**

_____. *Florida 1870.* Salt Lake City, UT: Accelerated Indexing Systems International, 1985. 221p.

_____. *Florida 1870 Mortality Schedule.* Bountiful, UT: Accelerated Indexing Systems, 1983. 60p.

_____. *Mortality Schedules Index, Online Edition.* Orem, UT: Ancestry.com, Inc., 1999. **http://www.ancestry.com**

U.S. Federal Population Census Schedules. 1870, M593, Microfilm Reel Nos. 128-133.

1880

Corley, Betty J. *Index, Yeoman(s), Yeaman(s), Youman(s), U.S. Census Index, 1850, 1860, 1880, Alabama, Florida, Kentucky, Louisiana, Maryland, Mississippi, Tennessee, Texas, Virginia, Includes Various Other Spellings.* Hyrum, UT: Author, 1988. 5p.

Jackson, Ronald Vern. *Florida 1880 Mortality Schedule.* Bountiful, UT: Accelerated Indexing Systems, 1983. 49p.

_____. *Mortality Schedules Index, Online Edition.* Orem, UT: Ancestry.com, Inc., 1999. **http://www.ancestry.com**

Mills, Donna Rachal. *Florida's Unfortunates, the 1880 Federal Census, Defective, Dependent and Delinquent Classes.* Tuscaloosa, AL: Mills Historical Press, 1993. 103p.

U.S. Federal Population Census Schedules. 1880, T9, Microfilm Reel Nos. 125-132.

U.S. Federal Population Census Schedules. 1880, Soundex. T743, 16 Microfilm Reels.

1885

Martin, William T., and Patricia Martin. *1885 Florida State Census Index.* Miami, FL: Author, 1991. 882p.

1890

Jackson, Ronald Vern. *Florida Census Index, Online Edition (Veterans Schedule; Naval Veterans Schedule)*. Orem, UT: Ancestry.com, Inc., 1999.
http://www.ancestry.com

1900

U.S. Federal Population Census Schedules. 1900, T623, Microfilm Reel Nos. 165-177.
U.S. Federal Population Census Schedules. 1900, Soundex. T1039, 59 Microfilm Reels.
U.S. Federal Population Census Schedules. 1900, Military & Naval Bases. T1081, Microfilm Reel Nos. 1838-1842.
U.S. Federal Population Census Schedules. 1900, Military & Naval Bases, Soundex. T1081, 32 Microfilm Reels.

1910

Cook — Cooke Every Name Index, 1910 Florida Miracode. Casselberry, FL: Quantic Inc., 1989. 22p.
Martin, William T., and Patricia Martin. *1910 Federal Census Index*. Miami, FL: Authors, 1989. Multivolume.
U.S. Federal Population Census Schedules. 1910, T624, Microfilm Reel Nos. 156-169.
U.S. Federal Population Census Schedules. 1910, Miracode. T1262, 84 Microfilm Reels.

1920

U.S. Federal Population Census Schedules. 1920, T625, Microfilm Reel Nos. 214-232.
U.S. Federal Population Census Schedules. 1920, Soundex. M1556, 74 Microfilm Reels.

Alachua County
1840

Pompey, Sherman Lee. *Index to the 1840 Census Records of Alachua, Calhoun, Dade, Escambia, Franklin, Hamilton, Hillsborough, Monroe, Mosquito (Orange), Nassau, Walton and Washington Counties, Florida Territory*. Charleston, OR: Pacific Specialities, 1974. 28p.

1850

Griffin, Myrtie Lou, and Roscoe Arnold Stallings. *Alachua County, Florida 1850 Census*. Homerville, GA: Huxford Genealogical Society. 33p.
USGenWeb Census Project. Florida, 1850 Alachua County. Slave Schedule.
ftp://ftp.rootsweb.com/pub/census/fl/alachua/1850/

1860

Griffin, Myrtie Lou, and Roscoe Arnold Stallings. *Alachua County, Florida 1860 Census*. Homerville, GA: Huxford Genealogical Society. 79p.
USGenWeb Census Project. Florida, 1860 Alachua County.
ftp://ftp.rootsweb.com/pub/census/fl/alachua/1860/

Benton County
1850

USGenWeb Census Project. Florida, 1850 Benton County. Slave Schedule.
ftp://ftp.rootsweb.com/pub/census/fl/benton/1850/

Bradford County
1860

Spencer, Elizabeth R., and Mary C. Parker. *Bradford (New River) County, Florida, 1860 U.S. Federal Census*. Orange Park FL: Author, 1978. 67p.

Brevard County
1860
USGenWeb Census Project. Florida, 1860 Brevard County.
ftp://ftp.rootsweb.com/pub/census/fl/brevard/1860/
1870
USGenWeb Census Project. Florida, 1870 Brevard County.
ftp://ftp.rootsweb.com/pub/census/fl/brevard/1870/

Calhoun County
1840
Pompey, Sherman Lee. *Index to the 1840 Census Records of Alachua, Calhoun, Dade, Escambia, Franklin, Hamilton, Hillsborough, Monroe, Mosquito (Orange), Nassau, Walton and Washington Counties, Florida Territory*. Charleston, OR: Pacific Specialities, 1974. 28p.

Clay County
1860, 1870
Spencer, Elizabeth R., and Mary C. Parker. *Clay County, Florida 1860 & 1870 U.S. Federal Censuses*. Orange Park, FL: Author 1978. 81p.
1910
Martin, Patricia Thomas. *1910 Census Index, Clay County, Florida*. Miami, FL: Author, 1989. 38p.

Columbia County
1850
1850 Florida Census, Columbia County. Jacksonville, FL: The Southern Genealogist's Exchange Society, 1974. 85p.
1860
Griffin, Myrtie Lou, and Roscoe Arnold Stallings. *Columbia County, Florida 1860 Census*. Homerville, GA: Huxford Genealogical Society. 66p.
Spencer, Elizabeth R., and Mary C. Parker. *Columbia County, Florida 1860 U.S. Federal Census*. Orange Park, FL: Author 1979. 70p.
1910
Martin, William T., and Patricia Martin. *1910 Census Index, Columbia County, Florida*. Miami, FL: Authors, 1990. 110p.

Dade County
1840
Pompey, Sherman Lee. *Index to the 1840 Census Records of Alachua, Calhoun, Dade, Escambia, Franklin, Hamilton, Hillsborough, Monroe, Mosquito (Orange), Nassau, Walton and Washington Counties, Florida Territory*. Charleston, OR: Pacific Specialities, 1974. 28p.
1850
Pompey, Sherman Lee. *The 1850 Census Records of Dade County, Florida*. Independence, CA: Historical & Genealogical Pub., 1965. 5p.
USGenWeb Census Project. Florida, 1850 Dade County.
ftp://ftp.rootsweb.com/pub/census/fl/dade/1850/
USGenWeb Census Project. Florida, 1850 Dade County. Slave Schedule.
ftp://ftp.rootsweb.com/pub/census/fl/dade/1850/
1860
USGenWeb Census Project. Florida, 1860 Dade County.
ftp://ftp.rootsweb.com/pub/census/fl/dade/1860/
1900
Stanley, Dorothy C., and Wava Rowe White. *Index to 1900 Census of Dade County, Florida*. West Palm Beach, FL: Seminole Chapter, DAR, 1979. 56p.

White, Wava Rowe. *1900 Census of Dade County, Florida, with Index Added*. West Palm Beach, FL: Author, 1981. 256p.

1910

Martin, Patricia. *1910 Census, Dade County, Florida*. Miami, FL: Author 1989. 115p.

DeSoto County
1910

Martin, William T., and Patricia Martin. *1910 Florida Federal Census Index, DeSoto County*. Miami, FL: Author, 1991. 65p.

Duval County
1850

USGenWeb Census Project. Florida, 1850 Duval County. (Partial).
ftp://ftp.rootsweb.com/pub/census/fl/duval/1850/
USGenWeb Census Project. Florida, 1850 Duval County. Slave Schedule.
ftp://ftp.rootsweb.com/pub/census/fl/duval/1850/

1910

Martin, William T., and Patricia Martin. *1910 Census Index, Duval County, Florida*. Miami, FL: Authors, 1997. 222p.

Escambia County
1840

Pompey, Sherman Lee. *Index to the 1840 Census Records of Alachua, Calhoun, Dade, Escambia, Franklin, Hamilton, Hillsborough, Monroe, Mosquito (Orange), Nassau, Walton and Washington Counties, Florida Territory*. Charleston, OR: Pacific Specialities, 1974. 28p.

1850

1850 Florida Census, Escambia County. Jacksonville, FL: The Southern Genealogist's Exchange Society, 1976. 75p.

1870

Thomes, Sidney Phoenix. *Every-name Index to the 1870, U.S. Census of Escambia County, Florida*. Pensacola, FL: West Florida Genealogical Society, 1985. 80p.

Franklin County
1840

Pompey, Sherman Lee. *Index to the 1840 Census Records of Alachua, Calhoun, Dade, Escambia, Franklin, Hamilton, Hillsborough, Monroe, Mosquito (Orange), Nassau, Walton and Washington Counties, Florida Territory*. Charleston, OR: Pacific Specialities, 1974. 28p.

1850

1850 Florida Census, Franklin County. Jacksonville, FL: The Southern Genealogist's Exchange Society, 1975. 29p.
USGenWeb Census Project. Florida, 1850 Franklin County. Slave Schedule.
ftp://ftp.rootsweb.com/pub/census/fl/franklin/1850/

1910

Martin, William T., and Patricia Martin. *1910 Census Index, Franklin County, Florida*. Miami, FL: Authors, 1991. 32p.

Hamilton County
1840

Pompey, Sherman Lee. *Index to the 1840 Census Records of Alachua, Calhoun, Dade, Escambia, Franklin, Hamilton, Hillsborough, Monroe, Mosquito (Orange), Nassau, Walton and Washington Counties, Florida Territory*. Charleston, OR: Pacific Specialities, 1974. 28p.

1850

Griffin, Myrtie Lou, and Roscoe Arnold Stallings. *1850 Census of Hamilton County, Florida*. Homerville, GA: Huxford Genealogical Society. 45p.

1860

Griffin, Myrtie Lou, and Roscoe Arnold Stallings. *Hamilton County, Florida 1860 Census*. Homerville, GA: Huxford Genealogical Society. 65p.

Hillsborough County
1840

Pompey, Sherman Lee. *Index to the 1840 Census Records of Alachua, Calhoun, Dade, Escambia, Franklin, Hamilton, Hillsborough, Monroe, Mosquito (Orange), Nassau, Walton and Washington Counties, Florida Territory*. Charleston, OR: Pacific Specialities, 1974. 28p.

1850

1850 Federal Census, Hillsborough County. Jacksonville, FL: Southern Genealogists' Exchange Society, 1975. 41p.

USGenWeb Census Project. Florida, 1850 Hillsborough County. Slave Schedule.

ftp://ftp.rootsweb.com/pub/census/fl/hillsborough/1850/

Holmes County
1850

1850 Florida Census, Homes County. Jacksonville, FL: The Southern Genealogist's Exchange Society, 1976. 27p.

USGenWeb Census Project. Florida, 1850 Holmes County. Slave Schedule.

ftp://ftp.rootsweb.com/pub/census/fl/holmes/1850/

1860, 1870

Bishop, Brenda C. *1860-1870 Holmes County, Florida Census*. Tallahassee, FL: Author, 1985. 24p.

Jackson County
1850

Nobles, Glen. *The Early Settlers of Jackson County; the Landholders, 1826-1893, the Voting Record of 1845, 1850 U.S. Census, and Stories and Reminiscences*. Grand Ridge, FL: Nobles Pub. Co., 1996. 96p.

1860

Bishop, Brenda C. *Jackson County, Florida 1860 Census*. Tallahassee, FL: Author, 1985. 38p.

Jefferson County
1850

Griffin, Myrtie Lou, and Roscoe Arnold Stallings. *Jefferson County, Florida 1850 Census*. Homerville, GA: Huxford Genealogical Society. 57p.

USGenWeb Census Project. Florida, 1850 Jefferson County.

ftp://ftp.rootsweb.com/pub/census/fl/jefferson/1850/

1860

Bishop, Brenda C. *Jefferson County, Florida 1860 Census*. Tallahassee, FL: Author, 1985. 27p.

Leon County
1825

Jackson, Ronald Vern. *Florida Census Index, Online Edition*. Orem, UT: Ancestry.com, Inc., 1999.

http://www.ancestry.com

_____. *Florida, Leon County, 1825 State Census Index*. North Salt Lake City, UT: Accelerated Indexing Systems, 1988. 59p.

Levy County
1850

USGenWeb Census Project. Florida, 1850 Levy County.
ftp://ftp.rootsweb.com/pub/census/fl/levy/1850/
USGenWeb Census Project. Florida, 1850 Levy County. Slave Schedule.
ftp://ftp.rootsweb.com/pub/census/fl/levy/1850/

Liberty County
1880
Shuler, Bernice G. *Index to the 1880 Liberty County, Florida U.S. Census*. Bristol, FL: Author, 1996. 26p.
1900
Shuler, Bernice G. *Index, 1900 Liberty County, Florida U.S. Census*. Bristol, FL: Author, 1996. 58p.
1910
Shuler, Bernice G. *Index, 1910 Liberty County, Florida U.S. Census*. Bristol, FL: Author, 1996. 88p.

Madison County
1850
Griffin, Myrtie Lou, and Roscoe Arnold Stallings. *Madison County, Florida 1850 Census*. Homerville, GA: Huxford Genealogical Society. 57p.
Madison County, Florida 1850 Census. Jacksonville, FL: Southern Genealogist's Exchange Society, 1973. 72p.
1860
Griffin, Myrtie Lou, and Roscoe Arnold Stallings. *Madison County, Florida 1860 Census*. Homerville, GA: Huxford Genealogical Society. 71p.

Manatee County
1860-1895
Schneider, Mabel. *Extractions from Manatee County Censuses of 1860, 1870, 1880, 1885, 1895*. Bradenton, FL: Manasota Genealogical Society, 1985. 321p.

Marion County
1850
1850 Florida Census, Marion County. Jacksonville, FL: The Southern Genealogist's Exchange Society, 1975. 51p.
USGenWeb Census Project. Florida, 1850 Marion County. Slave Schedule.
ftp://ftp.rootsweb.com/pub/census/fl/marion/1850/

Monroe County
1840
Pompey, Sherman Lee. *Index to the 1840 Census Records of Alachua, Calhoun, Dade, Escambia, Franklin, Hamilton, Hillsborough, Monroe, Mosquito (Orange), Nassau, Walton and Washington Counties, Florida Territory*. Charleston, OR: Pacific Specialities, 1974. 28p.
1850
1850 Florida Census, Monroe County. Jacksonville, FL: The Southern Genealogist's Exchange Society, 1976. 56p.

Nassau County
1840
Pompey, Sherman Lee. *Index to the 1840 Census Records of Alachua, Calhoun, Dade, Escambia, Franklin, Hamilton, Hillsborough, Monroe, Mosquito (Orange), Nassau, Walton and Washington Counties, Florida Territory*. Charleston, OR: Pacific Specialities, 1974. 28p.

1850

1850 Florida Census, Nassau County. Jacksonville, FL: The Southern Genealogist's Exchange Society, 1974. 29p.

1895

Jacksonville Genealogical Society. *1895 State Census, Nassau County, Florida.* Jacksonville, FL: Jacksonville Genealogical Society, 1976. 229p.

New River County
1860

Spencer, Elizabeth R., and Mary C. Parker. *Bradford (New River) County, Florida, 1860 U.S. Federal Census.* Orange Park FL: Author, 1978. 67p.

Orange County
1840

Pompey, Sherman Lee. *Index to the 1840 Census Records of Alachua, Calhoun, Dade, Escambia, Franklin, Hamilton, Hillsborough, Monroe, Mosquito (Orange), Nassau, Walton and Washington Counties, Florida Territory.* Charleston, OR: Pacific Specialities, 1974. 28p.

1850

Pompey, Sherman Lee. *The 1850 Census Records of Orange County, Florida.* Independence, CA: Historical and Genealogical Pub., 1966. 7p.

1860

USGenWeb Census Project. Florida, 1860 Orange County.
ftp://ftp.rootsweb.com/pub/census/fl/orange/1860/

Putnam County
1850

USGenWeb Census Project. Florida, 1850 Putnam County.
ftp://ftp.rootsweb.com/pub/census/fl/putnam/1850/

Rusk County
1850

USGenWeb Census Project. Florida, 1850 Rusk County. Slave Schedule.
ftp://ftp.rootsweb.com/pub/census/fl/rusk/1850/

Saint Augustine (Saint Johns County)
1784-1785

Feldman, Lawrence H. *The Last Days of British Saint Augustine, 1784-1785, a Spanish Census of the English Colony of East Florida.* Baltimore, MD: Genealogical Pub. Co., 1998. 116p.

Saint Johns County
1784-1785

Feldman, Lawrence H. *The Last Days of British Saint Augustine, 1784-1785, a Spanish Census of the English Colony of East Florida.* Baltimore, MD: Genealogical Pub. Co., 1998. 116p.

1850

1850 Florida Census, St. Johns County. Jacksonville, FL: The Southern Genealogist's Exchange Society, 1974. 40p.

USGenWeb Census Project. Florida, 1850 St. Johns County.
ftp://ftp.rootsweb.com/pub/census/fl/stjohns/1850/

Saint Lucie County
1850

Pompey, Sherman Lee. *The 1850 Census Records of St. Lucie County, Florida.* Independence, CA: Historical and Genealogical Pub., 1965. 4p.

USGenWeb Census Project. Florida, 1850 St. Lucie.
ftp://ftp.rootsweb.com/pub/census/fl/stlucie/1850/
USGenWeb Census Project. Florida, 1850 St. Lucie Slave Schedule.
ftp://ftp.rootsweb.com/pub/census/fl/stlucie/1850/

Wakulla County
1850
1850 Florida Census, Wakulla County. Jacksonville, FL: The Southern Genealogist's Exchange Society, 1975. 31p.

Walton County
1840
Pompey, Sherman Lee. *Index to the 1840 Census Records of Alachua, Calhoun, Dade, Escambia, Franklin, Hamilton, Hillsborough, Monroe, Mosquito (Orange), Nassau, Walton and Washington Counties, Florida Territory.* Charleston, OR: Pacific Specialities, 1974. 28p.
1850
USGenWeb Census Project. Florida, 1850 Walton County.
ftp://ftp.rootsweb.com/pub/census/fl/walton/1850/

Washington County
1840
Pompey, Sherman Lee. *Index to the 1840 Census Records of Alachua, Calhoun, Dade, Escambia, Franklin, Hamilton, Hillsborough, Monroe, Mosquito (Orange), Nassau, Walton and Washington Counties, Florida Territory.* Charleston, OR: Pacific Specialities, 1974. 28p.
1850
1850 Florida Census, Washington County. Jacksonville, FL: The Southern Genealogist's Exchange Society, 1975. 38p.

Georgia

Bode, Frederick A., and Donald E. Ginter. *Farm Tenancy and the Census in Antebellum Georgia.* Athens, GA: University of Georgia Press, 1987. 278p.

Pre-1820
Jackson, Ronald Vern. *Early American Series. Early Georgia, 1733-1819.* Bountiful, UT: Accelerated Indexing Systems, 1981. 514p.

1820
Barrow, Carol J. *Barrow Families in Georgia Census, 1820-1910.* Atlanta, GA: Author, 1990. 90p.
Georgia Historical Society. *Index to United States Census of Georgia for 1820.* Savannah, GA: The Society, 1963. 167p.
_____. 2nd ed. Baltimore, MD: Genealogical Publishing Co., 1969. 167p.
Jackson, Ronald Vern. *Georgia Census Index, Online Edition.* Orem, UT: Ancestry.com, Inc., 1999.
http://www.ancestry.com
_____, and Gary Ronald Teeples. *Georgia 1820 Census Index.* Bountiful, UT: Accelerated Indexing Systems, 1976. 76p.
U.S. Federal Population Census Schedules. 1820, M33, Microfilm Reel No. 5.

1830
Barrow, Carol J. *Barrow Families in Georgia Census, 1820-1910.* Atlanta, GA: Author, 1990. 90p.

Census Index: U.S. Selected States/Counties, 1830. Family Archive CD 315. Novato, CA: Broderbund Software. CD-ROM.

1830-1839 U.S. Census Indexes, Mid-Atlantic, South, Mid-West. Orem, UT: Automated Archives, 1993. CD-ROM.

Index to Heads of Families 1830 Census of Georgia. Albany, GA: Delwyn Associates, 1974. 323p.

Jackson, Ronald Vern. *Georgia Census Index, Online Edition*. Orem, UT: Ancestry.com, Inc., 1999. **http://www.ancestry.com**

_____, and Gary Ronald Teeples. *Georgia 1830 Census Index*. Bountiful, UT: Accelerated Indexing Systems, 1976. 127p.

Register, Alvaretta Kenan. *Index to the 1830 Census of Georgia*. Baltimore, MD: Genealogical Publishing Co., 1974. 520p.

U.S. Federal Population Census Schedules. 1830, M19, Microfilm Reel Nos. 16-21.

1838-1845

Townsend, Brigid S. *Indexes to Seven State Census Reports for Counties in Georgia, 1838-1845*. Atlanta, GA: Taylor Foundation, 1975. 152p.

1840

Barrow, Carol J. *Barrow Families in Georgia Census, 1820-1910*. Atlanta, GA: Author, 1990. 90p.

Census Index: U.S. Selected States/Counties, 1840. Family Archive CD 316. Novato, CA: Broderbund Software. CD-ROM.

Jackson, Ronald Vern. *Georgia Census Index, Online Edition*. Orem, UT: Ancestry.com, Inc., 1999. **http://www.ancestry.com**

_____, and Gary Ronald Teeples. *Georgia 1840 Census Index*. Bountiful, UT: Accelerated Indexing Systems, 1977. 175p.

Sheffield, Eileen, and Barbara Woods. *1840 Index to Georgia Census*. Baytown, TX: Authors, 1969; 1971. 381p.

U.S. Federal Population Census Schedules. 1840, M704, Microfilm Reel Nos. 37-53.

Woods, Barbara, and Eileen Sheffield. *1840 Index to Georgia Census*. Authors, 1969. 380p.

1845

Jackson, Ronald Vern. *Georgia Census Index, Online Edition (State Census)*. Orem, UT: Ancestry.com, Inc., 1999. **http://www.ancestry.com**

Townsend, Brigid S. *Indexes to Seven State Census Reports for Counties in Georgia, 1838-1845*. Atlanta, GA: Taylor Foundation, 1975. 152p.

1850

Barrow, Carol J. *Barrow Families in Georgia Census, 1820-1910*. Atlanta, GA: Author, 1990. 90p.

Census Index: U.S. Selected States/Counties, 1850. Family Archive CD 317. Novato, CA: Broderbund Software. CD-ROM.

Jackson, Ronald Vern. *Georgia Census Index, Online Edition*. Orem, UT: Ancestry.com, Inc., 1999. **http://www.ancestry.com**

_____. *Georgia 1850 Census Index*. Bountiful, UT: Accelerated Indexing Systems, 1976. 298p.

_____. *Georgia 1850 Slave Schedule Census Index*. Salt Lake City, UT: Accelerated Indexing Systems International, 1988. Unpgd.

_____. *Georgia 1850 Territorial Census Index*. Salt Lake City, UT: Accelerated Indexing Systems, 1979. 175p.

_____. *Mortality Schedules Index, Online Edition*. Orem, UT: Ancestry.com, Inc., 1999. **http://www.ancestry.com**

Otto, Rhea Cumming. *1850 Census of Georgia, Index to 25 Counties*. Savannah, GA: Author, 1975. 46p.

Shaw, Aurora Casteleiro. *1850 Georgia Mortality Schedules or Census*. Jacksonville, FL: Author, 1971. 43p.

U.S. Census Index Series, Alabama, Arkansas, Georgia, Florida, Louisiana, Mississippi, South Carolina, 1850. Orem, UT: Automated Archives, 1991. CD-ROM.

U.S. Federal Population Census Schedules. 1850, M432, Microfilm Reel Nos. 61-87.

U.S. Federal Population Census Schedules. 1850, M432, Slave Schedules, Microfilm Reel Nos. 88-96.

1860

Acord, Arlis, Martha S. Anderson, et. al. *An Index for the 1860 Federal Census of Georgia.* LaGrange, GA: Family Tree, 1986. 1,024p.

Barrow, Carol J. *Barrow Families in Georgia Census, 1820-1910.* Atlanta, GA: Author, 1990. 90p.

Census Index: U.S. Selected States/Counties, 1860. Family Archive CD 318. Novato, CA: Broderbund Software. CD-ROM.

Coursey, W. Tony, and Kenneth H. Thomas, Jr. *1860 Census of Georgia.* Camden County. Atlanta, GA: Authors, 1985. 46p.

Jackson, Ronald Vern. *Georgia Census Index, Online Edition.* Orem, UT: Ancestry.com, Inc., 1999.
http://www.ancestry.com

_____. *Georgia 1860.* North Salt Lake City, UT: Accelerated Indexing Systems International, 1986. 638p.

_____. *Georgia 1860 Mortality.* North Salt Lake City, UT: Accelerated Indexing Systems International, 1986. 70p.

_____. *Mortality Schedules Index, Online Edition.* Orem, UT: Ancestry.com, Inc., 1999.
http://www.ancestry.com

_____. *Georgia 1860 Slave Schedule Census Index.* North Salt Lake City, UT: Accelerated Indexing Systems International, 1990. 787p.

U.S. Federal Population Census Schedules. 1860, M653, Microfilm Reel Nos. 111-141.

U.S. Federal Population Census Schedules. 1860, M653, Slave Schedules, Microfilm Reel Nos. 142-153.

1870

Barrow, Carol J. *Barrow Families in Georgia Census, 1820-1910.* Atlanta, GA: Author, 1990. 90p.

Census Index: Georgia, 1870. Family Archive CD 291. Novato, CA: Broderbund Software. CD-ROM.

Census Index: U.S. Selected States/Counties, 1870. Family Archive CD 319. Novato, CA: Broderbund Software. CD-ROM.

Georgia 1870 Mortality Book Index. 60p.

Jackson, Ronald Vern. *Georgia Census Index, Online Edition.* Orem, UT: Ancestry.com, Inc., 1999.
http://www.ancestry.com

Steuart, Bradley W. *Georgia 1870 Census Index.* Bountiful, UT: Precision Indexing, 1990, 1991. 3 vols. CD-ROM.

U.S. Census Index Series, Georgia, 1870. Orem, UT: Automated Archives, 1994. CD-ROM.

U.S. Federal Population Census Schedules. 1870, M593, Microfilm Reel Nos. 134-184.

1880

Barrow, Carol J. *Barrow Families in Georgia Census, 1820-1910.* Atlanta, GA: Author, 1990. 90p.

U.S. Federal Population Census Schedules. 1880, T9, Microfilm Reel Nos. 133-172.

U.S. Federal Population Census Schedules. 1880, Soundex. T744, 86 Microfilm Reels.

1890

Jackson, Ronald Vern. *Georgia Census Index, Online Edition (Veterans Schedule).* Orem, UT: Ancestry.com, Inc., 1999.
http://www.ancestry.com

U.S. Federal Population Census Schedules. 1890, M407, Microfilm Reel No. 3.

U.S. Federal Population Census Schedules. 1890, Index. M496, 2 Microfilm Reels.

1900

Barrow, Carol J. *Barrow Families in Georgia Census, 1820-1910.* Atlanta, GA: Author, 1990. 90p.

U.S. Federal Population Census Schedules. 1900, T623, Microfilm Reel Nos. 178-230.
U.S. Federal Population Census Schedules. 1900, Soundex. T1040, 211 Microfilm Reels.
U.S. Federal Population Census Schedules. 1900, Military & Naval Bases. T1081, Microfilm Reel Nos. 1838-1842.
U.S. Federal Population Census Schedules. 1900, Military & Naval Bases, Soundex. T1081, 32 Microfilm Reels.

1910

Barrow, Carol J. *Barrow Families in Georgia Census, 1820-1910.* Atlanta, GA: Author, 1990. 90p.
U.S. Federal Population Census Schedules. 1910, T624, Microfilm Reel Nos. 170-220.
U.S. Federal Population Census Schedules. 1910, Soundex. T1263, 148 Microfilm Reels.
U.S. Federal Population Census Schedules. 1910, Separate Soundex for Cities of Atlanta, Augusta, Macon and Savannah, T1263, Microfilm Reel Nos. 149-174.

1920

U.S. Federal Population Census Schedules. 1920, 1920, T625, Microfilm Reel Nos. 233-286.
U.S. Federal Population Census Schedules. 1920, Soundex. M1557, 200 Microfilm Reels.

Appling County
1820
1820 United States Census, Appling County. Jacksonville, FL: Southern Genealogist's Exchange Quarterly. 23p.
1850
Huxford, Folks. *Appling County, Georgia, 1850 Census (With Index).* Jacksonville, FL: Southern Genealogist's Exchange Quarterly, 1964. 59p.
1860
Ingmire, Frances Terry. *Citizens of Appling County, Georgia, 1860.* Saint Louis, MO:Author. 56p.
Mobley, Biggers. *1860 Census of Appling County, Georgia.* Author. 77p.
1870
Stokes, Alvin. *Appling County, Georgia 1870 Census.* Homerville, GA: Huxford Genealogical Society. 76p.
1880
Stokes, Alvin. *Appling County, Georgia 1880 Census.* Milledgeville, GA: Boyd Pub. Co., 1995. 70p.
1910
Bohler, Kay, and Randall Walker. *Appling County, Georgia 1910 Census.* Homerville, GA: Huxford Genealogical Society. 91p.

Atlanta (De Kalb County)
1870
Jackson, Ronald Vern. *Atlanta, Augusta, & Savannah, Georgia 1870 Federal Census Index.* Salt Lake City, UT: Accelerated Indexing Systems International, 1990. 469p.
1910
U.S. Federal Population Census Schedules. Separate Soundex for Cities of Atlanta, Augusta, Macon and Savannah, T1263, Microfilm Reel Nos. 149-174.

Augusta (Richomond County)
1870
Jackson, Ronald Vern. *Atlanta, Augusta, & Savannah, Georgia 1870 Federal Census Index.* Salt Lake City, UT: Accelerated Indexing Systems International, 1990. 469p.
1910
U.S. Federal Population Census Schedules. Separate Soundex for Cities of Atlanta, Augusta, Macon and Savannah, T1263, Microfilm Reel Nos. 149-174.

Baker County

Census Records of Baker County, McIntosh County, Troup County. Morrow, GA: Genealogical Enterprises, 1969. 22p.

1850

Otto, Rhea Cumming. *1850 Census of Georgia*. Savannah, GA: Author, 1976. 45p.

1860

Ingmire, Frances Terry. *Citizens of Baker County, Georgia, 1860 Census Index*. San Antonio, TX: Ingmire. 27p.

Sweat, Faye. *1860 Census, Baker County, Georgia*. Albany, GA: Southwest Georgia Genealogical Society, 1985. 33p.

Baldwin County

1820

Tunnell, George Heard, Mrs. *Baldwin County, Georgia 1820 Census, 1850 Census*. Author, 1945.

1850

Otto, Rhea Cumming. *1850 Census of Georgia*. Savannah, GA: Author, 1994. 52p.

Tunnell, George Heard, Mrs. *Baldwin County, Georgia 1820 Census, 1850 Census*. Author, 1945.

Banks County

1860

Ingmire, Frances Terry. *Citizens of Banks County, Georgia, 1860 Census Index*. San Antonio, TX: Ingmire Pub., 1980. 70p.

Bartow County

1834

Hageness, MariLee Beatty. *1834 State Census, Cass — Bartow Counties*. Anniston, GA: MLH Research, 1994. 6p.

1850

Barnette, Mic. *1850 Census of Bartow County, Georgia (Formerly Cass)*. Shreveport, LA: J & W Enterprises, 1989. 282p.

Berrien County

1860

Dupree, James William. *1860 Census Berrien County, Georgia*. Homerville, GA: Huxford Genealogical Society. 57p.

Ingmire, Frances Terry. *Citizens of Berrien County, Georgia, 1860 Census*. San Antonio, TX: Ingmire Pub., 1989. 50p.

1870

Griffin, Myrtie Lou, and Roscoe Arnold Stallings. *1870 Census of Berrien County, Georgia*. Homerville, GA: Huxford Genealogical Society. 83p.

1880

Griffin, Myrtie Lou, and Roscoe Arnold Stallings. *1880 Census of Berrien County, Georgia*. Homerville, GA: Huxford Genealogical Society. 111p.

1900

Griffin, Myrtie Lou, and Roscoe Arnold Stallings. *1900 Census of Berrien County, Georgia*. Homerville, GA: Huxford Genealogical Society. 239p.

1920

Griffin, Myrtie Lou, and Roscoe Arnold Stallings. *1920 Census of Berrien County, Georgia*. Homerville, GA: Huxford Genealogical Society, 1987. 2 vols.

Bibb County

1850

1850 Bibb County, Georgia Census. Morrow, GA: Genealogical Enterprises, 1968. 137p.

Otto, Rhea Cumming. *1850 Census of Georgia*. Savannah, GA: Author, 1994. 105p.
1860
Ingmire, Frances Terry. *Citizens of Bibb County, Georgia, 1860 Census*. Saint Louis, MO: Author. Unpgd.

Bleckley County
1830-1860
Myrick, Victor Ray. *Census Records, 1830 through 1860, Pulaski and Bleckley Counties*. Cochran, GA: Author, 1976. 110p.

Brooks County
1860
Edmondson, John A. *1860 Census of Brooks County, Georgia*. Homerville, GA: Huxford Genealogical Society. 76p.
Ingmire, Frances Terry. *Citizens of Brooks County, Georgia, 1860 Census*. San Antonio, TX: Ingmire Pub., 1980. 53p.
1870
Griffin, Myrtie Lou, and Roscoe Arnold Stallings. *Brooks County, Georgia 1870 Census*. Homerville, GA: Huxford Genealogical Society, 1987. 72p.
1880
Griffin, Myrtie Lou, and Roscoe Arnold Stallings. *Brooks County, Georgia 1880 Census*. Homerville, GA: Huxford Genealogical Society, 1987. 104p.
1900
Craigmiles, Joe E. *1900 Brooks County Census Index*. Thomasville, GA: Author. 43p.

Bryan County
1830
Register, Alvaretta Kenan. *The Fifth Census of the United States, 1830, Bryan County, Georgia*. Statesboro, GA: Author, 1970. 6p.
1850
Otto, Rhea Cumming. *1850 Census of Georgia*. Savannah, GA: Author, 1975. 14p.
1860
Ingmire, Frances Terry. *Citizens of Bryan County, Georgia, 1860 Census*. Saint Louis, MO: Author. 28p.
Williams, E.L. *Bryan County, Georgia Census of 1860*. Homerville, GA: Huxford Genealogical Society, 1984. 42p.
1870
Georgia DAR. *1870 Census of Bryan County, Georgia*. Georgia DAR Genealogical Record Committee Report, v508. Archibald Bulloch Chapter, DAR, 1992. 142p.
Kelly, Huldah K. *Ninth Census of the United States, Bryan County, Georgia, 1870*. Statesboro, GA: Statesboro Regional Library, 1991, 174p.
1880
Kelly, Huldah K. *Tenth Census of the United States, Bryan County, Georgia, 1880*. Statesboro, GA: Statesboro Regional Library, 1990, 141p.

Bulloch County
1820
Register, Alvaretta Kenan. *The Fourth Census of the United States, 1820, Bulloch County, Georgia*. Norfolk, VA: Author, 1966. 9p.
1830
Register, Alvaretta Kenan. *The Fifth Census of the United States, 1830, Bulloch County, Georgia*. Norfolk, VA: Author, 1968. 57p.
1840
Register, Alvaretta Kenan. *The Sixth Census of the United States, 1840, Bulloch County, Georgia*. Norfolk, VA: Author, 1966. 19p.

1850

McMinus, J. *Bulloch County, Georgia 1850 Census, Heads of Household Index*. Homerville, GA: Huxford Genealogical Society. 7p.

Register, Alvaretta Kenan. *The Seventh Census of the United States, 1850, Bulloch County, Georgia*. Norfolk, VA: Author, 1968. 57p.

1860

Ingmire, Frances Terry. *Citizens of Bulloch County, Georgia, 1860 Census*. St. Louis, MO: Author, 1986. 59p.

Register, Alvaretta K. *1860 and 1870 Census of Bulloch County*, Georgia. Statesboro, GA: Author, 1976. 115p.

1870

Register, Alvaretta K. *1860 and 1870 Census of Bulloch County*, Georgia. Statesboro, GA: Author, 1976. 115p.

1880

Register, Alvaretta Kenan. *United States, Census of Bulloch County, Georgia 1880*. Statesboro, GA: Author. 174p.

1900

Kelly, Henry Russell. *Twelfth Census of the United States Bulloch County, Georgia, 1900*. Statesboro, GA: Statesboro Regional Library, 1986. 4 vols.

1910

Kelly, Henry Russell. *Thirteenth Census of the United States Bulloch County, Georgia, 1910*. Statesboro, GA: Statesboro Regional Library, 1989. 8 vols.

Burke County
1850

Otto, Rhea Cumming. *1850 Census of Georgia*. Savannah, GA: Author, 1975. 69p.

1860

Abbott-Braswell, Marjorie. *1860 Burke County, Georgia Census*. Augusta, GA: Author, 1998. 111p.

Georgia DAR. *1860 Census of Burke County, Georgia*. Georgia DAR Genealogical Records Committee Report v.509. Archibald Bulloch Chapter, DAR, 1992. 137p.

Griffin, Myrtie Lou, and Roscoe Arnold Stallings. *Burke County, Georgia 1860 Census*. Homerville, GA: Huxford Genealogical Society. 110p.

Ingmire, Frances Terry. *1860 Census of Burke County, Georgia*. St. Louis, MO: Author, 1987. 95p.

1870

Kelly, Huldah K. *1870 Census, Burke County, Georgia*. Statesboro, GA: Statesboro Regional Library, 1987. 2 vols.

1880

Kelly, Huldah K. *Tenth Census of the United States, Burke County, Georgia, 1880*. Statesboro, GA: Statesboro Regional Library, 1991, 1992. 4 vols.

Butts County
1830

McMinus, J. *Butts County, Georgia 1830 Census, Heads of Household Index*. San Antonio, TX: Family Adventurers. 7p.

1850

Otto, Rhea Cumming. *1850 Census of Georgia*. Savannah, GA: Author, 1976. 37p.

Camden County
1820

USGenWeb Census Project. Georgia, 1820 Camden County.
ftp://ftp.rootsweb.com/pub/census/ga/camden/1820/

1830

USGenWeb Census Project. Georgia, 1830 Camden County.
ftp://ftp.rootsweb.com/pub/census/ga/camden/1830/
1840

USGenWeb Census Project. Georgia, 1840 Camden County.
ftp://ftp.rootsweb.com/pub/census/ga/camden/1840/
1850

1850 Census of Camden County, Georgia. Homerville, GA: Huxford Genealogical Society. 21p.
Otto, Rhea Cumming. *1850 Census of Georgia.* Savannah, GA: Author, 1974. 27p.
USGenWeb Census Project. Georgia, 1850 Camden County.
ftp://ftp.rootsweb.com/pub/census/ga/camden/1850/
1860

Coursey, W. Tony, and Kenneth H. Thomas. *1860 Census of Georgia, Camden County.* Atlanta, GA: Author, 1985. 46p.

1880

Morris, Scott. *Camden County, Ceorgia, 1880 Census.* Homerville, GA: Huxford Genealogical Society. 21p.

Campbell County
1830, 1840

Cornell, Nancy Jones. *Campbell County, Georgia, 1830 and 1840 Census.* Riverdale, GA: Author, 1985. 26p.
1850

Otto, Rhea Cumming. *1850 Census of Georgia.* Savannah, GA: Author, 1976. 53p.
1860

Cornell, Nancy Jones. *1860 Census of Campbell County, Georgia.* Riverdale, GA: Author, 1990. 64p.

Carroll County
1830, 1840

McNinch, Ruth, and Mary Florence Word. *1830 & 1840 Federal Censuses of Carroll County, Georgia.* Carrollton, GA: Carroll County Genealogical Society, 1998. 60p.
1850

Cox, Clarice S., and Nell R. Yates. *Carroll County, Georgia 1850 Census.* Bowdon, GA: Author, 1981. 102p.
McNinch, Ruth, and Mary Florence Word. *1850 U.S. Census, Carroll County, Georgia.* Carrollton, GA: Carroll County Genealogical Society, 1997. 114p.
Otto, Rhea Cumming. *1850 Census of Georgia.* Savannah, GA: Author, 1984. 73p.
1860

Carroll County, Georgia Census 1860. Carrollton, GA: Carroll County Genealogical Society, 1982. 140p.
Ingmire, Frances Terry. *Citizens of Carroll County, Georgia, 1860 Census.* St. Louis, MO: Author, 1986. 96p.
1870

Carroll County, Georgia Census, 1870. LaGrange, GA: Family Tree, 1985. 172p.
1880

Gardner, Shirley M. *The 1880 Census of Carroll County, Georgia.* Carrollton, GA: Carroll County Genealogical Society, 1990. 223p.

Cass County
1834

Hageness, MariLee Beatty. *1834 State Census, Cass — Bartow Counties.* Anniston, GA: MLH Research, 1994. 6p.
1840

Ingmire, Frances Terry. *They Were There, Georgia County 1840 Census Index.* St. Louis, MO: Author. 24p.

1850

McMinus, J. *Cass County, Georgia 1850 Census, Heads of Household Index*. San Antonio, TX: Family Adventurers. 4p.

1860

Ingmire, Frances Terry. *Citizens of Cass County, Georgia 1860 Census Index*. St. Louis, MO: Author. 52p.

Catoosa County
1860

1860 United States, Catoosa County, Georgia. Ringgold, GA: Catoosa County Georgia Genealogical Society, 1994. Unpgd.

Ingmire, Frances Terry. *Citizens of Catoosa County, Georgia, 1860 Census*. Saint Louis, MO: Author, 1986. 20p.

Charlton County
1860

Griffin, Myrtie Lou, and Roscoe Arnold Stallings. *Charlton County, Georgia 1860 Census*. Homerville, GA: Huxford Genealogical Society. 24p.

1870

Griffin, Myrtie Lou, and Roscoe Arnold Stallings. *Charlton County, Georgia 1870 Census*. Homerville, GA: Huxford Genealogical Society. 30p.

1880

Griffin, Myrtie Lou, and Roscoe Arnold Stallings. *Charlton County, Georgia 1880 Census*. Homerville, GA: Huxford Genealogical Society. 35p.

1900

1900 Census of Charlton County, Georgia. Homerville, GA: Huxford Genealogical Society. 60p.

Chatham County
1845

Censuses for Georgia Counties, Taliaferro, 1827, Lumpkin, 1838, Chatham, 1845. Atlanta, GA: R. J. Taylor, Jr. Foundation, 1979. 57p.

1850

Otto, Rhea Cumming. *1850 Census of Georgia*. Savannah, GA: Author, 1975. 123p.

1860

1860 Census of Chatham County, Georgia. Savannah, GA: Georgia Historical Society, 1979. 436p.

Ingmire, Frances Terry. *Chatham County, Georgia, 1860 Index to Census*. St. Louis, MO: Author. 37p.

Chattooga County
1850

Griffith, Jessie June Brandon. *1850 Chattooga County, Georgia Census & Mortality Census*. Rossville, GA.: Author. 39p.

Lacy, Ruby. *Georgia, Chattooga County Census of 1850*. Ashland, OR: Author, 1983. 60p.

Otto, Rhea Cumming. *1850 Census of Georgia*. Savannah, GA: Author, 1978. 48p.

1870

Griffith, Jessie June Brandon. *1870 Census and Mortality Schedules of Chattooga County, Georgia, Plus Confederate Soldier Information, Where They Enlisted, Fought and Where They Died*. Fort Oglethorp, GA: Price. 102p.

Cherokee County
1834

Hageness, MariLee Beatty. *1834 State Census, Cherokee County, Georgia*. Anniston, AL: MLH Research, 1995. 6p.

1850

Otto, Rhea Cumming. *1850 Census of Georgia*. Savannah, GA: Author, 1976. 107p.
1860

Acord, Arlis L. *Cherokee County, Georgia, the 1860 Federal Census*. Alexandria, VA: Author, 1984. 56p.

Clarke County
1830

McMinus, J. *Clarke County, Georgia, 1830 Census, Heads of Household Index*. San Antonio, TX: Family Adventures. 10p.
1870

Jarvis, Grace Hemrick. *1850 Census, Clarke County, Georgia, (Seventh Census of the United States)*. Jacksonville, FL: Jacksonville Genealogical Society, 1981. 175p.

Clayton County
1860

Clayton County, Georgia, 1860 Census Including Slave and Mortality Census. Jonesboro, GA: Ancestors Unlimited, 1985. 84p.
Curry, Doris F. *Clayton County, Georgia 1860 Census*. Riverdale, GA: Author, 1978. 86p.
1870

Clayton County, Georgia, 1870 Census Including Slave and Mortality Census. Jonesboro, GA: Ancestors Unlimited, 1987. 105p.
Curry, Doris F. *Clayton County, Georgia 1870 Census*. Riverdale, GA: Author, 1978. 138p.
1880

1880 Census, Clayton County, Georgia. College Park, GA: Ancestors Unlimited, 1980. 162p.
1900

Curry, Doris F. *1900 U.S. Census, Clayton County, Georgia*. Riverdale, GA: Pea Ridge Publications, 1981. 320p.
1910

1910 U.S. Census of Clayton County, Georgia. Jonesboro, GA: Ancestors Unlimited, 1986. 217p.

Clinch County
1850

Griffin, Myrtie Lou, and Roscoe Arnold Stallings. *1850 Census of Clinch County, Georgia, the Portion of Lowndes County Made into Clinch County*. Homerville, GA: Huxford Genealogical Society. 10p.
Schunk, John Frederick. *1850 U.S. Census, Clinch County, Georgia*. Wichita, KS: S-K Publications, f1988. 27p.
1860

Clinch County, Georgia 1860 Census. Homerville, GA: Huxford Genealogical Society. 48p.
1870

1870 Census of Clinch County, Georgia. Homerville, GA: Huxford Genealogical Society. 78p.
1880

1880 Census of Clinch County, Georgia. Homerville, GA: Huxford Genealogical Society. 62p.
1900

Stokes, Mrs. A. J. *1900 Census, Clinch County, Georgia*. Homerville, GA: Huxford Genealogical Society. 110p.

Cobb County
1834

Hageness, MariLee Beatty. *Heads of Families, 1834 State Census, Cobb County, Georgia*. Author, 1995. 6p.
1840

Waters, Eleanor Tolliver. *Cobb County, Georgia, 1840 Census*. Marrietta, GA: Cobb County Genealogical Society, 1989. 46p.

1850

Otto, Rhea Cumming. *1850 Census of Georgia*. Savannah, GA: Author, 1984. 109p.

Coffee County
1860

Huxford, Folks. *Coffee County, Georgia, the Census of 1860*. Homerville, GA: Author, 1947. 50p.

Stokes, Alvin. *1860 Census of Coffee County, Georgia*. Homerville, GA: Huxford Genealogical Society. 42p.

1870

Gourley, Winifred Merier. *1870 Census of Coffee County, Georgia*. Douglas, GA: Author, 1983. 58p.

1880

Stokes, Alvin. *1880 Census of Coffee County, Georgia*. Homerville, GA: Huxford Genealogical Society. 77p.

Colquitt County
1870

Morris, Scott. *The Ninth Census of the United States of America, 1870, Colquitt County, Georgia*. Colquitt, GA: Colquitt County Genealogical Society, 1988. 34p.

1880

Morris, Scott. *The Ninth Census of the United States of America, 1880, Colquitt County, Georgia*. Colquitt, GA: Colquitt County Genealogical Society, 1989. 51p.

Columbia County
1850

Otto, Rhea Cumming. *1850 Census of Georgia*. Savannah, GA: Author, 1979. 40p.

Thiem, W. D., *1850 United States Census, Columbia County, Georgia*. San Angelo, TX: AAA Answering Service, 1969. 77p.

1859

Hageness, MariLee Beatty. *State Census 1859 Heads of Household, Columbia County, Georgia*. Author, 1995. 6p.

Cook County
1920

Stallings, Roscoe Arnold. *1920 Census of Cook County, Georgia*. Homerville, GA: Huxford Genealogical Society, 1987. 81p.

Coweta County
1830, 1840

Coweta County, Georgia Pioneers from the 1827 Land Lottery, 1830 Census and 1840 Census. Newnan, GA: Coweta County Genealogical Society, 1992. 154p.

1850

Otto, Rhea Cumming. *1850 Census of Georgia*. Savannah, GA: Author, 1981. 83p.

Steinback, Shirley Pitts. *1850 Coweta County, Georgia Census*. Newnan, GA: Coweta County Genealogical Society, 1991. 251p.

1860

Steinback, Shirley Pitts. *1860 Coweta County, Georgia Census*. Newnan, GA: Coweta County Genealogical Society, 1991. 121p.

1870

Steinback, Shirley Pitts. *The 1870 Census of Coweta County, Georgia*. Newnan, GA: Coweta County Genealogical Society, 1991. 251p.

Crawford County
1830, 1840
Howell, Addie Paramore, and William R. Henry. *Crawford County, Georgia Federal Census Records for 1830, 1840 and 1850*. Warner Robbins, GA: Central Georgia Genealogical Society, 1988. 121p.
1850
Howell, Addie Paramore, and William R. Henry. *Crawford County, Georgia Federal Census Records for 1830, 1840 and 1850*. Warner Robbins, GA: Central Georgia Genealogical Society, 1988. 121p.
Nottingham, Mrs. E. T. *1850 United States Census of Crawford, Georgia*. Author, 1945. 89p.
Otto, Rhea Cumming. *1850 Census of Georgia, Crawfod County, Nearly 4,400 Free Citizens*. Savannah, GA: Author, 1986. 43p.

Dade County
1840, 1850
Vance, Paul R. L. *Dade Pioneers 1840 and 1850 Census of Dade County, Georgia*. Author, 1970. 94p.

Decatur County
1850
USGenWeb Census Project. Georgia, 1850 Decatur County.
ftp://ftp.rootsweb.com/pub/census/ga/decatur/1850/
Varick, Floreda Duke, and Phyllis Rose Smith. *Decatur County, Georgia, 1850 Census*. Tallahassee, FL: Authors, 1978. 95p.

DeKalb County
1850
Otto, Rhea Cumming. *1850 Census of Georgia*. Savannah, GA: Author, 1979. 114p.

Dooly County
1850
Otto, Rhea Cumming. *1850 Census of Georgia*. Savannah, GA: Author, 1971. 77p.
_____. *1850 Census of Georgia, Dooly, Fayette, Floyd, Glynn and Jefferson Counties*. Savannah, GA: Author, 1973. 5 vols. in 1.
1860
Acord, Arlis L. *Dooly County, Georgia, the 1860 Federal Census*. Alexandria, VA: Author, 1984. 30p.

Douglas County
1900
Baggett, Joe. *Douglas County, Georgia 1900 United States Census*. Douglasville, GA: Author, 1981. 96p.

Dougherty County
1860
Sweat, Faye. *1860 Census, Dougherty County, Georgia, Abstracts*. Albany, GA: Southwest Georgia Genealogical Society, 1985. 46p.

Early County
1850
Otto, Rhea Cumming. *1850 Census of Georgia*. Savannah, GA: Author, 1970. 37p.
USGenWeb Census Project. Georgia, 1850 Early County.
ftp://ftp.rootsweb.com/pub/census/ga/early/1850/
1860
Acord, Arlis L. *Early and Echols Counties, Georgia, the 1860 Federal Census*. Alexandria, VA: Author, 1984. 21p.

Echols County
1860
Acord, Arlis L. *Early and Echols Counties, Georgia, the 1860 Federal Census*. Alexandria, VA: Author, 1984. 21p.
1880
Griffin, Myrtie Lou, and Roscoe Arnold Stallings. *Echols County, Georgia 1880 Census*. Homerville, GA: Huxford Genealogical Society. 42p.

Effingham County
1850
Otto, Rhea Cumming. *1850 Census of Effingham County, Georgia*. Savannah, GA: Author, 1970. 35p.
1860
Acord, Arlis L. *Effingham County, Georgia, the 1860 Federal Census*. Alexandria, VA: Author, 1984. 17p.

Elbert County
1820
Holloman, Ann Brown Clark. *Elbert County, Georgia 1820 Census*. Albany, GA: Author, 1995. 20p.
Wilcox, Irene Stillwell. *The Census Records of Elbert County, 1820-1860 and the 1850 Census of Wilkes County*. Easley, SC: Southern Historical Press, 1979. 138p.
1830, 1840
Wilcox, Irene Stillwell. *The Census Records of Elbert County, 1820-1860 and the 1850 Census of Wilkes County*. Easley, SC: Southern Historical Press, 1979. 138p.
1850
Otto, Rhea Cumming. *1850 Census of Georgia*. Savannah, GA: Author, 1970. 107p.
USGenWeb Census Project. Georgia, 1850 Elbert County. (Partial).
ftp://ftp.rootsweb.com/pub/census/ga/elbert/1850/
Wilcox, Irene Stillwell. *The Census Records of Elbert County, 1820-1860 and the 1850 Census of Wilkes County*. Easley, SC: Southern Historical Press, 1979. 138p.
1860
Wilcox, Irene Stillwell. *The Census Records of Elbert County, 1820-1860 and the 1850 Census of Wilkes County*. Easley, SC: Southern Historical Press, 1979. 138p.

Emanuel County
1850
Griffin, Myrtie Lou, and Roscoe Arnold Stallings. *Emanuel County, Georgia 1850 Census*. Homerville, GA: Huxford Genealogical Society. 72p.
Otto, Rhea Cumming. *1850 Census of Georgia*. Savannah, GA: Author, 1970. 55p.
1860
Griffin, Myrtie Lou, and Roscoe Arnold Stallings. *Emanuel County, Georgia 1860 Census*. Homerville, GA: Huxford Genealogical Society. 77p.
1870
Avant, David Alonz. *Ninth Census of the United States, Emanuel County, Georgia 1870*. Tallahasee, FL: Author, 1990. 164p.
USGenWeb Census Project. Georgia, 1850 Emanuel County.
ftp://ftp.rootsweb.com/pub/census/ga/emanuale/1850/
1880
Kelly, Hulda K. *Georgia 1880 Census, Emanuel County Index*. Statesboro, GA: Statesboro Regional Library, 1983. 43p.

Fannin County
1860
Casada, Helen Weaver. *1860 Fannin County, Georgia Census*. Charleston, TN: Author, 1987. 117p.

Ingmire, Frances Terry. *Citizens of Fannin County, Georgia, 1860 Census Index*. Saint Louis, MO: Author, 1986. 21p.

Poteet Pitts, Jennie Vee. *1860 Federal Census, Fannin County, Georgia*. Atlanta, GA: Author, 1986. 107p.

1870

Casada, Helen Weaver. *Fannin County, Georgia 1870 Census*. Charleston, TN: Author, 1991. 127p.

Poteet Pitts, Jennie Vee. *1870 Federal Census, Fannin County, Georgia*. Atlanta, GA: Author, 1986. 114p.

1880

Jones, Viola H. *Fannin County Georgia Census, 1880*. Louisville, TN: Author, 1987. 166p.

1900

Jones, Viola H. *Fannin County, Georgia Census, 1900*. Louisville, TN: Author, 1988. 244p.

1910

Jones, Viola H. *Fannin County, Georgia, Federal Census of 1910*. Louisville, TN: Author, 1990. 299p.

1920

Jones, Viola H. *Fannin County, Georgia, Federal Census of 1920*. Louisville, TN: Author, 1993. 277p.

Fayette County
1850

Otto, Rhea Cumming. *1850 Census of Georgia*. Savannah, GA: Author, 1973. 68p.

_____. *1850 Census of Georgia, Dooly, Fayette, Floyd, Glynn and Jefferson Counties*. Savannah, GA: Author, 1973. 5 vols. in 1.

Floyd County
1850

Otto, Rhea Cumming. *1850 Census of Georgia, Dooly, Fayette, Floyd, Glynn and Jefferson Counties*. Savannah, GA: Author, 1973. 5 vols. in 1.

1860

Anderson, Grover Calvin. *Floyd County, Georgia, 1860 Census*. McAlester, OK: Author, 1981. 262p.

Forsyth County
1834

Hageness, MariLee Beatty. *Heads of Families, 1834 State Census, Forsyth County, Georgia*. Author, 1995. 7p.

Parrish, Donna. *Census Index of Forsyth County, Georgia, 1834-1900*. Cumming, GA: Author, 1981. 155p.

1840

Ingmire, Frances Terry. *They Were There, Georgia County 1840 Census Index*. St. Louis, MO: Author. 16p.

1850

Parrish, Donna. *Census Index of Forsyth County, Georgia, 1834-1900*. Cumming, GA: Author, 1981. 155p.

1860

Ingmire, Frances Terry. *Citizens of Forsyth County, Georgia 1860 Census Index*. St. Louis, MO: Author, 1986. 31p.

_____. _____. Nacogdoches, TX: Author, 1995. 31p.

Parrish, Donna. *Census Index of Forsyth County, Georgia, 1834-1900*. Cumming, GA: Author, 1981. 155p.

1870-1900

Parrish, Donna. *Census Index of Forsyth County, Georgia, 1834-1900*. Cumming, GA: Author, 1981. 155p.

1910

Nalley, D.E. *Index, 1910 Census, Forsyth County, Georgia*. Washington, DC: Author, 1984. 69p.

Franklin County
1840

Ingmire, Frances Terry. *They Were There, Georgia County 1840 Census Index*. St. Louis, MO: Author, 1980. 26p.

1850

Franklin County, Georgia Census of 1850. DAR, McCall Genealogy Fund, 1941. Unpgd.

Otto, Rhea Cumming. *1850 Census of Georgia*. Savannah, GA: Author, 1976. 86p.
1860
Ingmire, Frances Terry. *Citizens of Franklin County, Georgia, 1860 Census Index*. Nacogdoches, TX: Ericson Books, 1986. 29p.

Fulton County
1860
Acord, Arlis L. *Fulton County, Georgia, the 1860 Federal Census*. Alexandria, VA: Author, 1985. 81p.
Ingmire, Frances Terry. *Fulton County, Georgia, 1860 Head of Household Census Index*. St. Louis, MO: Author, 1986. 68p.

Gilmer County
1840
Quarles, Anita. *Georgia, Gilmer County, 1840 U.S. Census*. Tunnel Hill, GA: Author. 21p.
Scates, Beulah Mae. *1840 Census of Gilmer County, Georgia*. Ada, OK: Pontotoc County Historical and Genealogical Society, 1973. 16p.
1850
1850 Federal Census, Gilmer County, Georgia. Atlanta, GA: R. J. Taylor, Jr. Foundation, 1978. 82p.
1860
Casada, Helen Weaver. *Gilmer County, Georgia 1860 Census*. Charleston, TN: Author, 1989. 172p.
Ingmire, Frances Terry. *Citizens of Gilmer County, Georgia, 1860 Census Index*. Saint Louis, MO: Author, 1986. 30p.
1870
Casada, Helen Weaver. *Gilmer County, Georgia 1870 Census*. Charleston, TN: Author, 1990. 150p.

Glynn County
1830, 1840
Stokes, Alvin. *Glynn County, Georgia 1830, 1840, 1850 Census*. Homerville, GA: Huxford Genealogical Society. 28p.
1850
Otto, Rhea Cumming. *1850 Census of Georgia*. Savannah, GA: Author, 1973. 11p.
_____. *1850 Census of Georgia, Dooly, Fayette, Floyd, Glynn and Jefferson Counties*. Savannah, GA: Author, 1973. 5 vols. in 1.
Stokes, Alvin. *Glynn County, Georgia 1830, 1840, 1850 Census*. Homerville, GA: Huxford Genealogical Society. 28p.
USGenWeb Census Project. Georgia, 1850 Glynn County.
ftp://ftp.rootsweb.com/pub/census/ga/glynn/1850/
1860
Coursey, W. Tony, and Kenneth H. Thomas, Jr. *1860 Census of Georgia, Glynn County*. Atlanta, GA: Authors, 1984. 37p.
Stokes, Alvin. *Glynn County, Georgia 1860 Census*. Homerville, GA: Huxford Genealogical Society. 21p.
1870
Stokes, Alvin. *Glynn County, Georgia 1870 Census*. Homerville, GA: Huxford Genealogical Society. 38p.
1880
Stokes, Alvin. *Glynn County, Georgia 1880 Census*. Homerville, GA: Huxford Genealogical Society, 1991. 44p.

Gordon County
1850
Otto, Rhea Cumming. *1850 Census of Georgia*. Savannah, GA: Author, 1974. 60p.
1860
Ingmire, Frances Terry. *Citizens of Gordon County, Georgia, 1860 Census Index*. Saint Louis, MO: Author, 1986. 39p.

Greene County
1850
Otto, Rhea Cumming. *1850 Census of Georgia*. Savannah, GA: Author, 1974. 61p.

Gwinnett County
1840
Ingmire, Frances Terry. *They Were There, Georgia County 1840 Census Index*. St. Louis, MO: Author. 27p.
1850
Nesbitt, Kate Duncan. *Gwinnett County, Georgia 1850 Census*. Lawrenceville, GA: Gwinnett Historical Society, 1986. 242p.
1860
Moore, John V. *Gwinnett County, Georgia 1860 Census*. Lawrenceville, GA: Gwinnett Historical Society, 1983. 322p.
1870
Frazier, Susan Robinson. *Gwinnett County, Georgia 1870 Census*. Lawrenceville, GA: Gwinnett Historical Society, 1986. 357p.

Habersham County
1840
Ingmire, Frances Terry. *They Were There, Georgia County 1840 Census Index*. St. Louis, MO: Author, 1980. 23p.
1860
Ingmire, Frances Terry. *Citizens of Habersham County, Georgia, 1860 Census Index*. Saint Louis, MO: Author, 1986. 22p.

Hall County
1850
Otto, Rhea Cumming. *1850 Census of Georgia*. Savannah, GA: Author, 1991. 74p.
1860
Ingmire, Frances Terry. *Citizens of Hall County, Georgia, 1860 Census Index*. Nagocdoches, TX: Author, 1995. 35p.

Hancock County
1830
USGenWeb Census Project. Georgia, 1830 Hancock County.
ftp://ftp.rootsweb.com/pub/census/ga/hancock/1830/
1840
USGenWeb Census Project. Georgia, 1840 Hancock County.
ftp://ftp.rootsweb.com/pub/census/ga/hancock/1840/
1850
Otto, Rhea Cumming. *1850 Census of Georgia*. Savannah, GA: Author, 1980. 45p.
Schunk, John Frederick. *1850 U.S. Census, Hancock County, Georgia*. Wichita, KS: S-K Publications, 1986. 51p.
USGenWeb Census Project. Georgia, 1850 Hancock County.
ftp://ftp.rootsweb.com/pub/census/ga/hancock/1850/

Haralson County
1860
Ingmire, Frances Terry. *Citizens of Haralson County, Georgia, 1860 Census Index*. Nacogdoches, TX: Ericson Books, 1986, 1995. 12p.
USGenWeb Census Project. Georgia, 1860 Haralson County.
ftp://ftp.rootsweb.com/pub/census/ga/haralson/1860/

1870

USGenWeb Census Project. Georgia, 1870 Haralson County.
ftp://ftp.rootsweb.com/pub/census/ga/haralson/1870/

Harris County
1850

Hawkins, Rhonda Leah. *1850 Census of Harris County, Georgia.* Marietta, GA: Author, 1998. 123p.

Hart County
1860

Holloman, Ann Brown Clark. *Hart County, Georgia 1860 Census, Including Slave Schedule and Mortality Schedule.* Albany, GA: Author, 1961, 1995. Unpgd.

1870

Parker, Harold Travis. *1870 Census of Hart County, Georgia.* Lavoria, GA: Author, 1979. 60p.

1880

Parker, Harold Travis. *1880 U.S. Census of Hart County, Georgia.* Lavonia, GA: Author, 1981. 148p.

Heard County
1840

USGenWeb Census Project. Georgia, 1840 Heard County.
ftp://ftp.rootsweb.com/pub/census/ga/heard/1840/

1850

Eller, Lynda S. *1850 Census, Heard County, Georgia.* Lanett, AL: Author, 1976. 60p.
USGenWeb Census Project. Georgia, 1850 Heard County.
ftp://ftp.rootsweb.com/pub/census/ga/heard/1850/

1860

Eller, Lynda S. *1860 Census, Heard County, Georgia.* Lanett, AL: Author, 1976. 69p.

1870

Eller, Lynda S. *1870 Census, Heard County, Georgia.* Lanett, AL: Author, 1977. 108p.

1880

Eller, Lynda S. *Heard County, Georgia, 1880 Census.* Lanett, AL: Author, 1978. 199p.

Henry County
1850

Hageness, MariLee Beatty. *Slaveowner Census, 1850, Henry County, Georgia.* Anniston, AL: MLH Research, 1995. 8p.

Otto, Rhea Cumming. *1850 Census of Georgia.* Savannah, GA: Author, 1979. 93p.

1860

Curry, Doris F. *Henry County, Georgia Census, 1860.* McDonough, GA: Genealogical Society of Henry & Clayton Counties. 116p.

1870

Turner, Freda R. *1870 Census Henry County, Georgia.* Roswell, GA: W.H. Wolfe Associates, 1995. 247p.

Houston County
1830

1830 Federal Census for Houston County, Georgia. Warner Robins, GA: Central Georgia Genealogical Society, 1986. 50p.

1840

Henry, William R. *1840 Federal Census for Houston County, Georgia.* Warner Robins, GA: Central Georgia Genealogical Society, 1986. 43p.

1850

Henry, William R. *1850 Federal Census for Houston County, Georgia.* Warner Robins, GA: Central Georgia Genealogical Society, 1986. 111p.

Otto, Rhea Cumming. *1850 Census of Georgia*. Savannah, GA: Author, 1979. 65p.
1860
Howell, Addie Paramore. *1860 Federal Census for Houston County, Georgia (Population Schedule)*. Warner Robbins, GA: Central Georgia Genealogical Society, 1986. 91p.

Irwin County
1820
Pompey, Sherman Lee. *Index to the 1820 Census Records of Irwin County, Georgia*. Charleston, OR: Pacific Specialities, 1974.
1850
Huxford, Folks. *Irwin County, Georgia United States Census 1850*. Homerville, GA: Author, 1946. 64p.
1860
Caves, Rachel Peterson. *1860 Census of Irwin County, Georgia*. Ocilla, GA: Author. 27p.
1870
Griffin, Myrtie Lou, and Roscoe Arnold Stallings. *Irwin County, Georgia 1870 Census*. Homerville, GA: Huxford Genealogical Society. 32p.
1880
Griffin, Myrtie Lou, and Roscoe Arnold Stallings. *Irwin County, Georgia 1880 Census*. Homerville, GA: Huxford Genealogical Society. 45p.

Jackson County
1850
Boyd, Terri B. *The 1850 Census of Jackson County, Georgia*. Huntsville, AL: Author, 1983. 155p.
Otto, Rhea Cumming. *1850 Census of Georgia*. Savannah, GA: Author, 1992. 67p.
1860
Boyd, Terri B. *The 1860 Census of Jackson County, Georgia*. Huntsville, AL: Author, 1984. 164p.

Jasper County
1820
USGenWeb Census Project. Georgia, 1820 Jasper County.
ftp://ftp.rootsweb.com/pub/census/ga/jasper/1820/
1850
Otto, Rhea Cumming. *1850 Census of Georgia*. Savannah, GA: Author, 1991. 43p.

Jefferson County
1820
USGenWeb Census Project. Georgia, 1820 Jefferson County.
ftp://ftp.rootsweb.com/pub/census/ga/jefferson/1820/
1830
USGenWeb Census Project. Georgia, 1830 Jefferson County.
ftp://ftp.rootsweb.com/pub/census/ga/jefferson/1830/
1840
USGenWeb Census Project. Georgia, 1840 Jefferson County.
ftp://ftp.rootsweb.com/pub/census/ga/jefferson/1840/
1850
Otto, Rhea Cumming. *1850 Census of Georgia*. Savannah, GA: Author, 1973. 54p.
_____. *1850 Census of Georgia, Dooly, Fayette, Floyd, Glynn and Jefferson Counties*. Savannah, GA: Author, 1973. 5 vols. in 1.
USGenWeb Census Project. Georgia, 1850 Jefferson County.
ftp://ftp.rootsweb.com/pub/census/ga/jefferson/1850/
1860
Griffin, Myrtie Lou, and Roscoe Arnold Stallings. *Jefferson County, Georgia 1860 Census*. Homerville, GA: Huxford Genealogical Society. 84p.

1870

Griffin, Myrtie Lou, and Roscoe Arnold Stallings. *Jefferson County, Georgia 1870 Census*. Homerville, GA: Huxford Genealogical Society. 88p.

Johnson County
1860

Georgia DAR. *Census and Index Records of Johnson and Montgomery Counties, Georgia*. Genealogical Records Committee Report, s2, v522. Georgia DAR, 1995. 106p.

1880

Kelly, Hulda K. *Eighth Census of the United States Johnson County, Georgia, 1860*. Statesboro, GA: Statesboro Regional Library, 1988. 56p.

Jones County
1840

Ingmire, Frances Terry. *They Were There, Georgia County 1840 Census Index*. St. Louis, MO: Author, 1986. 16p.

1850

1850 Census of Jones County, Georgia. Atlanta, GA: DAR, 1941.

1860

Ingmire, Frances Terry. *Citizens of Jones County, Georgia, 1860 Census Index*. Saint Louis, MO: Author, 1986. 16p.

Laurens County
1850

Otto, Rhea Cumming. *1850 Census of Georgia*. Savannah, GA: Author, 1973. 46p.

_____. *1850 Census of Georgia, Laurens, Lee, Liberty, Lincoln and Lumpkin Counties*. Savannah, GA: Author, 1973. 5 vols. in 1.

Lee County
1850

Otto, Rhea Cumming. *1850 Census of Georgia*. Savannah, GA: Author, 1973. 43p.

_____. *1850 Census of Georgia, Laurens, Lee, Liberty, Lincoln and Lumpkin Counties*. Savannah, GA: Author, 1973. 5 vols. in 1.

Liberty County
1850

Otto, Rhea Cumming. *1850 Census of Georgia, Laurens, Lee, Liberty, Lincoln and Lumpkin Counties*. Savannah, GA: Author, 1973. 5 vols. in 1.

_____. *1850 Census of Georgia, Liberty County, over 2,000 Free Citizens*. Savannah, GA: Author, 1971. 29p.

1860

Stokes, Alvin. *Liberty County, Georgia 1860 Census*. Homerville, GA: Huxford Genealogical Society. 46p.

1870

Griffin, Myrtie Lou, and Roscoe Arnold Stallings. *Liberty County, Georgia 1870 Census*. Homerville, GA: Huxford Genealogical Society. 89p.

Lincoln County
1800

Hudson, Frank Parker. *An 1800 Census for Lincoln County, Georgia*. Atlanta, GA: R. J. Taylor, Jr. Foundation, 1977. 135p.

1830

McMinus, J. *Lincoln County, Georgia 1830 Census, Heads of Household Index*. San Antonio, TX: Family Adventures. 5p.

USGenWeb Census Project. Georgia, 1830 Lincoln County.

ftp://ftp.rootsweb.com/pub/census/ga/lincoln/1830/

1850

Otto, Rhea Cumming. *1850 Census of Georgia*. Savannah, GA: Author, 1971. 31p.

_____. *1850 Census of Georgia, Laurens, Lee, Liberty, Lincoln and Lumpkin Counties*. Savannah, GA: Author, 1973. 5 vols. in 1.

Lowndes County
1850

Griffin, Myrtie Lou, and Roscoe Arnold Stallings. *1850 Census of Clinch County, Georgia, the Portion of Lowndes County Made into Clinch County*. Homerville, GA: Huxford Genealogical Society. 10p.

Huxford, Folks. *Lowndes County, Georgia United States Census of 1850*. Homerville, GA: Author, 1945. 100p.

1860

Williams, E. L. *Lowndes County, Georgia Census of 1860*. Homerville, GA: Huxford Genealogical Society, 1983. 74p.

1870

Stallings, Roscoe Arnold. *Lowndes County, Georgia, 1870 Census*. Homerville, GA: Huxford Genealogical Society. 76p.

1880

Griffin, Myrtie Lou, and Roscoe Arnold Stallings. *Lowndes County, Georgia 1880 Census*. Homerville, GA: Huxford Genealogical Society, 1986. 99p.

Lumpkin County
1834

Ingmire, Frances Terry. *1834 State Census of Lumpkin County, Georgia*. St. Louis, MO: Author. 8p.

1838

Censuses for Georgia Counties, Taliaferro, 1827, Lumpkin, 1838, Chatham, 1845. Atlanta, GA: R. J. Taylor, Jr. Foundation, 1979. 57p.

1850

Otto, Rhea Cumming. *1850 Census of Georgia*. Savannha, GA: Author, 1973. 100p.

_____. *1850 Census of Georgia, Laurens, Lee, Liberty, Lincoln and Lumpkin Counties*. Savannah, GA: Author, 1973. 5 vols. in 1.

1860

Ingmire, Frances Terry. *Citizens of Lumpkin County, Georgia, 1860 Census Index*. Saint Louis, MO: Author, 1986. 18p.

McDonough County
1890

U.S. Federal Population Census Schedules. 1890, M407, Microfilm Reel No. 3.

U.S. Federal Population Census Schedules. 1890, Index. M496, 2 Microfilm Reels.

McIntosh County

Census Records of Baker County, McIntosh County, Troup County. Morrow, GA: Genealogical Enterprises, 1969. 22p.

1850

Griffin, Myrtie Lou, and Roscoe Arnold Stallings. *1850 and 1860 Census of McIntosh County, Georgia*. Homerville, GA: Huxford Genealogical Society. Unpgd.

Otto, Rhea Cumming. *1850 Census of Georgia*. Savannah, GA: Author, 1974. 11p.; 1975. 16p.

USGenWeb Census Project. Georgia, 1850 McIntosh County.

ftp://ftp.rootsweb.com/pub/census/ga/mcintosh/1850/

1860

Griffin, Myrtie Lou, and Roscoe Arnold Stallings. *1850 and 1860 Census of McIntosh County, Georgia*. Homerville, GA: Huxford Genealogical Society. Unpgd.

1870, 1880

Griffin, Myrtie Lou, and Roscoe Arnold Stallings. *1870 and 1880 Census of McIntosh County, Georgia*. Homerville, GA: Huxford Genealogical Society. Unpgd.

Macon County
1840

Campbell, Davine Vining. *1840 Federal Census of Macon County, Georgia Population Schedule*. Warener Robbins, GA: Central Georgia Genealogical Society, 1989. 44p.

1850

Campbell, Davine Vining. *1850 Federal Census of Macon County, Georgia Population Schedules*. Warener Robbins, GA: Central Georgia Genealogical Society, 1989. 92p.; 1993. 97p.

Otto, Rhea Cumming. *1850 Census of Georgia*. Savannah, GA: Author, 1973. 52p.

1860

1860 Federal Census for Macon County, Georgia, Population Schedule. Warner Robins, GA: Central Georgia Genealogical Society, 1985. 64p.

1870

Campbell, Davine Vining. *1870 Federal Census of Macon County, Georgia White Population Schedules*. 1989. 92p.

1910

U.S. Federal Population Census Schedules. Separate Soundex for Cities of Atlanta, Augusta, Macon and Savannah, T1263, Microfilm Reel Nos. 149-174.

Madison County
1820

Berryman, Mary Love. *Madison County, Georgia, Censuses, 1820-1860*. Danielsville, GA: Heritage Papers, 1986. 429p.

USGenWeb Census Project. Georgia, 1820 Madison County.

ftp://ftp.rootsweb.com/pub/census/ga/madison/1820/

1830

Berryman, Mary Love. *Madison County, Georgia, Censuses, 1820-1860*. Danielsville, GA: Heritage Papers, 1986. 429p.

USGenWeb Census Project. Georgia, 1830 Madison County.

ftp://ftp.rootsweb.com/pub/census/ga/madison/1830/

1840

Berryman, Mary Love. *Madison County, Georgia, Censuses, 1820-1860*. Danielsville, GA: Heritage Papers, 1986. 429p.

USGenWeb Census Project. Georgia, 1840 Madison County.

ftp://ftp.rootsweb.com/pub/census/ga/madison/1840/

1850

Berryman, Mary Love. *Madison County, Georgia, Censuses, 1820-1860*. Danielsville, GA: Heritage Papers, 1986. 429p.

Cater, Mary and Joseph T. Maddox. *1850 U.S. Census Records, Madison, Upson Counties, Georgia, with Other Statistics Added*. Irwinton, GA: Author, 1980. 60p.

1860

Berryman, Mary Love. *Madison County, Georgia, Censuses, 1820-1860*. Danielsville, GA: Heritage Papers, 1986. 429p.

Marion County
1850
Otto, Rhea Cumming. *1850 Census of Georgia*. Savannah, GA: Author, 1974. 82p.

Meriwether County
1830
Lewis, Peggy McNair. *1830 Census Meriwether County, Georgia*. Hayden, AL: Author, 1992. 26p.
1850
Otto, Rhea Cumming. *1850 Census of Georgia*. Savannah, GA: Author, 1989. 81p.
USGenWeb Census Project. Georgia, 1850 Meriwether County.
ftp://ftp.rootsweb.com/pub/census/ga/meriwether/1850/

Mitchell County
1860
USGenWeb Census Project. Georgia, 1860 Mitchell County.
ftp://ftp.rootsweb.com/pub/census/ga/mitchell/1860/

Monroe County
1850
Otto, Rhea Cumming. *1850 Census of Georgia*. Savannah, GA: Author, 1975. 75p.
1860
Ingmire, Frances Terry. *Citizens of Monroe County, Georgia, 1860 Census Index*. Nacogdoches, TX: Ericson Books, 1986, 1995. 12p.
USGenWeb Census Project. Georgia, 1860 Monroe County.
ftp://ftp.rootsweb.com/pub/census/ga/monroe/1860/

Montgomery County
1850
Dwyer, Clifford S. *1850 Census, Montgomery County, Georgia*. Pensacola, FL: Author, 1993. 71p.
Otto, Rhea Cumming. *1850 Census of Georgia*. Savannah, GA: Author, 1975. 18p.
1860
Georgia DAR. *Census and Index Records of Johnson and Montgomery Counties, Georgia*. Genealogical Records Committee Report, s2, v522. Georgia DAR, 1995. 106p.
Griffin, Myrtie Lou, and Roscoe Arnold Stallings. *1860 Census of Montgomery County, Georgia*. Homerville, GA: Huxford Genealogical Society. 41p.
1880
Kelly, Hulda K. *Georgia 1880 Census, Montgomery County Index*. Statesboro, GA: Statesboro Regional Library, 1983. 49p.

Morgan County
1850
McMinus, J. *Morgan County, Georgia 1850 Census*. San Antonio, TX: Family Adventures. Unpgd.
Otto, Rhea Cumming. *1850 Census of Georgia*. Savannah, GA: Author, 1992. 39p.

Murray County
1850
Boggess, Polly. *Murray County, Georgia, Federal Census Report 1850 Index*. Dalton, GA: Crown Gardens and Archives. 25p.
1860
Boggess, Polly. *Murray County, Georgia, Federal Census Report 1860 Index*. Dalton, GA: Crown Gardens and Archives, 1984. 12p.

Ingmire, Frances Terry. *Citizens of Murray County, Georgia, 1860 Census Index*. Saint Louis, MO: Author, 1986. 24p.

Muscogee County
1850
Otto, Rhea Cumming. *1850 Census of Georgia*. Savannah, GA: Author, 1977. 111p.
1860
McGinnis, Callie B., Sandra K. Stratford, and John S. Lupold. *Muscogee County, Georgia, 1860 Census Index*. Columbus, GA: Yesteryear Research Associates, 1985. 25p.
1890
U.S. Federal Population Census Schedules. 1890, M407, Microfilm Reel No. 3.
U.S. Federal Population Census Schedules. 1890, Index. M496, 2 Microfilm Reels.

Oglethorpe County
Jackson, Ronald Vern. *Georgia Census Index, Online Edition*. Orem, UT: Ancestry.com, Inc., 1999.
http://www.ancestry.com
1800
Jackson, Ronald Vern. *Georgia, Oglethorpe County, 1800 Census Index*. Salt Lake City, UT: Accelerated Indexing Systems, 1979. 77p.
Warren, Mary B. *1800 Census of Oglethorpe County, Georgia, the Only Extant Census of 1800 within the State of Georgia*. Athens, GA: Author, 1965. 53p.
1850
Otto, Rhea Cumming. *1850 Census of Georgia*. Savannah, GA: Author, 1988. 46p.

Paulding County
1850
Richter, Sue Bright. *1850 Federal Census, Paulding County Georgia*. Madison, AL: Author, 1995. 206p.
1860
Austin, Jeannette Holland. *1860 Paulding County, Georgia Census*. Riverdale, GA: Author. 125p.
1870
Richter, Sue Bright. *1870 Federal Census, Paulding County Georgia*. Madison, AL: Author, 1995. 172p.

Pickins County
1860
Ingmire, Frances Terry. *Citizens of Pickens County, Georgia, 1860 Census Index*. Saint Louis, MO: Author, 1986. 20p.

Pierce County
1860
1860 Pierce County, Georgia. Homerville, GA: Huxford Genealogical Society. Unpgd.
1870
1870 Pierce County, Georgia. Homerville, GA: Huxford Genealogical Society. 38p.
1880
1880 Pierce County, Georgia. Homerville, GA: Huxford Genealogical Society. 58p.
1900
Walker, Randall M. *1900 Census of Pierce County, Georgia*. Homerville, GA: Huxford Genealogical Society. 58p.
1910
Walker, Randall M. *1910 Census of Pierce County, Georgia*. Homerville, GA: Huxford Genealogical Society. 80p.

Pike County
1850
Otto, Rhea Cumming. *1850 Census of Georgia*. Savannah, GA: Author, 1977. 86p.

Pulaski County
1830-1880
Myrick, Victor Ray. *Census Records, 1830 through 1860, Pulaski and Bleckley Counties*. Cochran, GA: Author, 1976. 110p.
_____. *Pulaski County, Georgia Census Records of White Families, 1830 through 1880*. Chester, GA: Author, 1986. 241p.

Putnam County
1850
Otto, Rhea Cumming. *1850 Census of Georgia*. Savannah, GA: Author, 1979. 37p.

Quitman County
1860
Harris, Sheryl Foster. *1860 Census, Quitman County, Georgia*. Albany, GA: Southwest Georgia Genealogical Society, 1988. 41p.

Rabun County
1830
Coleman, John Thomas. *1830 Census, Rabun County, Georgia*. Marietta, GA: Heritage Center. 14p.
1840
Coleman, John Thomas. *1840 Census, Rabun County, Georgia*. Marietta, GA: Heritage Center. 13p.
1850
Coleman, John Thomas. *1850 Census, Rabun County, Georgia*. Marietta, GA: Heritage Center, 1984. 64p.
1860
Coleman, John Thomas. *1860 Census, Rabun County, Georgia*. Marietta, GA: Heritage Center, 1985. 85p.
Ingmire, Frances Terry. *Citizens of Rabun County, Georgia, 1860 Census Index*. Saint Louis, MO: Author, 1986. 13p.
1870
Coleman, John Thomas. *1870 Census, Rabun County, Georgia*. Marietta, GA: Heritage Center, 1984. 86p.
1880
Coleman, John Thomas. *1880 Census, Rabun County, Georgia*. Marietta, GA: Heritage Center. Unpgd.
1900
Coleman, John Thomas. *1900 Census, Rabun County, Georgia*. Marietta, GA: Heritage Center. 143p.

Randolph County
1850
Otto, Rhea Cumming. *1850 Census of Georgia*. Savannah, GA: Author, 1976. 76p.
1860
Harris, Sheryl Foster. *1860 Census, Randolph County, Georgia*. Albany, GA: Southwest Georgia Genealogical Society, 1985. 99p.

Richmond County
1850
Richmond County, Georgia Census, 1850. Morrow, GA: Genealogical Enterprises. Unpgd.
Otto, Rhea Cumming. *1850 Census of Georgia*. Savannah, GA: Author, 1994. 127p.

Savannah (Chatham County)
1870
Jackson, Ronald Vern. *Atlanta, Augusta, & Savannah, Georgia 1870 Federal Census Index*. Salt Lake City, UT: Accelerated Indexing Systems International, 1990. 469p.
1910
U.S. Federal Population Census Schedules. Separate Soundex for Cities of Atlanta, Augusta, Macon and Savannah, T1263, Microfilm Reel Nos. 149-174.

Screven County
1830
Register, Alvaretta Kenan. *The Fifth Census of the United States, 1830, Screven County, Georgia*. Statesboro, GA: Author, 1970. 14p.
1850
Otto, Rhea Cumming. *1850 Census of Georgia*. Savannah, GA: Author, 1975. 34p.
1860
Griffin, Myrtie Lou, and Roscoe Arnold Stallings. *1860 Census of Screven County, Georgia*. Homerville, GA: Huxford Genealogical Society. 76p.
1870
Kelly, Hulda K. *Ninth Census of the United States, Screven County, Georgia 1870*. Statesboro, GA: Statesboro Regional Library, 1983. 49p.

Stewart County
1850
Otto, Rhea Cumming. *1850 Census of Georgia*. Savannah, GA: Author, 1977. 84p

Sumter County
1850
Otto, Rhea Cumming. *1850 Census of Georgia*. Savannah, GA: Author, 1977. 65p.
1860
USGenWeb Census Project. Georgia, 1860 Sumter County.
ftp://ftp.rootsweb.com/pub/census/ga/sumter/1860/

Talbot County
1850
Otto, Rhea Cumming. *1850 Census of Georgia*. Savannah, GA: Author, 1974. 98p.

Taliaferro County
1827
Censuses for Georgia Counties, Taliaferro, 1827, Lumpkin, 1838, Chatham, 1845. Atlanta, GA: R. J. Taylor, Jr., Foundation, 1979. 57p.
1850
Otto, Rhea Cumming. *1850 Census of Georgia*. Savannah, GA: Author, 1980. 23p.

Tattnall County
1820
1820 United States Census of Tattnall County, Georgia. Jacksonville, FL: Southern Genealogist's Exchange, 1960. 12p.
1850
Griffin, Myrtie Lou, and Roscoe Arnold Stallings. *Census of Tattnall County, Georgia for 1850*. Homerville, GA: Huxford Genealogical Society. 47p.
Otto, Rhea Cumming. *1850 Census of Georgia*. Savannah, GA: Author, 1971. 32p.

1860

Acord, Arlis L. *Tattnall County, Georgia, the 1860 Federal Census*. Author, 1984. 19p.

Oliver, Mary Frances Smith. *1860 Census of Georgia (Tattnall County)*. Glennville, GA: Author, 1982. 36p.

Stokes, Alvin. *1860 Census of Tattnall County, Georgia*. Homerville, GA: Huxford Genealogical Society. 61p.

1870

Stokes, Alvin. *1870 Census of Tattnall County, Georgia*. Homerville, GA: Huxford Genealogical Society. 68p.

1880

Georgia 1880 Census, Tattnall County Index. Statesboro, GA: Statesboro Regional Library, 1983. 17p.

Stokes, Alvin. *1880 Census of Tattnall County, Georgia*. Homerville, GA: Huxford Genealogical Society. 95p.

Taylor County
1850-1900

Childs, Essie Jones. *They Tarried in Taylor, 1860, 1870, 1880 & 1900 Census Records, County Records, Church Records & Family Records*. Warner Robins, GA: Central Georgia Genealogical Society, 1992. 396p.

Telfair County
1820

Shaw, Aurora C. *Index to 1820 Telfair County, Georgia, U.S. Census*. Jacksonville, FL: Southern Genealogist's Exchange Quarterly, 1960. 9p.

1850

Otto, Rhea Cumming. *1850 Census of Georgia, Telfair County, over 1,750 Free Citizens*. Author, 1970. 31p.

1860

Griffin, Myrtie Lou, and Roscoe Arnold Stallings. *Telfair County, Georgia 1860 Census*. Homerville, GA: Huxford Genealogical Society. 38p.

Thomas County
1830

Craigmiles, Joe E. *1830 Thomas County, Georgia Census*. Thomasville, GA: Author, 1989. 16p.

1840

Craigmiles, Joe E. *1840 Thomas County, Georgia Census*. Thomasville, GA: Author, 1989. 30p.

Towns County
1820-1850

Taylor, Jerry A. *Towns County, Georgia Census Records, 1820-1900*. Young Harris, GA: Author. 236p.

1860

Ingmire, Frances Terry. *Citizens of Towns County, Georgia, 1860 Census Index*. Saint Louis, MO: Author, 1986. 9p.

Taylor, Jerry A. *1860 Census Towns County, Georgia; 1870 Census Towns County, Georgia; 1880 Census, Towns County, Georgia; 1900 Census Towns County, Georgia*. Young Harris, GA: Author, 1988. 229p.

_____. *Towns County, Georgia Census Records, 1820-1900*. Young Harris, GA: Author. 236p.

1870-1900

Taylor, Jerry A. *1860 Census Towns County, Georgia; 1870 Census Towns County, Georgia; 1880 Census, Towns County, Georgia; 1900 Census Towns County, Georgia*. Young Harris, GA: Author, 1988. 229p.

_____. *Towns County, Georgia Census Records, 1820-1900*. Young Harris, GA: Author. 236p.

Troup County

Census Records of Baker County, McIntosh County, Troup County. Morrow, GA: Genealogical Enterprises, 1969. 22p.

1850
Otto, Rhea Cumming. *1850 Census of Georgia*. Savannah, GA: Author, 1978. 79p.

Twiggs County
1830, 1840
Myrick, Victor R. *Twiggs County, Georgia Census Records of White Families, 1830 through 1880*. Chester, GA: Author, 1986. 246p.
1850
Myrick, Victor R. *Twiggs County, Georgia Census Records of White Families, 1830 through 1880*. Chester, GA: Author, 1986. 246p.
Otto, Rhea Cumming. 1850 Census of Georgia. Savannah, GA: Author, 1980. 38p.
1860-1880
Myrick, Victor R. *Twiggs County, Georgia Census Records of White Families, 1830 through 1880*. Chester, GA: Author, 1986. 246p.

Union County
1834
Taylor, Jerry A. *Union County, Georgia Census Records, 1834-1850*. Young Harris, GA: Author. 150p.
1850
Otto, Rhea Cumming. *1850 Census of Georgia*. Savannah, GA: Author, 1980. 65p.
Taylor, Jerry A. *Union County, Georgia Census Records, 1834-1850*. Young Harris, GA: Author. 150p.
1860
Casada, Helen Weaver. *Union County, Georgia 1860 Census*. Charleston, TN: Author. 104p.
Ingmire, Frances Terry. *Citizens of Union County, Georgia, 1860 Census Index*. Saint Louis, MO: Author, 1986. 17p.
Wallis, Augustine Hunter. *The Eighth Census of the United States, Union County, Georgia, 1860*. Athens, GA: Author, 1991. 143p.
1870
Casada, Helen Weaver. *1870 Union County, Georgia Federal Census*. Charleston, TN: Author, 1991. 145p.

Upson County
1850
Cater, Mary, and Joseph T. Maddox. *1850 U.S. Census Records, Madison, Upson Counties, Georgia, with Other Statistics Added*. Irwinton, GA: Author, 1980. 60p.

Walker County
1850
Griffith, Jessie June Brandon. *Walker County, Georgia Census 1850*. Rossville, GA: Author, 1991. 126p.
Shaw, Ethel B., and Linda L. Criswell. *1850 Census of Walker County, Georgia*. Orange, CA: Author, 1971. 122p.
1860
Griffith, Jessie June Brandon. *1860 Walker County, Georgia Census, Mortality Records and Marriages*. Rossville, GA: Author, 1982. 178p.
Ingmire, Frances Terry. *Citizens of Walker County, Georgia, 1860 Census Index*. Saint Louis, MO: Author, 1986. 35p.
1870
Griffith, Jessie June Brandon. *1870 Census of Walker County, Georgia*. Fort Oglethorpe, GA: Jim & Barbara Price, 1984. 103p.

Walton County
1850
Otto, Rhea Cumming. *1850 Census of Georgia*. Savannah, GA: Author, 1987. 68p.

Ware County
1850

1850 Census of Ware County, Georgia. Homerville, GA: Huxford Genealogical Society. 114p.
1860
1860 Census of Ware County, Georgia. Homerville, GA: Huxford Genealogical Society. 43p.
USGenWeb Census Project. Georgia, 1860 Ware County.
ftp://ftp.rootsweb.com/pub/census/ga/ware/1860/
1870
1870 Census of Ware County, Georgia. Homerville, GA: Huxford Genealogical Society. 44p.
1880
Griffin, Myrtie Lou, and Roscoe Arnold Stallings. *Ware County, Georgia 1880 Census*. Homerville, GA: Huxford Genealogical Society. 30p.
1900
Walker, Randall M. *1900 Census of Ware County, Georgia*. Homerville, GA: Huxford Genealogical Society. 85p.

Warren County
1850

Otto, Rhea Cumming. *1850 Census of Georgia*. Savannah, GA: Author, 1974. 80p.
1860
Braswell, Marjorie Abbott. *1860 Warren County, Georgia Census with Added Information Included*. Hephizibah, GA: Author, 1983. 67p.
USGenWeb Census Project. Georgia, 1860 Warren County.
ftp://ftp.rootsweb.com/pub/census/ga/warren/1860/
1870
Griffin, Myrtie Lou, and Roscoe Arnold Stallings. *Warren County, Georgia 1870 Census*. Homerville, GA: Huxford Genealogical Society. 88p.

Washington County
1840

USGenWeb Census Project. Georgia, 1840 Washington County.
ftp://ftp.rootsweb.com/pub/census/ga/washington/1840/
1850
1850 Census of Washington County, Georgia. Homerville, GA: Huxford Genealogical Society. 81p.
Otto, Rhea Cumming. *1850 Census of Georgia*. Savannah, GA: Author, 1989. 59p.
USGenWeb Census Project. Georgia, 1850 Washington County.
ftp://ftp.rootsweb.com/pub/census/ga/washington/1850/
1860
Acord, Arlis L. *Washington County, Georgia the 1860 Federal Census*. Author, 1984. 37p.
USGenWeb Census Project. Georgia, 1860 Washington County.
ftp://ftp.rootsweb.com/pub/census/ga/washington/1860/
1890
Census, Washington County, 1890. Sanderville, GA: Washington County Historical Society. 106p.
Henry, William R. *1890 Federal Census, Court of Ordinary, Washington County, Georgia, Population Schedule*. Warner Robins, GA: Central Georgia Genealogical Society, 1994. 262p.

Wayne County
1850

Otto, Rhea Cumming. *1850 Census of Georgia*. Savannah, GA: Author, 1991. 12p.
Stokes, A.J. *Wayne County, Georgia 1850*. Homerville, GA: Huxford Genealogical Society. 20p.
1860
Stokes, A.J. *Wayne County, Georgia 1860*. Homerville, GA: Huxford Genealogical Society. 33p.

USGenWeb Census Project. Georgia, 1860 Wayne County.
ftp://ftp.rootsweb.com/pub/census/ga/wayne/1860/
1870
Stokes, A.J. *Wayne County, Georgia 1870*. Homerville, GA: Huxford Genealogical Society. 36p.
1880
Stokes, A.J. *Wayne County, Georgia 1880*. Homerville, GA: Huxford Genealogical Society. 79p.
1900
Stokes, A.J. *1900 Census of Wayne County, Georgia*. Homerville, GA: Huxford Genealogical Society. 148p.

White County
1860
Ingmire, Frances Terry. *Citizens of White County, Georgia, 1860 Census Index*. St. Louis, MO: Author, 1986. 13p.
USGenWeb Census Project. Georgia, 1860 White County.
ftp://ftp.rootsweb.com/pub/census/ga/white/1860/

Whitfield County
1860
Boggess, Polly. *Whitfield County, Georgia, Federal Census Report 1860 Index*. Dalton, GA: Crown Gardens and Archives. 19p.
Ingmire, Frances Terry. *Citizens of Whitfield County, Georgia*. St. Louis, MO: Author, 1986. 38p.
1870
Boggess, Polly. *Whitfield County, Georgia, Federal Census Report 1870 Index*. Dalton, GA: Whitfield-Murray Historical Society, 1991. 28p.

Wilcox County
1860
Griffin, Myrtie Lou, and Roscoe Arnold Stallings. *Wilcox County, Georgia 1860 Census*. Homerville, GA: Huxford Genealogical Society. 34p.

Wilkes County
1830
McMinus, J. *Wilkes County, Georgia, 1830 Census, Heads of Household Index*. San Antonio, TX: Family Adventures. 7p.
1840
Ingmire, Frances T. *1840 Wilkes County, Georgia Census Index*. Signal Mountain, TN: Mountain Press, 1999. 9p.
1850
Otto, Rhea Cumming. *1850 Census of Georgia*. Savannah, GA: Author, 1990. 39p.
Wilcox, Irene Stillwell. *The Census Records of Elbert County, 1820-1860 and the 1850 Census of Wilkes County*. Easley, SC: Southern Historical Press, 1979. 138p.
1860
Griffin, Myrtie Lou, and Roscoe Arnold Stallings. *Wilkes County, Georgia 1860 Census*. Homerville, GA: Huxford Genealogical Society. 70p.

Wilkinson County
1820
Myrick, Victor R. *Wilkinson County, Georgia Census Records of White Families, 1820 through 1880*. Chester, GA: Author, 1986. 277p.
USGenWeb Census Project. Georgia, 1820 Wilkinson County.
ftp://ftp.rootsweb.com/pub/census/ga/wilkinson/1820/

1830, 1840

Myrick, Victor R. *Wilkinson County, Georgia Census Records of White Families, 1820 through 1880*. Chester, GA: Author, 1986. 277p.

1850

Griffin, Myrtie Lou, and Roscoe Arnold Stallings. *Wilkinson County, Georgia 1850 Census*. Homerville, GA: Huxford Genealogical Society. 113p.

Myrick, Victor R. *Wilkinson County, Georgia Census Records of White Families, 1820 through 1880*. Chester, GA: Author, 1986. 277p.

Otto, Rhea Cumming. *1850 Census of Georgia*. Savannah, GA: Author, 1991. 56p.

1860

Griffin, Myrtie Lou, and Roscoe Arnold Stallings. *Wilkinson County, Georgia 1860 Census*. Homerville, GA: Huxford Genealogical Society. 112p.

Myrick, Victor R. *Wilkinson County, Georgia Census Records of White Families, 1820 through 1880*. Chester, GA: Author, 1986. 277p.

1870, 1880

Myrick, Victor R. *Wilkinson County, Georgia Census Records of White Families, 1820 through 1880*. Chester, GA: Author, 1986. 277p.

Worth County

1860

Sweat, Faye. *1860 Census, Worth County, Georgia, Abstracts*. Albany, GA: Southwest Georgia Genealogical Society, 1986. 44p.

1920

Jeffery, Alice. *Worth County, 1920 Census. Online Database*. Orem, UT: Ancestry.com, Inc., 1999. **http://www.ancestry.com**

Hawaii

Schmidt, Robert C. *The Missionary Censuses of Hawaii*. Honolulu, HI: Bernice Pauahi Bishop Museum, 1973. 49p.

1840-1844

Jackson, Ronald Vern. *Hawaii 1840-1843 Territorial Census Records*. North Salt Lake City, UT: Accelerated Indexing Systems International, 1986. Unpgd.

_____. *Hawaii, 1840-1844, Kingdom Census Index*. Salt Lake City, UT: Accelerated Indexing Systems International, 1986. 15, 19p.

1900

Jackson, Ronald Vern. *Hawaii Census Index, Online Edition*. Orem, UT: Ancestry.com, Inc., 1999. **http://www.ancestry.com**

_____. *Hawaii 1900, Pulama na Kupuna*. Salt Lake City, UT: Accelerated Indexing Systems International, 1989, 1999. 692p.

U.S. Federal Population Census Schedules. 1900, T623, Microfilm Reel Nos. 1833-1837.

U.S. Federal Population Census Schedules. 1900, Soundex. T1041, 30 Microfilm Reels.

U.S. Federal Population Census Schedules. 1900, Military & Naval Bases. T1081, Microfilm Reel Nos. 1838-1842.

U.S. Federal Population Census Schedules. 1900, Military & Naval Bases, Soundex. T1081, 32 Microfilm Reels.

1910

Jackson, Ronald Vern. *Hawaii Census Index, Online Edition*. Orem, UT: Ancestry.com, Inc., 1999.
http://www.ancestry.com
Hawaii 1910 Pulama na Kupuna, Cherish Our Ancestors. North Salt Lake City, UT: Accelerated Indexing Systems International, 1987. 756p.
U.S. Federal Population Census Schedules. 1910, T624, Microfilm Reel Nos. 1751-1755. (No Soundex/ Miracode Index was prepared by the Government for this State.)

1920

U.S. Federal Population Census Schedules. 1920, 1920, T625, Microfilm Reel Nos. 2033-2039.
U.S. Federal Population Census Schedules. 1920, Soundex. M1598, 24 Microfilm Reels.

Idaho

1860

Census Index: U.S. Selected States/Counties, 1860. Family Archive CD 318. Novato, CA: Broderbund Software. CD-ROM.

1863

Wood, Clara L. *First Census Report of the Marshall for Idaho Territory*. Author, 1938. Unpgd.

1870

Census Index: U.S. Selected States/Counties, 1870. Family Archive CD 319. Novato, CA: Broderbund Software. CD-ROM.
Idaho Territory Federal Population Schedules and Mortality Schedules. Boise, ID: Idaho Genealogical Society, 1973. 218p.
Jackson, Ronald Vern. *Idaho Census Index, Online Edition*. Orem, UT: Ancestry.com, Inc., 1999.
http://www.ancestry.com
_____. *Idaho 1870 Mortality Schedule*. Bountiful, UT: Accelerated Indexing Systems, 1980. 14p.
_____. *Idaho 1870 Territorial Census Index*. Salt Lake City, UT: Accelerated Indexing Systems, 1979. 187p.
_____. *Mortality Schedules Index, Online Edition*. Orem, UT: Ancestry.com, Inc., 1999.
http://www.ancestry.com
Pompey, Cherman Lee. *The 1870 Census Records of the Lincoln Valley, Oneida Territory, Idaho Territory*. Bakersfield, CA: Historical and Genealogical Pub. 7p.
U.S. Federal Population Census Schedules. 1870, M593, Microfilm Reel No. 185.

1880

Census Index: U.S. Selected States/Counties, 1880. Family Archive CD 320. Novato, CA: Broderbund Software. CD-ROM.
Idaho Territory Federal Population Schedules and Mortality Schedules. Boise, ID: Idaho Genealogical Society, 1976. 983p.
Jackson, Ronald Vern. *Idaho Census Index, Online Edition*. Orem, UT: Ancestry.com, Inc., 1999.
http://www.ancestry.com
_____. *Idaho 1880 Mortality Schedule*. Bountiful, UT: Accelerated Indexing Systems, 1979, 1999. 14p.
_____. *Idaho 1880 Territorial Census Index*. Salt Lake City, UT: Accelerated Indexing Systems, 1979. 400p.
_____. *Mortality Schedules Index, Online Edition*. Orem, UT: Ancestry.com, Inc., 1999.
http://www.ancestry.com

U.S. Federal Population Census Schedules. 1880, T9, Microfilm Reel No. 173.
U.S. Federal Population Census Schedules. 1880, Soundex. T745, 2 Microfilm Reels.

1890
Jackson, Ronald Vern. *Idaho Census Index, Online Edition (Veterans Schedules).* Orem, UT: Ancestry.com, Inc., 1999.
http://www.ancestry.com

1900
U.S. Federal Population Census Schedules. 1900, T623, Microfilm Reel Nos. 231-234.
U.S. Federal Population Census Schedules. 1900, Soundex. T1042, 19 Microfilm Reels.
U.S. Federal Population Census Schedules. 1900, Military & Naval Bases. T1081, Microfilm Reel Nos. 1838-1842.
U.S. Federal Population Census Schedules. 1900, Military & Naval Bases, Soundex. T1081, 32 Microfilm Reels.

1910
Family Tree Maker Census Index: Idaho, 1910. Family Archive CD 335. Novato, CA: Broderbund, 1996. CD-ROM.
Idaho State Federal Census Index, 1910. Boise, ID: Idaho Genealogical Society, 1991. 941p.
Upper Snake River Valley, Family History Center and McKay Library, Ricks College. *1910 Idaho Census Index.* Bountiful, UT: Precision Indexing, 1993. 1,245p.
_____. ACD 0025. Bountiful, UT: Heritage Quest, 1998. CD-ROM.
U.S. Federal Population Census Schedules. 1910, T624, Microfilm Reel Nos. 221-228. (No Soundex/Miracode Index was prepared by the Government for this State.)

1920
U.S. Federal Population Census Schedules. 1920, T625, Microfilm Reel Nos. 287-295.
U.S. Federal Population Census Schedules. 1920, Soundex. M1558, 33 Microfilm Reels.

Alturas County
1870
USGenWeb Census Project. Idaho, 1870 Alturas County.
ftp://ftp.rootsweb.com/pub/census/id/alturas/1870/

Boise County
1870
USGenWeb Census Project. Idaho, 1870 Boise County.
ftp://ftp.rootsweb.com/pub/census/id/boise/1870/

Fort Hall (Bingham County)
Teter, Thomas Benton. *1894 Census of the Bannock and Shoshone Indians of Fort Hall, Idaho.* Author. 30p.

Idaho County
1870
USGenWeb Census Project. Idaho, 1870 Idaho County.
ftp://ftp.rootsweb.com/pub/census/id/idaho/1870/

Lemhi County
1850
USGenWeb Census Project. Idaho, 1850 Lemhi County.
ftp://ftp.rootsweb.com/pub/census/id/lemhi/1850/

Nez Perce County
1870
USGenWeb Census Project. Idaho, 1870 Nez Perce County.
ftp://ftp.rootsweb.com/pub/census/id/nezperce/1870/

Oneida County
1870
USGenWeb Census Project. Idaho, 1870 Oneida County.
ftp://ftp.rootsweb.com/pub/census/id/oneida/1870/

Owyhee County
1870
USGenWeb Census Project. Idaho, 1870 Owyhee County.
ftp://ftp.rootsweb.com/pub/census/id/owyhee/1870/

Shoshone County
1870
USGenWeb Census Project. Idaho, 1870 Shoshone County.
ftp://ftp.rootsweb.com/pub/census/id/shoshone/1870/

Valley County
1920
Craig, Wesley W. *Surname Index and Selected Information from the 1920 Federal Population Census for Valley County, Idaho*. Cascade, ID: Valley County Genealogical Society, 1996. 52p.

Illinois

Norton, Margaret Cross. *Illinois Census Returns*. Springfield, IL: Illinois State Historical Library, 1934, 1935. 2 vols.

1787-1819
Jackson, Ronald Vern. *Early Illinois, 1787-1819*. Bountiful, UT: Accelerated Indexing Systems, 1980. Unpgd.

1810
Jackson, Ronald Vern. *Illinois, 1810*. North Salt Lake City, UT: Accelerated Indexing Systems International, 1987. Unpgd.
Whiteside, Don. *Whiteside(s), Names Listed in Illinois Censuses for Selected Counties, 1810-1880*. Edmonton, Alberta, Canada: University of Alberta, 1968. 65p.

1818
Jackson, Ronald Vern. *Illinois Census Index, Online Edition*. Orem, UT: Ancestry.com, Inc., 1999.
http://www.ancestry.com
_____. *Illinois, 1818*. North Salt Lake City, UT: Accelerated Indexing Systems International, 1987. 171p.

1820
Bohannan, Larry C. *Fourth Census of the United States 1820 Illinois Population Schedules*. Huntsville, AK: Century Enterprises, 1968.
Jackson, Ronald Vern. *Illinois Census Index, Online Edition*. Orem, UT: Ancestry.com, Inc., 1999.
http://www.ancestry.com

_____, and Gary Ronald Teeples. *Illinois 1820 Census Index*. Salt Lake City, UT: Accelerated Indexing Systems, 1977. 155p.

Norton, Margaret Cross. *Illinois Census Returns 1820*. Baltimore, MD: Genealogical Publishing Co., 1934, 1969.

_____. *Online Database Edition*. Orem, UT: Ancestry.com, Inc., 1999.
http://www.ancestry.com

U.S. Federal Population Census Schedules. 1820, M33, Microfilm Reel Nos. 11-12.

Volkel, Lowell M., and James V. Gill. *1820 Federal Census of Illinois*. Danville, IL: Heritage House, 1966. 79p.

Whiteside, Don. *Whiteside(s), Names Listed in Illinois Censuses for Selected Counties, 1810-1880*. Edmonton, Alberta, Canada: University of Alberta, 1968. 65p.

1825

Jackson, Ronald Vern. *Illinois Census Index, Online Edition*. Orem, UT: Ancestry.com, Inc., 1999.
http://www.ancestry.com

_____. *Illinois 1825*. Salt Lake City, UT: Accelerated Indexing Systems International, 1984. 31p.

1830

Census Index: U.S. Selected States/Counties, 1830. Family Archive CD 315. Novato, CA: Broderbund Software. CD-ROM.

1830-1839 U.S. Census Indexes, Mid-Atlantic, South, Mid-West. Orem, UT: Automated Archives, 1993. CD-ROM.

Gill, James V., and Maryan R. Gill. *Index to the 1830 Federal Census*. Danville, IL: Illiana Genealogical Pub. Co., 1968. 4 vols.

Illinois 1830 Census Index. Palmer, IL: Genie-Logic Enterprises, 1997. 237p.

Jackson, Ronald Vern. *Illinois Census Index, Online Edition*. Orem, UT: Ancestry.com, Inc., 1999.
http://www.ancestry.com

_____, and Gary Ronald Teeples. *Illinois 1830 Census Index*. Salt Lake City, UT: Accelerated Indexing Systems, 1976. 63p.

U.S. Federal Population Census Schedules. 1830, M19, Microfilm Reel Nos. 22-25.

Whiteside, Don. *Whiteside(s), Names Listed in Illinois Censuses for Selected Counties, 1810-1880*. Edmonton, Alberta, Canada: University of Alberta, 1968. 65p.

1835

Jackson, Ronald Vern. *Illinois Census Index, Online Edition*. Orem, UT: Ancestry.com, Inc., 1999.
http://www.ancestry.com

_____, and W. David Samuelson. *Illinois 1835 State Census Index*. North Salt Lake City, UT: Accelerated Indexing Systems International, 1984. 55p.

1840

Census Index: U.S. Selected States/Counties, 1840. Family Archive CD 316. Novato, CA: Broderbund Software. CD-ROM.

1840 United States Census Index, Mid-West, Great Lakes. Orem, UT: Automated Archives, 1994. CD-ROM.

Jackson, Ronald Vern. *Illinois Census Index, Online Edition*. Orem, UT: Ancestry.com, Inc., 1999.
http://www.ancestry.com

_____, and Gary Ronald Teeples. *Illinois 1840 Census Index*. Salt Lake City, UT: Accelerated Indexing Systems, 1977. 294p.

Wormer, Maxine E. *Illinois 1840 Census Index*. Thomson, IL: Heritage House, 1973-1979. 5 vols.

U.S. Federal Population Census Schedules. 1840, M704, Microfilm Reel Nos. 54-73.

Whiteside, Don. *Whiteside(s), Names Listed in Illinois Censuses for Selected Counties, 1810-1880*. Edmonton, Alberta, Canada: University of Alberta, 1968. 65p.

1850

Census Index: U.S. Selected States/Counties, 1850. Family Archive CD 317. Novato, CA: Broderbund Software. CD-ROM.

Census Microfilm Records: Illinois, 1850. Family Archive CD 301. Novato, CA: Broderbund Software. CD-ROM.

Jackson, Ronald Vern. *Illinois Census Index, Online Edition.* Orem, UT: Ancestry.com, Inc., 1999. **http://www.ancestry.com**

_____. *Illinois 1850 Mortality Schedule.* North Salt Lake City, UT: Accelerated Indexing Systems International, 1981. 152p.

_____. *Mortality Schedules Index, Online Edition.* Orem, UT: Ancestry.com, Inc., 1999. **http://www.ancestry.com**

_____, and Gary Ronald Teeples. *Illinois 1850 Census Index.* Salt Lake City, UT: Accelerated Indexing Systems, 1977. 192p.

U.S. Census Index Series, Iowa, Illinois, Michigan, Missouri, Minnesota, Wisconsin, 1850. Orem, UT: Automated Archives, 1992. CD-ROM.

U.S. Federal Population Census Schedules. 1850, M432, Microfilm Reel Nos. 134.

Volkel, Lowell M. *1850 Illinois Mortality Schedule.* Danville, IL: Author, 1972. 2 vols.

Whiteside, Don. *Whiteside(s), Names Listed in Illinois Censuses for Selected Counties, 1810-1880.* Edmonton, Alberta, Canada: University of Alberta, 1968. 65p.

1855

Jackson, Ronald Vern. *Illinois Census Index, Online Edition.* Orem, UT: Ancestry.com, Inc., 1999. **http://www.ancestry.com**

Taylor, Mrs. Harlin B. *Index to the 1855 State Census of DeKalb County, Illinois.* Decatur, IL: Vio-Lin Enterprises, 1972. 25p.

1860

Census Index: U.S. Selected States/Counties, 1860. Family Archive CD 318. Novato, CA: Broderbund Software. CD-ROM.

Federal Census Index Illinois 1860 South. West Jordan, UT: Genealogical Service, 1996. 2 vols.

Jackson, Ronald Vern. *Illinois Census Index, Online Edition.* Orem, UT: Ancestry.com, Inc., 1999. **http://www.ancestry.com**

_____. *Illinois 1860 Federal Census Index Addendum, Dewitt, Franklin, Wabash and Warren Counties.* West Jordan, UT: Genealogical Services, 1986; 1997. Unpgd.

_____. *Illinois 1860 Mortality Census Index.* Salt Lake City, UT: Accelerated Indexing Systems, 1988. 318p.

_____. *Illinois 1860 North, Federal Census Index.* Salt Lake City, UT: Accelerated Indexing Systems, 1986, 1997. 2 vols.

_____. *Illinois 1860 North, Addendum.* Salt Lake City, UT Accelerated Indexing Systems International, 1987. 134p.

_____. *Illinois 1860 South, Federal Census Index.* Salt Lake City, UT: Accelerated Indexing Systems, 1986, 1997. 772p.

U.S. Census Index Series, Illinois and Indiana, 1860. Orem, UT: Automated Archives, 1991. CD-ROM.

U.S. Federal Population Census Schedules. 1860, M653, Microfilm Reel Nos. 154-241.

Volkel, Lowell M. *1860 Illinois Mortality Schedule.* Indianapolis, IN: Heritage House, 1979. 5 vols.

Whiteside, Don. *Whiteside(s), Names Listed in Illinois Censuses for Selected Counties, 1810-1880.* Edmonton, Alberta, Canada: University of Alberta, 1968. 65p.

1870

Census Index: U.S. Selected States/Counties, 1870. Family Archive CD 319. Novato, CA: Broderbund Software. CD-ROM.

Jackson, Ronald Vern. *Illinois Census Index, Online Edition*. Orem, UT: Ancestry.com, Inc., 1999. **http://www.ancestry.com**

Steuart, Raeone Christensen. *Illinois 1870 Census Index*. Bountiful, UT: Heritage Quest, 1999. 5 vols. CD-ROM.

U.S. Federal Population Census Schedules. 1870, M593, Microfilm Reel Nos. 186-295.

Volkel, Lowell M. *1870 Illinois Mortality Schedule*. Indianapolis, IN: Heritage House, 1985. 5 vols.

Whiteside, Don. *Whiteside(s), Names Listed in Illinois Censuses for Selected Counties, 1810-1880*. Edmonton, Alberta, Canada: University of Alberta, 1968. 65p.

1880

Census Index: U.S. Selected States/Counties, 1880. Family Archive CD 320. Novato, CA: Broderbund Software. CD-ROM.

Frederick, Nancy Gubb. *The 1880 Illinois Census Index, Soundex Code O-200—O-240, the Code That Was Not Filmed*. Evanston, IL: Author, 1981. 287p.

U.S. Federal Population Census Schedules. 1880, T9, Microfilm Reel Nos. 174-262.

U.S. Federal Population Census Schedules. 1880, Soundex. T736, 143 Microfilm Reels.

Whiteside, Don. *Whiteside(s), Names Listed in Illinois Censuses for Selected Counties, 1810-1880*. Edmonton, Alberta, Canada: University of Alberta, 1968. 65p.

1890

Jackson, Ronald Vern. *Illinois Census Index, Online Edition*. Orem, UT: Ancestry.com, Inc., 1999. **http://www.ancestry.com**

Veterans' Schedules: U.S. Selected States, 1890. Family Archive CD 131. Novato, CA: Broderbund Software. CD-ROM.

1900

U.S. Federal Population Census Schedules. 1900, T623, Microfilm Reel Nos. 235-356.

U.S. Federal Population Census Schedules. 1900, Soundex. T1043, 479 Microfilm Reels.

U.S. Federal Population Census Schedules. 1900, Military & Naval Bases. T1081, Microfilm Reel Nos. 1838-1842.

U.S. Federal Population Census Schedules. 1900, Military & Naval Bases, Soundex. T1081, 32 Microfilm Reels.

1910

U.S. Federal Population Census Schedules. 1910, T624, Microfilm Reel Nos. 229-337.

U.S. Federal Population Census Schedules. 1910, Soundex. T1264, 491 Microfilm Reels.

1920

U.S. Federal Population Census Schedules. 1920, T625, Microfilm Reel Nos. 296-419.

U.S. Federal Population Census Schedules. 1920, Soundex. M1559, 509 Microfilm Reels.

Adams County
1830

Gill, James V., and Maryan R. Gill. *Index to the 1830 Federal Census, Greene, Morgan, Sangamon, Calhoun, Pike, Fulton, Knox, Henry, Adams, Hancock, Warren, Mercer, Peoria, Putnam, and Jo Daviess Counties, Illinois*. Danville, IL: Heritage House, 1970. 66p.

1850

1850 Census, Adams County, Illinois. Quincy, IL: Great River Genealogical Society, 1983, 1984. 3 vols.

Nelson, Thomas S., and Mildred C. Nelson. *The Census of Adams County, Illinois for the Year 1850 by Townships, Population Schedule of the Seventh Census of the United States*. Quincy, IL: Authors, 1972. 655p.

1860

1860 Census, Adams County, Illinois. Quincy, IL: Great River Genealogical Society, 1981, 1982. 6 vols.

Alexander County
1820

Dexter, Darrel. *Alexander County, Illinois Census Records*. Carterville, IL: Genealogical Society of Southern Illinois, 1991, 1993. 2 vols.

1830

Dexter, Darrel. *Alexander County, Illinois Census Records*. Carterville, IL: Genealogical Society of Southern Illinois, 1991, 1993. 2 vols.

Gill, James V. *Index to the 1830 Federal Census, Alexander, Pope, Union, Johnson, Jackson, Franklin, Perry, Randolph, Monroe, Washington, Marion, Jefferson, Hamilton and Gallatin Counties, Illinois*. Danville, IL: Heritage House, 1970. 57p.

1840

Dexter, Darrel. *Alexander County, Illinois Census Records*. Carterville, IL: Genealogical Society of Southern Illinois, 1991, 1993. 2 vols.

1850

Dexter, Darrel. *Alexander County, Illinois Census Records*. Carterville, IL: Genealogical Society of Southern Illinois, 1991, 1993. 2 vols.

Wormer, Maxine E. *Alexander County, Illinois, 1850 Census*. Thomson, IL: Heritage House. 31p.

1860

Dexter, Darrel. *Alexander County, Illinois Census Records*. Carterville, IL: Genealogical Society of Southern Illinois, 1991, 1993. 2 vols.

1870

Illinois 1870 Census Index, Alexander County. Palmer, IL: Genie-Logic, 1998. Unpgd.

Bond County
1830

Gill, James V. *An Index to the 1830 Federal Census, White, Edwards, Wabash, Wayne, Clay, Clinton, St. Clair, Madison, Bond, Fayette and Lawrence Counties, Illinois*. Danville, IL: Illiana Genealogical Pub. Co., 1968. 64p.

1840

Streleski, Nelda Skilbeck. *1840 United States Census of Bond County, Illinois*. Decatur, IL: Decatur Genealogical Society, 1979. 27p.

1850

Dugan, Mrs. Donald E., Harlin B. Taylor, Mrs. Lionel Hunter, Helen Brown, Linda Smith, and Bernice Disbrow. *1850 United States Census of Bond County, Illinois*. Decatur, IL: Decatur Genealogical Society, 1977. 124p.

1860

Collins, Mary E. *1860 United States Census of Bond County, Illinois*. Poplar Bluff, MO: Author 1982. 239p.

1870

McKean, Beutonne. *1870 Census of Bond County, Illinois*. Greenville, IL: Bond County Genealogical Society, 1989. 348p.

1880

Anthony, Nelda Neer. *United States Census, 1880, Bond County, Illinois*. Greenville, IL: Bond County Genealogical Society, 1988. 543p.

1900

Hawley, Carlos. *1900 United States Census of Bond County, Illinois*. Greenville, IL: Bond County Genealogical Society, 1995. 305p.

1910

Hawley, Carlos. *1910 United States Census of Bond County, Illinois*. Greenville, IL: Bond County Genealogical Society, 1995. 328p.

1920

Hawley, Carlos. *1920 United States Census of Bond County, Illinois*. Greenville, IL: Bond County Genealogical Society, 1995. 311p.

Boone County
1840

Johnson, Martin William. *1840 Boone County, Illinois Census Index*. Belvidere, IL: Author, 1989. 24p.

1850

Haskin, Harley. *1850 Federal Census of Boone County, Illinois*. Lebanon, OR: Author, 1981. 180p.

1860

Williams, Helen Maxwell. *1860 Federal Census, Boone County, Illinois*. Belvidere, IL: Author, 1986. 264p.

1870

Williams, Helen Maxwell. *1870 Federal Census, Boone County, Illinois*. Belvidere, IL: Author. 285p.

1880

Johnson, Martin William. *1880 Boone County, Illinois Census Index*. Belvidere, IL: Author. 393p.

1900

Johnson, Martin William. *Boone County, Illinois Census Surnames, 1900*. Belvidere, IL: Author. 393p.

Brown County
1850

Logsdon, Mary. *Brown County, Illinois Mortality Schedules, 1850, 1860, 1880*. Versailles Area Genealogical and Historical Society, 1985. 18p.

Robb, Ruth Flesher. *1850 Brown County, Illinois, Federal Census*. Lombard, IL: Author, 1983. 94p.

1860

Logsdon, Mary. *Brown County, Illinois Mortality Schedules, 1850, 1860, 1880*. Versailles Area Genealogical and Historical Society, 1985. 18p.

Winters, Lisa. *1860 United States Census, Brown County, Illinois*. Decatur, IL: Author, 1995. 250p.

1870

Logsdon, Mary. *Brown County, Illinois Mortality Schedules, 1850, 1860, 1880*. Versailles Area Genealogical and Historical Society, 1985. 18p.

Illinois 1870 Census Index, Brown County. Palmer, IL: Genie-Logic, 1997. 34p.

1880

Logsdon, Mary. *Brown County, Illinois Mortality Schedules, 1850, 1860, 1880*. Versailles Area Genealogical and Historical Society, 1985. 18p.

Bureau County
1850

The 1850 Federal Census of Bureau County, Illinois, with Index. Yakima, WA: Yakima Valley Genealogical Society, 1978. 181p.

1860

Lines, Jack Milton. *1860 Federal Census of Bureau County, Illinois with Index*. Yakima, WA: Yakima Valley Genealogical Society, 1985. 2 vols.

Calhoun County
1830

Gill, James V., and Maryan R. Gill. *Index to the 1830 Federal Census, Greene, Morgan, Sangamon, Calhoun, Pike, Fulton, Knox, Henry, Adams, Hancock, Warren, Mercer, Peoria, Putnam, and Jo Daviess Counties, Illinois*. Danville, IL: Heritage House, 1970. 66p.

1850

Wike, Mavis, and Linda S. Allison. *United States Census, 1850, Calhoun County, Illinois*. Decatur, IL: Decatur Genealogical Society, 1971, 1982. 68p.

1860

United States Census, Calhoun County, Illinois, 1860. Hardin, IL: Calhoun County Historical Society, 1984. 102p.

Carroll County
1850

Smith, Marjorie Corrine. *Carroll County, Illinois, Federal Census and Mortality Schedules for the Year 1850.* Forest Park, IL: Author, 1971. 60p.
1860

Davenport, David Paul. *1860 Census of Carroll County, Illinois, National Archives Microfilm Publication No. 653, Reel 159.* Urbana, IL: Author, 1983. 419p.

Cass County
1830

1830 Census Records for Morgan County, Illinois, Includes Cass and Scott Counties. Jacksonville, IL: Jacksonville Area Genealogical and Historical Society, 1980. Unpgd.
1835

1835 Illinois State Census, Morgan County, in 1835 Cass & Scott Counties Were Part of Morgan County. Jacksonville, IL: Jacksonville Area Genealogical & Historical Society, 1998. 2 vols.
1850

Fox, Janice Lovekamp. *An Index to the 1850 Census of Cass County, Illinois.* Author, 1970. 82p.
1855

Taylor, Mrs. Harlin B. *Index to the 1855 State Census of Cass County, Illinois.* Thomson, IL: Heritage House, 1972. 19p.
1870

Illinois 1870 Census Index, Cass County. Palmer, IL: Genie-Logic, 1997. 54p.
1880

Fox, Janice P. *1880 Federal Census of Cass County, Illinois.* Thomson, IL: Heritage House, 1977. 295p.

Champaign County
1840

Hupp, Mildred Fisher, and Nelda Skilbeck Streleski. *United States Census, 1840, Champaign County, Illinois.* Decatur, IL: Decatur Genealogical Society, 1975. 10p.
1850

Eberhart, Elsie Swartz. *1850 Census, Champaign County, Illinois.* Chicago, IL: Chicago Genealogical Society, 1971. 67p.

Roehm, Frances E. *Champaign County, Illinois 1850, a Historical Overview.* Urbana, IL: Author, 1986. 114p.

USGenWeb Census Project. Illinois, 1850 Champaign County.

ftp://ftp.rootsweb.com/pub/census/il/champaign/1850/
1860

1860 U.S. Federal Census of Champaign County, Illinois. Urbana, IL: Champaign County Genealogical Society, 1988. 364p.

Christian County
1840

Hauffe, Jean Parks. *United States Census, 1840 Christian County, Illinois.* Decatur, IL: Decatur Genealogical Society, 1975. 10p.
1850

Puckett, Martin. *1850 United States Census of Christian County, Illinois.* Decatur, IL: Decatur Genealogical Society, 1971. 64p.

1855

Gustafson, Carol Ruth. *Christian County, Illinois, 1855 & 1865 State Census Enumerations with Indexes.* Taylorville, IL: Christian County Genealogical Society, 1991. 144p.

1860

Hunter, Cheri Davis. *1860 United States Census of Christian County, Illinois.* Decatur, IL: Decatur Genealogical Society, 1983. 247p.

1865

Gustafson, Carol Ruth. *Christian County, Illinois, 1855 & 1865 State Census Enumerations with Indexes.* Taylorville, IL: Christian County Genealogical Society, 1991. 144p.

1870

1870 United States Census of Christian County, Illinois. Taylorville, IL: Christian County Genealogical Society, 1988. 311p.

Clark County

1830

Gill, James V. *Index to the 1830 Federal Census, Crawford, Edgar, Clark, Schuyler, McDonough, Vermillion, Macon, Shelby, Tazewell, Montgomery and Macoupin Counties.* Danville, IL: Heritage House, 1970. 50p.

1850

1850 United States Census of Clark County, Illinois. Marshall, IL: Clark County Genealogical Society, 1977. 197p.

USGenWeb Census Project. Illinois, 1850 Clark County.

ftp://ftp.rootsweb.com/pub/census/il/clark/1850/

1860

Turner, Betty. *1860 United States Census of Clark County, Illinois.* Marshall, IL: Clark County Genealogical Society, 1978. 314p.

1870

Surname Index to 1870 United States Census for Clark County, Illinois. Marshall, IL: Clark County Genealogical Society, 1979. 15p.

Clay County

Wingert, Mary. *Clay County Muster Roll and Military Census, Archives, Miscellaneous Roll #30-1380.* Claremont, IL: Richland County Genealogical & Historical Society, 1988. 55p.

1830

Gill, James V. *An Index to the 1830 Federal Census, White, Edwards, Wabash, Wayne, Clay, Clinton, St. Clair, Madison, Bond, Fayette and Lawrence Counties, Illinois.* Danville, IL: Illiana Genealogical Pub. Co., 1968. 64p.

1850

Wormer, Maxine E. *Clay County, Illinois, 1850 Census.* Thomson, IL: Heritage House.1973. 50p.

1860

McPeak, Becky. *1860 Census, Clay County, Illinois.* Louisville, IL: Clay County Genealogical Society, 1992. 213p.

Mortality Schedules, 1860, 1870, 1880. Olney, IL: Richland County Genealogical Society, 1978. 139p.

Scherer, Mary. *Clay County, Illinois, 1860 Census.* Olney, IL: Author, 1982. 182p.

1870

McPeak, Becky. *1870 Census, Clay County, Illinois.* Louisville, IL: Clay County Genealogical Society, 1988. 344p.

Mortality Schedules, 1860, 1870, 1880. Olney, IL: Richland County Genealogical Society, 1978. 139p.

1880

Mortality Schedules, 1860, 1870, 1880. Olney, IL: Richland County Genealogical Society, 1978. 139p.

Scherer, Mary. *1880 Clay County, Illinois Census, 10th U.S. Census, Transcribed from Microfilm T9 #181 & 182.* Olney, IL: Author, 1984. 323p.

1910

Taylor, Lola B. *1910 Census of Clay County, Illinois*. Olney, IL: Richland County Genealogical and Historical Society, 1990. 473p.

Clinton County
1830

Clinton County, Illinois 1830 Federal Census. Decatur, IL: Decatur Genealogical Society, 1980. 15p.

Gill, James V. *An Index to the 1830 Federal Census, White, Edwards, Wabash, Wayne, Clay, Clinton, St. Clair, Madison, Bond, Fayette and Lawrence Counties, Illinois*. Danville, IL: Illiana Genealogical Pub. Co., 1968. 64p.

1850

Wormer, Maxine E. *Clinton County, Illinois, 1850 Census*. Thomson, IL: Heritage House, 1973. 62p.

1860

Gentz, Harold L. *Index, Clinton County, Illinois, 1860 Census*. Carlyle, IL: Clinton County Historical Society, 1985. 129p.

Guttersohn, Mildred. *Clinton County, Illinois 1860 Census*. Carlyle, IL: Clinton County Genealogical Society, 1985. 116p.

Coles County
1850

Greeson, Mary. *U.S. Federal Census, 1850, Coles County, Illinois*. Charleston, IL: Coles County Genealogical Society, 1976. 176p.

1860

Talbott, Rose. *U.S. 1860 Census, Coles County, Illinois*. Charleston, IL: Coles County, Illinois Genealogical Society, 1979. 296p.

1870

Hartley, Kathy Cotterell. *United States Federal Census 1870, Coles County, Illinois*. Charleston, IL: Coles County Illinois Genelogical Society, 12993. 2 vols.

Cook County
1850

Lundberg, Gertrude W., and Bernice C. Richard. *Surname Index to the 1850 Federal Census of Chicago, Cook County, Illinois, a Bi-Centennial Project*. Chicago, IL: Genealogical Services & Publications, 1976. 66p.

_____. *Cook County, Illinois, 1850 Federal Census not Including the City of Chicago*. Chicago, IL: Genealogical Services & Publications, 1987. 306p.

1860

Jackson, Ronald Vern. *Illinois 1860 Cook County with Chicago Federal Census Index*. West Jordan, UT: Genealogical Services, 1986; 1997, 1999. 643p.

Richard, Bernice C. *1860 Federal Census Index of Cook County, Illinois*. Author, 1980.

1870

Census Index: Baltimore, Chicago, St. Louis, 1870. Family Archive CD 288. Novato, CA: Broderbund Software. CD-ROM.

Jackson, Ronald Vern. *Chicago, Cook County, Illinois 1870 Federal Census Index*. Salt Lake City, UT: Accelerated Indexing Systems International, 1988. 517p.

Steuart, Bradley W. *Chicago, Illinois (Including Cook County), 1870 Census Index*. Bountiful, UT: Precision Indexing, 1990. 1,216p.

1880

Jackson, Ronald Vern. *Chicago 1880, Cook County, Illinois Federal Census Index*. North Salt Lake City, UT: Accelerated Indexing Systems International, 1959. 2 vols.

_____. *Illinois Census Index, Online Edition*. Orem, UT: Ancestry.com, Inc., 1999.

http://www.ancestry.com

Swierenga, Robert P. *Dutch in Chicago and Cook County, 1880 Federal Census, an Alphabetical Index.* Kent, Ohio: Author, 1992. 123p.

U.S. Census Index, 1880, Cook County, Illinois. Orem, UT: Automated Archives, 1994. CD-ROM.
1900
Swierenga, Robert P. *Dutch in Chicago and Cook County, 1900 Federal Census.* Kent, Ohio: Author, 1992. 421p.

Crawford County
1830
Gill, James V. *Index to the 1830 Federal Census, Crawford, Edgar, Clark, Schuyler, McDonough, Vermillion, Macon, Shelby, Tazewell, Montgomery and Macoupin Counties.* Danville, IL: Heritage House, 1970. 50p.
1840
Bailey, Chris Harvey. *1840 Census of Crawford County, Illinois Index.* Author, 1976. 5p.
1850
USGenWeb Census Project. Illinois, 1850 Crawford County.
ftp://ftp.rootsweb.com/pub/census/il/crawford/1850/
1860-1880
Mortality Schedules, 1860, 1870, 1880. Olney, IL: Richland County Genealogical Society, 1978. 139p.
1900
1900 Census Index, Crawford County, Illinois. Robinson, IL: Crawford County Genealogical Society, 1984. 163p.

Cumberland County
1850
Puckett, Dolores. *1850 United States Census of Cumberland County, Illinois.* Author, 1969. 73p. 1860
1860 United States Census of Cumberland County, Illinois. Decatur, IL: Decatur Genealogical Society, 1983. 195p.
1870
Fletcher, James. *1870 United States Census of Cumberland County, Illinois.* Decatur, IL: Decatur Genealogical Society, 1986. 217p.

DeKalb County
1840
Records of DeKalb County, Illinois, Census, Taxable Lands, & School Lands, Year 1840. Sycamore, IL: Genealogical Society of DeKalb County, 1980. 57p.
1850
Richard, Bernice C. *1850 Federal Census of De Kalb County, Illinois.* Chicago, IL: Author, 1974. 185p.
1855
Taylor, Mrs. Harlin B. *Index to the 1855 State Census of De Kalb County, Illinois.* Decatur, IL: Author, 1972.
1860
Robinson, Marilyn. *DeKalb County, Illinois 1860 Census, Population Schedules of the Eighth Census of the United States.* Author, 1981. 269p.
1870
Marshall, Florence. *1870 Census County Index, De Kalb County, Illinois.* De Kalb, IL: Author, 1994. 149p.
_____. *1870 Census, Afton Township, DeKalb County, Illinois.* DeKalb, IL: Author, 1989. 46p.
_____. *1870 Census, Clinton Township, DeKalb County, Illinois.* DeKalb, IL: Author, 1989. Unpgd.
_____. *1870 Census, Cortland Township, DeKalb County, Illinois.* DeKalb, IL: Author, 1989. 164p.
_____. *1870 Census, DeKalb Township, DeKalb County, Illinois.* DeKalb, IL: Author, 1991. 274p.
1880
Marshall, Florence Houghton. *1880 Census Index DeKalb County, Illinois.* DeKalb, IL: Author, 1985. pp. 1494-1656.

_____. *1880 Census, Afton Township, DeKalb County, Illinois.* DeKalb, IL: Author, 1985. 52p.

_____. *1880 Census, Clinton Township, DeKalb County, Illinois.* DeKalb, IL: Author, 1985. Unpgd.

_____. *1880 Census, Cortland Township, DeKalb County, Illinois.* DeKalb, IL: Author, 1985. 195p.

_____. *1880 Census, DeKalb Township, DeKalb County, Illinois.* DeKalb, IL: Author, 1985. Unpgd.

_____. *1880 Census, Franklin Township, DeKalb County, Illinois.* DeKalb, IL: Author, 1985. Unpgd.

_____. *1880 Census, Genoa Township, DeKalb County, Illinois.* DeKalb, IL: Author, 1985. Unpgd.

_____. *1880 Census, Kingston Township, DeKalb County, Illinois.* DeKalb, IL: Author, 1985. Unpgd.

_____. *1880 Census, Malta Township, DeKalb County, Illinois.* DeKalb, IL: Author, 1989. Unpgd.

_____. *1880 Census, Mayfield Township, DeKalb County, Illinois.* DeKalb, IL: Author, 1985. Unpgd.

_____. *1880 Census, Milan Township, DeKalb County, Illinois.* DeKalb, IL: Author, 1985. Unpgd.

_____. *1880 Census, Paw Paw Township, DeKalb County, Illinois.* DeKalb, IL: Author, 1985. Unpgd.

_____. *1880 Census, Pierce Township, DeKalb County, Illinois.* DeKalb, IL: Author, 1985. 61p.

_____. *1880 Census, Shabbona Township, DeKalb County, Illinois.* DeKalb, IL: Author, 1985. Unpgd.

_____. *1880 Census, Somonauk Township, DeKalb County, Illinois.* DeKalb, IL: Author, 1985. Unpgd.

_____. *1880 Census, South Grove Township, DeKalb County, Illinois.* DeKalb, IL: Author, 1985. Unpgd.

_____. *1880 Census, Squaw Grove Township, DeKalb County, Illinois.* DeKalb, IL: Author, 1985. Unpgd.

_____. *1880 Census, Sycamore Township, DeKalb County, Illinois.* DeKalb, IL: Author, 1985. Unpgd.

_____. *1880 Census, Victor Township, DeKalb County, Illinois.* DeKalb, IL: Author, 1985. Unpgd.

1900

Marshall, Florence Houghton. *1900 Census, Afton Township, DeKalb County, Illinois.* DeKalb, IL: Author, 1986. 56p.

_____. *1900 Census, DeKalb City...Ward, DeKalb County, Illinois.* DeKalb, IL: Author, 1987-1988. 4 vols.

DeWitt County
1840

Hauffe, Jean Parks, Sandra Shellhammer, and Mildred Hupp. *United States Census, 1840, DeWitt County, Illinois.* Decatur, IL: Decatur Genealogical Society, 1975. 19p.

1850

Hauffe, Jean Parks. *1850 United States Census of DeWitt County, Illinois.* Decatur, IL: Decatur Genealogical Society, 1970. 97p.

1860

Jackson, Ronald Vern. *Illinois 1860 Federal Census Index Addendum, DeWitt, Franklin, Wabash and Warren Counties.* West Jordan, UT: Genealogical Services, 1986; 1997. Unpgd.

1870

1870 United States Federal Census, DeWitt County, Illinois. Clinton, IL: DeWitt County Genealogical Society, 1989. 210p.

Douglas County
1860

Brandenburg, Kathryn. *1860 Douglas County, Illinois Census.* Arcola, IL: Douglas County, Illinois Genealogical Society, 1980. 149p.

1870

The Douglas County, Illinois, 1870 Census Report. Douglas County Genealogical Society, 1984. 228p.

1880

The Douglas County, Illinois, 1880 Census Report. Tuscora, IL: Douglas County Genealogical Society. 290p.

DuPage County
1840

Robb, Ruth Flesher. *1840 DuPage County, Illinois Federal Census.* Lombard, IL: Author, 1978. 143p.

1850

Robb, Ruth Flesher. *1850 DuPage County, Illinois Federal Census*. Lombard, IL: Author, 1976. 197p.

1860

Robb, Ruth Flesher. *1860 DuPage County, Illinois Federal Census*. Lombard, IL: Author, 1983. 187p.

1870

Robb, Ruth Flesher. *1870 Dupage County, Illinois Federal Census*. Lombard, IL: Author, 1987. 214p.

Edgar County

1830

Gill, James V. *Index to the 1830 Federal Census, Crawford, Edgar, Clark, Schuyler, McDonough, Vermillion, Macon, Shelby, Tazewell, Montgomery and Macoupin Counties*. Danville, IL: Heritage House, 1970. 50p.

1850

Cary, Linda Perkinson. *1850 Edgar County, Illinois Census*. Paris, IL: Tresearch, 1993. Unpgd.

1860

Luebking, Sandra Hargreaves. *Edgar County, Illinois, 1860 Federal Population Census Transcription*. Paris, IL: Edgar County Genealogical Society, 1990. 367p.

1870

Hammond, Barbara L. *Edgar County, Illinois, an Extraction of the 1870 Census*. Paris, IL: Treesearch, 1993. 343p.

Edwards County

1825

Bond, Corene. *Edwards County, Illinois, 1825 State Census Record*. Author. 10p.

Swartz, Elsie R. *Edwards County, Illinois, 1825 Census, with Additions, Early History, Beginnings of Pioneers, Marriages and Lists from 1813 to 1880*. Chicago, IL: Ancestry Trails and Tails, 1973. 41p.

1830

Gill, James V. *An Index to the 1830 Federal Census, White, Edwards, Wabash, Wayne, Clay, Clinton, St. Clair, Madison, Bond, Fayette and Lawrence Counties, Illinois*. Danville, IL: Illiana Genealogical Pub. Co., 1968. 64p.

Streleski, Nelda Skilbeck. *Edwards County, Illinois 1830 Federal Census, Heads of Family Only*. Decatur, IL: Decatur Genealogical Society, 1968. 8p.

1850

1850 Federal and 1855 State Census, Edwards County, Illinois. Albion, IL: Edwards County Historical Society. 40p.

Smith, Marjorie. *1850 Census of Edwards County, Illinois*. Thomson, IL: Heritage House, 1972. 45p.

1855

1850 Federal and 1855 State Census, Edwards County, Illinois. Albion, IL: Edwards County Historical Society. 40p.

1860

1860 Census, Edwards County, Illinois. Albion, IL: Edwards County Historical Society, 1982. 118p.

Mortality Schedules, 1860, 1870, 1880. Olney, IL: Richland County Genealogical Society, 1978. 139p.

1865

1865 State Illinois Census of Edwards County. Albion, IL: Edwards County Historical Society, 1994. 52p.

Illinois DAR. *1865 State Census of Edwards County, Illinois*. Genealogical Records Committee Report, s2, v33. Bonpas Chapter, DAR, 1995. 52p.

1870

1870 Census, Edwards County, Illinois. Albion, IL: Edwards County Historical Society, 1986. 160p.

Mortality Schedules, 1860, 1870, 1880. Olney, IL: Richland County Genealogical Society, 1978. 139p.

1880

1880 Census by the United States of America of Edwards County, Illinois. Olney, IL: Richland County Genealogical and Historical Society, 1981. 183p.

Mortality Schedules, 1860, 1870, 1880. Olney, IL: Richland County Genealogical Society, 1978. 139p.

Effingham County

1840

Bounds, Eleanor. *1840-1850 Effingham County Census*. Effingham, IL: Effingham County Genealogical Society, 1985. 86p.

Hauffe, Jean Parks. *United States Census, 1840 Effingham County, Illinois*. Decatur, IL: Decatur Genealogical Society, 1975. 11p.

1850

Bounds, Eleanor. *1840-1850 Effingham County Census*. Effingham, IL: Effingham County Genealogical Society, 1985. 86p.

Daniels, Gene, and Darlene Daniels. *United States Census, 1850, Effingham County, Illinois*. Decatur, IL: Decatur Genealogical Society, 1974. 94p.

1860

1860 Census of Effingham County, Illinois. Effingham, IL: Effingham County Genealogical Society, 1981. 139p.

1860 Effingham County Census Index. Effingham, IL: Effingham County Genealogical Society, 1985. 42p.

Mortality Schedules, 1860, 1870, 1880. Olney, IL: Richland County Genealogical Society, 1978. 139p.

1870

1870 Effingham County Census Index. Effingham, IL: Effingham County Genealogical Society, 1985. 313p.

Mortality Schedules, 1860, 1870, 1880. Olney, IL: Richland County Genealogical Society, 1978. 139p.

1880

Bounds, Eleanor. *Effingham County, Illinois 1850 Census*. Effingham, IL: Effingham County Genealogical Society, 1990. 2 vols.

Mortality Schedules, 1860, 1870, 1880. Olney, IL: Richland County Genealogical Society, 1978. 139p.

Fayette Counties

1820

McCord, Alenia. *Fayette Facts, 1820, 1830, 1840, 1850, 1860 Census*. Vandalia, IL: Fayette County Genealogical Society, 1981. 164p.

1830

Gill, James V. *An Index to the 1830 Federal Census, White, Edwards, Wabash, Wayne, Clay, Clinton, St. Clair, Madison, Bond, Fayette and Lawrence Counties, Illinois*. Danville, IL: Illiana Genealogical Pub. Co., 1968. 64p.

McCord, Alenia. *Fayette Facts, 1820, 1830, 1840, 1850, 1860 Census*. Vandalia, IL: Fayette County Genealogical Society, 1981. 164p.

Middlesworth, Grace H. *Fayette County, Illinois, 1830 Federal Census*. 1969. 16p.

1840

McCord, Alenia. *Fayette Facts, 1820, 1830, 1840, 1850, 1860 Census*. Vandalia, IL: Fayette County Genealogical Society, 1981. 164p.

Middlesworth, Grace H. *Fayette County, Illinois, 1840 Federal Census*. 34p.

1850

McCord, Alenia. *Fayette Facts, 1820, 1830, 1840, 1850, 1860 Census*. Vandalia, IL: Fayette County Genealogical Society, 1981. 164p.

Middlesworth, Grace H. *United States Census, 1850, Fayette County, Illinois*. Decatur, IL: Decatur Genealogical Society, 1976. 157p.

1855

Gustafson, Carol B. *Fayette County, Illinois 1855 and 1865 State Census Enumeration with Indexes*. Vandalia, IL: Fayette County Genealogical Society, 1989. 174p.

1860

McCord, Alenia. *Fayette Facts, 1820, 1830, 1840, 1850, 1860 Census*. Vandalia, IL: Fayette County Genealogical Society, 1981. 164p.

_____. *Fayette Facts, 1860 Census*. Vandalia, IL: Fayette County Genealogical Society, 1981. 2 vols.

1865

Gustafson, Carol B. *Fayette County, Illinois 1855 and 1865 State Census Enumeration with Indexes*. Vandalia, IL: Fayette County Genealogical Society, 1989. 174p.

1870

McCord, Alenia. *Fayette Facts, 1870 Census*. Vandalia, IL: Fayette County Genealogical Society, 1981. 298p.

1880

McCord, Alenia. *Fayette Facts, 1880 Census*. Vandalia, IL: Fayette County Genealogical Society, 1982. 371p.

1900

1900 Census, Fayette County, Illinois. Vandalia, IL: Fayette County Genealogical Society. 3 vols.

Ford County
1860

Greenhagen, Lois C., Sharon Stenzel, and Ada A. Terwilliger. *Illinois, Ford County 1860 Census, from the National Archives Publication Microfilm No. 653, Roll No. 177*. Kewanee, IL: Henry County Genealogical Society, 1985. 40p.

Franklin County
1820

USGenWeb Census Project. Illinois, 1820 Franklin County.

ftp://ftp.rootsweb.com/pub/census/il/franklin/1820/

1830

Dorris, Susan Doxsie. *1830 Census, Franklin County, Illinois*. West Frankfort, IL: Author, 1993. 64p.

Gill, James V. *Index to the 1830 Federal Census, Alexander, Pope, Union, Johnson, Jackson, Franklin, Perry, Randolph, Monroe, Washington, Marion, Jefferson, Hamilton and Gallatin Counties, Illinois*. Danville, IL: Heritage House, 1970. 57p.

1840

Dorris, Susan Doxsie. *1840 Census, Franklin County, Illinois*. West Frankfort, IL: Author, 1994. 69p.

Rademacher, Frank. *1840 United States Census of Franklin County, Illinois*. Mt. Prospect, IL: Author, 1972. 67p.

1850

Rademacher, Frank. *1850 United States Census of Franklin County, Illinois*. Mt. Prospect, IL: Author. 136p.

1860

Jackson, Ronald Vern. *Illinois 1860 Federal Census Index Addendum, DeWitt, Franklin, Wabash and Warren Counties*. West Jordan, UT: Genealogical Services, 1986; 1997. Unpgd.

Melvin, Doreen Broy. *Tracing Surnames from the 1860 Franklin County Census*. West Frankfort, IL: Franklin County Genealogical Society. 66p.

Rademacher, Frank, and Carol Rademacher. *1860 United States Census of Franklin County, Illinois*. Mt. Prospect, IL: Author, 1973. 214p.

1870

Melvin, Doreen Broy. *Tracing Surnames from the 1870 Franklin County Census*. West Frankfort, IL: Franklin County Genealogical Society, 1994. 25p.

Rademacher, Frank. *1870 United States Census of Franklin County, Illinois*. Mt. Prospect, IL: Author, 1976. 306p.

1880

Summers, Charles T. *1880 Census, Franklin County, Illinois*. Springfield, IL: Author, 1983. 405p.

Fulton County
1830

Fulton County Historical & Genealogical Society Index to 1830 Census. Canton, IL: Fulton County Historical & Genealogical Society, 1980. 4 vols.

Gill, James V., and Maryan R. Gill. *Index to the 1830 Federal Census, Greene, Morgan, Sangamon, Calhoun, Pike, Fulton, Knox, Henry, Adams, Hancock, Warren, Mercer, Peoria, Putnam, and Jo Daviess Counties, Illinois*. Danville, IL: Heritage House, 1970. 66p.

1840

Regenos, Graydon W., and Ada Y. Regenos. *Census of 1840, Fulton County, Illinois*. Lewistown, IL: Fulton County Historical Society, 1974. 44p.

1850

1850 Census of Fulton County, Illinois, Census Information Plus Index. Fulton, IL: Fulton County Historical and Genealogical Society, 1978. 432p.

Schunk, John Frederick. *1850 United States Census, Fulton County, Illinois*. Wichita, KS: S-K Pub., 1986. 2 vols.

1860

Fulton County, Illinois, 1860 Federal Census. Normal, IL: McLean County Genealogical Society, 1990. 7 vols.

1870

The 1870 Census of Fulton County, Illinois. Canton, IL: Fulton County Historical & Genealogical Society, 1990. 13 vols.

USGenWeb Census Project. Illinois, 1870 Fulton County.
ftp://ftp.rootsweb.com/pub/census/il/fulton/1870/

Gallatin County

1820

USGenWeb Census Project. Illinois, 1820 Gallatin County.
ftp://ftp.rootsweb.com/pub/census/il/gallatin/1820/

1830

Gill, James V. *Index to the 1830 Federal Census, Alexander, Pope, Union, Johnson, Jackson, Franklin, Perry, Randolph, Monroe, Washington, Marion, Jefferson, Hamilton and Gallatin Counties, Illinois*. Danville, IL: Heritage House, 1970. 57p.

Gallatin County, Illinois, Federal Census of 1830. Harrisburg, IL: Saline County Genealogical Society, 1985. 25p.

USGenWeb Census Project. Illinois, 1830 Gallatin County.
ftp://ftp.rootsweb.com/pub/census/il/gallatin/1830/

1840

USGenWeb Census Project. Illinois, 1840 Gallatin County.
ftp://ftp.rootsweb.com/pub/census/il/gallatin/1840/

1850

Index to the 1850 Census of Gallatin County, Illinois. Pasco, WA: Tri-City Genealogical Society, 1972. 110p.

1860

Murphy, John V., and Mary Afton Anderson. *Gallatin County, Illinois, 1860, 8th United States Census, Transcribed from National Archives Microfilm Publication, Microcopy 653, Roll No. 180, Population Schedules of the Eighth Census of the United States, 1860, Illinois, Volume 14 (855-1062), Gallatin County*. Carrier Mills, IL: Authors, 1982. 123p.

1870

Gildehaus, Valerie Phillips. *1870 Gallatin County, Illinois, United States Census*. Utica, KY: McDowell Publications, 1991. 222p.

1880

McGrew, Joye I. *1880 Census, Gallatin County, Illinois*. Herod, IL: Silkscreen Printing, 1991. 330p.

1900

McGrew, Joye I., and Crystal McGrew. *1900 Gallatin County, Illinois, United States Census*. Ridgeway, IL: Author. 305p.

Galva (Henry County)
1900
Rodgers, David N. *1900 Galva, Illinois Census Index and Abstract*. Ames, IA: Rodgers Index Service, 1984. 45p.

Greene County
1830
1830 Census, Greene & Jersey, Illinois Index. Jerseyville, IL: Jersey County Genealogical Society, 1994. 25p.

Gill, James V., and Maryan R. Gill. *Index to the 1830 Federal Census, Greene, Morgan, Sangamon, Calhoun, Pike, Fulton, Knox, Henry, Adams, Hancock, Warren, Mercer, Peoria, Putnam, and Jo Daviess Counties, Illinois*. Danville, IL: Heritage House, 1970. 66p.

USGenWeb Census Project. Illinois, 1830 Greene County.

ftp://ftp.rootsweb.com/pub/census/il/greene/1830/
1840
King, George B. *1840 Census of Greene County, Illinois*. Carrollton, IL: Greene County, Illinois, Historical and Genealogical Society. 86p.

USGenWeb Census Project. Illinois, 1840 Greene County.

ftp://ftp.rootsweb.com/pub/census/il/greene/1840/
1850
Sheffer, Mabel Tucker. *1850 Greene County, Illinois Census*. Carrollton, IL: Greene County Historical & Genealogical Society. 109p.
1860
King, George B. *1860 Census of Greene County, Illinois*. Carrollton, IL: Greene County, Illinois, Historical and Genealogical Society, 1993. 339p.

Grundy County
1850
Richard, Bernice C. *1850 Federal Census of Grundy County, Illinois*. Author, 1978. 80p.
1860
1860 Federal Population Census, Grundy County, Illinois. Bolingbrook, IL: Northern Will County Genealogical Society, 1982. 266p.

Hamilton County
1830
Gill, James V. *Index to the 1830 Federal Census, Alexander, Pope, Union, Johnson, Jackson, Franklin, Perry, Randolph, Monroe, Washington, Marion, Jefferson, Hamilton and Gallatin Counties, Illinois*. Danville, IL: Heritage House, 1970. 57p.

USGenWeb Census Project. Illinois, 1830 Hamilton County.

ftp://ftp.rootsweb.com/pub/census/il/hamilton/1830/
1840
Rademacher, Frank, and Carol Rademacher. *1840 United States Census of Hamilton County, Illinois*. Mt. Prospect, IL: Author, 1972. 18p.

USGenWeb Census Project. Illinois, 1840 Hamilton County.

ftp://ftp.rootsweb.com/pub/census/il/hamilton/1840/
1850
Rademacher, Frank, and Carol Rademacher. *1850 United States Census of Hamilton County, Illinois*. Chicago, IL: Chicago Genealogical Society. 167p.

USGenWeb Census Project. Illinois, 1850 Hamilton County.

ftp://ftp.rootsweb.com/pub/census/il/hamilton/1850/
1860
Rademacher, Frank, and Carol Rademacher. *1860 United States Census of Hamilton County, Illinois*. Mt. Prospect, IL: Author, 1972. 23p.

1870

Rademacher, Frank, and Carol Sims Rademacher. *1870 United States Census of Hamilton County, Illinois*. Mount Prospect, IL: Author, 1981. 308p.

Hancock County
1830

Gill, James V., and Maryan R. Gill. *Index to the 1830 Federal Census, Greene, Morgan, Sangamon, Calhoun, Pike, Fulton, Knox, Henry, Adams, Hancock, Warren, Mercer, Peoria, Putnam, and Jo Daviess Counties, Illinois*. Danville, IL: Heritage House, 1970. 66p.

1840

Bole, Barbara. *Sixth Census of the United States, 1840, Hancock County, Illinois*. Tulsa, OK: Maudlin, 1974. 51p.

1850

Ballowe, Patricia Jewell, Violet Michaelis Jewell, and Carol Watkins Lundgren. *The 1850 Census of Illinois, Hancock County*. Richland, WA: Locust Grove Press, 1977. 298p.

1860

The 1860 Hancock County, Illinois, Census. Augusta, IL: Tri-County Genealogy Society, 1983. 3 vols.

Hardin County
1850

Richard, Bernice C. *1850 Federal Census of Hardin County, Illinois*. Chicago, IL: Author, 1977. 69p.

1860

Douglas, Mary Nelle. *Hardin County, Illinois, 1860 U.S. Census*. Owensboro, KY: McDowell Publications. 49p.

1870

Douglas, Mary Nelle. *Hardin County, Illinois, 1870 U.S. Census*. Elizabethtown, IL: Nelson Pub. Co., 1985. 112p.

1880

Gildehaus, Valerie. *Hardin County, Illinois 1880 U.S. Census Index*. Murphysboro, IL: Author, 1988. 17p.

1900

Gildehaus, Valerie. *Hardin County, Illinois 1900 U.S. Census Index*. Murphysboro, IL: Author, 1988. 20p.

Henderson County
1850

Richard, Bernice C. *1850 Federal Census of Henderson County, Illinois*. Chicago, IL: Author, 1977. 8p.

Henry County
1830

Gill, James V., and Maryan R. Gill. *Index to the 1830 Federal Census, Greene, Morgan, Sangamon, Calhoun, Pike, Fulton, Knox, Henry, Adams, Hancock, Warren, Mercer, Peoria, Putnam, and Jo Daviess Counties, Illinois*. Danville, IL: Heritage House, 1970. 66p.

1850

The 1850 Federal Census of Henry County, Illinois. Richland, WA: Tri-City Genealogical Society, 1976. 99p.

1860

Springstroh, Oriene. *The 1860 Federal Census of Henry County, Illinois*. Kewanee, IL: Henry County Genealogical Society, 1985. 531p.

Iroquois County
1840

Gocken, Cheryl. *1830 Vermillion County Census, 1840 Iroquois County Census with Index*. Watseka, IL: Iroquois County Genealogical Society, 1992. 55p.

1850

Ledoux, Albert H. *The French Canadian Families of Kankakee and Iroquois Counties, Illinois, Abstracts from the Federal Census 1850 through 1880.* Johnston, PA: Author, 1990. 2 vols.

Miller, Mary J. *U.S. Federal Census, 1850 Iroquois County, Illinois.* Watseka, IL: Iroquois County Genealogical Society, 1979. 42p.

1855

Gocken, Cheryl. *Iroquois County Surname Index, 1855 Illinois State Census.* Watseka, IL: Iroquois County Genealogical Society, 1994. 25p.

_____. *Iroquois County, Illinois State Census, 1855.* Watseka, IL: Iroquois County Genealogical Society, 1995. 85p.

1860

Garfield, Jannette. *1860 Federal Census of Iroquois County, Illinois.* Watseka, IL: Iroquois County Genealogical Society, 1983. 176p.

Ledoux, Albert H. *The French Canadian Families of Kankakee and Iroquois Counties, Illinois, Abstracts from the Federal Census 1850 through 1880.* Johnston, PA: Author, 1990. 2 vols.

1870

Garfield, Jannette. *Surname Index to 1870 Federal Census of Iroquois County, Illinois.* Watseka, IL: Iroquois County Genealogical Society, 1988. 67p.

Ledoux, Albert H. *The French Canadian Families of Kankakee and Iroquois Counties, Illinois, Abstracts from the Federal Census 1850 through 1880.* Johnston, PA: Author, 1990. 2 vols.

1880

Johnson, Florence S. *Surname Index to the 1880 Federal Census of Iroquois County, Illinois.* Watseka, IL: Iroquois County Genealogical Society, 1989. 98p.

Ledoux, Albert H. *The French Canadian Families of Kankakee and Iroquois Counties, Illinois, Abstracts from the Federal Census 1850 through 1880.* Johnston, PA: Author, 1990. 2 vols.

1900

Gocken, Cheryl. *1900 Iroquois County Census Index.* Watseka, IL: Iroquois County Genealogical Society, 1993. 258p.

Jackson County

1820

USGenWeb Census Project. Illinois, 1820 Jackson County.
ftp://ftp.rootsweb.com/pub/census/il/jackson/1820/

1830

Gill, James V. *Index to the 1830 Federal Census, Alexander, Pope, Union, Johnson, Jackson, Franklin, Perry, Randolph, Monroe, Washington, Marion, Jefferson, Hamilton and Gallatin Counties, Illinois.* Danville, IL: Heritage House, 1970. 57p.

1860

Eighth Census of the United States, 1860 Jackson County, Illinois, Federal Population Census. Murpheysboro, IL: Jackson County Historical Society, 1987. 153p.

Wright, John W. D. *Jackson County, Illinois Residents in 1850.* Carbondale, IL: Jackson County Historical Society, 1972. 64p.

1865

Neilson, Ann. *Illinois State Census, 1865 Jackson County, Illinois.* Murpheysboro, IL: Author. 68p.

1920

Armes, Beverly Spiller. *1920 United States Federal Census, Jackson County, Illinois, Elk Township.* West Frankfort, IL: Author, 1966. 83p.

Jasper County

1850

Huston, Patty. *1850 Census of Jasper County, Illinois and the 1835 & 1840 State Censuses of Jaspar County, Illinois.* Hidalgo, IL: Author. 46p.

1860

Mortality Schedules, 1860, 1870, 1880. Olney, IL: Richland County Genealogical Society, 1978. 139p.

1870

Mortality Schedules, 1860, 1870, 1880. Olney, IL: Richland County Genealogical Society, 1978. 139p.

Scherer, Mary. *Jasper County 1860 Census.* Olney, IL: Author, 1983. 159p.

1880

Mortality Schedules, 1860, 1870, 1880. Olney, IL: Richland County Genealogical Society, 1978. 139p.

1900

Jasper County, Illinois 1900 Federal Census. Newton, IL: Jasper County Historical & Genealogical Society, 1996. 577p.

Jefferson County
1820

Pompey, Sherman Lee. *Index to the 1820 Census Records of Jefferson and Union Counties, Illinois.* Charleston, OR: Pacific Specialities, 1974. 8p.

1830

Gill, James V. *Index to the 1830 Federal Census, Alexander, Pope, Union, Johnson, Jackson, Franklin, Perry, Randolph, Monroe, Washington, Marion, Jefferson, Hamilton and Gallatin Counties, Illinois.* Danville, IL: Heritage House, 1970. 57p.

1850

Wormer, Maxine E. *Jefferson County, Illinois, 1850 Census.* Thomson, IL: Heritage House, 1973. 2 vols.

1870

Clark, Linda Capps. *Jefferson County, Illinois 1870 Census.* Mt. Vernon, IL: LML Publications, 1996. 306p.

Jersey County
1830

1830 Census, Greene & Jersey, Illinois Index. Jerseyville, IL: Jersey County Genealogical Society, 1994. 25p.

1850

French, Robert L. *Jersey County 1850 Census.* Jerseyville, IL: Jersey County Genealogical Society, 1994. 132p

Index to the 1850 Census of Jersey County, Illinois. Yakima, WA: Yakima Valley Genealogical Society, 1976. 138p.

1860

Lines, Jack Milton. *1860 Federal Census of Jersey County, Illinois with Index.* Yakima, WA: Yakima Valley Genealogical Society, 1986. 223p.

Jo Daviess County
1830

Gill, James V., and Maryan R. Gill. *Index to the 1830 Federal Census, Greene, Morgan, Sangamon, Calhoun, Pike, Fulton, Knox, Henry, Adams, Hancock, Warren, Mercer, Peoria, Putnam, and Jo Daviess Counties, Illinois.* Danville, IL: Heritage House, 1970. 66p.

1850

Bostedt, Mrs. Raymond W. *Index to the 1850 Federal Census of Jo Daviess County.* Pp. 350-390.

Hansen, Robert. *1850 Census Index to Jo Daviess Illinois.* Galena, IL: Author, 1979. 56p.

1855

Hansen, Robert. *1855 State Census Index of Jo Daviess County, Illinois.* Galena, IL: Author, 1987. 77p.

1860

Hansen, Robert. *1860 Census Index to Jo Daviess County, Illinois.* Galena, IL: Author, 1979. 70p.

1870

Hansen, Robert. *Index to Jo Daviess County, Illinois, Federal Census for 1870.* Galena, IL: Author, 1982. 62p.

1880

Hansen, Robert. *1880 Census Index, Jo Daviess County, Illinois*. Galena, IL: Author, 1982. 61p.

1900

Hansen, Robert. *1900 Census Index to Jo Daviess Illinois*. Galena, IL: Author, 1982. 75p.

Johnson County

1830

Gill, James V. *Index to the 1830 Federal Census, Alexander, Pope, Union, Johnson, Jackson, Franklin, Perry, Randolph, Monroe, Washington, Marion, Jefferson, Hamilton and Gallatin Counties, Illinois*. Danville, IL: Heritage House, 1970. 57p.

1850

1850 Census, Johnson County, Illinois. Vienna, IL: Johnson County Genealogical and Historical Society, 1994. 120p.

Tri-City Genealogical Society. *The 1850 Federal Census of Johnson County, Illinois*. Richland, WA: Locust Grove Press, 1973. 83p.

1860

Johnson County, Illinois 1860 Census. Vienna, IL: Johnson County Genealogical and Historical Society, 1993. 199p.

1870

Mathis, Margaret. *Johnson County, Illinois 1870 Census*. Vienna, IL: Johnson County Genealogical and Historical Society, 1995. 231p.

1920

Sullins, Richard D. *1920 Federal Census, Johnson County, Illinois*. Vienna, IL: S and S Genealogists, 1996. Unpgd.

Kane County

1840

Eder, Linda Farroh. *1840 Kane County, Illinois Federal Census Index*. Elgin, IL: Author, 1979. 13p.

1850

Havlice, Patricia Pate. *1850 Census of Kane County, Illinois*. Author. 24p.

1860

Haller, Dolores. *1860 Kane County Census, Illinois*. Aurora, IL: Author, 1982. 454p.

Kankakee County

1850

Ledoux, Albert H. *The French Canadian Families of Kankakee and Iroquois Counties, Illinois, Abstracts from the Federal Census 1850 through 1880*. Johnston, PA: Author, 1990. 2 vols.

1860

First Census of Kankakee County, 1860. Kankakee, IL: Kankakee Valley Genealogical Society, 1985. 402p.

Ledoux, Albert H. *The French Canadian Families of Kankakee and Iroquois Counties, Illinois, Abstracts from the Federal Census 1850 through 1880*. Johnston, PA: Author, 1990. 2 vols.

1870, 1880

Ledoux, Albert H. *The French Canadian Families of Kankakee and Iroquois Counties, Illinois, Abstracts from the Federal Census 1850 through 1880*. Johnston, PA: Author, 1990. 2 vols.

Kendall County

1850

Dickson, Elmer George. *1850 Census of Kendall County, Illinois, with Supplemental Genealogical Data*. Chico, CA: Author, 1993. 244p.

Richard, Bernice C. *1850 Federal Census of Kendall County, Illinois*. Unpgd.

1855

Dickson, Elmer George. *Heads of Households, Illinois 1855, State Censuses of Kendall County*. Chico, CA: Author, 1991. 51p.

1860

Dickson, Elmer George. *1860 Census of Kendall County, Illinois, with Supplemental Genealogical Data.* Chico, CA: Author, 1993. 484p.

Wallace, Harriet E. *1860 Census of Kendall County, Illinois.* Urbana, IL: Author, 1984. 309p.

1865

Dickson, Elmer George. *Heads of Households, Illinois 1865, State Censuses of Kendall County.* Chico, CA: Author, 1991. 82p.

1870

Dickson, Elmer George. *1870 Census of Kendall County, Illinois, with Supplemental Genealogical Data.* Chico, CA: Author, 1994. 467p.

1880

Dickson, Elmer George. *1880 Census of Kendall County, Illinois, with Supplemental Genealogical Data.* Chico, CA: Author, 1994. 441p.

Kewanee County

1900

Rodgers, David N. *1900 Kewanee, Illinois Census Index & Abstract.* Ames, IA: Rodgers Index Service, 1984. 148p.

Knox County

1830

Gill, James V., and Maryan R. Gill. *Index to the 1830 Federal Census, Greene, Morgan, Sangamon, Calhoun, Pike, Fulton, Knox, Henry, Adams, Hancock, Warren, Mercer, Peoria, Putnam, and Jo Daviess Counties, Illinois.* Danville, IL: Heritage House, 1970. 66p.

1840

Holliday, Nathan. *Index 1850 Census of Knox County, Illinois, U.S. Census of 1840 for Knox County.* Galesburg, IL: Knox County Genealogical Society, 1977. 19p.

1850

Holliday, Nathan. *1850 Census of Knox County, Illinois.* Galesburg, IL: Knox County Genealogical Society, 1977. 137p.

1860

All Name Index to 1860 Federal Census of Knox County, Illinois. Galesburg, IL: Knox County Genealogical Society, 1982. 5 vols.

1870

Graham, Shirley Dredge. *1870 Federal Census, Knox County, Illinois.* Galesburg, IL: Knox County Genealogical Society, 1990, 1991. 2 vols.

1880

Waters, Lynn, and Shirley Dredge Graham. *1880 Federal Census, Knox County, Illinois.* Galesburg, IL: Knox County Genealogical Society, 1989. 5 vols.

1900

Graham, Shirley Dredge. *1900 Federal Census, Knox County, Illinois, Galesburg Township.* Galesburg, IL: Knox County Genealogical Society, 1993. 574p.

_____. *1900 Federal Census, Two All Name Indexes, Knox County, Illinois.* Galesburg, IL: Knox County Genealogical Society, 1994. 223p.

La Salle County

1850

1850 Federal Census of La Salle County, Illinois with Index. Yakima, WA: Yakima Valley Genealogical Society, 1978. 322p.

1855

Swanson, Jean E. *LaSalle County, Illinois, an Extraction of Names from the 1855 State Census.* Ottawa, IL: LaSalle County Genealogy Guild, 1987. 132p.

1860

La Salle County, Illinois 1860 Federal Census, Eighth Census of the United States, Roll 196. Ottawa, IL: La Salle County Genealogy Guild, 1993. 2 vols.

1870

La Salle County, Illinois, 1870 Federal Census Ninth Census of the United States. Ottawa, IL: La Salle County Genealogy Guild, 1996. 2 vols.

Lake County

1850

Thompson, Dorothy F. *1850 Census of Lake County, Illinois.* Evanston, IL: Author, 1976. 396p.

1860

1860 Census of Lake County, Illinois. Libertyville, IL: Lake County Genealogical Society, 1984. 238p.

1862

Roden, Joan. *Index to the 1862 Military Census of Lake County, Illinois.* Libertyville, IL: Lake County Genealogical Society, 1991. 96p.

1865

Dolph, Dorothy. *Illinois State Census, Lake County, 1865.* Libertyville, IL: Lake County Genealogical Society, 1989. 174p.

1870

1870 Census of Lake County, Illinois. Libertyville, IL: Lake County Genealogical Society, 1985. 4 vols.

1880

1880 Census of Lake County, Illinois. Libertyville, IL: Lake County Genealogical Society, 1987, 1988. 8 vols.

1900

1900 Census Lake County, Illinois. Vol. 8, Waukegan Township. Libertyville, IL: Lake County Genealogical Society, 1994, 1995. 8 vols.

Lawrence County

1830

Gill, James V. *An Index to the 1830 Federal Census, White, Edwards, Wabash, Wayne, Clay, Clinton, St. Clair, Madison, Bond, Fayette and Lawrence Counties, Illinois.* Danville, IL: Illiana Genealogical Pub. Co., 1968. 64p.

1840

Scherer, Mary. *Lawrence County 1840-1850 Census.* Olney, IL: Author, 1984. 117p.

1850

Miller, Marshall E. *1850 Federal Census Lawrence County, Illinois.* Author. 140p.

Scherer, Mary. *Lawrence County 1840-1850 Census.* Olney, IL: Author, 1984. 117p.

1860

Marlin, Aleen Thompson. *1860 Federal Census of Lawrence County, Illinois.* Olney, IL: Richland County Genealogical and Historical Society; 1982. 195p.

Mortality Schedules, 1860, 1870, 1880. Olney, IL: Richland County Genealogical Society, 1978. 139p.

1870

Mortality Schedules, 1860, 1870, 1880. Olney, IL: Richland County Genealogical Society, 1978. 139p.

Satterthwaite, Geraldine. *1870 Federal Census of Lawrence County, Illinois.* Bridgeport, IL: Author, 1982. 397p.

1880

Mortality Schedules, 1860, 1870, 1880. Olney, IL: Richland County Genealogical Society, 1978. 139p.

Lee County

1850

Smith, Marjorie. *Lee County, Illinois 1850 Census.* Thomason, IL: Heritage House, 1972. 66p.

Livingston County
1850

Livingston County, Illinois 1850 Federal Census. Normal, IL: Bloomington Normal Genealogical Society. 32p.

Logan County
1840

Shellhamer, Mrs. J. Dalen, Jean Hauffe, Mrs. Harlin B. Taylor. *United States 1840, Logan County, Illinois*. Decatur, IL: Decatur Genealogical Society, 1975. 12p.
1850
United States Census, 1850, Logan County, Illinois. Decatur, IL: Decatur Genealogical Society, 1976. 97p.
1860
1860 United States Federal Census, Logan County, Illinois. Lincoln, IL: Logan County Genealogical Society, 1981. 326p.

McDonough County
1830

1830 Census of McDonough County, Geographical Portion of Schuyler County, Illinois. Macomb, IL: McDonough County Genealogical Society, 1980. 7p.

Gill, James V. *Index to the 1830 Federal Census, Crawford, Edgar, Clark, Schuyler, McDonough, Vermillion, Macon, Shelby, Tazewell, Montgomery and Macoupin Counties*. Danville, IL: Heritage House, 1970. 50p.
1840
Grimm, Elizabeth. *1840 Census of United States for McDonough County, Illinois, from Microfilm Roll #65, M-704*. Macomb, IL: McDonough County Genealogical Society, 1982. 24p.
1850
Bates, Minnie Montanye, and Geraldine Hemp Mayhugh. *McDonough County, Illinois, 1850 Federal Census*. Owensboro, KY: McDowell Publications, 1981. 216p.

Solomon, Eileen. *Illinois, McDonough County 1850 Census*. Macomb, IL: McDonough County Genealogical Society, 1987. 194p.

USGenWeb Census Project. Illinois, 1850 McDonough (Partial).

ftp://ftp.rootsweb.com/pub/census/il/mcdonough/1850
1860
1860 United States Census of McDonough County, Illinois, Census Plus Surname Index. Macomb, IL: McDonough County Genealogical Society, 1981.

Solomon, Eileen. *Index for 1860 Census of McDonough County, Illinois*. Macomb, IL: McDonough County Genealogical Society, 1986. 23p.
1870
Solomon, Eileen. *Illinois, McDonough County 1870 Census*. Macomb, IL: McDonough County Genealogical Society, 1985. 520p.
1880
Solomon, Eileen. *Illinois: McDonough County 1880 Census*. Macomb, IL: McDonough County Genealogical Society, 1983. 549p.
1890
Grimm, E. *1890 Census, State of Illinois, County of McDonough, Township of Mound, Date, June, 1890*. Macomb, IL: McDonough County Genealogical Society. 47p.
1900
Harris, Marjorie Guy. *1900 Census McDonough County, Illinois, Emmet Township Enumerated by Emory Cole*. Macomb, IL: McDonough County Genealogical Society, 1995. 29p.

Martin, Elizabeth. *1900 Census McDonough County, Illinois, Hire Township*. Macomb, IL: McDonough County Genealogical Society, 1993. 28p.

_____. *1900 Census McDonough County, Illinois, New Salem Township*. Macomb, IL: McDonough County Genealogical Society, 1993. 37p.

Semonis, Sara Wisslead. *1900 Census McDonough County, Illinois, Blandinsville Township*. Macomb, IL: McDonough County Genealogical Society, 1995. 53p.

_____. *1900 Census McDonough County, Illinois, Hire Township*. Macomb, IL: McDonough County Genealogical Society, 1996. 29p.

_____. *1900 Census McDonough County, Illinois, Macomb Township, including Village of Bardolph*. Macomb, IL: McDonough County Genealogical Society, 1996. 35p.

McHenry County
1840
Bauer, Phyllis J. *McHenry County, Illinois 1840 Federal Census*. McHenry, IL: McHenry County Genealogical Society, 1986. 20p.
1850
Robb, Ruth Flesher. *1850 McHenry County, Illinois Federal Census*. Lombard, IL: Author, 1979. 177p.
1860
McHenry County, Illinois 1860 Federal Census. McHenry, IL: McHenry County Illinois Genealogical Society, 1986. 288p.

McLean County
1850
Gerwick, Verda. *1850 Federal Census, McLean County, State of Illinois*. Danville, IL: Heritage House, 1971. 112p.
1870
Stambazze, Dee Ann. *1870 McHenry County, Illinois Federal Census*. Crystal Lake, IL: McHenry County, Illinois Genealogical Society, 1992. 364p.

Macon County
1830
Gill, James V. *Index to the 1830 Federal Census, Crawford, Edgar, Clark, Schuyler, McDonough, Vermillion, Macon, Shelby, Tazewell, Montgomery and Macoupin Counties*. Danville, IL: Heritage House, 1970. 50p.

Streleski, Nelda Skilbeck. *Macon County, Illinois, 1830 Federal Census, Heads of Family Only*. 1968. 10p.
1840
Hauffe, Jean Parks, and Mildred Hupp. *United States Census, 1840, Macon County, Illinois*. Decatur, IL: Decatur Genealogical Society, 1975. 17p.
1850
Hauffe, Jean Parks. *1850 United States Census of Macon County, Illinois*. Decatur, IL: Decatur Genealogical Society, 1969. 78p.
1855
Hunter, Cheri Davis. *1855 Illinois State Census, Macon County*. Decatur, IL: Decatur Genealogical Society, 1986. 55p.
1860
Hunter, Cheri. *1860 United States Census of Macon County, Illinois*. Decatur, IL: Decatur Genealogical Society, 1977. 2 vols.

Macon County, Illinois Military Census, Militia Roll. Decatur, IL: Decatur Genealogical Society, 1991. 170p.
1861-1863
Macon County, Illinois Military Census, Militia Roll, 1861, 1862, 1863. Decatur, IL: Decatur Genealogical Society, 1990. 170p.
1870
1870 Macon County, Illinois Census. Decatur, IL: Decatur Genealogical Society, 1992.

Macoupin County

1830

Gill, James V. *Index to the 1830 Federal Census, Crawford, Edgar, Clark, Schuyler, McDonough, Vermillion, Macon, Shelby, Tazewell, Montgomery and Macoupin Counties*. Danville, IL: Heritage House, 1970. 50p.

1840

Sherman, Sharron K. *1840 United States Census of Macoupin County, Illinois*. Taylorsville, IL: 1984. 41p.

1850

Hess, Irvin David. *Abstract of the 1850 United States Census, Macoupin County, Illinois, and Surname Index*. Yuma, AZ: Author, 1972. 156p.

1860

Bradley, Littleton P. *Macoupin County, Illinois 1860 Federal Census*. St. Louis, MO: Author, 1984. 577p.

1870

Zimmer, Iris, and Cynthia Leonard. *Macoupin County, Illinois, 1870 Federal Census*. Staunton, IL: Leonard Data Quest, 1994. Unpgd.

Madison County

1820

Bauer, Phyllis J. *Madison County, Illinois 1820 Federal Census*. McHenry, IL: Author, 1994. 51p.

1830

Gill, James V. *An Index to the 1830 Federal Census, White, Edwards, Wabash, Wayne, Clay, Clinton, St. Clair, Madison, Bond, Fayette and Lawrence Counties, Illinois*. Danville, IL: Illiana Genealogical Pub. Co., 1968. 64p.

Streleski, Nelda Skilbeck, and Mrs. Harlin B. Taylor. *Madison County, Illinois 1830 Federal Census*. Decatur, IL: Decatur Genealogical Society, 1969. 31p.

1840

Bauer, Phyllis J., Roberta Smith, and Linda Stengele. *Madison County, Illinois 1840 Federal Census*. McHenry, IL: Author, 1986. 20p.

1845

Wasser, Elsie M. *1845 Census of Madison County, Illinois*. Edwardsville, IL: Author, 1985. 76p.

1855

Wasser, Elsie M. *1855 Census, Madison County, Illinois*. Author, 1995. 124p.

1860

Upton, Joy. *Madison County, Illinois 1860 Census*. Troy, IL: Author, 1986. 621p.

1880

Wasser, Elsie M., and Marie T. Eberle. *1880 Federal Census of Madison County, Illinois*. Edwardsville, IL: Madison County Genealogical Society, 1991. 945p.

Marion County

1830

Gill, James V. *Index to the 1830 Federal Census, Alexander, Pope, Union, Johnson, Jackson, Franklin, Perry, Randolph, Monroe, Washington, Marion, Jefferson, Hamilton and Gallatin Counties, Illinois*. Danville, IL: Heritage House, 1970. 57p.

1850

Wormer, Maxine E. *Marion County, Illinois, 1850 Census*. Thomson, IL: Heritage House, 1972. 135p.

1860

Wormer, Maxine E. *Marion County, Illinois 1860 Census*. Salem, IL: Marion County Genealogical & Historical Society, 1981. 150p.

1870

Wormer, Maxine E. *Marion County, Illinois 1870 Census*. Salem, IL: Marion County Genealogical & Historical Society, 1983. 193p.

1880

Wormer, Maxine E. *Marion County, Illinois, 1880 Census*. Salem, IL: Marion County Genealogical & Historical Society, 1985. 2 vols.

Marshall County
1850

Richard, Bernice C. *1850 Federal Census of Marshall County, Illinois*. Author, 1975. 124p.

1860

Raffensperger, Helen G. *1860 Federal Census, Marshall County, Illinois, Population 13,437; Copied from Microcopy 653, Roll 210, National Archives, Washington, D.C.* Henry, IL: Author, 1982. 155p.

1870

Swanson, Connie, and Helen Raffelsperger. *1870 Federal Census, Marshall County, Illinois, Population 16,956, Including 3098 Foreign Born Copied from Microcopy M593, Roll 254, National Archives, Washington, DC*. Henry, IL: Henry Historical and Genealogical Society of Henry, Illinois, 1987. 190p.

1880

Swanson, Connie, and Helen Raffensperger. *1880 Federal Census, Marshall County, Illinois, Population 15,055*. Henry, IL: Author, 1991. 167p.

Mason County
1850

Mason County, Illinois, 1850, 1860, 1870, 1880 Mortality Schedule. Havana, IL: Mason County History Project, 1993. 12p.

Mason County, Illinois, in 1850. Havana, IL: Mason County Members of The Church of Jesus Christ of Latter-day Saints, 1989. Unpgd.

Richard, Bernice C. *1850 Federal Census of Mason County, Illinois*. Author, 1978. pp. 285-425.

1855

Mason County, Illinois, the 1855 State Census. Havana, IL: Mason County Members of The Church of Jesus Christ of Latter-day Saints, 1988. 20p.

1860

Mason County, Illinois, 1850, 1860, 1870, 1880 Mortality Schedule. Havana, IL: Mason County History Project, 1993. 12p.

Mason County, Illinois 1860 Census Index. Havana, IL: Mason County History Project, 1993. 30p.

Todd, Sharon L. *The 1860 Census of Mason County, Illinois*. Stephenville, TX: Datatrace Systems, 1988. 362p.

1870

Mason County, Illinois, 1850, 1860, 1870, 1880 Mortality Schedule. Havana, IL: Mason County History Project, 1993. 12p.

1880

Mason County, Illinois, 1850, 1860, 1870, 1880 Mortality Schedule. Havana, IL: Mason County History Project, 1993. 12p.

Mason County, Illiniois, 1880 Federal Census Transcript and Index. Havana, IL: Mason County History Project, 1992. 243p.

Massac County
1850

Kansas City Branch Genealogical Library. *Massac County, Illinois 1850 Census*. Thomson, IL: Heritage House, 1976. 89p.

1855

1855 Illinois State Census of Massac County. Metropolis, IL: Massac County Genealogical Society, 1994. 76p.

1860

Artman, Pauline Tucker. *Annotated 1860 Census, Massac County, Illinois*. Evansville, IN: Evansville Bindery, 1992. 226p.

Menard County

1840

Hohimer, Margaret. *Federal Census, 1840, Menard County, Illinois*. Springfield, IL: Sangamon County Genealogical Society of Illinois, 1982. 35p.

1850

de Perez Galvez, Helen Bell. *1850 United States Census, Menard County, Illinois*. 111p.

1860

de Perez Galvez, Helen Bell. *1860 U.S. Census, Menard County, Illinois*. St. Louis, MO: Genealogical Research & Publications, 1977. 174p.

1865

Geary, Maxine, and Jeanne Weaver. *Menard County 1865 Illinois State Census*. Petersburg, IL: Weaver Genealogical Pubns., 1992. 43p.

1870

de Perez Galvez, Helen Bell. *1870 Menard County, Illinois, Census, and Menard County, Illinois, Mortality Schedule*. Springfield, IL: Author, 1983. 2 vols.

1880

Menard County, Illinois 1880 Federal Census Tenth Census of the United States, T9, Number 236. Springfield, IL: Gouchanour, 1984. 2 vols.

1910

Gochanour, Eileen Lynch. *1910 Menard County, Illinois Census, Thirteenth Census of the United States*. Springfield, IL: Author, 1984. 274p.

Mercer County

1830

Gill, James V., and Maryan R. Gill. *Index to the 1830 Federal Census, Greene, Morgan, Sangamon, Calhoun, Pike, Fulton, Knox, Henry, Adams, Hancock, Warren, Mercer, Peoria, Putnam, and Jo Daviess Counties, Illinois*. Danville, IL: Heritage House, 1970. 66p.

1850

Arvedson, Evelyn Houghton. *Alphabetical Index of Mercer County, Illinois, 1850 Census*. Author, 1975. 188p.; 1980.

1860

Garrett, Eulalia H. *Mercer County 1860 Census*. Davenport, IA: Richardson Sloane Genealogical Library, 1988. 230p.

1870

Garrett, Eulalia H. *Mercer County, Illinois 1870 Census, Original Transcription from United States Census Roll #260*. Author, 1998. 289, 123p.

1900

Garrett, Eulalia H. *Mercer County, Illinois 1900 Census, Original Transcription from United States Census Roll T623*. New Windsor, IL: Author, 1992. Unpgd.

Monroe County

1830

Gill, James V. *Index to the 1830 Federal Census, Alexander, Pope, Union, Johnson, Jackson, Franklin, Perry, Randolph, Monroe, Washington, Marion, Jefferson, Hamilton and Gallatin Counties, Illinois*. Danville, IL: Heritage House, 1970. 57p.

1860

Stewart, Ruth Weilbacher. *1860 Monroe County, Illinois, Federal Census*. Carterville, IL: Genealogy Society of Southern Illinois, 1998. 315p.

Montgomery County

1825

Sanders, Walter R. *1825 State Census of Montgomery County, Illinois*. Litchfield, IL: Author. 9p.

1830

Gill, James V. *Index to the 1830 Federal Census, Crawford, Edgar, Clark, Schuyler, McDonough, Vermillion, Macon, Shelby, Tazewell, Montgomery and Macoupin Counties*. Danville, IL: Heritage House, 1970. 50p.

Sanders, Walter R. *1830 State Census of Montgomery County, Illinois*. Litchfield, IL: Author, 1955. 14p.

1840

Sanders, Walter R. *1840 State Census of Montgomery County, Illinois*. Litchfield, IL: Author, 1955. 21p.

1850

Ingmire, Frances Terry. *1850 United States Census of Population Schedule, Montgomery County, Illinois*. St. Louis, MO: Author, 1980. 147p.

Sanders, Walter R. *1850 Census of Montgomery County, Illinois*. Litchfield, IL: Author, 1977. 49p.

1855

Sanders, Walter R. *1855 State Census of Montgomery County, Illinois*. Litchfield, IL: Author. 19p.

1860

Montgomery County, Illinois 1860 Census and Mortality Schedule. Litchfield, IL: Montgomery County Genealogical Society, 1982. Unpgd.

Morgan County

1830

1830 Census Records for Morgan County, Illinois, Includes Cass and Scott Counties. Jacksonville, IL: Jacksonville Area Genealogical and Historical Society, 1991. 85p.

Gill, James V., and Maryan R. Gill. *Index to the 1830 Federal Census, Greene, Morgan, Sangamon, Calhoun, Pike, Fulton, Knox, Henry, Adams, Hancock, Warren, Mercer, Peoria, Putnam, and Jo Daviess Counties, Illinois*. Danville, IL: Heritage House, 1970. 66p.

1835

1835 Illinois State Census, Morgan County, in 1835 Cass & Scott Counties Were Part of Morgan County. Jacksonville, IL: Jacksonville Area Genealogical & Historical Society, 1998. 2 vols.

1850

Hohimer, Margaret Sager, Eileen Lynch Gochanour, and Wanda Warkins Allers. *1850 Morgan County, Illinois Federal Census*. Springfield, IL: Ellen Lynch Gochanour, 1983. 2 vols.

USGenWeb Census Project. Illinois, 1850 Morgan County.

ftp://ftp.rootsweb.com/pub/census/il/morgan/1850/

1860

Gochanour, Eileen Lynch, and Wanda Warkins Allers. *Morgan County, Illinois 1860 Census, Eighth Census of the United States, M 653, Number 213*. Springfield, IL: Author, 1983. 306p.

1870

Gochanour, Eileen Lynch. *1870 Morgan County Census*. Springfield, IL, Author. 1985. 394p.

Moultree County

1850

Ray, Lora May. *1850 United States Census of Moultrie County, Illinois*. Decatur, IL: Decatur Genealogical Society. 70p.

1860

Ray, Lora May. *1860 United States Census of Moultrie County, Illinois*. Sullivan, IL: Moultrie County Historical and Genealogical Society, 1976. 125p.

1870

Ray, Lora May. *1870 United States Census of Moultrie County, Illinois*. Decatur, IL: Decatur Genealogical Society, 1980. 284p.

1880

Durbin, Sue, Mary E. Leeds, and Gertrude Dixon. *1880 United States Census of Moultrie County, Illinois*. Sullivan, IL: Moultrie County Historical & Genealogical Society, 1981. 3 vols.

Ogle County

1850

Richard, Bernice C. *1850 Federal Census of Ogle County, Illinois*. Chicago, IL: Author, 1974. 249p.

1860

Jackson, Ernest Harding. *Ogle County, Illinois 1860 Census and Indexes*. Oregon, IL: Ogle County Genealogical Society, 1990. Unpgd.

USGenWeb Census Project. Illinois, 1860 Ogle County.

ftp://ftp.rootsweb.com/pub/census/il/ogle/1860/

Peoria County

1830

Gill, James V., and Maryan R. Gill. *Index to the 1830 Federal Census, Greene, Morgan, Sangamon, Calhoun, Pike, Fulton, Knox, Henry, Adams, Hancock, Warren, Mercer, Peoria, Putnam, and Jo Daviess Counties, Illinois*. Danville, IL: Heritage House, 1970. 66p.

1850

O'Dell, Patti Combs. *1850 Peoria County, Illinois Census*. Author, 1972. 210p.

1860

1860 Census, Peoria County, Illinois. Peoria, IL: Peoria Genealogical Society, 1983. 18 vols.

1870

Peoria County, Illinois, 1870 Federal Census. Peoria, IL: Peoria Genealogical Society, 1996. 26 vols.

Perry County

1830

Gill, James V. *Index to the 1830 Federal Census, Alexander, Pope, Union, Johnson, Jackson, Franklin, Perry, Randolph, Monroe, Washington, Marion, Jefferson, Hamilton and Gallatin Counties, Illinois*. Danville, IL: Heritage House, 1970. 57p.

USGenWeb Census Project. Illinois, 1830 Perry County.

ftp://ftp.rootsweb.com/pub/census/il/perry/1830/

1840

USGenWeb Census Project. Illinois, 1840 Perry County.

ftp://ftp.rootsweb.com/pub/census/il/perry/1840/

1850

USGenWeb Census Project. Illinois, 1850 Perry County.

ftp://ftp.rootsweb.com/pub/census/il/perry/1850/

Wormer, Maxine E. *Perry County, Illinois 1850 Census*. Thomson, IL: Heritage House, 1973. 112p.

1860

Schick, Lee, Naomi Schick, and Ronald L. Schick. *Perry County, Illinois 1860 U.S. Census*. Hood River, OR: Authors, 1986. 218p.

USGenWeb Census Project. Illinois, 1860 Perry County.

ftp://ftp.rootsweb.com/pub/census/il/perry/1860/

Piatt County

1850

Federal Population Census and Mortality Schedule, 1850 Piatt County, Illinois. Monticello, IL: Piatt County Historical and Genealogical Society, 1984. 19p.

Hupp, Mildred Fisher. *1850 United States Census of Piatt County, Illinois*. Decatur, IL: Decatur Genealogical Society, 1978. 33p.

Piatt County 1855 and 1865 State Census and 1850, 1860, 1870, 1880 Federal Census Mortality Schedule. Monticello, IL: Piatt County Historical and Genealogical Society, 1985. 42p.

1860

Piatt County 1855 and 1865 State Census and 1850, 1860, 1870, 1880 Federal Census Mortality Schedule. Monticello, IL: Piatt County Historical and Genealogical Society, 1985. 42p.

Federal Population Census, 1860, Piatt County, Illinois. Monticello, IL: Piatt County Historical and Genealogical Society, 1981. 78p.

Winters, Lisa, Dorothy Dowdle, and Linda Redmond. *Piatt County, Illinois Agricultural Census*. Monticello, IL: Piatt County Historical & Genealogical Society, 1996. 90p.

1870

Federal Population Census, 1870, Piatt County, Illinois. Monticello, IL: Piatt County Historical and Genealogical Society, 1982. 118p.

Piatt County 1855 and 1865 State Census and 1850, 1860, 1870, 1880 Federal Census Mortality Schedule. Monticello, IL: Piatt County Historical and Genealogical Society, 1985. 42p.

1880

Federal Population Census, 1880, Piatt County, Illinois. Monticello, IL: Piatt County Historical and Genealogical Society, 1984. 262p.

Piatt County 1855 and 1865 State Census and 1850, 1860, 1870, 1880 Federal Census Mortality Schedule. Monticello, IL: Piatt County Historical and Genealogical Society, 1985. 42p.

1900

Federal Population Census, 1900, Piatt County, Illinois. Monticello, IL: Piatt County Historical and Genealogical Society, 1990. 248p.

1910

Federal Population Census, 1910, Piatt County, Illinois. Monticello, IL: Piatt County Historical and Genealogical Society, 1988. 226p.

1920

Federal Population Census 1920, Piatt County, Illinois. Monticello, IL: Piatt County Historical and Genealogical Society, 1997. 258p.

Pike County
1830

Gill, James V., and Maryan R. Gill. *Index to the 1830 Federal Census, Greene, Morgan, Sangamon, Calhoun, Pike, Fulton, Knox, Henry, Adams, Hancock, Warren, Mercer, Peoria, Putnam, and Jo Daviess Counties, Illinois*. Danville, IL: Heritage House, 1970. 66p.

1840

Hart, Virginia. *1840 Census Index for Pike County, Illinois*. 11p.

1850

Elgas, Barbara J. *1850 Federal Census, Pike County, Illinois, Persons Aged 50 and Over*. West Allis, WI: Janlen Enterprises, 1974. 12p.

Selby, Robert E., and Phyllis J. Selby. *1850 Census of Pike County, Illinois*. Kokomo, IN: Authors, 1979. 394p.

1860

Stead, George A. *Eighth Census of the United States, 1860, Illinois Pike County, Griggsville Township*. Oakland, CA: Author, 1972. 57p.

1880

Smith, Evelyn V. *1880 Federal Census of Pike County, Illinois, with Expanded Information*. 1985. 6 vols.

Pope County
1818-1850

Allen, Rickey. *Pope County, Illinois, Early Census Records, 1818-1850*. Golconda, IL: Author, 1995. 289p.

1830

Gill, James V. *Index to the 1830 Federal Census, Alexander, Pope, Union, Johnson, Jackson, Franklin, Perry, Randolph, Monroe, Washington, Marion, Jefferson, Hamilton and Gallatin Counties, Illinois*. Danville, IL: Heritage House, 1970. 57p.

1845

Lee, Judy Foreman, and Carolyn Cromeenes Foss. *Pope County, Illinois 1845, 1855, & 1865 State Census*. Newburgh, IN: Author, 1991. 105p.

1850
Allen, Rickey. *Pope County, Illinois, Early Census Records, 1818-1850*. Golconda, IL: Author, 1995. 289p.
Wormer, Maxine E. *Pope County, Illinois 1850 Census*. Thomson, IL: Heritage House, 1973. 50p.
1855
Lee, Judy Foreman, and Carolyn Cromeenes Foss. *Pope County, Illinois 1845, 1855, & 1865 State Census*. Newburgh, IN: Author, 1991. 105p.
1860
Allen, Ricky T. *1860 Federal Census & Mortality Schedule of Pope County, Illinois*. Decatur, IL: Bowers Press, 1983. 192p.
1865
Lee, Judy Foreman, and Carolyn Cromeenes Foss. *Pope County, Illinois 1845, 1855, & 1865 State Census*. Newburgh, IN: Author, 1991. 105p.
1870
Allen, Ricky T. *1870 Federal Census & Mortality Schedule of Pope County, Illinois*. Utica, KY: McDowell Publications, 1987. 191p.
1880
Allen, Ricky T. *1880 Federal Census & Mortality Schedule of Pope County, Illinois*. Utica, KY: McDowell Publications, 1990. 230p.

Pulaski County
1850
Wormer, Maxine E. *Pulaski County, Illinois 1850 Census*. Thomason, IL: Heritage House, 1972. 49p.
1860
Jenkins, Brenda Wetherington. *Pulaski County, Illinois, 1860 Federal Census*. Grand Chain, IL: Author, 1994. 68p.
1870
Illinois 1870 Census Index, Pulaski County. Palmer, IL: Genie-Logic Enterprises, 1997. Unpgd.
1880
Badgley, Glenna Conant, Wanda Atherton, and Martha W. McMunn. *Pulaski County Illinois, 1880 U.S. Census*. Utica, KY: McDowell Publications, 1986. 257p.
1910
Tellor, Floyd Junior. *Pulaski County, Illinois 1910 Head of Household Listing*. Buncombe, IL: From Generation to Generation, 1991. 24p.

Putnam County
1830
Gill, James V., and Maryan R. Gill. *Index to the 1830 Federal Census, Greene, Morgan, Sangamon, Calhoun, Pike, Fulton, Knox, Henry, Adams, Hancock, Warren, Mercer, Peoria, Putnam, and Jo Daviess Counties, Illinois*. Danville, IL: Heritage House, 1970. 66p.
1850
Wormer, Maxine E. *Putnam County, Illinois 1850 Census*. Thomson, IL: Heritage House, 1975. 47p.

Randolph County
1820
Jackson, Ronald Vern. *Illinois Census Index, Online Edition*. Orem, UT: Ancestry.com, Inc., 1999. http://www.ancestry.com
1825
Taylor, Mrs. Harlin B., and Mrs. Dorothy Dugan. *Census of Randolph County, Illinois, 1825*. Thomson, IL: Heritage House, 1972. 29p.
1830
Gill, James V. *Index to the 1830 Federal Census, Alexander, Pope, Union, Johnson, Jackson, Franklin, Perry, Randolph, Monroe, Washington, Marion, Jefferson, Hamilton and Gallatin Counties, Illinois*. Danville, IL: Heritage House, 1970. 57p.

1850

Crowder, Lola Frazer. *1850 Census of Randolph County, Illinois*. Author, 1998. 258p.

Index to the 1850 Randolph County, Illinois. Yakima, WA: Yakima Valley Genealogical Society, 1976. 215p.

1860

Schick, Lee, Naomi Schick, and Jack Milton Lines. *The 1860 Federal Census of Randolph County, Illinois*. Yakima, WA: Yakima Valley Genealogical Society, 1986. 313p.

Richland County

1850

Craddock, Dan A. *1850 Federal Census, County of Richland, State of Illinois*. Olney, IL: Craddock Title Service, 1968. 47p.

1860

1860 Census by the United States of America, of Richland County, Illinois. Olney, IL: Richland County Genealogical and Historical Society, 1980. 205p.

Mortality Schedules, 1860, 1870, 1880. Olney, IL: Richland County Genealogical Society, 1978. 139p.

1870

1870 Federal Census by the United States of America of Richland County, Illinois. Olney, IL: Richland County Genealogical & Historical Society, 1981. 270p.

Mortality Schedules, 1860, 1870, 1880. Olney, IL: Richland County Genealogical Society, 1978. 139p.

1880

1880 Census by the United States of America of Richland County, Illinois. Olney, IL: Richland County Genealogical Society, 1979. 331p.

Mortality Schedules, 1860, 1870, 1880. Olney, IL: Richland County Genealogical Society, 1978. 139p.

1900

1900 Census by the United States of America of Richland County, Illinois. Olney, IL: Richland County Genealogical and Historical Society, 1982. 431p.

1910

1910 Census by the United States of America of Richland County, Illinois. Olney, IL: Richland County Genealogical and Historical Society, 1986. 419p.

Rock Island County

1850

1850 Federal Population Census, Rock Island County, Illinois. Rock Island, IL: Blackhawk Genealogical Society, 1980. 205p.

1860

1860 Federal Population Census, Rock Island County, Illinois. Rock Island, IL: Blackhawk Genealogical Society, 1983. 72p.

1880

Pease, Janet Kathleen, and Virginia Heaton Horton. *Rock Island County, Illinois 1880 Census Index*. Rock Island, IL: Blackhawk Genealogical Society, 1995. 194p.

Saint Clair County

1830

Gill, James V. *An Index to the 1830 Federal Census, White, Edwards, Wabash, Wayne, Clay, Clinton, St. Clair, Madison, Bond, Fayette and Lawrence Counties, Illinois*. Danville, IL: Illiana Genealogical Pub. Co., 1968. 64p.

1840

Buecher, Robert. *St.Clair County, Illinois, 1840 Census*. Thomson, IL: Heritage House. 75p.

1860

Jetton, Kay F. *1860 Census St. Clair County, Illinois*. Decorah, IA: Anundsen, 1981. 2 vols.

1870

Buecher, Robert. *St.Clair County, Illinois, 1850 Census*. Thomson, IL: Heritage House, 1974. 2 vols.

Walsh, Diane Renner, and Allyson Monroe Tilton. *The 1870 Federal Census, St. Clair County, Illinois.* Belleville, IL: St. Clair County Genealogical Society, 1997. 449p.

Saline County
1850
The 1850 Federal Census of Saline County, Illinois. Richland, WA: Tri-City Genealogical Society, 1973. 111p.

USGenWeb Census Project. Illinois, 1850 Saline County.

ftp://ftp.rootsweb.com/pub/census/il/saline/1850/
1855
Murphy, John V. *Saline County 1855, Illinois State Census.* Carrier Mills, IL: Author, 1985. 28p.
1860
Anderson, Afton, and John V. Murphy. *Saline County, Illinois 1860, 8th United States Census.* Carrier Mills, IL: Authors, 1981. 139p.
1865
Murphy, John V. *Saline County 1865 Illinois State Census.* Carrier Mills, IL: Author, 1986. 46p.
1870
Moore, Bernard W. *1870 Federal Census, Saline County, Illinois.* Hartford, KY: McDowell Publications, 1978. 208p.
1880
Anderson, Afton, and John V. Murphy. *Saline County, Illinois 1880, 10th United States Census.* Carrier Mills, IL: Authors, 1983. 239p.
1900
Murphy, John V. *1900 U.S. Census, Brushy Township, Saline County, Illinois.* Carrier Mills, IL: Author, 1988. 43p.

Sangamon County
1830
Gill, James V., and Maryan R. Gill. *Index to the 1830 Federal Census, Greene, Morgan, Sangamon, Calhoun, Pike, Fulton, Knox, Henry, Adams, Hancock, Warren, Mercer, Peoria, Putnam, and Jo Daviess Counties, Illinois.* Danville, IL: Heritage House, 1970. 66p.

Marko, Ruth Zimmerli. *Federal Census 1830, Sangamon County, Illinois.* Springfield, IL: Sangamon County Genealogical Society of Illinois, 1979. 71p.
1840
Marko, Ruth Z. *Federal Census, 1840, Sangamon County, Illinois.* Springfield, IL: Sangamon County Genealogical Society of Illinois, 1980. 84p.
1850
1850 Population Census and 1850 Mortality Schedule, Sangamon County, Illinois. Springfield, IL: Sangamon County Genealogical Society, 1976. 232p.

USGenWeb Census Project. Illinois, 1850 Sangamon County.

ftp://ftp.rootsweb.com/pub/census/il/sangamon/1850/
1855
1855 State Census, Sangamon County, Illinois. Springfield, IL: Sangamon County Genealogical Society, 1990. 107p.
1860
Federal Census, 1860, of Sangamon County, Illinois. Springfield, IL: Sangamon County Genealogical Society, 1982. Unpgd.
1862, 1863
Military Census of Sangamon County, Illinois, in Pursuance of General Orders No. 99, of the War Department, and Instructions of the Adjutant General of the State of Illinois, 1862 and 1863. Springfield, IL: Sangamon County Genealogical Society, 1992. 196p.

1870

Gochanour, Eileen Lynch, and Wanda Warkins Allers. *1870 Sangamon County, Illinois Federal Census, Ninth Census of the United States, M593, Numbers 281 and 282.* Springfield, IL: Authors, 1985. 635p.

1880

1880 Federal Census, Sangamon County, Illinois. Springfield, IL: Sangamon County Genealogical Society, 1989. 4 vols.

Schuyler County

1830

Gill, James V. *Index to the 1830 Federal Census, Crawford, Edgar, Clark, Schuyler, McDonough, Vermillion, Macon, Shelby, Tazewell, Montgomery and Macoupin Counties.* Danville, IL: Heritage House, 1970. 50p.

1830 Census of McDonough County, Geographical Portion of Schuyler County, Illinois. Macomb, IL: McDonough County Genealogical Society, 1980. 7p.

1850

Chapman, Ruth L., and Lavina V. Walton. *Mortality Schedules of Schuyler County, Illinois, 1850, 1860, 1870, 1880.* Rushville, IL: Schuyler/Brown Historical and Genealogical Society, 1971. 19p.

Schunk, John Frederick. *1850 U.S. Census, Schuyler County, Illinois.* Wichita, KS: S-K Publications, 1990. Unpgd.

USGenWeb Census Project. Illinois, 1850 Schuyler County.
ftp://ftp.rootsweb.com/pub/census/il/schuyler/1850/

Walton, Lavina V. *1850 Census of Schuyler County, Illinois.* Rushville, IL: Schuyler/Brown Historical and Genealogical Society, 1971. 249p.

1860-1880

Chapman, Ruth L. and Lavina V. Walton. *Mortality Schedules of Schuyler County, Illinois, 1850, 1860, 1870, 1880.* Rushville, IL: Schuyler/Brown Historical and Genealogical Society, 1971. 19p.

Scott County

1830

1830 Census Records for Morgan County, Illinois, Includes Cass and Scott Counties. Jacksonville, IL: Jacksonville Area Genealogical and Historical Society, 1980. Unpgd.

1835

1835 Illinois State Census, Morgan County, in 1835 Cass & Scott Counties Were Part of Morgan County. Jacksonville, IL: Jacksonville Area Genealogical & Historical Society, 1998. 2 vols.

1850

Gochanour, Eileen Lynch, Margaret Hohimer, and Wanda Allers. *Illinois Census Scott County, 1850.* Springfield, IL: Wanda Allers, 1983. 100p.

Scott County, Iowa 1850 Federal Population Census, Early Marriages (1838-1851). Davenport, IA: Scott County, Iowa Genealogical Society. 208p.

1860

Gochanour, Eileen Lynch, Margaret Sager Hohimer, and Wanda Warkins Allers. *1860 Scott County, Illinois Federal Census.* Springfield, IL: Jacksonville Area Genealogical and Historical Society, 1983. 122p.

1870

Gochanour, Eileen Lynch, and Wanda Warkins Allers. *1870 Scott County, Illinois Census.* Springfield, IL: Authors, 1983. 2 vols.

1880

Gochanour, Eileen Lynch, Margaret Sager Hohimer, and Wanda Warkins Allers. *1880 Scott County, Illinois Federal Census, Tenth Census of the United States.* Springfield, IL: Authors, 1983. 2 vols.

Shelby County

1830

Gill, James V. *Index to the 1830 Federal Census, Crawford, Edgar, Clark, Schuyler, McDonough, Vermillion, Macon, Shelby, Tazewell, Montgomery and Macoupin Counties.* Danville, IL: Heritage House, 1970. 50p.

Hall, Trella. *United States Census, 1830, Shelby County, Illinois*. Decatur, IL: Decatur County Genealogical Society, 1969. 22p.

1840

Hall, Trella. *United States Census, 1840, Shelby County, Illinois*. Decatur, IL: Decatur County Genealogical Society, 1970. 36p.

1850

Daniels, Gene, and Darlene Daniels. *United States Census, 1850, Shelby County, Illinois*. Decatur, IL: Authors, 1970. 173p.

1850, 60, 70, 80 Mortality Schedule, Shelby County, Illinois. Shelbyville, IL: Shelby County Genealogical and Historical Society, 1982. 23p.

1855

Hapner, Phyllis, and Judy Graven. *1855 State Census, Shelby County, Illinois*. Shelbyville, IL: Authors, 1985. 38p.

1860

1850, 60, 70, 80 Mortality Schedule, Shelby County, Illinois. Shelbyville, IL: Shelby County Genealogical and Historical Society, 1982. 23p.

Graven, Judy, and Phyllis Hapner. *Shelby County, Illinois, 1860, Census Index*. Shelbyville, IL: Graven & Hapner, 1980. 376p.

USGenWeb Census Project. Illinois, 1860 Shelby County. (Partial).

ftp://ftp.rootsweb.com/pub/census/il/shelby/1860/

1870

1850, 60, 70, 80 Mortality Schedule, Shelby County, Illinois. Shelbyville, IL: Shelby County Genealogical and Historical Society, 1982. 23p.

United States Census, 1870, Shelby County, Illinois. Shelbyville, IL: Shelby County Historical and Genealogical Society, 1992. Unpgd.

1880

1850, 60, 70, 80 Mortality Schedule, Shelby County, Illinois. Shelbyville, IL: Shelby County Genealogical and Historical Society, 1982. 23p.

Hubbs, Mary. *1880 Census, Shelby County, Illinois*. Shelbyville, IL: Shelby County Historical and Genealogical Society, 1983, 1984. 2 vols.

USGenWeb Census Project. Illinois, 1880 Shelby County. (Partial).

ftp://ftp.rootsweb.com/pub/census/il/shelby/1880/

1910

1910 United States Census, Shelby County. Shelbyville, IL: Shelby County Historical and Genealogical Society. 3 vols.

Stark County

1850

Smith, Marjorie Corrine. *1850 Federal Census, Stark County, Illinois*. Chicago, IL: Chicago Genealogical Society, 1971. 81p.

1860

Berg, Irene Roberta Williams. *Population Schedules of the Eighth Census of the United States, 1860, Roll 229, Illinois, Volume 38 (767-993), Stark County*. Veradale, WA: Variable Business Services, 1982. 168p.

1870

Berg, Irene Roberta Williams. *Population Schedules of the Ninth Census of the United States, 1870, Roll 278, Illinois, Volume 51 (345-486), Stark County*. Veradale, WA: Variable Business Services, 1982. 212p.

1880

Berg, Irene Roberta Williams. *Population Schedules of the 10th Census of the United States, 1880, Roll 252, Illinois, Vol. 52, (345-447) Stark County*. Veradale, WA: Author, 1983. 218p.

1900

Berg, Irene Roberta Williams. *12th Census of Population 1900, Illinois, Vol. 148, Stark County, Ed's 129 to 137*. Veradale, WA: Variable Business Services. 135p.

Stephenson County
1850
Haver, Fern Rebecca, and George E. Morgan. *1850 Census of Stephenson County, Illinois*. West Covina, CA: Ewing Genealogical Services, 1973. 164p.

Tazewell County
1830
Gill, James V. *Index to the 1830 Federal Census, Crawford, Edgar, Clark, Schuyler, McDonough, Vermillion, Macon, Shelby, Tazewell, Montgomery and Macoupin Counties*. Danville, IL: Heritage House, 1970. 50p.
1850
Tazewell County, Illinois, 1850 Federal Census. Normal, IL: Bloomington Normal Genealogical Society, 1978. 2 vols.
1860
Tazewell County, Illinois, 1860 Census and Index, Eastern Half. Pekin, IL: Tazewell County Genealogical Society, 1984. 78p.
Western Half, Tazewell County, Illinois, 1860 Census and Index. Pekin, IL: Tazewell County Genealogical Society, 1986. 96p.

Union County
1820
Jackson, Ernest Harding. *Federal Census Index of Union County, Illinois, 1820-1880*. Rockford, IL: Author, 1978. 2 vols.
Pompey, Sherman Lee. *Index to the 1820 Census Records of Jefferson and Union Counties, Illinois*. Charleston, OR: Pacific Specialities, 1974.
1830
Gill, James V. *Index to the 1830 Federal Census, Alexander, Pope, Union, Johnson, Jackson, Franklin, Perry, Randolph, Monroe, Washington, Marion, Jefferson, Hamilton and Gallatin Counties, Illinois*. Danville, IL: Heritage House, 1970. 57p.
Jackson, Ernest Harding. *Federal Census Index of Union County, Illinois, 1820-1880*. Rockford, IL: Author, 1978. 2 vols.
1840
Jackson, Ernest Harding. *Federal Census Index of Union County, Illinois, 1820-1880*. Rockford, IL: Author, 1978. 2 vols.
1850
Jackson, Ernest Harding. *Federal Census Index of Union County, Illinois, 1820-1880*. Rockford, IL: Author, 1978. 2 vols.
Richard, Bernice C. *1850 Federal Census of Union County, Illinois*. Chicago, IL: Author, 1976. 195p.
1860-1880
Jackson, Ernest Harding. *Federal Census Index of Union County, Illinois, 1820-1880*. Rockford, IL: Author, 1978. 2 vols.

Vermillion County
Supplement to United States Census of Vermillion County, Illinois, Addenda and Errata. Danville, IL: Genealogical & Historical Society, 1979. 29p.
1830
Gill, James V. *Index to the 1830 Federal Census, Crawford, Edgar, Clark, Schuyler, McDonough, Vermillion, Macon, Shelby, Tazewell, Montgomery and Macoupin Counties*. Danville, IL: Heritage House, 1970. 50p.
Gocken, Cheryl. *1830 Vermillion County Census, 1840 Iroquois County Census with Index*. Watseka, IL: Iroquois County Genealogical Society, 1992. 55p.
1850
1850 United States Census of Vermillion County, Illinois. Danville, IL: Illiana Genealogical & Historical Society, 1973. 216p.

1850 Federal Population Census of Vermillion County, Illinois. Danville, IL: Illiana Genealogical & Historical Society, 1997. 327p.

1860

1860 Federal Population Census, Vermillion County, Illinois. Danville, IL: Illiana Genealogical & Historical Society, 1980. 387p.

USGenWeb Census Project. Illinois, 1860 Vermillion County.

ftp://ftp.rootsweb.com/pub/census/il/vermillion/1860/

1870

Gash, Donna. *1870 Federal Population Census Vermillion County, Illinois*. Danville, IL: Illiana Genealogical & Historical Society, 1997. 2 vols.

1880

1880 Federal Population Census, Vermillion County, Illinois. Danville, IL: Illiana Genealogical & Historical Society, 1995. 3 vols.

1920

Vermillion County, Illinois 1920 Census Index. Danville, IL: Illiana Genealogical & Historical Society, 1995. 267p.

Virden (Macoupin County)

1870, 1880

Bradley, Littleton P. *Virden, Illinois, 1870-1880 Federal Census*. St Louis, MO: Author, 1985. 114p.

1900

Bradley, Littleton P. *Virden, Illinois, 1900 Federal Census*. St Louis, MO: Author, 1985. 84p.

1910

Bradley, Littleton P. *Virden, Illinois, 1910 Federal Census*. St Louis, MO: Author, 1986. 143p.

1920

Bradley, Littleton P. *Virden, Illinois, 1920 Federal Census*. St Louis, MO: Author, 1995. 175p.

Wabash County

1830

Gill, James V. *An Index to the 1830 Federal Census, White, Edwards, Wabash, Wayne, Clay, Clinton, St. Clair, Madison, Bond, Fayette and Lawrence Counties, Illinois*. Danville, IL: Illiana Genealogical Pub. Co., 1968. 64p.

1850

Richard, Mrs. Bernice C. *1850 Federal Census of Wabash County, Illinois*. Chicago, IL: Chicago Genealogical Society, 1974. 120p.

1860

Jackson, Ronald Vern. *Illinois 1860 Federal Census Index Addendum, Dewitt, Franklin, Wabash and Warren Counties*. West Jordan, UT: Genealogical Services, 1986; 1997. Unpgd.

Mortality Schedules, 1860, 1870, 1880. Olney, IL: Richland County Genealogical Society, 1978. 139p.

Satterthwaite, Geraldine Keneipp. *1860 Federal Census of Wabash County, Illinois*. Author, 1981. 174p.

1870

Currie, William B., Dorothy Currie, and Carol Currie. *1870 Federal Census of Wabash County, Illinois, Microcopy M593, #286*. 167p.

Mortality Schedules, 1860, 1870, 1880. Olney, IL: Richland County Genealogical Society, 1978. 139p.

1880

Mortality Schedules, 1860, 1870, 1880. Olney, IL: Richland County Genealogical Society, 1978. 139p.

Warren County

1830

Gill, James V., and Maryan R. Gill. *Index to the 1830 Federal Census, Greene, Morgan, Sangamon, Calhoun, Pike, Fulton, Knox, Henry, Adams, Hancock, Warren, Mercer, Peoria, Putnam, and Jo Daviess Counties, Illinois*. Danville, IL: Heritage House, 1970. 66p.

1860

Jackson, Ronald Vern. *Illinois 1860 Federal Census Index Addendum, Dewitt, Franklin, Wabash and Warren Counties*. West Jordan, UT: Genealogical Services, 1986; 1997. Unpgd.

Warren County, Illinois, 1860 Federal Census. Monmouth, IL: Warren County Illinois Genealogical Society, 1984. 2 vols.

1870

Warren County, Illinois 1870 Federal Census. Monmouth, IL: Warren County Genealogical Society. 3 vols.

Washington County

1820

USGenWeb Census Project. Illinois, 1820 Washington County.

ftp://ftp.rootsweb.com/pub/census/il/washington/1820/

1830

Gill, James V. *Index to the 1830 Federal Census, Alexander, Pope, Union, Johnson, Jackson, Franklin, Perry, Randolph, Monroe, Washington, Marion, Jefferson, Hamilton and Gallatin Counties, Illinois*. Danville, IL: Heritage House, 1970. 57p.

1850

Wormer, Maxine E. *Washington County, Illinois, 1850 Census*. Thomson, IL: Heritage House, 1973. 81p.

USGenWeb Census Project. Illinois, 1850 Washington County.

ftp://ftp.rootsweb.com/pub/census/il/washington/1850/

1865

Bisenhauer, Inez Bost, and Donna Timpner Vuichard. *Washington County, Illinois 1865 State Census*. Carterville, IL: Genealogy Society of Southern Illinois, 1998. 160p.

Waukegan (Lake County)

1900

1900 Census Lake County, Illinois. Vol. 8, Waukegan Township. Mundelein, IL: Lake County Genealogical Society, 1995. 253p.

Wayne County

1830

Beeson, Betty Ann Butler. *1830 Federal Census of Wayne County, Illinois*. Fairfield, IL: Bland Books, 1982. 13p.

Gill, James V. *An Index to the 1830 Federal Census, White, Edwards, Wabash, Wayne, Clay, Clinton, St. Clair, Madison, Bond, Fayette and Lawrence Counties, Illinois*. Danville, IL: Illiana Genealogical Pub. Co., 1968. 64p.

1840

Beeson, Betty Ann Butler. *1840 Federal Census of Wayne County, Illinois*. Fairfield, IL: Bland Books, 1982. 27p.

1855

Beeson, Betty Ann Butler. *Wayne County, Illinois 1855 State Census*. Geff, IL: Beenson Enterprises, 1988. 61p.

1860

Beeson, Betty Ann Butler. *1860 Federal Census of Wayne County, Illinois*. Fairfield, IL: Bland Books, 1983. 2 vols.

Mortality Schedules, 1860, 1870, 1880. Olney, IL: Richland County Genealogical Society, 1978. 139p.

1865

Beeson, Betty Ann Butler. *Wayne County Illinois 1865 State Census*. Geff, IL: Beenson Enterprises, 1988. 88p.

1870

Beeson, Betty Ann Butler. *1870 Federal Census of Wayne County, Illinois*. Fairfield, IL: Bland Books, 1982. 2 vols.

Mortality Schedules, 1860, 1870, 1880. Olney, IL: Richland County Genealogical Society, 1978. 139p.

1880

Beeson, Betty Ann Butler. *1880 Federal Census of Wayne County, Illinois*. Geff, IL: Beenson Enterprises, 1985. 2 vols.

Mortality Schedules, 1860, 1870, 1880. Olney, IL: Richland County Genealogical Society, 1978. 139p.

White County
1830

Gill, James V. *An Index to the 1830 Federal Census, White, Edwards, Wabash, Wayne, Clay, Clinton, St. Clair, Madison, Bond, Fayette and Lawrence Counties, Illinois*. Danville, IL: Illiana Genealogical Pub. Co., 1968. 64p.

1850

Puckett, Martin. *1850 United States Census of White County, Illinois*. Decatur, IL: Decatur Genealogical Society, 1972. 203p.

1860

Shelton, Carl, and Elizabeth Myers. *1860 Federal Census of White County, Illinois*. Owensboro, KY: McDowell Pub., 1981. 142p.

1870

Myers, Elizabeth. *Population Schedules of the Ninth Census of the United States, 1870, Illinois, White County*. Utica, KY: McDowell Pub. 182p.

1880

Myers, Elizabeth. *1880 Tenth Census of the United States, White County, Illinois*. Utica, KY: McDowell, 1981. 513p.

1900

Myers, Elizabeth. *1900 12th Census of Population, White County, Illinois*. Carmi, IL: Shelton, 1981. 498p.

1910

Shelton, Carl, and Elizabeth Myers. *1910, 13th Census of Population, White County, Illinois*. Utica, KY: McDowell Publications, 1983. 491p.

Whiteside County
1850

Schunk, John Frederick. *1850 U.S. Census, Whiteside County, Illinois*. Wichita, KS: S-K Publications, 1989. Unpgd.

Smith, Dora Wilson. *Whiteside County, Illinois, 1850 Census*. Indianapolis, IN: Heritage House, 1977. 64p.

1860

1860 U.S. Federal Census and Mortality Schedule of Whiteside County, Illinois, Transcribed from 1860 Census Book from the Whiteside County Court House, Morrison, Illinois. 1984. 246p.

1865

Baar, Neva. *1865 State Census Whiteside County, Illinois*. Morrison, IL: Author, 1987. 123p.

1880

Baar, Neva. *1880 U.S. Federal Census of Whiteside County, Illinois, Transcribed from the Microfilm of the 1880 Census of Whiteside County, Illinois*. Morrison, IL: Author, 1986. 353p.

1900

1900 U.S. Federal Census of Whiteside County, Illinois, Transcribed from the Microfilm of the 1900 Census of Whiteside County, Illinois. 1988. 395p.

1910

Baar, Neva. *1910 U.S. Federal Census of Whiteside County, Illinois*. Morrison, IL: Author, 1991. 393p.

1920

1920 U.S. Federal Census of Whiteside County, Illinois. 1996. 441p.

Will County
1850

Lundberg, Gertrude. *Will County 1850 Census*. Homewood, IL: Root & Tree Pub., 1972. 18 vols.

_____. *Will County 1850 Census Mortality Schedules*. Homewood, IL: Root & Tree Pub., 1970. 13p.

1860

Allot, Millie Y. *1860 Federal Census, Will County, Illinois*. Wilmington, IL: Will/Grund Counties Genealogical Society, 1987. 2 vols.

Koukol, Winifred. *Surname Index to the Federal Census, 1860, Will County, Illinois*. Wilmington, IL: Will/Grundy Counties Genealogical Society, 1983. 43p.

Williamson County
1850

Hauffe, Jean Parks. *1850 United States Census of Williamson County, Illinois*. Decatur, IL: Decatur Genealogical Society, 1979. 149p.

1860

Hatfield, Jo Ann Ladd. *Williamson County, Illinois 1860 Federal Census*. Carterville, IL: Genealogical Society of Southern Illinois, 1987. 247p.

1870

Winget, Judith Walley. *Williamson County, Illinois, Census of 1870*. Owensboro, KY: Cook & McDowell Publications, 1980. 270p.

1880

Hoffard, Gay Roberson and Joyce Stephens Smith. *1880 (10th) Federal Census, Williamson County, Illinois, United States of America, Enumerated 1 June through 7 July*. Johnston City, IL: Author, 1991. 550p.

1900

Garr, F. Gene, and Margie Garr. *Williamson County, Illinois 1900 Federal Census Complete, Unabridged & Fully Indexed*. Mountain Home, AR: Author, 1996. 2 vols.

1910

Tellor, Floyd Junior. *The 1910 Census of Blairsville Township, Williamson County, Illinois*. Buncombe, IL: From Generation to Generation, 1991. 117p.

———. *Williamson County, Illinois 1910 Census Index*. Buncombe, IL: From Generation to Generation, 1990. 84p.

Winnebago County
1840

Jackson, Ernest Harding. *The 1840 Federal Census, Winnebago County, Illinois*. Rockford, IL: Author, 1983. 30p.

1850

Richard, Bernice C. *1850 Federal Census of Winnebago County, Illinois*. Chicago, IL: Chicago Genealogical Society, 1972. 300p.

1860

Jackson, Ernest Harding. *The 1860 Federal Census, Winnebago County, Illinois*. Rockford, IL: Author, 1983. 313p.

1870

Rowley, John D. *1870 Federal Census, Winnebago County, Illinois*. Mt. Vernon, IN: Windmill Pub., Inc., 1992. 2 vols.

1910

Rowley, John D. *1910 Federal Census, Winnebago County, Illinois*. Winnebago, IL: Author, 1996.

1920

Rowley, John D. *1920 Federal Census, Winnebago County*. Winnebago, IL: Author, 1996. Unpgd.

Woodford County
1850

Woodford County, Illinois, 1850 Federal Census. Normal, IL: Bloomington Normal Genealogical Society, 1979. 80p.

1860

Federal Census, Woodford County, Illinois. Normal, IL: McLean County Genealogical Society, 1994. 3 vols.

Indiana

1807

Census of Indiana Territory for 1807. Indianapolis, IN: Indiana Historical Society, 1980. 57p.

Fraustein, Rebah M. *Census of Indiana Territory for 1807.* Indianapolis, IN: Indiana Historical Society, 1989. 57p.

Jackson, Ronald Vern. *Indiana Census Index, Online Edition.* Orem, UT: Ancestry.com, Inc., 1999. **http://www.ancestry.com**

_____. *Indiana 1807 Census Index.* North Salt Lake City, UT: Accelerated Indexing Systems International, 1986. 44p.

1812

Jackson, Ronald Vern. *Indiana Census Index, Online Edition.* Orem, UT: Ancestry.com, Inc., 1999. **http://www.ancestry.com**

_____. *Indiana 1812 Census Index.* Salt Lake City, UT: AGES, 1988. 75p.

1820

Heiss, Willard C. *1820 Federal Census for Indiana.* Indianapolis, IN: Indiana Historical Society, 1966. 461p.

Jackson, Ronald Vern. *Indiana Census Index, Online Edition.* Orem, UT: Ancestry.com, Inc., 1999. **http://www.ancestry.com**

_____, Gary Ronald Teeples, and David Schaefermeyer. *Indiana 1820 Census Index.* Salt Lake City, UT: Accelerated Indexing Systems, 1976. 58p.

Morgan, Mary M. *The Indiana 1820 Enumeration of Males.* Indianapolis, IN: Family History Section, Indiana Historical Society, 1988. 173p.

U.S. Federal Population Census Schedules. 1820, M33, Microfilm Reel Nos. 13-15.

1830

Alig, Leona Tobey. *Index 1830 Federal Population Census for Indiana.* Indianapolis, IN: Indiana Historical Society, 1991. 245p.

Census Index: U.S. Selected States/Counties, 1830. Family Archive CD 315. Novato, CA: Broderbund Software. CD-ROM.

Jackson, Ronald Vern. *Indiana Census Index, Online Edition.* Orem, UT: Ancestry.com, Inc., 1999. **http://www.ancestry.com**

_____, and Gary Ronald Teeples. *Indiana 1830 Census Index.* Salt Lake City, UT: Accelerated Indexing Systems, 1976. 137p.

U.S. Federal Population Census Schedules. 1830, M19, Microfilm Reel Nos. 26-32.

1840

Census Index: U.S. Selected States/Counties, 1840. Family Archive CD 316. Novato, CA: Broderbund Software. CD-ROM.

1840 United States Census Index, Mid-West, Great Lakes. Orem, UT: Automated Archives, 1994. CD-ROM.

Indiana State Library. Genealogy Divsion. *Index, 1840 Federal Population Census, Indiana.* Indianapolis, IN: Author, 1975. 374p.

Jackson, Ronald Vern. *Indiana Census Index, Online Edition.* Orem, UT: Ancestry.com, Inc., 1999. **http://www.ancestry.com**

_____, and Gary Ronald Teeples. *Indiana 1840 Census Index.* Salt Lake City, UT: Accelerated Indexing Systems, 1976. 287p.

U.S. Federal Population Census Schedules. 1840, M704, Microfilm Reel Nos. 74-100.

1850

Census Index: U.S. Selected States/Counties, 1850. Family Archive CD 317. Novato, CA: Broderbund Software. CD-ROM.

Census Microfilm Records: Indiana, 1850. Family Archive CD 302. Novato, CA: Broderbund Software. CD-ROM.

Corley, Betty J. *Index, Yeoman(s), Yeaman(s), Youman(s), U.S. Census Index of Ohio and Indiana, 1850, 1860, 1880, 1900, 1910*. Hyrum, UT: Author, 1989. 15p.

Jackson, Ronald Vern. *Indiana Census Index, Online Edition*. Orem, UT: Ancestry.com, Inc., 1999. **http://www.ancestry.com**

_____. *Mortality Schedules Index, Online Edition*. Orem, UT: Ancestry.com, Inc., 1999. **http://www.ancestry.com**

_____, and Gary Ronald Teeples. *Indiana 1850 Census Index*. Salt Lake City, UT: Accelerated Indexing Systems, 1976. 628p.

_____. *Indiana 1850 Mortality Census Index*. Salt Lake City, UT: Accelerated Indexing Systems, 1979. 159p.

_____. *Mortality Schedule, Indiana 1850*. Bountiful, UT: Accelerated Indexing Systems, 1979. 159p.

U.S. Census Index Series, Indiana, Ohio, 1850. Orem, UT: Automated Archives, 1992. CD-ROM.

U.S. Federal Population Census Schedules. 1850, M432, Microfilm Reel Nos. 135-181.

Volkel, Lowell M. *1850 Indiana Mortality Schedule*. Danville, IL: Author, 1971. 118, 109, 106p.

1860

Census Index: Indiana, 1860. Family Archive CD 304. Novato, CA: Broderbund Software. CD-ROM.

Census Index: U.S. Selected States/Counties, 1860. Family Archive CD 318. Novato, CA: Broderbund Software. CD-ROM.

Corley, Betty J. *Index, Yeoman(s), Yeaman(s), Youman(s), U.S. Census Index of Ohio and Indiana, 1850, 1860, 1880, 1900, 1910*. Hyrum, UT: Author, 1989. 15p.

1860 Indiana Census Index. Indianapolis, IN: Indiana Historical Society, 1990. 60 microfiche.

Family Tree Maker. Census Records, Indiana. 1860 from the Indiana Historical Society. Family Archive CD 304. Novato, CA: Broderbund Software, 1997. CD-ROM.

Jackson, Ronald Vern. *Federal Census Index, 1860 Indiana, Marion County with Indianapolis*. West Jordan, UT: Genealogical Services, 1987; 1997. 499p.

_____. *Indiana Census Index, Online Edition*. Orem, UT: Ancestry.com, Inc., 1999. **http://www.ancestry.com**

_____. *Indiana 1860 North Federal Census Index Addendum, White and Whitley Counties*. West Jordan, UT: Genealogical Services, 1986; 1997.

_____. *Indiana, 1860 North Federal Census Index, Excluding Marion County*. Salt Lake City, UT: A.G.E.S., 1987. 739p.

_____. *Indiana 1860 South*. North Salt Lake City, UT: Accelerated Indexing Systems International, 1987. 991p.

_____. *Mortality Schedules Index, Online Edition*. Orem, UT: Ancestry.com, Inc., 1999. **http://www.ancestry.com**

_____. *U.S. Federal Census Index, Indiana 1860 South*. West Jordan, UT: Genealogical Services, 1987; 1998. 2 vols.

Kratz, Steven C. *Indiana 1860 Census Index, with Alternative Names, Ages and Birth Places*. Salt Lake City, UT: Kratz Indexing, 1986-1987. 2 vols.

U.S. Census Index Series, Illinois and Indiana, 1860. Orem, UT: Automated Archives, 1991. CD-ROM.

U.S. Federal Population Census Schedules. 1860, M653, Microfilm Reel Nos. 242-309.

1870

Census Index: U.S. Selected States/Counties, 1870. Family Archive CD 319. Novato, CA: Broderbund Software. CD-ROM.

Jackson, Ronald Vern. *Indiana Census Index, Online Edition*. Orem, UT: Ancestry.com, Inc., 1999. **http://www.ancestry.com**

Shook, Patricia M. Fox. *1870 Indiana Census Index*. Corona, CA: Author, 1986. 16 vols.

Steuart, Raeone Christensen. *Indiana 1870 Census Index*. Bountiful, UT: Heritage Quest, 1999. Vol. 5. CD-ROM.

U.S. Federal Population Census Schedules. 1870, M593, Microfilm Reel Nos. 296-373.

1880

Corley, Betty J. *Index, Yeoman(s), Yeaman(s), Youman(s), U.S. Census Index of Ohio and Indiana, 1850, 1860, 1880, 1900, 1910*. Hyrum, UT: Author, 1989. 15p.

Swierenga, Robert P. *Dutch in Indiana 1880 Federal Census, an Alphabetical Index*. Kent, OH: Author, 1994. 81p.

U.S. Federal Population Census Schedules. 1880, T9, Microfilm Reel Nos. 263-324.

U.S. Federal Population Census Schedules. 1880, Soundex. T747, 98 Microfilm Reels.

1890

Jackson, Ronald Vern. *Indiana Census Index, Online Edition (Veterans Schedules)*. Orem, UT: Ancestry.com, Inc., 1999.

http://www.ancestry.com

1900

Corley, Betty J. *Index, Yeoman(s), Yeaman(s), Youman(s), U.S. Census Index of Ohio and Indiana, 1850, 1860, 1880, 1900, 1910*. Hyrum, UT: Author, 1989. 15p.

Swierenga, Robert P. *Dutch in Indiana 1900 Federal Census, an Alphabetical Index*. Kent, OH: Author, 1994. 92p.

U.S. Federal Population Census Schedules. 1900, T623, Microfilm Reel Nos. 357-414.

U.S. Federal Population Census Schedules. 1900, Soundex. T1044, 252 Microfilm Reels.

U.S. Federal Population Census Schedules. 1900, Military & Naval Bases. T1081, Microfilm Reel Nos. 1838-1842.

U.S. Federal Population Census Schedules. 1900, Military & Naval Bases, Soundex. T1081, 32 Microfilm Reels.

1910

Corley, Betty J. *Index, Yeoman(s), Yeaman(s), Youman(s), U.S. Census Index of Ohio and Indiana, 1850, 1860, 1880, 1900, 1910*. Hyrum, UT: Author, 1989. 15p.

U.S. Federal Population Census Schedules. 1910, T624, Microfilm Reel Nos. 338-389. (No Soundex/Miracode Index was prepared by the Government for this State.)

1920

U.S. Federal Population Census Schedules. 1920, T625, Microfilm Reel Nos. 420-475.

U.S. Federal Population Census Schedules. 1920, Soundex, M1560, 230 Microfilm Reels.

Adams County
1850

Harter, Fayne Ellen. *1850 Federal Census of Adams County, Indiana*. Grabill, IN: Author, 1969. 224p.

USGenWeb Census Project. Indiana, 1850 Adams County.

ftp://ftp.rootsweb.com/pub/census/in/adams/1850/
1860

Kratz, Steven C. *Adams County, Indiana 1860 Census Index*. Salt Lake City, UT: Kratz Indexing, 1985. 29p.
1870, 1880

Werner, Betty Newland. *Index to Census of 1870 and 1880 Adams County, Indiana*. La Porte, IN: Author, 1990. 67p.

Allen County
1830

Rondot, Alfred Blase. *Allen County, Indiana 1830, 1840 Federal Census, with Resources*. Fort Wayne, IN: Allen County Genealogical Society, 1983. 582p.

1840

Rondot, Alfred Blase. *Allen County, Indiana 1830, 1840 Federal Census, with Resources*. Fort Wayne, IN: Allen County Genealogical Society, 1983. 582p.

Wilkens, Cleo Goff. *Index to the Sixth Census of the United States for Allen County, Indiana, 1840*. Fort Wayne, IN: Allen County-Fort Wayne Historical Society, 1958.

1850

Harter, Fayne Ellen. *1850 Federal Census of Allen County, Indiana, Indexed*. Grabill, IN: Author, 1968. 725p.

1860

Kratz, Steven C. *Allen County, Indiana 1860 Census Index*. Salt Lake City, UT: Kratz Indexing, 1995. 125p.

1910

Federal Census Index, Allen County, Indiana. Fort Wayne, IN: Allen County Genealogical Society of Indiana, 1999. 203p.

Bartholomew County
1860

Kratz, Steven C. *Bartholomew County, Indiana 1860 Census Index*. Salt Lake City, UT: Kratz Indexing, 1985. 56p.

1870

Shook, Patricia M. Fox. *1870 Bartholomew County, Indiana Census Index*. Anaheim, CA: Author, 1986. 48p.

Benton County
1850

USGenWeb Census Project. Indiana, 1850 Benton County. (Partial).
ftp://ftp.rootsweb.com/pub/census/in/benton/1850/

1860

Kratz, Steven C. *Benton County, Indiana 1860 Census Index*. Salt Lake City, UT: Kratz Indexing, 1985. 10p.

1870

Shook, Patricia M. Fox. *1870 Benton County, Indiana Census Index*. Anaheim, CA: Author, 1986. 14p.

Blackford County
1860

Kratz, Steven C. *Blackford County, Indiana 1860 Census Index*. Salt Lake City, UT: Kratz Indexing, 1985. 13p.

Boone County
1850

USGenWeb Census Project. Indiana, 1850 Boone County.
ftp://ftp.rootsweb.com/pub/census/in/boone/1850/

Walker, Marilyn S. *1850-1880 Mortality Boone County, Indiana*. Poland, IN: Author, 1991. 19p.

1860

Kratz, Steven C. *Boone County, Indiana 1860 Census Index*. Salt Lake City, UT: Kratz Indexing, 1986. 73p.

Walker, Marilyn S. *1850-1880 Mortality Boone County, Indiana*. Poland, IN: Author, 1991. 19p.

1870

Walker, Marilyn S. *1850-1880 Mortality Boone County, Indiana*. Poland, IN: Author, 1991. 19p.

_____. *1870 Census Boone County, Indiana*. Poland, IN: Author, 1991. 143p.

1880
Walker, Marilyn S. *1850-1880 Mortality Boone County, Indiana*. Poland, IN: Author, 1991. 19p.

Brown County
1840
Reeve, Helen H. *Brown County, Indiana Federal Census Index, 1840 through 1910*. Nashville, IN: Brown County Historical Society, 1988. 488p.
1850
Stultz, Carol Elkins. *1850 Brown County, Indiana Federal Census*. Danville, IN: Stultz Computer Services, 1987. Ungpd.
Reeve, Helen H. *Brown County, Indiana Federal Census Index, 1840 through 1910*. Nashville, IN: Brown County Historical Society, 1988. 488p.
1860
Kratz, Steven C. *Brown County, Indiana 1860 Census Index*. Salt Lake City, UT: Kratz Indexing, 1985. 14p.
Reeve, Helen H. *Brown County, Indiana Federal Census Index, 1840 through 1910*. Nashville, IN: Brown County Historical Society, 1988. 488p.
1870-1910
Reeve, Helen H. *Brown County, Indiana Federal Census Index, 1840 through 1910*. Nashville, IN: Brown County Historical Society, 1988. 488p.

Carroll County
1860
Kratz, Steven C. *Carroll County, Indiana 1860 Census Index*. Salt Lake City, UT: Kratz Indexing, 1985. 54p.
1880
Burton, Ann Mullin. *1880 Carroll County, Indiana, Federal Census Index*. Decatur, MI: Glyndwr Resources, 1997. 87p.

Cass County
1850
1850 Census, Cass County, Indiana. Mt. Vernon, IN: Windmill Publications, 1995. 195p.
1860
Kratz, Steven C. *Cass County, Indiana 1860 Census Index*. Salt Lake City, UT: Kratz Indexing, 1985. 57p.

Clark County
1820
Pompey, Sherman Lee. *Index to the 1820 Census Records of Silver Creek Township, Clark County; Columbia Township, DuBois County; Aurora, Laughey County; Decatur, Laughey County; Hartford Township, Randolph County; Warce Township, Randolph County; Wayne Township, Randolph County and Winchester, Randolph County, Indiana*. Charleston, OR: Pacific Specialties, 1974. 11p.
1860
Henley, Diane Eden. *Clark County, Indiana 1860 Census*. Jeffersonville, IN: Author, 1985. 132p.
Kratz, Steven C. *Clark County, Indiana 1860 Census Index*. Salt Lake City, UT: Kratz Indexing, 1985. 64p.

Clay County
1850
Selby, Robert E. *1850 Census of Clay County, Indiana*. Kokomo, IN: Author, 1976. 198p.
USGenWeb Census Project. Indiana, 1850 Clay County.
ftp://ftp.rootsweb.com/pub/census/in/clay/1850/
1860
Kratz, Steven C. *Clay County, Indiana 1860 Census Index*. Salt Lake City, UT: Kratz Indexing, 1986. 53p.

Clinton County
1850

Hammel, Ruth A., and Jane Rodenburger. *1850 Clinton County, Indiana Federal Census*. Lafayette, IN: Author, 1981. 245p.

1860

Kratz, Steven C. *Clinton County, Indiana 1860 Census Index*. Salt Lake City, UT: Kratz Indexing, 1985. 46p.

1866

Bohm, Joan Cox. *1866 Enumeration of White and Colored Males Age 21 and Over in Clinton County, Indiana*. Winter Garden, FL: Author. 61p.

1870

Bohm, Joan. *1870 Census of Clinton County, Indiana, for Michigan and Owen Townships*. Winter Garden, FL: Author.

_____. *1870 Census of Ross Township, Clinton County, Indiana, Index*. Frankfort, IN: Historic Pub. Co., 1991. 36p.

Grove, Helen E. *1870 Census of Clinton County, Indiana with Mortality Schedule*. Kokomo, IN: Author, 1994. 418p.

Crawford County
1850

Leistner, Doris. *Crawford County, Indiana 1850 Census*. Owensboro, KY: McDowell Publications, 1980. 168p.

1860

Kratz, Steven C. *Crawford County, Indiana 1860 Census Index*. Salt Lake City, UT: Kratz Indexing, 1985. 25p.

Leistner, Doris. *Crawford County, Indiana 1860 Census*. Utica, KY: McDowell Publications, 1987. 219p.

1900

Haycock, Hansel L. *1900 Census of Crawford County, Indiana*. Utica, KY: McDowell Pub., 1994. 308p.

Daviess County
1830

Hulen, Carol Johnson. *1830 Census for the Indiana Counties Daviess, Gibson, Greene, Knox, Martin, Pike and Sullivan*. Bicknell, IN: Author, 1985. 143p.

_____. *1830 Daviess County, Indiana Census*. Bicknell, IN: Author, 1986. 32p.

1850

Hulen, Carol Johnson. *Daviess County, Indiana 1850 Census and Marriages 1817-1849*. Bicknell, IN: Author, 1984. 292p.

1860

Kratz, Steven C. *Daviess County, Indiana 1860 Census Index*. Salt Lake City, UT: Kratz Indexing, 1986. 62p.

Decatur County
1820

Pompey, Sherman Lee. *Index to the 1820 Census Records of Silver Creek Township, Clark County; Columbia Township, DuBois County; Aurora, Laughey County; Decatur, Laughey County; Hartford Township, Randolph County; Warce Township, Randolph County; Wayne Township, Randolph County and Winchester, Randolph County, Indiana*. Charleston, OR: Pacific Specialties, 1974. 11p.

DeKalb County
1850

USGenWeb Census Project. Indiana, 1850 DeKalb County.
ftp://ftp.rootsweb.com/pub/census/in/dekalb/1850/

1860

Kratz, Steven C. *De Kalb County, Indiana 1860 Census Index*. Salt Lake City, UT: Kratz, 1985. Indexing, 1985. 33p.

Delaware County
1860

Kratz, Steven C. *Delaware County, Indiana 1860 Census Index*. Salt Lake City, UT: Kratz Indexing, 1985. 46p.

1870

Gray, Shawn. *1870 Delaware County, Indiana Census Book*. Muncie, IN: Author, 1996. 335p.

Shook, Patricia M. Fox. *1870 Delaware County, Indiana Census Index*. Anaheim, CA: Author, 1984. 55p.

DuBois County
1820

Pompey, Sherman Lee. *Index to the 1820 Census Records of Silver Creek Township, Clark County; Columbia Township, DuBois County; Aurora, Laughey County; Decatur, Laughey County; Hartford Township, Randolph County; Warce Township, Randolph County; Wayne Township, Randolph County and Winchester, Randolph County, Indiana*. Charleston, OR: Pacific Specialties, 1974. 11p.

1850

Manley, Kris, and Sharon Patmore. *1850 DuBois County, Indiana Federal Census*. Evansville, IN: Evansville Bindery, 1992. 154p.

1860

Kratz, Steven C. *DuBois County, Indiana 1860 Census Index*. Salt Lake City, UT: Kratz Indexing, 1986. 48p.

1870

Shook, Patricia M. Fox. *1870 Dubois County, Indiana Census Index*. Anaheim, CA: Author, 1986. 31p.

Elhart County
1850

Nunemaker, Ivan. *Elkhart County, Indiana 1850 Census with Index*. Wakarusa, IN: Author, 1983. 110p.

USGenWeb Census Project. Indiana, 1850 Elhart County.

ftp://ftp.rootsweb.com/pub/census/in/elkhart/1850/

1860

Kratz, Steven C. *Elkhart County, Indiana 1860 Census Index*. Salt Lake City, UT: Kratz Indexing, 1985. 65p.

Fayette County
1860

Kratz, Steven C. *Fayette County, Indiana 1860 Census Index*. Salt Lake City, UT: Kratz Indexing, 1985. 46p.

Floyd County
1870

Wolf, Shirley. *Index to the 1870 Census Floyd County, Indiana*. New Albany, IN: Southern Indiana Genealogical Society, 1989. 40p.

Fountain County
1860

Kratz, Steven C. *Fountain County, Indiana 1860 Census Index*. Salt Lake City, UT: Kratz Indexing, 1985. 60p.

Franklin County
1860

Kratz, Steven C. *Franklin County, Indiana 1860 Census Index*. Salt Lake City, UT: Kratz Indexing, 1986. 94p.

Fulton County
1850

Tombaugh, Jean C., and Wendell C. Tombaugh. *Fulton County, Indiana 1850 Census*. Rochester, IN: Tombaugh Pub. House, 1976. 229p.

USGenWeb Census Project. Indiana, 1850 Fulton County.

ftp://ftp.rootsweb.com/pub/census/in/fulton/1850/
1860

Kratz, Steven C. *Fulton County, Indiana 1860 Census Index*. Salt Lake City, UT: Kratz Indexing, 1985. 33p.

Tombaugh, Jean C., and Wendell C. Tombaugh. *Fulton County, Indiana 1860 Census*. Rochester, IN: Tombaugh Pub. House, 1977. 353p.

1870

Shook, Patricia M. Fox. *1870 Fulton County, Indiana Census Index*. Anaheim, CA: Author, 1984. 28p.

Tombaugh, Jean C., and Wendell C. Tombaugh. *Fulton County, Indiana 1870 Census*. Rochester, IN: Tombaugh Pub. House, 1977. 474p.

Gibson County
1830

Hulen, Carol Johnson. *1830 Census for the Indiana Counties Daviess, Gibson, Greene, Knox, Martin, Pike and Sullivan*. Bicknell, IN: Author, 1985. 143p.

Nolcox, Terry L. *1850 Federal Census Gibson County, Indiana*. Princeton, IN: Author, 1991. 253p.
1860

Barrett, Marilyn Mapes, and Charles Luther Barrett. *1860 Federal Census, Gibson County, Indiana*. Plainfield, IN: Barrett Research and Data Services, 1994. 340p.

Kratz, Steven C. *Gibson County, Indiana 1860 Census Index*. Salt Lake City, UT: Kratz Indexing, 1986. 67p.
1870

Barrett, Marilyn Mapes, and Charles Luther Barrett. *1870 Federal Census, Gibson County, Indiana*. Plainfield, IN: Barrett Research, 1996. 406p.

Shook, Patricia M. Fox. *1870 Gibson County, Indiana Census Index*. Anaheim, CA: Author, 1986. 35p.

Grant County
1860

Kratz, Steven C. *Grant County, Indiana 1860 Census Index*. Salt Lake City, UT: Kratz Indexing, 1986. 59p.

Greene County
1830

Hulen, Carol Johnson. *1830 Census for the Indiana Counties Daviess, Gibson, Greene, Knox, Martin, Pike and Sullivan*. Bicknell, IN: Author, 1985. 143p.
1850

Hunter, Albert Sinclair. *The 1850 Census of Greene County, Indiana*. Author, 1981. 2 vols.
1860

Wiles, Mary Lou, and Hubert Sims. *1860 Census, Greene County, Indiana*. Bloomington, IN: Author. 393p.

Hamilton County
1860

Kratz, Steven C. *Hamilton County, Indiana 1860 Census Index*. Salt Lake City, UT: Kratz Indexing, 1985. 62p.

Hancock County
1860
Kratz, Steven C. *Hancock County, Indiana 1860 Census Index*. Salt Lake City, UT: Kratz Indexing, 1985. 41p.

Harrison County
1810
Jackson, Ronald Vern. *Early Indiana Harrison County, 1810*. Bountiful, UT: Accelerated Indexing Systems, 1981. 6p.
1860
Kratz, Steven C. *Harrison County, Indiana 1860 Census Index*. Salt Lake City, UT: Kratz Indexing, 1985. 54p.

Hendricks County
1830
Kocher, Florence, Ruth Mitchell Pritchard, and Grace Cox. *Hendricks County, Indiana 1830 Census*. Stilesville, IN: Authors, 1977. 20p.

USGenWeb Census Project. Indiana, 1830 Hendricks County.
ftp://ftp.rootsweb.com/pub/census/in/hendricks/1830/
1840
USGenWeb Census Project. Indiana, 1840 Hendricks County.
ftp://ftp.rootsweb.com/pub/census/in/hendricks/1840/
1860
Kratz, Steven C. *Hendricks County, Indiana 1860 Census Index*. Salt Lake City, UT: Kratz Indexing, 1985. 46p.
1870
Hughes, Libbe, and Betty Bartley. *Index to the 1870 Census of Hendricks County, Indiana*. Kokomo, IN: Selby Pub. & Printing, 1984. 50p.

Henry County
1830
USGenWeb Census Project. Indiana, 1830 Henry County.
ftp://ftp.rootsweb.com/pub/census/in/henry/1830/

Howard County
1850
Schunk, John Frederick. *1850 U.S. Census Howard County, Indiana*. Wichita, KS: S-K Publications, 1986. Unpgd.

USGenWeb Census Project. Indiana, 1850 Howard County.
ftp://ftp.rootsweb.com/pub/census/in/howard/1850/
1860
Kratz, Steven C. *Howard County, Indiana 1860 Census Index*. Salt Lake City, UT: Kratz Indexing, 1985. 42p.
1870
Sheagley, Patricia Sue Bingaman. *1870 Census Index for Howard County, Indiana*. Kokomo, IN: Selby Pub. & Printing, 1993. 147p.
1880
Sheagley, Patricia Sue Bingaman. *1880 Census Index for Howard County, Indiana*. Kokomo, IN: Kokomo Howard County Public Library, Genealogy Department, 1995. 197p.

Huntington County
1860
Kratz, Steven C. *Huntington County, Indiana 1860 Census Index*. Salt Lake City, UT: Kratz Indexing, 1985. 53p.

Indianapolis (Marion County)
1830
Hecker, Edward J. *Names of Persons Enumerated in Marion County, Indiana at the Fifth Census, 1830*. Indianapolis, IN: Author, 1909. pp. 342-371.
1860
Jackson, Ronald Vern. *U.S. Federal Census Index, Indiana 1860, Marion County, with Indianapolis*. Salt Lake City, UT: Accelerated Indexing Systems International, 1987, 1997. 499p.
1870
Jackson, Ronald Vern. *Indianapolis, Indiana 1870 Federal Census Index*. Salt Lake City, UT: Accelerated Indexing Systems International, 1989. 559p.

Jackson County
1850
1850 Jackson County, Indiana U.S. Federal Census. Danville, IN: Stultz Computer Services, 1995. 213p.
1860
Stultz, Carol Elkins. *1860 Jackson County, Indiana Census*. Danville, IN: Stultz Computer Services, 1988. 2 vols.
1870
Stultz, Carol Elkins. *1870 United States Federal Census, Jackson County, Indiana with Index*. Brownstone, IN: Jackson County Genealogical Society, 1997. 455p.

Jasper County
1850
USGenWeb Census Project. Indiana, 1850 Jasper County.
ftp://ftp.rootsweb.com/pub/census/in/jasper/1850/
1860
Kratz, Steven C. *Jasper County, Indiana 1860 Census Index*. Salt Lake City, UT: Kratz Indexing, 1985. 17p.
1880
Indiana Works Progress Administration. *Index to Supplemental Record, Federal Census, 1880, Jasper County, Indiana, Taken June 1880, Letters A-Z*. Kokomo, IN: Shelby Pub., 1994. 118p.

Jay County
1860
Kratz, Steven C. *Jay County, Indiana 1860 Census Index*. Salt Lake City, UT: Kratz Indexing, 1985. 32p.

Jefferson County
1820
Ritchie, Betty M. *Jefferson County, Indiana Marriage Records, 1811-1831, 1820 Heads of Households Listed*. Madison, IN: Author. 56p.
1860
Kratz, Steven C. *Jefferson County, Indiana 1860 Census Index*. Salt Lake City, UT: Kratz Indexing, 1986. 110p.

Johnson County
1850
Allen, Lois. *Johnson County, Indiana 1850 Census*. Franklin, IN: Johnson County Historical Society, 1995. 405p.

1860

Kratz, Steven C. *Johnson County, Indiana 1860 Census Index*. Salt Lake City, UT: Kratz Indexing, 1986. 69p.

1880

Johnson County, Indiana 1880 Census as Filed with the County Auditor. Ft. Wayne, IN: Allen County Public Library, 1986. 321p.

Knox County

1830

Hulen, Carol Johnson. *1830 Census for the Indiana Counties Daviess, Gibson, Greene, Knox, Martin, Pike and Sullivan*. Bicknell, IN: Author, 1985. 143p.

1850

1850 Census, Knox County, Indiana. Vincennes, IN: Northwest Territory Genealogical Society, 1984. 224p.

1860

1860 Census Knox County, Indiana. Vincennes, IN: Northwest Territoy Genealogical Society, 1982. 333p.

1870

Hulen, Carol Johnson. *1870 Census, Knox County, Indiana*. Bicknell, IN: Author, 1985. 447p.

1880

Caballero, Conrad A. *1880 Census, Knox County, Indiana*. Vincennes, IN: Northwest Territory Genealogical Society, 1995. 516p.

1850 Census, Knox County, Indiana. Vincennes, IN: Lewis Historical Library, Vincennes University, 1984. 224p.

Kosciusko County

1840

Fawley, Caroline Conrad. *1840 Census Index of Kosciusko County, Indiana*. Pierceton, IN: Author, 1986. 10p.

USGenWeb Census Project. Indiana, 1840 Kosciusko County.

ftp://ftp.rootsweb.com/pub/census/in/kosciusko/1840/

1850

Fawley, Caroline Conrad. *1850 Census Index of Kosciusko County, Indiana*. Pierceton, IN: Author, 1986. 15p.

Moon, George. *Copy of Original 1850 Census, Kosciusko County, Indiana, Schedule I, Free Inhabitants*. Warsaw, IN: Kosciusko County Historical Society, 1991. 2 vols.

Priser, Marjorie. *1850 Census, Kosciusko County, Indiana*. Leesburg, IN: Pioneer Pub., 1987. 240p.

USGenWeb Census Project. Indiana, 1850 Kosciusko County.

ftp://ftp.rootsweb.com/pub/census/in/kosciusko/1850/

1860

Scheuer, Larry, and Cynthia Cochran Scheuer. *The Complete 1860 Federal Census of Kosciusko County, Indiana*. Warsaw, IN: Kosciusko County Historical Society, 1988. 325p.

1870

Scheuer, Larry, and Cynthia Cochran Scheuer. *Index to 1870 Federal Census of Kosciusko County, Indiana*. Warsaw, IN: Kosciusko County Historical Society, 1988. 402p.

Shook, Patricia M. Fox. *1870 Kosciusko County, Indiana Census Index*. Anaheim, CA: Author, 1986. 50p.

1880

Scheuer, Larry, and Cynthia Cochran Scheuer. *Index to 1880 Federal Census of Kosciusko County, Indiana*. Warsaw, IN: Kosciusko County Historical Society, 1988. 69p.

1900

Scheuer, Larry, and Cynthia Cochran Scheuer. *Index to 1900 Census of Kosciusko County, Indiana*. Warsaw, IN: Authors, 1988. 83p.

1910

Scheuer, Larry, and Cynthia Cochran Scheuer. *Index to 1910 Census of Kosciusko County, Indiana*. Warsaw, IN: Authors, 1988. 83p.

1920

Scheuer, Larry, and Cynthia Cochran Scheuer. *Index to the 1920 Federal Census of Kosciusko County, Indiana*. Warsaw, IN: Authors, 1993. 159p.

La Grange County
1860

Kratz, Steven C. *La Grange County, Indiana 1860 Census Index*. Salt Lake City, UT: Kratz Indexing, 1986. 50p.

Lake County
1860

Kratz, Steven C. *Lake County, Indiana 1860 Census Index*. Salt Lake City, UT: Kratz Indexing, 1985. 34p.
1870

Weaver, Betty Newland. *Index to 1870 United States Census Lake County, Indiana*. La Porte, IN: Author, 1990. 34p.

LaPorte County
1860

Kratz, Steven C. *La Porte County, Indiana 1860 Census Index*. Salt Lake City, UT: Kratz Indexing, 1985. 102p.
1870

Werner, Betty Newland. *Index to 1870 U.S. Census, La Porte County, Indiana*. LaPorte, IN: Author, 1987. 83p.
1880

Werner, Betty Newland. *Index to 1880 United States Census, La Porte County, Indiana*. La Porte, IN: Author, 1988. 98p.

Laughey County
1820

Pompey, Sherman Lee. *Index to the 1820 Census Records of Silver Creek Township, Clark County; Columbia Township, DuBois County; Aurora, Laughey County; Decatur, Laughey County; Hartford Township, Randolph County; Warce Township, Randolph County; Wayne Township, Randolph County and Winchester, Randolph County, Indiana*. Charleston, OR: Pacific Specialties, 1974. 11p.

Lawrence County
1820

USGenWeb Census Project. Indiana, 1820 Lawrence County.
ftp://ftp.rootsweb.com/pub/census/in/lawrence/1820/
1850

Stultz, Carol Elkins. *1850 Lawrence County, Indiana, United States Federal Census*. Danville, IN: Stultz Computer Services, 1988. 2 vols.
1860

Baker, Nancy. *1860 Lawrence County, Indiana Census*. Shoals, IN: Author, 1990. 2 vols.

Madison County
1830

1830-1840 U.S. Census, Madison County, Indiana. Wichita, KS: S.K. Publications, 1995. Unpgd.
Madison County, Indiana, 1830 Census. Savannah, MO: Andrew County Historical Society, 1980. 11p.
1840

1830-1840 U.S. Census, Madison County, Indiana. Wichita, KS: S.K. Publications, 1995. Unpgd.
1850

Madison County, Indiana 1850 Census Index. Anderson, IN: Anderson Public Library, 1986. 117p.

Schunk, John Frederick. *1850 U.S. Census Madison County, Indiana.* Wichita, KS: S-K Publications, 1986. Unpgd.

1860

Indiana Historical Society 1860 Indiana Census, County Madison. Indianapolis, IN: Indiana Historical Society, 1988. 150p.

Kratz, Steven C. *Madison County, Indiana 1860 Census Index.* Salt Lake City, UT: Kratz Indexing, 1985. 62p.

1870

Williamson, Jennifer. *1870 Census Madison County, Indiana.* Valparaiso, IN: Author, 1999. 152p.

1880

Williamson, Jennifer. *1880 Census Madison County, Indiana.* Valparaiso, IN: Author, 1998. 141p.

1900

Hunter, Darlene. *1900 Census of Park Place, Madison County, Indiana.* Anderson, IN: Anderson Public Library, 1986. 45p.

Marion County

1830

Hecker, Edward J. *Names of Persons Enumerated in Marion County, Indiana at the Fifth Census, 1830.* Indianapolis, IN: Author, 1909. pp. 342-371.

1860

Jackson, Ronald Vern. *U.S. Federal Census Index, Indiana 1860, Marion County, with Indianapolis.* Salt Lake City, UT: Accelerated Indexing Systems International, 1987, 1997. 499p.

Kratz, Steven C. *Marion County, Indiana 1860 Census Index.* Salt Lake City, UT: Kratz Indexing, 1986. 102p.

1870

Jackson, Ronald Vern. *Indianapolis, Indiana 1870 Federal Census Index.* Salt Lake City, UT: Accelerated Indexing Systems International, 1989. 559p.

Marshall County

1850

USGenWeb Census Project. Indiana, 1850 Marshall County.
ftp://ftp.rootsweb.com/pub/census/in/marshall/1850/

1860

Kratz, Steven C. *Marshall County, Indiana 1860 Census Index.* Salt Lake City, UT: Kratz Indexing, 1985. 45p.

Martin County

1830

Hulen, Carol Johnson. *1830 Census for the Indiana Counties Daviess, Gibson, Greene, Knox, Martin, Pike and Sullivan.* Bicknell, IN: Author, 1985. 143p.

Stiles, Mrs.Ruby H., Mrs. Dale Baker, Mrs. Russell S. Baker. *Martin County Indiana Handbook.* Authors, 1965. 100p.

1870

Martin County, Indiana 1870 Census. St. Louis, MO: St. Louis Genealogical Society, 1990. 240p.

1880

1880 Martin County, Indiana, Census. St. Louis, MO: St. Louis Genealogical Society, 1992, 2 vols.

Miami County

1840

Bakehorn, Ray. *1840-1850 Federal Population Census for Miami County, Indiana.* Peru, IN: American Pub., 1980. 249p.

1850

Bakehorn, Ray. *1840-1850 Federal Population Census for Miami County, Indiana*. Peru, IN: American Pub., 1980. 249p.

Wiles, Mary Lou. *1850 Census, Martin County, Indiana*. Bloomington, IN: Author. 152p.

1860

1860 Census of Martin County, Indiana, June 11, 1860 to September 11, 1860. St. Louis, MO: St. Louis Genealogical Society, 1990. 186p.

Kratz, Steven C. *Miami County, Indiana 1860 Census Index*. Salt Lake City, UT: Kratz Indexing, 1985. 60p.

Smith, Robert D. *1860 Federal Population Census for Miami County, Indiana*. Peru, IN: American Publishers, 1980. 374p.

1870

Smith, Robert D. *1870 Federal Population Census for Miami County, Indiana*. Peru, IN: American Publishers, 1978. 486p.

1880

1880 Martin County, Indiana Census. Shoals, IN: Martin County Genealogical Society. 2 vols.

1900

Pridemore, Jewel Marie, and Kay Hedrick. *Martin County 1900 Census*. Shoals, IN: Martin County Genealogical Society, 1995.

1910

Pridemore, Jewel Marie, and Deloris L. Sherfick. *Martin County, Indiana 1910 Census*. Shoals, IN: Martin County Genealogical Society, 1995. 2 vols.

Monroe County

1820-1840

Matson, Donald. *1820, 1830, 1840, & 1850 Census of Monroe County, Indiana*. Ellettsville, IN: Author, 1979. 330p.

1850

Kratz, Steven C. *Monroe County, Indiana 1850 Census Index*. Salt Lake City, UT: Kratz Indexing, 1985. 58p.

Matson, Donald. *1820, 1830, 1840, & 1850 Census of Monroe County, Indiana*. Ellettsville, IN: Author, 1979. 330p.

1860

Kratz, Steven C. *Monroe County, Indiana 1860 Census Index*. Salt Lake City, UT: Kratz Indexing, 1985. 38p.

Montgomery County

1850

Kratz, Steven C. *Montgomery County, Indiana 1850 Census Index*. Salt Lake City, UT: Kratz Indexing, 1986. 64p.

1860

Kratz, Steven C. *Montgomery County, Indiana 1860 Census Index*. Salt Lake City, UT: Kratz Indexing, 1986. 86p.

Morgan County

1830

USGenWeb Census Project. Indiana, 1830 Morgan County.
ftp://ftp.rootsweb.com/pub/census/in/morgan/1830

1840

USGenWeb Census Project. Indiana, 1840 Morgan County.
ftp://ftp.rootsweb.com/pub/census/in/morgan/1840/

1860

Kratz, Steven C. *Morgan County, Indiana 1860 Census Index*. Salt Lake City, UT: Kratz Indexing, 1985. 49p.

Newton County
1860

Kratz, Steven C. *Newton County, Indiana 1860 Census Index*. Salt Lake City, UT: Kratz Indexing, 1985. 13p.

USGenWeb Census Project. Indiana, 1860 Newton County.
ftp://ftp.rootsweb.com/pub/census/in/newton/1860/
1870

Shook, Patricia M. Fox. *1870 Newton County, Indiana Census Index*. Anaheim, CA: Author, 1986. 18p.

USGenWeb Census Project. Indiana, 1870 Newton County.
ftp://ftp.rootsweb.com/pub/census/in/newton/1870/

Noble County
1860

Kratz, Steven C. *Noble County, Indiana 1860 Census Index*. Salt Lake City, UT: Kratz Indexing, 1985. 51p.
1870

Shook, Patricia M. Fox. *1870 Noble County, Indiana Census Index*. Anaheim, CA: Author, 1986. 49p.

Treesh, Helen Lightfoot. *1870 Census Index, Noble County, Indiana*. Albion, IN: Noble County Genealogical Society. 54p.

Ohio County
1850

Selby, Robert E., and Phyllis J. Selby. *1850 Census of Ohio County, Indiana*. Kokomo, IN: Selby Pub. & Printing, 1981. 132p.
1860

Kratz, Steven C. *Ohio County, Indiana 1860 Census Index*. Salt Lake City, UT: Kratz Indexing, 1985. 19p.
1870

Shook, Patricia M. Fox. *1870 Ohio County, Indiana Census Index*. Anaheim, CA: Author, 1986. 19p.

Orange County
1850

1850 Orange County, Indiana Census, with Additions. Paoli, IN: Orange County Genealogical Society, 1996. 297p.
1860

Kratz, Steven C. *Orange County, Indiana 1860 Census Index*. Salt Lake City, UT: Kratz Indexing, 1986. 47p.
1870

Davis, Wilma, and Everett S. Davis. *1870 Federal Census Orange County, Indiana*. Paoli, IN: Orange County Genealogical Society. 327p.
1880

Davis, Wilma, and Everett S. Davis. *1880 Federal Census Orange County, Indiana*. Paoli, IN: Orange County Genealogical Society, 1996. 390p.
1910

Davis, Wilma, and Everett S. Davis. *1910 Federal Census Orange County, Indiana*. Paoli, IN: Orange County Genealogical Society, 1997. 472p.

Owen County
1820

Drescher, Deborah Lynn. *Owen County, Indiana, 1820 Census*. Spencer, IN: Author, 1993. 66p.

_____. *Owen County, Indiana 1820, 1830, 1840 Census*. Spencer, IN: Author, 1993. Unpgd.
1830, 1840

Drescher, Deborah Lynn. *Owen County, Indiana 1820, 1830, 1840 Census*. Spencer, IN: Author, 1993. Unpgd.

1850

Drescher, Deborah Lynn. *Owen County, Indiana, 1850 Census*. Spencer, IN: Author, 1992. 316p.

1860

Drescher, Deborah Lynn. *Owen County, Indiana, 1860 Census*. Spencer, IN: Author, 1999. 271p.

Kratz, Steven C. *Owen County, Indiana 1860 Census Index*. Salt Lake City, UT: Kratz Indexing, 1986. 59p.

1870

Fahs, Glorianne E. *Owen County, Indiana 1870 Federal Census Index*. Spencer, IN: Owen County Historical and Genealogical Society, 1994. 42p.

Palmer County

1860

Manley, Kristine, and Sharon Patmore. *1860 Perry County, Indiana Federal Census*. Evansville, IN: Evansville Bindery, 1997. 310p.

1870

Manley, Kristine, and Sharon Patmore. *1870 Perry County, Indiana Federal Census*. Evansville, IN: Evansville Bindery, 1998. 374p.

Parke County

1850

USGenWeb Census Project. Indiana, 1850 Parke County.

ftp://ftp.rootsweb.com/pub/census/in/parke/1850/

1860

Kratz, Steven C. *Parke County, Indiana 1860 Census Index*. Salt Lake City, UT: Kratz Indexing, 1986. 64p.

Perry County

1820-1840

Patmore, Sharon, and Kristine Manley. *1820, 1830, 1840 Spencer, Warrick, Perry Counties, Indiana Census Returns*. Chrisney, IN: Newspaper Abstracts, 1995. 171p.

1850

Wanhainen, Jeanne. *Perry County, Indiana, 1850 Census*. Utica, KY: McDowell Publications, 1982. 177p.

1900

Blue, Jean. *Perry County, Indiana, 1900 Federal Census Index*. Tell City, IN: Tell City Historical Society, 1985. 68p.

Zoll, Yvonne D. *Perry County, Indiana 1900 Census Index*. Clarksville, IN: Author, 1982. 17p.

_____. *Perry County, Indiana 1900 Federal Census*. Clarksville, IN: Author, 1982. 687p.

Pike County

1820

Cox, Eunice Evelyn Miner. *1820 Indiana Census, Pike County*. 10p.

1830

Hulen, Carol Johnson. *1830 Census for the Indiana Counties Daviess, Gibson, Greene, Knox, Martin, Pike and Sullivan*. Bicknell, IN: Author, 1985. 143p.

1850

Eldridge, Verl. *1850 Federal Census of Pike County, Indiana*. Booneville, IN: Halel, 1986. 164p.

1860

Hale, Clarice June. *1860 Federal Census of Pike County, Indiana*. Evansville, IN: Evansville Bindery, 1984. 268p.

Kratz, Steven C. *Pike County, Indiana 1860 Census Index*. Salt Lake City, UT: Kratz Indexing, 1985. 31p.

1870

Hale, Clarice June. *Pike County, Indiana, 1870 Federal Census, with 1870 Mortality Table*. Evansville, IN: Evansville Bindery, 1987. 265p.

1880

Hale, Clarice June. *1880 Federal Census of Pike County, Indiana, with 1880 Mortality Schedule*. Evansville, IN: Evansville Bindery, 1985. 387p.

1900

Hale, Clarice June. *Pike County, Indiana, 1900 Federal Census*. Evansville, IN: Evansville Bindery, 1990. 344p.

1910

Hale, Clarice June. *Pike County, Indiana, 1910 Federal Census*. Evansville, IN: Evansville Bindery, 1991. 316p.

Porter County
1850

Hiday, Nellie C. *1850 Federal Census, Porter County, Indiana*. Danville, IL: Heritage House, 1970. 107p.

USGenWeb Census Project. Indiana, 1850 Porter County.

ftp://ftp.rootsweb.com/pub/census/in/porter/1850/

1860

Kratz, Steven C. *Porter County, Indiana 1860 Census Index*. Salt Lake City, UT: Kratz Indexing, 1985. 40p.

Posey County
1820

Cox, Carroll O. *Posey County, Indiana 1820 Census*. Poseyville, IN: Author, 1996. 195p.

Weking, F. Woody. *Index of Names of Family Heads in 1820 Indiana Federal Census of Posey and Vanderburgh Counties, Indiana*. Evansville, IN: Author, 1951. 7p.

1850

Smith, Barbara Ramsey. *Posey County, Indiana 1850 Federal Census*. Jonesboro, IN: Author, 1982. 284p.

USGenWeb Census Project. Indiana, 1850 Posey County. (Partial).

ftp://ftp.rootsweb.com/pub/census/in/posey/1850/

1870

McConnell, Darlene. *Posey County, Indiana 1870 Federal Census*. Mt. Vernon, IN: Windmill Publications, 1994. 421p.

1880

Horager, Ilse Dorsch. *Tenth Census of the United States, State of Indiana, Posey County, 1880*. Evansville, IN: Evansville Bindery, 1992. 593p.

1910

Barrett, Lela M. *Thirteenth Census of the United States, State of Indiana, Posey County, 1910*. Author. 496p.

1920

McConnell, Darlene. *Posey County, Indiana 1920 U.S. Census Index*. Mt. Vernon, IN: Windmill Publications, 1996. 116p.

Pulaski County
1850

Burgess, Betty, and Julia Ann Binkley. *1850 Census of Pulaski County, Indiana, Added Genealogical Gleanings*. Winamac, IN: Author, 1972. 112p.

USGenWeb Census Project. Indiana, 1850 Pulaski County.

ftp://ftp.rootsweb.com/pub/census/in/pulaski/1850/

1860

Binkley, Julia Ann. *1860 Census of Pulaski County, Indiana*. Star City, IN: Author, 1980. 154p.

Kratz, Steven C. *Pulaski County, Indiana 1860 Census Index*. Salt Lake City, UT: Kratz Indexing, 1985. 17p.

Putnam County
1830

USGenWeb Census Project. Indiana, 1830 Putnam County.
ftp://ftp.rootsweb.com/pub/census/in/putnam/1830/
1860

Kratz, Steven C. *Putnam County, Indiana 1860 Census Index*. Salt Lake City, UT: Kratz Indexing, 1986. 78p.
1870

Shook, Patricia M. Fox. *1870 Putnam County, Indiana Census Index*. Anaheim, CA: Author, 1986. 50p.

Randolph County
1820

Pompey, Sherman Lee. *Index to the 1820 Census Records of Silver Creek Township, Clark County; Columbia Township, DuBois County; Aurora, Laughey County; Decatur, Laughey County; Hartford Township, Randolph County; Warce Township, Randolph County; Wayne Township, Randolph County and Winchester, Randolph County, Indiana*. Charleston, OR: Pacific Specialties, 1974. 11p.
1860

Kratz, Steven C. *Randolph County, Indiana 1860 Census Index*. Salt Lake City, UT: Kratz Indexing, 1985. 65p.

Ripley County
1860

Kratz, Steven C. *Ripley County, Indiana 1860 Census Index*. Salt Lake City, UT: Kratz Indexing, 1986. 81p.
Shook, Patricia M. Fox. *1860 Ripley County, Indiana Census Index*. Anaheim, CA: Author, 1983. 37p.
1870

Shook, Patricia M. Fox. *1870 Ripley County, Indiana Census Index*. Anaheim, CA: Author, 1984. 45p.

Rush County
1860

Kratz, Steven C. *Rush County, Indiana 1860 Census Index*. Salt Lake City, UT: Kratz Indexing, 1985. 63p.

St. Joseph County
1850

USGenWeb Census Project. Indiana, 1850 St. Joseph County.
ftp://ftp.rootsweb.com/pub/census/in/stjoseph/1850/
1860

Kratz, Steven C. *St. Joseph County, Indiana 1860 Census Index*. Salt Lake City, UT: Kratz Indexing, 1985. 68p.
1910

An Everyname Index to the 1910 Census of St. Joseph County, Indiana. South Bend, IN: South Bend Area Genealogical Society, 1992. Unpgd.

Scott County
1850

USGenWeb Census Project. Indiana, 1850 Scott County.
ftp://ftp.rootsweb.com/pub/census/in/scott/1850/
1860

Alguire, Joan L. *Scott County, Indiana 1860 Federal Census*. South Holland, IN: Alguire Abstracts, 1982. 155p.
Kratz, Steven C. *Scott County, Indiana 1860 Census Index*. Salt Lake City, UT: Kratz Indexing, 1985. 23p.
1870

Shook, Patricia M. Fox. *1870 Scott County, Indiana Census Index*. Anaheim, CA: Author, 1986. 21p.

Shelby County
1860
Kratz, Steven C. *Shelby County, Indiana 1860 Census Index*. Salt Lake City, UT: Kratz Indexing, 1986. 80p.

Spencer County
1820-1840
Patmore, Sharon and Kristine Manley. *1820, 1830, 1840 Spencer, Warrick, Perry Counties, Indiana Census Returns*. Chrisney, IN: Newspaper Abstracts, 1995. 171p.
1850
Manley, Kristine. *1850 Spencer County, Indiana Federal Census*. Evansville, IN: Evansville Bindery, 1988. 196p.
1860
Kratz, Steven C. *Spencer County, Indiana 1860 Census Index*. Salt Lake City, UT: Kratz Indexing, 1986. 70p.
Patmore, Sharon, and Kristine Manley. *1860 Spencer County, Indiana Federal Census*. Chrisney, IN: Newspaper Abstracts, 1992. 314p.
1870
Manley, Kristine, and Sharon Patmore. *1870 Spencer County, Indiana Federal Census*. Chrisney, IN: Newspaper Abstracts, 1994. 427p.
1880
Manley, Kristine, and Sharon Patmore. *1880 Spencer County, Indiana Federal Census*. Chrisney, IN: Authors, 1990. 504p.
1900
Manley, Kristine, and Sharon Patmore. *1900 Spencer County, Indiana Census Index*. Chrisney, IN: Author, 1995. 95p.

Stark County
1860
Kratz, Steven C. *Stark County, Indiana 1860 Census Index*. Salt Lake City, UT: Kratz Indexing, 1985. 8p.
1870
Kratz, Steven C. *Stark County, Indiana 1870 Census Index*. Salt Lake City, UT: Kratz Indexing, 1986. 15p.

Steuben County
1860
Kratz, Steven C. *Steuben County, Indiana 1860 Census Index*. Salt Lake City, UT: Kratz Indexing, 1985. 37p.

Sullivan County
1830
Hulen, Carol Johnson. *1830 Census for the Indiana Counties Daviess, Gibson, Greene, Knox, Martin, Pike and Sullivan*. Bicknell, IN: Author, 1985. 143p.
1850
Davis, Kathryn Hooper. *1850 Census, Sullivan County, Indiana*. Nacogdoches, TX: Ericson Books, 1993. 223p.
Sullivan County, Indiana, 1850 Census. Evansville, IN: Whipporwill Publications, 1987. 177p.
1860
Kratz, Steven C. *Sullivan County, Indiana 1860 Census Index*. Salt Lake City, UT: Kratz Indexing, 1986. 62p.
Miller, Ann. *1860 Federal Census, Sullivan County, Indiana*. Sandpoint, ID: Author, 1986. 223p.
1870
Miller, Ann. *1870 Federal Census, Sullivan County, Indiana*. Sandpoint, ID: Author, 1987. 241p.
1880
Roseberry, Janice. *1880 Census, Sullivan County, Indiana*. Sullivan, IN: Author, 1988. 400p.

Switzerland County
1820
Edgerton, Mildred Hester. *Switzerland County, Indiana Census for 1820*. Washington, DC: Author, 1963. 21p.
1860
Kratz, Steven C. *Switzerland County, Indiana 1860 Census Index*. Salt Lake City, UT: Kratz Indexing, 1986. 53p.

Tippecanoe County
1850
Hammel, Ruth Amanda, and Jean Rodenberger. *Tippecanoe County, Indiana Federal Census with 1850 Mortality Schedule and Notes of Early Marriages and Lives of Early Tippecanoe Families*. Lafayette, IN: Author. 468p.
1860
Kratz, Steven C. *Tippecanoe County, Indiana 1860 Census Index*. Salt Lake City, UT: Kratz Indexing, 1985. 119p.

Tipton County
1850
Freeman, Ruth. *Tipton County, Indiana Picture of a Pioneer People, Census 1850, Marriages 1844-1850, Wills 1844-1850*. Author, 1976. 99p.
1860
Henry, Marietta F. *Tipton County, Indiana, Census Index, 1860-1880*. Kokomo, IN: Selby Publishing & Printing, 1985. 45p.
_____. *Tipton County, Indiana, Census Index, 1860*. Kokomo, IN: Selby Publishing & Printing, 1984. 20p.
Kratz, Steven C. *Tipton County, Indiana 1860 Census Index*. Salt Lake City, UT: Kratz Indexing, 1985. 22p.
1870
Henry, Marietta F. *Tipton County, Indiana, Census Index, 1860-1880*. Kokomo, IN: Selby Publishing & Printing, 1985. 45p.
_____. *Tipton County, Indiana, Census Index, 1870*. Kokomo, IN: Selby Publishing & Printing, 1984. 33p.
Shook, Patricia M. Fox. *1870 Tipton County, Indiana Census Index*. Anaheim, CA: Author, 1986. 31p.
1880
Henry, Marietta F. *Tipton County, Indiana, Census Index, 1860-1880*. Kokomo, IN: Selby Publishing & Printing, 1985. 45p.
_____. *Tipton County, Indiana, Census Index, 1880*. Kokomo, IN: Selby Publishing & Printing, 1984. 45p.
1900
Henry, Marietta F. *1900 Tipton County, Indiana, Census Index*. Kokomo, IN: Selby Publishing & Printing, 1985. 488p.
_____. *Tipton County, Indiana, Census Index Combined, 1900-1910*. Kokomo, IN: Selby Publishing & Printing, 1988. 306p.
1910
Henry, Marietta F. *Tipton County, Indiana, Census Index Combined, 1900-1910*. Kokomo, IN: Selby Publishing & Printing, 1988. 306p.
1920
Henry, Marietta F. *Tipton County, Indiana, Census Index, 1920, Genealogical Data*. Kokomo, IN: Selby Publishing & Printing, 1993. 204p.

Union County
1860
Kratz, Steven C. *Union County, Indiana 1860 Census Index*. Salt Lake City, UT: Kratz Indexing, 1985. 27p.
Stevens, Mary Edith. *The 1860 Census of Union County, Indiana, Cross Referenced with the Marriage Records of the County and Other Genealogical Sources*. 3rd. ed. Flowery Branch, GA: Author, 1987. 208p.

1870

Shook, Patricia M. Fox. *1870 Union County, Indiana Census Index*. Anaheim, CA: Author, 1986. 16p.

Vanderburgh County
1820

Weking, F. Woody. *Index of Names of Family Heads in 1820 Indiana Federal Census of Posey and Vanderburgh Counties, Indiana*. Evansville, IN: Author, 1951. 7p.

1840

Dismore, Evelyn Pfingston. *Vanderburgh County, Indiana 1840 Census Heads of Households Only, Free White & Colored*. Gilbertsville, KY: E&T Publications, 1996. 40p.

1880

Tenbarge, Eleanor Glenn. *1880 Census of Vanderburgh County, Indiana*. Evansville, IN: Tri-State Genealogical Society, 1982. 1,037p.

Vermillion County
1860

Hammond, Barbara L. *1860 U.S. Census of Vermillion County, Indiana*. Paris, IL: Tresearch, 1994. 178p.

Kratz, Steven C. *Vermillion County, Indiana 1860 Census Index*. Salt Lake City, UT: Kratz Indexing, 1985. 32p.

Vigo County
1820

Brown, Immogene B. Hannan. *United States Census 1820 Vigo County, Indiana*. Terre Haute, IN: Wabash Valley Genealogical Society, 1977. 16p.

1830

Brown, Immogene B. Hannan. *United States Census 1830 Vigo County, Indiana*. Terre Haute, IN: Wabash Valley Genealogical Society, 1977. 39p.

1860

Kratz, Steven C. *Vigo County, Indiana 1860 Census Index*. Salt Lake City, UT: Kratz Indexing, 1986. 106p.

1870

Index to the 1870 Census of Vigo County, Indiana. Terre Haute, IN: Vigo County Public Library, 1985. Unpgd.

Wabash County
1840

Woodward, Ronald L. *1840 Census of Wabash County, Indiana*. Warsaw, IN: Scheuer, 1989. 27p.

1850

Woodward, Ronald L. *1850 Census of Wabash County, Indiana*. Warsaw, IN: Scheuer, 1990. 305p.

1860

Kratz, Steven C. *Wabash County, Indiana 1860 Census Index*. Salt Lake City, UT: Kratz Indexing, 1985. 62p.

1870

Woodward, Ronald L. *The Complete 1870 Federal Census of Wabash County, Indiana*. Rev. ed. Warsaw, IN: Scheuer, 1990. 2 vols.

Warren County
1850

USGenWeb Census Project. Indiana, 1850 Warren County.
ftp://ftp.rootsweb.com/pub/census/in/warren/1850/

1860

Kratz, Steven C. *Warren County, Indiana 1860 Census Index*. Salt Lake City, UT: Kratz Indexing, 1985. 46p.

Warrick County
1820-1840
Patmore, Sharon, and Kristine Manley. *1820, 1830, 1840 Spencer, Warrick, Perry Counties, Indiana Census Returns*. Chrisney, IN: Newspaper Abstracts, 1995. 171p.

1850
Smith, Barbara. *Warrick County, Indiana 1850 Census*. Jonesboro, IN: Author, 1980. 191p.

1860
Kratz, Steven C. *Warrick County, Indiana 1860 Census Index*. Salt Lake City, UT: Kratz Indexing, 1986. 55p.

Warrick County, Indiana 1860 Federal Census. Boonville, IN: Captain Jacob Warrick Chapter, DAR, 1981. 254p.

1880
Davidson, Zella. *Warrick County, Indiana 1880 Federal Census*. Boonville, IN: Captain Jacob Warrick Chapter, DAR, 1981. 2 vols.

1900
Patmore, Sharon, and Kristine Manley. *1900 Warrick County, Indiana Federal Census Index*. Chrisney, IN: Newspaper Abstracts, 1998. 134p.

Washington County
1850
Short, Helen Barret. *Federal Census 1850 Washington County, Indiana*. Salem, IN: Author, 1971. Unpgd.

1860
Bolding, James E., and Violet Cook. *1860 Census, Washington County, Indiana*. Salem, IN: Washington County Historical Society, 1994. 585p.

1870
McCoskey, Jim, and Sydne McCoskey. *Indiana 1870 Washington County Census*. Salem, IN: Washington County Historical Society, 1993. Unpgd.

1880
McCoskey, Jim, and Sydne McCoskey. *Indiana 1880 Washington County Census*. Salem, IN: Washington County Historical Society, 1993. 399p.

1900
Bolding, James E., Virginia Miller, and Eva Robertson. *1900 Census, Washington County, Indiana*. Salem, IN: Washington County Historical Society, 1996. 577p.

1910
1910 Census, Washington County, Indiana. Salem, IN: Washington County Historical Society, 1993. 625p.

Wayne County
1810
Jackson, Ronald Vern. *Indiana Census Index, Online Edition*. Orem, UT: Ancestry.com, Inc., 1999. **http://www.ancestry.com**

_____. *Indiana, Wayne County, 1810 Federal Census Index*. North Salt Lake City, UT: Accelerated Indexing Systems International, 1988. 55p.

1860
Indiana Historical Society 1860 Indiana Census, County Wayne. Indianapolis, IN: Indiana Historical Society, 1988. 268p.

Kratz, Steven C. *Wayne County, Indiana 1860 Census Index*. Salt Lake City, UT: Kratz Indexing, 1985. 118p.

1910
Dean, Arnold L. *1910 Wayne County, Indiana Census Index*. Richmond, IN: Author, 1994. 436p.

Wells County
1860
Kratz, Steven C. *Wells County, Indiana 1860 Census Index*. Salt Lake City, UT: Kratz Indexing, 1985. 30p.

1870

Manning, K. R. *1870 Wells County Census Index*. Bluffton, IN: Author, 1999. 271p.

White County
1850

Brewer, Pequetti Hunt. *White County, Indiana Index to 1850 White County Census*. Monticello, IN: Author, 1969. 28p.

USGenWeb Census Project. Indiana, 1850 White County.

ftp://ftp.rootsweb.com/pub/census/in/white/1850/

1860

Jackson, Ronald Vern. *Indiana 1860 North Federal Census Index Addendum, White and Whitley Counties*. West Jordan, UT: Genealogical Services, 1986; 1997.

Kratz, Steven C. *White County, Indiana 1860 Census Index*. Salt Lake City, UT: Kratz Indexing, 1985. 32p.

Whitley County
1850

Harter, Stuart. *1850 Federal Population Census of Whitley County, Indiana*. Churubusco, IN: Author, 1982. 149p.

1860

Harter, Stuart. *1860 Federal Population Census of Whitley County, Indiana*. Churubusco, IN: Author, 1982. 303p.

Jackson, Ronald Vern. *Indiana 1860 North Federal Census Index Addendum, White and Whitley Counties*. West Jordan, UT: Genealogical Services, 1986; 1997.

Kratz, Steven C. *Whitley County, Indiana 1860 Census Index*. Salt Lake City, UT: Kratz Indexing, 1985. 31p.

Iowa

1830

Census Index: U.S. Selected States/Counties, 1830. Family Archive CD 315. Novato, CA: Broderbund Software. CD-ROM.

Jackson, Ronald Vern. *Iowa Census Index, Online Edition*. Orem, UT: Ancestry.com, Inc., 1999.

http://www.ancestry.com

1836

Jackson, Ronald Vern, Gary Ronald Teeples, and David Schaefermeyer. *Iowa 1836 Territorial Census Index*. Salt Lake City, UT: Accelerated Indexing Systems, 1976. 35p.

1838

Jackson, Ronald Vern. *Iowa 1838 Territorial Census Index*. Bountiful, UT: Accelerated Indexing Systems, 1981, 1984. 2 vols.

1840

Census Index: U.S. Selected States/Counties, 1840. Family Archive CD 316. Novato, CA: Broderbund Software. CD-ROM.

1840 United States Census Index, Mid-West, Great Lakes. Orem, UT: Automated Archives, 1994. CD-ROM.

Jackson, Ronald Vern. *Iowa Census Index, Online Edition*. Orem, UT: Ancestry.com, Inc., 1999.

http://www.ancestry.com

————. *Iowa 1840 Territorial Census Index*. Salt Lake City, UT: Accelerated Indexing Systems, 1979. 116p.

Obert, Rowene T. *The 1840 Iowa Census*. Salt Lake City, UT: Author, 1968. 342p.
U.S. Federal Population Census Schedules. 1840, M704, Microfilm Reel Nos. 101-102.

1841-1849

Jackson, Ronald Vern. *Iowa Census Records, 1841-1849*. Salt Lake City, UT: Accelerated Indexing Systems, 1979. 2 vols.

1850

Census Index: U.S. Selected States/Counties, 1850. Family Archive CD 317. Novato, CA: Broderbund Software. CD-ROM.

Jackson, Ronald Vern. *Iowa Census Index, Online Edition*. Orem, UT: Ancestry.com, Inc., 1999.
http://www.ancestry.com

_____. *Mortality Schedules Index, Online Edition*. Orem, UT: Ancestry.com, Inc., 1999.
http://www.ancestry.com

_____, and Gary Ronald Teeples. *Iowa 1850 Census Index*. Salt Lake City, UT: Accelerated Indexing Systems, 1976. 115p.

Ross, Shirley Brodersen. *Iowa 1850 Census Mortality Schedule*. Jefferson, IA: Author, 1982. 62p.

U.S. Census Index Series, Iowa, Illinois, Michigan, Missouri, Minnesota, Wisconsin, 1850. Orem, UT: Automated Archives, 1992. CD-ROM.

U.S. Federal Population Census Schedules. 1850, M432, Microfilm Reel Nos. 182-189.

1851

Jackson, Ronald Vern. *Iowa Census Index, Online Edition*. Orem, UT: Ancestry.com, Inc., 1999.
http://www.ancestry.com

_____. *Iowa 1851 Census Index*. Salt Lake City, UT: Accelerated Indexing Systems, 1981. 167p.

1851-1859

Jackson, Ronald Vern. *Iowa 1851-1859*. North Salt Lake City, UT: Accelerated Indexing Systems, 1981. Unpgd.

1852

Jackson, Ronald Vern. *Iowa Census Index, Online Edition*. Orem, UT: Ancestry.com, Inc., 1999.
http://www.ancestry.com

_____. *Iowa 1852*. North Salt Lake City, UT: Accelerated Indexing Systems, 1988. 610p.

1860

Census Index: U.S. Selected States/Counties, 1860. Family Archive CD 318. Novato, CA: Broderbund Software. CD-ROM.

Jackson, Ronald Vern. *Federal Census Index, Iowa, 1860*. West Jordan, UT: Genealogical Services, 1987; 1997. 741p.

_____. *Iowa Census Index, Online Edition*. Orem, UT: Ancestry.com, Inc., 1999.
http://www.ancestry.com

_____. *Iowa 1860*. Salt Lake City, UT: Accelerated Indexing Systems International, 1987. 741p.

U.S. Federal Population Census Schedules. 1860, M653, Microfilm Reel Nos. 310-345.

1870

Census Index: U.S. Selected States/Counties, 1870. Family Archive CD 319. Novato, CA: Broderbund Software. CD-ROM.

Jackson, Ronald Vern. *Iowa Census Index, Online Edition*. Orem, UT: Ancestry.com, Inc., 1999.
http://www.ancestry.com

_____. *Iowa 1870*. Salt Lake City, UT: Accelerated Indexing Systems International, 1990. 2 vols.
U.S. Federal Population Census Schedules. 1870, M593, Microfilm Reel Nos. 374-427.

1880

U.S. Federal Population Census Schedules. 1880, T9, Microfilm Reel Nos. 325-371.
U.S. Federal Population Census Schedules. 1880, Soundex. T748, 78 Microfilm Reels.

1900

Ledoux, Albert H. *The French Canadian Families of the Plains and Upper Mountain States, Abstracts from the Federal Census of 1900*. Altoona, PA: Author, 1991. 2 vols.
U.S. Federal Population Census Schedules. 1900, T623, Microfilm Reel Nos. 415-468.
U.S. Federal Population Census Schedules. 1900, Soundex. T1045, 198 Microfilm Reels.
U.S. Federal Population Census Schedules. 1900, Military & Naval Bases. T1081, Microfilm Reel Nos. 1838-1842.
U.S. Federal Population Census Schedules. 1900, Military & Naval Bases, Soundex. T1081, 32 Microfilm Reels.

1910

U.S. Federal Population Census Schedules. 1910, T624, Microfilm Reel Nos. 390-430. (No Soundex/Miracode Index was prepared by the Government for this State.)

1920

U.S. Federal Population Census Schedules. 1920, T625, Microfilm Reel Nos. 476-521.
U.S. Federal Population Census Schedules. 1920, Soundex, M1561, 181 Microfilm Reels.

Adair County
1856
Mayes, Dorothy. *Adair County, 1856 Census Index*. Author. 8p.
1860
Adair County Census Index 1860-1900. Greenfield, IA: Greenfield Public Library. Card Index.
USGenWeb Census Project. Iowa, 1860 Adair County.
ftp://ftp.rootsweb.com/pub/census/ia/adair/1860/
1885
Mayes, Dorothy. *State Census Index, 1885*. Author. 30p.

Allamakee County
1850
1850 Federal Census Allamakee County, Iowa. Des Moines, IA: Iowa Genealogical Society, 1988. 17p.
USGenWeb Census Project. Iowa, 1850 Allamakee County.
ftp://ftp.rootsweb.com/pub/census/ia/allamakee/1850/
1860
USGenWeb Census Project. Iowa, 1860 Allamakee County.
ftp://ftp.rootsweb.com/pub/census/ia/allamakee/1860/

Appanoose County
1850
1850 Federal Census Appanoose County, Iowa. Des Moines, IA: Iowa Genealogical Society, 1975. 75p.
Index of Heads of Family 1850 Appanoose County Census. St. Louis, MO: Ingamire Pub. 11p.
Parker, Jimmy B. *1850 Mortality Schedules of Appanoose, Lucas and Pottawattamie Counties, Iowa*. Salt Lake City, UT: Genealogical Society of Utah, 1969. 7p.

USGenWeb Census Project. Iowa, 1850 Appanoose County.
ftp://ftp.rootsweb.com/pub/census/ia/appanoose/1850/
1860
1860 Federal Census Appanoose County, Iowa. Des Moines, IA: Iowa Genealogical Society, 1989. 3 vols.
1870
1870 Federal Census Appanoose County, Iowa. Des Moines, IA: Iowa Genealogical Society, 1990. 325p.
1880
1880 Federal Census Appanoose County, Iowa. Des Moines, IA: Iowa Genealogical Society, 1990. 245p.
1885
1885 State Census Appanoose County, Iowa. Des Moines, IA: Iowa Genealogical Society, 1991. 222p.
1895
1895 State Census Appanoose County, Iowa. Des Moines, IA: Iowa Genealogical Society, 1990. 483p.

Benton County
1850
1850 Federal Census Benton County, Iowa. Des Moines, IA: Iowa Genealogical Society, 1975. 16p.
1856
Benton County, Iowa Census, 1856 Iowa Index. Des Moines, IA: Iowa Genealogical Society, 2000. 139p.
1860
USGenWeb Census Project. Iowa, 1860 Benton County. (Partial).
ftp://ftp.rootsweb.com/pub/census/ia/benton/1860/

Black Hawk County
1850
Federal Census for Iowa, 1850 Black Hawk County. Des Moines, IA: Iowa Genealogical Society, 1975. 4p.
USGenWeb Census Project. Iowa, 1850 Black Hawk County.
ftp://ftp.rootsweb.com/pub/census/ia/blackhawk/1850/
1860
1860 Mortality Schedule for Black Hawk County, Iowa. Des Moines, IA: Iowa Genealogical Society, 1988.
    10p.

Boone County
1850
1850 Federal Census Boone County, Iowa. Webster City, IA: Hamilton Heritage Hunters. 22p.
1850 Federal Census for Iowa, Boone County. Des Moines, IA: Iowa Genealogical Society, 1975. 16p.
1895
1895 Federal Census Boone County, Iowa. Boone, IA: Boone County Genealogical Society. 2 vols.

Buchanan County
1850
Switzer, Harry M. *1850 Federal Census for Buchanan County, Iowa.* Des Moines, IA: Iowa Genealogical
    Society. 10p.
USGenWeb Census Project. Iowa, 1850 Buchanan County.
ftp://ftp.rootsweb.com/pub/census/ia/buchanan/1850/
1925
Wilken, Dale Wayne. *1925 Iowa Census, Buchanan.* Marion, IA: Author, 1995. 309p.

Calhoun County
1860
USGenWeb Census Project. Iowa, 1860 Calhoun County.
ftp://ftp.rootsweb.com/pub/census/ia/calhoun/1860/

Cedar County
1850

USGenWeb Census Project. Iowa, 1850 Cedar County.
ftp://ftp.rootsweb.com/pub/census/ia/cedar/1850/
1860
Kent, David L. *Index to the United States Census of 1860 Cedar County, Iowa.* Author, 1974. Unpgd.

Cerro Gordo County
1856

Rosenkild, Gertrude Kratzer. *1856 Cerro Gordo County, Iowa State Census.* Mason City, IA: North Central Iowa Genealogical Society, 1975. 16p.
1860
Federal Census for Iowa, 1860 Cerro Gordo County. Des Moines, IA: Iowa Genealogical Society, 1982. 23p.
Goranson, Rita. *The 1860, 1870, and 1880 Mortality Schedule for Cerro Gordo County, Iowa.* Mason City, IA: North Central Iowa Genealogical Society, 1985. 15p.
1870, 1880
Goranson, Rita. *The 1860, 1870, and 1880 Mortality Schedule for Cerro Gordo County, Iowa.* Mason City, IA: North Central Iowa Genealogical Society, 1985. 15p.
1925
Wellen, Margaret. *Every Name Index of Persons Enumerated, 1925 Iowa Census Cerro Gordo County.* Mason City, IA: Author. 2 vols.

Clarke County
1850

Federal Census for Iowa, 1850, Clarke County. Des Moines, IA: Iowa Genealogical Society, 1975. 2p.
USGenWeb Census Project. Iowa, 1850 Clarke County.
ftp://ftp.rootsweb.com/pub/census/ia/clarke/1850/

Clay County
1860

Pompey, Sherman Lee. *The 1860 Census Records of Clay County, Iowa.* Author, 1965. 2p.

Clayton County
1850

USGenWeb Census Project. Iowa, 1850 Clayton County.
ftp://ftp.rootsweb.com/pub/census/ia/clayton/1850/
1860
USGenWeb Census Project. Iowa, 1860 Clayton County. (Partial).
ftp://ftp.rootsweb.com/pub/census/ia/clayton/1860/

Clinton County
1850

Federal Census for Iowa, 1850, Clinton County. Des Moines, IA: Iowa Genealogical Society, 1983. 97p.

Dallas County
1850

Snedden, Howard, and Barbara Snedden. *Federal Census for Iowa, 1850, Dallas County.* Des Moines, IA: Iowa Genealogical Society, 1975. 20p.
_____. _____. 1981. 22p.

Davis County
1850

Federal Census for Iowa, 1850, Davis County. Des Moines, IA: Iowa Genealogical Society, 1984. 166p.

1856

Davis County Genealogical Society. *Davis County, Iowa 1856 Census.* Des Moines, IA: Genealogical Society, 1991. 3 vols.

1860

Davis County Genealogical Society. *1860 Census, Davis County, Iowa.* Des Moines, IA: Iowa Genealogical Society, 1988. 3 vols.

Decatur County
1850

Federal Census for Iowa, 1850, Decatur County. Des Moines, IA: Iowa Genealogical Society, 1975. 23p.
_____. 1982. 28p.

Delaware County
1840

Pompey, Sherman Lee. *Index to the 1840 Census of Delaware County, Iowa.* Charleston, OR: Pacific Specialities, 1974. 7p.

1850

Federal Census for Iowa, 1850, Delaware County. Des Moines, IA: Iowa Genealogical Society, 1988. 47p.

Des Moines
1836

Shambaugh, Benjamin F. *The First Census of the Original Counties of Dubuque and Des Moine (Iowa) Taken in July 1836.* Des Moines, IA: Historical Department of Iowa, 1897-1898. 2 vols.

1852

Des Moines County, Iowa Census, 1852 Iowa. Des Moines, IA: Iowa Genealogical Society, 1996. 45p.

1870

Des Moines County, Iowa Deaths, 1870 Mortality Schedule. Des Moines, IA: Iowa Genealogical Society, 1996. 41p.

Dubuque County
1836

Shambaugh, Benjamin F. *The First Census of the Original Counties of Dubuque and Des Moine (Iowa) Taken in July 1836.* Des Moines, IA: Historical Department of Iowa, 1897-1898. 2 vols.

1850

Federal Census for Iowa, 1850, Dubuque County. Des Moines, IA: Iowa Genealogical Society, 1975. 244p.

Fayette County
1850

1850 Federal Census Fayette County, Iowa. Des Moines, IA: Iowa Genealogical Society, 1975. 24p.

1860

USGenWeb Census Project. Iowa, 1860 Fayette County.
ftp://ftp.rootsweb.com/pub/census/ia/fayette/1860/

Franklin County
1856

Foster, Margaret. *Franklin County, Iowa Index to 1856 Special State Census.* Des Moines, IA: Iowa Genealogical Society, 1987. 8p.

Fremont County
1850

Schunk, John Frederick. *1850 U.S. Census Fremont County, Iowa*. Wichita, KS: S-K Publications. 64p.

1870

Harrison, Joan Fremont. *1870 Federal Census of Fremont County, Iowa*. Rapid City, SD: Author, 1970. 235p.

1885

Farwell, Walter. *Fremont County, an Index of the 1885 Iowa State Census*. Tipton, IA: Author, 1984. 61p.

Fulton County
1880

Broglin, Jana Sloan. *Index to the 1880 Fulton County, Ohio Census*. Decorah, IA: Anundsen, 1988. 97p.

Greene County
1856

1856 State Census Greene County, Iowa. Des Moines, IA: Iowa Genealogical Society, 1975. 30p.

1860

Greene County Genealogical Society. *Greene County, Iowa, Census, 1860 Federal Annotated*. Des Moines, IA: Iowa Genealogical Society, 1998. 66p.

Guthrie County
1860

Everyname Index to the 1860 Census of Guthrie County, Iowa. Jamaica, IA: Guthrie County Genealogical Society, 1993.

Tyler, Hazle A. *1860 Federal Census, Guthrie County, Iowa*. Springfield, MO: Author, 1985. 37p.

Hamilton County
1860

Tyler, Hazle A. *1860 Federal Census, Hamilton County, Iowa*. Springfield, MO: Author, 1985. 22p.

1870

1870 Federal Census Hamilton County, Iowa. Webster City, IA: Hamilton Heritage Hunters. 170p.

Henry County
1850

Colby, Ruth L. *Henry County, Iowa 1850 Census*. Author, 1977. 184p.

USGenWeb Census Project. Iowa, 1850 Henry County.

ftp://ftp.rootsweb.com/pub/census/ia/henry/1850/

1852

Henry County Genealogical Society. *Henry County, Iowa 1852 Special Census*. Des Moines, IA: Iowa Genealogical Society, 1989. 43p.

1854

Henry County Genealogical Society. *Henry County, Iowa 1854 Special Census*. Des Moines, IA: Iowa Genealogical Society, 1990. 42p.

1863

Henry County Genealogical Society. *Henry County, Iowa 1863 Special Census*. Des Moines, IA: Iowa Genealogical Society, 1989. 33p.

1869

Henry County Genealogical Society. *Henry County, Iowa 1869 Special Census*. Des Moines, IA: Iowa Genealogical Society, 1989. 41p.

1870

Henry County Genealogical Society. *Henry County, Iowa 1870 Special Census*. Des Moines, IA: Iowa Genealogical Society, 1989. 20p.

1925

Hayes, Edward R. *Henry County, Iowa Census, 1925 Iowa, Index*. Des Moines, IA: Iowa Genealogical Society, 1998. 111p.

Howard County
1860

Tyler, Hazle A. *1860 Federal Census, Howard County, Iowa*. Springfield, MO: Author, 1985. 39p.
1870

Tyler, Hazle A. *1870 Federal Census, Howard County, Iowa*. Springfield, MO: Author, 1985. 73p.
1880

Tyler, Hazle A. *1880 Federal Census, Howard County, Iowa*. Springfield, MO: Author, 1986. 203p.

Humboldt County
1870

Tyler, Hazle A. *1870 Federal Census, Humboldt County, Iowa*. Springfield, MO: Author, 1985. 34p.

Ida County
1885

Ida County Genealogical Society. *Ida County, Iowa, Census 1885 Index*. Des Moines, IA: Iowa Genealogical Society, 1996. 159p.

Iowa County
1850

1850 Federal Census Iowa County, Iowa. Des Moines, IA: Iowa Genealogical Society, 1988. 18p.
USGenWeb Census Project. Iowa, 1850 Iowa County.
ftp://ftp.rootsweb.com/pub/census/ia/iowa/1850/

Jasper County
1850

1850 Federal Census Jasper County, Iowa. Des Moines, IA: Iowa Genealogical Society, 1975. 27p.
USGenWeb Census Project. Iowa, 1850 Jasper County.
ftp://ftp.rootsweb.com/pub/census/ia/jasper/1850/

Jefferson County
1840

Baird, Verda Johnson. *1840, 1850 & 1856 Census Index, Jefferson County, Iowa*. Author, 1986. 165p.
Jefferson County, Iowa, Census 1840 Federal Census. Des Moines, IA: Iowa Genealogical Society, 1995. 50p.
1850

Baird, Verda Johnson. *1840, 1850 & 1856 Census Index, Jefferson County, Iowa*. Fairfield, IA: Author, 1986. 165p.
Jefferson County, Iowa Deaths, Mortality Schedule of Federal Census Records for 1850, 1860, 1870, 1880. Des Moines, IA: Iowa Genealogical Society, 1995. 42p.
1856

Baird, Verda Johnson. *1840, 1850 & 1856 Census Index, Jefferson County, Iowa*. Fairfield, IA: Author, 1986. 165p.
_____. *Jefferson County, Iowa, 1856 Census, Household Index*. Fairfield, IA: Author, 1986. 75p.
1860-1880

Jefferson County, Iowa Deaths, Mortality Schedule of Federal Census Records for 1850, 1860, 1870, 1880. Des Moines, IA: Iowa Genealogical Society, 1995. 42p.

Johnson County
1850

Iowa City Genealogical Society. *Index to Mortality Schedule, Johnson County, Iowa, 1850, 1860, 1870, 1880*. Des Moines, IA: Iowa Genealogical Society, 1983. 14p.

_____. *Johnson County, Iowa 1850 Census*. Des Moines, IA: Iowa Genealogical Society, 1991. 93, 43p.

1856

Johnson County, Iowa 1856 State Census. Des Moines, IA: Iowa Genealogical Society, 1994. 2 vols.

1860-1880

Iowa City Genealogical Society. *Index to Mortality Schedule, Johnson County, Iowa, 1850, 1860, 1870, 1880*. Des Moines, IA: Iowa Genealogical Society, 1983. 14p.

1885

Iowa City Genealogical Society. *Johnson County, Iowa 1885 Census*. Des Moines, IA: Iowa Genealogical Society, 1994. 177p.

Jones County
1850

1850 Federal Census Jones County, Iowa. Des Moines, IA: Iowa Genealogical Society, 1975. 75p.

Lee County
1850

1850 Census Index, Lee County, Iowa. Des Moines, IA: Iowa Genealogical Society, 1988. 138p.

1856

Beals, June. *The 1856 State Census of Lee County, Iowa*. Decorah, IA: Anundsen, 1987. 819p.

1860-1880

Lee County, Iowa Deaths, Mortality Schedules, 1860, 1870, 1880. Des Moines, IA: Iowa Genealogical Society, 1997. Unpgd.

Linn County
1850

1850 Federal Census Linn County, Iowa. Des Moines, IA: Iowa Genealogical Society, 1977. 139p.

Louisa County
1850

1850 Federal Census for Iowa, Louisa County. Des Moines, IA: Iowa Genealogical Society, 1975. 135p.

Lucas County
1850

1850 Federal Census for Lucas County, Iowa. Des Moines, IA: Iowa Genealogical Society, 1982. 13p.

Parker, Jimmy B. *1850 Mortality Schedules of Appanoose, Lucas and Pottawattamie Counties, Iowa*. Salt Lake City, UT: Genealogical Society of Utah, 1969. 7p.

1856

Lucas County Genealogical Society. *1856 Census of Lucas County, Iowa*. Des Moines, IA: Iowa Genealogical Society, 1987. 141p.

1860

Lucas County Genealogical Society. *Lucas County, Iowa 1860 Federal Census Index Every Name Index*. Des Moines, IA: Iowa Genealogical Society, 1997. 174p.

1870

Lucas County Genealogical Society. *Lucas County, Iowa 1870 Federal Census Index Every Name Index*. Des Moines, IA: Iowa Genealogical Society, 1997. 259p.

1880

Lucas County Genealogical Society. *Lucas County, Iowa 1880 Census*. Des Moines, IA: Iowa Genealogical Society, 1985. 3 vols.

1895

Lucas County Genealogical Society. *Lucas County, Iowa 1895 Census*. Des Moines, IA: Iowa Genealogical Society, 1993. 5 vols.

1925

Lucas County Genealogical Society. *Lucas County, Iowa Census Index to the 1925 State Census*. Des Moines, IA: Iowa Genealogical Society, 1995. 7 vols.

_____. *Lucas County, Iowa Census Index to the 1925 State Census Index*. Des Moines, IA: Iowa Genealogical Society, 1995. Unpgd.

Marion County

1850

Milledge, Ollie J. *1850 Head of Household Census Index, Marion County, Iowa*. Knoxville, IA: Marion County Genealogical Society, 1990. 10p.

1856

White, Iona Gomel. *Index, State Census, 1856, Marion County, Iowa*. Knoxville, IA: Author, 1990. 60p.

1860

Milledge, Ollie J. *Index of 1860 Marion County, Iowa Census*. Knoxville, IA: Marion County Genealogical Society, 1990. 20p.

1870

Milledge, Ollie J. *1870 Marion County, Iowa Census Index*. Knoxville, IA: Marion County Genealogical Society, 1990. 30p.

1880

Milledge, Ollie J. *1880 Marion County, Iowa Surname Index*. Knoxville, IA: Marion County Genealogical Society, 1990. 16p.

1885

Burton, June, and Lela B. Langstraat. *1885 Marion County, Iowa Census Index*. Knoxville, IA: Marion County Genealogical Society. 32p.

1895

Langstraat, Lela B. *1895 Marion County, Iowa Census Index*. Knoxville, IA: Marion County Genealogical Society. 26p.

1900

Milledge, Ollie J. *1900 Marion County, Iowa Surname Index*. Knoxville, IA: Marion County Genealogical Society. 35p.

1925

MacLeod, Ruth. *1925 Iowa State Census*. Knoxville, IA: Marion County Genealogical Society. 34p.

Marshall County

1850

1850 Federal Census for Iowa, Marshall County. Des Moines, IA: Iowa Genealogical Society, 1975. 11p.

1910

Snedden, Barbara A. *1910 Federal Census, Iowa Soldiers Home, Marshalltown, Iowa*. Des Moines, IA: Author, 1997. 26p.

Monroe County

1850

Monroe County Genealogical Society. *1850 Federal Census for Iowa, Monroe County*. Des Moines, IA: Iowa Genealogical Society, 1988. 66p.

_____. *Mortality Schedules Monroe County, Iowa for the Years Preceding the Census of 1850, 1860, 1870 and 1880*. Des Moines, IA: Iowa Genealogical Society, 1986. 15p.

1856

Monroe County, Iowa Census, 1856 Iowa Index to Head of Households. Des Moines, IA: Iowa Genealogical Society, 1997. 18p.

1860

Monroe County Genealogical Society. *1860 Federal Census for Iowa, Monroe County*. Des Moines, IA: Iowa Genealogical Society, 1986. 17p.

_____. *Mortality Schedules Monroe County, Iowa for the Years Preceding the Census of 1850, 1860, 1870 and 1880*. Des Moines, IA: Iowa Genealogical Society, 1986. 15p.

1870

Monroe County, Iowa Census, Index to 1870 Federal Census. Des Moines, IA: Iowa Genealogical Society, 1997. 32p.

_____. *Mortality Schedules Monroe County, Iowa for the Years Preceding the Census of 1850, 1860, 1870 and 1880*. Des Moines, IA: Iowa Genealogical Society, 1986. 15p.

1880

_____. *Mortality Schedules Monroe County, Iowa for the Years Preceding the Census of 1850, 1860, 1870 and 1880*. Des Moines, IA: Iowa Genealogical Society, 1986. 15p.

1895

Monroe County Genealogical Society. *List of Heads of Household, 1895 State Census*. Des Moines, IA: Iowa Genealogical Society, 1988. 37p.

Montgomery County
1856

Monroe County Genealogical Society. *1856 State Census Montgomery County, Iowa*. Des Moines, IA: Iowa Genealogical Society, 1984. 25p.

1860

Monroe County Genealogical Society. *1860 Census Montgomery County, Iowa*. Des Moines, IA: Iowa Genealogical Society, 1984. 52p.

1891

Montgomery County, Iowa Census, Town of Villisca, 1891. Des Moines, IA: Iowa Genealogical Society, 1997. 21p.

Muscatine County
1850

1850 Federal Census, Muscatine County. Des Moines, IA: Iowa Genealogical Society, 1977. 112p.

1910

Brossart, Marlin W. *1910 Federal Census of Muscatine County, Iowa*. Escondido, CA: Author, 1987. 374p.

Page County

Federal Census for Iowa, 1850, Page County. Des Moines, IA: Iowa Genealogical Society, 1975. 14p.

Plymouth County
1900

Northwest Iowa Genealogical Society. *1900 Federal Census Index, Plymouth County, Iowa*. Des Moines, IA: Iowa Genealogical Society, 1984. 128p.

1910

Northwest Iowa Genealogical Society. *1910 Federal Census Index, Plymouth County, Iowa*. Des Moines, IA: Iowa Genealogical Society, 1985. 153p.

Polk County
1850

1850 Federal Census for Polk County, Iowa. Des Moines, IA: Iowa Genealogical Society, 1977. 119p.; 1981. 112p.

1856

Pioneer Sons and Daughters Genealogical Society. *Polk County, Iowa 1856 State Census*. Des Moines, IA: Iowa Genealogical Society, 1994. Unpgd.

1885

Pioneer Sons and Daughters Genealogical Society. *Polk County, Iowa Census, 1885, Iowa, with Every Name Index*. Des Moines, IA: Iowa Genealogical Society, 1999. 8 vols.

Pottawattamie County
1850

Index to Pottawattamie County, Iowa 1850 Census. Salt Lake City, UT: Genealogical Society of Utah, 1966. 66p.

Parker, Jimmy B. *1850 Mortality Schedules of Appanoose, Lucas and Pottawattamie Counties, Iowa*. Salt Lake City, UT: Genealogical Society of Utah, 1969. 7p.

1870

Smith, Ione Rita Card. *Index, Pottawattamie County, Iowa, 1870 Census*. Elkhorn, NE: Author, 1985. Unpgd.

USGenWeb Census Project. Iowa, 1870 Pottawattamie County.

ftp://ftp.rootsweb.com/pub/census/ia/pottawattamie/1870/

1885

Botna Valley Genealogical Society. *1885 State Census of Pottawattamie County*. Des Moines, IA: Iowa Genealogical Society, 1990. 3 vols.

1895

1895 Iowa State Census of Pottawattamie County. Des Moines, IA: Iowa Genealogical Society, 1990. 4 vols.

Poweshiek County
1850

1850 Federal Census Poweshiek County, Iowa. Des Moines, IA: Iowa Genealogical Society, 1980. 15p.

Sac County
1860

Sac County Genealogical Society. *Index to 1860 Census, Sac County, Iowa*. Des Moines, IA: Iowa Genealogical Society, 1984. 6p.

1870

Sac County Genealogical Society. *Index to 1870 Census, Sac County, Iowa*. Des Moines, IA: Iowa Genealogical Society, 1984. 28p.

St. Clair County
1860

Jetton, Kay F. *1860 Census St. Clair County, Illinois*. Decorah, IA: Anundsen, 1981. 2 vols.

Scott County
1850

Scott County, Iowa 1850 Federal Population Census, Early Marriages (1838-1851). Davenport, IA: Scott County, Iowa Genealogical Society. 208p.

Tama County
1856

Tama County, Iowa 1856 Census. Des Moines, IA: Iowa Genealogical Society, 1987. 96p.

1860, 1870

Bidwell, Jean. *1860 and 1870 Mortality Schedule of Tama County, Iowa*. Des Moines, IA: Iowa Genealogical Society, 1985. 12p.

1885

Samuelson, W. David. *Tama 1885 State Census Index*. Salt Lake City, UT: Author, 1994. 117p.

Taylor County

O'Dell, Patti Combs. *Taylor County, Iowa, Census*. Clarinda, IA: Clarinda Pub. Co., 1975. 473p.
1850
Federal Census for Iowa 1850, Taylor County. Des Moines, IA: Iowa Genealogical Society, 1975. 5p.

Union County
1860, 1870
Saffell, Lester F. *1860 and 1870 Federal Census of Pleasant Township, Union County, Iowa*. Unpgd.

Van Buren County
1847
Harris, Vernon. *The 1847 Iowa Census, Van Buren County*. Des Moines, IA: Iowa Genealogical Society, 1996. 27p.
1850
Schunk, John Frederick. *1850 U.S. Census, Van Buren County, Iowa*. Wichita, KS: S-K Publications, 1986. Unpgd.
Van Buren County Genealogical Society. *Iowa, Van Buren County Census Mortality Schedules 1850, 1860, 1870, 1880*. Keosauqua, IA: Van Buren County Genealogy Society, 1994. 20p.
1860-1880
Van Buren County Genealogical Society. *Iowa, Van Buren County Census Mortality Schedules 1850, 1860, 1870, 1880*. Keosauqua, IA: Van Buren County Genealogy Society, 1994. 20p.
1925
Hayes, Edward R. *Van Buren County, Iowa Census 1925 Index*. Des Moines, IA: Iowa Genealogical Society, 1998. 96p.

Villisca (Montgomery County)
1891
Montgomery County, Iowa Census, Town of Villisca, 1891. Des Moines, IA: Iowa Genealogical Society, 1997. 21p.

Wapello County
1850
Wise, Darlene. *1850 Census Wapello County, Iowa*. Ottumwa, IA: Author, 1986. 189p.
1860
Wapello County Genealogical Society. *Wapello County, Iowa 1860 Federal Census*. Des Moines, IA: Iowa Genealogical Society, 1989. 3 vols.
1870
Wapello County Genealogical Society. *Wapello County, Iowa 1870 Federal Census*. Des Moines, IA: Iowa Genealogical Society, 1992. 4 vols.
1925
Wapello County Genealogical Society. *Wapello County, Iowa Census, 1925 Index*. Des Moines, IA: Iowa Genealogical Society, 1998. 2 vols.

Warren County
1850
Schunk, John Frederick. *1850 U.S. Census, Warren County, Iowa*. Wichita, KS: S-K Publications, 1986. Unpgd.
USGenWeb Census Project. Iowa, 1850 Warren County.
ftp://ftp.rootsweb.com/pub/census/ia/warren/1850/

Wallace, Betty. *Index to the 1850 Census of Warren County, Iowa*. Des Moines, IA: Author, 1977. 24p.
1853
McGlothlen, Ellen. *Special Iowa Census, Part of Warren County, Iowa 1853*. Des Moines, IA: Iowa Department of History, 1966. Unpgd.

Washington County
1849
Washington County Genealogical Society. *1849 Census Washington County, Iowa*. Des Moines, IA: Iowa Genealogical Society, 1984. 9p.
1850
Washington County Genealogical Society. *Washington County 1850 Census*. Des Moines, IA: Iowa Genealogical Society, 1985. Unpgd.
1925
Hayes, Edward R. W*ashington County, Iowa Census, 1925 Iowa Index. D*es Moines, IA: Iowa Genealogical Society, 1999. 141p.

Wayne County
1850
Schunk, John Frederick. *1850 U.S. Census Wayne County, Iowa*. Wichita, KS: S-K Publications. 20p.
Seaton, Myrna. *Wayne County, Iowa 1850 Census*. Des Moines, IA: Iowa Genealogical Society. 8p.
USGenWeb Census Project. Iowa, 1850 Wayne County.
ftp://ftp.rootsweb.com/pub/census/ia/wayne/1850/
1856
Wayne County Genealogical Society. *1856 State Census, Wayne County, Iowa*. Des Moines, IA: Iowa Genealogical Society, 1985. 27p.
1860
Wayne County Genealogical Society. *1860 Census, Wayne County, Iowa*. Des Moines, IA: Iowa Genealogical Society, 1985. 62p.
1870
Janson, Helen. *1870 Census Wayne County, Iowa*. Author, 1960. 271p.
1880
Wayne County Genealogical Society. *Wayne County, Iowa 1880 Census Index*. Des Moines, IA: Iowa Genealogical Society, 1994. 105p.
1885
Wayne County Genealogical Society. *Wayne County, Iowa Census Index to 1885 Wayne County, Iowa State Census*. Des Moines, IA: Iowa Genealogical Society, 1998. 90p.
1895
Wayne County, Iowa Census 1895 State Index. Des Moines, IA: Iowa Genealogical Society, 1999. 189p.

Webster County
1856
1856 State Census, Webster County, Iowa. Webster City, IA: Hamilton Heritage Hunters. 97p.
1860
Webster County Genealogical Society. *Webster County, Iowa 1860 Census*. Des Moines, IA: Iowa Genealogical Society, 1989. 68p.
1870
Webster County Genealogical Society. *Webster County, Iowa 1870 Federal Census*. Des Moines, IA: Iowa Genealogical Society, 1991. 90p.
1880
Webster County Genealogical Society. *Webster County, Iowa 1880 State Census*. Des Moines, IA: Iowa Genealogical Society, 1994. 2 vols.

1885

Webster County Genealogical Society. *Webster County, Iowa 1885 State Census*. Des Moines, IA: Iowa Genealogical Society, 1990. 6 vols.

1895

Webster County Genealogical Society. *Webster County, Iowa 1895 State Census*. Des Moines, IA: Iowa Genealogical Society, 1991. 6 vols.

1925

Webster County Genealogical Society. *Webster County, Iowa 1925 State Census*. Des Moines, IA: Iowa Genealogical Society, 1995. 95p.

Winnishiek County

1850

Winnishiek County, Iowa 1850 Census. Des Moines, IA: Iowa Genealogical Society, 1980. 13p.

1870

Richmond, Mary Huber. *Winnishiek County, Iowa Index to 1870 Federal Census*. Des Moines, IA: Iowa Genealogical Society, 1991. 87p.

Woodbury County

1846

Powell, Peggy Maybury, and MaryAnn Haafke. *1846 Iowa Census of Woodbury County*. Sioux City, IA: Woodbury County Genealogcial Society, 1994. 17p.

1860

Woodbury County Genealogical Society. *1860 Federal Census Index Woodbury County, Iowa*. Des Moines, IA: Iowa Genealogical Society, 1986. 9p.

1880

Mitchell, Ethel. *1880 Federal Census Woodbury County, Iowa*. Sioux City, IA: Woodbury County Genealogical Society, 1994. 3 vols.

Kansas

1850

Census Index: U.S. Selected States/Counties, 1850. Family Archive CD 317. Novato, CA: Broderbund Software. CD-ROM.

Jackson, Ronald Vern. *Kansas Census Index, Online Edition*. Orem, UT: Ancestry.com, Inc., 1999.

http://www.ancestry.com

1855

The Census of the Territory of Kansas, February, 1855, with Index and Map of Kansas Election Districts in 1854. Knightstown, IN: Bookmark, 1973. 74 microfilm.

Dunbar, Bobbie. *Kansas Territory Census, 1855-1858; Shawnee Indians 1857 Census and Land Records of the Shawnees*. Richland, MO: Author, 1992. 93p.

Heiss, Willard C. *The Census of the Territory of Kansas, February, 1855, with Index and Map of Kansas Election Districts in 1854*. Knightstown, IN: Eastern Indiana Pub., Co., 1968. 38p.

Jackson, Ronald Vern. *Kansas Census Index, Online Edition (Territorial Census)*. Orem, UT: Ancestry.com, Inc., 1999.

http://www.ancestry.com

_____, and Gary Ronald Teeples. *Kansas 1855 Territorial Census Index*. Salt Lake City, UT: Accelerated Indexing Systems, 1977. 105p.

1856

Jackson, Ronald Vern. *Kansas Census Index, Online Edition (Territorial Census)*. Orem, UT: Ancestry.com, Inc., 1999.
http://www.ancestry.com

1857

Jackson, Ronald Vern. *Kansas Census Index, Online Edition (Territorial Census)*. Orem, UT: Ancestry.com, Inc., 1999.
http://www.ancestry.com
_____. *Kansas 1856-1858*. North Salt Lake City, UT: Accelerated Indexing Systems International, 1987. 318p.

1858

Jackson, Ronald Vern. *Kansas Census Index, Online Edition (Territorial Census)*. Orem, UT: Ancestry.com, Inc., 1999.
http://www.ancestry.com
_____. *Kansas 1856-1858*. North Salt Lake City, UT: Accelerated Indexing Systems International, 1987. 318p.

1859

Jackson, Ronald Vern. *Kansas Census Index, Online Edition (Territorial Census)*. Orem, UT: Ancestry.com, Inc., 1999.
http://www.ancestry.com
_____. *Kansas 1859*. North Salt Lake City, UT: Accelerated Indexing Systems International, 1988. 422p.

1860

Census Index: U.S. Selected States/Counties, 1860. Family Archive CD 318. Novato, CA: Broderbund Software. CD-ROM.
Jackson, Ronald Vern. *Kansas Census Index, Online Edition*. Orem, UT: Ancestry.com, Inc., 1999.
http://www.ancestry.com
_____. *Kansas 1860 Mortality Schedule*. Bountiful, UT: Accelerated Indexing Systems, 1980. 20p.
_____. *Mortality Schedules Index, Online Edition*. Orem, UT: Ancestry.com, Inc., 1999.
http://www.ancestry.com
_____, and Gary Ronald Teeples. *Kansas 1860 Territorial Census Index*. Salt Lake City, UT: Accelerated Indexing Systems, 1978. 153p.
Mortality Schedule of the Territory of Kansas. Topeka, KS: Topeka Genealogical Society. 44p.
Robertsson, Clara Hamlett. *Kansas Territorial Settlers of 1860 Who Were Born in Tennessee, Virginia, North Carolina and South Carolina*. Baltimore, MD: Genealogical Publishing Co., 1976. 187p.
U.S. Federal Population Census Schedules. 1860, M653, Microfilm Reel Nos. 346-352.

1870

Census Index: U.S. Selected States/Counties, 1870. Family Archive CD 319. Novato, CA: Broderbund Software. CD-ROM.
Franklin, Helen, and Thelma Carpenter. *1870 Mortality Schedule of Kansas*. Topeka, KS: Topeka Genealogical Society, 1974. 234p.
Jackson, Ronald Vern. *Kansas 1870*. Salt Lake City, UT: Accelerated Indexing Systems International, 1987. 524p.
_____. *Mortality Schedules Index, Online Edition*. Orem, UT: Ancestry.com, Inc., 1999.
http://www.ancestry.com
_____. *Mortality Schedule, Kansas 1870*. Bountiful, UT: Accelerated Indexing Systems, 1979. Unpgd.
U.S. Federal Population Census Schedules. 1870, M593, Microfilm Reel Nos. 428-443.

1880

Carpenter, Thelma, and Helen Franklin. *1880 Mortality Schedules of Kansas*. Topeka, KS: Topeka Genealogical Society, 1973. 143p.

Jackson, Ronald Vern. *Mortality Schedules Index, Online Edition*. Orem, UT: Ancestry.com, Inc., 1999.
http://www.ancestry.com

_____. *Mortality Schedule, Kansas 1880*. Bountiful, UT: Accelerated Indexing Systems, 1979. 190p.

U.S. Federal Population Census Schedules. 1880, T9, Microfilm Reel Nos. 372-400.

U.S. Federal Population Census Schedules. 1880, Soundex. T749, 51 Microfilm Reels.

1890

Jackson, Ronald Vern. *Kansas Census Index, Online Edition (Veterans Schedules)*. Orem, UT: Ancestry.com, Inc., 1999.
http://www.ancestry.com

1900

Ledoux, Albert H. *The French Canadian Families of the Plains and Upper Mountain States, Abstracts from the Federal Census of 1900*. Altoona, PA: Author, 1991. 2 vols.

U.S. Federal Population Census Schedules. 1900, T623, Microfilm Reel Nos. 469-505.

U.S. Federal Population Census Schedules. 1900, Soundex. T1046, 147 Microfilm Reels.

1910

U.S. Federal Population Census Schedules. 1910, T624, Microfilm Reel Nos. 431-461.

U.S. Federal Population Census Schedules. 1910, Miracode INdex, T1265, 145 Microfilm Reels.

1920

U.S. Federal Population Census Schedules. 1920, T625, Microfilm Reel Nos. 522-556.

U.S. Federal Population Census Schedules. 1920, Soundex. M1562, 129 Microfilm Reels.

Allen County
1870

Kratz, Steven C. *Allen County, Kansas 1870 Census*. Salt Lake City, UT: Kratz Indexing, 1987. 32p.

Anderson County
1870

Kratz, Steven C. *Anderson County, Kansas 1870 Census*. Salt Lake City, UT: Kratz Indexing, 1987. 24p.

Atchison County
1865

Ostertag, John A. *1865 Kansas State Census for Atchison County, Kansas*. Atchison, KS: Atchison County Genealogical Society, 1991. 179p.

1870

Kratz, Steven C. *Atchison County, Kansas 1870 Census*. Salt Lake City, UT: Kratz Indexing, 1987. 78p.

1895

1895 Kansas State Census for the City of Atchison, Kansas. Atchison, KS: Atchison County Genealogical Society, 1997. 276p.

Breckenridge County
1860

USGenWeb Census Project. Kansas, 1860 Breckenridge County.
ftp://ftp.rootsweb.com/pub/census/ks/breckenridge/1860/

Brown County
1860

Brown County, Kansas, 1860 Federal Census. Springfield, MO: Catlett, 1986. 41p.
1870

Kratz, Steven C. *Brown County, Kansas 1870 Census.* Salt Lake City, UT: Kratz Indexing, 1987. 30p.
1880

Brown, Evelyn J. *1880 Federal Census Brown County, Kansas.* Manhattan, KS: Riley County Genealogical Society, 1975. Unpgd.

Butler County
1860

Kansas Federal Census, 1860 Butler, Otoe, Hunter, 1870 Butler. Springfield, MO: Catlett, 1987. 63p.
USGenWeb Census Project. Kansas, 1860 Butler County.
ftp://ftp.rootsweb.com/pub/census/ks/butler/1860/
1865

Kansas DAR. *1865 Census, Butler County, Kansas.* Genealogical Records Committee Report. Series 2, v 45. Kansas DAR, 1996.
1870

Kansas Federal Census, 1860 Butler, Otoe, Hunter, 1870 Butler. Springfield, MO: Catlett, 1987. 63p.
Kratz, Steven C. *Butler County, Kansas 1870 Census.* Salt Lake City, UT: Kratz Indexing, 1987. 17p.

Chase County
1870

Kratz, Steven C. *Chase County, Kansas 1870 Census.* Salt Lake City, UT: Kratz Indexing, 1987. 10p.

Clay County
1860

Brown, Evelyn J. *1860 Federal Census Clay County, Kansas Territory.* Manhattan, KS: Riley County Genealogical Society, 1988. 5p.
1870

Kratz, Steven C. *Clay County, Kansas 1870 Census.* Salt Lake City, UT: Kratz Indexing, 1987. 14p.
1880

Darby, Earl Gilbert. *1880 Federal Census, Clay County, Kansas.* Manhattan, KS: Riley County Genealogical Society, 1973. 216p.

Cloud County

Kratz, Steven C. *Cloud County, Kansas 1870 Census.* Salt Lake City, UT: Kratz Indexing, 1987. 12p.

Coffey County
1859

Christy, Wanda Houck. *1859 Census of Coffey County, Kansas.* Burlington, KS: Author, 1985. 59p.
1860

Christy, Wanda Houck. *1860 Census of Coffey County, Kansas.* Burlington, KS: Author, 1985. 59p.
1870

Kratz, Steven C. *Coffey County, Kansas 1870 Census.* Salt Lake City, UT: Kratz Indexing, 1987. 29p.

Cowley County
1870

Kratz, Steven C. *Cowley County, Kansas 1870 Census.* Salt Lake City, UT: Kratz Indexing, 1987. 8p.

Crawford County
1870

Kratz, Steven C. *Crawford County, Kansas 1870 Census*. Salt Lake City, UT: Kratz Indexing, 1988. 36p.

Davis County
1860

Brown, Evelyn J. *1860 Federal Census Davis County, Kansas Territory*. Manhattan, KS: Riley County Genealogical Society, 1988. 22p.

1870

Brown, Evelyn J. *1870 Davis County, Kansas Census*. Manhattan, KS: Riley County Genealogical Society, 1982. 50p.

Kratz, Steven C. *Davis County, Kansas 1870 Census*. Salt Lake City, UT: Kratz Indexing, 1988. 30p.

1880

Darby, Earl Gilbert. *1880 Federal Census, Davis County, Kansas*. Manhattan, KS: Riley County Genealogical Society, 1970. Unpgd.

Dickinson County
1880

Darby, Earl Gilbert. *1880 Federal Census Dickinson County, Kansas*. Manhattan, KS: Riley County Genealogical Society, 1975. Unpgd.

Doniphan County
1860

Ostertag, John A., and Enid Ostertag. *1860 Federal Census of Doniphan County, Kansas, Fully Indexed!*. St. Joseph, MO: Author, 1991. 145p.

1870

Ostertag, John A., and Enid Ostertag. *1870 Federal Census of Doniphan County, Kansas*. St. Joseph, MO: Author, 1992. 247p.

1900

Ostertag, John A., and Enid Ostertag. *1900 Federal Census of Doniphan County, Kansas*. St. Joseph, MO: Author, 1998. 339p.

Douglas County
1875

1875 Douglas County, Kansas Census. Lawrence, KS: Douglas County Genealogical Society, 1985. Unpgd.

Ellis County
1870

Kratz, Steven C. *Ellis County, Kansas 1870 Census*. Salt Lake City, UT: Kratz Indexing, 1987. 16p.

Ellsworth County
1870

Kratz, Steven C. *Ellsworth County, Kansas 1870 Census*. Salt Lake City, UT: Kratz Indexing, 1987. 10p.

1880

Darby, Earl Gilbert. *1880 Federal Census Ellsworth County, Kansas*. Manhattan, KS: Riley County Genealogical Society, 1970. 152p.

Ford County
1870

Kratz, Steven C. *Ford County, Kansas 1870 Census*. Salt Lake City, UT: Kratz Indexing, 1987. 5p.

Franklin County
1880
Carpenter, Thelma, and Helen Franklin. *1880 Mortality Schedules of Franklin and Osage Counties of Kansas*. Topeka, KS: Topeka Genealogical Society. 36p.

Godfrey County
1860
Pompey, Sherman Lee. *The 1860 Census Records of Godfrey and Wilson Counties, Kansas Territory*. Bakersfield, CA: Historical and Genealogical Pub. Co. 2p.

Greenwood County
1865
Harrell, Leta Ellen Watts, and Katheryn Ann Brooks Griffith. *Greenwood County, Kansas, 1865 Kansas State Census, Complete Family Information and Complete Index for Greenwood County, Kansas*. Hamilton, KS: Relatively Searching, 1992. 33p.
1870
Burris, Gary W. *Index to the Ninth United States Census of Greenwood County, Kansas*. Author, 1988. 81p.
Kratz, Steven C. *Greenwood County, Kansas 1870 Census*. Salt Lake City, UT: Kratz Indexing, 1987. 17p.

Howard County
1870
Kratz, Steven C. *Howard County, Kansas 1870 Census*. Salt Lake City, UT: Kratz Indexing, 1987. 13p.

Hunter County
1860
Pompey, Sherman Lee. *The 1860 Census Records of Hunter County, Kansas Territory*. Bakersfield, CA: Historical and Genealogical Pub. Co., 5p.

Jefferson County
1875
1875 Census Index of Jefferson County, Kansas. Oskaloosa, KS: Jefferson County Genealogical Society, 1984. 218p.
1885
Index to Jefferson County, Kansas 1885 Census. Oskaloosa, KS: Jefferson County Genealogical Society, 1989. 238p.

Jewell County
1870
Roberts, Diana Ousley. *1870 Jewell County, Kansas Census*. McMinnville, OR: Yamhill County Genealogical Society, 1981. 11p.

Lane County
1920
Carter, Gloria Bogart. *1920 Census of Lane County, Kansas*. Springfield, MO: Author, 1992. 97p.

Leavenworth County
1885
Spindler, Rita Benge. *Index, Kansas State Census, 1885, Leavenworth County, Kansas*. Leavenworth, KS: Leavenworth County Genealogical Society, 1996. 128p.

Madison County
1860

USGenWeb Census Project. Kansas, 1860 Madison County.
ftp://ftp.rootsweb.com/pub/census/ks/madison/1860/

Marion County
1860
Pompey, Sherman Lee. *The 1860 Census Records of Marion County, Kansas Territory.* Bakersfield, CA: Historical and Genealogical Pub. Co., 1966. 3p.
1870
Wiebe, Raymond F. *Marion County, Kansas Census, 1870.* Author, 1983. 33p.
1880
Darby, Earl Gilbert. *1880 Federal Census, Marion County, Kansas.* Manhattan, KS: Riley County Genealogical Society, 1974. 213p.

Marshall County
1880

Darby, Earl Gilbert. *1880 Federal Census, Marshall County, Kansas.* Manhattan, KS: Riley County Genealogical Society, 1973. 278p.

Meade County
1880

Aiken, Gladys Lee. *1880 Census Meade and Wichita Census Kansas.* Lawrence, KS: Author. 27p.

Mitchell County
1880

Darby, Earl Gilbert. *1880 Federal Census, Mitchell County, Kansas.* Manhattan, KS: Riley County Genealogical Society, 1975. 258p.

Montgomery County
1880

Darby, Earl Gilbert. *1880 Federal Census, Montgomery County, Kansas.* Manhattan, KS: Riley County Genealogical Society, 1971. Unpgd.
Van Dyne, Robert A. *West Cherry Township, Montgomery County, Kansas, 1880-1900.* Salina, KS: Author, 1987. 162p.
1900
Van Dyne, Robert A. *West Cherry Township, Montgomery County, Kansas, 1880-1900.* Salina, KS: Author, 1987. 162p.

Morris County
1880

Darby, Earl Gilbert. *1880 Federal Census, Morris County, Kansas.* Manhattan, KS: Riley County Genealogical Society, 1974. 160p.

Nemaha County
1860

USGenWeb Census Project. Kansas, 1860 Nemaha County.
ftp://ftp.rootsweb.com/pub/census/ks/nemaha/1860/
1880
Darby, Earl Gilbert. *1880 Federal Census, Nemaha County, Kansas.* Manhattan, KS: Riley County Genealogical Society, 1976. 216p.

Norton County
1885
Chojnowski, Pat. *Aldine Township, Norton County, Kansas, Kansas State Census 1885*. Clayton, KS: Norton County Genealogical Society, 1987. 47p.

Osage County
1880
Carpenter, Thelma, and Helen Franklin. *1880 Mortality Schedules of Franklin and Osage Counties of Kansas*. Topeka, KS: Topeka Genealogical Society. 36p.

Osborne County
1870
Kratz, Steven C. *Osborne County, Kansas 1870 Census*. Salt Lake City, UT: Kratz Indexing, 1987. 1p.

Ottawa County
1865
Cunningham, Mona M. *Saline County, Kansas 1865 Census and Ottawa County, Kansas Existing 1865 Census*. Salina, KS: Smoky Valley Genealogical Society and Library, 1987. 12p.
1870
Kratz, Steven C. *Ottawa County, Kansas 1870 Census*. Salt Lake City, UT: Kratz Indexing, 1987. 14p.

Pawnee County
1870
Kratz, Steven C. *Pawnee County, Kansas 1870 Census*. Salt Lake City, UT: Kratz Indexing, 1987. 3p.

Phillips County
1875
Jones, Yvonne Fortney. *Phillips County, Kansas, 1875, State Census, Alphabetized*. Decorah, IA: Anundsen, 1982. 57p.

Pottawatomie County
1860
Cunningham, Annie, and Evelyn J. Brown. *1860 Kansas Territory Census of Pottawatomie County*. Manhattan, KS: Riley County Genealogical Society, 1982. 15p.
1865
1865 Kansas State Census of Pottawatomie County. Atchison, KS: Riley County Genealogical Society, 1982. 22p.
1870
Kratz, Steven C. *Pottawatomie County, Kansas 1870 Census*. Salt Lake City, UT: Kratz Indexing, 1987. 40p.
1880
Darby, Earl Gilbert. *1880 Federal Census, Pottawatomie County, Kansas*. Manhattan, KS: Riley County Genealogical Society, 1970. 293p.
1900
Brown, Evelyn J. *Pottawatomie County, Kansas 1900 Federal Census Abstract*. Manhattan, KS: Riley County Genealogical Society, 1994.

Reno County
1880
1880 Census Reno County, Kansas. Hutchinson, KS: Reno County Genealogical Society, 1989. 239p.

Republic County
1870
Kratz, Steven C. *Republic County, Kansas 1870 Census*. Salt Lake City, UT: Kratz Indexing, 1987. 6p.
1880
Darby, Earl Gilbert. *1880 Federal Census, Republic County, Kansas*. Manhattan, KS: Riley County Genealogical Society, 1977. 264p.

Rice County
1870
Kratz, Steven C. *Rice County, Kansas 1870 Census*. Salt Lake City, UT: Kratz Indexing, 1987. 1p.

Riley County
1855-1865
Darby, Earl Gilbert. *1855, 1857, 1860, 1865 Riley County, Kansas Census*. Manhattan, KS: Riley County Genealogical Society. 34p.
1870
Darby, Earl Gilbert. *1870 Census, Riley County, Kansas*. Manhattan, KS: Riley County Genealogical Society, 1970. 93p.
Kratz, Steven C. *Riley County, Kansas 1870 Census*. Salt Lake City, UT: Kratz Indexing, 1987. 24p.
1875
Darby, Earl Gilbert. *1875 State Census, Riley County, Kansas*. Manhattan, KS: Riley County Genealogical Society, 1969. 121p.
_____. *People Either Born in Ohio or Coming from Ohio to Kansas as Enumerated in the Riley County, Kansas, 1875 State Census*. Manhattan, KS: Author, 1970. 23p.
1880
Darby, Earl Gilbert. *1880 Census, Riley County, Kansas*. Manhattan, KS: Riley County Genealogical Society, 1969. 193p.
_____. *People Born in Ohio Who Were Enumerated in the 1880 Riley County, Kansas Census*. Manhattan, KS: Author, 1970. 35p.
1885
Darby, Earl Gilbert. *1885 State Census, Riley County, Kansas*. Manhattan, KS: Riley County Genealogical Society, 1976. 212p.
1895
Brown, Evelyn J. *1895 Kansas State Census, Riley County*. Manhattan, KS: Riley County Genealogical Society, 1978. 125p.
1900
1900 Riley County, Kansas Census Index. Manhattan, KS: Riley County Genealogical Society, 1985. 68p.
1915
Riley County, Kansas, 1915 State Census Abstract. Manhattan, KS: Riley County Genealogical Society, 1990. 459p.

Russell County
1870
Kratz, Steven C. *Russell County, Kansas 1870 Census*. Salt Lake City, UT: Kratz Indexing, 1987. 2p.

Saline County
Saline County, Kansas Census Index. Salina, KS: Smoky Valley Genealogical Society, 1980. 18p.
1865
Census Index, Saline County, Kansas, 1865 State, 1870 Federal, 1875 State. Salina, KS: Smoky Valley Genealogical Society, 1980. 26p.
Cunningham, Mona M. *Saline County, Kansas 1865 Census and Ottawa County, Kansas Existing 1865 Census*. Salina, KS: Smoky Valley Genealogical Society and Library, 1987. 12p.

1870

Census Index, Saline County, Kansas, 1865 State, 1870 Federal, 1875 State. Salina, KS: Smoky Valley Genealogical Society, 1980. 26p.

Cunningham, Mona M., and LaDeene Wickersham. *1870 Federal Census, Saline County, Kansas with Surname Index*. Salina, KS: Smoky Valley Genealogical Society and Library, 1990. 82p.

Salina Public Library. *Kansas Census, City of Salina 1870 Index*. Salina, KS: Smoky Valley Genealogical Society. 18p.

1875

Census Index, Saline County, Kansas, 1865 State, 1870 Federal, 1875 State. Salina, KS: Smoky Valley Genealogical Society, 1980. 26p.

Salina Public Library. *Kansas Census, City of Salina 1875 Index*. Salina, KS: Smoky Valley Genealogical Society. 5p.

Sedgwick County
1870

1870 Sedgwick County Census. Wichita, KS: Midwest Historical and Genealogical Society. 32p.

1875

1875 Census for Sedgwick County, Kansas. Wichita, KS: Midwest Historical & Genealogical Society, 1984. 186p.

1880

USGenWeb Census Project. Kansas, 1880 Sedgwick County.

ftp://ftp.rootsweb.com/pub/census/ks/sedgwick/1880/

1900

Sickmon, Anita, and Bill Pennington. *Sedgwick County, Kansas Federal Census Index, 1900*. Wichita, KS: Authors, 1993. 310p.

Shawnee County
1860

Mowak, Christine M. *1860 Shawnee County, Kansas Territorial Census*. West Allis, WI: Janlen Enterprises, 1973. 67p.

Wabaunsee County
1860

Brown, Evelyn J. *1860 Kansas Territory Census of Wabaunsee*. Manhattan, KS: Riley County Genealogical Society, 1982. 11p.

1865

1865 Kansas State Census of Wabaunsee County. Atchison, KS: Riley County Genealogical Society, 1982. 12p.

1870

Brown, Evelyn J. *1870 Kansas Territory Census of Wabaunsee*. Manhattan, KS: Riley County Genealogical Society, 1984. 30p.

1880

Darby, Earl Gilbert. *1880 Census, Wabaunsee County, Kansas*. Manhattan, KS: Riley County Genealogical Society, 1970. 153p.

Brown, Evelyn J. *1880 Kansas Territory Census of Wabaunsee*. Manhattan, KS: Riley County Genealogical Society, 1971. Unpgd.

Washington County
1860

Brown, Evelyn J. *1860 Federal Census of Washington County, Kansas Territory*. Manhattan, KS: Riley County Genealogical Society, 1988. 9p.

1880

Darby, Earl Gilbert. *1880 Federal Census Washington County, Kansas*. Manhattan, KS: Riley County Genealogical Society, 1971. Unpgd.

Wichita County
1880

Aiken, Gladys Lee. *1880 Census Meade and Wichita Census Kansas*. Lawrence, KS: Author. 27p.

Wilson County
1855

Index, 1885 State Census for Wilson County, Kansas, Heads of Households and Those with Different Surnames Living with Them. Neodesha, KS: Heritage Genealogical Society, 1983.

1860

Pompey, Sherman Lee. *The 1860 Census Records of Godfrey and Wilson Counties, Kansas Territory*. Bakersfield, CA: Historical Gen. Pub. Co. 2p.

USGenWeb Census Project. Kansas, 1860 Wilson County.

ftp://ftp.rootsweb.com/pub/census/ks/wilson/1860/

1875

Index, 1875 Kansas State Census, Wilson County, Kansas. Neodesha, KS: Heritage Genealogical Society. 22p.

1880

1880 Wilson County, Kansas Federal Census Index. Neodesha, KS: Heritage Genealogical Society, 1976. 33p.

1885

Index, 1885 Kansas State Census, Wilson County, Kansas. Neodesha, KS: Heritage Genealogical Society, 1983. 40p.

1895

Index, 1895 Kansas State Census, Wilson County, Kansas. Neodesha, KS: Heritage Genealogical Society, 1982. 41p.

1900

Index, 1900 Wilson County, Kansas, Federal Census. Neodesha, KS: Heritage Genealogical Society, 1986. 44p.

1905

Index, 1905 Kansas State Census, Wilson County, Kansas. Neodesha, KS: Heritage Genealogical Society, 1987. 54p.

Woodson County
1859

Christy, Wanda. *1859 Woodson County, Kansas Census*. Burlington, KS: Coffey County Genealogical Society, 1985. 8p.

Kentucky

Nave, Doris, and Barbara Augspurger. *Kentucky Frontiersmen Located in Census and County Records*. Midway, KY: Authors, 1981. 3 vols.

1800

Abell, William Russell. *Abell, Abel, Able Surnames in the Federal Census of Kentucky, 1800-1850*. Des Moines, IA: Author, 1983. 21p.

1810

Abell, William Russell. *Abell, Abel, Able Surnames in the Federal Census of Kentucky, 1800-1850*. Des Moines, IA: Author, 1983. 21p.

Bell, Annie Walker Burns. *Third Census of the United States 1810 State of Kentucky*. Washington, DC: Author, 1933. 7 vols.

Jackson, Ronald Vern. *Kentucky Census Index, Online Edition*. Orem, UT: Ancestry.com, Inc., 1999. **http://www.ancestry.com**

_____. *Kentucky 1810 Census*. Bountiful, UT: Accelerated Indexing Systems, 1978. 882p.

U.S. Federal Population Census Schedules, 1810. M252, Microfilm Reel Nos. 5-9.

Volkel, Lowell M. *An Index to the 1810 Federal Census of Kentucky*. Springfield, IL: Author, 1971. 4 vols.

Wagstaff, Ann T. *Index to the 1810 Census of Kentucky*. Baltimore, MD: Genealogical Publishing Co., 1980. 230p.

1820

Abell, William Russell. *Abell, Abel, Able Surnames in the Federal Census of Kentucky, 1800-1850*. Des Moines, IA: Author, 1983. 21p.

Clift, Garrett Glenn. *Second Census of Kentucky 1800*. Baltimore, MD: Genealogical Publishing Co., 1966. 333p.

Felldin, Jeanne Robey. *The 1820 Census of Kentucky*. Baltimore, MD: Genealogical Pub. Co., 1981. 318p.

Jackson, Ronald Vern. *Kentucky Census Index, Online Edition*. Orem, UT: Ancestry.com, Inc., 1999. **http://www.ancestry.com**

_____, and Gary Ronald Teeples. *Kentucky 1820 Census Index*. Salt Lake City, UT: Accelerated Indexing Systems, 1976. 168p.

U.S. Federal Population Census Schedules. 1820, M33, Microfilm Reel Nos. 16-29.

Volkel, Lowell M. *An Index to the 1820 Federal Census of Kentucky*. Thomson, IL: Heritage House, 1974. 4 vols.

1830

Abell, William Russell. *Abell, Abel, Able Surnames in the Federal Census of Kentucky, 1800-1850*. Des Moines, IA: Author, 1983. 21p.

Census Index: U.S. Selected States/Counties, 1830. Family Archive CD 315. Novato, CA: Broderbund Software. CD-ROM.

1830-1839 U.S. Census Indexes, Mid-Atlantic, South, Mid-West. Orem, UT: Automated Archives, 1993. CD-ROM.

Jackson, Ronald Vern. *Kentucky Census Index, Online Edition*. Orem, UT: Ancestry.com, Inc., 1999. **http://www.ancestry.com**

_____, and Gary Ronald Teeples. *Kentucky 1830 Census Index*. Salt Lake City, UT: Accelerated Indexing Systems, 1976. 206p.

Smith, Dora Wilson. *Kentucky 1830 Census Index*. Thomson, IL: Heritage House, 1973. 6 vols.

U.S. Federal Population Census Schedules. 1830, M19, Microfilm Reel Nos. 33-42.

1840

Abell, William Russell. *Abell, Abel, Able Surnames in the Federal Census of Kentucky, 1800-1850*. Des Moines, IA: Author, 1983. 21p.

Census Index: U.S. Selected States/Counties, 1840. Family Archive CD 316. Novato, CA: Broderbund Software. CD-ROM.

1840 United States Census Index, Mid-West, Great Lakes. Orem, UT: Automated Archives, 1994. CD-ROM.

Jackson, Ronald Vern. *Kentucky Census Index, Online Edition*. Orem, UT: Ancestry.com, Inc., 1999. **http://www.ancestry.com**

_____, and Gary Ronald Teeples. *Kentucky 1840 Census Index*. Salt Lake City, UT: Accelerated Indexing Systems, 1978. 250p.

Minix, Sharroll K. *1840 Special Federal Census of Kentucky Pensioners of Revolutionary or Military Service.* Salyersville, KY: Magoffin County Historical Society, 1983. 28p.

U.S. Federal Population Census Schedules. 1840, M704, Microfilm Reel Nos. 103-126.

1850

Abell, William Russell. *Abell, Abel, Able Surnames in the Federal Census of Kentucky, 1800-1850.* Des Moines, IA: Author, 1983. 21p.

Census Index: U.S. Selected States/Counties, 1850. Family Archive CD 317. Novato, CA: Broderbund Software. CD-ROM.

Census Microfilm Records: Kentucky, 1850. Family Archive CD 303. Novato, CA: Broderbund Software. CD-ROM.

Corley, Betty J. *Index, Yeoman(s), Yeaman(s), Youman(s), U.S. Census Index, 1850, 1860, 1880, Alabama, Florida, Kentucky, Louisiana, Maryland, Mississippi, Tennessee, Texas, Virginia, Includes Various Other Spellings.* Hyrum, UT: Author, 1988. 5p.

Jackson, Ronald Vern. *Kentucky Census Index, Online Edition.* Orem, UT: Ancestry.com, Inc., 1999.
http://www.ancestry.com

_____. *Mortality Schedules Index, Online Edition.* Orem, UT: Ancestry.com, Inc., 1999.
http://www.ancestry.com

_____, and Gary Ronald Teeples. *Kentucky 1850 Census Index.* Salt Lake City, UT: Accelerated Indexing Systems, 1976. 469p.

_____. *Kentucky 1850 Slave Schedule Census Index.* North Salt Lake City, UT: Accelerated Indexing Systems International, 1990. 665p.

McDowell, Samuel. *A Surname Index to the 1850 Federal Population Census of Kentucky, Microfilm Publication Number M432*, Roll Number 190-222. Hartford, KY: Author, 1974. 33 vols.

Parrish, Verle Hamilton. *1850 Census Index of Eastern Kentucky.* Stamping Ground, KY: Author, 1973. Unpgd.

Sistler, Barbara. *1850 Census, Central Kentucky, Counties of Boyle, Casey, Green, Lincoln, Marion, Mercer, Rockcastle and Taylor.* Nashville, TN: Byron Sistler & Associates, 1996. 494p.

_____. *1850 Census, East Central Kentucky, Counties of Clark, Estill, Fayette, Garrard, Jessamine, Madison, Montgomery and Owsley.* Nashville, TN: Byron Sistler & Associates, 1995. 563p.

_____. *1850 Census, Kentucky, Head of Household Index.* Nashville, TN: Byron Sistler & Associates, 1995. 452p.

_____. Nashville, TN: Byron Sistler & Associates, 1996. 625p.

_____. *1850 Census, North Central Kentucky, Counties of Anderson, Bullitt, Franklin, Nelson, Shelby, Spencer, Washington and Woodford.* Nashville, TN: Byron Sistler & Associates, 1995. 574p.

_____. *1850 Census, North East Kentucky, Counties of Bath, Bourbon, Fleming, Lewis, Mason and Nichols.* Nashville, TN: Byron Sistler & Associates, 1995. 563p.

_____. *1850 Census, Northern Kentucky, Part I Counties of Carroll, Gallatin, Harrison, Henry, Oldham, Owen, Scott, and Trimble.* Nashville, TN: Byron Sistler & Associates, 1996. 494p.

_____. *1850 Census, Northern Kentucky, Part II Counties of Boone, Bracken, Campbell, Grant, Kenton, and Pendleton.* Nashville, TN: Byron Sistler & Associates, 1996. 563p.

_____. *1850 Census, West Central Kentucky, Counties of Breckenridge, Butler, Edmonson, Grayson, Hancock, Hardin, Hart, LaRue and Meade.* Nashville, TN: Byron Sistler & Associates, 1995. 486p.

U.S. Census Index Series, Kentucky and Tennessee, 1850. Orem, UT: Automated Archives, 1991. CD-ROM.

U.S. Federal Population Census Schedules. 1850, M432, Microfilm Reel Nos. 190-222.

U.S. Federal Population Census Schedules. 1850, M432, Slave Schedules, Microfilm Reel Nos. 223-228.

1860

Census Index: U.S. Selected States/Counties, 1860. Family Archive CD 318. Novato, CA: Broderbund Software. CD-ROM.

Corley, Betty J. *Index, Yeoman(s), Yeaman(s), Youman(s), U.S. Census Index, 1850, 1860, 1880, Alabama, Florida, Kentucky, Louisiana, Maryland, Mississippi, Tennessee, Texas, Virginia, Includes Various Other Spellings.* Hyrum, UT: Author, 1988. 5p.

Jackson, Ronald Vern. *Kentucky Census Index, Online Edition.* Orem, UT: Ancestry.com, Inc., 1999. **http://www.ancestry.com**

_____. *Kentucky 1860 East.* Salt Lake City, UT: Accelerated Indexing Systems, 1988. 1,175p.

_____. *Kentucky 1860 East Federal Census Index.* West Jordan, UT: Genealogical Services, 1988, 1997.

_____. *Kentucky 1860 Mortality Schedule, Federal Census Index.* Salt Lake City, UT: Accelerated Indexing Systems, 1984. 162p.

_____. *Kentucky 1860 West.* Salt Lake City, UT: Accelerated Indexing Systems, 1987. 1,289p.

_____. _____. West Jordan, UT: Genealogical Services, 1987, 1997. 1,289p.

_____. *Mortality Schedules Index, Online Edition.* Orem, UT: Ancestry.com, Inc., 1999. **http://www.ancestry.com**

U.S. Federal Population Census Schedules. 1860, M653, Microfilm Reel Nos. 353-400.

U.S. Federal Population Census Schedules. 1860, M653, Slave Schedules, Microfilm Reel Nos. 401-406.

1870

Census Index: U.S. Selected States/Counties, 1870. Family Archive CD 319. Novato, CA: Broderbund Software. CD-ROM.

Jackson, Ronald Vern. *Kentucky Census Index, Online Edition.* Orem, UT: Ancestry.com, Inc., 1999. **http://www.ancestry.com**

_____. *Kentucky 1870 Federal Census Index East.* Salt Lake City, UT: Accelerated Indexing Systems, 1988. 702p.

_____. *Kentucky 1870 Federal Census Index West.* Salt Lake City, UT: Accelerated Indexing Systems, 1988. 876p.

U.S. Federal Population Census Schedules. 1870, M593, Microfilm Reel Nos. 444-504.

1880

Corley, Betty J. *Index, Yeoman(s), Yeaman(s), Youman(s), U.S. Census Index, 1850, 1860, 1880, Alabama, Florida, Kentucky, Louisiana, Maryland, Mississippi, Tennessee, Texas, Virginia, Includes Various Other Spellings.* Hyrum, UT: Author, 1988. 5p.

U.S. Federal Population Census Schedules. 1880, T9, Microfilm Reel Nos. 401-446.

U.S. Federal Population Census Schedules. 1880, Soundex. T750, 83Microfilm Reels.

1890

Dilts, Bryan Lee. *1890 Kentucky Census Index of Civil War Veterans or Their Widows.* Salt Lake City, UT: Index Pub. Co., 1984. 135p.

Jackson, Ronald Vern. *1890 Kentucky Census Index, Special Schedule of the Eleventh Census (1890) Enumerating Union Veterans and of Union Veterans of the Civil War.* Salt Lake City, UT: Accelerated Indexing Systems, 1984. 2 vols.

_____. *Kentucky Census Index, Online Edition (Veterans Schedules).* Orem, UT: Ancestry.com, Inc., 1999. **http://www.ancestry.com**

U.S. Federal Population Census Schedules, Special Schedule, Enumerating Union Veterans and Widows of Union Veterans of the Civil War. 1890, M123, Microfilm Reel No. 1-3.

Veterans' Schedules: U.S. Selected States, 1890. Family Archive CD 131. Novato, CA: Broderbund Software. CD-ROM.

1900

U.S. Federal Population Census Schedules. 1900, T623, Microfilm Reel Nos. 506-555.

U.S. Federal Population Census Schedules. 1900, Soundex. T1047, 198 Microfilm Reels.

1910

U.S. Federal Population Census Schedules. 1910, T624, Microfilm Reel Nos. 462-506.

U.S. Federal Population Census Schedules. 1910, Miracode Index, T1266, 194 Microfilm Reels.

1920

Sizemore, Darlene. *1920 Kentucky Sizemores*. Dayton, OH: Author, 1992. 35p.

U.S. Federal Population Census Schedules. 1920, T625, Microfilm Reel Nos. 557-602.

U.S. Federal Population Census Schedules. 1920, Soundex. M1563, 180 Microfilm Reels.

Adair County

1810

Lawson, Rowena. *Adair County, Kentucky, 1810-1840 Censuses*. Bowie, MD: Heritage Books, 1986. 69p.

Simmons, Don. *Adair County, Kentucky Census 1810*. Murray, KY: Author, 1974. 27p.

Watson, Michael C. *Adair County, Kentucky 1810 Federal Census 1802, 1805, 1810 Tax Lists*. Columbia, KY: Author, 87p.

1820-1840

Lawson, Rowena. *Adair County, Kentucky, 1810-1840 Censuses*. Bowie, MD: Heritage Books, 1986. 69p.

1850

Flowers, Mrs. Randy H., and Michael C. Watson. *1850 Census of Adair County, Kentucky*. Columbia, KY: Adair County Genealogical Society, 1986. 111p.

Sistler, Barbara. *1850 Census, South Central Kentucky, Counties of Adair, Allen, Barren, Clinton, Cumberland and Monroe*. Nashville, TN: Byron Sistler & Associates, 1992. 382p.

1860

Smith, Randolph N. *Federal Mortality Census Schedules, 1860, 1870, 1880, Abstract and Index, Adair, Clinton, Cumberland, Metcalfe, Monroe Counties, Kentucky*. Burkesville, KY: Author, 1975. 51p.

Watson, Michael C. *1860 Census of Adair County, Kentucky*. Columbia, KY: Author, 1988. 120p.

1870

Smith, Randolph N. *Federal Mortality Census Schedules, 1860, 1870, 1880, Abstract and Index, Adair, Clinton, Cumberland, Metcalfe, Monroe Counties, Kentucky*. Burkesville, KY: Author, 1975. 51p.

Watson, Michael C. *Adair County, Kentucky Census Index for 1870 and 1880*. Columbia, KY: Author, 1989. 17p.

1880

Smith, Randolph N. *Federal Mortality Census Schedules, 1860, 1870, 1880, Abstract and Index, Adair, Clinton, Cumberland, Metcalfe, Monroe Counties, Kentucky*. Burkesville, KY: Author, 1975. 51p.

Watson, Michael C. *Adair County, Kentucky Census Index for 1870 and 1880*. Columbia, KY: Author, 1989. 17p.

1900

England, Beverly A. *1900 Census of Adair County, Kentucky*. Columbia, KY: Author, 1995. 395p.

Allen County

1820

Jackson, Martha Werst. *The Federal Census of Allen County, Kentucky for 1820*. Scottsville, KY: Author, 1984. 25p.

Lawson, Rowena. *Allen County, Kentucky, 1820-1840 Censuses*. Bowie, MD: Heritage Books, 1987. 51p.

1830

Jackson, Martha Werst. *The 1830 Census of Allen County, Kentucky*. Scottsville, KY: Author, 1996. 25p.

Lawson, Rowena. *Allen County, Kentucky, 1820-1840 Censuses*. Bowie, MD: Heritage Books, 1987. 51p.

1840

Lawson, Rowena. *Allen County, Kentucky, 1820-1840 Censuses*. Bowie, MD: Heritage Books, 1987. 51p.

1850

Jackson, Martha Werst. *The Federal Census of Allen County, Kentucky for 1850*. Scottsville, KY: Author, 1998. 57p.

Simmons, James. *Allen County, Kentucky Federal 1850 Census*. Glasgow, KY: Gorin Genealogical Pub., 1991. 175p.

Sistler, Barbara. *1850 Census, South Central Kentucky, Counties of Adair, Allen, Barren, Clinton, Cumberland and Monroe*. Nashville, TN: Byron Sistler & Associates, 1992. 382p.

1880

Jackson, Martha Werst. *The 1880 Census of Allen County, Kentucky*. Scottsville, KY: Author, 1996. 112p.

Anderson County

Anderson County, Kentucky Census Index. Mosheim, TN: Rowe, 1980. 4 vols.

1830, 1840

Lawson, Rowena. *Anderson County, Kentucky, 1830-1850 Censuses*. Bowie, MD: Heritage Books, 1987. 78p.

1850

Lawson, Rowena. *Anderson County, Kentucky, 1830-1850 Censuses*. Bowie, MD: Heritage Books, 1987. 78p.

Sanders, Faye Sea. *Washington, Mercer and Anderson Counties, Kentucky Mortality Schedules for 1850, 1860, 1870, 1880. Also Deaths Reported in 1874-1878 Vital Statistics*. Louisville, KY: Author. 61p.

1860-1880

Sanders, Faye Sea. *Washington, Mercer and Anderson Counties, Kentucky Mortality Schedules for 1850, 1860, 1870, 1880. Also Deaths Reported in 1874-1878 Vital Statistics*. Louisville, KY: Author. 61p.

Ballard County

1850

Sistler, Barbara. *1850 Census, Western Kentucky, Counties of Ballard, Caldwell, Calloway, Fulton, Graves, Hickman, Livingston, Marshall and McCracken*. Nashville, TN: Byron Sistler & Associates, 1993. 452p.

1860

Simmons, Don. *Ballard County, Kentucky Census of 1860*. Melber, KY: Simmons Historical Pub., 1987. 142p.

1870

Birchfield, Steven A. *Ballard County, Kentucky Census of 1870*. Melber, KY: Simmons Historical Publications. 208p.

Barren County

1810

Burns, Annie Walker. *Census of 1810 of Barren County, Kentucky*. Annapolis, MD: Author. 31p.

Carter, Genevieve L. *1810 Census Barren County*. Sedalia, MO: Author. 22p.

Gorin, Sandra K. Laughery. *Barren County, Kentucky Census Records 1810, 1820, 1830, 1840 Alphabetically Presented with Censuses Merged in Chronological Order*. Glasgow, KY: Gorin Genealogical Pub., 1992. 182p.

Hubble Anna Joy Munday. *Barren County, Kentucky 1810 Census*. Whitefish, MT: Author, 1976. 14p.

Lawson, Rowena. *Barren County, Kentucky, 1810-1840 Censuses*. Bowie, MD: Heritage Books, 1986. 113p.

McGhee, Lucy Kate. *United States Census, 1810, Barren County, Kentucky, County Seat Glasgow; Campbell County, Kentucky, County Seat, Newport and Alexandria; Caldwell County, Kentucky, County Seat, Princeton; Casey County, Kentucky, County Seat Liberty*. Washington, DC: Author, 1958. 130p.

1820

Barren County, Kentucky 1820 Census. Twain Harte, CA: G-N Pubns., 1985. 14p.

Gorin, Sandra K. Laughery. *Barren County, Kentucky Census Records 1810, 1820, 1830, 1840 Alphabetically Presented with Censuses Merged in Chronological Order*. Glasgow, KY: Gorin Genealogical Pub., 1992. 182p.

Lawson, Rowena. *Barren County, Kentucky, 1810-1840 Censuses*. Bowie, MD: Heritage Books, 1986. 113p.

Merrell, B.J. *1820 Federal Census of Barren County, Kentucky*. Tulsa, OK: Author, 1987. 28p.

1830

Gorin, Sandra K. Laughery. *Barren County, Kentucky Census Records 1810, 1820, 1830, 1840 Alphabetically Presented with Censuses Merged in Chronological Order*. Glasgow, KY: Gorin Genealogical Pub., 1992. 182p.

Lawson, Rowena. *Barren County, Kentucky, 1810-1840 Censuses*. Bowie, MD: Heritage Books, 1986. 113p.

1840

Gorin, Sandra K. Laughery. *Barren County, Kentucky Census Records 1810, 1820, 1830, 1840 Alphabetically Presented with Censuses Merged in Chronological Order.* Glasgow, KY: Gorin Genealogical Pub., 1992. 182p.

Lawson, Rowena. *Barren County, Kentucky, 1810-1840 Censuses.* Bowie, MD: Heritage Books, 1986. 113p.

1850

Froggett, Judy. *United States Census Barren County, Kentucky, 1850.* Greensburg, KY: Green County Public Library, 1984. 318p.

Gorin, Sandra K. *Barren County, Kentucky 1850 Census.* Glasgow, KY: Gorin Genealogial Publishing, 1995. 253p.

Merell, B.J. *1850 Federal Census, Barren County, Kentucky.* Tulsa, OK: Author, 1987. 3 vols.

Peden, Eva Coe. *1850 Barren County, Kentucky Census.* Glasgow, KY: Gorin Genealogical Pub., 1991. 331p.

Sistler, Barbara. *1850 Census, South Central Kentucky, Counties of Adair, Allen, Barren, Clinton, Cumberland and Monroe.* Nashville, TN: Byron Sistler & Associates, 1992. 382p.

1860

Harrison, H. Dane. *1860 Barren County, Kentucky Census.* Glasgow, KY: Gorin Genealogical Pub., 1994. 169p.

Merrell, B. J. *1860 Federal Census, Barren County, Kentucky.* Tulsa, OK: Author, 1991. 3 vols.

1870

Harrison, H. Dane. *1870 Barren County, Kentucky Census.* Glasgow, KY: Gorin Genealogical Pub., 1994. 453p.

Bath County
1820-1840

Lawson, Rowena. *Bath County, Kentucky 1820-1840 Censuses.* Bowie, MD: Heritage Books, 1986. 67p.

Bell County
1870

Nolan, Gertrude, and Janette Nolan. *The 1870 Bell County Census.* Lexington, KY: American Pub. Co., 1987. 81p.

1880

Deaton, Garland. *1880 Census Bell County, Kentucky.* Middlesboro, KY: Bell County Historical Society, 1996. Unpgd.

1890

Cox, Eunice Evelyn. *Bell County, Kentucky 1890 Special Census.* Ellensburg, WA: Ancestree House, 1979. 8p.

1900

Deaton, Garland. *1900 Census Bell County, Kentucky.* Middlesboro, KY: Bell County Historical Society, 1996. Unpgd.

Minton, Vestina Laws. *Bell County, Kentucky Census, 1900.* Harrogate, TN: Author, 1989. 356p.

1910

Deaton, Garland. *1910 Census Bell County, Kentucky.* Middlesboro, KY: Bell County Historical Society, 1991. 410p.

Boone County
1810

Lawson, Rowena. *Boone County, Kentucky, 1810-1840 Censuses.* Bowie, MD: Heritage Books, 1986. 68p.

USGenWeb Census Project. KY, 1810 Boone County.

ftp://ftp.rootsweb.com/pub/census/ky/boone/1810/

1820

Lawson, Rowena. *Boone County, Kentucky, 1810-1840 Censuses.* Bowie, MD: Heritage Books, 1986. 68p.

USGenWeb Census Project. KY, 1820 Boone County.
ftp://ftp.rootsweb.com/pub/census/ky/boone/1820/
Worrel, Stephen William. *Northern Kentucky Towns Census of 1819-1820.* Falls Church, VA: Author, 1993.
    12p.
1830, 1840
Lawson, Rowena. *Boone County, Kentucky, 1810-1840 Censuses.* Bowie, MD: Heritage Books, 1986. 68p.
1850
Lawson, Rowena. *Boone County, Kentucky, 1850 Census.* Bowie, MD: Heritage Books, 1986. 93p.

Bourbon County
1850
Hubble, Anna Joy Munday. *Bourbon County, Kentucky, 1850 Census.* Whitefish, MT: Author, 1986. 56p.

Bracken County
1850
McDowell, Samuel Riley. *A Surname Index to the 1850 Federal Population Census of Kentucky, Bracken,
    Breathitt, Breckinridge and Bullitt Counties.* Richland, IN: Author, 1975. 71p.
USGenWeb Census Project. Kentucky, 1850 Bracken County.
ftp://ftp.rootsweb.com/pub/census/ky/bracken/1850/

Breathitt County
1840
Banks, Homer. *1840 Breathitt County, Kentucky Census.* Cincinnati, OH: Author, 1987. 18p.
1840 Census Breathitt County, Kentucky. Quicksand, KY: Breathitt County Historical Society, 1990. 14p.
1850
Cunagin, Judy Murray. *1850 Breathitt County, Kentucky Census with Heads of Household Index.* Indianapo-
    lis, IN: Author, 1990. Unpgd.
1850 Census Breathitt County, Kentucky. Quicksand, KY: Breathitt County Historical Society, 1990. 42p.
Little, Harley S. *Breathitt County, Kentucky, Census 1850.* Dayton, OH: Author, 1973. Unpgd.
McDowell, Samuel Riley. *A Surname Index to the 1850 Federal Population Census of Kentucky, Bracken,
    Breathitt, Breckinridge and Bullitt Counties.* Richland, IN: Author, 1975. 71p.
Perry, Zandra Addington. *1850 and 1870 Census, Breathitt County, Kentucky.* Ermine, KY: Author. 113p.
1860
Breathitt County 1860 U.S. Census. Jackson, KY: Breathitt County Historical Society, 1983. 59p.
Wireman, Connie Arnett. *1860 Breathitt County, Kentucky Census.* Salyersville, KY: Magoffin County His-
    torical Society. 78p.
1870
Hurst, John C. *1870 Census Breathitt County, Kentucky.* Jackson, KY: Breathitt County Historical Society,
    1983. 58p.
Perry, Zandra Addington. *1850 and 1870 Census, Breathitt County, Kentucky.* Ermine, KY: Author. 113p.
1880
Hurst, John C. *1880 Census, Breathitt County, Kentucky.* Jackson, KY: Breathitt County Historical Society,
    1970. Unpgd.
1900
1900 Census Breathitt County, Kentucky. Quicksand, KY: Breathitt County Historical Society, 1990. 132p.
1910
Herald, Nancy E. *1910 Census Breathitt County, Kentucky.* Jackson, KY: Breathitt County Historical Soci-
    ety, 1991. 234p.

Breckinridge County
1810-1840
Hinton, Virginia, and Shirley Pile. *Breckenridge County, Kentucky 1800 Tax Lists; 1810, 1820, 1830, 1840
    Census.* Vine Grove, KY: Ancestral Trails Historical Society, 1996. 188p.

1850

Leftwich, Holly. *Breckinridge County, Kentucky, 1850 Census*. Owensboro, KY: West-Central Kentucky Family Research Assn., 1976. 141p.

McDowell, Samuel Riley. *A Surname Index to the 1850 Federal Population Census of Kentucky, Bracken, Breathitt, Breckinridge and Bullitt Counties*. Richland, IN: Author, 1975. 71p.

1860

Boucher, Avery. *1860 Census, Breckinridge County, Kentucky, Microcopy 653, Roll 358*. Vine Grove, KY: Ancestral Trails Historical Society, 1981. 181p.

1870

McManaway, Robert D. *Breckinridge County, Kentucky, 1870 Census*. Utica, KY: McDowell Publications, 1983. 204p.

Bullitt County

1810

Darnell, Betty Rolwing. *1810 Census and 1810 Tax List, Bullitt County, Kentucky*. Mt. Washington, KY: Author, 1988. 21p.

Hubble, Anna Joy Munday. *Bullitt County, Kentucky, 1810 Kentucky Census*. Whitefish, MT: Author. Unpgd.

Walker, Annie Burns. *Third Census of the United States for the County of Bullitt, State of Kentucky*. Washington, DC: Author, 1934. 24p.

1820

Darnell, Betty Rolwing. *1820 Census, Bullitt County, Kentucky*. Mt. Washington, KY: Author, 1989. 22p.

1830

Darnell, Betty Rolwing. *1830 Census, Bullitt County, Kentucky*. Mt. Washington, KY: Author, 1989. 33p.

1840

Darnell, Betty Rolwing. *1840 Census, Bullitt County, Kentucky*. Mt. Washington, KY: Author, 1989. 29p.

1850

Blue, James. *Bullitt County, Kentucky Census of 1850*. Melber, KY: Simmons Historical Publications, 1997. 103p.

Crume, Betty A. *Bullitt County, Kentucky 1850 Federal Census*. Lubbock, TX: Author. 57p.

McDowell, Samuel Riley. *A Surname Index to the 1850 Federal Population Census of Kentucky, Bracken, Breathitt, Breckinridge and Bullitt Counties*. Richland, IN: Author, 1975. 71p.

Wright, Joan June. *1850 Census, Bullitt County, Kentucky, Microcopy No. M432, Roll No. 193*. Vine Grove, KY: Ancestral Trails Historical Society, 1981. 88p.

1860

Sabetti, Mary L. *Bullitt County, Kentucky 1870 Census*. Mt. Washington, KY: Author, 1993. 151p.

Wright, Joan Leslie, and Patricia Susan Dodson. *1860 Census, Bullitt County, Kentucky, Microcopy No. M653, Roll No. 358*. Brooks, KY: Authors, 1981. 141p.

1880

Darnell, Betty Rolwing. *Bullitt County, Kentucky, 1880 Census*. Mt. Washington, KY: Author, 1992. 175p.

1900

Darnell, Betty Rolwing. *Bullitt County, Kentucky 1900 Census, Copied from Microfilm #T653-511*. Mt. Washington, KY: Author, 1997.

Butler County

1810

USGenWeb Census Project. Kentucky, 1810 Butler County.
ftp://ftp.rootsweb.com/pub/census/ky/butler/1810/

1850

Leftwich, Holly. *Butler County, Kentucky, 1850 Census*. Owensboro, KY: West-Central Kentucky Family Research Assn., 1975. 77p.

1860

Butler County, Kentucky 1860 Census. Morgantown, KY: Butler County Historical & Genealogical Society, 1983. 189p.

USGenWeb Census Project. Kentucky, 1860 Butler County.
ftp://ftp.rootsweb.com/pub/census/ky/butler/1860/
1870
Haun, Weynette Parks. *1870 Butler County, Kentucky, Federal Census.* Durham, NC: Raper, 1974. 102p.
1880
Butler County, Kentucky, 1880 Census. Morgantown, KY: Butler County Historical and Genealogical Society, 1977. 289p.

Caldwell County
1810
Federal Census of Caldwell County, Kentucky, 1810, 1820, 1830, 1840. Madisonville, KY: Hopkins County Genealogical Society, 1976. 220p.
Jones, Thomas Harold. *Caldwell County, Kentucky Census of 1810.* Melber, KY: Simmons Historical Pub., 1977. 16p.
McGhee, Lucy Kate. *United States Census, 1810, Barren County, Kentucky, County Seat Glasgow; Campbell County, Kentucky, County Seat, Newport and Alexandria; Caldwell County, Kentucky, County Seat, Princeton; Casey County, Kentucky, County Seat Liberty.* Washington, DC: Author, 1958. 130p.
1820
Federal Census of Caldwell County, Kentucky, 1810, 1820, 1830, 1840. Madisonville, KY: Hopkins County Genealogical Society, 1976. 220p.
Simmons, Don. *Caldwell County, Kentucky Census of 1820.* Melber, KY: Simmons Historical Pub., 1987. 26p.
1830
Federal Census of Caldwell County, Kentucky, 1810, 1820, 1830, 1840. Madisonville, KY: Hopkins County Genealogical Society, 1976. 220p.
Simmons, Don. *Caldwell County, Kentucky Census of 1830.* Melber, KY: Simmons Historical Pub., 1977. 25p.
1840
Federal Census of Caldwell County, Kentucky, 1810, 1820, 1830, 1840. Madisonville, KY: Hopkins County Genealogical Society, 1976. 220p.
Jones, Thomas Harold. *Caldwell County, Kentucky Census of 1840.* Melber, KY: Simmons Historical Pub., 1977. 34p.
1850
Sistler, Barbara. *1850 Census, Western Kentucky, Counties of Ballard, Caldwell, Calloway, Fulton, Graves, Hickman, Livingston, Marshall and McCracken.* Nashville, TN: Byron Sistler & Associates, 1993. 452p.
Willhite, A. B. *Caldwell County, Kentucky 1850 Federal Census.* Russellville, KY: Author, 1997. 179p.
1860
1860 Federal Census Caldwell County, Kentucky. Madisonville, KY: Hopkins County Genealogical Society, 1977. 193p.
1870
McDowell, Samuel Riley. *1870 Federal Census Caldwell County, Kentucky.* Madisonville, KY: Hopkins County Genealogical Society. 258p.
1880
Monks, Sue. *1880 Caldwell County, Kentucky, Federal Census.* Princeton, KY: Caldwell County Historical Society, 1997. 268p.
1900
Monks, Sue, and Brenda Joyce Jerome. *Caldwell County, Kentucky, 1900 Federal Census.* Princeton, KY: Caldwell County, Kentucky Historical Society, 1998. 315p.

Calloway County
1830
Hatcher, Danny R. *The Jackson Purchase, Calloway County, Kentucky, 1830 Census.* Murray, KY: Author, 1969. 25p.

Simmons, Don. *Jackson Purchase, 1830 Census of Kentucky Consisting of the First Four Original Counties of Calloway, Graves, Hickman and McCracken.* Murray, KY: Author, 1974 Unpgd.

1840

Simmons, Don. *Calloway County, Kentucky Census of 1840.* Murray, KY: Author, 1974. 34p.

1850

Sistler, Barbara. *1850 Census, Western Kentucky, Counties of Ballard, Caldwell, Calloway, Fulton, Graves, Hickman, Livingston, Marshall and McCracken.* Nashville, TN: Byron Sistler & Associates, 1993. 452p.

Stilley, Van A. *Calloway County, Kentucky, Census of 1850.* Melber, KY: Simmons Historical Publications, 1995. 78p.

1860

Simmons, Don. *Calloway County, Kentucky Census of 1860.* Melber, KY: Simmons Historical Pub., 1989. 129p.

1870

Williams, Patricia Ramsey. *Calloway County, Kentucky Census of 1870.* Melber, KY: Simmons Historical Publications, 1996. 169p.

Campbell County

1810

Gladden, Sanford Charles. *Heads of Families Census of 1810 Campbell County, Kentucky.* Author, 1965. 9p.

McGhee, Lucy Kate. *United States Census, 1810, Barren County, Kentucky, County Seat Glasgow; Campbell County, Kentucky, County Seat, Newport and Alexandria; Caldwell County, Kentucky, County Seat, Princeton; Casey County, Kentucky, County Seat Liberty.* Washington, DC: Author, 1958. 130p.

Wieck, Dorothy L. *Campbell County, Kentucky Census Index, 1810, 1820, 1830.* Covington, KY: Kenton County Historical Society, 1987. 64p.

1820

Gladden, Sanford Charles. *Heads of Families Census of 1820 Campbell County, Kentucky.* Author, 1965. 21p.

Wieck, Dorothy L. *Campbell County, Kentucky Census Index, 1810, 1820, 1830.* Covington, KY: Kenton County Historical Society, 1987. 64p.

Worrel, Stephen William. *Northern Kentucky Towns Census of 1819-1820.* Falls Church, VA: Author, 1993. 12p.

1830

Gladden, Sanford Charles. *Heads of Families Census of 1830 Campbell County, Kentucky.* Author, 1965. 29p.

Wieck, Dorothy L. *Campbell County, Kentucky Census Index, 1810, 1820, 1830.* Covington, KY: Kenton County Historical Society, 1987. 64p.

1840

Gladden, Sanford Charles. *Heads of Families Census of 1840 Campbell County, Kentucky.* Author, 1965. 17p.

1850

Gladden, Sanford Charles. *Heads of Families Census of 1850 Campbell County, Kentucky.* Author, 1965. 48p.

1860

Brennan, Ronald. *Index to the 1860 Census, Campbell County, Kentucky.* Wilder, KY: Author, 1980. 53p.

Gladden, Sanford Charles. *Heads of Families Census of 1860 Campbell County, Kentucky.* Author, 1965. 9p.

1870

Brennan, Ronald. *Surname Index 1870 Census, Campbell County, Kentucky, Plus Atlas and City Directories.* Wilder, KY: Author, 1980. 31p.

1880

Brennan, Ronald. *Surname Index 1880 Census, Campbell County, Kentucky.* Wilder, KY: Author, 1980. 99p.

1900

Brennan, Ronald. *Surname Index 1900 Census, Campbell County, Kentucky, Including City Directories.* Wilder, KY: Author, 1983. 197p.

1910

Brennan, Ronald.*Campbell County, Kentucky, Surname Index to the 1910 Census*. Wilder, KY: Author, 1987. 124p.

Carter County
1850

Atkins, Oscar Thomas. *Carter County, Kentucky Families, 1850, Information from Several Sources, Including the Carter County Federal Census for 1850, the Microfilm Copies of the Originals Being on File in the National Archives in Washington, D.C., from Tax Records, Marriage Records, Other Census Records, and from the Files and Library of the Writer*. Williamson, WV: Author, 1997. 135p.

1880

Crawford, Charles Wann. *1880 Census Carter County, Kentucky*. Muscatine, IA: Author, 1997. 222p.

Casey County
1810

Black, Patty. *Casey County, Kentucky Census, 1810, 1820, 1830, 1840*. Hustonville, KY: Author. 69p.

Burns, Annie Walker. *Third Census of the United States, County of Casey, State of Kentucky*. Washington, DC: Author, 1935. 31p.

Cornett, Faye Bastin Paevey. *People of Early Casey County, Kentucky, Deed Index and Will Index of Casey County, 1806-1850; Revolutionary War and War of 1812 Soldiers, 1810 Casey County Census; Coleman, Durham, and Hatter 1806-1910 Genealogy, and Selected Other Family Histories*. Liberty, KY: Corbett, 1992. 263p.

McGhee, Lucy Kate. *United States Census, 1810, Barren County, Kentucky, County Seat Glasgow; Campbell County, Kentucky, County Seat, Newport and Alexandria; Caldwell County, Kentucky, County Seat, Princeton; Casey County, Kentucky, County Seat Liberty*. Washington, DC: Author, 1958. 130p. 1820

1820-1840

Black, Patty. *Casey County, Kentucky Census, 1810, 1820, 1830, 1840*. Hustonville, KY: Author. 69p.

1850

Thomas, Gladys Cotham. *1850 Census of Casey County, Kentucky*. Liberty, KY: Bicentennial Heritage Corp., 1979. 152p.

1860

Austin, Bert A. *1860 Census Casey County, Kentucky*. Liberty, KY: Casey County Public Library, 1990. 156p.

Black, Patty. *Mortality Schedule of Casey County, Kentucky for 1860, 1870, 1880 Census Years*. Hustonville, KY: Author. 13p.

1870

Black, Patty. *Casey County, Kentucky 1870 Census and Mortality Schedule*. Hustonville, KY: Author. 139p.

_____. *Mortality Schedule of Casey County, Kentucky for 1860, 1870, 1880 Census Years*. Hustonville, KY: Author. 13p.

1880

Black, Patty. *Mortality Schedule of Casey County, Kentucky for 1860, 1870, 1880 Census Years*. Hustonville, KY: Author. 13p.

Sanders, Carol Lee. *1880 Casey County, Kentucky Census*. Blue Ash, OH: Author, 1986. 310p.

Christian County
1810

Burns, Annie Walker. *Third Census of the United States, Christian County, Kentucky*. Washington, DC: Author, 1934. 56p.

Simmons, Don. *Christian County, Kentucky, Census of 1810*. Melber, KY: Simmons Historical Pub., 1974. 33p.

1820, 1830

Christian County, Kentucky Census Records, 1820, 1830, 1840. Hopkinsville, KY: Christian County Genealogical Society, 1995. 85p.

1840

Christian County, Kentucky Census Records, 1820, 1830, 1840. Hopkinsville, KY: Christian County Genealogical Society, 1995. 85p.

Federal Census of Christian County, Kentucky, 1860. Madisonville, KY: Hopkins County Genealogical Society, 1978. 324p.

1850

Jones, Thomas Harold. *Christian County, Kentucky 1850 Federal Census*. Edwardsville, IL: Author, 1968. 258p.

Sistler, Barbara. *1850 Census, South West Kentucky, Counties of Christian, Logan, Simpson, Todd, Trigg and Warren*. Nashville, TN: Byron Sistler & Associates, 1993. 442p.

Whillhite, A.B. *Christian County, Kentucky 1850 Federal Census*. Russellville, KY: Author. 215p.

1860

Federal Census of Christian County, Kentucky 1860. Madisonville, KY: Hopkins County Genealogical Society, 1978. 324p.

Willhite, A.B. *Christian County, Kentucky 1860 Federal Census*. Russellville, KY: Author, 1994. 142p.

1870

Willhite, A.B. *Christian County, Kentucky 1870 Federal Census*. Russellville, KY: Author, 1995. 278p.

Willis, Laura. *Christian County, Kentucky Census of 1870*. Hopkinsville, KY: Christian County Genealogical Society, 1996. 323p.

1880

Cain, Shirley West. *1880 Federal Census of Christian County, Kentucky*. Hopkinsville, KY: Author, 1981. 395p.

1900

Willhite, A.B. *Christian County, Kentucky 1900 Federal Census*. Russellville, KY: Author, 1996. 704p.

Clark County

1840

Norris, William V. *1840 U.S. Census, Clark County, Kentucky, (From U.S. Census Microfilm), and Index, with Slave Summary*. Jacksonville, FL: Author, 1983. pp. 257-297.

1860

Norris, William V. *1860 U.S. Census, Clark County, Kentucky*. Jacksonville, FL: Author, 1981, 1983. 165p.

Clay County

1810

McGhee, Lucy Kate. *Clay County, Kentucky 1810 Census*. Author, 1959. 28p.

Welch, James E. *Clay County 1810 and 1820*. Oneida, KY: Mountaineer Press, 1986. 57p.

1820

Welch, James E. *Clay County 1810 and 1820*. Oneida, KY: Mountaineer Press, 1986. 57p.

1850

Sistler, Barbara. *1850 Census, Southeastern Kentucky, Counties of Clay, Harlan, Knox, Laurel, Pulaski, Russell, Wayne and Whitley*. Nashville, TN: Byron Sistler & Associates, 1993. 412p.

Welch, James Edward, Sr. *Clay County, 1850*. Oneida, KY: Mountaineer Press, 1984. 122p.

1860

Welch, James E. *Clay County 1860*. Oneida, KY: Mountaineer Press, 1984. 152p.

1870

Welch, James Edward, Sr. *Clay County, 1870*. Ozark, MO: Yates Pub. Co., 1986. 196p.

1880

Welch, James E. *Clay County 1880*. Oneida, KY: Mountaineer Press, 1988. 291p.

1900

1900 Clay County, Kentucky Census. Manchester, KY: Clay County Genealogical and Historical Society, 1997. 2 vols.

1910

Collett, Beverly. *Clay County 1910*. Ozark, MO: Dogwood Print, 1988. 2 vols.

1920

1920 Clay County, Kentucky Census. Manchester, KY: Clay County Genealogical and Historical Society, 1997. 2 vols.

Clinton County

1840

Farmer, Jane Frogue, and Frances E. Parker. *Clinton County, Kentucky Census, 1840-1850, Abstracts and Index*. Sun City, CA: Authors, 1978. 55p.

1850

Farmer, Jane Frogue, and Frances E. Parker. *Clinton County, Kentucky Census, 1840-1850, Abstracts and Index*. Sun City, CA: Authors, 1978. 55p.

Peden, Eva Coe. *1850 Census of Clinton County, Kentucky*. Glasgow, KY: Gorin Genealogical Pub., 1992. 61p.

Sistler, Barbara. *1850 Census, South Central Kentucky, Counties of Adair, Allen, Barren, Clinton, Cumberland and Monroe*. Nashville, TN: Byron Sistler & Associates, 1992. 382p.

1860

Farmer, Jane Frogue, and Frances E. Parker. *Clinton County, Kentucky Census, 1860, Abstracts and Index*. Sun City, CA: Author, 1979. 71p.

Smith, Randolph N. *Federal Mortality Census Schedules, 1860, 1870, 1880, Abstract and Index, Adair, Clinton, Cumberland, Metcalfe, Monroe Counties, Kentucky*. Burkesville, KY: Author, 1975. 51p.

1870

Farmer, Jane Frogue, and Frances E. Parker. *Clinton County, Kentucky Census, 1870, Abstracts and Index*. Sun City, CA: Authors, 1980. 83p.

Smith, Randolph N. *Federal Mortality Census Schedules, 1860, 1870, 1880, Abstract and Index, Adair, Clinton, Cumberland, Metcalfe, Monroe Counties, Kentucky*. Burkesville, KY: Author, 1975. 51p.

1880

Farmer, Jane Frogue, and Frances E. Parker. *Clinton County, Kentucky Census, 1880, Abstracts and Index*. Sun City, CA: Authors, 1982. 117p.

Smith, Randolph N. *Federal Mortality Census Schedules, 1860, 1870, 1880, Abstract and Index, Adair, Clinton, Cumberland, Metcalfe, Monroe Counties, Kentucky*. Burkesville, KY: Author, 1975. 51p.

1900

Farmer, Jane Frogue, and Frances E. Parker. *Clinton County, Kentucky Census, 1900, Abstracts and Index*. Sun City, CA: Author, 1985. 143p.

1910

Conner, Eva Burchett. *1910 Census, Clinton County, Kentucky, Abstract and Index*. Albany, KY: Author, 1988. 155p.

Crittenden County

1850

Hammers, Marian G. *1850 Crittenden County, Kentucky Census*. Madisonville, KY: Hopkins County Genealogical Society, 1976. 124p.

Sistler, Barbara. *1850 Census, North West Kentucky Counties of Crittenden, Daviess, Henderson, Hopkins, Muhlenberg, Ohio and Union*. Nashville, TN: Byron Sistler & Associates, 1994. 497p.

1860

Crittenden County, Kentucky 1860 Federal Census. Marion, KY: Crittenden County Genealogical Society, 1994. 190p.

1870

The Crittenden County, Kentucky 1870 Federal Census. Marion, KY: Crittenden County Genealogical Society, 1996. 235p.

Drake, Ruth Crider. *Crittenden County, Kentucky 1870 Federal Census*. Ault, CO: Author. 124p.

1880

Drennan, Juanita Walker. *Crittenden County, Kentucky Census of 1880*. Ledbetter, KY: Author, 1992. 248p.

1910

Drennan, Juanita Walker. *Crittenden County, Kentucky Census of 1910*. Ledbetter, KY: Author, 1994. 254p.

Cumberland County
1800-1840

Smith, Randolph N. *Cumberland County, Kentucky Census Index and Abstracts, 1800-1850*. Burkesville, KY: Author, 1975. 232p.

1850

Peden, Sue Elender. *1850 Cumberland County, Kentucky Alphabetical Census*. Glasgow, KY: Gorin Genealogical Pub., 1992. 146p.

Sistler, Barbara. *1850 Census, South Central Kentucky, Counties of Adair, Allen, Barren, Clinton, Cumberland and Monroe*. Nashville, TN: Byron Sistler & Associates, 1992. 382p.

Smith, Randolph N. *Cumberland County, Kentucky Census Index and Abstracts, 1800-1850*. Burkesville, KY: Author, 1975. 232p.

1860

Smith, Randolph N. *1860 Census, Cumberland County, Kentucky Abstract and Index*. Burkesville, KY: Author, 1975. 150p.

_____. *Federal Mortality Census Schedules, 1860, 1870, 1880, Abstract and Index, Adair, Clinton, Cumberland, Metcalfe, Monroe Counties, Kentucky*. Burkesville, KY: Author, 1975. 51p.

1870

Smith, Randolph N. *1870 Census, Cumberland County, Kentucky Abstract and Index*. Burkesville, KY: Author, 1975. 189p.

_____. *Federal Mortality Census Schedules, 1860, 1870, 1880, Abstract and Index, Adair, Clinton, Cumberland, Metcalfe, Monroe Counties, Kentucky*. Burkesville, KY: Author, 1975. 51p.

1880

Smith, Randolph N. *1880 Census, Cumberland County, Kentucky Abstract and Index*. Burkesville, KY: Author, 1975. 225p.

_____. *Federal Mortality Census Schedules, 1860, 1870, 1880, Abstract and Index, Adair, Clinton, Cumberland, Metcalfe, Monroe Counties, Kentucky*. Burkesville, KY: Author, 1975. 51p.

1900

Smith, Randolph N. *1900 Census, Cumberland County, Kentucky Abstract and Index*. Burkesville, KY: Author, 1979. 289p.

1910

Smith, Randolph N. *1910 Census, Cumberland County, Kentucky Abstract and Index*. Burkesville, KY: Author, 1984. 281p.

Daviess County
1850

Daviess County, Kentucky, 1850 Census, Annotated. Owensboro, KY: West-Central Kentucky Family Research Assn., 1974. 147p.

McDowell, Samuel Riley. *A Surname Index to the 1850 Federal Population Census of Kentucky, Daviess, Edmonson and Estill Counties*. Richland, IN: Author, 1975. 50p.

Sistler, Barbara. *1850 Census, North West Kentucky Counties of Crittenden, Daviess, Henderson, Hopkins, Muhlenberg, Ohio and Union*. Nashville, TN: Byron Sistler & Associates, 1994. 497p.

USGenWeb Census Project. Kentucky, 1850 Daviess County.
ftp://ftp.rootsweb.com/pub/census/ky/daviess/1850/

1860

McManaway, Robert D. *Daviess County, Kentucky 1860 Census*. Utica, KY: Author, 1988. 196p.

1870

McManaway, Robert D. *1870 Census of Daviess County, Kentucky*. Utica, KY: Author, 1980. 294p.

1880

Ford, Nancy H. *Daviess County, Kentucky, 1880 Census*. Owensboro, KY: Cook & McDowell Publications, 1980. 614p.

1920

Stanley, Mary. *Daviess County, Kentucky 1920 Census*. Online Database. Orem, UT: Ancestry.com, Inc., 1999.

http://www.ancestry.com

Edmonson County

Rajewich, Kathleen. *Population Census of Edmonson County, Kentucky*. Brownsville, KY: Author, 1995. 2 vols.

1850

Edmonson County, Kentucky 1850 Census. Owensboro, KY: West-Central Kentucky Family Research Assn., 1978. 84p.

McDowell, Samuel Riley. *A Surname Index to the 1850 Federal Population Census of Kentucky, Daviess, Edmonson and Estill Counties*. Richland, IN: Author, 1975. 50p.

USGenWeb Census Project. Kentucky, 1850 Edmonson County.

ftp://ftp.rootsweb.com/pub/census/ky/edmonson/1850/

Elliott County

1870

Barker, Charles A. *1870 Elliott County, Kentucky Census*. Ashland, KY: Author, 1988. 116p.

1880

Barker, Charles A. *1880 Elliott County, Kentucky Census*. Ashland, KY: Author, 1988. 174p.

Estill County

1810

Edwards, Eva Dean, and Sandra Winkler Rose. *Estill County, Kentucky Census, 1810 through 1820*. Irvine, KY: Edwards & Rose Genealogical Heritage, 1986. 58p.

Hubble, Anna Joy Munday. *Estill County, Kentucky, 1810 Census*. Whitefish, MT: Author, 1978. 8p.

1820

Edwards, Eva Dean, and Sandra Winkler Rose. *Estill County, Kentucky Census, 1810 through 1820*. Irvine, KY: Edwards & Rose Genealogical Heritage, 1986. 58p.

Estill County, Kentucky 1820 Census. Twain Harte, CA: G-N Publications, 1985. 8p.

Hubble, Anna Joy Munday. *Estill County, Kentucky, 1820 Census*. Whitefish, MT: Author, 1979. 23p.

1830, 1840

Edwards, Eva Dean, and Sandra Winkler Rose. *Estill County, Kentucky Census, 1830 through 1840*. Irvine, KY: Edwards & Rose Genealogical Heritage, 1986. pp. 59-171.

1850

Edwards, Eva Dean, and Sandra Winkler Rose. *Estill County, Kentucky Census, 1850*. Irvine, KY: Edwards & Rose Genealogical Heritage, 1986. pp. 172-395.

Hubble, Anna Joy Munday. *Estill County, Kentucky, 1850 Census*. Whitefish, MT: Author, 1980. 56p.

McDowell, Samuel Riley. *A Surname Index to the 1850 Federal Population Census of Kentucky, Daviess, Edmonson and Estill Counties*. Richland, IN: Author, 1975. 50p.

1860

Crowe, James. *The 1860 Census of Estill County*. Irvine, KY: Estill County Tribune, 1981, 1985. 74p.

1870

Patrick, Tracy R. *The 1870 Federal Census of Estill County, Kentucky*. Irvine, KY: Estill County Tribune, 1984, 1992. 78p.

1880

Patrick, Tracy R. *The 1880 Federal Census of Estill County, Kentucky*. Irvine, KY: Estill County Tribune, 1987, 1992. 86p.

1890

Patrick, Tracy R. *1890 Soldier Census of Powell and Estill Counties Kentucky*. Irvine, KY: Estill County Tribune. 9p.

1900

Puckett, Edward. *The 1900 Federal Census of Estill County, Kentucky*. Irvine, KY: Estill County Tribune, 1992. 87p.

1910

Pitts, Mabel. *1910 Census, Estill County, Kentucky*. Irvine, KY: Estill County Tribune, 1987. 119p.

1920

Wise, William E. *1920 Estill County, Kentucky, Census*. Ravenna, KY: Author, 1995. 166p.

Fayette County

1810

Lawson, Rowena. *Fayette County, Kentucky, 1810-1840 Censuses*. Bowie, MD: Heritage Books, 1986. 148p.

1820

Fayette County, Kentucky 1820 Census. Twain Harte, CA: G-N Publications, 1985. 21p.

Lawson, Rowena. *Fayette County, Kentucky, 1810-1840 Censuses*. Bowie, MD: Heritage Books, 1986. 148p.

1850

1850 Fayette County, Kentucky Census. Lexington, KY: Fayette County Genealogical Society, 1992. 289p.

McDowell, Samuel Riley. *A Surname Index to the 1850 Federal Population Census of Kentucky Fayette and Fleming Counties*. Richland, IN: Author, 1975. 86p.

Fleming County

1850

Cowan, Jane. *Fleming County, Kentucky, 1850 Census, Microcopy 432, Household Number, Roll 199, District I, Pages 1-141, Index, District II Pages 1-68, Index*. Author, 1991. Unpgd.

_____, and Bill Courtney. *Fleming County, Kentucky, 1850 Census*. Author, 1986. Unpgd.

McDowell, Samuel Riley. *A Surname Index to the 1850 Federal Population Census of Kentucky Fayette and Fleming Counties*. Richland, IN: Author, 1975. 86p.

1870

Cowan, Jane. *Fleming County, Kentucky 1870 Ninth Census of United States, Microcopy 593, Roll 461*. Author, 1996. 622p.

1880

Grady, Evie Ruth Hill. *Blacks Living in Fleming County, Kentucky, Federal Census, 1880*. Cincinnati, OH: Author, 1983. 34p.

1900

Grady, Evie Ruth Hill. *Blacks Living in Fleming County, Kentucky, Federal Census, 1900*. Cincinnati, OH: Author, 1983. 34p.

Floyd County

1810

Floyd County, Kentucky 1810 Census. Helena, MT: Rosemarie Spradlin, 1985. 22p.

1820

Mullins, Betty R. *1820 Federal Census Floyd County, Kentucky*. Clintwood, VA: Author, 1989. 57p.

1840

Clinton, Mrs. Bob G. *1840 Census of Floyd County, Kentucky*. East Alton, IL: Author, 1982. 23p.

Wireman, Connie Arnett. *1840 Floyd County, Kentucky Census*. Salyersville, KY: Magoffin County Historical Society, 1991. 63p.

1850

Parrish, Verle Hamilton. *1850 Census of Floyd County, Kentucky*. Stamping Ground, KY: Author. 130p.

1860

Shepard, Clarence E. *1860 Census, Floyd County, Kentucky*. Dayton, OH: Author, 1977. 79p.

1870

Shepard, Clarence E. *1870 Census, Floyd County, Kentucky*. Dayton, OH: Author, 1977. 86p.

1880

Parrish, Verle Hamilton. *1880 Census of Floyd County, Kentucky*. Prestonsburg, KY: Skeens, 1988. 226p.

Wireman, Connie Arnett. *1840 Floyd County, Kentucky Census*. Salyersville, KY: Magoffin County Historical Society, 1991. 242p.

Franklin County
1810-1840
Lawson, Rowena. *Franklin County, Kentucky, 1810-1840 Censuses*. Bowie, MD: Heritage Books, 1986. 73p.
1860
Gantley, Anita Chinn. *Franklin County, Kentucky, 1860 Census*. Frankfort, KY: Author, 1982. 2 vols.

Fulton County
1850
Simmons, Don. *1850 Census of Fulton County, Kentucky*. Melber, KY: Simmons Historical Pub., 1983. 72p.
Sistler, Barbara. *1850 Census, Western Kentucky, Counties of Ballard, Caldwell, Calloway, Fulton, Graves, Hickman, Livingston, Marshall and McCracken*. Nashville, TN: Byron Sistler & Associates, 1993. 452p.
1860
Livingston, Donald L. *Fulton County, Kentucky 1860 Census*. Fulton, KY: Fulton County Genealogical Society, 1989. 104p.
1870
Fulton County Census 1870. Fulton, KY: Fulton County Genealogical Society, 1993. 274p.

Gallatin County
1820
Gallatin County, Kentucky 1820 Census. Twain Harte, CA: G-N Publications, 1985. 11p.

Garrard County
1810
Hubble, Anna Joy Munday. *Garrard County, Kentucky, 1810 Census*. Whitefish, MT: Author, 1984. 15p.
1820-1840
Vockery, Bill, and Kathy Vockery. *1820, 1830, 1840 Federal Census of Garrard County, Kentucky*. Richmond, KY: Authors, 1990. 143p.
1850
Cornelius, Wilma J. *Garrard County, Kentucky, Census of 1850*. Lancaster, KY: Author. Unpgd.
McDowell, Samuel Riley. *A Surname Index to the 1850 Federal Census of Kentucky, Garrard, Grant and Graves Counties*. Hartford, KY: Author, 1977. 64p.
1860
Vockery, Bill, and Kathy Vockery. *1860 Federal Census Garrard County, Kentucky*. Richmond, KY: Authors, 1989. 103p.
1870
Kurtz, J. M. *Garrard County, Kentucky, Census of 1870*. Lancaster, KY: Garrard County Historical Society, 1990. 229p.
1880
Kurtz, Harold J. *1880 Census of Garrard County, Kentucky*. Lancaster, KY: Garrard County Historical Society, 1989. 281p.
1900
Kurtz, Harold J. *1900 Census of Garrard County, Kentucky*. Lancaster, KY: Garrard County Historical Society, 1992. 302p.

Grant County
1820
Grant County, Kentucky 1820 Census. Twain Harte, CA: G-N Publications, 1986. 5p.

1830

Bickers, Robert L. *Grant County, Kentucky Heads of Families 1830 Census*. Hyrum, UT: Author, 1993. 16p.

1850

McDowell, Samuel Riley. *A Surname Index to the 1850 Federal Census of Kentucky, Garrard, Grant and Graves Counties*. Hartford, KY: Author, 1977. 64p.

1860

Osborne, Lee K. *Transcript of the Grant County, Kentucky 1860 Census*. San Jose, CA: Arrow Software, 1986. 193p.

Graves County

1830

Simmons, Don. *Jackson Purchase, 1830 Census of Kentucky Consisting of the First Four Original Counties of Calloway, Graves, Hickman and McCracken*. Murray, KY: Author, 1974 Unpgd.

1840

Simmons, Don. *Graves County, Kentucky Census of 1840*. Melber, KY: Simmons Historical Pub., 1971. 24p.

1850

McDowell, Samuel Riley. *A Surname Index to the 1850 Federal Census of Kentucky, Garrard, Grant and Graves Counties*. Hartford, KY: Author, 1977. 64p.

Simmons, Don. *Census of Graves County, Kentucky, 1850*. Melber, KY: Simmons Historical Pub., 1954. 209p.

Sistler, Barbara. *1850 Census, Western Kentucky, Counties of Ballard, Caldwell, Calloway, Fulton, Graves, Hickman, Livingston, Marshall and McCracken*. Nashville, TN: Byron Sistler & Associates, 1993. 452p.

1860

Dennis, Lennie C. *1860 Grayson County, Kentucky, Census, Eighth Census of the United States, Copied from Microfilm #653, Roll #369, Vol. #9 (1-537), Graves and Grayson Counties*. Lewisburg, KY: Author, 1986. 125p.

Record, Pat. *Graves County, Kentucky Census of 1860*. Benton, KY: Author, 1979. 207p.

Simmons, Don. *Graves County, Kentucky, Agricultural Census of 1860*. Melber, KY: Simmons Historical Pub., 1990. 56p.

Smith, Barbara Ramsey. *Graves County, Kentucky Expanded Census of 1860*. Melber, KY: Simmons Historical Pub., 1997. 247p.

1870

Simmons, Don. *Graves County, Kentucky Census of 1870*. Melber, KY: Simmons Historical Pub., 1983. 327p.

1880

Austin, Dorothy, Anna Laura Griffith, and Don Simmons. *Graves County, Kentucky Census of 1880*. Melber, KY: Simmons Historical Pub., 1987. 269p.

1910

Austin, Dorothy, and Anna Laura Griffith. *Graves County, Kentucky Census of 1910*. Melber, KY: Simmons Historical Publications, 1992. 343p.

1920

Austin, Dorothy. *Graves County, Kentucky, Census of 1920*. Mayfield, KY: Graves County Genealogical Society, 1997. 369p.

Grayson County

1810

Nacke, Judy. *Grayson County, Kentucky, 1810-1840 Censuses and 1815, 1825 & 1834 Tax Lists*. Utica, KY: McDowell Publications, 1986. 83p.

USGenWeb Census Project. Kentucky, 1810 Grayson County.

ftp://ftp.rootsweb.com/pub/census/ky/grayson/1810/

1820-1840

Nacke, Judy. *Grayson County, Kentucky, 1810-1840 Censuses and 1815, 1825 & 1834 Tax Lists*. Utica, KY: McDowell Publications, 1986. 83p.

1850

Ford, Nancy H. *Grayson County, Kentucky, 1850 Census*. Owensboro, KY: West-Central Kentucky Family Research Assn., 1974. 97p.

McDowell, Samuel Riley. *A Surname Index to the 1850 Federal Population Census of Kentucky*. Richland, IN: Author, 1974. 72p.

1860

Dennis, Lennie C. *1860 Grayson County, Kentucky, Census, Eighth Census of the United States, Copied from Microfilm #653, Roll #369, Vol. #9 (1-537), Graves and Grayson Counties*. Lewisburg, KY: Author, 1986. 125p.

1880

Dennis, Lennie C. *Grayson County, Kentucky 1880 Federal Census*. Utica, KY: McDowell Publications, 1990. 243p.

1900

Dennis, Lennie C. *Grayson County, Kentucky, 1900 Federal Census*. Lewisburg, KY: Author, 1995. 274p.

Green County
1850

Lind, Ruth Marcum. *United States Census, Green County, Kentucky, 1850-1860*. Dinuba, CA: Author, 1975. 300p.

McDowell, Samuel Riley. *A Surname Index to the 1850 Federal Population Census of Kentucky*. Richland, IN: Author, 1974. 72p.

1860

Lind, Ruth Marcum. *United States Census, Green County, Kentucky, 1850-1860*. Dinuba, CA: Author, 1975. 300p.

1870

Wilson, DeWayne. *1870 Census Green County, Kentucky*. Campbellsville, KY: Author, 1995. 205p.

Greenup County
1820

Hardiman, Richard. *United States Census, 1820 Greenup County, Kentucky*. Author, 1981. 18p.

1840

Hardiman, Richard. *United States Census, 1840 Greenup County, Kentucky*. Author, 1983. 28p.

1850

Jackson, Evelyn. *1850 Census of Greenup County, Kentucky*. Ashland, KY: Eastern Kentucky Genealogical Society, 1988. 300p.

1880

Schlaudt, Billee Hammond. *1880 Census Greenup County, Kentucky*. Houston, TX: Author, 1986. 420p.

Hancock County
1850

Ford, Nancy H. *Hancock County, Kentucky, 1850 Census*. Owensboro, KY: West-Central Kentucky Family Research Assn., 1974. 50p.

McDowell, Samuel Riley. *A Surname Index to the 1850 Federal Population Census of Kentucky*. Richland, IN: Author, 1974. 72p.

1860

Phillips, Claribel. *1860 Census of Hancock County, Kentucky*. Utica, KY: McDowell Pub., 1982. 133p.

1870

McManaway, Robert D. *1870 Census of Hancock County, Kentucky*. Utica, KY: McDowell Publications, 1982. 81p.

1880

Phillips, Claribel. *Hancock County, Kentucky 1880 Federal Census*. Hawesville, KY: Genealogical Society of Hancock County, 1991. 240p.

1900

Bruner, Harlan Keith. *1900 Federal Census of Hancock County Kentucky*. Hawesville, KY: Author, 1992. 260p.

1920

Bruner, Harlan Keith. *1920 Federal Census of Hancock County Kentucky*. Hawesville, KY: Author, 1993. 292p.

Hardin County

1850

Crabb, Katharine Sturgeon. *1850 Census of Hardin County, Kentucky*. Vine Grove, KY: Ancestral Trails Historical Society, 1979. 236p.

McDowell, Samuel Riley. *A Surname Index to the 1850 Federal Population Census of Kentucky*. Richland, IN: Author, 1975. 64p.

1870

Deardorff, Jennie. *1870 Census of Hardin County, Kentucky*. Vine Grove, KY: Ancestral Trails Historical Society, 1983. 254p.

Harlan County

1820

Fee, Holly. *1820 Harlan County, Kentucky Census and Tax List Annotated*. Harlan, KY: Genealogical Society of Harlan County, Kentucky, 1984. 50p.

1850

Hiday, Nellie C. *1850 Census, Harlan County, Kentucky*. Thomson, IL: Heritage House, 1972. 45p.

McDowell, Samuel Riley. *A Surname Index to the 1850 Federal Population Census of Kentucky*. Richland, IN: Author, 1975. 64p.

Sistler, Barbara. *1850 Census, Southeastern Kentucky, Counties of Clay, Harlan, Knox, Laurel, Pulaski, Russell, Wayne and Whitley*. Nashville, TN: Byron Sistler & Associates, 1993. 412p.

1860

Fee, Holly. *1860 Harlan Census, Transcription, Notation & Cross-reference to Harlan Connections*. Harlan, KY: Footprints Publications & Research, 1989. 103p.

1870

Nolan, Gertrude, and Janette Nolan. *The 1870 Harlan County Census*. Evansville, IN: Whipporwill Pub., 1987. 195p.

1880

Fee, Holly. *1880 Census of Harlan Census*. Harlan, KY: Footprints Publications & Research, 1987. 91p.

1900

Fee, Holly. *1900 Census of Harlan County, Kentucky*. Harlan, KY: Footprints Publications & Research, 1992. 193p.

Pope, Helen. *1900 Census of Harlan County, Kentucky*. London, KY: Author, 1982. 240p.

1910

Trail, Kathryn Howard. *1910 Census of Harlan County*. Harlan, KY: Harlan Heritage Seekers. 239p.

Harrison County

1810

Schunk, John Frederick. *1810 Census, Harrison County, Kentucky*. Wichita, KS: Author, 1986. 21p.

1850

McDowell, Samuel Riley. *A Surname Index to the 1850 Federal Population Census of Kentucky*. Richland, IN: Author, 1975. 64p.

Hart County

1820

Hart County, Kentucky 1820 Census. Twain Harte, CA: G-N Pubns., 1985. 8p.

1830

Gorin, Sandra Kaye Laughery. *1830 Hart County, Kentucky Census*. Glasgow, KY: Gorin Genealogical Pub., 1995. 26p.

1840

Gorin, Sandra Kaye Laughery. *1840 Hart County, Kentucky Census*. Glasgow, KY: Gorin Genealogical Pub., 1995. 33p.

1850

Crabb, Katharine Sturgeon. *1850 Census of Hart County, Kentucky*. Vine Grove, KY: Ancestral Trails Historical Society, 1979. 140p.

McDowell, Samuel Riley. *A Surname Index to the 1850 Federal Population Census of Kentucky*. Richland, IN: Author, 1975. 71p.

1870

Hawley, Carlos. *Hart County, Kentucky 1870 Census*. Greenville, IL: Bond County Genealogical Society, 1996. 228p.

1880

Hawley, Carlos. *Hart County, Kentucky 1880 Census*. Greenville, IL: Bond County Genealogical Society, 1996. 315p.

1900

Hawley, Carlos. *Hart County, Kentucky 1900 Census*. Greenville, IL: Bond County Genealogical Society, 1996. 338p.

Henderson County

1850

Sistler, Barbara. *1850 Census, North West Kentucky Counties of Crittenden, Daviess, Henderson, Hopkins, Muhlenberg, Ohio and Union*. Nashville, TN: Byron Sistler & Associates, 1994. 497p.

1870

McManaway, Robert D. *Henderson County, Kentucky, 1870 Census*. Owensboro, KY: Cook-McDowell Publications, 1981. 241p.

Henry County

1860

Winburn, C. Marie. *1860 Census, Henry County, Kentucky*. Eminence, KY: Author, 1996. 100p.

1870

Winburn, C. Marie. *1870 Census, Henry County, Kentucky*. Eminence, KY: Author, 1997. 150p.

Hickman County

1830

Simmons, Don. *Jackson Purchase, 1830 Census of Kentucky Consisting of the First Four Original Counties of Calloway, Graves, Hickman and McCracken*. Murray, KY: Author, 1974 Unpgd.

1840

Simmons, Don. *1840 Census of Hickman County, Kentucky*. Murray, KY: Author, 1974. 34p.

1850

McDowell, Samuel Riley. *A Surname Index to the 1850 Federal Population Census of Kentucky*. Richland, IN: Author, 1977. 85p.

Simmons, Don. *1850 Census of Hickman County, Kentucky*. Murray, KY: Author, 1972. 87p.

Sistler, Barbara. *1850 Census, Western Kentucky, Counties of Ballard, Caldwell, Calloway, Fulton, Graves, Hickman, Livingston, Marshall and McCracken*. Nashville, TN: Byron Sistler & Associates, 1993. 452p.

1860

Simmons, Don, and Dorothy Austin. *Hickman County, Kentucky Census of 1860*. Melber, KY: Simmons Historical Pub., 1987. 101p.

1870

Goodgion, Roland E., and Ernestine Goodgion. *1870 Census, Hickman County, Kentucky*. Murray, KY: Authors, 1976. 176p.

Hopkins County
1810-1840

1810, 1820, 1830 and 1840 Census of Hopkins County, Kentucky. Madisonville, KY: Hopkins County Genealogical Society, 1970. 180p.

1850

Cox, Evelyn May, and Lalla F. McCulley. *1850 Census of Hopkins County, Kentucky*. Authors. 2 vols.

McDowell, Samuel Riley. *A Surname Index to the 1850 Federal Population Census of Kentucky*. Richland, IN: Author, 1975. 64p.

Sistler, Barbara. *1850 Census, North West Kentucky Counties of Crittenden, Daviess, Henderson, Hopkins, Muhlenberg, Ohio and Union*. Nashville, TN: Byron Sistler & Associates, 1994. 497p.

1860

Potter, Dorothy Williams. *1860 Federal Census of Hopkins County, Kentucky*. Tullahoma, TN: Author, 1967. Unpgd.; 1974. 144p.

1870

Federal Census Hopkins County, Kentucky 1870. Madisonville, KY: Hopkins County Genealogical Society, 1973. 353p.

1880

1880 Federal Census, Hopkins County, Kentucky. Madisonville, KY: Hopkins County Genealogical Society, 1974. 557p.

Jackson County
1860

Cunagin, Judy Murray. *1860 Jackson County, Kentucky Census, with Surname Index*. Indianapolis, IN: Author, 1990. Unpgd.

Sasser, June. *1860 Jackson County, Kentucky Census*. McKee, KY: Author, 1981. 35p.

Jefferson County
1810-1830

Louisville and Jefferson County, Kentucky Census 1810, 1820, 1830. Louisville, KY: Louisville Genealogical Society, 1991. 281p.

1850

1850 Census of Jefferson County, Kentucky. Louisville, KY: Louisville Genealogical Society, 1993. 270p.

1850 Census of Louisville, Districts 1 & 2, Jefferson County, Kentucky. Louisville, KY: Louisville Genealogical Society, 1995. 444p.

McDowell, Samuel Riley. *A Surname Index to the 1850 Federal Population Census of Kentucky*. Richland, IN: Author, 1975. 64p.

Sistler, Barbara. *1850 Census, Jefferson County, Kentucky*. Nashville, TN: Byron Sistler & Associates, 1996. 613p.

Jessamine County
1810

Hubble, Anna Joy Munday. *Jessamine County, Kentucky 1810 Census, Including Surnames of the 1850 and 1880 Census of Jessamine County, Kentucky*. Whitefish, MT: Author, 1984. 20p.

1850

Hubble, Anna Joy Munday. *Jessamine County, Kentucky 1810 Census, Including Surnames of the 1850 and 1880 Census of Jessamine County, Kentucky*. Whitefish, MT: Author, 1984. 20p.

Vockery, Bill, and Kathy Vockery. *1850 Federal Census of Jessamine County*. Richmond, KY: Authors, 1990. 94p.

1860

Vockery, Bill, and Kathy Vockery. *1860 Federal Census of Jessamine County*. Richmond, KY: Authors. 79p.

1880

Hubble, Anna Joy Munday. *Jessamine County, Kentucky 1810 Census, Including Surnames of the 1850 and 1880 Census of Jessamine County, Kentucky*. Whitefish, MT: Author, 1984. 20p.

Johnson County

1850

Ward, Billie Edyth. *1850 Federal Census of Johnson County, Kentucky*. Paintsville, KY: Johnson County Historical Society, 1990. 39p.

1860

Ward, Billie Edyth. *1860 Federal Census of Johnson County, Kentucky*. Paintsville, KY: Johnson County Historical Society, 1992. 49p.

1900

Salyer, Ruth. *1900 Census, Johnson County, Kentucky*. Paintsville, KY: Johnson County Historical Society, 1981. 293p.

1910

Salyer, Ruth. *1910 Census, Johnson County, Kentucky*. Staffordsville, KY: Author. 418p.

1920

Salyer, Ruth. *1920 Census, Johnson County, Kentucky*. Staffordsville, KY: Author, 1993. 285p.

Kenton County

Wieck, Dorothy L. *Census Index for Kenton County, Kentucky*. Covington, KY: Kenton County Historical Society, 1983.

1820

Worrel, Stephen William. *Northern Kentucky Towns Census of 1819-1820*. Falls Church, VA: Author, 1993. 12p.

1840

Gladden, Sanford Charles. *Heads of Families, Census of 1840 Kenton County, Kentucky*. Covington, KY: Kenton County Historical Society, 1965. 26p.

1850

Gladden, Sanford Charles. *Heads of Families, Census of 1850 Kenton County, Kentucky*. Covington, KY: Kenton County Historical Society, 1966. 58p.

1860

Wieck, Dorothy L. *1860 Census Index for Kenton County, Kentucky*. Covington, KY: Kenton County Historical Society, 1983. 156p.

1870

Wieck, Dorothy L. *1870 Census Index for Kenton County, Kentucky*. Covington, KY: Author, 1986. 204p.

1880

Gladden, Sanford Charles, and Dorothy L. Wieck. *Kenton County, Kentucky Census of 1880*. Covington, KY: Kenton County Historical Society, 1990. 2 vols.

1900

Harris, Theodore H.H. *Afro-American Residents of Kenton County, Kentucky, the 1900 Kenton County, Kentucky Census*. Covington, KY: Author, 1991. 17p.

Knott County

1900

Perry, Sherry Mate. *1900 Census Knott County, Kentucky*. Whitesburg, KY: Letcher County Historical & Genealogical Society. 268p.

Shepard, Clarence E. *Index to 1900 Census of Knott County, Kentucky*. Dayton, OH: Author, 1988. 21p.

1910

Perry, Sherry. *Knott County, Kentucky 1910 Census*. Oberlin, OH: Author. 257p.

1920

Knott County, Kentucky 1920 Census. Whitesburg, KY: Letcher County Historical and Genealogical Society. 325p.

Knox County
1840

Logan, Virginia J., and Maxine H. Jones. *1840 Knox County, Kentucky, Census*. Louisville, KY: Knox County Genealogical Society, 1980. 47p.

1850

McDowell, Samuel Riley. *A Surname Index to the 1850 Federal Population Census of Kentucky*. Hartford, KY: Author, 1977. 63p.

Sistler, Barbara. *1850 Census, Southeastern Kentucky, Counties of Clay, Harlan, Knox, Laurel, Pulaski, Russell, Wayne and Whitley*. Nashville, TN: Byron Sistler & Associates, 1993. 412p.

1860

Jones, Maxine H. *1860 Knox County, Kentucky, Census*. Louisville, KY: Knox County Genealogical Society, 1982. 75p.

1870

Gallagher, Glen. *1870 United States Census Knox County, Kentucky*. Kingwood, TX: Author, 1984. 50p.

Jones, Maxine H. *1870 Knox County, Kentucky, Census*. Louisville, KY: Knox County Genealogical Society, 1984. 141p.

1880

Jones, Maxine H. *1880 Knox County, Kentucky, Census*. Louisville, KY: Knox County Genealogical Society, 1986. 190p.

1890

Masterson, Elizabeth Hammons. *1890 Knox County, Kentucky Census*. Louisville, KY: Knox County Genealogical Society, 1980. 19p.

1900

Jones, Maxine H. *1900 Knox County, Kentucky, Census*. Louisville, KY: Knox County Genealogical Society, 1988. 2 vols.

Larue County
1850

Jones, Mary Josephine. *Larue County, Kentucky 1850 Census*. Vine Grove, KY: Ancestral Trails Historical Society, 1982. 97p.

McDowell, Samuel Riley. *A Surname Index to the 1850 Federal Population Census of Kentucky*. Hartford, KY: Author, 1977. 63p.

1860

The Annotated 1860 Larue County Census. Vine Grove, KY: Ancestral Trails Historical Society, 1993. 110p.

1880

Benningfield, Edward. *Larue County, Kentucky, 1880 Census*. Utica, KY: McDowell Pub., 1984. 163p.

Laurel County
1830

Ferguson, Penny. *Laurel County, Kentucky Federal Census, 1830*. London, KY: Laurel County, Kentucky Historical Society, 1986. 13p.

_____. *Laurel County, Kentucky Federal Census, 1830 & 1840*. London, KY: Laurel County, Kentucky Historical Society, 1986. 28p.

1840

Ferguson, Penny. *Laurel County, Kentucky Federal Census, 1830 & 1840*. London, KY: Laurel County, Kentucky Historical Society, 1986. 28p.

1850

McDowell, Samuel Riley. *A Surname Index to the 1850 Federal Population Census of Kentucky*. Hartford, KY: Author, 1977. 63p.

Pope, Geneva Green, Sadie Wells Stidham, and Wilma Parker Johnson. *Seventh Census of the United States, 1850 Laurel County, Kentucky, with Marriages and Vital Statistics*. London, KY: Laurel County Historical Society, 1984. 93p.

Sistler, Barbara. *1850 Census, Southeastern Kentucky, Counties of Clay, Harlan, Knox, Laurel, Pulaski, Russell, Wayne and Whitley*. Nashville, TN: Byron Sistler & Associates, 1993. 412p.

1860

Pope, Geneva Green, and Wilma Parker Johnson. *Eighth Census of the United States, 1860, Laurel County, Kentucky*. London, KY: Laurel County Historical Society, 1983. 130p.

1870

Proffitt, Deborah. *1870 Laurel County, Kentucky Census*. London, KY. Laurel County Historical Society, 1984. 161p.

1880

Proffitt, Deborah. *1880 Laurel County, Kentucky Census*. London, KY. Author, 1987. 205p.

1890

Proffitt, Deborah. *1890 Laurel County, Kentucky Special Federal Census*. London, KY: Author, 1987. 22p.

1900

Hopper, Carol F. *12th Census of Population, 1900, Kentucky, Vol. 46, Laurel County, Enumeration Districts 147-159*. Lily, KY: Author, 1987. 387p.

1910

Thirteenth Census of the United States 1910 Laurel County, Kentucky. London, KY: Laurel County Historical Society, 1988. 600p.

1920

1920 Laurel County, Kentucky Census. London, KY: Laurel County Historical Society, 1996. Unpgd.

Lawrence County

1840

Clinton, Mrs. Bob G. *1840 Census of Lawrence County, Kentucky*. East Alton, IL: Author, 1982. 17p.

1850

McDowell, Samuel Riley. *A Surname Index to the 1850 Federal Population Census of Kentucky*. Hartford, KY: Author, 1977. 63p.

1860

Muncy, Opal Mae Hughes. *1860 Federal Census of Lawrence County, Kentucky*. Louisa, KY: Author, 1983. 172p.

1870

Gallagher, Glen. *1870 United States Census Lawrence County, Kentucky*. Decatur, AL: Author, 1984. 53p.

Muncy, Opal Mae Hughes. *1870 Federal Census of Lawrence County, Kentucky*. Louisa, KY: Author, 1982. 202p.

1900

Muncy, Opal Mae Hughes. *1900 Federal Census of Lawrence County, Kentucky*. Louisa, KY: Author, 1986. 470p.

1910

Muncy, Opal Mae Hughes. *1910 Federal Census of Lawrence County, Kentucky*. Louisa, KY: Author. 488p.

Lee County

1870

Seal, Myrna Gulley. *Lee County, Kentucky Records 1870 Census*. Connersville, IN: Author, 1986. 48p.

Workman, Velma Ballard. *Lee and Letcher County, Kentucky Census, 1870*. Minden City, MI: G&H Enterprise, 1984. 140p.

1880

Hayes, Margaret Millar. *Lee County, Kentucky 1880 Annotated Census, Including the 1880 Mortality Schedule*. Bowie, MD: Heritage Books, 1993. 165p.

Leslie County
1880
Cunagin, Judy Murray. *1880 Leslie County, Kentucky Census Record with Head of Household Index*. Indianapolis, IN: Author, 1992. 106p.
1900
Sizemore, Darlene. *1900 Leslie County, Kentucky Census, Transcribed from National Archives Microfilm T623, Roll #538*. Dayton, OH: Author, 1992. 255p.
1910
Brinkmeier, Hermina. *1910 Census, Leslie County, Kentucky*. Author, 1997. Unpgd.

Letcher County
1850
Griffith, Dorothy Amburgey. *1850 & 1880 U.S. Censuses, Letcher County, Kentucky*. St. Louis, MO: Genealogical Research & Publications, 1977. 49p.
_____. *1850 United States Census Letcher County, Kentucky*. Clintwood, VA: Mullins Printing, 1970. 24p.
McDowell, Samuel Riley. *A Surname Index to the 1850 Federal Population Census of Kentucky*. Hartford, KY: Author, 1977. 63p.
Mullins, Billie Hill. *Letcher County, Kentucky 1850 Federal Census*. Logan, WV: Author, 1997. 65p.
USGenWeb Census Project. Kentucky, 1850 Letcher County.
ftp://ftp.rootsweb.com/pub/census/ky/letcher/1850/
1860
Horne, Helen P. *1860 Letcher County, Kentucky, Federal Census, with Every-name Index*. Hazard, KY: Author, 1983. 62p.
1870
Hall, Elizabeth Anne. *1870 Census of Letcher County, Kentucky*. Clintwood, VA: Mullins Printing, 1989. 76p.
Johnson, Wilma Parker. *1870 U.S. Census, Letcher County, Kentucky*. Whitesburg, KY: Letcher County Historical and Genealogical Society, 1995. 166p.
Workman, Velma Ballard. *Lee and Letcher County, Kentucky Census, 1870*. Minden City, MI: G&H Enterprise, 1984. 140p.
1880
Griffith, Dorothy Amburgey. *1850 & 1880 U.S. Censuses, Letcher County, Kentucky*. St. Louis, MO: Genealogical Research & Publications, 1977. 49p.
_____, and Ruby Rigor Herrick. *Indexed Transcription of 1880 United States, Letcher County, Kentucky Including Knott County*. St. Louis, MO: St. Louis Genealocial Society. 64p.
Johnson, Wilma Parker. *1880 U.S. Census, Letcher County, Kentucky*. Whitesburg, KY: Letcher County Historical and Genealogical Society, 1995. 270p.
1900
Cunagin, Judy Murray. *1900 Letcher County, Kentucky Census, with Heads of Household Index*. Indianapolis, IN: Author, 1991. 2 vols.
1910
Perry, Zandra Addington. *1910 Letcher County, Kentucky Census*. Ermine, KY: Author. 239p.

Lewis County
1850
McDowell, Samuel Riley. *A Surname Index to the 1850 Federal Population Census of Kentucky*. Richland, IN: Author, 1975. 32p.
1860
1860 Federal Census of Lewis County, Kentucky. Vanceburg, KY: Lewis County Historical Society. 174p.
Logan, Bruce Elmer. *Federal Census of Lewis County Kentucky 1860*. Wheelersburg, OH: Author, 1996. Unpgd.
1870
Lewis County, Kentucky 1870 Census Record. Vanceburg, KY: Lewis County Historical Society. 167p.
Workman, Velma Ballard. *Lewis County, Kentucky, 1870 Census Record*. Canton, MI: Author, 1984. 165p.

1880

Workman, Velma Ballard. *Lewis County, Kentucky, 1880 Census Record*. Canton, MI: Author, 1984. 244p.

1900

1900 Federal Census of Lewis County, Kentucky. Vanceburg, KY: Lewis County Historical Society.

1910

1910 Federal Census of Lewis County, Kentucky. Vanceburg, KY: Lewis County Historical Society. 370p.

Lincoln County

1810

Burns, Annie Walker. *Third Census of the United States, Lincoln County, Kentucky*. Washington, DC: Author, 1936. 21p.

Hubble, Anna Joy Munday. *Lincoln County, Kentucky 1810 Census*. Whitefish, MT: Author. 9p.

1820

Langley, Elizabeth B. *Lincoln County, Kentucky 1820 Census*. Billings, MO: Author, 1968. 11p.

1850

Dunn, Shirley, Dorothy A. Griffith, and Marilyn A. Haag. *Lincoln County, Kentucky Marriages, 1850-1900 & 1850 U.S. Census*. St. Louis, MO: Genealogical Research and Productions, 1980. 132p.

McDowell, Samuel Riley. *A Surname Index to the 1850 Federal Population Census of Kentucky*. Richland, IN: Author, 1975. 32p.

Livingston County

1810

Simmons, Don. *Livingston County, Kentucky Census of 1810*. Melber, KY: Author, 1974. 14p.

1820, 1830

Simmons, Don. *Livingston County, Kentucky Census of 1820, 1830*. Melber, KY: Author, 1983. 37p.

1840

Clinton, Bob G., *1840 Census of Livingston County, Kentucky*. East Alton, IL: Author, 1985. 32p.

Hunt, Phyllis Driskill. *Livingston County, Kentucky Census, 1840*. Ledbetter, KY: Author, 1992. 56p.

1850

Drennan, Juanita Walker. *1850 Census of Livingston County, Kentucky*. Smithland, KY: Author, 1980. 126p.

McDowell, Samuel Riley. *A Surname Index to the 1850 Federal Population Census of Kentucky*. Richland, IN: Author, 1975. 32p.

Sistler, Barbara. *1850 Census, Western Kentucky, Counties of Ballard, Caldwell, Calloway, Fulton, Graves, Hickman, Livingston, Marshall and McCracken*. Nashville, TN: Byron Sistler & Associates, 1993. 452p.

1860

Drennan, Juanita Walker. *1860 Census of Livingston County, Kentucky*. Smithland, KY: Author, 1987. 131p.

_____. 2nd ed. Ledbetter, KY: Author, 1991. 140p.

1870

Hunt, Phyllis Driskill, and Juanita Walker Drennan. *1870 Census, Livingston County, Kentucky*. Ledbetter, KY: Authors, 1991. 183p.

1880

Drennan, Juanita Walker. *Livingston County, Kentucky Census of 1880*. Ledbetter, KY: Author, 1992. 231p.

1900

Drennan, Juanita Walker, and Phyllis Driskill Hunt. *Livingston County, Kentucky Census of 1900*. Ledbetter, KY: Author, 1992. 227p.

1920

Drennan, Juanita Walker. *Livingston County, Kentucky Census of 1920*. Ledbetter, KY: Author, 1994. 211p.

Logan County

1820, 1830

Simmons, Don, and Laura Willis. *Logan County, Kentucky Census and Tax Lists, 1820 and 1830*. Melber, KY: Simmons Historical Publications, 1995. 140p.

1840

Vanderpool, Montgomery. *1840 Logan County, Kentucky Census*. Russellville, KY: Author, 1985. 195p.

1850

McDowell, Samuel Riley. *A Surname Index to the 1850 Federal Population Census of Kentucky*. Richland, IN: Author, 1982. 35p.

Sistler, Barbara. *1850 Census, South West Kentucky, Counties of Christian, Logan, Simpson, Todd, Trigg and Warren*. Nashville, TN: Byron Sistler & Associates, 1993. 442p.

Todd, James W. *Logan County, Kentucky, 1850 Census*. Owensboro, KY: West-Central Kentucky Family Research Assn., 1978. 180p.

Vanderpool, Montgomery. *1850 Logan County, Kentucky Census*. Russellville, KY: Author, 1988. 171p.

1860

Willhite, A. B. *Logan County, Kentucky 1860 Federal Census*. Russellville, KY: Author. 143p.

1870

Vanderpool, Montgomery. *1870 Logan County, Kentucky Census*. Russellville, KY: Author, 1989. 507p.

1880

Vanderpool, Montgomery. *1880 Logan County, Kentucky Census*. Russellville, KY: Author, 1986. 543p.

1900

Vanderpool, Montgomery. *1900 Logan County, Kentucky Census*. Russellville, KY: Author, 1990. 579p.

1920

Vanderpool, Montgomery. *1920 Logan County, Kentucky Census*. Russellville, KY: Author, 1994. 185p.

Louisville (Jefferson County)
1810-1830

Louisville and Jefferson County, Kentucky Census 1810, 1820, 1830. Louisville, KY: Louisville Genealogical Society, 1991. 281p.

1850

McDowell, Samuel Riley. *A Surname Index to the 1850 Federal Population Census of Kentucky, City of Louisville Districts 3 and 4*. Hartford, KY: Author, 1977. 127p.

1850 Census of Louisville, Districts 1 & 2, Jefferson County, Kentucky. Louisville, KY: Louisville Genealogical Society, 1995. 444p.

Lyon County
1860

Jones, Thomas Harold. *Lyon County, Kentucky 1860 Federal Census*. Owensboro, KY: Cook McDowell Pub., 1980. 97p.

McCracken County
1830

Simmons, Don. *Jackson Purchase, 1830 Census of Kentucky Consisting of the First Four Original Counties of Calloway, Graves, Hickman and McCracken*. Murray, KY: Author, 1974 Unpgd.

1840

Simmons, Don. *The 1840 Census of McCracken County, Kentucky*. Murray, KY: Simmons Historical Pub., 1972. 19p.

1850

McDowell, Samuel Riley. *A Surname Index to the 1850 Federal Population Census of Kentucky*. Richland, IN: Author, 1982. 35p.

Simmons, Don. *The 1850 Census of McCracken County, Kentucky*. Murray, KY: Simmons Historical Pub., 1974. 108p.

Sistler, Barbara. *1850 Census, Western Kentucky, Counties of Ballard, Caldwell, Calloway, Fulton, Graves, Hickman, Livingston, Marshall and McCracken*. Nashville, TN: Byron Sistler & Associates, 1993. 452p.

McCreary County
1920

Whitis, Alma Coffey. *McCreary County, Kentucky 1920 Census*. Apple Valley, CA: Bork, 1995. 480p.

McLean County
1860

McLean County, Kentucky, 1860 Census, Annotated. Owensboro, KY: West-Central Kentucky Family Research Assn., 1978. 108p.

1870

McManaway, Robert D. *McLean County, Kentucky, 1870 Census*. Owensboro, KY: West Central Kentucky Family Research, 1979. 84p.

1880

McManaway, Robert D. *McLean County, Kentucky, 1880 Census*. Utica, KY: McDowell, 1988. 153p.

Madison County
1810

Hubble, Anna Joy Munday. *Madison County, Kentucky, 1810 Census, this Census Was Transcribed from the Microfilm of the Original 1810 Census of Madison County, Kentucky, a Surname Index Has Been Added for Your Convenience*. Whitefish, MT: Author, 1976. 28p.

Schunk, John Frederick. *1810 Census, Madison County, Kentucky*. Wichita, KS: Author, 1986. 46p.

1820

Hubble, Anna Joy Munday. *Madison County, Kentucky, 1820 Census*. Whitefish, MT: Author, 1977. 35p.

1830

Hubble, Anna Joy Munday. *Madison County, Kentucky, 1830 Census*. Whitefish, MT: Author, 1978. 37p.

1840

Hubble, Anna Joy Munday. *Madison County, Kentucky, 1840 Census*. Whitefish, MT: Author, 1979. 33p.

1850

Hubble, Anna Joy Munday. *Madison County, Kentucky, 1850 Census, This Census Was Transcribed from the Microfilm of the Original 1850 Census of Madison County, Kentucky, a Surname Index Has Been Added for Your Convenience*. Whitefish, MT: Author, 1976. 227p.

McDowell, Samuel Riley. *A Surname Index to the 1850 Federal Population Census of Kentucky*. Richland, IN: Author, 1982. 35p.

1860

Hubble, Anna Joy Munday. *Madison County, Kentucky, 1860 Census*. Whitefish, MT: Author, 1985. 108p.

1870

Vockery, Bill, and Kathy Vockery. *1870 Federal Census of Madison County, Kentucky*. Richmond, KY: Authors, 1979. 244p.

1880

Grady, Evie Ruth Hill. *Inhabitants of Madison County, Kentucky, 1880 Federal Census*. Cincinnati, OH: Author, 1985. 4 vols.

Magoffin County
1860

Magoffin County, Kentucky 1860 Census. Salyersville, KY: Magoffin County Historical Society, 1990. 63p.

Shepard, Clarence E *1860 Census, Magoffin County, Kentucky*. Dayton, OH: Author, 1977. 39p.

1870

Shepard, Clarence E *1870 Census, Magoffin County, Kentucky*. Dayton, OH: Author, 1977. 48p.

Wireman, Connie Arnett. *1870 Magoffin County, Kentucky Census*. Salyersville, KY: Magoffin County Historical Society. 1993. 130p.

1880

Shepard, Clarence E *1880 Census, Magoffin County, Kentucky*. Dayton, OH: Author, 1977. 163p.

1890

1890 Special Census, Surviving Union Veterans and Widows of the Civil War in Magoffin County, Kentucky. Salyersville, KY: Magoffin County Historical Society, 1982. 13p.

1900

Dolan, Katie Prater Arnett, David Risner, and Connie Arnett Wiremen. *1900 Magoffin County, Kentucky Census.* Salyersville, KY: Magoffin County Historical Society, 1984. 288p.

1910

Preston, Nadine Hamilton, and Connie Arnett Wireman. *The 1910 Magoffin County, Kentucky, Census.* Salyersville, KY: Magoffin County Historical Society, 1986. 320p.

1920

Wireman, Connie Arnett. *1920 Magoffin County, Kentucky Census.* Salyersville, KY: Magoffin County Historical Society, 1992. 355p.

Marion County

1860

Benningfield, Arland W. *1860 Marion County, Kentucky Federal Census.* Louisville, KY: Author, 1996. 158p.

1880

Bertram, Dianna F. *1880 Federal Census, Marion County, Kentucky.* Louisville, KY: Author, 1991. 404p.

Marshall County

1850

Simmons, Don. *Marshall County, Kentucky, Census of 1850.* Melber, KY: Simmons Historical Pub., 1984. 83p.

Sistler, Barbara. *1850 Census, Western Kentucky, Counties of Ballard, Caldwell, Calloway, Fulton, Graves, Hickman, Livingston, Marshall and McCracken.* Nashville, TN: Byron Sistler & Associates, 1993. 452p.

USGenWeb Census Project. Kentucky, 1870 Marshall County.

ftp://ftp.rootsweb.com/pub/census/ky/marshall/1870/

1860

Simmons, Don. *Marshall County, Kentucky, Census of 1860.* Melber, KY: Simmons Historical Pub., 1986. 127p.

1870

Simmons, Don. *Marshall County, Kentucky, Census of 1870.* Melber, KY: Simmons Historical Pub., 1985. 168p.

1880

Lewis, Elvira Breezeel. *Marshall County, Kentucky Families of 1880.* Benton, KY: Author, 1992. 245p.

1900

Dismore, Evelyn Pfingston. *Marshall County, Kentucky Census 1900.* Gilbertsville, KY: Author, 1989. 281p.

1910

Lee, Leslie C. *1910 Marshall County, Kentucky Census.* Gilbertsville, KY: Author, 1991. 2 vols.

1920

Dismore, Evelyn Pfingston. *Marshall County, Kentucky Census 1920.* Gilbertville, KY: Author, 1994. 171p.

Martin County

1880

Ward, Billie Edyth. *Martin County Census, 1880, Revised and Annotated.* Boons Camp, KY: Author, 1987. 58p.

1900

Ward, Billie Edyth. *Martin County Federal Census for 1900.* Boons Camp, KY: Author, 1987. 112p.

1910

Ward, Billie Edyth. *Federal Census of Martin County Census, 1910.* Boons Camp, KY: Author. 62p.

Mason County
1850

Kendall, Margaret M. G. *Irish in the 1850 Mason County, Kentucky Federal Census*. Maysville, KY: Mason County Museum, 1980. 30p.

1870

Grady, Evie Ruth Hill. *Blacks Living in Mason County, Kentucky, Federal Census, 1870*. Cincinnati, OH: Author, 1983. 33p.

1880

Grady, Evie Ruth Hill. *1880 Mason County, Kentucky Federal Census, Black Inhabitants*. Cincinnati, OH: Author, 1984. 87p.

1900

Grady, Evie Ruth Hill. *1900 Mason County, Kentucky Federal Census, Black Inhabitants*. Cincinnati, OH: Author, 1984. 83p.

Meade County
1850

McDowell, Samuel Riley. *A Surname Index to the 1850 Federal Population Census of Kentucky*. Richland, IN: Author, 1974. 67p.

Sims, Shelly. *1850 Census, Meade County, Kentucky*. Vine Grove, KY: Ancestral Trails Historical Society, 1984. 101p.

1860

Boucher, Mrs. Avery. *1860 Census, Meade County, Kentucky, Microcopy 653, Roll 386*. Vine Grove, KY: Ancestral Trails Historical Society, 1978. 118p.

1870

Miller, Wathena Kennedy. *Meade County, Kentucky, 1870 Census*. Vine Grove, KY: Ancestral Trails Historical Society, 1991. 201p.

1880

Newton, Jane Meador. *Meade County, Kentucky 1880 Census*. Vine Grove, KY: Ancestral Trails Historical Society, 1995. 239p.

Menifee County
1870-1890

Ingram, Barbara W. *Menifee County Census 1870, 1880, 1890*. Frenchburg, KY: Author, 1985, 1989. 63p.

1900

Sorrell, Irma, and Barbara W. Ingram. *1900 Menifee County Census*. Frenchburg, KY: Author, 1982. 98p.

1910

Ingram, Barbara W. *Menifee County Census 1910*. Frenchburg, KY: Author, 1989. 63p.

Mercer County
1789, 1800

Yenne, Betty J. *Mercer County, Kentucky Census Records 1789, 1800, 1820 and Tax List 1795*. Fort Wayne, KY: Fort Wayne Public Library, 1965. 90p.

1810

Hubble, Anna Joy Munday. *Mercer County, Kentucky, 1810 Census*. Whitefish, MT: Author, 1987. 19p.

McGhee, Lucy Kate. *Mercer County, Kentucky 1810 United States Census*. Harrodsburg, KY: Author. 104p.

1820

Yenne, Betty J. *Mercer County, Kentucky Census Records 1789, 1800, 1820 and Tax List 1795*. Fort Wayne, KY: Fort Wayne Public Library, 1965. 90p.

1850

McDowell, Samuel Riley. *A Surname Index to the 1850 Federal Population Census of Kentucky*. Richland, IN: Author, 1974. 67p.

Sanders, Faye Sea. *1850 Federal Census, Mercer County, Kentucky*. Louisville, KY: Author, 1983. 131p.

_____. *Washington, Mercer and Anderson Counties, Kentucky Mortality Schedules for 1850, 1860, 1870, 1880. Also Deaths Reported in 1874-1878 Vital Statistics*. Louisville, KY: Author. 61p.

1860

Sanders, Faye Sea. *1860 Federal Census, Mercer County, Kentucky*. Louisville, KY: Author, 1988. 121p.

_____. *Washington, Mercer and Anderson Counties, Kentucky Mortality Schedules for 1850, 1860, 1870, 1880. Also Deaths Reported in 1874-1878 Vital Statistics*. Louisville, KY: Author. 61p.

1870

Sanders, Faye Sea. *Washington, Mercer and Anderson Counties, Kentucky Mortality Schedules for 1850, 1860, 1870, 1880. Also Deaths Reported in 1874-1878 Vital Statistics*. Louisville, KY: Author. 61p.

Webb, Donna Jean. *1870 Federal Census Mercer County, Kentucky*. Lexington, KY: Author, 1993. 173p.

1880

Sanders, Faye Sea. *Washington, Mercer and Anderson Counties, Kentucky Mortality Schedules for 1850, 1860, 1870, 1880. Also Deaths Reported in 1874-1878 Vital Statistics*. Louisville, KY: Author. 61p.

Webb, Donna Jean. *1880 Federal Census Mercer County, Kentucky*. Lexington, KY: Author, 1994. 199p.

1900

Webb, Donna Jean. *1900 Federal Census Mercer County, Kentucky*. Lexington, KY: Author, 1995. 231p.

1910

Webb, Donna Jean. *1910 Federal Census, Mercer County, Kentucky*. Lexington, KY: Author, 1995. 249p.

Metcalfe County
1860

Edwards, Dennis L. *Metcalfe County, Kentucky, 1860 Census*. Edmonton, KY: Author, 1982. 109p.

Smith, Randolph N. *Federal Mortality Census Schedules, 1860, 1870, 1880, Abstract and Index, Adair, Clinton, Cumberland, Metcalfe, Monroe Counties, Kentucky*. Burkesville, KY: Author, 1975. 51p.

1870

Aiken, Gladys Lee. *1870 Census Metcalfe County, Kentucky*. Lawrence, KS: Author, 1976. 214p.

Smith, Randolph N. *Federal Mortality Census Schedules, 1860, 1870, 1880, Abstract and Index, Adair, Clinton, Cumberland, Metcalfe, Monroe Counties, Kentucky*. Burkesville, KY: Author, 1975. 51p.

1880

Smith, Randolph N. *Federal Mortality Census Schedules, 1860, 1870, 1880, Abstract and Index, Adair, Clinton, Cumberland, Metcalfe, Monroe Counties, Kentucky*. Burkesville, KY: Author, 1975. 51p.

Monroe County
1820

Phillips, Oma Dee. *1820 Federal Census, Monroe County, Kentucky*. Lamesa, TX: Author, 1976. 13p.

Headrick, Marcella P. *1820 Cenus*. Tompkinsville, KY: Author. 17p.

1850

McDowell, Samuel Riley. *A Surname Index to the 1850 Federal Population Census of Kentucky*. Richland, IN: Author, 1974. 67p.

Sistler, Barbara. *1850 Census, South Central Kentucky, Counties of Adair, Allen, Barren, Clinton, Cumberland and Monroe*. Nashville, TN: Byron Sistler & Associates, 1992. 382p.

Willhite, A. B. *1850 Federal Census, Monroe County, Kentucky*. Russellville, KY: Author, 1997. 130p. (4396 Coopertown Road, Russellville, KY 42276-9806).

1860

Smith, Randolph N. *Federal Mortality Census Schedules, 1860, 1870, 1880, Abstract and Index, Adair, Clinton, Cumberland, Metcalfe, Monroe Counties, Kentucky*. Burkesville, KY: Author, 1975.

1870

Aiken, Gladys Lee. *1870 Census Monroe County, Kentucky*. Lawrence, KS: Author, 1976. 212p.

Headrick, Marcella. *1870 Monroe County Census, Head of Families*. Tompkinsville, KY: Author. 63p.

Smith, Randolph N. *Federal Mortality Census Schedules, 1860, 1870, 1880, Abstract and Index, Adair, Clinton, Cumberland, Metcalfe, Monroe Counties, Kentucky*. Burkesville, KY: Author, 1975.

1880

Headrick, Marcella P. *1880 Census*. Tompkinsville, KY: Author. 432p.

Smith, Randolph N. *Federal Mortality Census Schedules, 1860, 1870, 1880, Abstract and Index, Adair, Clinton, Cumberland, Metcalfe, Monroe Counties, Kentucky*. Burkesville, KY: Author, 1975.

Montgomery County
1810
Dunn, Thelma M. *Montgomery County, Kentucky County Clerk Tax Assessment Records, 1806-1807-1808-1809-1810 & the 1810 U.S. Census Record*. Atoka, TN: Author, 1996. 62p.
Lawson, Rowena. *Montgomery County, Kentucky, 1810-1840 Censuses*. Bowie, MD: Heritage Books, 1985. 60p.
1820-1840
Lawson, Rowena. *Montgomery County, Kentucky, 1810-1840 Censuses*. Bowie, MD: Heritage Books, 1985. 60p.
1850
Lawson, Rowena. *Montgomery County, Kentucky, 1850 Census*. Bowie, MD: Heritage Books, 1986. 70p.
McDowell, Samuel Riley. *A Surname Index to the 1850 Federal Population Census of Kentucky*. Richland, IN: Author, 1975. 55p.
1870
Aiken, Gladys Lee. *1870 Census Montgomery County, Kentucky*. Lawrence, KS: Author, 1976. 208p.

Morgan County
1830, 1840
Lawson, Rowena. *Morgan County, Kentucky, 1830-1850 Censuses*. Bowie, MD: Heritage Books, 1987. 90p.
Nickell, Joe, and Ella T. Nickell. *Morgan County, Kentucky Genealogical Source Book, with the 1830-1840 Censuses and More, Including Index of Confederate Pension Applications, a Complete List of Kentucky Counties with Dates of Formation and Parent Counties and Data on Vital Statistics, Libraries, County Records, Published Genealogies ...* . West Liberty, KY: Authors, 1980. 75p.
1850
Lawson, Rowena. *Morgan County, Kentucky, 1830-1850 Censuses*. Bowie, MD: Heritage Books, 1987. 90p.
McDowell, Samuel Riley. *A Surname Index to the 1850 Federal Population Census of Kentucky*. Richland, IN: Author, 1975. 55p.
Schaller, Alice. *Morgan County, Kentucky 1850 Census*. Casheon, WI: Author, 1993. 82p.
1870
Minix, Sharroll K. *1860 Morgan County, Kentucky Census*. Salyersville, KY: Magoffin County Historical Society, 1984. 230p.
1900
Lewis, Rexford Gardner. *Morgan County, Kentucky 1900 Census*. Buffalo Grove, IL: Author. Unpgd.
1910
Lewis, Rexford Gardner. *Morgan County, Kentucky 1910 Census*. Buffalo Grove, IL: Author. Unpgd.

Muhlenberg County
1850
Hammers, Marian Georgia Duvall. *1850 Census of Muhlenberg County, Kentucky*. Madisonville, KY: Hopkins County Genealogical Society, 1969. 136p.
McDowell, Samuel Riley. *A Surname Index to the 1850 Federal Population Census of Kentucky*. Richland, IN: Author, 1975. 55p.
Sistler, Barbara. *1850 Census, North West Kentucky Counties of Crittenden, Daviess, Henderson, Hopkins, Muhlenberg, Ohio and Union*. Nashville, TN: Byron Sistler & Associates, 1994. 497p.
1860
Hammers, Marian G. *1860 Muhlenberg County, Kentucky Census*. Madisonville, KY: Hopkins County Genealogical Society, 1978. 98p.
1870
Hammers, Marian G. *1870 Census, Muhlenberg County, Kentucky*. Muhlenberg, KY: Muhlenberg County Genealogical Society, 1983. 129p.

1880

Hammers, Marian G., Brenda Collier Doss, and Kathy Elaine Kemp. *1880 Muhlenberg County, Kentucky Census*. Central City, KY: Muhlenberg County Genealogical Society, 1987. 259p.

1900

Doss, Brenda Collier. *Muhlenberg County, Kentucky 1900 Census*. Greeenville, KY: Author, 1988. 315p.

Muncie County
1880

Muncy, Opal Mae Hughes. *1880 Federal Census of Lawrence County, Kentucky*. Louisa, KY: Author, 1980. 301p.

Nelson County
1810-1830

Lawson, Rowena. *Nelson County, Kentucky 1810-1840 Censuses*. Bowie, MD: Heritage Books, 1984. 40p.

1840

1840 Federal Census, Nelson County, Kentucky. Bardstown, KY: Nelson County Genealogical Round Table, 1984. 99p.

Lawson, Rowena. *Nelson County, Kentucky 1810-1840 Censuses*. Bowie, MD: Heritage Books, 1984. 40p.

1850

Lawson, Rowena. *Nelson County, Kentucky, 1850 Census*. Bowie, MD: Heritage Books, 1985. 88p.

McDowell, Samuel Riley. *A Surname Index to the 1850 Federal Population Census of Kentucky*. Richland, IN: Author, 1975. 79p.

1860

Nelson County, Kentucky 1860 Federal Census. Bardstown, KY: Nelson County Genealogical Society. 197p.

Swigart, Katharine L. *1860 Federal Census, Nelson County, Kentucky*. Cuyahoga Falls, OH: Author, 1971. 2 vols.

1870

McManaway, Robert D. *Nelson County, Kentucky, 1870 Census*. Utica, KY: McDowell Pub., 1985. 193p.

1880

1880 Federal Census, Nelson County, Kentucky. Bardstown, KY: Nelson County Genealogical Society, 1986. 413p.

Nicholas County
1810

Lawson, Rowena. *Nicholas County, Kentucky 1810-1840 Censuses*. Bowie, MD: Heritage Books, 1984. 55p.

USGenWeb Census Project. Kentucky, 1810 Nicholas County.

ftp://ftp.rootsweb.com/pub/census/ky/nicholas/1810/

1820-1840

Lawson, Rowena. *Nicholas County, Kentucky 1810-1840 Censuses*. Bowie, MD: Heritage Books, 1984. 55p.

USGenWeb Census Project. Kentucky, 1840 Nicholas County.

ftp://ftp.rootsweb.com/pub/census/ky/nicholas/1840/

1850

Lawson, Rowena. *Nicholas County, Kentucky, 1850 Census*. Bowie, MD: Heritage Books, 1983. 92p.

McDowell, Samuel Riley. *A Surname Index to the 1850 Federal Population Census of Kentucky*. Richland, IN: Author, 1975. 79p.

Sharp, John L. *Nicholas County, Kentucky 1850 Census*. Kuttawa, KY: Author, 1978. 186p.

USGenWeb Census Project. Kentucky, 1850 Nicholas County.

ftp://ftp.rootsweb.com/pub/census/ky/nicholas/1850/

Ohio County
1810

Lawson, Rowena. *Ohio County, Kentucky 1810-1840 Censuses*. Bowie, MD: Heritage Books, 1984. 40p.

USGenWeb Census Project. Kentucky, 1810 Ohio County.
ftp://ftp.rootsweb.com/pub/census/ky/ohio/1810/
1820
Lawson, Rowena. *Ohio County, Kentucky 1810-1840 Censuses.* Bowie, MD: Heritage Books, 1984. 40p.
USGenWeb Census Project. Kentucky, 1820 Ohio County.
ftp://ftp.rootsweb.com/pub/census/ky/ohio/1820/
1830
Lawson, Rowena. *Ohio County, Kentucky 1810-1840 Censuses.* Bowie, MD: Heritage Books, 1984. 40p.
USGenWeb Census Project. Kentucky, 1830 Ohio County.
ftp://ftp.rootsweb.com/pub/census/ky/ohio/1830/
1840
Lawson, Rowena. *Ohio County, Kentucky 1810-1840 Censuses.* Bowie, MD: Heritage Books, 1984. 40p.
USGenWeb Census Project. Kentucky, 1840 Ohio County.
ftp://ftp.rootsweb.com/pub/census/ky/ohio/1840/
1850
Lawson, Rowena. *Ohio County, Kentucky, 1850 Census.* Bowie, MD: Heritage Books, 1984. 87p.
McDowell, Samuel Riley. *A Surname Index to the 1850 Federal Population Census of Kentucky.* Richland, IN: Author, 1975. 79p.
Ohio County, Kentucky, 1850 Census. Owensboro, KY: West-Central Kentucky Family Research Assn., 1974. 127p.
Sistler, Barbara. *1850 Census, North West Kentucky Counties of Crittenden, Daviess, Henderson, Hopkins, Muhlenberg, Ohio and Union.* Nashville, TN: Byron Sistler & Associates, 1994. 497p.
USGenWeb Census Project. Kentucky, 1850 Ohio County.
ftp://ftp.rootsweb.com/pub/census/ky/ohio/1850/
1860
O'Brien, Bobbie Hamilton. *Ohio County Kentucky 1860 Census, an in Depth Study of the Census and Marriage Records of Ohio County.* Owensboro, KY: Cook & McDowell Pubs., 1981. 262p.
1870
McManaway, Robert D. *Ohio County, Kentucky 1870 Census.* Utica, KY: McDowell Pub., 1982. 178p.

Oldham County
1850
McDowell, Samuel Riley. *A Surname Index to the 1850 Federal Population Census of Kentucky.* Richland, IN: Author, 1982. 33p.

Owen County
1850
McDowell, Samuel Riley. *A Surname Index to the 1850 Federal Population Census of Kentucky.* Richland, IN: Author, 1982. 33p.

Owsley County
1850
McDowell, Samuel Riley. *A Surname Index to the 1850 Federal Population Census of Kentucky.* Richland, IN: Author, 1982. 33p.
Smith, Robert L. *Owsley County, Kentucky, 1850 Census.* Cincinnati, OH: Author, 1995. 100p.
1860
McGraw, Karen Caudill. *1860 Owsley County Census.* Cincinnati, OH: Author. 60p.
Smith, Robert L. *Owsley County, Kentucky, 1860 Census.* Cincinnati, OH: Author, 1995. 146p.
1870
Seal, Myrna Gulley. *Owsley County, Kentucky, Records, 1870 Census.* Connersville, IN: Author, 1986. 54p.
Smith, Robert L. *Owsley County, Kentucky, 1870 Census.* Cincinnati, OH: Author, 1995. 120p.

1880

Hayes, Margaret Millar. *Owsley County, Kentucky, 1880 Annotated Census.* Bowie, MD: Heritage Books, 1994. 218p.

_____. _____. 1996. 220p.

Helton, Helen C. *1880 Census Owsley County, Kentucky.* Akron, OH: Author, 1978. 61p.

Smith, Robert L. *Owsley County, Kentucky, 1880 Census.* Cincinnati, OH: Author, 1995. 158p.

1900

Smith, Robert L. *Owsley County, Kentucky, 1900 Census.* Cincinnati, OH: Author, 1995. 188p.

1910

Smith, Robert L. *Owsley County, Kentucky 1910 Census.* Cincinnati, OH: Author, 1995. 203p.

1920

Smith, Robert L. *Owsley County, Kentucky 1920 Census.* Cincinnati, OH: Author, 1920. 206p.

Pendleton County
1810

Schunk, John Frederick. *1810 Census, Pendleton County, Kentucky.* Wichita, KS: Author, 1986. 11p.

USGenWeb Census Project. Kentucky, 1810 Pendleton County.

ftp://ftp.rootsweb.com/pub/census/ky/pendleton/1810/

1820

USGenWeb Census Project. Kentucky, 1820 Pendleton County.

ftp://ftp.rootsweb.com/pub/census/ky/pendleton/1820/

1830

USGenWeb Census Project. Kentucky, 1830 Pendleton County.

ftp://ftp.rootsweb.com/pub/census/ky/pendleton/1830/

1840

USGenWeb Census Project. Kentucky, 1840 Pendleton County.

ftp://ftp.rootsweb.com/pub/census/ky/pendleton/1840/

1850

McDowell, Samuel Riley. *A Surname Index to the 1850 Federal Population Census of Kentucky.* Richland, IN: Author, 1982. 33p.

Nagle, Eric C. *1850 Federal Census of Pendleton County, Kentucky.* Falmouth, KY: Pendleton County Historical and Genealogical Society, 1994. 68p.

Perry County
1830, 1840

Perry County, Kentucky Records, 1830 and 1840 Census. Hazard, KY: Perry County Genealogical and Historical Society, 1984. Unpgd.

1850

McDowell, Samuel Riley. *A Surname Index to the 1850 Federal Population Census of Kentucky.* Richland, IN: Author, 1982. 33p.

Perry County, Kentucky Records, 1850 Census, Vital Statistics 1852-1859. Hazard, KY: Perry County Genealogical and Historical Society, 1982. 90p.

1860

Inman, Robert Wesley, and Gloria Kay Vandiver Inman. *1860 Perry County, Kentucky, Federal Census with Every-name Index.* Anchorage, AK: Authors, 1980. 62p.

Johnson, Mrs. John O. *Perry County, Kentucky Records, 1860 Census.* Hazard, KY: Perry County Genealogical and Historical Society, 1988. Unpgd.

1870

Perry County, Kentucky Records, 1870 Census. Hazard, KY: Perry County Genealogical and Historical Society, 1984. 68p.

1880

Cunagin, Judy Murray. *Perry County, Kentucky Census Records, 1880.* Indianapolis, IN: Author, 1986. 154p.

1890, 1900

Cunagin, Judy Murray. *1900 Perry County, Kentucky Census, with Heads of Household Index, Special 1890 Census for Perry County, Kentucky, Enumerating Soldiers, Sailors or Widows*. Indianapolis, IN: Author, 1986. 247p.

1910

Cunagin, Judy Murray. *Perry County, Kentucky Census, with Heads of Household Index, 1910, Book I*. Indianapolis, IN: Author, 1990. 2 vols.

1920

Cunagin, Judy Murray. *1920 Perry County, Kentucky Census Record, with Head of Household Index*. Indianapolis, IN: Author, 1993. 2 vols.

Pike County

1830

Atkins, Oscar Thomas. *Pike County, Kentucky 1830, Taken in Part from the Federal Census of Pike County, Kentucky for 1830, and from Tax Lists, Other Census Records, Marriage Records and from the Library and Files of the Compiler*. Williamson, WV: Author, 1995. 25p.

Stewart, Jesse. *Complete Index to Federal Census, Pike County, Kentucky, 1830-1920*. Grundy, VA: Author. Unpgd.

1840

Atkins, Oscar Thomas. *Pike County, Kentucky, 1840, Taken in Part from the Federal Census of Pike County, Kentucky, for 1840 and from Tax Lists, other Census Records, Marriage Records and from the Library and Files of the Compiler*. Williamson, WV: Author, 1995. 32p.

Stewart, Jesse. *Complete Index to Federal Census, Pike County, Kentucky, 1830-1920*. Grundy, VA: Author. Unpgd.

_____, and Leah Stewart. *1840 Federal Census of Pike County, Kentucky*. Grundy, VA: Authors, 1984. 24p.

1850

Atkins, Oscar Thomas. *Pike County, Kentucky Families, Being Information Extracted and Digested from the 1850 Federal Census of Pike County, Kentucky, from Microfilm Copies of Originals Which Are on File in the National Archives in Washington, D.C.* Williamson, WV: East Kentucky, Southern West Virginia Family Records, 1994-1997. 4 vols.

Honaker, Dewey R. *1850 Census of Pike County, Kentucky*. Pikeville, KY: Author, 1970. Unpgd.

McDowell, Samuel Riley. *A Surname Index to the 1850 Federal Population Census of Kentucky*. Richland, IN: Author, 1977. 61p.

Mullins, Billie Hill. *Pike County, Kentucky 1850 Federal Census*. Logan, WV: Author. 156p.

Stewart, Jesse. *Complete Index to Federal Census, Pike County, Kentucky, 1830-1920*. Grundy, VA: Author. Unpgd.

USGenWeb Census Project. Kentucky, 1850 Pike County.

ftp://ftp.rootsweb.com/pub/census/ky/pike/1850/

1860

Honaker, Dewey R. *1860 Census of Pike County, Kentucky*. Pikeville, KY: Author, 1974. 115p.

Mullins, Billie Hill. *Pike County, Kentucky 1860 Federal Census with Genealogical Annotations*. Logan, WV: Author, 1997. 186p.

Stewart, Jesse. *Complete Index to Federal Census, Pike County, Kentucky, 1830-1920*. Grundy, VA: Author. Unpgd.

_____, and Leah Stewart. *1860 Federal Census Pike County, Kentucky*. Grundy, VA: Author. 126p.

1870

Robinson, Lewis, Teresa Robinson, and Mrs. E.N. Venters. *1870 Federal Census of Pike County, Kentucky*. Pikesville, KY: Author, 1981. 123p.

Stewart, Jesse. *Complete Index to Federal Census, Pike County, Kentucky, 1830-1920*. Grundy, VA: Author. Unpgd.

_____, and Leah Stewart. *1870 Federal Census Pike County, Kentucky*. Grundy, VA: Author. 118p.

1880

Robinson, Lewis, and Teresa Robinson. *1880 Federal Census of Pike County, Kentucky*. Pikeville, KY: Authors, 1981. 303p.

Stewart, Jesse. *Complete Index to Federal Census, Pike County, Kentucky, 1830-1920*. Grundy, VA: Author. Unpgd.

1900

Stewart, Jesse. *Complete Index to Federal Census, Pike County, Kentucky, 1830-1920*. Grundy, VA: Author. Unpgd.

_____, and Leah Stewart. *1900 Federal Census of Pike County, Kentucky*. Grundy, VA: Authors, 1984. 556p.

1910

Stewart, Jesse. *Complete Index to Federal Census, Pike County, Kentucky, 1830-1920*. Grundy, VA: Author. Unpgd.

_____, and Leah Stewart. *1910 Federal Census of Pike County, Kentucky*. Grundy, VA: Authors, 1985. 2 vols.

1920

Atkins, Oscar Thomas. *Big Creek, Kentucky 1920*. Williamston, WV: Author, 1992. 49p.

_____. *Blackberry Creek, Kentucky 1920*. Williamston, WV: Author, 1993. 53p.

_____. *Old Pond Families, Kentucky 1920*. Williamston, WV: Author, 1992. 222p.

Stewart, Jesse. *Complete Index to Federal Census, Pike County, Kentucky, 1830-1920*. Grundy, VA: Author. Unpgd.

Powell County
1860

Patrick, Tracy R. *1860 Census Powell County, Kentucky*. Irvine, KY: Estill County Tribune, 1981. 26p.

Wonn, Mildred. *The 1860 Census of Powell County, Kentucky*. Owingsville, KY: Author, 1981. 31p.

1870

Patrick, Tracy R. *1870 Census Powell County, Kentucky*. Irvine, KY: Estill County Tribune, 1988. 27p.

1880

Morton, Lynn Douglas. *1880 Census Powell County, Kentucky*. Stanton, KY: Author, 1994. 83p.

1890

Patrick, Tracy R. *1890 Soldier Census of Powell and Estill Counties Kentucky*. Irvine, KY: Estill County Tribune. 9p.

1900

Morton, Douglas. *1900 Census, Powell County, Kentucky*. Stanton, KY: Author. 164p.

1910

Hensley, Chuckie Hall. *Powell County, Kentucky, 1910 Census*. Utica, KY: McDowell Publications, 1986. 134p.

1920

Morton, Douglas. *1920 Census, Powell County, Kentucky*. Stanton, KY: Author, 1993. 91p.

Pulaski County
1810

Census Index, 1810, 1820, 1830, 1840, 1890, Pulaski County, Kentucky. Somerset, KY: Pulaski County Historical Society, 1982. 47p.

Stultz, Carol Elkins. *1810 Pulaski and Rockcastle Counties, Kentucky Federal Census, Complete*. Danville, IN: Stultz Computer Services, 1988. 32p.

1820-1840

Census Index, 1810, 1820, 1830, 1840, 1890, Pulaski County, Kentucky. Somerset, KY: Pulaski County Historical Society, 1982. 47p.

1850

Pulaski County, Kentucky, 1850 Census. Somerset, KY: Pulaski County Historical Society, 1976. 306p.

Sistler, Barbara. *1850 Census, Southeastern Kentucky, Counties of Clay, Harlan, Knox, Laurel, Pulaski, Russell, Wayne and Whitley*. Nashville, TN: Byron Sistler & Associates, 1993. 412p.

1860

Pulaski County, Kentucky, 1860 Census. Somerset, KY: Pulaski County Historical Society, 1988. 342p.

1870

Pulaski County, Kentucky, 1870 Census. Somerset, KY: Pulaski County Historical Society, 1980. 395p.

1880

Pulaski County, Kentucky, 1880 Census. Somerset, KY: Pulaski County Historical Society, 1992. 394p.

1890

Census Index, 1810, 1820, 1830, 1840, 1890, Pulaski County, Kentucky. Somerset, KY: Pulaski County Historical Society, 1982. 47p.

1900

1900 Census, Pulaski County, Kentucky. Somerset, KY: Pulaski County Historical Society, 1987. 2 vols.

Rockcastle County

Bonham, Jeanne Snodgrass, and Patricia Heylmann Hiatt. *Rockcastle County, Kentucky State Vital Statistics and Federal Census Mortality Schedules, Official Records from the 1800s*. Greenwood, IN: High Grass Pub., 1992. 339p.

1810

Hubble, Anna Joy Munday. *Rockcastle County, Kentucky, 1810 Census, 1815 Tax List, 1820 Census*. Whitefish, MT: Author, 1979. 16p.

Stultz, Carol Elkins. *1810 Pulaski and Rockcastle Counties, Kentucky Federal Census, Complete*. Danville, IN: Stultz Computer Services, 1988. 32p.

1850

Hubble, Anna Joy Munday. *Rockcastle County, Kentucky, 1850 Census, 1815 Tax List, 1820 Census*. Whitefish, MT: Author, 1980. 43p.

McDowell, Samuel Riley. *A Surname Index to the 1850 Federal Population Census of Kentucky*. Richland, IN: Author, 1977. 61p.

1870

Cummins, Shirley, and Alberta Hasty. *Rockcastle County, Kentucky, 1870 Census, Population Schedule of the Ninth Census of the United States, Copied from Microfilm #593, Roll 497*. Mt. Vernon, KY: Rockcastle County Historical Society, 1985. 209p.

1880

Ashley, Linda Ramsey. *1880 Census Rockcastle County, Kentucky*. Lexington, KY: Author, 1974. Unpgd.

Bonham, Jeanne Snodgrass. *Rockcastle County, Kentucky 1880 Federal Census*. Mt. Vernon, KY: Rockcastle County Historical Society, 1995. 174p.

Loftin, Bennie Lou Coffey. *1880 Federal Census of Rockcastle County, Kentucky*. Kiowa, OK: Author, 1988. 155p.

1900

Bonham, Jeanne Snodgrass, and Patricia Heylmann Hiatt. *Rockcastle County, Kentucky 1900 Federal Census, Rockcastle County, Kentucky, Twelfth Census of the United States, Schedule No. 1, Population*. Greenwood, IN: High Grass Pub., 1993. 321p.

Rowan County

1860

Curtis, Mary G., and Alethea B. Read. *The 1860 Census of Rowan County, Kentucky*. Santa Rosa, CA: Author, 1976. 39p.

Russell County

1830, 1840

Roy, Emogene McFarland. *Russell County, Kentucky 1830-1840 Census*. Russell Springs, KY: Author, 1987. 69p.

1850

Crume, Barney D., *Russell County, Kentucky 1850 Federal Census*. 56p.

McDowell, Samuel Riley. *A Surname Index to the 1850 Federal Population Census of Kentucky*. Richland, IN: Author, 1977. 61p.

Roy, Emogene McFarland. *Russell County, Kentucky 1850 Census*. Russell Springs, KY: Author, 1987. 109p.

Shepherd, Irma Miller. *1850 Census, Russell County, Kentucky*. Lake Oswego, OR: Author, 1999. 247p.

Sistler, Barbara. *1850 Census, Southeastern Kentucky, Counties of Clay, Harlan, Knox, Laurel, Pulaski, Russell, Wayne and Whitley*. Nashville, TN: Byron Sistler & Associates, 1993. 412p.

1860

Garner, James D. *1860 Russell County, Kentucky Census Record, Including Full Name Census Index, over 650 Maiden Names Indexed, Occupations Index, List of Slaveholders, List of "Married within One Year."* Bowling Green, KY: JayLib Publications, 1986. 81p.

Hopper, Carol F. *Population Schedule of the Eighth Census of the United States, 1860, Russell County, Kentucky*. Lily, KY: Author, 1988. 54p.

Shepherd, Irma Miller. *1860 Census Russell County, Kentucky*. Lake Oswego, OR: Author, 1999. 287p.

1870

Roy, Emogene McFarland. *Russell County, Kentucky 1870 Census*. Russell Springs, KY: Author, 1987. 104p.

Shepherd, Irma Miller. *1870 Census Russell County, Kentucky*. Lake Oswego, OR: Author, 1999. 310p.

1880

Shepherd, Irma Miller. *1880 Census, Russell County, Kentucky*. Lake Oswego, OR: Author, 1997. 316p.

1900

Roy, Emogene McFarland. *Russell County, Kentucky 1900 Census*. Russell Springs, KY: Author, 1989. 263p.

Shepherd, Irma Miller. *Twelfth Census of the United States, Schedule No. 1, 1900 Population of Russell County, Kentucky*. Lake Oswego, OR: Author, 1999. 420p.

1910

Shepherd, Irma Miller. *Thirteenth Census of the United States, 1910 Population of Russell*. Lake Oswego, OR: Author, 1998. 2 vols.

1920

Shepherd, Irma Miller. *Fourteenth Census of the United States, 1920 Population*. Lake Oswego, OR: Author, 1998. 2 vols.

Scott County

1810

Burns, Annie Walker. *Third Census of the United States, Scott County, Kentucky*. Washington, DC: Author, 1935. 53p.

Hubble, Anna Joy Munday. *Scott County, 1810 Kentucky Census*. Whitefish, MT: Author. 10p.

1850

McDowell, Samuel Riley. *A Surname Index to the 1850 Federal Population Census of Kentucky*. Owensboro, KY: Author, 1982. 35p.

Schunk, John Frederick. *1850 U.S. Census, Scott County, Kentucky*. Wichita, KS: S-K Publications, 1990. 532p.

Shelby County

1850

McDowell, Samuel Riley. *A Surname Index to the 1850 Federal Population Census of Kentucky*. Owensboro, KY: Author, 1982. 35p.

1870

McManaway, Robert D. *Shelby County, Kentucky, 1870 Census*. Utica, KY: McDowell Pub., 1986. 245p.

Simpson County

1820

Jackson, Martha Werst. *The Federal Census of Simpson County, Kentucky for 1820*. Scottsville, KY: Author, 1985. 38p.

Simpson County, Kentucky Records, the Census of 1820 and 1830, Family Bible Entries, Cemetery Headstone Inscriptions, Revolutionary War Veteran Pensions Indexed. Frankfort, KY: Simpson County Historical Society, 1975. 455p.

1830

Simpson County, Kentucky Records, the Census of 1820 and 1830, Family Bible Entries, Cemetery Headstone Inscriptions, Revolutionary War Veteran Pensions Indexed. Frankfort, KY: Simpson County Historical Society, 1975. 455p.

1850

McDowell, Samuel Riley. *A Surname Index to the 1850 Federal Population Census of Kentucky.* Owensboro, KY: Author, 1982. 35p.

Sistler, Barbara. *1850 Census, South West Kentucky, Counties of Christian, Logan, Simpson, Todd, Trigg and Warren.* Nashville, TN: Byron Sistler & Associates, 1993. 442p.

Steers, Dorothy Donnell. *Simpson County, Kentucky 1850 Census and Tax List.* Franklin, KY: Author, 1984. 141p.

USGenWeb Census Project. Kentucky, 1850 Simpson County.
ftp://ftp.rootsweb.com/pub/census/ky/simpson/1850/

1860

Denning, Michael. *1860 Simpson County, Kentucky Census.* Gallatin, TN: Author, 1996. 152p.

Spencer County
1830

Darnell, Betty Rolwing. *1830 Census, Spencer County, Kentucky.* Mt. Washington, KY: Author, 1989. 33p.

1840

Darnell, Betty Rolwing. *1840 Census, Spencer County, Kentucky.* Mt. Washington, KY: Author, 1989. 27p.

1850

Darnell, Betty Rolwing. *1850 Census, Spencer County, Kentucky.* Mt. Washington, KY: Author, 1990. 57p.

McDowell, Samuel Riley. *A Surname Index to the 1850 Federal Population Census of Kentucky.* Richland, IN: Author, 1975. 72p.

USGenWeb Census Project. Kentucky, 1850 Spencer County.
ftp://ftp.rootsweb.com/pub/census/ky/spencer/1850/

Taylor County
1850

Benningfield, Edward. *The 1850 Census of Taylor County, Kentucky.* Campbellsville, KY: Taylor County Historical Society, 1983. 98p.

McDowell, Samuel Riley. *A Surname Index to the 1850 Federal Population Census of Kentucky.* Richland, IN: Author, 1975. 72p.

Wilson, DeWayne. *Mortality Schedules Taylor County, 1850, 1860, 1870, 1880.* Campbellsville, KY: Author, 1994. 19p.

1860

Sullivan, Gwynette Turner. *The 1860 Census of Taylor County, Kentucky.* Campbellsville, KY: Taylor County Historical Society, 1988. 128p.

Wilson, DeWayne. *Mortality Schedules Taylor County, 1850, 1860, 1870, 1880.* Campbellsville, KY: Author, 1994. 19p.

1870

Wilson, DeWayne. *1870 Census of Taylor County, Kentucky.* Campbellsville, KY: Author, 1992. 180p.

Wilson, DeWayne. *Mortality Schedules Taylor County, 1850, 1860, 1870, 1880.* Campbellsville, KY: Author, 1994. 19p.

1880

Wilson, DeWayne. *Mortality Schedules Taylor County, 1850, 1860, 1870, 1880.* Campbellsville, KY: Author, 1994. 19p.

Todd County

1820

Jones, Thomas Harold. *Todd County, Kentucky Census of 1820*. Melber, KY: Simmons Historical Pub., 1987. 17p.

1830

Jones, Thomas Harold. *Todd County, Kentucky Census of 1830*. Melber, KY: Simmons Historical Pub., 1977. 21p.

1840

Jones, Thomas Harold. *Todd County, Kentucky Census of 1840*. Melber, KY: Simmons Historical Pub., 1977. 25p.

1850

McDowell, Samuel Riley. *A Surname Index to the 1850 Federal Population Census of Kentucky*. Richland, IN: Author, 1975. 72p.

Sistler, Barbara. *1850 Census, South West Kentucky, Counties of Christian, Logan, Simpson, Todd, Trigg and Warren*. Nashville, TN: Byron Sistler & Associates, 1993. 442p.

Willhite, A. B. *Todd County, Kentucky 1850 Federal Census*. Russellville, KY: Author, 1996. 165p.

1860

Willhite, A. B. *Todd County, Kentucky 1860 Federal Census*. Russellville, KY: Author. 123p.

1870

Willhite, A. B. *Todd County, Kentucky 1870 Federal Census*. Russellville, KY: Author, 1988. 137p.

1880

Willnite, A. B. *Todd County, Kentucky 1880 Federal Census*. Russellville, KY: Author, 1999. 316p.

1900

Willhite, A. B. *Todd County, Kentucky 1900 Federal Census*. Russellville, KY: Author, 1991. 201p.

1920

Willhite, A. B. *Todd County, Kentucky 1920 Federal Census*. Russellville, KY: Author, 1996. 187p.

Trigg County

1820, 1830

Simmons, Don. *Trigg County, Kentucky Census of 1820 and 1830*. Melber, KY: Simmons Historical Pub., 1987. 28p.

1840

Willis, Laura. *Trigg County, Kentucky, Census and Tax List of 1840*. Melber, KY: Simmons Historical Publications, 1995. 53p.

1850

McDowell, Samuel Riley. *A Surname Index to the 1850 Federal Population Census of Kentucky*. Richland, IN: Author, 1975. 72p.

Simmons, Don. *Trigg County, Kentucky, Census of 1850*. Melber, KY: Simmons Historical Pub., 1989. Unpgd.

Sistler, Barbara. *1850 Census, South West Kentucky, Counties of Christian, Logan, Simpson, Todd, Trigg and Warren*. Nashville, TN: Byron Sistler & Associates, 1993. 442p.

1860

Simmons, Don. *Trigg County, Kentucky, Census of 1860*. Melber, KY: Simmons Historical Pub., 1983. 96p.

1870

Simmons, Don. *Trigg County, Kentucky, Census of 1870*. Melber, KY: Simmons Historical Pub., 1993. 241p.

1880

Taylor, Pete. *Trigg County, Kentucky 1880 Families*. Melber, KY: Simmons Historical Pub., 1996. 189p.

1900

Jones, Thomas Harold. *Trigg County, Kentucky Census of 1900 Federal Census*. Utica, KY: McDowell, 1984. 388p.

1920

Blue, James L. *Trigg County, Kentucky Census of 1920*. Melber, KY: Simmons Historical Pub., 1997. 234p.

Trimble County
1850
Thompson, Donna Stark. *1850 Census, Trimble County, Kentucky, with Mortality Schedule*. Frankfort, KY: Author, 1985. 116p.
1860
Thompson, Donna Stark. *1860 Census, Trimble County, Kentucky, with Mortality Schedule*. Frankfort, KY: Author, 1985. 119p.
1870
Thompson, Donna Stark. *1870 Census, Trimble County, Kentucky, with Mortality Schedule*. Frankfort, KY: Author, 1986. 125p.
1880
1880 Census Trimble County, Kentucky. Bedford, KY: Trimble County Historical Society, 1993. 169p.
1900
1900 Trimble County, Kentucky, Census. Pendleton, KY: Trimble County Historical Society, 1995. 175p.
1910
Trimble County, Kentucky 1910 Census. Pendleton, KY: Trimble County Historical Society, 1995. 161p.

Union County
1810
Blue, James L. *The Census of the United States, Union County, Kentucky, 1810*. Morganfield, KY: Heady, 1988. Unpgd.
1850
Blue, James L. *1850 Union County, Kentucky U.S. Census*. Morganfield, KY: Heady. Unpgd.

1850 Federal Census, Union County, Kentucky. Madisonville, KY: Hopkins County Genealogical Society, 1976. 153p.

Sistler, Barbara. *1850 Census, North West Kentucky Counties of Crittenden, Daviess, Henderson, Hopkins, Muhlenberg, Ohio and Union*. Nashville, TN: Byron Sistler & Associates, 1994. 497p.
1860
Blue, James L. *The Census of the United States in the Year 1860, Union County, Kentucky*. Morganfield, KY: Heady, 1988. 249p.
1870
Blue, James L. *The Census of the United States in the Year 1870, Union County, Kentucky*. Morganfield, KY: Heady, 1990. Unpgd.
1880
Heady, Peyton. *The 1880 Census, Union County, Kentucky*. Morganfield, KY: Author, 1993. 324p.
1900
Blue, James L. *The Census of the United States, 1900, Union County, Kentucky*. Morganfield, KY: Peyton Heady, 1997. 466p.
1910
Blue, James L. *1910 Union County, Kentucky U.S. Federal Census*. Morganfield, KY: Heady. Unpgd.
1920
Blue, James L. *The Census of the United States, 1920. Union County, Kentucky*. Morganfield, KY: Peyton Heady, 1996. Inpgd.

Warren County
1810
Lawson, Rowena. *Warren County, Kentucky, 1810-1840 Censuses*. Bowie, MD: Heritage Books, 1986. 97p.

McGhee, Lucy Kate. *Warren County, Kentucky, 1810 United States Census*. Washington, DC: Author, 1958. 93p.

Reid, Patricia Ennis. *1810 Warren County, Kentucky Census*. Bowling Green, KY: Author, 1992. 81p.

Thomas, Helen Gilmore Smith. *1810 Census Warren County, Kentucky*. Bowling Green, KY: Author. 92p.
1820-1840
Lawson, Rowena. *Warren County, Kentucky, 1810-1840 Censuses*. Bowie, MD: Heritage Books, 1986. 97p.

1850

Crume, Mrs. Barney D. *Warren County, Kentucky 1850 Federal Census*. Author. 120p.

Rabold, Mary Moltenberry. *Census 1850 Warren County, Kentucky*. Bowling Green, KY: Author, 1970. 205p.

Reid, Patricia Ennis. *Warren County, Kentucky 1850 Census*. Bowling Green, KY: Author, 1993. 327p.

Sistler, Barbara. *1850 Census, South West Kentucky, Counties of Christian, Logan, Simpson, Todd, Trigg and Warren*. Nashville, TN: Byron Sistler & Associates, 1993. 442p.

1860

Reid, Patricia Ennis. *Warren County, Kentucky 1860 Census*. Bowling Green, KY: Author, 1986. 386p.

1870

Gorin, Michelle Bartley. *1870 Warren County, Kentucky Black Census, They Won't Be Forgotten*. Glasgow, KY: Gorin Genealogical Pub., 1997. 154p.

Reid, Patricia Ennis. *Index to 1870 Warren County, Kentucky Census*. Bowling Green, KY: Author, 1986. 64p.

Washington County

1810

Burns, Annie Walker. *Third Census of the United States, Washington County, Kentucky*. Washington, DC: Author, 1935. 68p.

Lawson, Rowena. *Washington County, Kentucky, 1810-1840 Censuses*. Bowie, MD: Heritage Books, 1986. 112p.

1820-1840

Lawson, Rowena. *Washington County, Kentucky, 1810-1840 Censuses*. Bowie, MD: Heritage Books, 1986. 112p.

1850

Crume, Mrs. Barney D. *Washington County, Kentucky 1850 Federal Census*. Lubbock, TX: Author. 103p.

McDowell, Samuel Riley. *A Surname Index to the 1850 Federal Population Census of Kentucky*. Utica, KY: Author, 1977. 44p.

Sanders, Faye Sea. *Washington, Mercer and Anderson Counties, Kentucky Mortality Schedules for 1850, 1860, 1870, 1880. Also Deaths Reported in 1874-1878 Vital Statistics*. Louisville, KY: Author. 61p.

1860

Sanders, Faye Sea. *Washington, Mercer and Anderson Counties, Kentucky Mortality Schedules for 1850, 1860, 1870, 1880. Also Deaths Reported in 1874-1878 Vital Statistics*. Louisville, KY: Author. 61p.

1870

Sanders, Faye Sea. *1870 Federal Census, Washington County, Kentucky*. Louisville, KY: Author, 1987. 147p.

_____. *Washington, Mercer and Anderson Counties, Kentucky Mortality Schedules for 1850, 1860, 1870, 1880. Also Deaths Reported in 1874-1878 Vital Statistics*. Louisville, KY: Author. 61p.

1880

Sanders, Faye Sea. *1880 Federal Census, Washington County, Kentucky*. Louisville, KY: Author, 1990. 127p.

_____. *Washington, Mercer and Anderson Counties, Kentucky Mortality Schedules for 1850, 1860, 1870, 1880. Also Deaths Reported in 1874-1878 Vital Statistics*. Louisville, KY: Author. 61p.

1900

Sanders, Faye Sea. *1900 Federal Census, Washington County, Kentucky*. Louisville, KY: Author, 1991. 139p.

1910

Sanders, Faye Sea. *1910 Federal Census, Washington County, Kentucky*. Louisville, KY: Author, 1994. 154p.

Wayne County

1810

Burns, Annie Walker. *Third Census of the United States, County of Wayne, State of Kentucky*. Washington, DC: Author, 1934. 52p.

Carter, Mrs. J. R. *1810 Census, Wayne County, Kentucky*. Sedalia, MO: Author, 1966. 16p.

Crawford, Andrew J. *Index, Wayne County, Kentucky Population Census, Head of Families, 1810-1880*. New Carlisle, OH: Graphic Printing, 1976. 138p.

Lawson, Rowena. *Wayne County, Kentucky 1810-1840 Censuses*. Bowie, MD: Heritage Books, 1988. 73p.
1820
Crawford, Andrew J. *Index, Wayne County, Kentucky Population Census, Head of Families, 1810-1880*. New Carlisle, OH: Graphic Printing, 1976. 138p.
Lawson, Rowena. *Wayne County, Kentucky 1810-1840 Censuses*. Bowie, MD: Heritage Books, 1988. 73p.
1830
Crawford, Andrew J. *Index, Wayne County, Kentucky Population Census, Head of Families, 1810-1880*. New Carlisle, OH: Graphic Printing, 1976. 138p.
High, Jessye Ann. *1830 Census, Wayne County, Kentucky*. Sunnyvale, CA: Author, 1972. 40p.
Lawson, Rowena. *Wayne County, Kentucky 1810-1840 Censuses*. Bowie, MD: Heritage Books, 1988. 73p.
1840
Crawford, Andrew J. *Index, Wayne County, Kentucky Population Census, Head of Families, 1810-1880*. New Carlisle, OH: Graphic Printing, 1976. 138p.
Lawson, Rowena. *Wayne County, Kentucky 1810-1840 Censuses*. Bowie, MD: Heritage Books, 1988. 73p.
1850
Crawford, Andrew J. *Index, Wayne County, Kentucky Population Census, Head of Families, 1810-1880*. New Carlisle, OH: Graphic Printing, 1976. 138p.
McDowell, Samuel Riley. *A Surname Index to the 1850 Federal Population Census of Kentucky*. Utica, KY: Author, 1977. 44p.
Sanders, Faye Sea. *1850 Federal Census, Washington County, Kentucky*. Louisville, KY: Author, 1982. 103p.
_____. *Washington, Mercer and Anderson Counties, Kentucky Mortality Schedules for 1850, 1860, 1870, 1880, also Deaths Reported in 1874-1878, Vital Statistics, Washington, Mercer and Anderson Counties, Kentucky*. Louisville, KY: Author. 61p.
Sistler, Barbara. *1850 Census, Southeastern Kentucky, Counties of Clay, Harlan, Knox, Laurel, Pulaski, Russell, Wayne and Whitley*. Nashville, TN: Byron Sistler & Associates, 1993. 412p.
1860
Crawford, Andrew J. *Index, Wayne County, Kentucky Population Census, Head of Families, 1810-1880*. New Carlisle, OH: Graphic Printing, 1976. 138p.
Sanders, Faye Sea. *1860 Federal Census, Washington County, Kentucky*. Louisville, KY: Author, 1982. 109p.
_____. *Washington, Mercer and Anderson Counties, Kentucky Mortality Schedules for 1850, 1860, 1870, 1880, also Deaths Reported in 1874-1878, Vital Statistics, Washington, Mercer and Anderson Counties, Kentucky*. Louisville, KY: Author. 61p.
Whitis, Mrs. Alma Coffey. *Wayne County, Kentucky 1860 Census*. Apple Valley, CA: Bork, 1990. Unpgd.
1870
Crawford, Andrew J. *Index, Wayne County, Kentucky Population Census, Head of Families, 1810-1880*. New Carlisle, OH: Graphic Printing, 1976. 138p.
Sanders, Faye Sea. *Washington, Mercer and Anderson Counties, Kentucky Mortality Schedules for 1850, 1860, 1870, 1880, also Deaths Reported in 1874-1878, Vital Statistics, Washington, Mercer and Anderson Counties, Kentucky*. Louisville, KY: Author. 61p.
Whitis, Mrs. Alma Coffey. *Wayne County, Kentucky 1870 Census*. Apple Valley, CA: Bork, 1990. Unpgd.
1880
Crawford, Andrew J. *Index, Wayne County, Kentucky Population Census, Head of Families, 1810-1880*. New Carlisle, OH: Graphic Printing, 1976. 138p.
Sanders, Faye Sea. *Washington, Mercer and Anderson Counties, Kentucky Mortality Schedules for 1850, 1860, 1870, 1880, also Deaths Reported in 1874-1878, Vital Statistics, Washington, Mercer and Anderson Counties, Kentucky*. Louisville, KY: Author. 61p.
Whitis, Mrs. Alma Coffey. *Wayne County, Kentucky 1880 Census*. Apple Valley, CA: Bork, 1990. Unpgd.
1900
Whitis, Mrs. Alma Coffey. *Wayne County, Kentucky 1900 Census*. Apple Valley, CA: Bork, 1990. Unpgd.
1910
Sanders, Faye Sea. *1910 Washington County, Kentucky Census*. Louisville, KY: Author, 1994. 183p.
Whitis, Mrs. Alma Coffey. *Wayne County, Kentucky 1910 Census*. Apple Valley, CA: Bork, 1990. Unpgd.
1920
Whitis, Mrs. Alma Coffey. *Wayne County, Kentucky 1920 Census*. Apple Valley, CA: Bork, 1995. 2 vols.

Webster County
1860
1860 Federal Census, Webster County, Kentucky. Madisonville, KY: Hopkins County Genealogical Society, 1975. 139p.
1870
Federal Census of Webster County, Kentucky, 1870. Madisonville, KY: Hopkins County Genealogical Society, 1979. 318p.
1880
Hammers, Marian G. *Federal Census of Webster County, Kentucky, 1880*. Madisonville, KY: Hopkins County Genealogical Society, 1984. 393p.
1920
Blue, James L. *Webster County, Kentucky Census of 1920*. Melber, KY: Simmons Historical Pubs., 1996. 365p.

Whitley County
1820
USGenWeb Census Project. Kentucky, 1820 Whitley County.
ftp://ftp.rootsweb/com/pub/census/ky/whitley/1820/
Withers, Sharon Mayne. *Whitley County, Kentucky 1820 Census, 1819 Tax Book*. Louisville, KY: Knox County Genealogical Society, 1987. 33p.
1850
Cook, Kathleen *Stanfield. Index of 1850 Whitley County, Kentucky Federal Census, Annotated Version*. Astoria, IL: Stevens Pub. Co., 1986. 117p.
Hopper, Carol F., and Linda C. Jones. *Population Schedule of the Seventh Census of the United States 1850 Whitley County, Kentucky*. Lily, KY: Author, 1986. 78p.
Sistler, Barbara. *1850 Census, Southeastern Kentucky, Counties of Clay, Harlan, Knox, Laurel, Pulaski, Russell, Wayne and Whitley*. Nashville, TN: Byron Sistler & Associates, 1993. 412p.
1860
Hopper, Carol F. *Population Schedule of the Eighth Census of the United States, 1860, Whitley County, Kentucky*. Lily, KY: Author, 1987. 100p.
1870
Hopper, Carol F. *Population Schedule of the Ninth Census of the United States, 1870, Whitley County, Kentucky*. Lily, KY: Author, 1987. 92p.

Wolfe County
1880
Bogar, Mary Lou. *1880 Census of Wolfe County, Kentucky*. Kansas, MO: Author, 1983. 133p.
Horne, Helen P. *Wolfe County, Kentucky 1880 Census*. Hazard, KY: Author, 1990. 72p.
1900
Spencer, Kay A. *1900 Wolfe County, Kentucky Census*. Hazard, KY: Author, 1993. 115p.
1910
Spencer, Kay A. *1910 Wolfe County, Kentucky Census*. Novi, MI: Author. 126p.
1920
Bays, Carole. *1920 Wolfe County Census*. Dayton, OH: Author. 119p.

Woodford County
1810-1840
Lawson, Rowena. *Woodford County, Kentucky, 1810-1840 Censuses*. Bowie, MD: Heritage Books, 1987. 75p.
1850
Wilson, Dona Adams. *Woodford County, Kentucky, 1850 U.S. Census*. Versailles, KY: Woodford County Historical Society Library and Museum, 1998. 138p.

1860

Nave, Doris, and Barbara Augspurger. *1860 Census, Woodford County, Kentucky*. Midway, KY: Author, 1981. 69p.

1870

Manley, Doris N., and Mabel H. Bain. *1870 Woodford County, Kentucky Federal Census*. Frankfort, KY: Author, 1986. 157p.

Louisiana

Childs, Marieta. North Louisiana Census Reports. New Orleans, LA: Polyanthos, 1975. 3 vols.

Feldman, Lawrence H. *Anglo Americans in Spanish Archives, Lists of Anglo American Settlers in the Spanish Colonies of America*. Baltimore, MD: Genealogical Publishing Co., 1991. 349p.

Jackson, Ronald Vern. *Early Louisiana*. North Salt Lake City, UT: Accelerated Indexing Systems International, 1981.

1699-1732

Maduell, Charles Rene. *The Census Tables for the French Colony of Louisiana from 1699 through 1732*. Baltimore, MD: Genealogical Publishing Co., 1972. 171p.

1770-1798

Robichaux, Albert J. *Colonial Settlers along Bayou Lafourche, Louisiana Census Records 1770-1798*. Harvey, LA: Author, 1974. 219p.

_____. *Louisiana Census and Militia Lists, Vol. 1, 1770-1789, German Coast, New Orleans, below New Orleans and Lafouche*. New Orleans, LA: Polyanthos, 1973. 161p.

1777

De Ville, Winston. *Southwest Louisiana Families in 1777, Census Records of Attakapas and Opelousas Posts*. Ville Platte, LA: Author, 1987. Unpgd.

_____. *St. Gabriel Settlers, the 1777 Census of Iberville District in the Province of Louisiana*. Ville Platte, LA: Author, 1987.

1784

De Ville, Winston. *Valenzuela in the Province of Louisiana a Census of 1784*. Ville Platte, LA: Author, 1987. 6p.

1793

De Ville, Winston. *New Feliciana in the Province of Louisiana a Guide to the Census of 1793*. Ville Platte, LA: Author, 1987. 8p.

1810

Ardoin, Robert Bruce L. *Louisiana Census Records 1810 & 1820*. Baltimore, MD: Genealogical Publishing Co., 1977. 3 vols.

Federal Census of 1810, Territory of Orleans, Excluding the Parish of Orleans. Baton Rouge, LA: Lousiana Genealogical & Historical Society, 1961. 26p.

Jackson, Ronald Vern. *Louisiana Census Index, Online Edition*. Orem, UT: Ancestry.com, Inc., 1999. **http://www.ancestry.com**

_____, and Gary Ronald Teeples. *Louisiana 1810 Census Index*. Salt Lake City, UT: Accelerated Indexing Systems, 1976. 151p.

Roux, Vincent M. *Louisiana's Households of Free People of Color Residing Outside of Orleans Parish & the City of New Orleans in 1810 & 1820*. San Francisco, CA: Author, 195. 72p.

U.S. Federal Population Census Schedules, 1810. M252, Microfilm Reel No. 10.

1820

Ardoin, Robert Bruce L. *Louisiana Census Records 1810 & 1820*. Baltimore, MD: Genealogical Publishing Co., 1977. 3 vols.

Jackson, Ronald Vern. *Louisiana Census Index, Online Edition*. Orem, UT: Ancestry.com, Inc., 1999. **http://www.ancestry.com**

_____, and Gary Ronald Teeples. *Louisiana 1820 Census Index*. Salt Lake City, UT: Accelerated Indexing Systems, 1976. 33p.

Roux, Vincent M. *Louisiana's Households of Free People of Color Residing Outside of Orleans Parish & the City of New Orleans in 1810 & 1820*. San Francisco, CA: Author, 195. 72p.

U.S. Federal Population Census Schedules. 1820, M33, Microfilm Reel Nos. 30-32.

1830

Census Index: U.S. Selected States/Counties, 1830. Family Archive CD 315. Novato, CA: Broderbund Software. CD-ROM.

1830-1839 U.S. Census Indexes, Mid-Atlantic, South, Mid-West. Orem, UT: Automated Archives, 1993. CD-ROM.

Jackson, Ronald Vern. *Louisiana Census Index, Online Edition*. Orem, UT: Ancestry.com, Inc., 1999. **http://www.ancestry.com**

_____, and Gary Ronald Teeples. *Louisiana 1830 Census Index*. Salt Lake City, UT: Accelerated Indexing Systems, 1976. 48p.

U.S. Federal Population Census Schedules. 1830, M19, Microfilm Reel Nos. 43-45.

1840

Census Index: U.S. Selected States/Counties, 1840. Family Archive CD 316. Novato, CA: Broderbund Software. CD-ROM.

Ingmire, Frances Terry. *1840 Louisiana State Wide Census Index*. Signal Mountain, TN: Mountain Press, 1997. 264p.

Jackson, Ronald Vern. *Louisiana Census Index, Online Edition*. Orem, UT: Ancestry.com, Inc., 1999. **http://www.ancestry.com**

_____, and Gary Ronald Teeples. *Louisiana 1840 Census Index*. Salt Lake City, UT: Accelerated Indexing Systems, 1976. 81p.

U.S. Federal Population Census Schedules. 1840, M704, Microfilm Reel Nos. 127-135.

1850

Census Index: U.S. Selected States/Counties, 1850. Family Archive CD 317. Novato, CA: Broderbund Software. CD-ROM.

Census Microfilm Records: Alabama, Arkansas, Louisiana and Mississippi, 1850. Family Archive CD 453. Novato, CA: Broderbund Software. CD-ROM.

Corley, Betty J. *Index, Yeoman(s), Yeaman(s), Youman(s), U.S. Census Index, 1850, 1860, 1880, Alabama, Florida, Kentucky, Louisiana, Maryland, Mississippi, Tennessee, Texas, Virginia, Includes Various Other Spellings*. Hyrum, UT: Author, 1988. 5p.

Jackson, Ronald Vern. *Louisiana Census Index, Online Edition*. Orem, UT: Ancestry.com, Inc., 1999. **http://www.ancestry.com**

_____. *Louisiana 1850 Census Index*. Salt Lake City, UT: Accelerated Indexing Systems, 1988. 405p.

_____. *Louisiana 1850 Slave Schedule Census Index*. Salt Lake City, UT: Accelerated Indexing Systems International, 1988. 405p.

_____. *Mortality Schedules Index, Online Edition*. Orem, UT: Ancestry.com, Inc., 1999. **http://www.ancestry.com**

_____. *Mortality Schedule Louisiana 1850*. Bountiful, UT: Accelerated Indexing Systems, 1979. 81p.

U.S. Census Index Series, Alabama, Arkansas, Georgia, Florida, Louisiana, Mississippi, South Carolina, 1850. Orem, UT: Automated Archives, 1991. CD-ROM.

U.S. Federal Population Census Schedules. 1850, M432, Microfilm Reel Nos. 229-241.

U.S. Federal Population Census Schedules. 1850, M432, Slave Schedules, Microfilm Reel Nos. 242-247.

1860

Census Index: U.S. Selected States/Counties, 1860. Family Archive CD 318. Novato, CA: Broderbund Software. CD-ROM.

Corley, Betty J. *Index, Yeoman(s), Yeaman(s), Youman(s), U.S. Census Index, 1850, 1860, 1880, Alabama, Florida, Kentucky, Louisiana, Maryland, Mississippi, Tennessee, Texas, Virginia, Includes Various Other Spellings*. Hyrum, UT: Author, 1988. 5p.

Jackson, Ronald Vern. *Louisiana Census Index, Online Edition*. Orem, UT: Ancestry.com, Inc., 1999. **http://www.ancestry.com**

_____. *Louisiana 1860 Census Index*. Salt Lake City, UT: Accelerated Indexing Systems, 1985. 507p.

_____. _____. West Jordan, UT: Genealogical Services, 1985, 1997.

_____. *Louisiana 1860 Slave Schedules Index*. Salt Lake City, UT: Accelerated Indexing Systems International, 1988. 431p.

_____. *Mortality Schedules Index, Online Edition*. Orem, UT: Ancestry.com, Inc., 1999. **http://www.ancestry.com**

U.S. Census Index, 1860, Alabama, Arkansas, Florida, Louisiana, Mississippi, South Carolina. Orem, UT: Automated Archives, 1992. 1 CD-ROM.

U.S. Federal Population Census Schedules. 1860, M653, Microfilm Reel Nos. 407-426.

U.S. Federal Population Census Schedules. 1860, M653, Slave Schedules, Microfilm Reel Nos. 427-431.

1870

Census Index: U.S. Selected States/Counties, 1870. Family Archive CD 319. Novato, CA: Broderbund Software. CD-ROM.

Jackson, Ronald Vern. *Louisiana Census Index, Online Edition*. Orem, UT: Ancestry.com, Inc., 1999. **http://www.ancestry.com**

_____. *Louisiana 1870*. North Salt Lake City, UT: Accelerated Indexing Systems International, 1987. 2 vols.

_____. *Louisiana 1870 Federal Census Index*. West Jordan, UT: Genealogical Services, 1987, 1996. 846p.

U.S. Federal Population Census Schedules. 1870, M593, Microfilm Reel Nos. 505-535.

1880

Corley, Betty J. *Index, Yeoman(s), Yeaman(s), Youman(s), U.S. Census Index, 1850, 1860, 1880, Alabama, Florida, Kentucky, Louisiana, Maryland, Mississippi, Tennessee, Texas, Virginia, Includes Various Other Spellings*. Hyrum, UT: Author, 1988. 5p.

Fenerty, Patricia Ann. *1880 Census of New Orleans*. New Orleans, LA: Padraigeen Pub., 1991.

U.S. Federal Population Census Schedules. 1880, T9, Microfilm Reel Nos. 447-474.

U.S. Federal Population Census Schedules. 1880, Soundex. T751, 55 Microfilm Reels.

1890

Dilts, Bryan Lee. *1890 Louisiana Census Index of Civil War Veterans or Their Widows*. Salt Lake City, UT: Index Pub., 1984. 68p.

Jackson, Ronald Vern. *1890 Louisiana Census Index, Special Schedule of the Eleventh Census (1890) Enumerating Union Veterans and of Union Veterans of the Civil War*. Salt Lake City, UT: Accelerated Indexing Systems, 1984. 126p.

_____. *Louisiana Census Index, Online Edition, (Veterans Schedules)*. Orem, UT: Ancestry.com, Inc., 1999. **http://www.ancestry.com**

U.S. Federal Population Census Schedules, Special Schedule, Enumerating Union Veterans and Widows of Union Veterans of the Civil War. 1890, M123, Microfilm Reel No. 4-5.

Veterans' Schedules: U.S. Selected States, 1890. Family Archive CD 131. Novato, CA: Broderbund Software. CD-ROM.

1900

U.S. Federal Population Census Schedules. 1900, T623, Microfilm Reel Nos. 556-586.

U.S. Federal Population Census Schedules. 1900, Soundex. T1048, 146 Microfilm Reels.

1910

U.S. Federal Population Census Schedules. 1910, T624, Microfilm Reel Nos. 507-535.

U.S. Federal Population Census Schedules. 1910, Soundex. T1267, 132 Microfilm Reels.

U.S. Federal Population Census Schedules. 1910, Separate Miracode Index for Cities of New Orleans and Shreveport, Microfilm Reel Nos. 79-132.

1911

Burns, Loretta Elliott. *1911 Louisiana Census, Confederate Veterans or Widows.* Pasadena, TX: C&L Printing, 1995. 98p.

Jenks, Houston C. *1911 Louisiana Census, Confederate Veterans or Widows.* Baton Rouge, LA: Author, 1989. 115p.

1920

U.S. Federal Population Census Schedules. 1920, T625, Microfilm Reel Nos. 603-636.

U.S. Federal Population Census Schedules. 1920, Soundex. M1564, 135 Microfilm Reels.

Ascension Parish
1810
USGenWeb Census Project. Louisiana, 1810 Ascension Parish.
ftp://ftp.rootsweb.com/pub/census/la/ascension/1810/
1840
Ingmire, Frances Terry. *1840 Census Index, Ascension Parish, Louisiana.* San Antonio, TX: Author, 1987. 7p.
1850
Butler, Rita Babin. *Ascension Parish, Louisiana, 1850 Census, Annotated, and Slave Schedule.* Gonzales, LA: Author, 1992. 172p.
1860
Westerman, A.B. *1860 Census, Ascension Parish, Louisiana.* Thibodaux, LA: Author, 1982. 140p.
1890
Butler, Rita Babin. *Ascension Parish, Louisiana, 1890 U.S. Census.* Baton Rouge, LA: Oracle Press, 1983. 256p.

Assumption Parish
1850
Toups, Kenneth Bourgeois. *1850 Census of Assumption Parish, Louisiana.* Mobile, AL: Author, 1986. 164p.
1860
USGenWeb Census Project. Louisiana, 1860 Assumption Parish.
ftp://ftp.rootsweb.com/pub/census/la/assumption/1860/
Westerman, Audrey B. *1860 Census, Assumption Parish, Louisiana.* Thibodaux, LA: Author, 1983. 195p.
1870
1870 Census of Assumption Parish, Louisiana. Houma, LA: Terrebonne Genealogical Society, 1985. 332p.

1880

Morrison, Phoebe Chauvin, and Wilma Boudreaux Boudreaux. *Census, 1 June 1880, Assumption Parish Louisiana* . Thibodaux, LA: A.B. Westerman, 1991. 328p.

Attakapas (Assumption Parish)
1771

De Ville, Winston. *Attakapas Post, the Census of 1771*. Ville Platte, LA: Author, 1986. 16p.
1777

De Ville, Winston. *Southwest Louisiana Families in 1777, Census Records of Attakapas and Opelousas Posts*. Ville Platte, LA: Author, 1987. 31p.
1785

De Ville, Winston. *Southwest Louisiana Families in 1785, the Spanish Census of the Posts of Attakapas and Opelousas*. Ville Platte, LA: Author, 1991. Unpgd.

Avoyelles Parish
1820

Felldin, Jeanne Robey. *The 1820 United States Census Index, the Louisiana Parishes of Avoyelles, Catahoula, Concordia, Feliciana, Iberville, Natchitoches, and West Baton Rouge*. Tomball, TX: Genealogical Publications, 1976. 23p.

Baton Rouge (East Baton Rouge Parish)
1782

DeVille, Winston. *The Baton Rouge Census of 1782*. Ville Platte, LA: Author, 1987. 4p.

Bienville Parish
1850

Brooks, Mary. *1850 Census Records, Louisiana, Bienville Parish*. San Angelo, TX: Author, 1996. 2 vols.

Caddo Parish
1840

Ingmire, Frances Terry. *1840 Census Index, Caddo Parish, Louisiana*. San Antonio, TX: Author, 1987. 10p.
1850

Boyett, Jeanie Knox, and Joyce Shannon Bridges. *1850 Caddo Parish Louisiana Census*. Shreveport, LA: Authors, 1988. 70p.

Brooks, Mary. *1850 Census Records, Louisiana, Caddo Parish*. San Angelo, TX: Author, 1996. 2 vols.

Calcasieu Parish
1840

Seymour, Geneva Bailey. *1840 Census of Calcasieu Parish, Louisiana*. Lubbock, TX: Author, 1982. 24p.
1850

Seymour, Geneva Bailey. *1850 Census of Calcasieu Parish, Louisiana*. Cecilia, LA: Hebert Publications, 1980. 96p.
1860

Seymour, Geneva Bailey. *1860 Census of Calcasieu Parish, Louisiana*. Eunice, LA: Hebert Publications, 1980. 156p.
1870

Seymour, Geneva Bailey. *1870 Census of Calcasieu Parish, Louisiana*. Cecilia, LA: Hebert Publications, 1982. 209p.

Caldwell Parish
1850

Brooks, Mary. *1850 Census Records, Louisiana, Caldwell Parish, Concordia Parish*. San Angelo, TX: Author, 1996. Unpgd.

Cameron Parish
1870
Seymour, Geneva Bailey. *1870 Census of Cameron Parish, Louisiana.* Cecilia, LA: Hebert Publications, 1983. 52p.

Catahoula Parish
1810
Roberts, Ed, and Mattie M. Somerville. *1810 Census of the Northeast Louisiana Parishes of Ouachita, Catahoula, and Concordia.* Monroe, LA: Northeast Louisiana Genealogical Society, 1975. 15p.

USGenWeb Census Project. Louisiana, 1810 Catahoula Parish.

ftp://ftp.rootsweb.com/pub/census/la/catahoula/1810/
1820
Felldin, Jeanne Robey. *The 1820 United States Census Index, the Louisiana Parishes of Avoyelles, Catahoula, Concordia, Feliciana, Iberville, Natchitoches, and West Baton Rouge.* Tomball, TX: Genealogical Publications, 1976. 23p.
1850
Knight, Carol Young. *1850 Census of Catahoula Parish, Louisiana.* Aledo, TX: Author, 1984. 87p.
1870
1870 Census Index, Catahoula Parish, Louisiana. Harrisonburg, LA: Catahoula Parish Library, 1985. 194p.

Claiborne Parish
1830-1850
Head, Wanda Volentine. *Claiborne Parish, Louisiana 1830, 1840 and 1850 Censuses with 1850 Mortality Schedule and Slave Holders.* Shreveport, LA: J&W Enterprises, 1996. 165p.

Concordia Parish
1810
Roberts, Ed, and Mattie M. Somerville. *1810 Census of the Northeast Louisiana Parishes of Ouachita, Catahoula, and Concordia.* Monroe, LA: Northeast Louisiana Genealogical Society, 1975. 15p.

USGenWeb Census Project. Louisiana, 1810 Concordia Parish.

ftp://ftp.rootsweb.com/pub/census/la/concordia/1810/
1820
Felldin, Jeanne Robey. *The 1820 United States Census Index, the Louisiana Parishes of Avoyelles, Catahoula, Concordia, Feliciana, Iberville, Natchitoches, and West Baton Rouge.* Tomball, TX: Genealogical Publications, 1976. 23p.
1850
Brooks, Mary. *1850 Census Records, Louisiana, Caldwell Parish, Concordia Parish.* San Angelo, TX: Author, 1996. Unpgd.

DeSoto Parish
Davis, Kathryn Hooper. *1850 Census DeSoto Parish, Louisiana.* Nacogdoches, TX: Ericson Books, 1996. 88p.

Donaldsonville Parish
1840
Ingmire, Frances Terry. *1840 Census Index, Donaldsonville Parish, Louisiana.* San Antonio, TX: Author, 1987. 3p.

East Baton Rouge Parish
1810
USGenWeb Census Project. Louisiana, 1810 E-Baton Rouge Parish.

ftp://ftp.rootsweb.com/pub/census/la/e-batonrough/1810/

1820

*USGen*Web Census Project. Louisiana, 1820 E-Baton Rouge Parish.
ftp://ftp.rootsweb.com/pub/census/la/e-batonrouge/1820/

1830

Johnson, Donald W., Mrs. M. Earl Denham, and Mrs. Warren Strickland. *1830 Enumeration Census of East Baton Rouge Parish*. Baton Rouge, LA: Baton Rouge Genealogical and Historical Society, 1974. 13p.

1850

Slaton, Claude B. *East Baton Rouge Parish, Louisiana Mortality Schedules, 1850, 1860, 1870, 1880*. Baker, LA: Folk Finders, 1983. 92p.

1860

Lipscomb, Billie, and Mary Lou Loudon. *Surname Index, 1860 Census, East Baton Rouge Parish, Louisiana*. Baton Rouge, LA: East Baton Rouge Parish Library, 1983. 58p.

Slaton, Claude B. *East Baton Rouge Parish, Louisiana Mortality Schedules, 1850, 1860, 1870, 1880*. Baker, LA: Folk Finders, 1983. 92p.

1870, 1880

Slaton, Claude B. *East Baton Rouge Parish, Louisiana Mortality Schedules, 1850, 1860, 1870, 1880*. Baker, LA: Folk Finders, 1983. 92p.

East Feliciana Parish
1820

Felldin, Jeanne Robey. *The 1820 United States Census Index, the Louisiana Parishes of Avoyelles, Catahoula, Concordia, Feliciana, Iberville, Natchitoches, and West Baton Rouge*. Tomball, TX: Genealogical Publications, 1976. 23p.

1830

Johnson, Donald W. *1830 East Feliciana Parish, Louisiana Census*. Zachary, LA: Author, 1975. 17p.

1840

Slaton, Claude B. *The 1840 Census' of East and West Feliciana Parishes of Louisiana*. Clinton, LA: J & W Enterprises, 1986. 76p.

1850

Johnson, Donald W. *1850 East Feliciana Parish, Louisiana Census*. Zachary, LA: Author, 1975. 156p.

Florida Parish
1820

Sanders, Mary Elizabeth. *An Index to the 1820 Census of Louisiana's Florida Parishes and 1812 St. Tammany Parish Tax List*. Lafayette, LA: Author, 1972. 34p.

Iberville Parish
1777

DeVille, Winston. *St. Gabriel Settlers, the 1777 Census of Iberville District in the Province of Louisiana*. Ville Platte, LA: Author, 1987. 12p.

1820

Felldin, Jeanne Robey. *The 1820 United States Census Index, the Louisiana Parishes of Avoyelles, Catahoula, Concordia, Feliciana, Iberville, Natchitoches, and West Baton Rouge*. Tomball, TX: Genealogical Publications, 1976. 23p.

1878

Riffel, Judy. *1878 Iberville Parish Census*. Baton Rouge, LA: Comité des Archives de la Louisiane, 1991. 200p.

Jefferson Parish
1840

Ingmire, Frances Terry. *1840 Census Index, Jefferson Parish, Louisiana*. San Antonio, TX: Author, 1987. 9p.

1850

Boling, Yvette Guillot, and Mary Alice Trosclair Duffard. *1850 Federal Census, Jefferson Parish, Louisiana*. Jefferson, LA: Authors, 1986. 395p.

Lafourche Parish
1770-1798

Robichaux, Albert J. *Colonial Settlers along Bayou Lafourche, Louisiana Census Records, 1770-1798*. Harvey, LA: Author, 1974. 219p.

1810

Westerman, Audrey B. *First Land Owners and 1810 Annotated Census of Lafourche Interior Parish, Louisiana*. Houma, LA: Terrebonne Genealogical Society, 1995. Unpgd.

1850

Westerman, Audrey B. *Lafourche Parish, Louisiana Census 1850*. Thibodaux, LA: Nicholls State University Press, 1979. 120p.

1860

Toups, Kenneth Bourgeois. *1860 Census Lafourche Parish*. Thibodaux, LA: Author, 1986. 224p.

1880

Chauvin, Phillip. *1880 U.S. Census, Lafourche Parish, Louisiana*. Houma, LA: Terrebonne Genealogical Society, Inc., 1999. 200p.

1900

Census of the Tenth Ward of Lafourche Parish, 1900. Golden Meadow, LA: Société des Cajuns, 1985. 67p.

Lincoln Parish
1880

Richardson, Marcia Duncan. *Lincoln Parish, Louisiana 1880 Census*. Shreveport, LA: J&W Enterprises, 1989. 105p.

Livingston Parish
1840

Cambre, Mercy Aydell. *1840 Enumeration Census of Livingston Parish, Louisiana*. Baton Rouge, LA: Author, 1976. 16p.

1850

1850 U.S. Census, Livingston Parish, Louisiana. Livingston, LA: Edward Livingston Historical Assn., 1979. 145p.

Kerns, Gloria Lambert, and Claude B. Slaton. *Livingston Parish, Louisiana Mortality and Slave Schedules 1850, 1860, 1870, 1880*. Baker, LA: Folk Finders. 30p.

1860

Aucoin, Barbara. *1860 U.S. Census of Livingston Parish, Louisiana*. Livingston, LA: Edward Livingston Historical Assn., 1977. 170p.

Kerns, Gloria Lambert, and Claude B. Slaton. *Livingston Parish, Louisiana Mortality and Slave Schedules 1850, 1860, 1870, 1880*. Baker, LA: Folk Finders. 30p.

1870

1870 U.S. Census of Livingston Parish, Louisiana. Livingston, LA: Edward Livingston Historical Assn., 1980. 218p.

Kerns, Gloria Lambert, and Claude B. Slaton. *Livingston Parish, Louisiana Mortality and Slave Schedules 1850, 1860, 1870, 1880*. Baker, LA: Folk Finders. 30p.

1880

1880 U.S. Census of Livingston Parish, Louisiana. Livingston, LA: Edward Livingston Historical Assn., 1983. 2 vols.

Kerns, Gloria Lambert, and Claude B. Slaton. *Livingston Parish, Louisiana Mortality and Slave Schedules 1850, 1860, 1870, 1880*. Baker, LA: Folk Finders. 30p.

1900

1900 U.S. Census, Livingston Parish, Louisiana. Livingston, LA: Edward Livingston Historical Assn., 1985. 2 vols.

_____. _____. 1993. 326p.

1910

Livingston Parish, Louisiana, the 1910 Federal Census and the 1911 School Census. Livingston, LA: Edward Livingston Historical Association, 1995. 262p.

1920

Livingston Parish, Louisiana, the 1920 Federal Census. Livingston, LA: Edward Livingston Historical Association, 1997. 248p.

Natchitoches Parish

Mills, Elizabeth S. *Natchitoches Colonials, Censuses, Military Rolls, and Tax Lists, 1722-1803.* Chicago, IL: Adams Press, 1981. 148p.

1810

USGenWeb Census Project. Louisiana, 1810 Natchitoches Parish.

ftp://ftp.rootsweb.com/pub/census/la/natchitoches/1810/

1820

Felldin, Jeanne Robey. *The 1820 United States Census Index, the Louisiana Parishes of Avoyelles, Catahoula, Concordia, Feliciana, Iberville, Natchitoches, and West Baton Rouge.* Tomball, TX: Genealogical Publications, 1976. 23p.

_____. *The 1820 United States Census Index, Natchitoches Parish, Louisiana.* Tomball, TX: Genealogical Publications, 1976. 5p.

Orleans Parish

1820

USGenWeb Census Project. Louisiana, 1820 Orleans Parish.

ftp://ftp.rootsweb.com/pub/census/la/orleans/1820/

1910

U.S. Federal Population Census Schedules. 1910, Separate Miracode Index for Cities of New Orleans and Shreveport, Microfilm Reel Nos. 79-132.

Ouachita Parish

1810

Roberts, Ed, and Mattie M. Somerville. *1810 Census of the Northeast Louisiana Parishes of Ouachita, Catahoula, and Concordia.* Monroe, LA: Northeast Louisiana Genealogical Society, 1975. 15p.

USGenWeb Census Project. Louisiana, 1810 Ouachita Parish.

ftp://ftp.rootsweb.com/pub/census/la/ouachita/1810/

1820

Roberts, Ed, and Mattie M. Somerville. *1820 Census of the Northeast Louisiana Parishes of Ouachita, Catahoula, and Concordia.* Monroe, LA: Northeast Louisiana Genealogical Society, 1975. 13p.

Plaquemines Parish

1810

USGenWeb Census Project. Louisiana, 1810 Plaquemines Parish.

ftp://ftp.rootsweb.com/pub/census/la/plaquemines/1810/

1820

USGenWeb Census Project. Louisiana, 1820 Plaquemines Parish.

ftp://ftp.rootsweb.com/pub/census/la/plaquemines/1820/

1850

Menge, Margaret A. *Plaquemines Parish, Louisiana Census, 1850.* New Orleans, LA: Author. 91p.

1920

Stringfield, William R. *United States Census 1920, Plaquemines Parish, Louisiana.* Greenville, SC: Blossom Press, 1993. 187p.

Point Coupee Parish
1745

Barron, Bill. *Census of Pointe Coupee, Louisiana, 1745.* New Orleans, LA: Polyanthos, 1978. 106p.
1810

USGenWeb Census Project. Louisiana, 1810 Point Couppee Parish. ftp://ftp.rootsweb.com/pub/census/la/ pointecouppee/1810/

Rapides Parish

De Ville, Winston. *Rapides Post on Red River, Census and Military Documents for Central Louisiana, 1769-1800.* Ville Platte, LA: Author, 1985. 47p.
1810

USGenWeb Census Project. Louisiana, 1810 Rapides Parish.
ftp://ftp.rootsweb.com/pub/census/la/rapides/1810/
1850

McManus, Jane Parker. *Rapides Parish, Louisiana 1850 Census.* Seattle, WA: Author, 1978. 136p.
1870

Dill, Harry F. *African American Inhabitants of Rapides Parish, Louisiana, 1 June - 4 September 1870.* Bowie, MD: Heritage Books, 1998. 373p.

Sabine Parish
1850

Sandel, Elias Wesley. *Early Sabine Parish, Including the 1850 Sabine Parish Census and Early Towns.* Author, 1972. Unpgd.
1860

Davis, Kathryn Hooper. *1860 Census, Sabine Parish, Louisiana.* Nacogdoches, TX: Ericson Books, 1996. 100p.

1860 Census, Sabine Parish, Louisiana. Nacogdoches, TX: Ericson Books, 1996. 100p.
1870

Davis, Kathryn Hooper. *1870 Census, Sabine Parish, Louisiana.* Nacogdoches, TX: Ericson Books, 1996. 121p.

1870 Census, Sabine Parish, Louisiana. Nacogdoches, TX: Ericson Books, 1996. 121p.
1880

Davis, Kathryn Hooper. *1880 Census, Sabine Parish, Louisiana.* Nacogdoches, TX: Ericson Books, 1996. 125p.
1900

Davis, Kathryn Hooper. *1900 Census, Sabine Parish, Louisiana.* Nacogdoches, TX: Ericson Books, 1996. 258p.

Saint Bernard Parish
1810

USGenWeb Census Project. Louisiana, 1810 St. Bernard Parish.
ftp://ftp.rootsweb.com/pub/census/la/stbernard/1810/
1870

Donnelly, Deborah Hoover, and Sally Embry Viada. *1870 Census, St. Bernard Parish, State of Louisiana.* Chalmette, LA: St. Bernard Genealogical Society, 1984. 104p.

Saint Charles Parish
1810
USGenWeb Census Project. Louisiana, 1810 St. Charles Parish.
ftp://ftp.rootsweb.com/pub/census/la/stcharles/1810/

Saint Domingue
1688-1720
De Ville, Winston. *St. Domingue, Census Records and Military Lists, 1688-1720.* Ville Platte, LA: Author, 1988. Unpgd.

Saint Helena Parish
1830
1830 Enumeration Census of St. Helena Parish, Louisiana. Zachary, LA: Author, 1975. 13p.
1850
Johnson, Donald W. *Louisiana, Saint Helena Parish, 1850 U.S. Census.* Zachary, LA: Author, 1975. 94p.
1880
1880 U.S. Census of St. Helena Parish, Louisiana. Greensburg, LA: St. Helena Historical Association, 1991. 464p.
1900
1900 United States Census for St. Helena Parish, Louisiana. Greensburg, LA: St. Helena Historical Association, 1991. 2 vols.
1910
1910 United States Census for St. Helena Parish Louisiana. Amite, LA: St. Helena Historical Association, 1996. 3 vols.

Saint James Parish
1777
De Ville, Winston. *The Parish of St. James in the Province of Louisiana, Genealogical Abstracts from the Spanish Census of 1777.* Ville Platte, LA: Author, 1987. 23p.
1810
USGenWeb Census Project. Louisiana, 1810, St. James Parish.
ftp://ftp.rootsweb.com/pub/census/la/stjames/1810/
1840
Ingmire, Frances Terry. *1840 Census Index, St. James Parish, Louisiana.* San Antonio, TX: Author, 1987. 9p.
1850, 1860
Oubre, Elton J. *St. James Parish, Louisiana, 1850 & 1860 Census.* Thibodaux, LA: Nicholls State University Library, 1983. 180p.

Saint John the Baptist Parish
1810
Maurin, Michael J. *U.S. Census of 1850, St. John the Baptist Parish, Louisiana.* Destrehan, LA: German-Acadian Coast, Historical & Genealogical Society, 1983. 71p.
USGenWeb Census Project. Louisiana, 1810 St. John the Baptist Parish.
ftp://ftp.rootsweb.com/pub/census/la/stjohn/1810/

Saint Landry Parish
1777
De Ville, Winston. *Southwest Louisiana Families in 1777, Census Records of Attakapas and Opelousas Posts.* Ville Platte, LA: Author, 1987. 31p.
1781
De Ville, Winston. *Opelousas Post, the Census of 1771.* Ville Platte, LA: Author, 1986. 17p.

1785

De Ville, Winston. *Southwest Louisiana Families in 1785, the Spanish Census of the Posts of Attakapas and Opelousas*. Ville Platte, LA: Author, 1991. Unpgd.

1810

USGenWeb Census Project. Louisiana, 1810 Opelousas Parish.
ftp://ftp.rootsweb.com/pub/census/la/opelousas/1810/

1850

Young, John Austin. *1850 Census, St. Landry Parish, Louisiana*. Basile, LA: Author, 1992. 292p.

1860

Young, John Austin. *1860 Census, St. Landry Parish, Louisiana*. Basile, LA: Author, 1992. 307p.

Saint Mary Parish
1860

Businelle, Lynda J. *The 1860 St. Mary Parish Census, Including the 1870 St. Mary Parish Mortality Schedules*. Morgan City, LA: Author, 1986. 82p.

Saint Tammany Parish

Ingmire, Frances Terry. *1840 Census Index, St. Tammany Parish, Louisiana*. San Antonio, TX: Author, 1987. 9p.

Shreveport (Caddo Parish)
1910

U.S. Federal Population Census Schedules. 1910, Separate Miracode Index for Cities of New Orleans and Shreveport, Microfilm Reel Nos. 79-132.

Tangipahoa Parish
1870

Sandel, Elias Wesley, and Mary E. Sandel. *Early Tangipahoa Parish, Including the 1870 (1st) Census, Confederate Soldiers, Towns, Old Families, Voters, Pensioners, Parish Officials, Excerpts from Old Newspapers, the First Schools*. Author, 1984. 359p.

1900

Perrin, James Morris. *1900 Census Tangipahoa Parish, Louisiana, an Index of all Surnames Listed on the 1900 Census*. Hammond, LA: Author, 1982. 23p.

1910

Perrin, James Morris. *1910 Census Tangipahoa Parish, Louisiana, an Index of all Surnames Listed on the 1910 Census*. Hammond, LA: Author, 1983. 46p.

Sandel, Mary E., and Edward Sandel. *Italian Immigrants in the 1910 U.S. Census of Tangipahoa Parish, Louisiana*. Roseland, LA: Tabor-Lucas Publications, 1993. 158p.

Terrebonne Parish
1770-1798

Robichaux, Albert J. *Colonial Settlers along Bayou Lafourche, Louisiana Census Records, 1770-1798*. Harvey, LA: Author, 1974. 219p.

1810

Westerman, Audrey B. *First Land Owners and 1810 Annotated Census of Lafourche Interior Parish, Louisiana*. Houma, LA: Terrebonne Genealogical Society, 1995. Unpgd.

1840

Morrison, Phoebe Chauvin. *1840 Census of Terrebonne Parish, Louisiana*. Houma, LA: Terrebonne Genealogical Society, 1988. 94p.

1850

Horvath, Dorothea. *1850 Census of Terrebonne Parish, Louisiana*. Houma, LA: Terrebonne Genealogical Society, 1985. 198p.

1860

Morrison, Phoebe Chauvin. *Reannotated 1860 Census of Terrebonne Parish, Louisiana, June 4, 1860*. Houma, LA: Terrebonne Genealogical Society, 1992. 163p.

The Terrebonne Parish 1860 Census, June 4, 1860. Houma, LA: Terrebonne Genealogical Society, 1983. 134p.

1870

United States Terrebonne Parish 1870. Houma, LA: Terrebonne Genealogical Society, 1986. 405p.

1880

Horvath, Dorothea. *1850 Census of Terrebonne Parish, Louisiana, with Annotations*. Houma, LA: Terrebonne Genealogical Society, 1985. 198p.

1900

Boudreaux, Wilma Boudreaux, and Phoebe Chauvin Morrison. *Census, 1 June 1900, Terrebonne Parish, Louisiana*. Thibodaux, LA: Westerman, 1989. 2 vols.

1910

Chauvin, Phillip. *1910 Census, Terrebonne Parish, Louisiana, Wards 1, 2, 3*. Houma, LA: Terrebonne Genealogical Society, Inc., 1983. 289p.

_____. *1910 Census, Terrebonne Parish, Louisiana, Wards 4-10*. Houma, LA: Terrebonne Genealogical Society, Inc., 1984. pp. 291-652.

Union Parish
1839-1865

Dill, Harry Francis. *Some Slaveholders and Their Slaves, Union Parish, Louisiana, 1839-1865*. Bowie, MD: Heritage Books, 1997. 195p.

1850

Butler, Catherine Bradley. *Union Parish, Louisiana, United States Census of 1850*. Monroe, LA: Northeast Louisiana Genealogical Society, 1977. 82p.

1865

Dill, Harry Francis. *Some Slaveholders and Their Slaves, Union Parish, Louisiana, 1839-1865*. Bowie, MD: Heritage Books, 1997. 195p.

Vernon Parish
1880

McManus, Jane P. *1880 Vernon Parish, Louisiana U.S. Census Population Schedules*. Pineville, LA: Parker Enterprises, 1988. 181p.

Washington Parish
1830

Johnson, Donald W., Mrs. Walter Moss, and Mrs. Warren Strickland. *1830 Enumeration Census of Washington Parish, Louisiana*. Baton Rouge, LA: Baton Rouge Genealogical and Historical Society, 1975. 12p.

West Baton Rouge Parish
1820

Felldin, Jeanne Robey. *The 1820 United States Census Index, the Louisiana Parishes of Avoyelles, Catahoula, Concordia, Feliciana, Iberville, Natchitoches, and West Baton Rouge*. Tomball, TX: Genealogical Publications, 1976. 23p.

West Feliciana Parish
1820

Felldin, Jeanne Robey. *The 1820 United States Census Index, the Louisiana Parishes of Avoyelles, Catahoula, Concordia, Feliciana, Iberville, Natchitoches, and West Baton Rouge*. Tomball, TX: Genealogical Publications, 1976. 23p.

1830

Johnson, Donald W. *1830 Enumeration Census of West Feliciana Parish, Louisiana.* Zachary, LA: Author, 1976. 14p.

1840

Slaton, Claude B. *The 1840 Census' of East and West Feliciana Parishes of Louisiana.* Clinton, LA: J & W Enterprises, 1986. 76p.

1850

Johnson, Donald W. *West Feliciana Parish, Louisiana, Census 1850.* Zachary, LA: Author, 1976. 101p.

Winn Parish
1860

Womack, Annette Carpenter. *1860 Federal Census of Winn Parish, Louisiana and 1860 Mortality Schedule for Winn Parish, Louisiana.* Natchitoches, LA: Courier Publication, 1984. 127p.

Maine

1790

U.S. Bureau of the Census. *Heads of Families at the First Census of the United States Taken in the Year 1790, Maine.* Washington, DC: Government Printing Office, 1908. 105p.

_____. _____. Spartanburg, SC: Reprint Co., 1963. 105p.

_____. _____. *Online Database Edition.* Orem, UT: Ancestry.com, Inc., 1999.

http://www.ancestry.com

_____. *U.S. Federal Population Census Schedules*, 1790. T498, Microfilm Reel No. 1.

1790 Census of Maine. Camden, ME: Picton Press, 1995. 124p.

U.S. Federal Population Census Schedules, 1790. M637, Microfilm Reel No. 2.

1800

Jackson, Ronald Vern. *Maine Census Index, Online Edition.* Orem, UT: Ancestry.com, Inc., 1999.

http://www.ancestry.com

_____, Gary Ronald Teeples, and David Schaefermeyer. *Maine 1800 Census Index.* Salt Lake City, UT: Accelerated Indexing Systems, 1974. 107p.

Steuart, Raeone Christensen. *Maine 1800 Census Index.* Bountiful, UT: Heritage Quest, 2000. 156p.

_____. *United States 1800 Census Index.* Bountiful, UT: Heritage Quest, 2000. 4 vols. CD-ROM.

U.S. Federal Population Census Schedules, 1800. M32, Microfilm Reel Nos. 6-8.

1810

Jackson, Ronald Vern. *Maine Census Index, Online Edition.* Orem, UT: Ancestry.com, Inc., 1999.

http://www.ancestry.com

_____, Gary Ronald Teeples, and David Schaefermeyer. *Maine 1810 Census Index.* Salt Lake City, UT: Accelerated Indexing Systems, 1976. 86p.

U.S. Census Index Series, New England, New York, 1810. Orem, UT: Automated Archives, 1992. CD-ROM.

U.S. Federal Population Census Schedules, 1810. M252, Microfilm Reel Nos. 11-12.

1820

Jackson, Ronald Vern. *Maine Census Index, Online Edition.* Orem, UT: Ancestry.com, Inc., 1999.

http://www.ancestry.com

_____, and Gary Ronald Teeples. *Maine 1820 Census Index.* Bountiful, UT: Accelerated Indexing Systems, 1976. 118p.

U.S. Federal Population Census Schedules. 1820, M33, Microfilm Reel Nos. 33-39.

1830

Census Index: U.S. Selected States/Counties, 1830. Family Archive CD 315. Novato, CA: Broderbund Software. CD-ROM.

Jackson, Ronald Vern. *Maine Census Index, Online Edition.* Orem, UT: Ancestry.com, Inc., 1999.
http://www.ancestry.com

_____, and Gary Ronald Teeples. *Maine 1830 Census Index.* Bountiful, UT: Accelerated Indexing Systems, 1977. 170p.

U.S. Census Index, 1830-1839, New England, New York, Pennsylvania. Orem, UT: Automated Archives, 1992. 1 CD-ROM.

U.S. Federal Population Census Schedules. 1830, M19, Microfilm Reel Nos. 46-52.

1840

Census Index: U.S. Selected States/Counties, 1840. Family Archive CD 316. Novato, CA: Broderbund Software. CD-ROM.

Jackson, Ronald Vern. *Maine Census Index, Online Edition.* Orem, UT: Ancestry.com, Inc., 1999.
http://www.ancestry.com

_____, and Gary Ronald Teeples. *Maine 1840 Census Index.* Bountiful, UT: Accelerated Indexing Systems, 1978. 210p.

U.S. Federal Population Census Schedules. 1840, M704, Microfilm Reel Nos. 136-155.

1850

Census Index: U.S. Selected States/Counties, 1850. Family Archive CD 317. Novato, CA: Broderbund Software. CD-ROM.

Jackson, Ronald Vern. *Maine Census Index, Online Edition.* Orem, UT: Ancestry.com, Inc., 1999.
http://www.ancestry.com

_____, and Gary Ronald Teeples. *Maine 1850 Census Index.* Salt Lake City, UT: Accelerated Indexing Systems, 1978. 404p.

U.S. Census Index Series, New England, 1850. Orem, UT: Automated Archives, 1991. CD-ROM.

U.S. Federal Population Census Schedules. 1850, M432, Microfilm Reel Nos. 248-276.

1860

Census Index: U.S. Selected States/Counties, 1860. Family Archive CD 318. Novato, CA: Broderbund Software. CD-ROM.

Federal Census Index, Maine 1860. West Jordan, UT: Genealogical Services, 1991, 1997. 3 vols.

U.S. Census Index, 1860, Maine. Orem, UT: Automated Archives, 1994. CD-ROM.

Jackson, Ronald Vern. *Federal Census Index, Maine 1860.* West Jordan, UT: Genealogical Services, 1991, 1997.

_____. *Maine Census Index, Online Edition.* Orem, UT: Ancestry.com, Inc., 1999.
http://www.ancestry.com

Savage, Nellie P., and William H. Blue. *Washington Pioneers from the State of Maine, 1860-1870.* Seattle, WA: Seattle Genealogical Society, 1989. 85p.

U.S. Federal Population Census Schedules. 1860, M653, Microfilm Reel Nos. 432-455.

1870

Census Index: U.S. Selected States/Counties, 1870. Family Archive CD 319. Novato, CA: Broderbund Software. CD-ROM.

Jackson, Ronald Vern. *Maine Census Index, Online Edition.* Orem, UT: Ancestry.com, Inc., 1999.
http://www.ancestry.com

_____, and Gary Ronald Teeples. *Maine 1870 Census Index.* Salt Lake City, UT: Accelerated Indexing Systems, 1991. 925p.

Savage, Nellie P., and William H. Blue. *Washington Pioneers from the State of Maine, 1860-1870.* Seattle, WA: Seattle Genealogical Society, 1989. 85p.

Steuart, Raeone Christensen. *Maine 1870 Census Index*. Bountiful, UT: Heritage Quest, 2000. 2 vols.

_____. *Maine, New Hampshire and Vermont 1810 Census Index*. Bountiful, UT: Heritage Quest, 2000. CD-ROM.

U.S. Federal Population Census Schedules. 1870, M593, Microfilm Reel Nos. 536-565.

1880

U.S. Federal Population Census Schedules. 1880, T9, Microfilm Reel Nos. 475-492.

U.S. Federal Population Census Schedules. 1880, Soundex. T752, 29 Microfilm Reels.

1890

Dilts, Bryan Lee. *1890 Maine Census Index of Civil War Veterans or Their Widows*. Salt Lake City, UT: Index Pub., 1984. 156p.

Jackson, Ronald Vern. *Federal Census Index, Maine 1890, Union Veterans*. West Jordan, UT: Genealogical Services, 1996. 441p.

_____. *Maine Census Index, Online Edition (Veterans Schedules)*. Orem, UT: Ancestry.com, Inc., 1999.
http://www.ancestry.com

U.S. Federal Population Census Schedules, Special Schedule, Enumerating Union Veterans and Widows of Union Veterans of the Civil War. 1890, M123, Microfilm Reel No. 6-7.

Veterans' Schedules: U.S. Selected States, 1890. Family Archive CD 131. Novato, CA: Broderbund Software. CD-ROM.

1900

U.S. Federal Population Census Schedules. 1900, T623, Microfilm Reel Nos. 587-603.

U.S. Federal Population Census Schedules. 1900, Soundex. T1049, 79 Microfilm Reels.

1910

U.S. Federal Population Census Schedules. 1910, T624, Microfilm Reel Nos. 536-548. (No Soundex/Miracode Index was prepared by the Government for this State.)

1920

U.S. Federal Population Census Schedules. 1920, T625, Microfilm Reel Nos. 637-651.

U.S. Federal Population Census Schedules. 1920, Soundex. M1565, 67 Microfilm Reels.

Bradford (Penobscott County)
1900
Corliss, Stephen L. *Twelfth Census of the United States, Bradford Town, 1900*. Author, 1995. 22p.

Cumberland County
1860
Jackson, Ronald Vern. *Maine 1860 Federal Census Index, Cumberland County*. Salt Lake City, UT: Accelerated Indexing Systems International, 1990. 55p.

Orrington (Penobscot County)
1790-1900
Swett, David Livingstone. *Census and Cemetery Records of Orrington, Penobscot County, Maine 1790-1900*. Camden, ME: Picton Press, 1996. 677p.
1838-1893
Swett, David Livingstone. *School Records and Agricultural Censuses and Bounties of Orrington, Penobscot County, Maine, 1838-1893*. Camden, ME: Picton Press, 1997. 698p.

York County
1850
Frost, John Eldridge. *York County, Maine Mortality Schedules, United States Census 1850, 1860, 1870.* Author, 1987. 64p.
1860
Frost, John Eldridge. *York County, Maine Mortality Schedules, United States Census 1850, 1860, 1870.* Author, 1987. 64p.
Index to the York County, Maine 1860 Census. Ogunquit, ME: York County Genealogical Society, 1993. 2 vols.
1870
Frost, John Eldridge. *York County, Maine Mortality Schedules, United States Census 1850, 1860, 1870.* Author, 1987. 64p.

Maryland

Wilkins, William N. *Maryland Census Records.* Baltimore, MD: Author, 1945. 155p.

1776
Carothers, Bettie Stirling. *1776 Census of Maryland.* Lutherville, MD: Author, 1972. 212p.

1778
Carothers, Bettie Stirling. *1778 Census of Maryland.* Lutherville, MD: Author. 54p.

1790
Jackson, Ronald Vern. *Maryland Census Index, Online Edition.* Orem, UT: Ancestry.com, Inc., 1999.
http://www.ancestry.com
U.S. Bureau of the Census. *Heads of Families at the First Census of the United States Taken in the Year 1790, Maryland.* Washington, DC: Government Printing Office, 1907. 189p.
_____. _____. Spartanburg, SC: Reprint Co., 1964. 189p.
_____. _____. Baltimore, MD: Genealogical Publishing Co., 1965. 189p.
_____. _____. Bountiful, UT: Accelerated Indexing Systems, 1978. 189p.
_____. _____. *Online Database Edition.* Orem, UT: Ancestry.com, Inc., 1999.
http://www.ancestry.com
_____. *U.S. Federal Population Census Schedules*, 1790. T498, Microfilm Reel No. 3.
U.S. Federal Population Census Schedules, 1790. M637, Microfilm Reel No. 3.

1800
Jackson, Ronald Vern. *Maryland Census Index, Online Edition.* Orem, UT: Ancestry.com, Inc., 1999.
http://www.ancestry.com
_____, and Gary Ronald Teeples. *Maryland 1800 Census Index.* Salt Lake City, UT: Accelerated Indexing Systems, 1973. 153p.
Steuart, Raeone Christensen. *Maryland 1800 Census Index.* Bountiful, UT: Heritage Quest, 2000. 243p.
_____. *United States 1800 Census Index.* Bountiful, UT: Heritage Quest, 2000. 4 vols. CD-ROM.
U.S. Federal Population Census Schedules, 1800. M32, Microfilm Reel Nos. 9-12.
Volkel, Charlotte A. *An Index to the 1800 Federal Census of Maryland.* Author, 1967. 4 vols.

1801
Jackson, Ronald Vern. *Maryland 1801 Census.* Bountiful, UT: Accelerated Indexing Systems, 1976. 104p.

1810

Jackson, Ronald Vern. *Maryland Census Index, Online Edition.* Orem, UT: Ancestry.com, Inc., 1999. **http://www.ancestry.com**

_____, and Gary Ronald Teeples. *Maryland 1810 Census Index.* Salt Lake City, UT: Accelerated Indexing Systems, 1976. 104p.

U.S. Federal Population Census Schedules, 1810. M252, Microfilm Reel Nos. 13-16.

1820

Jackson, Ronald Vern. *Maryland Census Index, Online Edition.* Orem, UT: Ancestry.com, Inc., 1999. **http://www.ancestry.com**

_____, and Gary Ronald Teeples. *Maryland 1820 Census Index.* Salt Lake City, UT: Accelerated Indexing Systems, 1977. 123p.

Parks, Gary W. *Index to the 1820 Census of Maryland and Washington, D.C..* Baltimore, MD: Genealogical Publishing Co., 1986. 274p.

U.S. Federal Population Census Schedules. 1820, M33, Microfilm Reel Nos. 40-46.

1830

Census Index: U.S. Selected States/Counties, 1830. Family Archive CD 315. Novato, CA: Broderbund Software. CD-ROM.

1830-1839 U.S. Census Indexes, Mid-Atlantic, South, Mid-West. Orem, UT: Automated Archives, 1993. CD-ROM.

Jackson, Ronald Vern. *Maryland Census Index, Online Edition.* Orem, UT: Ancestry.com, Inc., 1999. **http://www.ancestry.com**

_____, and Gary Ronald Teeples. *Maryland 1830 Census Index.* Salt Lake City, UT: Accelerated Indexing Systems, 1976, 1978. 119p.

U.S. Federal Population Census Schedules. 1830, M19, Microfilm Reel Nos. 53-58.

1832

Hynson, Jerry M. *Free African Americans of Maryland 1832, Including Allegany, Anne Arundel, Calvert, Caroline, Cecil, Charles, Dorchester, Frederick, Kent, Montgomery, Queen Ann's, and St. Mary's Counties.* Westminster, MD: Family Line Publications, 1998. 161p.

1840

Census Index: U.S. Selected States/Counties, 1840. Family Archive CD 316. Novato, CA: Broderbund Software. CD-ROM.

Jackson, Ronald Vern. *Maryland Census Index, Online Edition.* Orem, UT: Ancestry.com, Inc., 1999. **http://www.ancestry.com**

_____, and Gary Ronald Teeples. *Maryland 1840 Census Index.* Salt Lake City, UT: Accelerated Indexing Systems, 1977. 164p.

U.S. Federal Population Census Schedules. 1840, M704, Microfilm Reel Nos. 156-172.

1850

Census Index: U.S. Selected States/Counties, 1850. Family Archive CD 317. Novato, CA: Broderbund Software. CD-ROM.

Corley, Betty J. *Index, Yeoman(s), Yeaman(s), Youman(s), U.S. Census Index, 1850, 1860, 1880, Alabama, Florida, Kentucky, Louisiana, Maryland, Mississippi, Tennessee, Texas, Virginia, Includes Various Other Spellings.* Hyrum, UT: Author, 1988. 5p.

Dryden, Ruth T. *State of Maryland Mortality Schedules, 1850 and 1860.* San Diego, CA: Author. 231p.

Jackson, Ronald Vern. *Maryland Census Index, Online Edition.* Orem, UT: Ancestry.com, Inc., 1999. **http://www.ancestry.com**

_____, and Gary Ronald Teeples. *Maryland 1850 Census Index*. Salt Lake City, UT: Accelerated Indexing Systems, 1976. 444p.

_____. *Maryland 1850 Slave Schedule Census Index*. Salt Lake City, UT: Accelerated Indexing Systems International, 1988. 288p.

U.S. Census Index Series, Virginia, West Virginia, Maryland, North Carolina and the District of Columbia, 1850. Orem, UT: Automated Archives, 1991. CD-ROM.

U.S. Federal Population Census Schedules. 1850, M432, Microfilm Reel Nos. 277-299.

U.S. Federal Population Census Schedules. 1850, M432, Slave Schedules, Microfilm Reel Nos. 300-302.

1860

Corley, Betty J. *Index, Yeoman(s), Yeaman(s), Youman(s), U.S. Census Index, 1850, 1860, 1880, Alabama, Florida, Kentucky, Louisiana, Maryland, Mississippi, Tennessee, Texas, Virginia, Includes Various Other Spellings*. Hyrum, UT: Author, 1988. 5p.

Dryden, Ruth T. *State of Maryland Mortality Schedules, 1850 and 1860*. San Diego, CA: Author. 231p.

Jackson, Ronald Vern. *Federal Census Index, Maryland 1860, Except Baltimore County*. West Jordan, UT: Genealogical Services, 1996. 403p.

_____. *Maryland Census Index, Online Edition*. Orem, UT: Ancestry.com, Inc., 1999.

http://www.ancestry.com

U.S. Census Index, 1860, District of Columbia, Maryland, North Carolina, Virginia, West Virginia. Orem, UT: Automated Archives, 1992. CD-ROM.

U.S. Federal Population Census Schedules. 1860, M653, Microfilm Reel Nos. 456-483.

U.S. Federal Population Census Schedules. 1860, M653, Slave Schedules, Microfilm Reel Nos. 484-485.

1870

Jackson, Ronald Vern. *Federal Census Index, Maryland, 1870, Baltimore County*. West Jordan, UT: Genealogical Services, 1993, 1996. 709p.

Riley, Janet Wilson. *Eastern Shore, Mortality Schedule 1870*. Silver Spring, MD: Family Line, 1985. 59p.

Steuart, Raeone Christensen. *Maryland 1870 Census Index*. Bountiful, UT: Heritage Quest, 1997. 2 vols.

_____. *Maryland and District of Columbia 1870 Census Index*. Bountiful, UT: Heritage Quest, 2000. CD-ROM.

U.S. Federal Population Census Schedules. 1870, M593, Microfilm Reel Nos. 566-599.

1880

Corley, Betty J. *Index, Yeoman(s), Yeaman(s), Youman(s), U.S. Census Index, 1850, 1860, 1880, Alabama, Florida, Kentucky, Louisiana, Maryland, Mississippi, Tennessee, Texas, Virginia, Includes Various Other Spellings*. Hyrum, UT: Author, 1988. 5p.

Riley, Janet Wilson. *Mortality Schedule of the Eastern Shore of Maryland 1880*. Silver Spring, MD: Family Line, 1986. 53p.

U.S. Federal Population Census Schedules. 1880, T9, Microfilm Reel Nos. 493-518.

U.S. Federal Population Census Schedules. 1880, Soundex. T753, 47 Microfilm Reels.

1890

Dilts, Bryan Lee. *1890 Maryland Census Index of Civil War Veterans or Their Widows*. Salt Lake City, UT: Index Pub., 1984. 69p.

Jackson, Ronald Vern. *Maryland Census Index, Online Edition (Veterans Schedules)*. Orem, UT: Ancestry.com, Inc., 1999.

http://www.ancestry.com

_____. *Maryland 1890 Veterans*. Salt Lake City, UT: Accelerated Indexing Systems, 1990. 323p.

Powell, Jody. *Eastern Shore of Maryland, 1890 Census of Civil War Veterans*. Roanoke, TX: Author, 1993. 112p.

Veterans' Schedules: U.S. Selected States, 1890. Family Archive CD 131. Novato, CA: Broderbund Software. CD-ROM.

1900

U.S. Federal Population Census Schedules. 1900, T623, Microfilm Reel Nos. 604-630.
U.S. Federal Population Census Schedules. 1900, Soundex. T1050, 127 Microfilm Reels.

1910

Davis White, Jeanne S. *People of Polonia, the 1910 Census, Maryland*. Baltimore, MD: Historyk Press, 1993. 4 vols.
Hollowak, Thomas L. *Polish Heads of Household in Maryland, an Index to the 1910 Census*. Westminster, MD: Family Line Publications, 1990. 74p.
U.S. Federal Population Census Schedules. 1910, T624, Microfilm Reel Nos. 549-570. (No Soundex/Miracode Index was prepared by the Government for this State.)

1920

U.S. Federal Population Census Schedules. 1920, T625, Microfilm Reel Nos. 652-678.
U.S. Federal Population Census Schedules. 1920, Soundex. M1566, 126 Microfilm Reels.

Allegheny County
1800

Cupler, Margaret Durst. *Allegany County, Maryland 1800 Census*. Arlington, VA: Maryland Genealogical Society, 1971. 21p.
Volkel, Charlotte A., Lowell M. Volkel, and Timothy Q. Wilson. *An Index to the 1800 Federal Census of Allegheny, Anne Arundel, Calvert Counties and the City of Baltimore, State of Maryland*. Danville, IL: Authors, 1967. Unpgd.
1832

Hynson, Jerry M. *Free African Americans of Maryland 1832, Including Allegany, Anne Arundel, Calvert, Caroline, Cecil, Charles, Dorchester, Frederick, Kent, Montgomery, Queen Ann's, and St. Mary's Counties*. Westminster, MD: Family Line Publications, 1998. 161p.

Anne Arundel County
1800

Volkel, Charlotte A., Lowell M. Volkel, and Timothy Q. Wilson. *An Index to the 1800 Federal Census of Allegheny, Anne Arundel, Calvert Counties and the City of Baltimore, State of Maryland*. Danville, IL: Authors, 1967. Unpgd.
1832

Hynson, Jerry M. *Free African Americans of Maryland 1832, Including Allegany, Anne Arundel, Calvert, Caroline, Cecil, Charles, Dorchester, Frederick, Kent, Montgomery, Queen Ann's, and St. Mary's Counties*. Westminster, MD: Family Line Publications, 1998. 161p.
1850

Powell, John W. *1850 Census Anne Arundel County, Maryland, Including Howard District*. Pasadena, MD: Anne Arundel Genealogical Society, 1991. 529p.
1860

Jones, Barbara and Avlyn Conley. *Index to 1860 Census of Anne Arundel County, Maryland*. Riva, MD: Author, 1986. 70p.

Baltimore City and County
1800

Volkel, Charlotte A., Lowell M. Volkel, and Timothy Q. Wilson. *An Index to the 1800 Federal Census of Allegheny, Anne Arundel, Calvert Counties and the City of Baltimore, State of Maryland*. Danville, IL: Authors, 1967. Unpgd.
1850

USGenWeb Census Project. Maryland, 1850 Baltimore County.
ftp://ftp.rootsweb.com/pub/census/md/baltimore/1850/

1860

Jackson, Ronald Vern. *Federal Census Index, Maryland 1860, Baltimore County with City of Baltimore.* West Jordan, UT: Genealogical Services, 1988; 1997. 391p.

Reamy, Bill, and Martha Reamy. *1860 Census of Baltimore City.* Silver Spring, MD: Family Line, 1987. 2 vols.

1870

Census Index: Baltimore, Chicago, St. Louis, 1870. Family Archive CD 288. Novato, CA: Broderbund Software. CD-ROM.

Baltimore, Maryland 1870 Census Index, City of Baltimore and Baltimore County. Bountiful, UT: Precision Indexing, 1996. 744p.

Jackson, Ronald Vern. *Federal Census Index, Maryland, 1870, Baltimore County.* West Jordan, UT: Genealogical Services, 1996, 1993. 709p.

Calvert County
1800

Calvert County, Maryland 1800 Census. Baltimore, MD: Maryland Historical Society, 1965. 18p.

Volkel, Charlotte A., Lowell M. Volkel, and Timothy Q. Wilson. *An Index to the 1800 Federal Census of Allegheny, Anne Arundel, Calvert Counties and the City of Baltimore, State of Maryland.* Danville, IL: Authors, 1967. Unpgd.

1810

Calvert County, Maryland 1810 Census. Sunderland, MD: Calvert County Genealogical Newsletter. 18p.

1830

Calvert County, Maryland 1830 Census. Sunderland, MD: Calvert County Genealogical Newsletter. 11p.

1832

Hynson, Jerry M. *Free African Americans of Maryland 1832, Including Allegany, Anne Arundel, Calvert, Caroline, Cecil, Charles, Dorchester, Frederick, Kent, Montgomery, Queen Ann's, and St. Mary's Counties.* Westminster, MD: Family Line Publications, 1998. 161p.

1840

Calvert County, Maryland 1840 Census. Sunderland, MD: Calvert County Genealogical Newsletter. 12p.

1850

Calvert County, Maryland 1850 Census. Sunderland, MD: Calvert County Genealogical Newsletter, 1987. 61p.

1860

Calvert County, Maryland 1860 Census. Sunderland, MD: Calvert County Genealogical Newsletter. 65p.

1870

Calvert County, Maryland 1870 Census. Sunderland, MD: Calvert County Genealogical Newsletter. 77p.

1880

Calvert County, Maryland 1880 Census. Sunderland, MD: Calvert County Genealogical Newsletter, 1987. 67p.

1900

Calvert County, Maryland 1900 Census. Sunderland, MD: Calvert County Genealogical Newsletter, 1987. 65p.

1910

Calvert County, Maryland 1910 Census. Sunderland, MD: Calvert County, Maryland Genealogical Newsletter. 84p.

1920

O'Brien, Jerry, and Mildred Bowen O'Brien. *The 1920 Census, Calvert County.* Authors, 1992. 70p.

Caroline County
1800

Caroline County, Maryland 1800 Census. Baltimore, MD: Maryland Genealogical Society, 1972. 26p.

Volkel, Charlotte A., Lowell M. Volkel, and Timothy Q. Wilson. *An Index to the 1800 Federal Census of Caroline, Cecil, Charles, Frederick and Kent Counties, State of Maryland.* Danville, IL: Authors, 1968. 95p.

1820

Wright, Frederick Edward. *Caroline County, 1820 Census.* Silver Spring, MD: Author, 1973. 48p.

1832

Hynson, Jerry M. *Free African Americans of Maryland 1832, Including Allegany, Anne Arundel, Calvert, Caroline, Cecil, Charles, Dorchester, Frederick, Kent, Montgomery, Queen Ann's, and St. Mary's Counties.* Westminster, MD: Family Line Publications, 1998. 161p.

1860

Wright, Frederick Edward. *Caroline County, 1860 Census.* Silver Spring, MD: Author, 1973. 161p.

Carroll County

1850

Index to 1850 Census of Carroll County, Maryland. Westminster, MD: Carroll County Public Library, 1978. 74p.

1860

Carroll County, Maryland, 1860, Census Index. Westminster, MD: Genealogy Department. Volunteers, Carroll County Public Library, 1990. 177p.

Cecil County

1693

Craig, Peter Stebbins. *The 1693 Census of the Swedes on the Delaware Family Histories of the Swedish Lutheran Church Members Residing in Pennsylvania, Delaware, West New Jersey and*

Cecil County, Maryland, 1638-1693. Studies in Swedish American Genealogy No. 3. Winter Park, FL: SAG Publications, 1993. 213p.

1800

Cecil County, Maryland 1800 Census. Baltimore, MD: Maryland Genealogical Society, 1972. 24p.

Volkel, Charlotte A., Lowell M. Volkel, and Timothy Q. Wilson. *An Index to the 1800 Federal Census of Caroline, Cecil, Charles, Frederick and Kent Counties, State of Maryland.* Danville, IL: Authors, 1968. 95p.

1832

Hynson, Jerry M. *Free African Americans of Maryland 1832, Including Allegany, Anne Arundel, Calvert, Caroline, Cecil, Charles, Dorchester, Frederick, Kent, Montgomery, Queen Ann's, and St. Mary's Counties.* Westminster, MD: Family Line Publications, 1998. 161p.

1850

Patton, Robert J. *Cecil County, Maryland 1850 Federal Census, July 3, 1850 to October 9, 1850, 4000 Households.* Arlington, VA: Author, 1996. 357p.

Charles County

1800

Charles County, Maryland 1800 Census. Baltimore, MD: Maryland Genealogical Society, 1967. 42p.

Volkel, Charlotte A., Lowell M. Volkel, and Timothy Q. Wilson. *An Index to the 1800 Federal Census of Caroline, Cecil, Charles, Frederick and Kent Counties, State of Maryland.* Danville, IL: Authors, 1968. 95p.

1832

Hynson, Jerry M. *Free African Americans of Maryland 1832, Including Allegany, Anne Arundel, Calvert, Caroline, Cecil, Charles, Dorchester, Frederick, Kent, Montgomery, Queen Ann's, and St. Mary's Counties.* Westminster, MD: Family Line Publications, 1998. 161p.

1850

Davis, Linda D. *The 1850 Census of Charles County, Maryland.* Mechanicsville, MD: Author, 1983. 213p.

1860

Nelson, Richard T., Jr. *The 1860 Census of Charles County, Maryland*. Leonardtown, MD: Saint Mary's County Historical Society. 203p.

1870

Nelson, Richard T., Jr. *The 1870 Census of Charles County, Maryland*. Leonardtown, MD: Saint Mary's County Historical Society, 1998. 454p.

Dorchester County

1776

Powell, Judy. *1776, 1790 Dorchester; 1790 Worcester Census of Maryland*. Roanoke, TX: Author, 1991. 58p.

1790

Powell, Judy. *1776, 1790 Dorchester; 1790 Worcester Census of Maryland*. Roanoke, TX: Author, 1991. 58p.

USGenWeb Census Project. Maryland, 1790 Dorchester County.

ftp://ftp.rootsweb.com/pub/census/md/dorchester/1790/

1800

Volkel, Charlotte A., Lowell M. Volkel, and Timothy Q. Wilson. *An Index to the 1800 Federal Census of Dorchester, Harford, Montgomery, Prince Georges and Queen Anne Counties, State of Maryland*. Danville, IL: Authors, 1968. Unpgd.

1810

Moxey, Debra Smith. *The 1810 Census of Dorchester County, Maryland*. Madison, MD: Author, 1987. 52p.

1820

Powell, Jody. *Dorchester County, Maryland 1820 Census*. Roanoke, TX: Author, 1993. 60p.

1830

Moxey, Debra Smith. *The 1830 Census of Dorchester County, Maryland*. Madison, MD: Author, 1984. 108p.

1832

Hynson, Jerry M. *Free African Americans of Maryland 1832, Including Allegany, Anne Arundel, Calvert, Caroline, Cecil, Charles, Dorchester, Frederick, Kent, Montgomery, Queen Ann's, and St. Mary's Counties*. Westminster, MD: Family Line Publications, 1998. 161p.

1840

Powell, Jody. *Dorchester County, Maryland 1840 Census*. Roanoke, TX: Author, 1993. 119p.

1850

Moxey, Debra Smith. *1850 Census of Dorchester County, Maryland*. Silver Spring, MD: Family Line Publications, 1984. 113p.

1860

Molisani, Jackie. *1860 Census of Dorchester County, Maryland*. Silver Spring, MD: Family Line Publications, 1984. 140p.

1870

Moxey, Debra Smith. *The 1870 Census of Dorchester County, Maryland*. Madison, MD: Author, 1991. 165p.

1880

Moxey, Debra Smith. *The 1880 Census of Dorchester County, Maryland*. Madison, MD: Author, 1994. 386p.

Frederick County

1800

Seubold, Helen Winters, and Frank H. Seubold. *Frederick County, Maryland 1800 Census*. Baltimore, MD: Maryland Genealogical Society, 1977. Unpgd.

Volkel, Charlotte A., Lowell M. Volkel, and Timothy Q. Wilson. *An Index to the 1800 Federal Census of Caroline, Cecil, Charles, Frederick and Kent Counties, State of Maryland*. Danville, IL: Authors, 1968. 95p.

1832

Hynson, Jerry M. *Free African Americans of Maryland 1832, Including Allegany, Anne Arundel, Calvert, Caroline, Cecil, Charles, Dorchester, Frederick, Kent, Montgomery, Queen Ann's, and St. Mary's Counties*. Westminster, MD: Family Line Publications, 1998. 161p.

1850

Hitselberger, Mary Fitzhugh, and John Philip Dern. *Bridge in Time, the Complete 1850 Census of Frederick County, Maryland*. Redwood City, CA: Monocacy Book Co., 1978. 686p.

Harford County

1800

Harford County, Maryland 1800 Census. 1972.

Volkel, Charlotte A., Lowell M. Volkel, and Timothy Q. Wilson. *An Index to the 1800 Federal Census of Dorchester, Harford, Montgomery, Prince Georges and Queen Anne Counties, State of Maryland*. Danville, IL: Authors, 1968.

1810

Carothers, Bettie Stirling. *Index to the 1810 Federal Census of Harford County, Maryland*. Chesterfield, MO: Author, 1972. 28p.

Howard County

1850

Powell, John W. *1850 Census Anne Arundel County, Maryland, Including Howard District*. Pasadena, MD: anne Arundel Genealogical Society, 1991. 529p.

Kent County

1790

USGenWeb Census Project. Maryland, 1790 Kent County.

ftp://ftp.rootsweb.com/pub/census/md/kent/1790/

1800

Volkel, Charlotte A., Lowell M. Volkel, and Timothy Q. Wilson. *An Index to the 1800 Federal Census of Caroline, Cecil, Charles, Frederick and Kent Counties, State of Maryland*. Danville, IL: Authors, 1968. 95p.

1832

Hynson, Jerry M. *Free African Americans of Maryland 1832, Including Allegany, Anne Arundel, Calvert, Caroline, Cecil, Charles, Dorchester, Frederick, Kent, Montgomery, Queen Ann's, and St. Mary's Counties*. Westminster, MD: Family Line Publications, 1998. 161p.

Montgomery County

1790

USGenWeb Census Project. Maryland, 1790 Montgomery County.

ftp://ftp.rootsweb.com/pub/census/md/montgomery/1790/

1800

Montgomery County, Maryland 1800 Census. Westminister, MD: Family Line Publications, 1972. 29p.

Volkel, Charlotte A., Lowell M. Volkel, and Timothy Q. Wilson. *An Index to the 1800 Federal Census of Dorchester, Harford, Montgomery, Prince Georges and Queen Anne Counties, State of Maryland*. Danville, IL: Authors, 1968. Unpgd.

1810

Carothers, Bettie Stirling. *Index to the 1810 Federal Census of Montgomery County, Maryland*. Chesterfield, MO: Author, 1972. 32p.

1832

Hynson, Jerry M. *Free African Americans of Maryland 1832, Including Allegany, Anne Arundel, Calvert, Caroline, Cecil, Charles, Dorchester, Frederick, Kent, Montgomery, Queen Ann's, and St. Mary's Counties*. Westminster, MD: Family Line Publications, 1998. 161p.

1850

Hurley, William Neal, Jr. *Montgomery County, Maryland 1850 Census*. Bowie, MD: Heritage Books, Inc., 1998. 359p.

1860

Hurley, William Neal, Jr. *Montgomery County, Maryland 1860 Census*. Bowie, MD: Heritage Books, Inc., 1998. 364p.

1870

Hurley, William Neal, Jr. *1870 Population Census of Montgomery County, Maryland*. Bowie, MD: Heritage Books, Inc., 1999. 556p.

Neimeyer, David. *Index of the 1870 Federal Census of Montgomery County, Maryland*. Rockville, MD: Author, 1998. 50p.

Prince Georges County
1790

USGenWeb Census Project. Maryland, 1790 Prince Georges County.
ftp://ftp.rootsweb.com/pub/census/md/princegeorges/1790/

1800

Prince George's County, Maryland, 1800 Census. Baltimore, MD: Maryland Genealogical Society. 40p.

Volkel, Charlotte A., Lowell M. Volkel, and Timothy Q. Wilson. *An Index to the 1800 Federal Census of Dorchester, Harford, Montgomery, Prince Georges and Queen Anne Counties, State of Maryland*. Danville, IL: Authors, 1968. Unpgd.

1850

1850 Census of Prince George's County, Maryland. Bowie, MD: Prince George's County Genealogical Society, 1978. 160p.

Queen Anne County
1790

USGenWeb Census Project. Maryland, 1790 Queen Anne County.
ftp://ftp.rootsweb.com/pub/census/md/queenanne/1790/

1800

Queen Anne County, Maryland 1800 Census. Baltimore, MD: Maryland Genealogical Society, 1972. 34p.

Volkel, Charlotte A., Lowell M. Volkel, and Timothy Q. Wilson. *An Index to the 1800 Federal Census of Dorchester, Harford, Montgomery, Prince Georges and Queen Anne Counties, State of Maryland*. Danville, IL: Authors, 1968. Unpgd.

1832

Hynson, Jerry M. *Free African Americans of Maryland 1832, Including Allegany, Anne Arundel, Calvert, Caroline, Cecil, Charles, Dorchester, Frederick, Kent, Montgomery, Queen Ann's, and St. Mary's Counties*. Westminster, MD: Family Line Publications, 1998. 161p.

1850

Kidd, Anne Covington. *Queen Anne's County 1850 Census*. Silver Spring, MD: Family Line Publications, 1987. 116p.

Saint Mary's County
1790

The First Census, the 1790 Census, Saint Mary's County, Maryland. Leonardtown, MD: St. Mary's County Historical Society. 26p.

USGenWeb Census Project. Maryland, 1790 St. Mary's County.
ftp://ftp.rootsweb.com/pub/census/md/stmarys/1790/

1800

Volkel, Charlotte A., Lowell M. Volkel, and Timothy Q. Wilson. *An Index to the 1800 Federal Census of Saint Mary's, Somerset, Talbot, Washington and Worchester Counties, State of Maryland*. Danville, IL: Authors, 1968. 84p.

1810
The Third Census, the 1810 Census of St. Mary's County, Maryland. Leonardtown, MD: St. Mary's County Historical Society, 1998. 35p.

1832
Hynson, Jerry M. *Free African Americans of Maryland 1832, Including Allegany, Anne Arundel, Calvert, Caroline, Cecil, Charles, Dorchester, Frederick, Kent, Montgomery, Queen Ann's, and St. Mary's Counties*. Westminster, MD: Family Line Publications, 1998. 161p.

1850
The 1850 Census of St. Mary's County, Maryland. Leonardtown, MD: St. Mary's County Historical Society, 1979. 226p.

1860
Colleary, Shirley Evans, Harvey L. Lineback, David Roberts. *The 1860 Census of St. Mary's County, Maryland*. Author, 1982. 258p.

1870
The 1870 Census of St. Mary's County, Maryland. Leonardtown, MD: St. Mary's County Historical Society, 1991. 749p.

1880
Nelson, Richard T., Jr. *Saint Mary's County, Maryland 1880 Census Index*. Author, 1994. 56p.

Reno, Linda Davis. *1880 Census, St. Mary's County, Maryland*. Mechanicsville, MD: Author. 2 vols.

1900
Reno, Linda Davis. *1900 Census, St. Mary's County, Maryland*. Mechanicsville, MD: Author, 1994. 218p.

1910
The 1910 Census of St. Mary's County, Maryland. Leonardtown, MD: St. Mary's County Historical Society, 1997. 484p.

Somerset County
1800
Volkel, Charlotte A., Lowell M. Volkel, and Timothy Q. Wilson. *An Index to the 1800 Federal Census of Saint Mary's, Somerset, Talbot, Washington and Worchester Counties, State of Maryland*. Danville, IL: Authors, 1968. 84p.

1810-1840
Powell, Jody. *Somerset County, Maryland, 1810, 1820, 1840 Census*. Roanoke, TX: Author, 1991. 200p.

1850
Dryden, Ruth T. *Somerset County, Maryland, 1850*. Silver Spring, MD: Family Line Publications, 1985. 254p.

USGenWeb Census Project. Maryland, 1850 Somerset County.

ftp://ftp.rootsweb.com/pub/census/md/somerset/1850/

1860
Barnes, John C. *Maryland Somerset County 1860 Census*. San Diego, CA: Dryden, 1988. 317p.

Crockett Tabb, Nancy. *1860 Census of Somerset County, Maryland*. Silver Spring, MD: Family Line Publications, 1985. 156p.

1870
Barnes, John C. *Maryland Somerset County 1870 Census*. San Diego, CA: Dryden, 1988. 228p.

1880
Powell, Jody. *Somerset County, Maryland 1880 Census*. Roanoke, TX: Author, 1991. 302p.

Talbot County
1790
USGenWeb Census Project. Maryland, 1790 Talbot County.

ftp://ftp.rootsweb.com/pub/census/md/talbot/1790/

1800
Wilson, George Branford. *Talbot County, Maryland 1800 Census*. Baltimore, MD: Maryland Genealogical Society, 1991. 32p.

Volkel, Charlotte A., Lowell M. Volkel, and Timothy Q. Wilson. *An Index to the 1800 Federal Census of Saint Mary's, Somerset, Talbot, Washington and Worchester Counties, State of Maryland*. Danville, IL: Authors, 1968. 84p.

1850

Seymour, Helen E. *1850 Federal Census, Talbot County, Maryland*. St. Michaels, MD: Author, 1997. 88p.

USGenWeb Census Project. Maryland, 1850 Talbot County.

ftp://ftp.rootsweb.com/pub/census/md/talbot/1850/

1860

Riley, Janet Wilson. *1860 Census of Talbot County, Maryland*. Family Line Publications, 1985. 102p.

1870

Seymour, Helen E. *1870 Federal Census, Talbot County, Maryland*. St. Michaels, MD: Author, 1996. 143p.

1880

Seymour, Helen E. *1880 Federal Census, Talbot County, Maryland*. St. Michaels, MD: Author, 1997. 209p.

Washington County
1800

Clark, Raymond B. *Washington County, Maryland 1800 Census*. St. Michael's, MD: Author, 1964. 64p.

Morrow, Dale Walton, and Deborah Jensen Morrow. *Washington County, Maryland Complete Census 1800*. Center, MD: Traces, 1983. 24p.

Volkel, Charlotte A., Lowell M. Volkel, and Timothy Q. Wilson. *An Index to the 1800 Federal Census of Saint Mary's, Somerset, Talbot, Washington and Worchester Counties, State of Maryland*. Danville, IL: Authors, 1968. 84p.

Wicomico County
1870

Barnes, John C. *Maryland, Wicomico County 1870 Census*. San Diego, CA: Dryden, 1988. 239p.

Worchester County
1800

Scott, Mrs. F. Paul. *Worchester County, Maryland 1800 Census*. Baltimore, MD: Maryland Genealogical Society. 44p.

USGenWeb Census Project. Maryland, 1800 Worchester County.

ftp://ftp.rootsweb.com/pub/census/md/worchester/1800/

Volkel, Charlotte A., Lowell M. Volkel, and Timothy Q. Wilson. *An Index to the 1800 Federal Census of Saint Mary's, Somerset, Talbot, Washington and Worchester Counties, State of Maryland*. Danville, IL: Authors, 1968. 84p.

1810

Scott, Mrs. F. Paul. *Worchester County, Maryland 1810 Census*. Baltimore, MD: Maryland Genealogical Society, 1983. 26p.

1830

Powell, Jody. *Worcester County, Maryland, 1830 Census*. Roanoke, TX: Author, 1992. 129p.

1840

Powell, Jody. *Worcester County, Maryland, 1840 Census*. Roanoke, TX: Author, 1992. 124p.

1850

Dryden, Ruth T. *Worcester County, Maryland 1850 Census*. Silver Spring, MD: Family Line. 174p.

1860

Barnes, John C. *Maryland,Worcester County 1860 Census*. San Diego, CA: Dryden, 1988. 266p.

1870

Barnes, John C. *Maryland,Worcester County 1870 Census*. San Diego, CA: Dryden, 1988. 265p.

1880

Barnes, John C. *Maryland,Worcester County 1880 Census*. San Diego, CA: Dryden, 1992. 314p.

Massachusetts

Childress, Nancy Porter. *Massachusetts Porters from 1790-1850 Census*. Phoenix, AZ: Author, 1996. 128p.

1790

Jackson, Ronald Vern. *Massachusetts Census Index, Online Edition*. Orem, UT: Ancestry.com, Inc., 1999. **http://www.ancestry.com**

U.S. Bureau of the Census. *Heads of Families at the First Census of the United States Taken in the Year 1790. Massachusetts*. Washington, DC: Government Printing Office, 1908. 363p.

_____. _____. Bountiful, UT: Accelerated Indexing Systems, 1978. 363p.

_____. _____. *Online Database Edition*. Orem, UT: Ancestry.com, Inc., 1999. **http://www.ancestry.com**

_____. _____. *U.S. Federal Population Census Schedules*, 1790. T498, Microfilm Reel No. 1.

U.S. Federal Population Census Schedules, 1790. M637, Microfilm Reel No. 4.

1800

Bentley, Elizabeth Petty. *Index to the 1800 Census of Massachusetts*. Baltimore, MD: Genealogical Pub. Co., 1978. 305p.

Jackson, Ronald Vern. *Massachusetts Census Index, Online Edition*. Orem, UT: Ancestry.com, Inc., 1999. **http://www.ancestry.com**

_____, and Gary Ronald Teeples. *Massachusetts 1800 Census Index*. Salt Lake City, UT: Accelerated Indexing Systems, 1973. 250p.

Steuart, Raeone Christensen. *Massachusetts 1800 Census Index*. Bountiful, UT: Heritage Quest, 2000. 400p.

_____. *United States 1800 Census Index*. Bountiful, UT: Heritage Quest, 2000. 4 vols. CD-ROM.

U.S. Federal Population Census Schedules, 1800. M32, Microfilm Reel Nos. 13-19.

1810

Jackson, Ronald Vern. *Massachusetts Census Index, Online Edition*. Orem, UT: Ancestry.com, Inc., 1999. **http://www.ancestry.com**

_____, and Gary Ronald Teeples. *Massachusetts 1810 Census Index*. Salt Lake City, UT: Accelerated Indexing Systems, 1976. 192p.

_____. *Federal Census Index, Massachusetts 1810*. West Jordan, UT: Genealogical Services, 1997. 192p.

U.S. Census Index Series, New England, New York, 1810. Orem, UT: Automated Archives, 1992. CD-ROM.

U.S. Federal Population Census Schedules, 1810. M252, Microfilm Reel Nos. 17-22.

1820

Jackson, Ronald Vern. *Massachusetts Census Index, Online Edition*. Orem, UT: Ancestry.com, Inc., 1999. **http://www.ancestry.com**

_____, and Gary Ronald Teeples. *Massachusetts 1820 Census Index*. Salt Lake City, UT: Accelerated Indexing Systems, 1976. 222p.

U.S. Federal Population Census Schedules. 1820, M33, Microfilm Reel Nos. 47-55.

1830

Census Index: U.S. Selected States/Counties, 1830. Family Archive CD 315. Novato, CA: Broderbund Software. CD-ROM.

Jackson, Ronald Vern. *Massachusetts Census Index, Online Edition*. Orem, UT: Ancestry.com, Inc., 1999. **http://www.ancestry.com**

_____, and Gary Ronald Teeples. *Massachusetts 1830 Census Index*. Salt Lake City, UT: Accelerated Indexing Systems, 1976. 274p.

U.S. Census Index, 1830-1839, New England, New York, Pennsylvania. Orem, UT: Automated Archives, 1992. 1 CD-ROM.

U.S. Federal Population Census Schedules. 1830, M19, Microfilm Reel Nos. 59-68.

1840

Census Index: U.S. Selected States/Counties, 1840. Family Archive CD 316. Novato, CA: Broderbund Software. CD-ROM.

Jackson, Ronald Vern. *Massachusetts Census Index, Online Edition*. Orem, UT: Ancestry.com, Inc., 1999. **http://www.ancestry.com**

_____, and Gary Ronald Teeples. *Massachusetts 1840 Census Index*. Salt Lake City, UT: Accelerated Indexing Systems, 1978. 344p.

U.S. Census Index Series, New England, New York, 1840. Orem, UT: Automated Archives, 1992. CD-ROM.

U.S. Federal Population Census Schedules. 1840, M704, Microfilm Reel Nos. 173-202.

1850

Census Microfilm Records: Massachusetts, 1850. Family Archive CD 307. Novato, CA: Broderbund Software. CD-ROM.

Jackson, Ronald Vern. *Massachusetts Census Index, Online Edition*. Orem, UT: Ancestry.com, Inc., 1999. **http://www.ancestry.com**

_____, and Gary Ronald Teeples. *Massachusetts 1850 Census Index*. Salt Lake City, UT: Accelerated Indexing Systems, 1978. 934p.

U.S. Census Index Series, New England, 1850. Orem, UT: Automated Archives, 1991. CD-ROM.

U.S. Federal Population Census Schedules. 1850, M432, Microfilm Reel Nos. 503-345.

1860

Census Index: U.S. Selected States/Counties, 1860. Family Archive CD 318. Novato, CA: Broderbund Software. CD-ROM.

Jackson, Ronald Vern. *Massachusetts Census Index, Online Edition*. Orem, UT: Ancestry.com, Inc., 1999. **http://www.ancestry.com**

_____. *Massachusetts 1860 North Federal Census Index, Berkshire, Franklin, Hampden, Hampshire, Worcester*. West Jordan, UT: Genealogical Services, 1992, 1997. 2 vols.

_____. *Massachusetts 1860 South Federal Census Index, Bristol, Dukes, Essex, Middlesex, Nantucket, Norfolk, Plymouth*. West Jordan, UT: Genealogical Services, 1992, 1997. 906p.

U.S. Census Index, 1860, Massachusetts. Orem, UT: Automated Archives, 1994. CD-ROM.

U.S. Federal Population Census Schedules. 1860, M653, Microfilm Reel Nos. 486-534.

1870

Census Index Massachusetts 1870. Family Archive CD 284. Novato, CA: Broderbund, 1997. CD-ROM.

Census Index: U.S. Selected States/Counties, 1870. Family Archive CD 319. Novato, CA: Broderbund Software. CD-ROM.

Steuart, Raeone Christensen. *Massachusetts 1870 Census Index*. Bountiful, UT: Heritage Quest, 2000. CD-ROM.

U.S. Federal Population Census Schedules. 1870, M593, Microfilm Reel Nos. 600-659.

1880

U.S. Federal Population Census Schedules. 1880, T9, Microfilm Reel Nos. 519-568.

U.S. Federal Population Census Schedules. 1880, Soundex. T754, 70 Microfilm Reels.

1890

Dilts, Bryan Lee. *1890 Massachusetts Census Index of Civil War Veterans or Their Widows*. Salt Lake City, UT: Index Pub., 1985. 222p.

Jackson, Ronald Vern. *Massachusetts Census Index, Online Edition (Veterans Schedules)*. Orem, UT: Ancestry.com, Inc., 1999. **http://www.ancestry.com**

Steuart, Raeone Christensen. *Massachusetts 1890 Veterans Census Index*. Bountiful, UT: Heritage Quest, 1999. 280 p. CD-ROM.

U.S. Federal Population Census Schedules, Special Schedule, Enumerating Union Veterans and Widows of Union Veterans of the Civil War. 1890, M123, Microfilm Reel No. 11-16.

1900

U.S. Federal Population Census Schedules. 1900, T623, Microfilm Reel Nos. 698-758.

U.S. Federal Population Census Schedules. 1900, Soundex. T1051, 314 Microfilm Reels.

1910

Mariner, Mary Lou, and Patricia Roughan Bellows. *A Research Aid for the Massachusetts 1910 Federal Census*. Sudbury, MA: Computerized Assistance, 1988. 115p.

U.S. Federal Population Census Schedules. 1910, T624, Microfilm Reel Nos. 571-633. (No Soundex/Miracode Index was prepared by the Government for this State.)

1920

U.S. Federal Population Census Schedules. 1920, T625, Microfilm Reel Nos. 679-752.

U.S. Federal Population Census Schedules. 1920, Soundex. M1567, 326 Microfilm Reels.

Berkshire County
1830
Shepard, Elmer I. *Fifth Census of Berkshire County, 1830*. Author. Unpgd.
1860
Jackson, Ronald Vern. *Massachusetts 1860 North Federal Census Index, Berkshire, Franklin, Hampden, Hampshire, Worcester*. West Jordan, UT: Genealogical Services, 1992, 1997. 2 vols.
1900
USGenWeb Census Project. Massachusetts, 1900 Berkshire County.
ftp://ftp.rootsweb.com/pub/census/ma/berkshire/1900/

Boston (Suffolk County)
1845
Shattuck, Lemuel. *Report to the Committee of the City Council Appointed to Obtain the Census of Boston for the Year 1845*. New York, NY: Arno Press, 1976. 179p.
1860
Jackson, Ronald Vern. *Massachusetts 1860 Suffolk County, Includes City of Boston*. West Jordan, UT: Genealogical Services, 1992, 1996. 359p.

Bristol County
1860
Jackson, Ronald Vern. *Massachusetts 1860 South Federal Census Index, Bristol, Dukes, Essex, Middlesex, Nantucket, Norfolk, Plymouth*. West Jordan, UT: Genealogical Services, 1992, 1997. 906p.

Cheshire (Berkshire County)
1900-1920
Halvorsen, Alice. *Census, 1900-1920, Cheshire, Massachusetts. Online Database Edition*. Orem, UT: Ancestry.com, Inc., 1999.
http://www.ancestry.com

Dukes County
1860
Jackson, Ronald Vern. *Massachusetts 1860 South Federal Census Index, Bristol, Dukes, Essex, Middlesex, Nantucket, Norfolk, Plymouth.* West Jordan, UT: Genealogical Services, 1992, 1997. 906p.

Essex County
1860
Jackson, Ronald Vern. *Massachusetts 1860 South Federal Census Index, Bristol, Dukes, Essex, Middlesex, Nantucket, Norfolk, Plymouth.* West Jordan, UT: Genealogical Services, 1992, 1997. 906p.

Franklin County
1860
Jackson, Ronald Vern. *Massachusetts 1860 North Federal Census Index, Berkshire, Franklin, Hampden, Hampshire, Worcester.* West Jordan, UT: Genealogical Services, 1992, 1997. 2 vols.

Hampden County
1860
Jackson, Ronald Vern. *Massachusetts 1860 Hampden County Federal Census Index.* West Jordan, UT: Genealogical Services, 1992. 508p.

_____. *Massachusetts 1860 North Federal Census Index, Berkshire, Franklin, Hampden, Hampshire, Worcester.* West Jordan, UT: Genealogical Services, 1992, 1997. 2 vols.
1870
Jackson, Ronald Vern. *Hampden County, Massachusetts 1870 Federal Census.* North Salt Lake City, UT: Accelerated Indexing Services International, 1991. 912p.

Hampshire County
1860
Jackson, Ronald Vern. *Massachusetts 1860 North Federal Census Index, Berkshire, Franklin, Hampden, Hampshire, Worcester.* West Jordan, UT: Genealogical Services, 1992, 1997. 2 vols.

Hancock (Berkshire County)
1790-1920
Halvorsen, Alice. *Census for the Town of Hancock, 1790-1920. Online Database Edition.* Orem, UT: Ancestry.com, Inc., 1999.
http://www.ancestry.com

Lanesboro (Berkshire County)
1790-1920
Lyon, Maurice. *Heads of Families Index, Federal Census, Lanesboro Census Index, 1790-1920. Online Database Edition.* Orem, UT: Ancestry.com, Inc., 1999.
http://www.ancestry.com

Middlesex County
1860
Jackson, Ronald Vern. *Massachusetts 1860 South Federal Census Index, Bristol, Dukes, Essex, Middlesex, Nantucket, Norfolk, Plymouth.* West Jordan, UT: Genealogical Services, 1992, 1997. 906p.

Nantucket County
1860
Jackson, Ronald Vern. *Massachusetts 1860 South Federal Census Index, Bristol, Dukes, Essex, Middlesex, Nantucket, Norfolk, Plymouth.* West Jordan, UT: Genealogical Services, 1992, 1997. 906p.

Norfolk County
1860
Jackson, Ronald Vern. *Massachusetts 1860 South Federal Census Index, Bristol, Dukes, Essex, Middlesex, Nantucket, Norfolk, Plymouth*. West Jordan, UT: Genealogical Services, 1992, 1997. 906p.

Peru (Berkshire County)
1790-1920
Halvorsen, Alice. *Census for the Town of Peru, 1790-1920. Online Database Edition*. Orem, UT: Ancestry.com, Inc., 1999.
http://www.ancestry.com

Plymouth County
1860
Jackson, Ronald Vern. *Massachusetts 1860 South Federal Census Index, Bristol, Dukes, Essex, Middlesex, Nantucket, Norfolk, Plymouth*. West Jordan, UT: Genealogical Services, 1992, 1997. 906p.

Provincetown (Barnstable County)
1790-1840
Ferguson, Edith P. *The 1790-1840 Federal Censuses, Provincetown, Barnstable County, Massachusetts, a Verbatim Transcription with Index*. Bowie, MD: Heritage Books, 1983. 123p.
1850
Ferguson, Edith P. *The 1850 Federal Census, Provincetown, Barnstable County, Massachusetts, a Verbatim Transcription with Index*. Bowie, MD: Heritage Books, 1983. 145p.
1860
Ferguson, Edith P. *The 1860 Federal Census, Provincetown, Barnstable County, Massachusetts, a Verbatim Transcription with Index*. Bowie, MD: Heritage Books, 1984. 122p.

Randolph (Norfolk County)
1850
Poole, J. R. *Randolph, Massachusetts, Index to Family Names in the Census of 1850*. Author, 1978.

Suffolk County
1845
Shattuck, Lemuel. *Report to the Committee of the City Council Appointed to Obtain the Census of Boston for the Year 1845*. New York, NY: Arno Press, 1976. 179p.
1860
Jackson, Ronald Vern. *Massachusetts 1860 Suffolk County, Includes City of Boston*. West Jordan, UT: Genealogical Services, 1992, 1996. 359p.

Webster (Worcester County)
1870
Gonsalves, Joanne M. *1870 U.S. Census, Webster, Worcester County, Massachusetts. Online Database Edition*. Orem, UT: Ancestry.com, Inc., 1999.
http://www.ancestry.com

West Boylston (Worcester County)
1870
Gonsalves, Joanne M. *1870 U.S. Census, West Boylston, Worcester County, Massachusetts. Online Database Edition*. Orem, UT: Ancestry.com, Inc., 1999.
http://www.ancestry.com

West Brookfield (Worcester County)
1870
Gonsalves, Joanne M. *1870 U.S. Census, West Brookfield, Worcester County, Massachusetts. Online Database Edition.* Orem, UT: Ancestry.com, Inc., 1999.
http://www.ancestry.com

Westborough (Worcester County)
1870
Gonsalves, Joanne M. *1870 U.S. Census, Westborough, Worcester County, Massachusetts. Online Database Edition.* Orem, UT: Ancestry.com, Inc., 1999.
http://www.ancestry.com

Westminster (Worcester County)
1870
Gonsalves, Joanne M. *1870 U.S. Census, Westminster, Worcester County, Massachusetts. Online Database Edition.* Orem, UT: Ancestry.com, Inc., 1999.
http://www.ancestry.com

Winchendon (Worcester County)
1870
Gonsalves, Joanne M. *1870 U.S. Census, Winchendon, Worcester County, Massachusetts. Online Database Edition.* Orem, UT: Ancestry.com, Inc., 1999.
http://www.ancestry.com

Worcester County
1860
Jackson, Ronald Vern. *Massachusetts 1860 North Federal Census Index, Berkshire, Franklin, Hampden, Hampshire, Worcester.* West Jordan, UT: Genealogical Services, 1992, 1997. 2 vols.
1870
Gonsalves, Joanne M. *1870 U.S. Census, Webster, Worcester County, Massachusetts. Online Database Edition.* Orem, UT: Ancestry.com, Inc., 1999.
http://www.ancestry.com
_____. *1870 U.S. Census, West Boylston, Worcester County, Massachusetts. Online Database Edition.* Orem, UT: Ancestry.com, Inc., 1999.
http://www.ancestry.com
_____. *1870 U.S. Census, West Brookfield, Worcester County, Massachusetts. Online Database Edition.* Orem, UT: Ancestry.com, Inc., 1999.
http://www.ancestry.com
_____. *1870 U.S. Census, Westborough, Worcester County, Massachusetts. Online Database Edition.* Orem, UT: Ancestry.com, Inc., 1999.
http://www.ancestry.com
_____. *1870 U.S. Census, Westminster, Worcester County, Massachusetts. Online Database Edition.* Orem, UT: Ancestry.com, Inc., 1999.
http://www.ancestry.com
_____. *1870 U.S. Census, Winchendon, Worcester County, Massachusetts. Online Database Edition.* Orem, UT: Ancestry.com, Inc., 1999.
http://www.ancestry.com
1910
USGenWeb Census Project. Massachusetts, 1910 Worcester County. (Partial).
ftp://ftp.rootsweb.com/pub/census/ma/worcester/1910/

Michigan

Jackson, Ronald Vern. *Early Michigan Census Records*. Bountiful, UT: Accelerated Indexing Systems, 1976. 58p.

Sourcebook of Michigan Census, County Histories and Vital Records. Lansing, MI: Library of Michigan, 1986. 176p.

1710

Russell, Donna Valley. *Michigan Censuses, 1710-1830, under the French, British, and Americans*. Detroit, MI: Detroit Society for Genealogical Research, 1982. 291p.

1820

Jackson, Ronald Vern. *Michigan 1820 Index Census*. Salt Lake City, UT: Accelerated Indexing Systems International, 1981. 104p.

U.S. Federal Population Census Schedules. 1820, M33, Microfilm Reel No. 56.

Wiedeman, Ruby, and Larry Bohannan. *Fourth Census of the United States 1820, Michigan Population Schedules*. Huntsville, AR: Century Enterprises, 1968. 32p.

1827

Jackson, Ronald Vern. *Michigan Census Index, Online Edition*. Orem, UT: Ancestry.com, Inc., 1999. **http://www.ancestry.com**

_____, W. David Samuelsen, and Scott D. Rosenkilke. *Michigan 1827 Census Index*. Salt Lake City, UT: Accelerated Indexing Systems, 1984. 21p.

1830

Census Index: U.S. Selected States/Counties, 1830. Family Archive CD 315. Novato, CA: Broderbund Software. CD-ROM.

1830 Federal Census, Territory of Michigan. Detroit, MI: Detroit Society for Genealogical Research, 1970. 150p.

1830-1839 U.S. Census Indexes, Mid-Atlantic, South, Mid-West. Orem, UT: Automated Archives, 1993. CD-ROM.

Jackson, Ronald Vern, and Gary Ronald Teeples. *Michigan 1830 Census Index*. Salt Lake City, UT: Accelerated Indexing Systems, 1976. 78p.

Russell, Donna Valley. *Michigan Censuses, 1710-1830, under the French, British, and Americans*. Detroit, MI: Detroit Society for Genealogical Research, 1982. 291p

U.S. Federal Population Census Schedules. 1830, M19, Microfilm Reel No. 69.

1837

Jackson, Ronald Vern. *Michigan 1837 Census Index*. Bountiful, UT: Accelerated Indexing Systems, 1984. 29p.

1840

Census Index: U.S. Selected States/Counties, 1840. Family Archive CD 316. Novato, CA: Broderbund Software. CD-ROM.

1840 United States Census Index, Mid-West, Great Lakes. Orem, UT: Automated Archives, 1994. CD-ROM.

Jackson, Ronald Vern. *Michigan Census Index, Online Edition*. Orem, UT: Ancestry.com, Inc., 1999. **http://www.ancestry.com**

_____, and Gary Ronald Teeples. *Michigan 1840 Census Index*. Salt Lake City, UT: Accelerated Indexing Systems, 1977. 92p.

McGlynn, Estelle A. *Index to 1840 Federal Population Census of Michigan*. Detroit, MI: Detroit Society for Genealogical Research, 1977. 165p.
U.S. Federal Population Census Schedules. 1840, M704, Microfilm Reel Nos. 203-212.

1845
Jackson, Ronald Vern. *Michigan Census Index, Online Edition*. Orem, UT: Ancestry.com, Inc., 1999.
http://www.ancestry.com

1850
Census Index: U.S. Selected States/Counties, 1850. Family Archive CD 317. Novato, CA: Broderbund Software. CD-ROM.
Corley, Betty J. *Index, Yeoman(s), Yeaman(s), Youman(s), U.S. Census Index, Minnesota, Wisconsin, Michigan, 1850, 1860, 1880 Includes Various Other Spellings*. Hyrum, UT: Author, 1988. 6p.
Jackson, Ronald Vern. *Michigan Census Index, Online Edition*. Orem, UT: Ancestry.com, Inc., 1999.
http://www.ancestry.com
_____. *Michigan 1850 Census Index*. West Jordan, UT: Genealogical Services, 1978, 1997. 58p.
_____. *Mortality Schedules Index, Online Edition*. Orem, UT: Ancestry.com, Inc., 1999.
http://www.ancestry.com
_____, and Gary Ronald Teeples. *Michigan 1850 Census Index*. Salt Lake City, UT: Accelerated Indexing Systems, 1978. 299p.
Michigan Genealogical Council. *Index to the 1850 Federal Population Census of Michigan*. Lansing, MI: Michigan State Society, DAR and the Michigan Genealogical Council, 1976. 463p.
Pate, Joan. *Michigan 1850 Mortality Schedule, for the State*. Birmingham, MI: Oakland County Genealogical Society, 1996. 150p.
U.S. Census Index Series, Iowa, Illinois, Michigan, Missouri, Minnesota, Wisconsin, 1850. Orem, UT: Automated Archives, 1992. CD-ROM.
U.S. Federal Population Census Schedules. 1850, M432, Microfilm Reel Nos. 346-366.
Williams, Ethel W. *Michigan Mortality Record for Year Ending June 1, 1850*. Author, 1961. 127p.

1860
Benson, Toni I. *1860 Michigan Federal Mortality Abstracts*. Decatur, MI: F-Ami-Lee Pub., 1998. Unpgd.
Jackson, Ronald Vern. *Michigan Census Index, Online Edition*. Orem, UT: Ancestry.com, Inc., 1999.
http://www.ancestry.com
_____. *Michigan 1860 Census Index*. West Jordan, UT: Genealogical Services, 1988, 1997. 923p.
Corley, Betty J. *Index, Yeoman(s), Yeaman(s), Youman(s), U.S. Census Index, Minnesota, Wisconsin, Michigan, 1850, 1860, 1880 Includes Various Other Spellings*. Hyrum, UT: Author, 1988. 6p.
Sawyer, Evelyn M. *Index to 1860 Michigan Census for the Northern Lower Peninsula*. Grand Rapids, MI: Western Michigan Genealogical Society, 1987. Unpgd.
U.S. Federal Population Census Schedules. 1860, M653, Microfilm Reel Nos. 535-566.
U.S. Federal Population Census Schedules. 1870, M593, Microfilm Reel Nos. 660-715.

1870
Jackson, Ronald Vern. *Michigan Census Index, Online Edition*. Orem, UT: Ancestry.com, Inc., 1999.
http://www.ancestry.com
Michigan 1870 Census Index. Lansing, MI: Library of Michigan, 1991- . 7 vols.

1880
Corley, Betty J. *Index, Yeoman(s), Yeaman(s), Youman(s): U.S. Census Index, Minnesota, Wisconsin, Michigan, 1850, 1860, 1880 Includes Various Other Spellings*. Hyrum, UT: Author, 1988. 6p.
U.S. Federal Population Census Schedules. 1880, T9, Microfilm Reel Nos. 569-614.
U.S. Federal Population Census Schedules. 1880, Soundex. T754, 70 Microfilm Reels.

1890

Dilts, Bryan Lee. *1890 Michigan Census Index of Civil War Veterans or Their Widows*. Salt Lake City, UT: Index Publications, 1985. 236p.

Steuart, Raeone Christensen. *Michigan 1890 Veterans Census Index*. Bountiful, UT: Heritage Quest, 1999. 321p.

U.S. Federal Population Census Schedules, Special Schedule, Enumerating Union Veterans and Widows of Union Veterans of the Civil War. 1890, M123, Microfilm Reel No. 17-21.

Veterans' Schedules: U.S. Selected States, 1890. Family Archive CD 131. Novato, CA: Broderbund Software. CD-ROM.

1900

U.S. Federal Population Census Schedules. 1900, T623, Microfilm Reel Nos. 698-755.

U.S. Federal Population Census Schedules. 1900, Soundex. T1052, 259 Microfilm Reels.

1910

Cook, Cooke Every Name Index, 1910, Michigan Miracode. Casselberry, FL: Quantic, 1989. 100p.

U.S. Federal Population Census Schedules. 1910, T624, Microfilm Reel Nos. 634-688.

U.S. Federal Population Census Schedules. 1910, Miracode Index. T1268, 253 Microfilm Reels.

1920

U.S. Federal Population Census Schedules. 1920, T625, Microfilm Reel Nos. 753-821.

U.S. Federal Population Census Schedules. 1920, Soundex. M1568, 291 Microfilm Reels.

Allegan County
1840

Monteith, Ruth Marian Robbins. *1840 Census Allegan County, Michigan*. Lucinda Hinsdale Stone Chapter, DAR, 1962. 53p.

1850

Monteith, Ruth Marian Robbins. *1850 Census Allegan County, Michigan*. Hannah McIntosh Chapter, DAR, 1942. 144p.

1860

Monteith, Ruth Marian Robbins. *1860 Census Allegan County, Michigan*. Hannah McIntosh Chapter DAR, 1956. 144p.

1870

Monteith, Ruth Marian Robbins. *1870 Census Allegan County, Michigan*. Lucina Hinsdale Stone Chapter, DAR, 1963. 3 vols.

Antrim County
1860, 1870

Player, Margaret, and Jay Player. *Index to the Eighth Federal Census 1860, the Ninth Federal Census 1870, Antrim County, Michigan*. Traverse City, MI: Grand Traverse Area Genealogical Society, 1990. 50p.

Barry County
1850

Monteith, Ruth Robbins. *Census of 1850, Barry County, Michigan*. Author, 1956. 141p.

1860

Sawyer, Evelyn M. *Index to the 1860 Barry County, Michigan Census*. Author, 1989. 38p.

Benzie County
1870

Player, Margaret, and Jay Player. *Index to the Ninth Federal Census 1870, Benzie County, Michigan*. Traverse City, MI: Grand Traverse Area Genealogical Society, 1990. 46p.

Berrian County
1830
Pompey, Sherman Lee. *Index to the 1830 Census Records of Berrian, Cass, Crawford and Van Buren Counties in the Michigan Territory*. Charleston, OR: Pacific Specialities, 1974. 6p.
1860
1860 Berrien County, Michigan Census. Niles, MI: Four Flags Area Genealogical Society, 1987. 342p.
1880
1880 Berrien County, Michigan Federal Census Index. Decatur, MI: Glyndwr Resources, 1995. 189p.

Branch County
1854, 1874
Branch County, Michigan State Census for 1854 and 1874. Coldwater, MI: Branch County Genealogical Society, 1995. 110p.

Cass County
1830
Pompey, Sherman Lee. *Index to the 1830 Census Records of Berrian, Cass, Crawford and Van Buren Counties in the Michigan Territory*. Charleston, OR: Pacific Specialities, 1974. 6p.
1860
1860 Cass County, Michigan, Census Index. Decatur, MI: Glyndwr Resources, 1986. 56p.
1870
1870 Cass County, Michigan, Census Index. Decatur, MI: Glyndwr Resources, 1990. 76p.
1880
1880 Cass County, Michigan, Federal Census Index. Decatur, MI: Glyndwr Resources, 1995. 113p.

Chippewa County
1850
Monteith, Ruth Robbins. *Census of 1850 Chippewa County, Michigan*. Author, 1956. 25p.

Clinton County
1870
Bohm, Joan. *1870 Census of Clinton County, Indiana, for Michigan and Owen Townships*. Winter Garden, FL: Author.

Crawford County
1820
Pompey, Sherman Lee. *Index to the 1820 Census of Crawford and Oakland Counties in the Michigan Territory*. Charleston, OR: Pacific Specialities, 1974. 3p.
1830
Pompey, Sherman Lee. *Index to the 1830 Census Records of Berrian, Cass, Crawford and Van Buren Counties in the Michigan Territory*. Charleston, OR: Pacific Specialities, 1974.

Detroit (Wayne County)
1860
Stuart, Donna Valley. *Index to the 1860 Federal Population Census of Detroit and Wayne County, Michigan*. Detroit, MI: Detroit Society for Genealogical Research, 1979. 172p.
1870
Jackson, Ronald Vern. *Detroit, Michigan 1870 Federal Census Index*. Salt Lake City, UT: Accelerated Indexing Systems International, 1990. 528p.

Eaton County

1840

Halsey, Drouscella Perry. *Index to 1840 Census, Eaton County, Michigan*. Charlotte, MI: Eaton County Genealogical Society, 1991. 9p.

1845

Jackson, Ronald Vern. *Michigan 1845, State Census, St. Joseph County, Lenawee County, Washtenaw County, Eaton County*. North Salt Lake City, UT: Accelerated Indexing Systems International, 1988. 280p.

1850

All-name Index to the 1850 Federal Census for Eaton County, Michigan. Charlotte, MI: Eaton County Genealogical Society, 1993. 124p.

1870

USGenWeb Census Project. Michigan, 1870 Eaton County.
ftp://ftp.rootsweb.com/pub/census/mi/eaton/1870/

Erie (Monroe County)

1880

1876 Township Plat Map, Includes Index and 1880 Federal Census Index, Includes Census of Erie Township, Monroe County, Michigan. Monroe, MI: Genealogical Society of Monroe County, Michigan, 1995. 124p.

Fruitland (Muskegon County)

Burns, Matthew W. *State Censuses of Fruitland Township, Muskegon County, Michigan*. Muskegon, MI: Author, 1995. 34p.

Genesee County

1840

1840 Census and Evolution of Genesee County, Michigan. Flint, MI: Flint Genealogical Society, 1982. 78p.

1860

1860 Census of Genesee County, Michigan. Flint, MI: Flint Genealogical Society, 1982. 247p.

1880

Ladd, Dale. *1880 Federal Census, Genesee County, Michigan an Every-Name Index*. Flint, MI: Flint Genealogical Society, 1997. 655p.

Grand Rapids (Kent County)

Sawyer, Evelyn M. *1894 Michigan Census, Grand Rapids, Ward One*. Author, 1988. 53p.

Grand Traverse County

1860

Player, Margaret, and Jay Player. *Index to the Eighth Federal Census, 1860, Grand Traverse County, Michigan*. Traverse City, MI: Grand Traverse Area Genealogical Society, 1989. 29p.

1870

Player, Margaret, and Jay Player. *Index to the Ninth Federal Census, 1870, Grand Traverse County, Michigan*. Traverse City, MI: Grand Traverse Area Genealogical Society, 1989. 93p.

Gratiot County

1860

1860 Federal Census of Gratiot County, Michigan. Ithica, MI: Gratiot County Historical Society. 94p.

Hillsdale County
1860
Hillsdale County, Michigan, 1860 Federal Census Index. Lansing, MI: Southern Michigan Genealogical Society, 1985. 169p.
1870
Hillsdale County, Michigan, 1870 Federal Census Index. Allen, MI: Southern Michigan Genealogical Society, 1990. 214p.
1880
Hillsdale County, Michigan, 1880 Federal Census Index. Lansing, MI: Southern Michigan Genealogical Society, 1987. 221p.
1894
Hillsdale County, Michigan, 1894 State Census Index. Lansing, MI: Southern Michigan Genealogical Society, 1989. 208p.

Houghton County
1850
Monteith, Ruth Robbins. *Michigan Census 1850 Counties of Houghton, Marquette, Michillimackenac, Schollcraft, Ontonagon*. Author, 1956.

Huron County
1850
Montieth, Ruth Robbins. *1850 Census, Huron County, Mason County, Midland County, Newaygo County, Oceana County, Tuscola County, Michigan*. Author, 1956.

Ingham County
1850
Hammel, George Lee. *Federal Census of 1850, Ingham County, Michigan*. East Lansing, MI: State Library, 1948. 234p.

Ionia County
1850
Montieth, Ruth Robbins. *Census of 1850 Ionia County, Michigan*. Author, 1956. 210p.

Iosco County
1890
Sherman, Alonzo Joseph. *1890 Census, Surviving Soldiers, Sailors, Marines, and Widows, Iosco County, Michigan*. Oscoda, MI: Huron Shore Genealogical Society, 1994. 22p.

Isabella County
1860
Burwash, Mytra Wilsey. *Isabella's First Census, 1860*. Mt. Pleasant, MI: Author, 1936. 9p.

Kalamazoo County
1837
Jackson, Ronald Vern. *Michigan Census Index, Online Edition*. Orem, UT: Ancestry.com, Inc., 1999. http://www.ancestry.com
1860-1890
Index to the United States Census of Kalamazoo County, Michigan, 1860, 1870, 1880 and the Veterans Rolls for 1890. Kalamazoo, MI: Kalamazoo Valley Genealogical Society and the Kalamazoo Public Library, 1986. 216p.

Kalkaska County
1870
Player, Margaret, and Jay Player. *Index to the Ninth Federal Census, 1870 Kalkaska County, Michigan.* Traverse City, MI: Grand Traverse Area Genealogical Society, 1990. 10p.

Kent County
1860
Kent County, Michigan 1860, Census Index & Heads of Families in the Federal Census. Grand Rapids, MI: Western Michigan Genealogical Society, 1986. 71p.
1870
Jackson, Ronald Vern. *Kent & Saginaw Counties, Michigan 1870 Federal Census.* North Salt Lake City, UT: Accelerated Indexing Systems International, 1991. 911p.
1870 Census Index to the Townships of Kent County, Michigan. 1996. 98p.
1880
Sawyer, Evelyn M. *Index, 1880 Kent County, Michigan Federal Census.* Author, 1998. 246p.
1884
Index to the 1884 State Census of Kent County, Michigan. Grand Rapids, MI: Western Michigan Genealogical Society, 1990. 309p.
1894
Sawyer, Evelyn M. *Index to the 1894 State Census, Kent County, Michigan.* Author, 1992. Unpgd.

Keweenaw County
1870
USGenWeb Census Project. Michigan, 1870 Keweenaw County.
ftp://ftp.rootsweb.com/pub/census/mi/keweenaw/1870/

Lapeer County
1850
USGenWeb Census Project. Michigan, 1850 Lapeer County.
ftp://ftp.rootsweb.com/pub/census/mi/lapeer/1850/
1870
Ellis, J. Dee. *1870 Census Index, Lapeer County, Michigan.* Holland, MI: Author, 1990. 52p.

Leelanau County
1860
Player, Margaret. *Index to the Eighth Federal Census 1860 Leelanau County, Michigan.* Traverse, MI: Grand Traverse Area Genealogical Society, 1990. 47p.
1870
Player, Margaret. *Index to the Ninth Federal Census 1870 Leelanau County, Michigan.* Traverse, MI: Grand Traverse Area Genealogical Society, 1990. 93p.

Lenawee County
1845
Jackson, Ronald Vern. *Michigan 1845, State Census, St. Joseph County, Lenawee County, Washtenaw County, Eaton County.* North Salt Lake City, UT: Accelerated Indexing Systems International, 1988. 280p.

Livingston County
1840
1840 Federal Census, Livingston County, Michigan. Howell, MI: Livingston County Genealogical Society, 1990. 51p.

1850

Kellogg, Lucy May. *Livingston County, Michigan 1850 Census Index*. Brighton, MI: Author, 1972. 167p.

King, Kernie L. *1850 Federal Census, Livingston County, Michigan*. Howell, MI: Livingston County Genealogical Society, 1992. 294p.

1860

King, Kernie L. *1860 Federal Census and Mortality Schedule, Livingston County, Michigan*. Howell, MI: Livingston County Genealogical Society, 1993. 373p.

1870

King, Kernie L. *1870 Federal Census and Mortality Schedule, Livingston County, Michigan*. Howell, MI: Livingston County Genealogical Society, 1995. 342p.

1880

King, Kernie L. *1880 Federal Census and Mortality Schedule, Livingston County, Michigan*. Howell, MI: Livingston County Genealogical Society, 1997. 464p.

Livonia (Wayne County)
1870

The 1870 U.S. Federal Population Census for the Township of Livonia, County of Wayne, State of Michigan, Completely Transcribed and Indexed from the Microfilmed Census Schedules Including an 1876 Township Landowners Map with a Complete Index. Livonia, MI: Western Wayne County Genealogical Society, 1980. 74p.

Losco County
1880

USGenWeb Census Project. Michigan, 1880 Losco County. (Partial).
ftp://ftp.rootsweb.com/pub/census/mi/losco/1880/

Macomb County
1880

Worrell, Donald E., Jr. *Index to the 1880 Federal Population Census of Macomb County, Michigan*. Detroit, MI: Detroit Society for Genealogical Research, 1980, 98p.

Manitou County
1860-1880

Player, Margaret, and Jay Player. *Index to the Eighth Federal Census, 1860, the Ninth Federal Census, 1870, the Tenth Federal Census, 1880, Manitou County, Michigan*. Traverse City, MI: Grand Traverse Area Genealogical Society, 1990. 74p.

Marquette County
1850

Bellows, Betty Marie. *Mortality Census Extractions, Marquette County, Michigan 1850, 1860, 1870, 1880*. Marquette, MI: Diadem Research Co. 98p.

1850 and 1860 United States Census, Marquette County, Michigan. Marquette, MI: Diadem Research, Co., 1989. 46p.

Monteith, Ruth Robbins. *Michigan Census 1850 Counties of Houghton, Marquette, Michillimackenac, Schollcraft, Ontonagon*. Author, 1956.

USGenWeb Census Project. Michigan, 1850 Marquette County.
ftp://ftp.rootsweb.com/pub/census/mi/marquette/1850/

1860

Bellows, Betty Marie. *Mortality Census Extractions, Marquette County, Michigan 1850, 1860, 1870, 1880*. Marquette, MI: Diadem Research Co. 98p.

1850 and 1860 United States Census, Marquette County, Michigan. Marquette, MI: Diadem Research, Co. 46p.

1870, 1880

Bellows, Betty Marie. *Mortality Census Extractions, Marquette County, Michigan 1850, 1860, 1870, 1880.* Marquette, MI: Diadem Research Co. 98p.

Mason County
1850

Montieth, Ruth Robbins. *1850 Census, Huron County, Mason County, Midland County, Newaygo County, Oceana County, Tuscola County, Michigan.* Author, 1956.

1860

Native American, Federal Census Indexes with Special Lists, Mason County and Oceana County, Michigan, 1860-1920. Unpgd.

Symonds, Marilyn Hawley. *Mason County, Michigan 1860 Federal Census.* Lansing, MI: Author, 1965. 47p.

1870

Native American, Federal Census Indexes with Special Lists, Mason County and Oceana County, Michigan, 1860-1920. Unpgd.

Symonds, Marilyn Hawley. *Mason County, Michigan 1870 Federal Census.* Lansing, MI: Author, 1965. 181p.

1880

Native American, Federal Census Indexes with Special Lists, Mason County and Oceana County, Michigan, 1860-1920. Unpgd.

Schneider, Marilyn Hawley. *Transcript and Index of 1880 Federal Census for Mason County, Michigan.* Ludington, MI: Author, 1986. 350p.

1900-1920

Native American, Federal Census Indexes with Special Lists, Mason County and Oceana County, Michigan, 1860-1920. Unpgd.

Michillimachenac County
1850

Monteith, Ruth Robbins. *Michigan Census 1850 Counties of Houghton, Marquette, Michillimackenac, Schollcraft, Ontonagon.* Author, 1956.

Midland County
1850

Midland County, Michigan Census Records 1850-1894, a Listing of All Persons Appearing on the Official Census Rolls. Midland, MI: Midland Genealogical Society, 1983. 438p.

Montieth, Ruth Robbins. *1850 Census, Huron County, Mason County, Midland County, Newaygo County, Oceana County, Tuscola County, Michigan.* Author, 1956.

1860

USGenWeb Census Project. Michigan, 1860 Midland County.
ftp://ftp.rootsweb.com/pub/census/mi/midland/1860/

Missaukee County
1870

USGenWeb Census Project. Michigan, 1870 Missaukee County.
ftp://ftp.rootsweb.com/pub/census/mi/missaukee/1870/

Monroe County
1860

USGenWeb Census Project. Michigan, 1860 Monroe County. (Partial).
ftp://ftp.rootsweb.com/pub/census/mi/monroe/1860/

1880

Vidolich, John R., and Lois Ann Vidolich. *Monroe County, Michigan 1880 Federal Census Index, Townships and City Wards*. Monroe, MI: Genealogical Society of Monroe County, Michigan, 1996. 85p.

Muskegon County
1860

Miller, Sharon L. *1860 United States Census, Muskegon County, Michigan, First Census of Muskegon County, Schedule 1*. Muskegon, MI: Author, 1985. 136p.

1890

Miller, Sharon L. *1890 United States Census Schedule Enumerating Union Veterans and Widows of Union Veterans of the Civil War in Muskegon County, Michigan*. Muskegon, MI: Author, 1984. 40p.

Newaygo County
1850

Montieth, Ruth Robbins. *1850 Census, Huron County, Mason County, Midland County, Newaygo County, Oceana County, Tuscola County, Michigan*. Author, 1956.

1884

Sawyer, Evelyn M. *Index to the 1884 Newaygo County, Michigan State Census*. Hudsonville, MI: Author, 1997. 65p.

1894

Sawyer, Evelyn M. *Index to the 1894 Newaygo County, Michigan State Census*. Hudsonville, MI: Author, 1997. 61p.

Oakland County
1820

Pompey, Sherman Lee. *Index to the 1820 Census of Crawford and Oakland Counties in the Michigan Territory*. Charleston, OR: Pacific Specialities, 1974. 3p.

1845

Pate, Joan. *State Census of Oakland County, Michigan for the Year 1845*. Birmingham, MI: Oakland County Genealogical Society, 1985. 290p.

1860

Pate, Joan. *1860 Federal Census and Mortality Schedule, Oakland County, Michigan*. Birmingham, MI: Oakland County Genealogical Society, 1988. 689p.

1890

Pate, Joan. *Oakland County, Michigan, Eleventh Census of the United States, 1890*. Birmingham, MI: Oakland County Genealogical Society, 1994. 112p.

Oceana County
1850

Montieth, Ruth Robbins. *1850 Census, Huron County, Mason County, Midland County, Newaygo County, Oceana County, Tuscola County, Michigan*. Author, 1956.

1860-1920

Native American, Federal Census Indexes with Special Lists, Mason County and Oceana County, Michigan, 1860-1920. Unpgd.

Ontonagon County
1850

Monteith, Ruth Robbins. *Michigan Census 1850 Counties of Houghton, Marquette, Michillimackenac, Schollcraft, Ontonagon*. Author, 1956.

Osceola County
1880
1880 Federal Census Surname Index, Osceola County, Michigan. Reed City, MI: Reed City Area Genealogical Society, 1991. 81p.

Otsego County
1880
Marrs, Donna M. *1880 Federal Census Index Otsego County, Michigan*. Gaylord, MI: Gaylord Fact Finders Genealogical Society, 1994. 35p.
1890
Marrs, Donna M. *1890 Federal Census Index to Schedules Enumerating Union Veterans and Widows of Union Veterans of the Civil War, Otesgo County, Michigan*. Gaylord, MI: Gaylord Fact Finders Genealogical Society, 1995. 5p.

Ottawa County
1840, 1850
Sawyer, Evelyn M. *Every Name Georgetown Township, Ottawa County, Michigan Federal Census Records, 1840 thru 1880*. Author, 1996. 90p.
1860
Sawyer, Evelyn M. *Every Name Georgetown Township, Ottawa County, Michigan Federal Census Records, 1840 thru 1880*. Author, 1996. 90p.
_____. *Index, 1860 Ottawa County, Michigan Federal Census*. Author. 46p.
1870, 1880
Sawyer, Evelyn M. *Every Name Georgetown Township, Ottawa County, Michigan Federal Census Records, 1840 thru 1880*. Author, 1996. 90p.
1884
Sawyer, Evelyn M. *Index 1884 Ottawa County, State Census Michigan*. Author, 1996. 77p.
_____. *The Residents of the Townships of Allendale, Blendon, Georgetown, Jamestown and Zeeland of Ottawa County, Michigan from the 1884 State Census*. Author, 1996. 115p.
1900, 1910
Sawyer, Evelyn M. *Residents of Georgetown Township, Ottawa County, Michigan from the Federal Census, 1900-1910*. Author, 1996. 81p.

Saginaw County
1850
Monteith, Ruth Robbins. *Census of 1850 Saginaw County, Michigan*. Author, 1956. 74p.
1860
Saginaw County, Michigan, 1860 Federal Census Index. Saginaw, MI: Saginaw Genealogical Society. 1993. 478p.
1870
Jackson, Ronald Vern. *Kent & Saginaw Counties, Michigan 1870 Federal Census*. North Salt Lake City, UT: Accelerated Indexing Systems International, 1991. 911p.

Saint Clair County
1845
Index to the 1845 State Census of St. Clair County, Michigan, Heads of Families and Names of White Males over Twenty-one. Port Huron, MI: St. Clair County Family History Group, 1990. 78p.
Lewis, Ruth Ziegenmeyer. *1845 State Census of St. Clair County, Michigan*. Lansing, MI: Author, 1996. Unpgd.
1850
Monteith, Ruth Robbins. *Census of 1850 Saint Clair County, Michigan*. Author, 1957. 279p.

1870

Surname Index of the 1870 Federal Census of St. Clair County, Michigan. Port Huron, MI: St. Clair County Family History Group, 1990. 89p.

Saint Joseph County
1845

Jackson, Ronald Vern. *Michigan 1845, State Census, St. Joseph County, Lenawee County, Washtenaw County, Eaton County.* North Salt Lake City, UT: Accelerated Indexing Systems International, 1988. 280p.

Williams, Bette. *1845 State Census, St. Joseph County, Michigan.* Kalamazoo, MI: Author, 1968. 53p.
1850

Silliman, Sue Imogene. *Federal Census of 1850, St. Joseph County, Michigan.* Three Rivers, MI: Three Rivers Free Public Library, 1949. 343p.

Sanilac County
1850

Monteith, Ruth Robbins. *Census of 1850 Sanilac County, Michigan.* Author, 1956.

Schollcraft County
1850

Monteith, Ruth Robbins. *Michigan Census 1850 Counties of Houghton, Marquette, Michillimackenac, Schollcraft, Ontonagon.* Author, 1956.

Shiawassee County
1860

Hazelton, Frances Herber. *1860 Census, Shiawassee County, Michigan.* Vernon, MI: Author, 1991. 156p.

Libby, Louise. *Shiawassee County, Michigan, 1860 Federal Census.* Lansing, MI: Lansing Chapter, DAR, 1952. 406p.

Monteith, Ruth Robbins. *Census of 1860 Shiawassee County, Michigan.* Author, 1956.
1870

Hazelton, Frances Herber. *1870 Census, Shiawassee County, Michigan.* Vernon, MI: Author, 1990. 34p.
1880

Hazelton, Frances Herber. *1880 Census, Shiawassee County, Michigan.* Vernon, MI: Author, 1988. 517p.

Tuscola County
1850

Montieth, Ruth Robbins. *1850 Census, Huron County, Mason County, Midland County, Newaygo County, Oceana County, Tuscola County, Michigan.* Author, 1956.

Van Buren County
1830

Pompey, Sherman Lee. *Index to the 1830 Census Records of Berrian, Cass, Crawford and Van Buren Counties in the Michigan Territory.* Charleston, OR: Pacific Specialities, 1974. 6p.
1840, 1850

Corliss, Lois Streeter. *1840 and 1850 Federal Census, Van Buren County, Michigan.* South Haven, MI: Author, 1951. 164p.
1860

Corliss, Lois Streeter. *1860 Federal Census, Van Buren County, Michigan.* South Haven, MI: Author, 1953. 304p.

1860 Van Buren County, Michigan, Census Index. Decatur, MI: Glyndwr Resources, 1986. 49p.
1870

Corliss, Lois Streeter. *1870 Federal Census, Van Buren County, Michigan.* South Haven, MI: Author, 1953. 161p.

Van Buren County, Michigan 1870 Census Index. Decatur, MI: Van Buren Regional Genealogical Society, 1991. 328p.

1880

1880 Van Buren County, Michigan, Federal Census Index. Decatur, MI: Glyndwr Resources, 1995. 159p.

Washtenaw County
1845

Jackson, Ronald Vern. *Michigan 1845, State Census, St. Joseph County, Lenawee County, Washtenaw County, Eaton County*. North Salt Lake City, UT: Accelerated Indexing Systems International, 1988. 280p.

1870

USGenWeb Census Project. Michigan, 1870 Washtenaw County.
ftp://ftp.rootsweb.com/pub/census/mi/washtentaw/1870/

1894

Sarah Caswell Angell Chapter, DAR. *Index of 1894 State Census for Washtenaw County, Michigan*. Ann Arbor, MI: Genealogical Society of Washtenaw County, Michigan, 1984. 225p.

Wayne County
1860

Stuart, Donna Valley. *Index to the 1860 Federal Population Census of Detroit and Wayne County, Michigan*. Detroit, MI: Detroit Society for Genealogical Research, 1979. 172p.

Minnesota

Bakeman, Mary Hawker. *A Guide to the Minnesota State Census Microfilm*. Brooklyn Park, MN: Park Genealogical Books, 1992. 14p.

1830

Census Index: U.S. Selected States/Counties, 1830. Family Archive CD 315. Novato, CA: Broderbund Software. CD-ROM.

1840

Census Index: U.S. Selected States/Counties, 1840. Family Archive CD 316. Novato, CA: Broderbund Software. CD-ROM.

1840 United States Census Index, Mid-West, Great Lakes. Orem, UT: Automated Archives, 1994. CD-ROM.

Jackson, Ronald Vern. *Minnesota 1840*. North Salt Lake City, UT: Accelerated Indexing Systems International, 1982. 55p.

1849

Jackson, Ronald Vern. *Minnesota Census Index, Online Edition*. Orem, UT: Ancestry.com, Inc., 1999.
http://www.ancestry.com

_____. *Minnesota 1849 Census Index*. North Salt Lake City, UT: Accelerated Indexing Systems International, 1982. 55, 82p.

1850

Census Index: U.S. Selected States/Counties, 1850. Family Archive CD 317. Novato, CA: Broderbund Software. CD-ROM.

Corley, Betty J. *Index, Yeoman(s), Yeaman(s), Youman(s), U.S. Census Index, Minnesota, Wisconsin, Michigan, 1850, 1860, 1880 Includes Various Other Spellings*. Hyrum, UT: Author, 1988. 6p.

Harpole, Patricia C., and Mary D. Nagle. *Minnesota Territorial Census, 1850*. St. Paul, MN: Minnesota Historical Society, 1972. 115p.

Jackson, Ronald Vern. *Minnesota Census Index, Online Edition*. Orem, UT: Ancestry.com, Inc., 1999.
    http://www.ancestry.com
_____. *Minnesota 1850 Census Index*. Bountiful, UT: Accelerated Indexing Systems, 1981. 133p.
_____. *Minnesota 1850 Mortality Schedule*. Bountiful, UT: Accelerated Indexing Systems, 1981. 35p.
_____. *Mortality Schedules Index, Online Edition*. Orem, UT: Ancestry.com, Inc., 1999.
    http://www.ancestry.com
U.S. Census Index Series, Iowa, Illinois, Michigan, Missouri, Minnesota, Wisconsin, 1850. Orem, UT: Auto-
    mated Archives, 1992. CD-ROM.
U.S. Federal Population Census Schedules. 1850, M432, Microfilm Reel No. 367.

1860
Census Index: U.S. Selected States/Counties, 1860. Family Archive CD 318. Novato, CA: Broderbund Soft-
    ware. CD-ROM.
Corley, Betty J. *Index, Yeoman(s), Yeaman(s), Youman(s), U.S. Census Index, Minnesota, Wisconsin, Michi-
    gan, 1850, 1860, 1880 Includes Various Other Spellings*. Hyrum, UT: Author, 1988. 6p.
Finnell, Arthur Louis. *Index to the 1860 Minnesota Mortality Schedule*. Marshall, MN: Author, 1978. 17p.
Jackson, Ronald Vern. *Minnesota Census Index, Online Edition*. Orem, UT: Ancestry.com, Inc., 1999.
    http://www.ancestry.com
_____. *Minnesota 1860 Census Index*. North Salt Lake City, UT: Accelerated Indexing Systems Interna-
    tional, 1980. 397p.
_____. *Mortality Schedule, Minnesota 1860*. Bountiful, UT: Accelerated Indexing Systems, 1979. 7p.
Meissner, Dennis E. *Guide to the Use of the 1860 Minnesota Population Census Schedules and Index*.
    St. Paul, MN: Division of Archives and Manuscripts; Minnesota Historical Society, 1978. 21p.
U.S. Federal Population Census Schedules. 1860, M653, Microfilm Reel Nos. 567-576.

1865
*Inventory to a Microfilm Edition of the Minnesota State Population Census Schedules, 1865, 1875, 1885,
    1895, 1905*. St. Paul, MN: Minnesota Historical Society, Division of Archives & Manuscripts, 1977.
    5 vols.

1870
Census Index: U.S. Selected States/Counties, 1870. Family Archive CD 319. Novato, CA: Broderbund Soft-
    ware. CD-ROM.
Corley, Betty J. *Index, Yeoman(s), Yeaman(s), Youman(s), U.S. Census Index, Minnesota, Wisconsin, Michi-
    gan, 1850, 1860, 1880 Includes Various Other Spellings*. Hyrum, UT: Author, 1988. 6p.
Jackson, Ronald Vern. *Minnesota Census Index, Online Edition*. Orem, UT: Ancestry.com, Inc., 1999.
    http://www.ancestry.com
_____. *Minnesota 1870 Census Index*. Salt Lake City, UT: Accelerated Indexing Systems International,
    1979. 1,095p.
_____. *Minnesota 1870 Mortality Schedule*. Bountiful, UT: Accelerated Indexing Systems, 1980. 26p.
_____. *Mortality Schedules Index, Online Edition*. Orem, UT: Ancestry.com, Inc., 1999.
    http://www.ancestry.com
U.S. Federal Population Census Schedules. 1870, M593, Microfilm Reel Nos. 716-719; T132, Microfilm
    Reel Nos. 1-13.

1875
*Inventory to a Microfilm Edition of the Minnesota State Population Census Schedules, 1865, 1875, 1885,
    1895, 1905*. St. Paul, MN: Minnesota Historical Society, Division of Archives & Manuscripts, 1977.
    5 vols.

1880
Jackson, Ronald Vern. *Minnesota Census Index, Online Edition*. Orem, UT: Ancestry.com, Inc., 1999.
    http://www.ancestry.com

_____. *Minnesota 1880*. Salt Lake City, UT: Accelerated Indexing Systems International, 1986. 2 vols.

_____. *Mortality Schedule, Minnesota 1880*. Bountiful, UT: Accelerated Indexing Systems, 1979. Unpgd.

U.S. Federal Population Census Schedules. 1880, T9, Microfilm Reel Nos. 615-638.

U.S. Federal Population Census Schedules. 1880, Soundex. T756, 37 Microfilm Reels.

1885

Inventory to a Microfilm Edition of the Minnesota State Population Census Schedules, 1865, 1875, 1885, 1895, 1905. St. Paul, MN: Minnesota Historical Society, Division of Archives & Manuscripts, 1977. 5 vols.

1890

Dilts, Bryan Lee. *1890 Minnesota Census Index of Civil War Veterans or Their Widows*. Salt Lake City, UT: Index Publications, 1985. 96p.

Jackson, Ronald Vern. *Minnesota Census Index, Online Edition (Veterans Schedules)*. Orem, UT: Ancestry.com, Inc., 1999.

http://www.ancestry.com

Johnson, Martin William. *Wisconsin and Minnesota Veterans Census 1890*. Belvidere, IL: Author.

Steuart, Raeone Christensen. *Minnesota 1890 Veterans Census Index*. Bountiful, UT: Heritage Quest, 1999. 141p.

U.S. Federal Population Census Schedules. 1890, M407, Microfilm Reel No. 3.

U.S. Federal Population Census Schedules. 1890, Index. M496, 2 Microfilm Reels.

U.S. Federal Population Census Schedules, Special Schedule, Enumerating Union Veterans and Widows of Union Veterans of the Civil War. 1890, M123, Microfilm Reel Nos. 22-25.

1895

Inventory to a Microfilm Edition of the Minnesota State Population Census Schedules, 1865, 1875, 1885, 1895, 1905. St. Paul, MN: Minnesota Historical Society, Division of Archives & Manuscripts, 1977. 5 vols.

1900

Warren, James W. *Minnesota 1900 Census Mortality Schedule*. St.Paul, MN: Warren Research & Marketing, 1992. 120p.

1905

Inventory to a Microfilm Edition of the Minnesota State Population Census Schedules, 1865, 1875, 1885, 1895, 1905. St. Paul, MN: Minnesota Historical Society, Division of Archives & Manuscripts, 1977. 5 vols.

1910

U.S. Federal Population Census Schedules. 1910, T624, Microfilm Reel Nos. 689-730. (No Soundex/Miracode Index was prepared by the Government for this State.)

1920

U.S. Federal Population Census Schedules. 1920, T625, Microfilm Reel Nos. 822-867.

U.S. Federal Population Census Schedules. 1920, Soundex. M1569, 174 Microfilm Reels.

Aitkin County
1860

Pompey, Sherman Lee. *The 1860 Census of Aitkin, Itasca, Mille Lacs, Murray, Buchanan, Cottonwood, Jackson, Kanabec Counties, Minnesota*. Independence, CA: Historical and Genealogical Pub. Co., 1966. Unpgd.

Anoka County
1857
Elrite, Lucille O. *Anoka County, Minnesota 1857 Census*. Anoka, MN: Anoka County Genealogical Society, 1992. 29p.

Buchanan County
1860
Pompey, Sherman Lee. *The 1860 Census of Aitkin, Itasca, Mille Lacs, Murray, Buchanan, Cottonwood, Jackson, Kanabec Counties, Minnesota*. Independence, CA: Historical and Genealogical Pub. Co., 1966. Unpgd.

Chisago County
1865
Liedman, Jay W. *Index to the 1865 Minnesota State Census for Chisago County*. Roseville, MN: Park Genealogical Books, 1998. 62p.

Cottonwood County
1860
Pompey, Sherman Lee. *The 1860 Census of Aitkin, Itasca, Mille Lacs, Murray, Buchanan, Cottonwood, Jackson, Kanabec Counties, Minnesota*. Independence, CA: Historical and Genealogical Pub. Co., 1966. Unpgd.

Freeborn County
1910
Surname Index to the 1910 US Census for Freeborn County, Minnesota. Albert Lea, MN: Freeborn County Genealogical Society, 1994. 199p.

Itasca County
1850
Pompey, Sherman Lee. *The 1850 Census Records of Itasca, Wahnahta, Mankahta Counties Minnesota Territory*. Independence, CA: Historical and Genealogical Pub. Co., 1966. Unpgd.
1860
Pompey, Sherman Lee. *The 1860 Census of Aitkin, Itasca, Mille Lacs, Murray, Buchanan, Cottonwood, Jackson, Kanabec Counties, Minnesota*. Independence, CA: Historical and Genealogical Pub. Co., 1966. Unpgd.

Jackson County
1857
Pompey, Sherman Lee. *The 1857 Census Records of Jackson County, Minnesota*. Independence, CA: Historical and Genealogical Society, 1965. 8p.
1860
Pompey, Sherman Lee. *The 1860 Census of Aitkin, Itasca, Mille Lacs, Murray, Buchanan, Cottonwood, Jackson, Kanabec Counties, Minnesota*. Independence, CA: Historical and Genealogical Pub. Co., 1966. Unpgd.
_____. *1860 Census Records of Jackson and Kanabec Counties*. Independence, CA: Historical and Genealogical Society, 1965. 6p.

Kanabec County
1860
Pompey, Sherman Lee. *The 1860 Census of Aitkin, Itasca, Mille Lacs, Murray, Buchanan, Cottonwood, Jackson, Kanabec Counties, Minnesota*. Independence, CA: Historical and Genealogical Pub. Co., 1966. Unpgd.

_____. *1860 Census Records of Jackson and Kanabec Counties*. Independence, CA: Historical and Genea-
logical Society, 1965. 6p.

Mankahta County
1850
Pompey, Sherman Lee. *The 1850 Census Records of Itasca, Wahnahta, Mankahta Counties, Minnesota Territory*. Independence, CA: Historical and Genealogical Pub. Co., 1966. Unpgd.

Mille Lacs County
1860
Pompey, Sherman Lee. *The 1860 Census of Aitkin, Itasca, Mille Lacs, Murray, Buchanan, Cottonwood,
Jackson, Kanabec Counties, Minnesota*. Independence, CA: Historical and Genealogical Pub. Co., 1966.
Unpgd.

Murray County
1860
Pompey, Sherman Lee. *The 1860 Census of Aitkin, Itasca, Mille Lacs, Murray, Buchanan, Cottonwood,
Jackson, Kanabec Counties, Minnesota*. Independence, CA: Historical and Genealogical Pub. Co., 1966.
Unpgd.
1870
USGenWeb Census Project. Minnesota, 1870 Murray County.
ftp://ftp.rootsweb.com/pub/census/mn/murray/1870/

Nobles County
1900
USGenWeb Census Project. Minnesota, 1900 Nobles County.
ftp://ftp.rootsweb.com/pub/census/mn/nobles/1900/

Northfield (Rice County)
1920
Kurth, Ann A. *Northfield, Rice County, Minnesota 1920 Federal Census Records. Online Database Edition*.
Orem, UT: Ancestry.com, Inc., 1999.
http://www.ancestry.com

Olmstead County
1857
1857 Territorial Census of Olmstead County. Rochester, MN: Olmstead Genealogical Society, 1995. 342p.

Rice County
1900, 1910
Dalby, John. *Rice County, Minnesota Census Records, 1900-1910. Online Database Edition*. Orem, UT:
Ancestry.com, Inc., 1999.
http://www.ancestry.com
1920
Kurth, Ann A. *Northfield, Rice County, Minnesota 1920 Federal Census Records. Online Database Edition*.
Orem, UT: Ancestry.com, Inc., 1999.
http://www.ancestry.com

Wabasha County
1900
USGenWeb Census Project. Minnesota, 1900 Wabasha County.
ftp://ftp.rootsweb.com/pub/census/mn/wabasha/1900/

Wahnahta County
1850
Pompey, Sherman Lee. *The 1850 Census Records of Itasca, Wahnahta, Mankahta Counties, Minnesota Territory*. Independence, CA: Historical and Genealogical Pub. Co., 1966. Unpgd.

White Bear Lake
1850-1910
White Bear Lake, Minnesota, Census Surname Index, 1850-1910. White Bear Lake, MN: White Bear Lake Genealogical Society, 1992. 154p.

Wright County
1890
U.S. Federal Population Census Schedules. 1890, M407, Microfilm Reel No. 3.
U.S. Federal Population Census Schedules. 1890, Index. M496, 2 Microfilm Reels.

Mississippi

Feldman, Lawrence H. *Anglo Americans in Spanish Archives, Lists of Anglo American Settlers in the Spanish Colonies of America*. Baltimore, MD: Genealogical Publishing Co., 1991. 349p.

1805
Jackson, Ronald Vern. *Mississippi Census Index, Online Edition*. Orem, UT: Ancestry.com, Inc., 1999. **http://www.ancestry.com**
_____. *Mississippi 1805 Census Index*. North Salt Lake City, UT: Accelerated Indexing Systems International, 1988. 10p.

1808
Strickland, Jean, and Patricia N. Edwards. *Residents of the Southeastern Mississippi Territory, Census, Tax Rolls and Petitions*. Moss Point, MS: Author, 1989; 1995. 234p.

1810
Jackson, Ronald Vern. *Mississippi Census Index, Online Edition*. Orem, UT: Ancestry.com, Inc., 1999. **http://www.ancestry.com**
_____. *Mississippi 1810*. Salt Lake City, UT: Accelerated Indexing Systems International, 1983. 79p.
Strickland, Jean, and Patricia N. Edwards. *Residents of the Southeastern Mississippi Territory, Census, Tax Rolls and Petitions*. Moss Point, MS: Author, 1989; 1995.

1818
Jackson, Ronald Vern. *Mississippi Census Index, Online Edition*. Orem, UT: Ancestry.com, Inc., 1999. **http://www.ancestry.com**
_____. *Mississippi 1818 Census Index*. North Salt Lake City, UT: Accelerated Indexing Systems International, 1986. 21p.

1820
Gillis, Irene S. *Mississippi 1820 Census*. Baton Rouge, LA: Author, 1963. 147p.
Jackson, Ronald Vern. *Mississippi Census Index, Online Edition*. Orem, UT: Ancestry.com, Inc., 1999. **http://www.ancestry.com**
_____, Gary Ronald Teeples, and David Schaefermeyer. *Mississippi 1820 Census Index*. Bountiful, UT: Accelerated Indexing Systems International, 1976. 124p.

_____. *Mississippi, 1820-1825, Covering 1820, 1822, 1823, 1824, 1825*. North Salt Lake City, UT: Accelerated Indexing Systems International, 1986. 161, 58p.

McEllhiney, Wilda Blewett. *1820 Census of Mississippi*. Tuscaloosa, AL: Willo Pub. Co., 1964. 201p.

Mississippi Terry Records, 1810 Census (Index), 1820 Census (Index), 1830 and 1840 Censuses, 1850 and 1860 Censuses, Mississippi Marriages to 1920. Enid, OK: Terry Family Historian. 47p.

U.S. Federal Population Census Schedules. 1820, M33, Microfilm Reel Nos. 57-58.

1822-1825

Jackson, Ronald Vern. *Mississippi Census Index, Online Edition*. Orem, UT: Ancestry.com, Inc., 1999. **http://www.ancestry.com**

_____. *Mississippi, 1820-1825, Covering 1820, 1822, 1823, 1824, 1825*. North Salt Lake City, UT: Accelerated Indexing Systems International, 1986. 161, 58p.

1830

Census Index: U.S. Selected States/Counties, 1830. Family Archive CD 315. Novato, CA: Broderbund Software. CD-ROM.

1830-1839 U.S. Census Indexes, Mid-Atlantic, South, Mid-West. Orem, UT: Automated Archives, 1993. CD-ROM.

Gillis, Irene S. *Mississippi 1830 Census*. Shreveport, LA: Author, 1972. 521p.

Jackson, Ronald Vern. *Mississippi Census Index, Online Edition*. Orem, UT: Ancestry.com, Inc., 1999. **http://www.ancestry.com**

_____, and Gary Ronald Teeples. *Mississippi 1830 Census Index*. Bountiful, UT: Accelerated Indexing Systems International, 1976. 28p.

_____. *Mississippi 1830, 1837*. North Salt Lake City, UT: Accelerated Indexing Systems International, 1986. 63p.

Mississippi Terry Records, 1810 Census (Index), 1820 Census (Index), 1830 and 1840 Censuses, 1850 and 1860 Censuses, Mississippi Marriages to 1920. Enid, OK: Terry Family Historian. 47p.

U.S. Federal Population Census Schedules. 1830, M19, Microfilm Reel Nos. 70-71.

1831

Wiltshire, Betty Couch. *Choctaw and Chickasaw Early Census Records*. Carrollton, MS: Pioneer Pub., 1997. 174p.

1835

Baker, Imogene. *Cherokee Indians Index, Micro-copy #T496, Roll #1, Census Roll of Cherokee Indians East of the Mississippi and Index to Roll, 1835*. Ellington, MO: Reynolds County Genealogical & Historical Society, 1986. 21p.

Felldin, Jeanne Robey. *Index to the 1835 Census of the Cherokee Indians East of the Mississippi River, Excerpted from National Archives Microfilm Publication No. T-496*. Tomball, TX: Genealogical Publications, 1976. 15p.

1837

Jackson, Ronald Vern. *Mississippi Census Index, Online Edition*. Orem, UT: Ancestry.com, Inc., 1999. **http://www.ancestry.com**

_____. *Mississippi 1830, 1837*. North Salt Lake City, UT: Accelerated Indexing Systems International, 1986. 63p.

Wiltshire, Betty Couch. *Choctaw and Chickasaw Early Census Records*. Carrollton, MS: Pioneer Pub., 1997. 174p.

1839

Wiltshire, Betty Couch. *Choctaw and Chickasaw Early Census Records*. Carrollton, MS: Pioneer Pub., 1997. 174p.

1840

Census Index: U.S. Selected States/Counties, 1840. Family Archive CD 316. Novato, CA: Broderbund Software. CD-ROM.

Coyle, Thomas E., and Bernice D. Coyle. *Mississippi 1840 Census, Compiled from the 1840 United States Census of Mississippi.* 2nd ed. Lewisville, TX: Coyle Data Co., 1991. 2 vols.

Jackson, Ronald Vern. *Mississippi Census Index, Online Edition.* Orem, UT: Ancestry.com, Inc., 1999. **http://www.ancestry.com**

_____. *Mississippi 1840 Census Index.* Bountiful, UT: Accelerated Indexing Systems, 1983. 389p.

_____. *Mississippi 1840, 1841.* North Salt Lake City, UT: Accelerated Indexing Systems International, 1986. 177p.

Mississippi Index to the United States Census of 1840. Tustin, CA: G.A.M. Publications, 1970. 2 vols.

Mississippi Terry Records, 1810 Census (Index), 1820 Census (Index), 1830 and 1840 Censuses, 1850 and 1860 Censuses, Mississippi Marriages to 1920. Enid, OK: Terry Family Historian. 47p.

Platt, Gwen, Annabel Lannart, and Marian Peer. *Mississippi Northern District, Index to the United States Census of 1840.* Santa Anna, CA: GAM Publications, 1978. 185p.

_____. *Mississippi Southern District, Index to the United States Census of 1840.* Santa Anna, CA: GAM Publications, 1970. 185p.

U.S. Federal Population Census Schedules. 1840, M704, Microfilm Reel Nos. 213-219.

1841

Jackson, Ronald Vern. *Mississippi Census Index, Online Edition.* Orem, UT: Ancestry.com, Inc., 1999. **http://www.ancestry.com**

_____. *Mississippi 1840, 1841.* North Salt Lake City, UT: Accelerated Indexing Systems International, 1986. 177p.

1845

Jackson, Ronald Vern. *Mississippi Census Index, Online Edition.* Orem, UT: Ancestry.com, Inc., 1999. **http://www.ancestry.com**

_____. *Mississippi 1845.* North Salt Lake City, UT: Accelerated Indexing Systems International, 1986. 169p.

1850

Census Microfilm Records: Alabama, Arkansas, Louisiana and Mississippi, 1850. Family Archive CD 453. Novato, CA: Broderbund Software. CD-ROM.

Corley, Betty J. *Index, Yeoman(s), Yeaman(s), Youman(s), U.S. Census Index, 1850, 1860, 1880, Alabama, Florida, Kentucky, Louisiana, Maryland, Mississippi, Tennessee, Texas, Virginia, Includes Various Other Spellings.* Hyrum, UT: Author, 1988. 5p.

Gillis, Irene S. *Mississippi 1850 Census, Surname Index.* Shreveport, LA: Author, 1972. 521p.

_____. *Mississippi 1850 Mortality Schedules.* Shreveport, LA: Author, 1973. 59p.

Jackson, Ronald Vern. *Mississippi Census Index, Online Edition.* Orem, UT: Ancestry.com, Inc., 1999. **http://www.ancestry.com**

_____. *Mississippi 1850 Slave Schedules Index.* Salt Lake City, UT: Accelerated Indexing Systems, 1988. 465p.

_____. *Mortality Schedules Index, Online Edition.* Orem, UT: Ancestry.com, Inc., 1999. **http://www.ancestry.com**

_____. *Mortality Schedule Mississippi 1850.* Bountiful, UT: Accelerated Indexing Systems, 1979. 40p.

_____, and Gary Ronald Teeples. *Mississippi 1850 Census Index.* North Salt Lake City, UT: Accelerated Indexing Systems International, 1977. 199p.

Mississippi Terry Records, 1810 Census (Index), 1820 Census (Index), 1830 and 1840 Censuses, 1850 and 1860 Censuses, Mississippi Marriages to 1920. Enid, OK: Terry Family Historian. 47p.

U.S. Census Index Series, Alabama, Arkansas, Georgia, Florida, Louisiana, Mississippi, South Carolina, 1850. Orem, UT: Automated Archives, 1991. CD-ROM.

U.S. Federal Population Census Schedules. 1850, M432, Microfilm Reel Nos. 368-382.
U.S. Federal Population Census Schedules. 1850, M432, Slave Schedules, Microfilm Reel Nos. 383-390.

1853

Jackson, Ronald Vern. *Mississippi Census Index, Online Edition*. Orem, UT: Ancestry.com, Inc., 1999. **http://www.ancestry.com**

_____. *Mississippi 1853 State Census Index*. North Salt Lake City, UT: Accelerated Indexing Systems International, 1988. 251p.

1860

Bonner, Kathryn Rose. *Mississippi 1860 U.S. Census Index. Indexing Heads of Households, and All Others with a Different Surname, within Said Household, Including Hotels, Boarding Establishments, Railroad Camps, Schools, Military Posts, etc.* Marianna, AR: Author, 1983. 3 vols.

Census Index: U.S. Selected States/Counties, 1860. Family Archive CD 318. Novato, CA: Broderbund Software. CD-ROM.

Corley, Betty J. *Index, Yeoman(s), Yeaman(s), Youman(s), U.S. Census Index, 1850, 1860, 1880, Alabama, Florida, Kentucky, Louisiana, Maryland, Mississippi, Tennessee, Texas, Virginia, Includes Various Other Spellings*. Hyrum, UT: Author, 1988. 5p.

Jackson, Ronald Vern. *Mississippi Census Index, Online Edition*. Orem, UT: Ancestry.com, Inc., 1999. **http://www.ancestry.com**

_____. *Mississippi 1860 Mortality Schedule*. North Salt Lake City, UT: Accelerated Indexing Systems International, 1981. 149p.

_____. *Mississippi 1860 Mortality Schedule Census Index*. North Salt Lake City, UT: Accelerated Indexing Systems International, 1981. 149p.

_____. *Mississippi 1860 Slave Schedule*. North Salt Lake City, UT:Accelerated Indexing Systems International, 1990. 528p.

_____. *Mortality Schedules Index, Online Edition*. Orem, UT: Ancestry.com, Inc., 1999. **http://www.ancestry.com**

U.S. Census Index, 1860, Alabama, Arkansas, Florida, Louisiana, Mississippi, South Carolina. Orem, UT: Automated Archives, 1992. 1 CD-ROM.

U.S. Federal Population Census Schedules. 1860, M653, Microfilm Reel Nos. 577-594.

U.S. Federal Population Census Schedules. 1860, M653, Slave Schedules, Microfilm Reel Nos. 595-604.

1866

Jackson, Ronald Vern. *Mississippi Census Index, Online Edition*. Orem, UT: Ancestry.com, Inc., 1999. **http://www.ancestry.com**

_____. *Mississippi 1866 State Census Index*. North Salt Lake City, UT: Accelerated Indexing Systems International, 1988. 158p.

1870

Jackson, Ronald Vern. *Mississippi Census Index, Online Edition*. Orem, UT: Ancestry.com, Inc., 1999. **http://www.ancestry.com**

_____. *Mississippi 1870 Federal Census Index*. North Salt Lake City, UT: Accelerated Indexing Systems International, 1988. 979p.

_____. *Mississippi 1870 Mortality Schedule*. Bountiful, UT: Accelerated Indexing Systems, 1981. 126p.

_____. *Mortality Schedules Index, Online Edition*. Orem, UT: Ancestry.com, Inc., 1999. http://www.ancestry.com

U.S. Federal Population Census Schedules. 1870, M593, Microfilm Reel Nos. 720-826.

1880

Corley, Betty J. *Index, Yeoman(s), Yeaman(s), Youman(s), U.S. Census Index, 1850, 1860, 1880, Alabama, Florida, Kentucky, Louisiana, Maryland, Mississippi, Tennessee, Texas, Virginia, Includes Various Other Spellings*. Hyrum, UT: Author, 1988. 5p.

Jackson, Ronald Vern. *Mortality Schedules Index, Online Edition*. Orem, UT: Ancestry.com, Inc., 1999.
http://www.ancestry.com
U.S. Federal Population Census Schedules. 1880, T9, Microfilm Reel Nos. 639-670.
U.S. Federal Population Census Schedules. 1880, Soundex. T757, 69 Microfilm Reels.

1890

Dilts, Bryan Lee. *1890 Mississippi Census Index of Civil War Veterans or Their Widows*. Salt Lake City, UT: Index Publications, 1985. 45p.
Jackson, Ronald Vern. *1890 Census Index*. North Salt Lake City, UT: Accelerated Indexing Systems International, 1985. 96p.
_____. *Mississippi Census Index, Online Edition (Veterans Schedules)*. Orem, UT: Ancestry.com, Inc., 1999.
http://www.ancestry.com
Steuart, Raeone Christensen. *Mississippi 1890 Veterans Census Index*. Bountiful, UT: Heritage Quest, 1999. 45p.
U.S. Federal Population Census Schedules, Special Schedule, Enumerating Union Veterans and Widows of Union Veterans of the Civil War. 1890, M123, Microfilm Reel No. 26.
Veterans' Schedules: U.S. Selected States, 1890. Family Archive CD 131. Novato, CA: Broderbund Software. CD-ROM.

1900

U.S. Federal Population Census Schedules. 1900, T623, Microfilm Reel Nos. 799-835.
U.S. Federal Population Census Schedules. 1900, Soundex. T1054, 155 Microfilm Reels.

1910

U.S. Federal Population Census Schedules. 1910, T624, Microfilm Reel Nos. 731-765.
U.S. Federal Population Census Schedules. 1910, Soundex. T1269, 118 Microfilm Reels.

1920

U.S. Federal Population Census Schedules. 1920, T625, Microfilm Reel Nos. 868-901.
U.S. Federal Population Census Schedules. 1920, Soundex. M1570, 123 Microfilm Reels.

Adams County
1886

Natchez City, Adams County, Mississippi, 1886 Census. Pride, LA: F & M Enterprises, 1994. 174p.
Shumway, Bob, Sarah Shumway, and Serena Abbess Haymong. *1886 Natchez, Adams County, Mississippi Census Black Families*. Pride, LA: F & M Enterprises, 1994. 262p.

Amite County
1850

USGenWeb Census Project. Mississippi, 1850 Amite County.
ftp://ftp.rootsweb.com/pub/census/ms/amite/1850/
1860

Burns, Loretta Elliott, and Kaaran L. Randall. *Amite County, Mississippi 1860 Surname Index*. Pasadena, TX: B& R Publications, 1976. 11p.
Haymon, Serena Abbess. *Amite County, Mississippi 1880 United States Census, Black Families*. Greenwell Springs, LA: Author, 1994. 364p.

Attala County
1900

Hart, James W., and Lillian Noles Hart. *Index, 1900 Census Attala County, Mississippi*. Hot Springs, AR: Authors, 1980. 68p.

Bainbridge County
1823

Sandel, Mary Eleanor. *Bainbridge County, Mississippi, 1823 Census and History*. Author, 1992. 10p.

Bolivar County
1850

USGenWeb Census Project. Mississippi, 1850 Bolivar County.
ftp://ftp.rootsweb.com/pub/census/ms/bolivar/1850/
1860

Green, John C. *1860 Federal Population Census, Bolivar County, Mississippi*. Alexandria, VA: Author, 1984. 65p.

Chickasaw County
1840

USGenWeb Census Project. Mississippi, 1840 Chickasaw County.
ftp://ftp.rootsweb.com/pub/census/ms/chickasaw/1840/
1860

Felldin, Jeanne Robey and Charlotte Magee Tucker. *The 1860 Census of Chickasaw County, Mississippi*. Tomball, TX: Genealogical Publications, 1978. 185p.

Clairborne County
1860

Burns, Loretta Elliott. *Claiborne County, Mississippi 1860*. Pasadena, TX: B & R Publications, 1976. 2p.

Clarke County

Strickland, Jean. *Clarke County, Mississippi, Tax Rolls and Census, 1835-1866*. Moss Point, MS: Author, 1990. 186p.

Coahoma County
1850

USGenWeb Census Project. Mississippi, 1850 Coahoma County.
ftp://ftp.rootsweb.com/pub/census/ms/coahoma/1850/

Copiah County
1850

USGenWeb Census Project. Mississippi, 1850 Copiah County.
ftp://ftp.rootsweb.com/pub/census/ms/copiah/1850/
1860

Burns, Loretta Elliott, and Kaaran L. Randall. *Copiah County, Mississippi 1860 Surname Index*. Pasadena, TX: B & R Publications, 1976. 16p.

Covington County
1820-1850

Edwards, Patricia N., and Jean Strickland. *Covington County, Mississippi, 1820, 1830, 1840 and 1850 Federal Census, 1841 State Census*. Moss Point, MS: Authors, 1987. 110 p.
1850

USGenWeb Census Project. Mississippi, 1850 Covington County.
ftp://ftp.rootsweb.com/pub/census/ms/covington/1850/

DeSoto County
1840

USGenWeb Census Project. Mississippi, 1840 DeSoto County.
ftp://ftp.rootsweb.com/pub/census/ms/desoto/1840/

1850

Scott, Mildred M. *De Soto County, Mississippi 1850 Census, Northern Division*. Hernando, MS: Genealogical Society of De Soto County, 1995. 221p.

1870

Index 1870 Federal Census, DeSoto County, Mississippi. Hernando, MS: Genealogical Society of DeSoto County, Mississippi, 1984. 36p.

1880

Scott, Mildred M. *DeSoto County, Mississippi 1880 Federal Census Index, White Only*. Hernando, MS: Genealogical Society of DeSoto County, 1993. 37p.

1900

Scott, Mildred M. *DeSoto County, Mississippi 1900 Federal Census Index, White Only*. Hernando, MS: Genealogical Society of DeSoto County, 1993. 30p.

1910

Scott, Mildred M. *DeSoto County, Mississippi 1910 Federal Census Index, White Only*. Hernando, MS: Genealogical Society of DeSoto County, 1993. 26p.

Franklin County

1850

Johnston, Jewel Dixon. *1850 Franklin County, Mississippi, U.S. Census*. Mount Pleasant, TX: Author, 1986. 60p.

Freeman County

Freeman, Hobbs. *Early Jefferson County, Mississippi Records*. Vicksburg, MS: Vicksburg Genealogical Society, 1991. Unpgd.

Greene County

1820

USGenWeb Census Project. Mississippi, 1820 Greene County.
ftp://ftp.rootsweb.com/pub/census/ms/greene/1820/

1830

USGenWeb Census Project. Mississippi, 1830 Greene County.
ftp://ftp.rootsweb.com/pub/census/ms/greene/1830/

1840

USGenWeb Census Project. Mississippi, 1840 Greene County.
ftp://ftp.rootsweb.com/pub/census/ms/greene/1840/

Hancock County

1840

Eddington, Bettye Jane. *1840 Hancock County Census*. Biloxi, MS: Mississippi Coast Historical & Genealogical Society, 1976. 83p.

1870

Carvin, Ernest Anthony. *Hancock County 1870 Mississippi*. Belford, NJ: Author, 1983. 119p.

1880

Carvin, Ernest Anthony. *Hancock County Census of 1880*. Belford, NJ: Author, 1980. 202p.

Harrison County

1850

Guice, Julia Cook. *Harrison County, Mississippi 1850 Census, 1850 Mortality*. Biloxi, MS: Mississippi Coast Historical & Genealogical Society, 1972. 96p.

USGenWeb Census Project. Mississippi, 1850 Harrison County.
ftp://ftp.rootsweb.com/pub/census/ms/harrison/1850/

1860

Guice, Julia Cook. *Harrison County, Mississippi 1860 Census*. Biloxi, MS: Mississippi Coast Historical & Genealogical Society, 1982. 109p.

1870

Guice, Julia Cook. *Harrison County, Mississippi 1870 Census*. Biloxi, MS: Mississippi Coast Historical & Genealogical Society, 1981. 166p.

1880

Carvin, Ernest Anthony. *Harrison County Census of 1880*. Belford, NJ: Author, 1979. 245p.

Hinds County
1860

Burns, Loretta Elliott, and Kaaran L. Randall. *Hinds County Mississippi, 1860, Surname Index*. Pasadena, TX: B and R Publications, 1976. 28p.

Holmes County
1850

USGenWeb Census Project. Mississippi, 1850 Holmes County.
ftp://ftp.rootsweb.com/pub/census/ms/holmes/1850/

Issaquena County
1850

USGenWeb Census Project. Mississippi, 1850 Issaquena County.
ftp://ftp.rootsweb.com/pub/census/ms/issaquena/1850/

1860

Burns, Loretta Elliott, and Kaaran L. Randall. *Issaquena County, Mississippi 1860 Surname Index*. Pasadena, TX: B& R Publications, 1976. 15p.

Itawamba County
1850

1850 Census, Itawamba County, Mississippi. Tupelo, MS: Genealogical Press. 164p.

1860

Platt, Gwen. *1860 Federal Census of Itawamba County, Mississippi*. North Little Rock, AR: GAM Publications, 1978. 185p.

1870

Platt, Gwen. *1870 Federal Census, Itawamba County, Mississippi*. Dunnellon, FL: Author, 1982. 155p.

Jackson County
1820

USGenWeb Census Project. Mississippi, 1820 Jackson County.
ftp://ftp.rootsweb.com/pub/census/ms/jackson/1820/

1830

USGenWeb Census Project. Mississippi, 1830 Jackson County.
ftp://ftp.rootsweb.com/pub/census/ms/jackson/1830/

1840

USGenWeb Census Project. Mississippi, 1840 Jackson County.
ftp://ftp.rootsweb.com/pub/census/ms/jackson/1840/

1860

USGenWeb Census Project. Mississippi, 1860 Jackson County.
ftp://ftp.rootsweb.com/pub/census/ms/jackson/1860/

Jasper County
1840

Edwards, Patricia N. *Jasper County, Mississippi*. Moss Point, MS: P.N. Edwards, 1986. 176p.
USGenWeb Census Project. Mississippi, 1840 Jasper County.
ftp://ftp.rootsweb.com/pub/census/ms/jasper/1840/
1850

Edwards, Patricia N. *Jasper County, Mississippi*. Moss Point, MS: P.N. Edwards, 1986. 176p.
USGenWeb Census Project. Mississippi, 1850 Jasper County.
ftp://ftp.rootsweb.com/pub/census/ms/jasper/1850/
1866

Edwards, Patricia N. *Jasper County, Mississippi*. Moss Point, MS: P.N. Edwards, 1986. 176p.

Jefferson County
1805

Jackson, Ronald Vern. *Mississippi Census Index, Online Edition*. Orem, UT: Ancestry.com, Inc., 1999.
http://www.ancestry.com

Jones County
1830

USGenWeb Census Project. Mississippi, 1830 Jones County.
ftp://ftp.rootsweb.com/pub/census/ms/jones/1830/
1840

USGenWeb Census Project. Mississippi, 1840 Jones County.
ftp://ftp.rootsweb.com/pub/census/ms/jones/1840/
1850

USGenWeb Census Project. Mississippi, 1850 Jones County.
ftp://ftp.rootsweb.com/pub/census/ms/jones/1850/

Lafayette County
1840, 1850

Truett, Earl A. *1840 U.S. Federal Census, Lafayette County & Yalobusha County, Mississippi; also Index to 1850 U. S. Census, Lafayette County, Mississippi*. Oxford, MS: Author, 1981. 39p.
1870

Truett, Earl A., and Sybil Metts Hill. *1870 Census, Lafayette County, Mississippi*. Oxford, MS: Author, 1990. 491p.

Lauderdale County
1840

Edmiston, Fred W. *Lauderdale County, Mississippi 1840 Census*. Meridian, MS: Lauderdale County Department of Archives & History, 1988. 63p.
1853

Strickland, Ben, and Jean Strickland. *Lauderdale County, Mississippi, 1835-1848 Tax Rolls, 1853 State Census*. Moss Point, MS: Author, 1986. 221p.

Lawrence County
1820

USGenWeb Census Project. Mississippi, 1820 Lawrence County.
ftp://ftp.rootsweb.com/pub/census/ms/lawrence/1820/
1830

USGenWeb Census Project. Mississippi, 1830 Lawrence County.
ftp://ftp.rootsweb.com/pub/census/ms/lawrence/1830/

Lee County
1870
Collins, Mertice Finley. *1870 Lee County, Mississippi, Census*. Tupelo, MS: Author, 1985. 201p.

Lincoln County
1910
Perrin, James Morris. *1910 Census, Lincoln County, Mississippi, an Index to All Surnames Listed on the 1910 Census*. Hammond, LA: Author, 1984. 29p.

Marshall County
1840
Carlton, Marie Haven. *1840 Census Index, Marshall County, Mississippi*. Senatobia, MS: Tate County Mississippi Genealogical and Historical Society, 1995. 24p.

Monroe County
1850
Mann, Lillian. *1850 Census, Monroe County, Mississippi*. Aberdeen, MS: Author, 1976. 94p.

Natchez (Adams County)
1886
Natchez City, Adams County, Mississippi, 1886 Census. Pride, LA: F & M Enterprises, 1994. 174p.
Shumway, Bob, Sarah Shumway, and Serena Abbess Haymong. *1886 Natchez, Adams County, Mississippi Census Black Families*. Pride, LA: F & M Enterprises, 1994. 262p.

Neshoba County
1860
Sanders, Delores Pickering, and Lynda Harvey. *Neshoba County, Mississippi 1860 Census*. Forest, MS: Authors. 118p.

Newton County
1860
Morse, Bonnie. *Newton County, Mississippi 1860 Census and Slave Schedule*. Mobile, AL: Author, 1984. 257p.

Noxubee County
1860
Sanders, Delores Pickering, and Lynda Harvey. *Noxubee County, Mississippi 1860 Census*. Forest, MS: Authors. 97p.
USGenWeb Census Project. Mississippi, 1860 Noxubee County.
ftp://ftp.rootsweb.com/pub/census/ms/noxubee/1860/

Pike County
1850
USGenWeb Census Project. Mississippi, 1850 Pike County.
ftp://ftp.rootsweb.com/pub/census/ms/pike/1850/

Pontotoc County
1850
USGenWeb Census Project. Mississippi, 1850 Pontotoc County.
ftp://ftp.rootsweb.com/pub/census/ms/pontotoc/1850/

Saint Stephens

Strickland, Ben, and Jean Strickland. *Records of Choctaw Trading Post, St. Stephens, Mississippi Territory.* Moss Point, MS: Authors, 1984. 2 vols.

Scott County

1830

Felldin, Jeanne Robey, and Charlotte Magee Tucker. *1830 Census of Scott County, Mississippi, with an Added Surname Index.* Tomball, TX: Genealogical Publications, 1978. 139p.

1840

USGenWeb Census Project. Mississippi, 1840 Scott County.

ftp://ftp.rootsweb.com/pub/census/ms/scott/1840/

1860

Felldin, Jeanne Robey, and Charlotte Magee Tucker. *The 1860 Census of Scott County, Mississippi, with an Added Surname Index.* Tomball, TX: Genealogical Publications, 1978.

Simpson County

1830

USGenWeb Census Project. Mississippi, 1830 Simpson County.

ftp://ftp.rootsweb.com/pub/census/ms/simpson/1830/

1840

USGenWeb Census Project. Mississippi, 1840 Simpson County.

ftp://ftp.rootsweb.com/pub/census/ms/simpson/1840/

1860

Felldin, Jeanne Robey. *1860 Census of Simpson County, Mississippi, with an Added Surname Index.* Tomball, TX: Genealogical Publications, 1978. 95p.

Smith County

1834

Strickland, Jean, and Patricia N. Edwards. *Smith County, Mississippi Census and Tax Rolls, 1834.* Moss Point, MS: Ben Strickland, 1997. 239p.

1850

USGenWeb Census Project. Mississippi, 1850 Smith County.

ftp://ftp.rootsweb.com/pub/census/ms/smith/1850/

1860

Felldin, Jeanne Robey, and Charlotte Magee Tucker. *The 1860 Census of Smith County, Mississippi, with an Added Surname Index.* Tomball, TX: Genealogical Publications, 1978. 141p.

Sunflower County

1850

USGenWeb Census Project. Mississippi, 1850 Sunflower County.

ftp://ftp.rootsweb.com/pub/census/ms/sunflower/1850/

Tallahatchie County

1841

USGenWeb Census Project. Mississippi, 1841 Tallahatchie County.

ftp://ftp.rootsweb.com/pub/census/ms/tallahatchie/1841/

1850

USGenWeb Census Project. Mississippi, 1850 Tallahatchie County.

ftp://ftp.rootsweb.com/pub/census/ms/tallahatchie/1850/

Tate County

Loftiss, Betty Arnold. *Tate County, Mississippi Confederate Soldiers Pension Records with Their Census Genealogy Records.* Coldwater, MS, 1994. 186p.

Tishomingo County
1840

USGenWeb Census Project. Mississippi, 1840 Tishomingo County.
ftp://ftp.rootsweb.com/pub/census/ms/tishomingo/1840/

Tunica County
1840

USGenWeb Census Project. Mississippi, 1840 Tunica County.
ftp://ftp.rootsweb.com/pub/census/ms/tunica/1840/
1850

USGenWeb Census Project. Mississippi, 1850 Tunica County.
ftp://ftp.rootsweb.com/pub/census/ms/tunica/1850/

Warren County
1820

USGenWeb Census Project. Mississippi, 1820 Warren County.
ftp://ftp.rootsweb.com/pub/census/ms/warren/1820/
1850

USGenWeb Census Project. Mississippi, 1850 Warren County.
ftp://ftp.rootsweb.com/pub/census/ms/warren/1850/

Wayne County
1820

Strickland, Ben, and Patricia N. Edwards. *Wayne County, Mississippi, 1820, 1830, 1840 & 1850 Federal Census, 1821-1829 Tax Rolls*. Moss Point, MS: Author, 1988. 178p.
USGenWeb Census Project. Mississippi, 1820 Wayne County.
ftp://ftp.rootsweb.com/pub/census/ms/wayne/1820/
1830

Strickland, Ben, and Patricia N. Edwards. *Wayne County, Mississippi, 1820, 1830, 1840 & 1850 Federal Census, 1821-1829 Tax Rolls*. Moss Point, MS: Author, 1988. 178p.
USGenWeb Census Project. Mississippi, 1830 Wayne County.
ftp://ftp.rootsweb.com/pub/census/ms/wayne/1830/
1831-1833

Strickland, Jean, and Patricia N. Edwards. *Wayne County, Mississippi, 1831-1844 Tax Rolls and Agricultural Census*. Moss Point, MS: Authors, 1991. 200p.
1840

Strickland, Ben, and Patricia N. Edwards. *Wayne County, Mississippi, 1820, 1830, 1840 & 1850 Federal Census, 1821-1829 Tax Rolls*. Moss Point, MS: Author, 1988. 178p.
USGenWeb Census Project. Mississippi, 1840 Wayne County.
ftp://ftp.rootsweb.com/pub/census/ms/wayne/1840
1850

Strickland, Ben, and Patricia N. Edwards. *Wayne County, Mississippi, 1820, 1830, 1840 & 1850 Federal Census, 1821-1829 Tax Rolls*. Moss Point, MS: Author, 1988. 178p.
USGenWeb Census Project. Mississippi, 1850 Wayne County.
ftp://ftp.rootsweb.com/pub/census/ms/wayne/1850/

Wilkinson County
1805

Jackson, Ronald Vern. *Mississippi Census Index, Online Edition*. Orem, UT: Ancestry.com, Inc., 1999.
http://www.ancestry.com

Winston County

1850

USGenWeb Census Project. Mississippi, 1850 Winston County.
ftp://ftp.rootsweb.com/pub/census/ms/winston/1850/

1880

Taunton, Louis. *1880 Census of Winston County, Mississippi.* Louisville, MS: Taunton Publishers. 194p.

Yalobusha County

1840

Truett, Earl A. *1840 U.S. Federal Census, Lafayette County & Yalobusha County, Mississippi; also Index to 1850 U. S. Census, Lafayette County, Mississippi.* Oxford, MS: Author, 1981. 39p.

Yazoo County

1850

Roos, Diane Fyans. *Yazoo County, Mississippi, 1850 U.S. Census and Marriages.* Bowie, MD: Heritage Books, 1990. 135p.

Missouri

Feldman, Lawrence H. *Anglo Americans in Spanish Archives, Lists of Anglo American Settlers in the Spanish Colonies of America.* Baltimore, MD: Genealogical Publishing Co., 1991. 349p.

1820

Jackson, Ronald Vern. *Missouri 1820.* North Salt Lake City, UT: Accelerated Indexing Systems International, 1981. 51p.

1830

Census Index: U.S. Selected States/Counties, 1830. Family Archive CD 315. Novato, CA: Broderbund Software. CD-ROM.

Glazner, Capitola Hensley. *An Index to Fifth Census of the United States, 1830, Population Schedules, State of Missouri.* Hot Springs, AR: Author, 1966. 191p.

Jackson, Ronald Vern. *Missouri Census Index, Online Edition.* Orem, UT: Ancestry.com, Inc., 1999.
http://www.ancestry.com

_____. *Missouri 1830 Census Index.* Bountiful, UT: Accelerated Indexing Systems, 1976. 47p.

U.S. Federal Population Census Schedules. 1830, M19, Microfilm Reel Nos. 72-73.

1840

Census Index: U.S. Selected States/Counties, 1840. Family Archive CD 316. Novato, CA: Broderbund Software. CD-ROM.

1840 United States Census Index, Mid-West, Great Lakes. Orem, UT: Automated Archives, 1994. CD-ROM.

Jackson, Ronald Vern. *Missouri Census Index, Online Edition.* Orem, UT: Ancestry.com, Inc., 1999.
http://www.ancestry.com

_____, and Gary Ronald Teeples. *Missouri 1840 Census Index.* Bountiful, UT: Accelerated Indexing Systems, 1976. 131p.

Missouri Census of 1840. Riverside, CA: Ancestor's Attic, 1977.

Nelson, Frances R., and Gwen Brouse. *The Index to the Federal Census of Missouri for 1840, a Guide to the County by County Enumeration.* Riverside, CA: Ancestor's Attic, 1977. 3 vols.

U.S. Federal Population Census Schedules. 1840, M704, Microfilm Reel Nos. 220-233.

1850

Census Index: U.S. Selected States/Counties, 1850. Family Archive CD 317. Novato, CA: Broderbund Software. CD-ROM.

Ellsberry, Elizabeth Prather. *Johnson Surname, Taken from 89 Different 1850 and 1860 Missouri Federal Censuses*. Chillicothe, MO: Author. 48p.

Jackson, Ronald Vern. *Missouri Census Index, Online Edition*. Orem, UT: Ancestry.com, Inc., 1999. http://www.ancestry.com

_____. *Missouri 1850 Slave Schedules, Federal Census Index.*West Jordan, UT: Genealogical Services, 1988; 1996. 388p.

_____, and Gary Ronald Teeples. *Missouri 1850 Census Index*. Bountiful, UT: Accelerated Indexing Systems, 1976. 409p.

Pompey, Sherman Lee. *Missourians in the 1850 Census of Yolo County, California*. Bakersfield, California Historical and Genealogical Pub. Co., 1965. 4p.

U.S. Census Index Series, Iowa, Illinois, Michigan, Missouri, Minnesota, Wisconsin, 1850. Orem, UT: Automated Archives, 1992. CD-ROM.

U.S. Federal Population Census Schedules. 1850, M432, Microfilm Reel Nos. 391-421.

U.S. Federal Population Census Schedules. 1850, M432, Slave Schedules, Microfilm Reel Nos. 422-424.

1860

Ellsberry, Elizabeth Prather. *Johnson Surname, Taken from 89 Different 1850 and 1860 Missouri Federal Censuses*. Chillicothe, MO: Author. 48p.

Jackson, Ronald Vern. *Missouri Census Index, Online Edition*. Orem, UT: Ancestry.com, Inc., 1999. http://www.ancestry.com

_____. *Missouri 1860 Census Index*. West Jordan, UT: Genealogical Services, 1986, 1997. 2 vols.

_____. *Missouri 1860 Slave Schedule*. North Salt Lake City, UT: Accelerated Indexing Systems International, 1990. 456p.

_____. *Mortality Schedules Index, Online Edition*. Orem, UT: Ancestry.com, Inc., 1999. http://www.ancestry.com

_____. *U.S. Federal Census Index, Missouri 1860 Mortality Schedules*. West Jordan, UT: Genealogical Services, 1984. 52p.

U.S. Federal Population Census Schedules. 1860, M653, Microfilm Reel Nos. 507-660.

U.S. Federal Population Census Schedules. 1860, M653, Slave Schedules, Microfilm Reel Nos. 661-664.

1870

1870 Missouri North, Federal Census Index. West Jordan, UT: Genealogical Services, 1981, 1989, 1996. 793p.

Jackson, Ronald Vern. *Missouri Census Index, Online Edition*. Orem, UT: Ancestry.com, Inc., 1999. http://www.ancestry.com

_____. *Missouri, North 1870 Federal Census Index*. Bountiful, UT: Accelerated Indexing Systems, 1989. 793p.

_____. *Missouri, South 1870 Federal Census Index*. Bountiful, UT: Accelerated Indexing Systems, 1990. 953p.

Pompey, Sherman Lee. *Missourians in the San Francisco, California Death Records 1848-1863; Missourians in the 1870 Mortality Census Records of California; Missourians in the Death Records of California; Missourians in the Death Records of Marysville, Yuma County, California, 1870-1900*. Bakersfield, CA: Historical & Genealogical Pub. 7p.

Steuart, Raeone Christensen. *Missouri 1870 Census Index*. Bountiful, UT: Heritage Quest, 1999. 4 vols. CD-ROM

1880

U.S. Federal Population Census Schedules. 1880, T9, Microfilm Reel Nos. 671-741.

U.S. Federal Population Census Schedules. 1880, Soundex. T758, 114 Microfilm Reels.

1890

DeGood, Harold. *An Index, Civil War Veterans and Widows, 1890 Census*. Columbia, MO: Missouri State Genealogical Association, 1994. 3 vols.

Dilts, Bryan Lee. *1890 Missouri Census Index of Civil War Veterans or Their Widows*. Salt Lake City, UT: Index Publications, 1985.

_____. 2nd ed. Bountiful, UT:Precision Indexing, 1993. 304p.

U.S. Federal Population Census Schedules, Special Schedule, Enumerating Union Veterans and Widows of Union Veterans of the Civil War. 1890, M123, Microfilm Reel Nos. 27-34.

1900

U.S. Federal Population Census Schedules. 1900, T623, Microfilm Reel Nos. 836-908.

U.S. Federal Population Census Schedules. 1900, Soundex. T1055, 300 Microfilm Reels.

1910

U.S. Federal Population Census Schedules. 1910, T624, Microfilm Reel Nos. 766-828.

U.S. Federal Population Census Schedules. 1910, Miracode Index, T12, 285 Microfilm Reels.

1920

U.S. Federal Population Census Schedules. 1920, T625, Microfilm Reel Nos. 902-966.

U.S. Federal Population Census Schedules. 1920, Soundex. M1571, 269 Microfilm Reels.

Adair County
1850
Ellsberry, Elizabeth Prather. *1850 Census Records of Adair County, Missouri*. Chillicothe, MO: Author. 93p.
1860
Treadway, Gladys L. *1860 Adair County, Missouri, Census*. Gatesville, TX: Author, 1988, 105p.
1870
Treadway, Gladys L. *1870 Adair County, Missouri Census*. Bettendorf, IA: Author, 1992. 123p.

Andrew County
1850
Ellsberry, Elizabeth Prather. *1850 Census Records of Andrew County, Missouri*. Chillicothe, MO: Author. 111p.

Hodges, Nadine, and Mrs. Howard W. Woodruff. *Andrew County, Missouri Federal Census of 1850*. Authors, 1968. 98p.

Special Schedule of the Eleventh Census (1890) Enumerating Union Veterans and Widows of Union Veterans of the Civil War, Andrew County, Missouri; Mortality Schedule, Andrew County, Missouri, 1850, 1860, 1870, 1880. Savannah, MO: Andrew County Historical Society. 36p.
1860
Marcum, Martha. *1860 Census, Andrew County, Missouri*. Savannah, MO: Author. 118p.

Special Schedule of the Eleventh Census (1890) Enumerating Union Veterans and Widows of Union Veterans of the Civil War, Andrew County, Missouri; Mortality Schedule, Andrew County, Missouri, 1850, 1860, 1870, 1880. Savannah, MO: Andrew County Historical Society. 36p.
1870, 1880
Special Schedule of the Eleventh Census (1890) Enumerating Union Veterans and Widows of Union Veterans of the Civil War, Andrew County, Missouri; Mortality Schedule, Andrew County, Missouri, 1850, 1860, 1870, 1880. Savannah, MO: Andrew County Historical Society. 36p.

Atchison County
1850
Ellsberry, Elizabeth Prather. *1850 Federal Census for Atchison County, Missouri*. Chillicothe, MO: Author. 22p.

White, Iona Gomel. *Every Name Index to 1850 Federal Census for Atchison County, Missouri*. Ames, IA: Johnston, 1998. 19p.

1860

Ellsberry, Elizabeth Prather. *1860 Federal Census for Atchison County, Missouri*. Chillicothe, MO: Author. 62p.

White, Iona Gomel. *Every Name Index to 1860 Federal Census for Atchison County, Missouri*. Ames, IA: Johnston, 1998. 10p.

1870

White, Iona Gomel. *Every Name Index to 1870 Federal Census for Atchison County, Missouri*. Ames, IA: Johnston, 1998. 15p.

1880

White, Iona Gomel. *Every Name Index to 1880 Federal Census for Atchison County, Missouri*. Ames, IA: Johnston, 1998. 30p.

1900

White, Iona Gomel. *Every Name Index to 1900 Federal Census for Atchison County, Missouri*. Ames, IA: Johnston, 1998. 33p.

Audrain County
1840

Nelson, Frances R., and Gwen Brouse. *1840, Missouri Census, 1840, Reel I, Audrain, Barry, Benton, Boone and Buchanan Counties*. Riverside, CA: Authors, 1975. 165p.

1850

Ellsberry, Elizabeth Prather. *1850 Federal Census for Audrain County, Missouri*. Chillicothe, MO: Author. 38p.

1860

Ellsberry, Elizabeth Prather. *1860 Federal Census for Audrain County, Missouri*. St. Louis, MO: Ingmire Pub. 91p.

1870

1870 Federal Census Audrain County, Missouri. Mexico, MO: Audrain County Area Genealogical Society, 1997. Unpgd.

Barry County
1840

Nelson, Frances R., and Gwen Brouse. *1840, Missouri Census, 1840, Reel I, Audrain, Barry, Benton, Boone and Buchanan Counties*. Riverside, CA: Authors, 1975. 165p.

1850

Ellsberry, Elizabeth Prather. *1850 Federal Census for Barry County, Missouri*. Chillicothe, MO: Author. 43p.

1860

Ellsberry, Elizabeth Prather. *1860 Federal Census for Barry County, Missouri*. Chillicothe, MO: Author. 101p.

1870

Lamp, Lisa. *1870 Federal Census, Barry County, Missouri*. Monett, MO: Author, 1994. 131p.

Barton County
1860

Kunkel, Joan. *1860 Federal Census, Barton County, Missouri*. Carthage, MO: Author. 14p.

1870

Kunkel, Joan. *1870 Barton County, Missouri Census*. Carthage, MO: Author, 1984. 40p.

Bates County
1850

Ellsberry, Elizabeth Prather. *1850 Federal Census for Bates County, Missouri*. St. Louis, MO: Ingmire Pub. 46p.

Benton County
1840
Carter, Mrs. J. R. *Missouri Census Records of Four Counties for 1840, Cooper County, Riveso or Henry County, Platte County, Benton County*. Author. 76p.

Census of Benton County, Missouri, 1840 and 1850, Listed by Townships. Clinton, MO: Printery, 1969. 70p.

Nelson, Frances R., and Gwen Brouse. *1840, Missouri Census, 1840, Reel I, Audrain, Barry, Benton, Boone and Buchanan Counties*. Riverside, CA: Authors, 1975. 165p.

1850
Census of Benton County, Missouri, 1840 and 1850, Listed by Townships. Clinton, MO: Printery, 1969. 70p.

Ellsberry, Elizabeth Prather. *1850 Federal Census for Benton County, Missouri*. St. Louis, MO: Ingmire Pub. 59p.

1876
Williams, Jacqueline Hogan, and Betty Harvey Williams. *1876 Benton County, Missouri State Census*. Warrensburg, MO: Authors, 1969. 119p.

Bollinger County
1860
Ellsberry, Elizabeth Prather. *1860 Federal Census for Barry County, Missouri*. Chillicothe, MO: Author, 87p.

1870
Byerley, Donna. *1870 Federal Census Bollinger County, Missouri*. Brownsville, OR: Author. 163p.

Boone County
1840
Nelson, Frances R., and Gwen Brouse. *1840, Missouri Census, 1840, Reel I, Audrain, Barry, Benton, Boone and Buchanan Counties*. Riverside, CA: Authors, 1975. 165p.

1850
Ellsberry, Elizabeth Prather. *1850 Federal Census for Boone County, Missouri*. Chillicothe, MO: Author. 141p.

1860
Ellsberry, Elizabeth Prather. *1860 Federal Census for Boone County, Missouri*. Chillicothe, MO: Author. Unpgd.

Buchanan County
1840
Nelson, Frances R., and Gwen Brouse. *1840, Missouri Census, 1840, Reel I, Audrain, Barry, Benton, Boone and Buchanan Counties*. Riverside, CA: Authors, 1975. 165p.

1850
Ellsberry, Elizabeth Prather. *Buchanan County, Missouri 1850 Federal Census*. Chillicothe, MO: Author, 1970. 147p.

1860
Nelson, Frances R., and Betty R. Jackson. *1860, Buchanan County, Missouri, 1860, Printed Copy and Index to the Eighth Federal Census, 1860*. Riverside, CA: Authors, 1974. 2 vols.

Butler County
1860
Ellsberry, Elizabeth Prather. *1860 Federal Census, Butler County, Missouri*. Chillicothe, MO: Author. 38p.

Felldin, Jeanne Robey. *1860 United States Census, Butler County, Missouri*. Tomball, TX: Genealogical Publications, 1976.

1870
Glass, Therma, and Betty Hanks. *1870 Butler County, Missouri Federal Census*. Broseley, MO: Authors, 1983. 128p.

1876

McManus, Thelma S., and Robert E. Parkin. *1876 State Census, Butler County, Missouri*. St. Louis, MO: Genealogical Research & Publications, 1981. 80p.

Caldwell County
1840

Nelson, Frances R., and Gwen Brouse. *The Missouri Census of 1840, Caldwell, Callaway, Carroll, Cape Girardeau, Chariton and Clark Counties, Reel 221*. Riverside, CA: Authors, 1975. 171p.

1850

Ellsberry, Elizabeth Prather. *1850 Federal Census for Caldwell County, Missouri*. Chillicothe, MO: Author. 26p.

1860

Ellsberry, Elizabeth Prather. *1860 Federal Census, Caldwell County, Missouri*. Chillicothe, MO: Author. 63p.

Callaway County
1844

Bartels, Carolyn M. *Callaway County, Missouri State Census, 1844*. Shawnee Mission, KS: Author, 1989. 89p.

1850

Ellsberry, Elizabeth Prather. *1850 Federal Census for Callaway County, Missouri*. Chillicothe, MO: Author, 196. 121p.

1860

Ellsberry, Elizabeth Prather. *1860 Federal Census of Callaway County, Missouri*. Chillicothe, MO: Author. Unpgd.

Camden County
1850

Ellsberry, Elizabeth Prather. *1850 Federal Census for Camden County, Missouri*. Chillicothe, MO: Author. 27p.

Cape Girardeau County
1840

Nelson, Frances R., and Gwen Brouse. *The Missouri Census of 1840, Caldwell, Callaway, Carroll, Cape Girardeau, Chariton and Clark Counties, Reel 221*. Riverside, CA: Authors, 1975. 171p.

1880

1880 Federal Census, Cape Girardeau County, Missouri. 2 vols.

Carroll County
1840

Nelson, Frances R., and Gwen Brouse. *The Missouri Census of 1840, Caldwell, Callaway, Carroll, Cape Girardeau, Chariton and Clark Counties, Reel 221*. Riverside, CA: Authors, 1975. 171p.

1850

Ellsberry, Elizabeth Prather. *1850 Federal Census for Carroll County, Missouri*. Chillicothe, MO: Author. 63p.

USGenWeb Census Project. Missouri, 1850 Carroll County.
ftp://ftp.rootsweb.com/pub/census/mo/carroll/1850/

Cass County
1860

Cass County, Missouri, 1860 Federal Census. Harrisonville, MO: Cass County Historical Society, 1982. 122p.

Cedar County
1850
Ellsberry, Elizabeth Prather. *1850 Federal Census for Cedar County, Missouri*. Chillicothe, MO: Author. 43p.
1860
Ammerman, Betty Beason. *Federal Census of Cedar County, Missouri, 1860*. Greenfield, MO: Dade County, Missouri Historical Society, 1978. 79p.
1870
Looney, Janice Soutee. *1870 Cedar County, Missouri Federal Census*. Walnut Grove, MO: Author, 1996. 115p

Chariton County
1840
Nelson, Frances R., and Gwen Brouse. *The Missouri Census of 1840, Caldwell, Callaway, Carroll, Cape Girardeau, Chariton and Clark Counties, Reel 221*. Riverside, CA: Authors, 1975. 171p.
1850
Ellsberry, Elizabeth Prather. *1850 Federal Census for Chariton County, Missouri*. Chillicothe, MO: Author. 76p.
USGenWeb Census Project. Missouri, 1850 Chariton County.
ftp://ftp.rootsweb.com/pub/census/mo/chariton/1850/

Christian County
1860
Buckley, Sandra Johns. *Christian County, Missouri, 1860 Federal Census*. Willard, MO: Author, 1989. 82p.
1870
Christian County, Missouri, 1870 Federal Census. Springfield, MO: Ozarks Genealogical Society, 1984. 73p.
1890
Union Soldiers & Widows, 1890 Special Federal Census, Index to Christian, Dade, Dallas, Polk and Taney Counties of Missouri. Springfield, MO: Ozarks Genealogical Society, 1980. 75p.
_____. Rev. ed. Springfield, MO: Ozarks Genealogical Society, 1989. 109p.
1910
Wilson, Maxine. *Christian County, Missouri, 1910 Federal Census*. Ozark, MO: Author, 1985. 2 vols.

Clark County
1840
Nelson, Frances R., and Gwen Brouse. *The Missouri Census of 1840, Caldwell, Callaway, Carroll, Cape Girardeau, Chariton and Clark Counties, Reel 221*. Riverside, CA: Authors, 1975. 171p.
1850
Ellsberry, Elizabeth Prather. *1850 Federal Census of Clark County, Missouri*. Chillicothe, MO: Author. 67p.

Clay County
1840
Nelson, Frances R., and Gwen Brouse. *The Missouri Census of 1840, Reel #222, Clay, Clinton, Cole and Cooper Counties*. Riverside, CA: Authors, 1975. 150p.
1850
Hodges, Nadine. *Clay County, Missouri, Federal Census Records of 1850*. Kansas City, MO: Author. 100p.
1860
1860 Federal Census, Clay County, Missouri. Liberty, MO: Genealogical Society of Liberty, 1985. 89p.
1880
1880 Federal Census, Clay County, Missouri. Liberty, MO: Clay County Archives & Historical Library. 382p.

Clinton County
1840
Nelson, Frances R., and Gwen Brouse. *The Missouri Census of 1840, Reel #222, Clay, Clinton, Cole and Cooper Counties*. Riverside, CA: Authors, 1975. 150p.
1860
Swearing, Joyce Anderson. *1860 Clinton County, Missouri Census*. Lawton, MO: Author. 168p.

Cole County
1830
Pompey, Sherman Lee. *Index to the 1830 Census of Cole County, Missouri*. Kingsburg, CA: Pacific Specialties, 1971. Unpgd.
1840
Nelson, Frances R., and Gwen Brouse. *The Missouri Census of 1840, Reel #222, Clay, Clinton, Cole and Cooper Counties*. Riverside, CA: Authors, 1975. 150p.
1850
Ellsberry, Elizabeth Prather. *1850 Federal Census for Cole County, Missouri*. Chillicothe, MO: Author. 80p.

Cooper County
1840
Carter, Mrs. J. R. *Missouri Census Records of Four Counties for 1840, Cooper County, Riveso or Henry County, Platte County, Benton County*. Author. 76p.
Nelson, Frances R., and Gwen Brouse. *The Missouri Census of 1840, Reel #222, Clay, Clinton, Cole and Cooper Counties*. Riverside, CA: Authors, 1975. 150p.
1850
Ellsberry, Elizabeth Prather. *1850 Federal Census for Cooper County, Missouri*. Chillicothe, MO: Author. 121p.

Crawford County
1850
Ellsberry, Elizabeth Prather. *1850 Federal Census for Crawford County, Missouri*. Chillicothe, MO: Author. 66p.

Dade County
1850
Ellsberry, Elizabeth Prather. *Dade County, Missouri 1850 Federal Census*. Chillicothe, MO: Author. 51p.
1860
Ellsberry, Elizabeth Prather. *1860 Federal Census for Dade County, Missouri*. Chillicothe, MO: Author. 87p.
Smith, Pauline. *Federal Census of Dade County, Missouri, 1860*. Greenfield, MO: Dade County Missouri Historical Society, 1974. 78p.
1870
McConnell, Don. *Federal Census of Dade County, Missouri, 1870*. Greenfield, MO: Dade County Missouri Historical Society, 1974. 101p.
1880
Federal Census of Dade County, Missouri, 1880. Greenfield, MO: Dade County Missouri Historical Society, 1975. 145p.
1890
Union Soldiers & Widows, 1890 Special Federal Census, Index to Christian, Dade, Dallas, Polk and Taney Counties of Missouri. Springfield, MO: Ozarks Genealogical Society, 1980. 75p.
_____. Rev. ed. Springfield, MO: Ozarks Genealogical Society, 1989. 109p.

Dallas County
1850
Ellsberry, Elizabeth Prather. *Dallas County, Missouri 1850 Federal Census*. Chillicothe, MO: Author. 46p.
1860
Ellsberry, Elizabeth Prather. *1860 Federal Census for Dallas County, Missouri*. Chillicothe, MO: Author. 76p.
1890
Union Soldiers & Widows, 1890 Special Federal Census, Index to Christian, Dade, Dallas, Polk and Taney Counties of Missouri. Springfield, MO: Ozarks Genealogical Society, 1980. 75p.
_____. Rev. ed. Springfield, MO: Ozarks Genealogical Society, 1989. 109p.

Daviess County
1850
Ellsberry, Elizabeth Prather. *1850 Federal Census for Daviess County, Missouri*. Chillicothe, MO: Author. 65p.
1860
Ellsberry, Elizabeth Prather. *1860 Federal Census, Daviess County, Missouri*. Chillicothe, MO: Author. 116p.

Dekalb County
1850
Ellsberry, Elizabeth Prather. *1850 Dekalb County, Missouri Census*. Chillicothe, MO: Author, 1960. 67p.

Dodge County
1850
Ellsberry, Elizabeth Prather. *1850 Federal Census of Dodge County, Missouri*. Chillicothe, MO: Author. 6p.

Douglas County
1870
Weber, Nancie Todd. *1870 Douglas County, Missouri, Wood, Richland Townships in Texas County*. El Segundo, CA: Author, 1992. 70p.
1880
Wilson, Maxine. *Douglas County, Missouri, 1880 Federal Census*. Ozark, MO: Author, 1986. 161p.

Franklin County
1810
Ellsberry, Elizabeth Prather. *1810 Federal Census for Franklin County, Missouri*. Chillicothe, MO: Author. 13p.
1830
Pompey, Sherman Lee. *Index to the 1830 Census of Franklin County, Missouri*. Charleston, OR: Pacific Specialities, 1974. Unpgd.
1850
Ellsberry, Elizabeth Prather. *1850 Federal Census for Franklin County, Missouri*. Chillicothe, MO: Author. 128p.

Gasconade County
1840
Brawley, Joyce I. *The Missouri Census of 1840 Gasconade County*. Riverside, CA: Author, 1977. 112p.
1850
Ellsberry, Elizabeth Prather. *1850 Federal Census Gasconade County, Missouri*. Chillicothe, MO: Author, 1973. 66p.

Gentry County
1860
Ellsberry, Elizabeth Prather. *1850 Federal Census of Gentry County, Missouri*. Chillicothe, MO: Author. 54p.

Greene County
1840
Brawley, Joyce I. *The Missouri Census of 1840*. Riverside, CA: Author, 1977. 146p.
Greene County, Missouri, First Federal Census, 1840. Springfield, MO: Ozarks Genealogical Society, 1987. 50p.
1850
Ellsberry, Elizabeth Prather. *Greene County, Missouri, 1850 Federal Census*. Chillicothe, MO: Author. 84p.
1860
Greene County, Missouri, 1860 Federal Census. Springfield, MO: Ozarks Genealogical Society, 1984. 117p.
1870
Greene County, Missouri, 1870 Federal Census. Springfield, MO: Ozarks Genealogical Society, 1986. 221p.
1876
Carter, Gloria Bogart. *An Index to 1876 Census of Greene County, Missouri*. Greene County Archives Bulletin, No. 16. Springfield, MO: Greene County Archives and Records Center, 1992. 202p.

Grundy County
1850
Ellsberry, Elizabeth Prather. *1850 Federal Census for Grundy County, Missouri*. Chillicothe, MO: Author, 1969. 39p.
USGenWeb Census Project. Missouri, 1850 Grundy County.
ftp://ftp.rootsweb.com/pub/census/mo/grundy/1850/
1860
Ellsbery, Elizabeth Prather. *1860 Federal Census for Grundy County, Missouri*. Chillicothe, MO: Author. 97p.
1890
Cox, E. Evelyn. *Grundy County, Missouri 1890 Special Census*. Ellensburg, WA: Ancestree House, 1979. Unpgd.

Harrison County
1850
Ellsberry, Elizabeth Prather. *1850 Federal Census of Harrison County, Missouri*. Chillicothe, MO: Author. 28p.
1890
Graham, Margery M. *Harrison County, Missouri 1890 Special Census Schedule*. MO: Author, 1990. 86p.

Henry County
1840
Carter, Mrs. J. R. *Missouri Census Records of Four Counties for 1840, Cooper County, Riveso or Henry County, Platte County, Benton County*. Author. 76p.
1850
Ellsberry, Elizabeth Prather. *1850 Federal Census for Henry County, Missouri*. Chillicothe, MO: Author, 1972. 44p.

Hickory County
1850
Ellsberry, Elizabeth Prather. *1850 Federal Census for Hickory County, Missouri*. Chillicothe, MO: Author. 28p.

1860

Ellsberry, Elizabeth Prather. *1860 Federal Census for Hickory County, Missouri.* Chillicothe, MO: Author. 59p.

1870

Looney, Janice Soutee. *1870 Hickory County, Missouri Federal Census.* Walnut Grove, MO: Author, 1996. 74p.

Holt County

1850

Ellsberry, Elizabeth Prather. *1850 Federal Census for Holt County, Missouri.* Chillicothe, MO: Author, 1969. 51p.

Hodges, Nadine. *Holt County, Missouri, Census of 1850.* Kansas City, MO: Author, 1967. 56p.

USGenWeb Census Project. Missouri, 1850 Holt County.

ftp://ftp.rootsweb.com/pub/census/mo/holt/1850/

USGenWeb Census Project. Missouri, 1850 Holt County Slave Schedule.

ftp://ftp.rootsweb.com/pub/census/mo/holt/1850/slav.txt

1860

Ellsberry, Elizabeth Prather. *1860 Federal Census for Holt County, Missouri.* Chillicothe, MO: Author. 82p.

Hodges, Nadine. *Holt County, Missouri, Census of 1850.* Kansas City, MO: Author, 1967. 56p.

1876

1876 Holt County, Missouri Special Census. St. Joseph, MO: Northwest Missouri Genealogy Society, 1981. 195p.

Howard County

1840

Nelson, Frances R., and Gwen Brouse. *The Missouri Census of 1840, Reel #224, Howard, Jackson, Jefferson, Johnson and Lafayette Counties.* Riverside, CA: Authors, 1976. 168p.

1850

Ellsberry, Elizabeth Prather. *1850 Federal Census for Howard County, Missouri.* Chillicothe, MO: Author. 116p.

Howell County

1870

Buckley, Sandra. *1870 Federal Census, Howell County, Missouri.* Willard, MO: Author, 1989. 52p.

1880

Griffith, Carolyn. *1880 Howell County, Missouri Census. Online Database Edition.* Orem, UT: Ancestry.com, Inc., 1998.

http://www.ancestry.com

1910

Thornton, Velvie Gene. *1910 Federal Census of Howell County, Missouri.* Shawnee, KS: Author, 1996. 2 vols.

Iron County

1870

Beasley, Mildred Sutton McAdoo. *Iron County, Missouri 1870 Census.* Oklahoma DAR Genealogical Records Committee Report, s2 v13. Gore, OK: Talking Leaves Chapter, DAR, 1990. 138p.

Jackson County

1840

Nelson, Frances R., and Gwen Brouse. *The Missouri Census of 1840, Reel #224, Howard, Jackson, Jefferson, Johnson and Lafayette Counties.* Riverside, CA: Authors, 1976. 168p.

1870

Jackson, Ronald Vern. *Federal Census Index, Missouri 1870, St. Louis and Jackson Counties, with Cities of St. Louis and Kansas City*. West Jordan, UT: Genealogical Services, 1997. 600p.

1910

1910 Federal Census and Index Jackson County, Missouri, City of Independence and the Rest of Blue Township Outside Independence. Independence, MO: C.B. Barr, 1983. 168p.

Jasper County

1850

Ellsberry, Elizabeth Prather. *1850 Federal Census for Jasper County, Missouri*. Chillicothe, MO: Author. 52p.

Jefferson County

1840

Nelson, Frances R., and Gwen Brouse. *The Missouri Census of 1840, Reel #224, Howard, Jackson, Jefferson, Johnson and Lafayette Counties*. Riverside, CA: Authors, 1976. 168p.

Johnson County

1840

Nelson, Frances R., and Gwen Brouse. *The Missouri Census of 1840, Reel #224, Howard, Jackson, Jefferson, Johnson and Lafayette Counties*. Riverside, CA: Authors, 1976. 168p.

1850

Ellsberry, Elizabeth Prather. *1850 Federal Census for Johnson County, Missouri*. Chillicothe, MO: Author. 81p.

Williams, Jacqueline Hogan, and Betty Harvey Williams. *1850 Federal Census, Johnson County, Missouri*. Author, 1969. 104p.

1860

USGenWeb Census Project. Missouri, 1860 Johnson County.
ftp://ftp.rootsweb.com/pub/census/mo/johnson/1860/

Kansas City (Jackson County)

1870

Jackson, Ronald Vern. *Federal Census Index, Missouri 1870, St. Louis and Jackson Counties, with Cities of St. Louis and Kansas City*. West Jordan, UT: Genealogical Services, 1997. 600p.

Knox County

1850

Ellsberry, Elizabeth Prather. *1850 Federal Census for Knox County, Missouri*. Chillicothe, MO: Author. 32p.

1860

Knox County, Missouri, 1860 Census Index. Shelbyville, MO: Wilham Genealogical Research & Pub., 1988. 15p.

1870

Dromey, John H. *Partial Index to the 1870 Census of Knox County, Missouri, an Aid in Locating Surnames on the Microfilm*. Baring, MO: Author, 1983. 38p.

Knox County, Missouri, 1870 Census Index. Shelbyville, MO: Wilham Genealogical Research & Pub., 1988. 17p.

Langley, Elizabeth B. *Knox County, Missouri Index to 1850 Census*. Author, 1968. 9p.

LaClede County

1850

Ellsberry, Elizabeth Prather. *1850 Federal Census for LaClede County, Missouri*. Chillicothe, MO: Author. 30p.

Lafayette County
1840

Nelson, Frances R., and Gwen Brouse. *The Missouri Census of 1840, Reel #224, Howard, Jackson, Jefferson, Johnson and Lafayette Counties*. Riverside, CA: Authors, 1976. 168p.

1850

Ellsberry, Elizabeth Prather. *1850 Federal Census for Lafayette County, Missouri*. Chillicothe, MO: Author, 1970. 117p.

1860

Brunetti, Marty Helm. *1860 Federal Census, Lafayette County, Missouri*. Odessa, MO: Author, 1982.

Lawrence County
1850

Ellsberry, Elizabeth Prather. *1850 Federal Census for Lawrence County, Missouri*. Chillicothe, MO: Author. 69p.

USGenWeb Census Project. Missouri, 1850 Lawrence County.

ftp://ftp.rootsweb.com/pub/census/mo/lawrence/1850/

Lewis County
1850

Ellsberry, Elizabeth Prather. *1850 Federal Census for Lewis County, Missouri*. Chillicothe, MO: Author, 1993. 73p.

USGenWeb Census Project. Missouri, 1850 Lewis County.

ftp://ftp.rootsweb.com/pub/census/mo/lewis/1850/

1860

USGenWeb Census Project. Missouri, 1860 Lewis County.

ftp://ftp.rootsweb.com/pub/census/mo/1860/

1870

USGenWeb Census Project. Missouri, 1870 Lewis County.

ftp://ftp.rootsweb.com/pub/census/mo/lewis/1870/

1880

USGenWeb Census Project. Missouri, 1880 Lewis County.

ftp://ftp.rootsweb.com/pub/census/mo/lewis/1880/

Lincoln County
1850

Ellsberry, Elizabeth Prather. *1850 Federal Census for Lincoln County, Missouri*. Chillicothe, MO: Author, 1996. 93p.

Linn County
1850

Ellsberry, Elizabeth Prather. *1850 Federal Census for Linn County, Missouri*. Chillicothe, MO: Author. 47p.

1860

Ellsberry, Elizabeth Prather. *1860 Federal Census for Linn County, Missouri*. Chillicothe, MO: Author. 107p.

1870

Ellsberry, Elizabeth Prather. *1850 Federal Census for Linn County, Missouri*. Chillicothe, MO: Author, 1972. 2 vols.

Livingston County
1850

Ellsberry, Elizabeth Prather. *1850 Federal Census for Livingston County, Missouri*. Chillicothe, MO: Author. 51p.

1860

Ellsberry, Elizabeth Prather. *1860 Federal Census of Livingston County, Missouri*. Chillicothe, MO: Author. 87p.

McDonald County
1850

Ellsberry, Elizabeth Prather. *1850 Federal Census of McDonald County, Missouri*. Chillicothe, MO: Author. 26p.

1860

Ellsberry, Elizabeth Prather. *1860 Federal Census of McDonald County, Missouri*. Chillicothe, MO: Author. 51p.

1870

Looney, Janice Soutee. *1870 McDonald County, Missouri Federal Census*. Walnut Grove, MO: Author, 1996. 67p

1880

Looney, Janice Soutee. *1880 McDonald County, Missouri Federal Census*. Walnut Grove, MO: Author, 1996. 166p.

Macon County
1840

Petty, Gerald M. *Composite Index of the 1840 & 1850 United States Censuses of Macon County, Missouri*. Author, 1969. 32p.

1850

Ellsberry, Elizabeth Prather. *1850 Federal Census for Macon County, Missouri*. Chillicothe, MO: Author. 77p.

Petty, Gerald M. *Composite Index of the 1840 & 1850 United States Censuses of Macon County, Missouri*. Author, 1969. 32p.

Madison County
1850

Ellsberry, Elizabeth Prather. *1850 Federal Census of Madison County, Missouri*. Chillicothe, MO: Author. 66p.

USGenWeb Census Project. Missouri, 1850 Madison County. (Partial).

ftp://ftp.rootsweb.com/pub/census/mo/madison/1850/

Marceline (Linn County)
1900

Couch, May Bartee. *1900 City of Marceline, Missouri Census*. Marceline, MO: Author, 1987. 67p.

Maries County
1860

Hodge, Wanda. *1860 Federal Census, Maries County, Missouri*. Rolla, MO: Author, 1986. 83p.

Marion County
1830

Pompey, Sherman Lee. *Index to the 1830 Census of Marion County, Missouri*. Charleston, OR: Pacific Specialities, 1974. Unpgd.

1850

Ellsberry, Elizabeth Prather. *1850 Federal Census for Marion County, Missouri*. Chillicothe, MO: Author. 120p.

Marion County Missouri 1850 Census. Shelbyville, MO: Wilhelm Genealogical Research & Pub., 1992. 113p.

Mercer County
1850

Ellsberry, Elizabeth Prather. *1850 Federal Census for Mercer County, Missouri*. Chillicothe, MO: Author. 36p.

1860

Ellsberry, Elizabeth Prather. *1860 Federal Census for Mercer County, Missouri*. Chillicothe, MO: Author. 116p.

Miller County
1840

McKinley, Robert L. *1840 Census of Miller County, Missouri with Annotations*. Bowie, MD: Heritage Books, Inc., 1997. 467p.

1850

Ellsberry, Elizabeth Prather. *Miller County, Missouri, 1850 Federal Census*. Chillicothe, MO: Author. 46p.

1860

Ellsberry, Elizabeth Prather. *1860 Federal Census of Miller County, Missouri*. Chillicothe, MO: Author. 84p.

Mississippi County
1850

Ellsberry, Elizabeth Prather. *1850 Federal Census for Mississippi County, Missouri*. Chillicothe, MO: Author. 35p.

1860

Feezor, Joan Tinsley. *1860 Census of Mississippi County, Missouri*. Charleston, MO: Mississippi County Genealogical Society, 1988. 56p.

1870

Darnell, Betty Rolwing. *1870 Census, Mississippi County, Missouri*. Bloomfield, MO: Author, 1987. 57p.

1900

Mississippi County Genealogical Society. *1900 Census Mississippi County, Missouri*. Ozark, MO: Dogwood Pub. Co., 1995. Unpgd.

Missouri County
1850

Ellsberry, Elizabeth Prather. *1850 Federal Census for Missouri County, Missouri*. Chillicothe, MO: Author. 39p.

Moniteau County
1850

Apperson, Debra Jill. *The Seventh Census of the United States of America, This Being the 1850 Census of Moniteau County, Missouri*. Reseda, CA: Apperson Family Publications, 1978. 70p.

Monroe County
1850

Ellsberry, Elizabeth Prather. *1850 Federal Census of Monroe County, Missouri*. Chillicothe, MO: Author. 131p.

1860

Monroe County, Missouri, 1860 Census Index. Shelbyville, MO: Wilham Genealogical Research & Pub., 1988. 22p.

1870

Monroe County, Missouri, 1870 Census Index. Shelbyville, MO: Wilham Genealogical Research & Pub., 1988. 28p.

Montgomery County
1850

Ellsberry, Elizabeth Prather. *1850 Federal Census for Montgomery County, Missouri*. Chillicothe, MO: Author. 56p.

1876

1876 Census, Montgomery County, Missouri. Jefferson City, MO: Mid-Missouri Genealogical Society, Inc., 1996. 191p.

New Madrid County
1860

Ellsberry, Elizabeth Prather. *1860 Federal Census of New Madrid County, Missouri*. Chillicothe, MO: Author. 54p.

Newton County
1850

Ellsberry, Elizabeth Prather. *1850 Federal Census for Newton County, Missouri*. Chillicothe, MO: Author. 51p.

Nodaway County
1850

Ellsberry, Elizabeth Prather. *1850 Federal Census of Nodaway County, Missouri*. Chillicothe, MO: Author. 28p.

1860

Ellsberry, Elizabeth Prather. *1860 Federal Census, Nodaway County, Missouri*. Chillicothe, MO: Author. 66p.

Oregon County
1860

Ellsberry, Elizabeth Prather. *1860 Federal Census for Oregon County, Missouri*. Chillicothe, MO: Author. 38p.

Osage County
1850

Ellsberry, Elizabeth Prather. *1850 Federal Census Osage County, Missouri*. Chillicothe, MO: Author. 102p.

Ozark County
1850

Ellsberry, Elizabeth Prather. *1850 Federal Census for Ozark County, Missouri*. Chillicothe, MO: Author. 39p.

Weber, Nancie Todd. *Ozark County, Missouri in 1850*. Rev. ed. Canyon Lake, CA: Author, 1997. 86p.

1860

Ellsberry, Elizabeth Prather. *1860 Federal Census for Ozark County, Missouri*. Chillicothe, MO: Author. 31p.

Weber, Nancie Todd. *Ozark County, Missouri in 1860*. Canyon Lake, CA: Author, 1997. 53p.

1880

Looney, Janice Soutee. *Ozark County, Missouri 1880 Federal Census*. Walnut Grove, MO: Author, 1995. 135p.

Perry County
1850

Ellsberry, Elizabeth Prather. *1850 Federal Census for Perry County, Missouri*. Chillicothe, MO: Author. 85p.

1860

Sanders, Thomas Burgee, Helen Ward Sanders, and Jessie Manche Bueckman. *1860 Federal Census, Perry County, Missouri*. Perryville, MO: Perry County Historical Society, 1984.

1876

County of Perry, State of Missouri, 1876. Perryville, MO: Perry County Historical Society, 1989. 75p.

1880

Beck, Mary Neblett. *1880 Federal Census, Perry County, Missouri*. Jefferson City, MO: Mid-Missouri Genealogical Society.

Pettis County

1850

USGenWeb Census Project. Missouri, 1850 Pettis County.
ftp://ftp.rootsweb.com/pub/census/mo/pettis/1850/

Pike County

1850

Ellsberry, Elizabeth Prather. *1850 Federal Census for Pike County, Missouri*. Chillicothe, MO: Author. 131p.

Platte County

1840

Carter, Mrs. J. R. *Missouri Census Records of Four Counties for 1840, Cooper County, Riveso or Henry County, Platte County, Benton County*. Author. 76p.

Murray, Betty Runner. *Platte County, Missouri Records, 1839-1849; 1840 Federal Census, Sale of Sixteenth Section, 1842 Land Records and Tax Lists of 1839, 1847, and 1849*. Platte City, MO: Platte County Historical Society, 1993. 297p.

1850

Ellsberry, Elizabeth Prather. *1850 Federal Census for Platte County, Missouri*. Chillicothe, MO: Author. 2 vols.

1870

Murray, Betty R. *Platte County, Missouri 1870 Federal Census*. Platte City, MO: Platte County Historical Society, 1996. 276p.

Polk County

1840

Brawley, Joyce I. *The Missouri Census of 1840*. Riverside, CA: Author, 1977. 147-193p.

1850

Ellsberry, Elizabeth Prather. *1850 Federal Census for Polk County, Missouri*. Chillicothe, MO: Author. 72p.

1860

Polk County, Missouri, 1860 Federal Census (Transcribed from Microcopy Number 653, Roll Number 641). Springfield, MO: Ozarks Genealogical Society, 1985. 102p.

1870

Polk County, Missouri, 1870 Federal Census (Transcribed from Microcopy Number 593, Roll Number 800). Springfield, MO: Ozarks Genealogical Society, 1986. 127p.

1890

Union Soldiers & Widows, 1890 Special Federal Census, Index to Christian, Dade, Dallas, Polk and Taney Counties of Missouri. Springfield, MO: Ozarks Genealogical Society, 1980. 75p.

_____. Rev. ed. Springfield, MO: Ozarks Genealogical Society, 1989. 109p.

Pulaski County

1850

Ellsberry, Elizabeth Prather. *1850 Federal Census for Pulaski County, Missouri*. Chillicothe, MO: Author. 51p.

1860
Tyler, Hazle A. *1860 Federal Census, Pulaski County, Missouri*. Springfield, MO: Author. 53p.
1900
Gammon, Sharon. *Index to the 1900 Census of Pulaski County, Missouri*. Sherman, TX: Author, 1983.
1910
1910 Federal Census, Pulaski County, Missouri. Crocker, MO: Genealogy Society of Pulaski County, Missouri, 1987. 352p.

Putnam County
1850
Ellsberry, Elizabeth Prather. *1850 Federal Census for Putnam County, Missouri*. Chillicothe, MO: Author. 21p.

Ralls County
1850
Ellsberry, Elizabeth Prather. *1850 Federal Census for Ralls County, Missouri*. Chillicothe, MO: Author. 62p.
1860
Ellsberry, Elizabeth Prather. *1860 Federal Census of Ralls County, Missouri*. Chillicothe, MO: Author. 89p.

Randolph County
1830, 1840
Petty, Gerald McKinney. *Composite Index of the 1830, 1840, 1850, 1860, 1870 & 1880 United States Censuses of Randolph County, Missouri*. Columbus, OH: Author, 1970. 138p.
1850
Ellsberry, Elizabeth Prather. *1850 Federal Census for Randolph County, Missouri*. Chillicothe, MO: Author. 89p.
Petty, Gerald McKinney. *Composite Index of the 1830, 1840, 1850, 1860, 1870 & 1880 United States Censuses of Randolph County, Missouri*. Columbus, OH: Author, 1970. 138p.
1860
Ellsberry, Elizabeth Prather. *1860 Federal Census Randolph County, Missouri*. Chillicothe, MO: Author. 108p.
Hodges, Nadine, and Mrs. Howard W. Woodruff. *Randolph County, Missouri, Federal Census of 1850*. Kansas City, MO: Authors, 1968. 79p.
Petty, Gerald McKinney. *Composite Index of the 1830, 1840, 1850, 1860, 1870 & 1880 United States Censuses of Randolph County, Missouri*. Columbus, OH: Author, 1970. 138p.
1870, 1880
Petty, Gerald McKinney. *Composite Index of the 1830, 1840, 1850, 1860, 1870 & 1880 United States Censuses of Randolph County, Missouri*. Columbus, OH: Author, 1970. 138p.

Ray County
1830
Ellsberry, Elizabeth Prather. *1830 Ray County Census, Ray County, Missouri*. Chillicothe, MO: Author. 23p.
The Ray County 1830 Federal Census with Name Index. Richmond, MO: Ray County, Missouri Genealogical Association, 1996. 35p.
1850
Ellsberry, Elizabeth Prather. *1850 Federal Census for Ray County, Missouri*. Chillicothe, MO: Author. 113p.
Hodges, Nadine. *Ray County, Missouri Federal Census of 1850*. Kansas City, MO: Author. 115p.
Woods, Fred D. *The Ray County 1850 Federal Census with Name Index*. Richmond, MO: Ray County, Missouri Genealogical Association, 1996. 223p.
1860
Ellsbery, Elizabeth Prather. *1860 Federal Census for Ray County, Missouri*. Chillicothe, MO: Author. 2 vols.

Reynolds County
1860
Ellsberry, Elizabeth Prather. *1860 Federal Census of Reynolds County, Missouri*. Chillicothe, MO: Author. 42p.
1870
Ellsberry, Elizabeth Prather. *1850 Federal Census for Reynolds County, Missouri*. Chillicothe, MO: Author. 48p.
1876
Preissle, Edward, and Millie Albert Preissle. *1876 Census, Reynolds County, Missouri*. Houston, MO: Authors, 1984. 100p.

Ripley County
1850
Ellsberry, Elizabeth Prather. *1850 Federal Census for Ripley County, Missouri*. Chillicothe, MO: Author. 37p.

USGenWeb Census Project. Missouri, 1850 Ripley County.
ftp://ftp.rootsweb.com/pub/census/mo/ripley/1850/
1860
Ellsberry, Elizabeth Prather. *1860 Federal Census of Ripley County, Missouri*. Chillicothe, MO: Author. 47p.
Felldin, Jeanne Robey, and Charlotte Magee Tucker. *The 1860 Census of Ripley County, Missouri*. Tomball, TX: Genealogical Publications, 1978. 101p.
1870
Ellsberry, Elizabeth Prather. *1870 Federal Census for Ripley County, Missouri*. Chillicothe, MO: Author. 40p.

Riveso County
1840
Carter, Genevieve L. *Missouri Census Records of Four Counties for 1840, Cooper County, Riveso or Henry County, Platte County, Benton County*. Sedalia, MO: Author. 76p.

St. Charles County
1850
Ellsberry, Elizabeth Prather. *1850 Federal Census of St. Charles County, Missouri*. Chillicothe, MO: Author. 135p.
1852
Buschmeyer, Mary Ethel. *1852 State Census, St. Charles County, Missouri*. Author, 1985. 69p.

St. Clair County
1850
Ellsberry, Elizabeth Prather. *St. Clair County, Missouri 1850 Federal Census*. Chillicothe, MO: Author, 1972. 39p.

St. Francois County
1850
Ellsberry, Elizabeth Prather. *1850 Federal Census for St. Francois County, Missouri*. Chillicothe, MO: Author. 53p.
1860
Ellsberry, Elizabeth Prather. *1860 Federal Census for St. Francois County, Missouri*. Chillicothe, MO: Author, 1986. 83p.

Sainte Genevieve County
1840

Brawley, Joyce I. *The Missouri Census of 1840*. Riverside, CA: Author, 1977. 63-84p.

1850

Bishop, Bernadine LaRose, and Dorothy Amburgy Griffith. *1850 Census, Sainte Genevieve County, Missouri, Population Schedule, Mortality Schedule, Slave Schedule*. St. Louis, MO: St. Louis Genealogical Society, 1991. 62p.

1860

Ellsberry, Elizabeth Prather. *1860 Federal Census for St. Genevieve County, Missouri*. Chillicothe, MO: Author. 97p.

St. Louis County
1850

Index of 1850 U.S. Census, St. Louis and St. Louis County, Missouri. St. Louis, MO: St. Louis Genealogical Society, 1969. Unpgd.

1860

Jackson, Ronald Vern. *Missouri 1860 St. Louis County Federal Census Index*. Salt Lake City, UT: AGES, 1987. 958p.

St. Louis and St. Louis County, Missouri Index to 1860 Federal Census. St. Louis, MO: St. Louis Genealogical Society, 1984. 4 vols.

1870

Census Index: Baltimore, Chicago, St. Louis, 1870. Family Archive CD 288. Novato, CA: Broderbund Software. CD-ROM.

Jackson, Ronald Vern. *Federal Census Index, Missouri 1870, St. Louis and Jackson Counties, with Cities of St. Louis and Kansas City*. West Jordan, UT: Genealogical Services, 1997. 600p.

Steuart, Bradley W. *St. Louis, Missouri 1870 Census Index*. Bountiful, UT: Precision Indexing, 1989. 1,181p.

Saline County
1850

Ellsberry, Elizabeth Prather. *1850 Federal Census for Saline County, Missouri*. Chillicothe, MO: Author. 79p.

USGenWeb Census Project. Missouri, 1850 Saline County.

ftp://ftp.rootsweb.com/pub/census/mo/saline/1850/

1860

Ellsberry, Elizabeth Prather. *1860 Federal Census of Saline County, Missouri*. Chillicothe, MO: Author. 127p.

Schuyler County
1850

1850 Census Schuyler County, Missouri. Downing, MO: M & B Ancestor Chasers. Unpgd.

Ellsberry, Elizabeth Prather. *Schuyler County, Missouri 1850 Federal Census*. Chillicothe, MO: Author. 43p.

Missouri DAR. *Schuyler County, Missouri, 1850 Census & Mortality Schedule Report*. Genealogical Records Committee Report, s2, v273, MO: Missouri DAR, 1994. Unpgd.

USGenWeb Census Project. Missouri, 1850 Schuyler County.

ftp://ftp.rootsweb.com/pub/census/mo/schuyler/1850/

USGenWeb Census Project. Missouri, 1850 Schuyler County. Slave Schedule.

ftp://ftp.rootsweb.com/pub/census/mo/schuyler/1850/slave.txt

1860

1860 Census & Mortality Schedule of Schuyler County, Missouri. Downing, MO: M & B Ancestor Chasers. Unpgd.

Missouri DAR. *Schuyler County, Missouri, 1860 Census & Mortality Schedule Report.* Genealogical Records Committee Report, s2, v274. MO: Missouri DAR, 1994. Unpgd.

Scotland County
1850
Ellsberry, Elizabeth Prather. *1850 Federal Census Scotland County, Missouri.* Chillicothe, MO: Author. 48p.
1860
1860 Census of Scotland County, Missouri. St. Louis, MO: Wilma Walker Dunlap. 177p.

Scott County
1850
USGenWeb Census Project. Missouri, 1850 Scott County.
ftp://ftp.rootsweb.com/pub/census/mo/scott/1850/
1860
Ellsberry, Elizabeth Prather. *1860 Federal Census Scott County, Missouri.* Chillicothe, MO: Author. 65p.

Shannon County
1850
Ellsberry, Elizabeth Prather. *1850 Federal Census for Shannon County, Missouri.* Chillicothe, MO: Author. 17p.
1860
Ellsberry, Elizabeth Prather. *1860 Federal Census of Shannon County, Missouri.* Chillicothe, MO: Author. 30p.

Shelby County
1850
Ellsberry, Elizabeth Prather. *1850 Federal Census for Shelby County, Missouri.* Chillicothe, MO: Author. 51p.
1860
Ellsberry, Elizabeth Prather. *1860 Federal Census of Shelby County, Missouri.* Chillicothe, MO: Author. 85p.
1870
Shelby County, Missouri, 1870 Census Index. Shelbyville, MO: Wilham Genealogical Research & Pub., 1988. 13p.
1880
Shelby County, Missouri, 1880 Census Index. Shelbyville, MO: Wilham Genealogical Research & Pub., 1988. 29p.
1900
Shelby County, Missouri, 1900 Census Index. Shelbyville, MO: Wilham Genealogical Research & Pub., 1988. 24p.

Stoddard County
1850
Ellsberry, Elizabeth Prather. *1850 Federal Census for Stoddard County, Missouri.* Chillicothe, MO: Author. 53p.
1860
Ellsberry, Elizabeth Prather. *1860 Federal Census of Stoddard County, Missouri.* Chillicothe, MO: Author. 93p.

Sullivan County
1850
Ellsberry, Elizabeth Prather. *1850 Federal Census for Sullivan County, Missouri.* Chillicothe, MO: Author. 37p.

USGenWeb Census Project. Missouri, 1850 Sullivan County.
ftp://ftp.rootsweb.com/pub/census/mo/sullivan/1850/
1860
Ellsberry, Elizabeth Prather. *1860 Federal Census Sullivan County, Missouri.* Chillicothe, MO: Author. Unpgd.
1870
Ellsberry, Elizabeth Prather. *1870 Federal Census for Sullivan County, Missouri.* Chillicothe, MO: Author. 2 vols.

Taney County
1840
Brawley, Joyce I. *The Missouri Census of 1840.* Riverside, CA: Author, 1977. 116p.
1850
Ellsberry, Elizabeth Prather. *1850 Federal Census for Taney County, Missouri.* Chillicothe, MO: Author. 55p.
Langley, Elizabeth B. *The County of Taney, State of Missouri, Seventh Census of the United States.* Billings, MO: Author, 1968. 57p.
1860
Ellsbery, Elizabeth Prather. *1860 Federal Census for Taney County, Missouri.* Chillicothe, MO: Author. 45p.
1870
1870 Taney County Missouri Census. Point Lookout, MO: White River Valley Historical Society, 1990. 110p.
Looney, Janice Soutee. *1870 Taney County, Missouri Federal Census.* Walnut Grove, MO: Author, 1992. 57p.
1890
Union Soldiers & Widows, 1890 Special Federal Census, Index to Christian, Dade, Dallas, Polk and Taney Counties of Missouri. Springfield, MO: Ozarks Genealogical Society, 1980. 75p.
————. Rev. ed. Springfield, MO: Ozarks Genealogical Society, 1989. 109p.

Texas County
1850
Ellsberry, Elizabeth Prather. *1850 Federal Census for Texas County, Missouri.* Chillicothe, MO: Author. 30p.
Mayfield, J. Hoyle. *1890 Special Census of Union Veterans and Widows, Also 1850, 1860, 1870, 1880 Mortality Schedules of Texas County, Missouri.* Houston, TX: Texas County, Missouri Genealogical & Historical Society, 1996. 60p.
1860
Ellsberry, Elizabeth Prather. *1860 Federal Census of Texas County, Missouri.* Chillicothe, MO: Author. 77p.
Mayfield, J. Hoyle. *1890 Special Census of Union Veterans and Widows, Also 1850, 1860, 1870, 1880 Mortality Schedules of Texas County, Missouri.* Houston, TX: Texas County, Missouri Genealogical & Historical Society, 1996. 60p.
1870
Ellsbery, Elizabeth Prather. *1860 Federal Census for Texas County, Missouri.* Chillicothe, MO: Author. 77p.
Mayfield, J. Hoyle. *1890 Special Census of Union Veterans and Widows, Also 1850, 1860, 1870, 1880 Mortality Schedules of Texas County, Missouri.* Houston, TX: Texas County, Missouri Genealogical & Historical Society, 1996. 60p.
Weber, Nancie Todd. *1870 Douglas County, Missouri, Wood, Richland Townships in Texas County.* El Segundo, CA: Author, 1992. 70p.
1876
Preissle, Edward, and Millie Preissle. *1876 Census, County of Texas, State of Missouri Books One and Two (Indexed).* Houston, MO: Texas County Missouri Genealogical Society, 1983. 180p.
1880, 1890
Mayfield, J. Hoyle. *1890 Special Census of Union Veterans and Widows, Also 1850, 1860, 1870, 1880 Mortality Schedules of Texas County, Missouri.* Houston, TX: Texas County, Missouri Genealogical & Historical Society, 1996. 60p.

1900

Melton, Mildred Fourt, and Neva N. Bryant. *1900 Federal Census of Texas County, Missouri*. Houston, MO: Author. Unpgd.

Warren County
1850

Ellsberry, Elizabeth Prather. *1850 Federal Census for Warren County, Missouri*. Chillicothe, MO: Author, 1970. 65p.

1860

Ellsberry, Elizabeth Prather. *1860 Federal Census of Warren County, Missouri*. Chillicothe, MO: Author. 108p.

Washington County
1860

Ellsberry, Elizabeth Prather. *1860 Federal Census of Washington County, Missouri*. Chillicothe, MO: Author. 116p.

Wayne County
1850

Ellsberry, Elizabeth Prather. *1850 Federal Census for Wayne County, Missouri*. Chillicothe, MO: Author. 56p.

Washington County
1850

Ellsberry, Elizabeth Prather. *1850 Federal Census for Washington County, Missouri*. Chillicothe, MO: Author. 99p.

Webster County
1900

Cunningham, Mary Bean. *1900 Federal Census, Webster County, Missouri*. Springfield, MO: Author, 1988. 2 vols.

Worth County
1870

Ray, Mrs. William K. *1870 Federal Census and 1870 Mortality Schedule, Worth County, Missouri*. Columbia, MO: Missouri State Genealogical Association. 59p.

1876

Worth County, Missouri 1876 Special Census. St. Joseph, MO: Northwest Missouri Genealogical Society, 1996. 98p.

Wright County
1850

Ellsberry, Elizabeth Prather. *1850 Federal Census for Wright County, Missouri*. Chillicothe, MO: Author. 42p.

1860

Ellsberry, Elizabeth Prather. *1860 Federal Census for Wright County, Missouri*. Chillicothe, MO: Author. 62p.

1900

Carter, Gloria Bogart. *Wright County, Missouri 1900 Federal Census*. Springfield, MO: Author, 1986. 2 vols.

Montana

1850

Census Index: U.S. Selected States/Counties, 1850. Family Archive CD 317. Novato, CA: Broderbund Software. CD-ROM.

1860

Bell, Margery H. *1860 Census, Bitter Root Valley & Ponderay Mountains, Area of Washington Territory Now in the State of Montana.* Author. 13p.

Census Index: U.S. Selected States/Counties, 1860. Family Archive CD 318. Novato, CA: Broderbund Software. CD-ROM.

Jackson, Ronald Vern. *Montana 1860 Territorial Census Index.* Bountiful, UT: Accelerated Indexing Systems, 1982. 55, 6p.

_____. _____. West Jordan, UT: Genealogical Services, 1982, 1997.

Morgan, Sue Powell. *Montana 1860, U.S. Territorial Census Index.* West Jordan, UT: Genealogical Services, 1999. Unpgd.

1870

Census Index: U.S. Selected States/Counties, 1870. Family Archive CD 319. Novato, CA: Broderbund Software. CD-ROM.

Jackson, Ronald Vern. *Montana Census Index, Online Edition.* Orem, UT: Ancestry.com, Inc., 1999. **http://www.ancestry.com**

_____. *Montana 1870 Territorial Census Index.* Bountiful, UT: Accelerated Indexing Systems, 1979. 241p.

_____. *Mortality Schedules Index, Online Edition.* Orem, UT: Ancestry.com, Inc., 1999. **http://www.ancestry.com**

_____, Wylma Winmill, and Shirley P. Zachrison. *Montana 1870 Mortality Schedule.* Bountiful, UT: Accelerated Indexing Systems, 1981. 20p.

Marshall, Thelma Leasure. *Montana Territory 1870 Census Index.* Great Falls, MT: Licini's Print Shop, 1979. 184p.

Strombo, Cathryn J. *1870 Montana Census, Cedar Creek Mines. 1880 Montana Census, District 92.* Superior, MT: Author, 1976. Unpgd.

U.S. Federal Population Census Schedules. 1870, M593, Microfilm Reel No. 827.

1880

1880 Montana Territory Census Index. Lewistown, MT: Lewistown Genealogical Society, 1987. 365p.

Jackson, Ronald Vern. *Montana Census Index, Online Edition.* Orem, UT: Ancestry.com, Inc., 1999. **http://www.ancestry.com**

_____. *Montana 1880 Census Index.* Bountiful, UT: Accelerated Indexing Systems, 1985. 468p.

_____. *Mortality Schedules Index, Online Edition.* Orem, UT: Ancestry.com, Inc., 1999. **http://www.ancestry.com**

Strombo, Cathryn J. *1870 Montana Census, Cedar Creek Mines. 1880 Montana Census, District 92.* Superior, MT: Author, 1976. Unpgd.

U.S. Federal Population Census Schedules. 1880, T9, Microfilm Reel No. 742.

U.S. Federal Population Census Schedules. 1880, Soundex. T759, 2 Microfilm Reels.

1890

Jackson, Ronald Vern. *Montana Census Index, Online Edition.* Orem, UT: Ancestry.com, Inc., 1999. **http://www.ancestry.com**

_____. *1890 Montana Census Index, Special Schedule of the Eleventh Census (1890) Enumerating Union Veterans and of Union Veterans of the Civil War.* Salt Lake City, UT: Accelerated Indexing Systems, 1984. 46p.

_____. _____. North Salt Lake City, UT: Accelerated Indexing Systems International, 1984. 40p.

U.S. Federal Population Census Schedules, Special Schedule, Enumerating Union Veterans and Widows of Union Veterans of the Civil War. 1890, M123, Microfilm Reel No. 35.
Veterans' Schedules: U.S. Selected States, 1890. Family Archive CD 131. Novato, CA: Broderbund Software. CD-ROM.

1900

Ledoux, Albert H. *The French Canadian Families of the Plains and Upper Mountain States, Abstracts from the Federal Census of 1900.* Altoona, PA: Author, 1991. 2 vols.
U.S. Federal Population Census Schedules. 1900, T623, Microfilm Reel Nos. 909-915.
U.S. Federal Population Census Schedules. 1900, Soundex. T1056, 40 Microfilm Reels.

1910

U.S. Federal Population Census Schedules. 1910, T624, Microfilm Reel Nos. 829-837. (No Soundex/Miracode Index was prepared by the Government for this State.)

1920

U.S. Federal Population Census Schedules. 1920, T625, Microfilm Reel Nos. 967-978.
U.S. Federal Population Census Schedules. 1920, Soundex. M1572, 46 Microfilm Reels.

Beaverhead County
1910
Darling, P. B. *Index 1910 Census: Beaverhead County, Montana.* Dillon, MT: Author, 1999. 122p.

Custer County
1920
1920 Census Index, Custer County, Montana. Miles City, MT: Miles City Genealogical Society, 1994. 235p.

Fergus County
1900
1900 Federal Census Index, Fergus County, Montana. Lewistown, MT: Lewistown Genealogical Society, 1982. 69p.
1910
Quiring, Mary Ann. *1910 Federal Census Index, Fergus County, Montana.* Lewistown, MT: Lewistown Genealogical Society, 1984. 169p.

Missoula County
1880
Missoula County, Montana Territory, 1880 Census and Index. Missoula, MT: Family History Library, The Church of Jesus Christ of Latter-day Saints, Missoula, MT Stake, 1979. 103p.

Powell County
1910
Powell County 1910 Census Index, Including Montana State Prison. Deer Lodge, MT: Powell County Genealogy Society. 84p.

Ravalli County
1910
Ravalli County 1910 U.S. Census. Hamilton, MT: Bitter Root Genealogical Society, 1985. 264p.

Nebraska

1854-1856

Cox, E. Evelyn. *Nebraska Territory Census Records for the Years of 1854, 1855, 1856.* Ellensburg, WA: Kittitas County Genealogical Society. 3 vols.

Jackson, Ronald Vern. *Nebraska Census Index, Online Edition.* Orem, UT: Ancestry.com, Inc., 1999. **http://www.ancestry.com**

_____. *1854, 1855, 1856 Nebraska Territorial Census Index.* Bountiful, UT: Accelerated Indexing Systems, 1980. 57p.

1860

Census Index: U.S. Selected States/Counties, 1860. Family Archive CD 318. Novato, CA: Broderbund Software. CD-ROM.

Cox, Evelyn. *1860 Nebraska Territory Census, County Index.* Ellenburg, WA: Author, 1973. 592p.

_____. *1860 Nebraska Territory Census, Index to Heads-of-families.* Ellensburg, WA: Ancestree House, 1979. 251p.

Jackson, Ronald Vern. *Mortality Schedules Index, Online Edition.* Orem, UT: Ancestry.com, Inc., 1999. **http://www.ancestry.com**

_____, and Gary Ronald Teeples. *Nebraska 1860 Territorial Census Index.* Bountiful, UT: Accelerated Indexing Systems, 1978. 70p.

_____, Wylma Winmill, and Shirley P. Zachrison. *Nebraska 1860 Mortality Schedule.* Bountiful, UT: Accelerated Indexing Systems, 1980. 16p.

James, Jane Emerson. *Eighth Census of the United States, 1860: Nebraska Territory Mortality Schedules.* Huntsville, AR: Century Enterprises, 1972. 24p.

U.S. Federal Population Census Schedules. 1860, M653, Microfilm Reel No. 665.

1870

Cox, E. Evelyn. *1870 Nebraska Census.* Ellensburg, WA: Ancestree House, 1979. Unpgd.

Jackson, Ronald Vern. *Mortality Schedules Index, Online Edition.* Orem, UT: Ancestry.com, Inc., 1999. **http://www.ancestry.com**

_____. *Nebraska Census Index, Online Edition.* Orem, UT: Ancestry.com, Inc., 1999. **http://www.ancestry.com**

_____. *Nebraska 1870 Census Index.* North Salt Lake City, UT: Accelerated Indexing Systems, 1985. 56p.

U.S. Federal Population Census Schedules. 1870, M593, Microfilm Reel Nos. 828-833.

1880

Jackson, Ronald Vern. *Mortality Schedules Index, Online Edition.* Orem, UT: Ancestry.com, Inc., 1999. **http://www.ancestry.com**

_____, Wylma Winmill, Shirley P. Zachrison. *Nebraska 1880 Mortality Schedule.* Bountiful, UT: Accelerated Indexing Systems, 1981. 105p.

U.S. Federal Population Census Schedules. 1880, T9, Microfilm Reel Nos. 743-757.

U.S. Federal Population Census Schedules. 1880, Soundex. T760, 22 Microfilm Reels.

1890

U.S. Federal Population Census Schedules, Special Schedule, Enumerating Union Veterans and Widows of Union Veterans of the Civil War. 1890, M123, Microfilm Reel No. 36-38.

Veterans' Schedules: U.S. Selected States, 1890. Family Archive CD 131. Novato, CA: Broderbund Software. CD-ROM.

1900

Ledoux, Albert H. *The French Canadian Families of the Plains and Upper Mountain States, Abstracts from the Federal Census of 1900.* Altoona, PA: Author, 1991. 2 vols.

U.S. Federal Population Census Schedules. 1900, T623, Microfilm Reel Nos. 916-942.
U.S. Federal Population Census Schedules. 1900, Soundex. T1057, 107 Microfilm Reels.

1910

U.S. Federal Population Census Schedules. 1910, T624, Microfilm Reel Nos. 838-857. (No Soundex/Miracode
Index was prepared by the Government for this State.)

1920

U.S. Federal Population Census Schedules. 1920, T625, Microfilm Reel Nos. 979-1003.
U.S. Federal Population Census Schedules. 1920, Soundex. M1573, 96 Microfilm Reels.

Buffalo County
1885

Smith, Luaine. *1885 Mortality Census, Buffalo County, Nebraska*. Author, 1987. 14p.

Cedar County
1870

USGenWeb Census Project. Nebraska, 1870 Cedar County.
ftp://ftp.rootsweb.com/pub/census/ne/cedar/1870/

Custer County
1880

Strombo, Cathryn J. *Index to the 1880 Census of Custer County, Nebraska*. Superior, MT: Author, 1977.
88p.

Douglas County
1910

An Index to the 1910 Federal Population Census of Douglas County (City of Omaha). Lincoln, NE: Nebraska State Genealogical Society, 1996. Unpgd.

Fillmore County
1870

USGenWeb Census Project. Nebraska, 1870 Fillmore County.
ftp://ftp.rootsweb.com/pub/census/ne/fillmore/1870/

Fort Laramie
1860

USGenWeb Census Project. Nebraska, 1860 Fort Laramie.
ftp://ftp.rootsweb.com/pub/census/ne/fort-laramie/1860/

Franklin County
1900

USGenWeb Census Project. Nebraska, 1900 Franklin County.
ftp://ftp.rootsweb.com/pub/census/ne/franklin/1900/

Howard County
1880

Fairbairn, Marian Anderson. *1880 Federal Census Index, Howard County, Nebraska*. Jefferson, IA: Author,
1985. 44p.

Johnson County
1910
Marshall, Audrey Morris. *An Index to Johnson County, Nebraska 1910 Federal Population Census.* Lincoln, NE: Nebraska State Genealogical Society, 1989. 61p.

Kearney County
1910
Marshall, Audrey Morris. *An Index to Kearney County, Nebraska 1910 Federal Population Census.* Lincoln, NE: Nebraska State Genealogical Society, 1990. 55p.

Keith County
1885
Hughes, Phyllis Pankonin. *1885 Keith County, Nebraska State Census Index, Includes Only People Who Later Became Residents of Perkins County, Nebraska.* Boulder, CO: Author, 1985. 3p.
1910
Marshall, Audrey Morris. *An Index to the 1910 Federal Population Census of the Nebraska Counties of Keith, Keya Paha, Kimball, Logan and Loup.* Lincoln, NE: Nebraska State Genealogical Society, 1991. 62p.

Keya Paha County
1910
Marshall, Audrey Morris. *An Index to the 1910 Federal Population Census of the Nebraska Counties of Keith, Keya Paha, Kimball, Logan and Loup.* Lincoln, NE: Nebraska State Genealogical Society, 1991. 62p.

Kimball County
1900
Kimball County, Nebraska 1900 Census Index. Kimball, NE: Plains Genealogical Society, 1987. 7p.
1910
Marshall, Audrey Morris. *An Index to the 1910 Federal Population Census of the Nebraska Counties of Keith, Keya Paha, Kimball, Logan and Loup.* Lincoln, NE: Nebraska State Genealogical Society, 1991. 62p.

Knox County
1880
Romberg, Jacquelyn. *Knox County, Nebraska 1880 Census Index.* Lincoln, NE: Nebraska State Genealogy Society, 1993. 160p.
1910
Marshall, Audrey Morris. *An Index to Knox County, Nebraska 1910 Federal Population Census.* Lincoln, NE: Nebraska State Genealogical Society, 1991. 81p.

Lancaster County
1910
Marshall, Audrey Morris. *An Index to the 1910 Federal Population Census for Lancaster County, Nebraska 1910.* Lincoln, NE: Nebraska State Genealogical Society, 1992. Unpgd.

Lincoln County
1880
Rowley, Charlene. *1880 Federal Census Index, Lincoln County, Nebraska.* Lincoln, NE: Nebraska State Genealogical Society, 1996. 34p.

1885

Pressnall, Gloria. *1885 Lincoln County Nebraska State Census*. North Platte, NE: North Platte Genealogy Society, 1987. 150, 56p.

1910

Marshall, Audrey Morris. *Lincoln County, Nebraska 1910 Census Index*. Lincoln, NE: Nebraska State Genealogical Society, 1994. 86p.

Logan County
1910

Marshall, Audrey Morris. *An Index to the 1910 Federal Population Census of the Nebraska Counties of Keith, Keya Paha, Kimball, Logan and Loup*. Lincoln, NE: Nebraska State Genealogical Society, 1991. 62p.

Loup County
1910

Marshall, Audrey Morris. *An Index to the 1910 Federal Population Census of the Nebraska Counties of Keith, Keya Paha, Kimball, Logan and Loup*. Lincoln, NE: Nebraska State Genealogical Society, 1991. 62p.

McPherson County
1910

Marshall, Audrey M. *1910 Federal Population Census, an Index of McPherson, Merrick and Morrill Counties, Nebraska*. Lincoln, NE: Nebraska State Genealogical Society, 1996. 91p.

Merrick County
1910

Marshall, Audrey M. *1910 Federal Population Census, an Index of McPherson, Merrick and Morrill Counties, Nebraska*. Lincoln, NE: Nebraska State Genealogical Society, 1996. 91p.

Morrill County
1910

Marshall, Audrey M. *1910 Federal Population Census, an Index of McPherson, Merrick and Morrill Counties, Nebraska*. Lincoln, NE: Nebraska State Genealogical Society, 1996. 91p.

Nuckolls County
1870

USGenWeb Census Project. Nebraska, 1870 Nuckolls.
ftp://ftp.rootsweb.com/pub/census/ne/nuckolls/1870/

Pawnee County
1910

Marshall, Audrey Morris. *An Index to Pawnee County, Nebraska 1910 Federal Population Census*. Lincoln, NE: Nebraska State Genealogical Society, 1989. 62p.

Perkins County
1900

Hughes, Phyllis Pankonin. *Perkins County, Nebraska, 1900 and 1910 Census Index, Including the 1890 Civil War Census Index and Earliest Pioneers to Perkins County, Nebraska and Perkins County Miscellanea*. Boulder, CO: Author, 1984. 97p.

1910

Hughes, Phyllis Pankonin. *Perkins County, Nebraska, 1900 and 1910 Census Index, Including the 1890 Civil War Census Index and Earliest Pioneers to Perkins County, Nebraska and Perkins County Miscellanea*. Boulder, CO: Author, 1984. 97p.

Marshall, Audrey Morris. *An Index to Perkins County, Nebraska 1910 Federal Population Census*. Lincoln, NE: Nebraska State Genealogical Society, 1990. 17p.

Platte County
1870

USGenWeb Census Project. Nebraska, 1870 Platte County.
ftp://ftp.rootsweb.com/pub/census/ne/platte/1870/

Red Willow County
1880

Brooks, Gail I. *The 10th Census of the United States of America, 1880 Red Willow County, Nebraska*. Arcata, CA: Gibson Computers and Pub., 1986. 137p.

Richardson County
1854

Pompey, Sherman Lee. *Index to the 1854 State Census of Richardson County, Nebraska, Territory*. Charleston, OR: Pacific Specialities, 1974. 4p.

1890

1890 Special Census, Richardson County, Nebraska. Ellensburg, WA: Ancestree House, 1979. 19p.

Washington County
1885

Nebraska DAR. *Washington County, Nebraska 1885 Census*. Genealogical Records Committee Report, s2 v15. Omaha, NE: Sylvia L. Nimmo Chapter, DAR. 97p.

Wayne County
1880

USGenWeb Census Project. Nebraska, 1880 Wayne County.
ftp://ftp.rootsweb.com/pub/census/ne/wayne/1880/

Winnebago County
1870

USGenWeb Census Project. Nebraska, 1870 Winnebago.
ftp://ftp.rootsweb.com/pub/census/ne/winnebago/1870/

Nevada

1860

Census Index: U.S. Selected States/Counties, 1860. Family Archive CD 318. Novato, CA: Broderbund Software. CD-ROM.

Jackson, Ronald Vern. *Mortality Schedules Index, Online Edition*. Orem, UT: Ancestry.com, Inc., 1999.
http://www.ancestry.com

_____. *Nevada Census Index, Online Edition*. Orem, UT: Ancestry.com, Inc., 1999.
http://www.ancestry.com

_____. *Nevada 1860 Territorial Census Index*. Bountiful, UT: Accelerated Indexing Systems, 1981. 86p.

U.S. Federal Population Census Schedules. 1860, M653, Microfilm Reel No. 1314.

1870

Census Index: U.S. Selected States/Counties, 1870. Family Archive CD 319. Novato, CA: Broderbund Software. CD-ROM.

Jackson, Ronald Vern. *Mortality Schedules Index, Online Edition*. Orem, UT: Ancestry.com, Inc., 1999.
http://www.ancestry.com

_____. *Nevada Census Index, Online Edition*. Orem, UT: Ancestry.com, Inc., 1999.
http://www.ancestry.com

_____. *Nevada 1870 Territorial Census Index*. Salt Lake City, UT: Accelerated Indexing Systems, 1979. 531p.

_____. _____. West Jordan, UT: Genealogical Services, 1979, 1997.

U.S. Federal Population Census Schedules. 1870, M593, Microfilm Reel Nos. 834-835.

1875

Census of the Inhabitants of the State of Nevada, 1875. Carson City, NV: Hill, 1877. 2 vols.

Index to the 1875 Nevada Census. Carson City, NV: Nevada State Library, 1978. 75 microfiche.

1880

Census Index: U.S. Selected States/Counties, 1880. Family Archive CD 320. Novato, CA: Broderbund Software. CD-ROM.

Jackson, Ronald Vern. *Mortality Schedules Index, Online Edition*. Orem, UT: Ancestry.com, Inc., 1999.
http://www.ancestry.com

_____. *Nevada Census Index, Online Edition*. Orem, UT: Ancestry.com, Inc., 1999.
http://www.ancestry.com

_____. *Nevada 1880 Territorial Census Index*. Bountiful, UT: Accelerated Indexing Systems, 1979. 793p.

U.S. Federal Population Census Schedules. 1880, T9, Microfilm Reel Nos. 758-759.

U.S. Federal Population Census Schedules. 1880, Soundex. T761, 3 Microfilm Reels.

1890

Jackson, Ronald Vern. *1890 Nevada Census Index, Special Schedule of the Eleventh Census, 1890, Enumerating Union Veterans and of Union Veterans of the Civil War (This Index Includes Every Name Listed on the Census Record)*. Salt Lake City, UT: Accelerated Indexing Systems International, 1983. 62p.

_____. *Nevada Census Index, Online Edition Veterans Schedules*. Orem, UT: Ancestry.com, Inc., 1999.
http://www.ancestry.com

U.S. Federal Population Census Schedules, Special Schedule, Enumerating Union Veterans and Widows of Union Veterans of the Civil War. 1890, M123, Microfilm Reel No. 39.

Veterans' Schedules: U.S. Selected States, 1890. Family Archive CD 131. Novato, CA: Broderbund Software. CD-ROM.

1900

Jackson, Ronald Vern. *Nevada Census Index, Online Edition*. Orem, UT: Ancestry.com, Inc., 1999.
http://www.ancestry.com

_____. *Nevada 1900*. North Salt Lake City, UT: Accelerated Indexing Systems, 1986. 252p.

U.S. Federal Population Census Schedules. 1900, T623, Microfilm Reel Nos. 943.

U.S. Federal Population Census Schedules. 1900, Soundex. T1058, 52 Microfilm Reels.

1910

Dilts, Bryan Lee. *1910 Nevada Census Index, Heads of Households and Other Surnames in Household Index*. Salt Lake City, UT: Index Publishing, 1984. 169p.

Jackson, Ronald Vern. *Nevada Census Index, Online Edition*. Orem, UT: Ancestry.com, Inc., 1999.
http://www.ancestry.com

_____. *Nevada 1910 Census Index*. Bountiful, UT: Accelerated Indexing Systems, 1984. 555p.

Steuart, Bradley. *Nevada 1910 Census Index*. Bountiful, UT: Heritage Quest, 1999. 271p.

U.S. Federal Population Census Schedules. 1910, T624, Microfilm Reel Nos. 858-859. (No Soundex/Miracode Index was prepared by the Government for this State.)

1920
U.S. Federal Population Census Schedules. 1920, T625, Microfilm Reel Nos. 1004-1005.
U.S. Federal Population Census Schedules. 1920, Soundex. M1574, 39 Microfilm Reels.

New Hampshire

Bunker, Paul Delmont. *The Bunkers of New Hampshire; Being Copies of All Records Contained in the Federal Censuses of 1790-1850 Inclusive Which Refer to Members of the Bunker Family, Taken from the Original Records of the Census Bureau, Washington, DC.* Washington, DC: Author, 1931. 25p.
Jackson, Ronald Vern. *Early New Hampshire.* Bountiful, UT: Accelerated Indexing Systems, 1981. Unpgd.

1633-1699
Holbrook, Jay Mack. *New Hampshire Residents, 1633-1699.* Oxford, MA: Holbrook Research Institute, 1979. 209p.

1730
Holbrook, Jay Mack. *New Hampshire 1732 Census.* Oxford, MA: Holbrook Research Institute, 1981. 75p.

1776
Holbrook, Jay Mack. *New Hampshire 1776 Census.* Oxford, MA: Holbrook Research Institute, 1976. 164p.

1790
Jackson, Ronald Vern. *New Hampshire Census Index, Online Edition.* Orem, UT: Ancestry.com, Inc., 1999. **http://www.ancestry.com**
_____. *New Hampshire 1790, Vermont 1790 Federal Census Indexes.* North Salt Lake City, UT: Accelerated Indexing Systems International, 1990. 252p.
U.S. Bureau of the Census. *Heads of Families at the First Census of the United States Taken in the Year 1790, New Hampshire.* Washington, DC: Government Printing Office, 1908.
_____. _____. Baltimore, MD: Genealogical Pub. Co., 1973. 146p.
_____. _____. Bountiful, UT: American Genealogical Lending Library, 1993. 146p.
_____. _____. *Online Database Edition.* Orem, UT: Ancestry.com, Inc., 1999.
http://www.ancestry.com
_____. *U.S. Federal Population Census Schedules,* 1790. T498, Microfilm Reel No. 1.
U.S. Federal Population Census Schedules, 1790. M637, Microfilm Reel No. 5.

1800
Gill, James V., and Maryan R. Gill. *New Hampshire 1800.* Thomson, IL Author. 3 vols.
Jackson, Ronald Vern. *New Hampshire Census Index, Online Edition.* Orem, UT: Ancestry.com, Inc., 1999.
http://www.ancestry.com
_____, and Gary Ronald Teeples. *New Hampshire 1800 Census Index.* Bountiful, UT: Accelerated Indexing Systems, 1974. 110p.
Steuart, Raeone Christensen. *New Hampshire 1800 Census Index.* Bountiful, UT: Heritage Quest, 2000. 156p.
_____. *United States 1800 Census Index.* Bountiful, UT: Heritage Quest, 2000. 4 vols. CD-ROM.
Threlfall, John Brooks. *Heads of Families at the Second Census of the United States Taken in the Year 1800, New Hampshire.* Madison, WI, 1973. 222p.
U.S. Federal Population Census Schedules, 1800. M32, Microfilm Reel Nos. 20.

1810

Jackson, Ronald Vern. *New Hampshire Census Index, Online Edition.* Orem, UT: Ancestry.com, Inc., 1999. **http://www.ancestry.com**

_____, and Gary Ronald Teeples. *New Hampshire 1810 Census Index.* Bountiful, UT: Accelerated Indexing Systems, 1976. 86p.

U.S. Federal Population Census Schedules, 1810. M252, Microfilm Reel Nos. 23-25.

1820

Jackson, Ronald Vern. *New Hampshire Census Index, Online Edition.* Orem, UT: Ancestry.com, Inc., 1999. **http://www.ancestry.com**

_____, and Gary Ronald Teeples. *New Hampshire 1820 Census Index.* Bountiful, UT: Accelerated Indexing Systems, 1976. 66p.

U.S. Federal Population Census Schedules. 1820, M33, Microfilm Reel Nos. 59-61.

1830

Census Index: U.S. Selected States/Counties, 1830. Family Archive CD 315. Novato, CA: Broderbund Software. CD-ROM.

Jackson, Ronald Vern. *New Hampshire Census Index, Online Edition.* Orem, UT: Ancestry.com, Inc., 1999. **http://www.ancestry.com**

_____, and Gary Ronald Teeples. *New Hampshire 1830 Census Index.* Bountiful, UT: Accelerated Indexing Systems, 1977. 165p.

U.S. Census Index, 1830-1839, New England, New York, Pennsylvania. Orem, UT: Automated Archives, 1992. 1 CD-ROM.

U.S. Federal Population Census Schedules. 1830, M19, Microfilm Reel Nos. 74-78.

1837

Jackson, Ronald Vern. *New Hampshire Census Index, Online Edition.* Orem, UT: Ancestry.com, Inc., 1999. **http://www.ancestry.com**

1840

Census Index: U.S. Selected States/Counties, 1840. Family Archive CD 316. Novato, CA: Broderbund Software. CD-ROM.

Jackson, Ronald Vern. *New Hampshire Census Index, Online Edition.* Orem, UT: Ancestry.com, Inc., 1999. **http://www.ancestry.com**

_____, and Gary Ronald Teeples. *New Hampshire 1840 Census Index.* Bountiful, UT: Accelerated Indexing Systems, 1976. 129p.

U.S. Census Index Series, New England, New York, 1840. Orem, UT: Automated Archives, 1992. CD-ROM.

U.S. Federal Population Census Schedules. 1840, M704, Microfilm Reel Nos. 234-246.

1850

Jackson, Ronald Vern. *Mortality Schedules Index, Online Edition.* Orem, UT: Ancestry.com, Inc., 1999. **http://www.ancestry.com**

_____. *New Hampshire Census Index, Online Edition.* Orem, UT: Ancestry.com, Inc., 1999. **http://www.ancestry.com**

_____, and Gary Ronald Teeples. *New Hampshire 1850 Census Index.* Bountiful, UT: Accelerated Indexing Systems, 1978. 268p.

U.S. Census Index Series, New England, 1850. Orem, UT: Automated Archives, 1991. CD-ROM.

U.S. Federal Population Census Schedules. 1850, M432, Microfilm Reel Nos. 425-441.

1860

Census Index: U.S. Selected States/Counties, 1860. Family Archive CD 318. Novato, CA: Broderbund Software. CD-ROM.

Jackson, Ronald Vern. *New Hampshire Census Index, Online Edition*. Orem, UT: Ancestry.com, Inc., 1999.
http://www.ancestry.com
_____. *New Hampshire 1860 U.S. Federal Census Index*. West Jordan, UT: Genealogical Services, 1986, 1997. 1,097p.
U.S. Federal Population Census Schedules. 1860, M653, Microfilm Reel Nos. 666-681.

1870

Steuart, Raeone Christensen. *New Hampshire 1870 Census Index*. Bountiful, UT: Heritage Quest, 2000. 702p.
_____. *Maine, New Hampshire and Vermont 1870 Census Index*. Bountiful, UT: Heritage Quest, 2000. CD-ROM.
U.S. Federal Population Census Schedules. 1870, M593, Microfilm Reel Nos. 836-850.

1880

U.S. Federal Population Census Schedules. 1880, T9, Microfilm Reel Nos. 760-769.
U.S. Federal Population Census Schedules. 1880, Soundex. T762, 13 Microfilm Reels.

1890

Jackson, Ronald Vern. *1890 New Hampshire Census Index, Special Schedule of the Eleventh Census, 1890, Enumerating Union Veterans and of Union Veterans of the Civil War (This Index Includes Every Name Listed on the Census Record)*. Salt Lake City, UT: Accelerated Indexing Systems International, 1985. 169p.
_____. *New Hampshire Census Index, Online Edition*. Orem, UT: Ancestry.com, Inc., 1999.
http://www.ancestry.com
U.S. Federal Population Census Schedules, Special Schedule, Enumerating Union Veterans and Widows of Union Veterans of the Civil War. 1890, M123, Microfilm Reel No. 40.
Veterans' Schedules: U.S. Selected States, 1890. Family Archive CD 131. Novato, CA: Broderbund Software. CD-ROM.

1900

U.S. Federal Population Census Schedules. 1900, T623, Microfilm Reel Nos. 944-952.
U.S. Federal Population Census Schedules. 1900, Soundex. T1059, 52 Microfilm Reels.

1910

U.S. Federal Population Census Schedules. 1910, T624, Microfilm Reel Nos. 860-866. (No Soundex/Miracode Index was prepared by the Government for this State.)

1920

U.S. Federal Population Census Schedules. 1920, T625, Microfilm Reel Nos. 1006-1014.
U.S. Federal Population Census Schedules. 1920, Soundex. M1575, 39 Microfilm Reels.

Cheshire County
1800

Gill, James V. *An Index to the 1800 Federal Census of Cheshire County, State of New Hampshire*. Danville, IL: Illiana Genealogical, 1967. 54p.

Grafton County
1800

Gill, Maryan R. *An Index to the 1800 Federal Census of Grafton and Hillsborough Counties, State of New Hampshire*. Danville, IL: Illiana Genealogical, 1972. 88p.

Hillsborough County
1800
Gill, Maryan R. *An Index to the 1800 Federal Census of Grafton and Hillsborough Counties, State of New Hampshire*. Danville, IL: Illiana Genealogical, 1972. 88p.
1850
Brown, Ann L. Nichols. *1850 Census, Hillsborough County, New Hampshire, Including Population and Mortality Schedules*. Bowie, MD: Heritage Books, 1992-1993. 2 vols.

Lempster (Sullivan County)
Stevens, Jessica W. *Lempster, New Hampshire, Inhabitants from Incorporation in 1767 through the 1900 Federal Census*. St. Petersburg, FL: Author, 1995. 135p.

Milford (Hillsborough County)
1910
Belt, Thomas. *Index to the Milford, New Hampshire Listings for the 13th Census, 1910*. Milford, NH: Author, 1910. 40p.

Rockingham County
1800
Gill, Maryan R. *An Index to the 1800 Federal Census of Rockingham and Strafford Counties, State of New Hampshire*. Danville, IL: Author, 1973. 84p.

Strafford County
1800
Gill, Maryan R. *An Index to the 1800 Federal Census of Rockingham and Strafford Counties, State of New Hampshire*. Danville, IL: Author, 1973. 84p.

New Jersey

Jackson, Ronald Vern, Altha Polson, and Shirley P. Zachrison. *Early New Jersey*. Bountiful, UT: Accelerated Indexing Systems. Unpgd.
Stryker Rodda, Kenn. *Revolutionary Census of New Jersey, an Index, Based on Ratables, of the Inhabitants of New Jersey during the Period of the American Revolution*. Cottonport, LA: Polyanthos, 1972. 248p.
_____. Lambertville, NJ: Hunterdon House, 1986. 413p.

1693
Craig, Peter Stebbins. *The 1693 Census of the Swedes on the Delaware Family Histories of the Swedish Lutheran Church Members Residing in Pennsylvania, Delaware, West New Jersey and Cecil County, Maryland, 1638-1693*. Studies in Swedish American Genealogy No. 3. Winter Park, FL: SAG Publications, 1993. 213p.

1790
Jackson, Ronald Vern. *1790 Census Index, Miscellaneous Sources*. North Salt Lake City, UT: Accelerated Indexing Systems, 1990. Unpgd.
U.S. Federal Population Census Schedules, 1790. M637. Records did not survive for this State.

1793
Norton, James S. *New Jersey in 1793, an Abstract and Index to the 1793 Militia Census of the State of New Jersey*. Salt Lake City, UT: Author, 1973. 515p.

1830

Census Index: U.S. Selected States/Counties, 1830. Family Archive CD 315. Novato, CA: Broderbund Software. CD-ROM.

Jackson, Ronald Vern. *New Jersey Census Index, Online Edition.* Orem, UT: Ancestry.com, Inc., 1999. **http://www.ancestry.com**

_____. *New Jersey 1830 Census.* Bountiful, UT: Accelerated Indexing Systems, 1974. 253p.

U.S. Federal Population Census Schedules. 1830, M19, Microfilm Reel Nos. 79-83.

1840

Census Index: U.S. Selected States/Counties, 1840. Family Archive CD 316. Novato, CA: Broderbund Software. CD-ROM.

Jackson, Ronald Vern. *New Jersey Census Index, Online Edition.* Orem, UT: Ancestry.com, Inc., 1999. **http://www.ancestry.com**

_____, and Gary Ronald Teeples. *New Jersey 1840 Census Index.* Bountiful, UT: Accelerated Indexing Systems, 1978. 164p.

Tanco, Barbrae Owens. *The 1850 Census Together with Index, New Jersey, Including the 1840 List of Revolutionary and Military Pensioners.* Ft. Worth, TX: Millican Press, 1973.

U.S. Federal Population Census Schedules. 1840, M704, Microfilm Reel Nos. 247-262.

1850

George, Shirley J., and Sandra E. Glenn. *New Jersey 1850 Mortality Schedule Index.* Columbus, NJ: G. & G. Genealogical Book Co., 1982. 85p.

Jackson, Ronald Vern. *Federal Census Index New Jersey 1850 Mortality Schedules.* West Jordan, UT: Genealogical Services, 1988, 1998. 114p.

_____. *Mortality Schedules Index, Online Edition.* Orem, UT: Ancestry.com, Inc., 1999. **http://www.ancestry.com**

_____. *New Jersey Census Index, Online Edition.* Orem, UT: Ancestry.com, Inc., 1999. **http://www.ancestry.com**

_____. *New Jersey 1850 Slave Schedule Census.* Salt Lake City, UT: Accelerated Indexing Systems International, 1988. Unpgd.

_____, and Gary Ronald Teeples. *New Jersey 1850 Census Index.* Bountiful, UT: Accelerated Indexing Systems, 1976. 386p.

Tanco, Barbrae Owens. *The 1850 Census Together with Index, New Jersey, Including the 1840 List of Revolutionary and Military Pensioners.* Ft. Worth, TX: Millican Press, 1973. 2 vols.

U.S. Census Index Series, Pennsylvania, Delaware and New Jersey, 1850. Orem, UT: Automated Archives, 1991. CD-ROM.

U.S. Federal Population Census Schedules. 1850, M432, Microfilm Reel Nos. 442-465.

U.S. Federal Population Census Schedules. 1850, M432, Slave Schedules, Microfilm Reel No. 466.

1860

Census Index: U.S. Selected States/Counties, 1860. Family Archive CD 318. Novato, CA: Broderbund Software. CD-ROM.

Jackson, Ronald Vern. *1860 New Jersey North, Federal Census Index.* West Jordan, UT: Genealogical Services, 1986, 1997.

_____. *New Jersey Census Index, Online Edition.* Orem, UT: Ancestry.com, Inc., 1999. **http://www.ancestry.com**

_____. *New Jersey 1860 North.* North Salt Lake City, UT: Accelerated Indexing Systems International, 1987. 581p.

_____. *New Jersey South 1860, Federal Census Index.* West Jordan, UT: Genealogical Services, 1986. 433p.

U.S. Census Index, 1860, Delaware, New Jersey and Pennsylvania. Orem, UT: Automated Archives, 1992. CD-ROM.

U.S. Federal Population Census Schedules. 1860, M653, Microfilm Reel Nos. 682-711.

1865

Martin, Barbara Hankins. *Index, Historical Collections of New Jersey, Past and Present, Containing a General Collection of the Most Interesting Facts, Traditions, Biographical Sketches, Anecdotes, Etc., Relating to the History and Antiquities, with Geographical Descriptions, of All the Important Places in the State, and the State Census of All the Towns in 1865.* Spartanburg, SC: Reprint Co., 1986. 32p.

1870

Delaware and New Jersey 1870 Census Index Extracted from the Original U.S. Federal Census Schedules. ACD 0033. Bountiful, UT: Heritage Quest, 1998. CD-ROM.

Jackson, Ronald Vern. *New Jersey Census Index, Online Edition.* Orem, UT: Ancestry.com, Inc., 1999.
http://www.ancestry.com

Steuart, Raeone Christensen. *New Jersey 1870 Census Index.* Bountiful, UT: Heritage Quest, 1998. 2 vols.

_____. *Delaware and New Jersey 1870 Census Index.* Bountiful, UT: Heritage Quest, 2000. CD-ROM.

U.S. Federal Population Census Schedules. 1870, M593, Microfilm Reel Nos. 851-892.

1880

U.S. Federal Population Census Schedules. 1880, T9, Microfilm Reel Nos. 770-801.
U.S. Federal Population Census Schedules. 1880, Soundex. T763, 49 Microfilm Reels.

1890

Jackson, Ronald Vern. *New Jersey Census Index, Online Edition (Veterans Schedules).* Orem, UT: Ancestry.com, Inc., 1999.
http://www.ancestry.com

_____. *New Jersey 1890.* Salt Lake City, UT: Accelerated Indexing Systems International, 1990, 1998. 397p.

U.S. Federal Population Census Schedules. 1890, M407, Microfilm Reel No. 3.
U.S. Federal Population Census Schedules. 1890, Index. M496, 2 Microfilm Reels.
U.S. Federal Population Census Schedules, Special Schedule, Enumerating Union Veterans and Widows of Union Veterans of the Civil War. 1890, M123, Microfilm Reel Nos. 41-43.
Veterans' Schedules: U.S. Selected States, 1890. Family Archive CD 131. Novato, CA: Broderbund Software. CD-ROM.

1900

U.S. Federal Population Census Schedules. 1900, T623, Microfilm Reel Nos. 953-998.
U.S. Federal Population Census Schedules. 1900, Soundex. T1060, 203 Microfilm Reels.

1910

U.S. Federal Population Census Schedules. 1910, T624, Microfilm Reel Nos. 867-912. (No Soundex/Miracode Index was prepared by the Government for this State.)

1920

U.S. Federal Population Census Schedules. 1920, T625, Microfilm Reel Nos. 1015-1073.
U.S. Federal Population Census Schedules. 1920, Soundex. M1576, 253 Microfilm Reels.

Atlantic County
1850

Tanco, Barbrae Owens. *The 1850 Census Together with Index, Atlantic, Burlington, and Bergen Counties, New Jersey Including the 1840 List of Revolutionary and Military Pensioners Residing in Those Counties.* Fort Worth, TX: Millican Press, 1973. 1,029p.

USGenWeb Census Project. New Jersey, 1850 Atlantic County.
ftp://ftp.rootsweb.com/pub/census/nj/atlantic/1850/

Burlington County
1850

Tanco, Barbrae Owens. *The 1850 Census Together with Index, Atlantic, Burlington, and Bergen Counties, New Jersey Including the 1840 List of Revolutionary and Military Pensioners Residing in Those Counties*. Fort Worth, TX: Millican Press, 1973. 1,029p.

Cumberland County
1800

Jackson, Ronald Vern. *New Jersey Census Index, Online Edition*. Orem, UT: Ancestry.com, Inc., 1999. **http://www.ancestry.com**

_____, and Gary Ronald Teeples. *New Jersey 1800 Cumberland County Census Index*. Bountiful, UT: Accelerated Indexing Systems, 1977. 42p.

Essex County
1870

Jackson, Ronald Vern. *New Jersey 1870 Essex County Federal Census Index*. North Salt Lake City, UT: Accelerated Indexing Systems International, 1990, 1996. 2 vols.

Gloucester County
1850

Tanco, Barbrae Owens. *The 1850 Census Together with Index, Gloucester, Hunterdon and Hudson Counties, New Jersey, Including the 1840 List of Revolutionary and Military Pensioners Residing in Those Counties*. Fort Worth, TX: Millican Press, 1974. 1,009p.

Hoboken (Hudson County)
1850

Askea, Doris Anderson. *1850 Hoboken, New Jersey, Census*. Kernersville, NC: Author, 1995. 70p.
1870

Jackson, Ronald Vern. *Hoboken and Jersey City, New Jersey 1870 Federal Census Index*. North Salt Lake City, UT: Accelerated Indexing Systems International, 1989. 617p.

Hudson County
1850

Tanco, Barbrae Owens. *The 1850 Census Together with Index, Gloucester, Hunterdon and Hudson Counties, New Jersey, Including the 1840 List of Revolutionary and Military Pensioners Residing in Those Counties*. Fort Worth, TX: Millican Press, 1974. 1,009p.
1890

U.S. Federal Population Census Schedules. 1890, M407, Microfilm Reel No. 3.
U.S. Federal Population Census Schedules. 1890, Index. M496, 2 Microfilm Reels.

Hunterdon County
1850

Ivie, Joseph B. *Index, 1830 Federal Census, Hunterdon County, New Jersey*. Warren, NJ: Author, 1975. 147p.
Tanco, Barbrae Owens. *The 1850 Census Together with Index, Gloucester, Hunterdon and Hudson Counties, New Jersey, Including the 1840 List of Revolutionary and Military Pensioners Residing in Those Counties*. Fort Worth, TX: Millican Press, 1974. 1,009p.

Jersey City (Hudson County)
1870

Jackson, Ronald Vern. *Hoboken and Jersey City, New Jersey 1870 Federal Census Index*. North Salt Lake City, UT: Accelerated Indexing Systems International, 1989. 617p.

Mercer County
1870

Jackson, Ronald Vern. *Federal Census Index, New Jersey 1870 Mercer County, with the City of Trenton.* West Jordan, UT: Genealogical Services, 1990, 1997. 507p.

Morris County
1885

Sass, John Andrew. *The 1885 New Jersey State Census for Morristown, Morris County, New Jersey Index.* Morristown, NJ: Morris Area Genealogy Society, Joint Free Public Library of Morristown and Morris Township, 1996. 70p.

Newark (Essex County)
1910

Cross Index to Selected City Streets and Enumeration Districts, 1910 Census, Newark, New Jersey. Washington, DC: National Archives and Records Service, 1987. Microfiche.

Passaic County
1870

Jackson, Ronald Vern. *New Jersey 1870, Passaic County Federal Census Index.* Salt Lake City, UT: AGES, 1990. 466p.

Salem County
1860

Gibson, Florence H. *Salem County, New Jersey Census, 1860.* Woodbury, NJ: Gloucester County Historical Society, 1991. 531p.

Somerset County
1830

Ivie, Joseph B. *Index, 1830 Federal Census, Somerset County, New Jersey.* Warren, NJ: Author, 1973. 75p.

Warren County
1850

USGenWeb Census Project. New Jersey, 1850 Warren County.
ftp://ftp.rootsweb.com/pub/census/nj/warren/1850/

New Mexico

De Leon, Arnoldo. *Tejanos and the Numbers Game, a Socio-historical Interpretation from the Federal Censuses, 1850-1900.* Albuquerque, NM: University of New Mexico Press, 1989. 119p.

Federal Census, Territory of New Mexico and Territory of Arizona. Washington, DC: Government Printing Office, 1965. 253p.

_____. *Online Database Edition.* Orem, UT: Ancestry.com, Inc., 1999.
http://www.ancestry.com

1750

Olmsted, Virginia Langham. *Spanish and Mexican Censuses of New Mexico, 1750-1830.* Albuquerque, NM: New Mexico Genealogical Society, 1981. 305p.

1790

Olmstead, Virginia Langham. *Spanish and Mexican Colonial Censuses of New Mexico, 1790, 1823, 1845.* Albuquerque, NM: New Mexico Genealogical Society, 1975. 303p.

1821

Esterly, Patricia Black. *Census of 1821, New Mexico Province, Santa Fe Parish.* Albuquerque, NM: New Mexico Genealogical Society, 1994.164p.

1823

Olmstead, Virginia Langham. *Spanish and Mexican Colonial Censuses of New Mexico, 1790, 1823, 1845.* Albuquerque, NM: New Mexico Genealogical Society, 1975. 303p.

1830

Olmstead, Virginia Langham. *Spanish and Mexican Censuses of New Mexico, 1750-1830.* Albuquerque, NM: New Mexico Genealogical Society, 1981. 305p.

1840

Census Index: U.S. Selected States/Counties, 1840. Family Archive CD 316. Novato, CA: Broderbund Software. CD-ROM.

1845

Olmstead, Virginia Langham. *Spanish and Mexican Colonial Censuses of New Mexico, 1790, 1823, 1845.* Albuquerque, NM: New Mexico Genealogical Society, 1975. 303p.

1850

Census Index: U.S. Selected States/Counties, 1850. Family Archive CD 317. Novato, CA: Broderbund Software. CD-ROM.
Jackson, Ronald Vern. *New Mexico Census Index, Online Edition.* Orem, UT: Ancestry.com, Inc., 1999. **http://www.ancestry.com**
_____, and Gary Ronald Teeples. *New Mexico 1850 Census Index.* Bountiful, UT: Accelerated Indexing Systems, 1978. 50p.
U.S. Federal Population Census Schedules. 1850, M432, Microfilm Reel Nos. 46-470.
Windham, Margaret Leonard. *New Mexico 1850 Territorial Census.* Albuquerque, NM: New Mexico Genealogical Society, 1976. 4 vols.

1860

Federal Census, Territory of New Mexico and Territory of Arizona. Washington, DC: Government Printing Office, 1965. 253p.
Jackson, Ronald Vern. *New Mexico Census Index, Online Edition.* Orem, UT: Ancestry.com, Inc., 1999. **http://www.ancestry.com**
_____, and Gary Ronald Teeples. *Arizona 1860 Territorial Census Index.* Bountiful, UT: Accelerated Indexing Systems, 1978. 80, 36p.
_____. *New Mexico 1860 Census Index.* Bountiful, UT: Accelerated Indexing Systems, 1980. 203p.
U.S. Federal Population Census Schedules. 1860, M653, Microfilm Reel Nos. 712-716.

1870

Census Index: U.S. Selected States/Counties, 1870. Family Archive CD 319. Novato, CA: Broderbund Software. CD-ROM.
Jackson, Ronald Vern. *New Mexico Census Index, Online Edition.* Orem, UT: Ancestry.com, Inc., 1999. **http://www.ancestry.com**
_____. *New Mexico 1870 Census Index.* Salt Lake City, UT: Accelerated Indexing Systems International, 1978. 2 vols.
Surname Index Guides to 1870 and 1900 New Mexico Counties. Albuquerque, NM: Turpen Enterprizes, 1985-1986. 2 vols.
U.S. Federal Population Census Schedules. 1870, M593, Microfilm Reel Nos. 893-897.

1880

U.S. Federal Population Census Schedules. 1880, T9, Microfilm Reel Nos. 802-804.
U.S. Federal Population Census Schedules. 1880, Soundex. T764, 6 Microfilm Reels.

1890

Jackson, Ronald Vern. *U.S. Federal Census Index New Mexico 1890 Union Veterans and Windows Schedules*. West Jordan, UT: Genealogical Services, 1998. 72p.
U.S. Federal Population Census Schedules, Special Schedule, Enumerating Union Veterans and Widows of Union Veterans of the Civil War. 1890, M123, Microfilm Reel No. 44.

1900

Surname Index Guides to 1870 and 1900 New Mexico Counties. Albuquerque, NM: Turpen Enterprizes, 1985-1986. 2 vols.
U.S. Federal Population Census Schedules. 1900, T623, Microfilm Reel Nos. 999-1003.
U.S. Federal Population Census Schedules. 1900, Soundex. T1061, 23 Microfilm Reels.

1910

U.S. Federal Population Census Schedules. 1910, T624, Microfilm Reel Nos. 913-919. (No Soundex/Miracode Index was prepared by the Government for this State.)

1920

U.S. Federal Population Census Schedules. 1920, T625, Microfilm Reel Nos. 1074-1080.
U.S. Federal Population Census Schedules. 1920, Soundex. M1577, 31 Microfilm Reels.

Fort Union County
1860-1880

Myers, Harry C. *La Junta Precinct No. 11 and the Area Surrounding Fort Union, Mora and San Miguel Counties, New Mexico, 1860, 1870, 1880 Federal Census Enumeration*. Albuquerque, NM: New Mexico Genealogical Society, 1993. 154p.

Miguel County
1860-1880

Myers, Harry C. *La Junta Precinct No. 11 and the Area Surrounding Fort Union, Mora and San Miguel Counties, New Mexico, 1860, 1870, 1880 Federal Census Enumeration*. Albuquerque, NM: New Mexico Genealogical Society, 1993. 154p.

Mora County
1860-1880

Myers, Harry C. *La Junta Precinct No. 11 and the Area Surrounding Fort Union, Mora and San Miguel Counties, New Mexico, 1860, 1870, 1880 Federal Census Enumeration*. Albuquerque, NM: New Mexico Genealogical Society, 1993. 154p.

San Juan County
1910

Jameson, Norma H. *San Juan County, New Mexico, 1910 Census Index*. Bloomfield, NM: Totah Tracers Genealogical Society. 50p.
New Mexico DAR. *Index, San Juan County, New Mexico 1910 Census*. Genealogical Records Committee Report, s2, v16. New Mexico DAR, 1993. Unpgd.

New York

Putman, Warren Thomas. *The Putman-Putnam Index, Federal Census, State of New York, 1790 through 1860*. Rio Linda, CA: Author, 1989. Unpgd.

1790

Eichholz, Alice, and James M. Rose. *Free Black Heads of Households in the New York State Federal Census, 1790-1830*. Gale Genealogy and Local History Series, No. 14. Detroit, MI: Gale Research, 1981. 301p.

Jackson, Ronald Vern. *New York Census Index, Online Edition*. Orem, UT: Ancestry.com, Inc., 1999. **http://www.ancestry.com**

_____. *New York 1790 Federal Census Index*. North Salt Lake City, UT: Accelerated Indexing Systems International, 1990. 970p.

U.S. Bureau of the Census. *Heads of Families at the First Census of the United States Taken in the Year 1790, New York*. Washington, DC: Government Printing Office, 1908. 308p.

_____. _____. Bountiful, UT: American Genealogical Lending Library, 1993. 308p.

_____. _____. North Salt Lake City, UT: Accelerated Indexing Systems International, 1990. 308p.

_____. _____. *Online Database Edition*. Orem, UT: Ancestry.com, Inc., 1999. **http://www.ancestry.com**

_____. *U.S. Federal Population Census Schedules*, 1790. T498, Microfilm Reel No. 2.

U.S. Federal Population Census Schedules, 1790. M637, Microfilm Reel No. 6.

1800

Armstrong, Barbara Kay. *Index to the 1800 Census of New York*. Baltimore, MD: Genealogical Pub. Co., 1984. 432p.

_____. Baltimore, MD: Clearfield, 1996. 432p.

Eichholz, Alice, and James M. Rose. *Free Black Heads of Households in the New York State Federal Census, 1790-1830*. Gale Genealogy and Local History Series, No. 14. Detroit, MI: Gale Research, 1981. 301p.

Jackson, Ronald Vern. *New York Census Index, Online Edition*. Orem, UT: Ancestry.com, Inc., 1999. **http://www.ancestry.com**

_____, and Gary Ronald Teeples. *New York 1800 Census Index*. Bountiful, UT: Accelerated Indexing Systems, 1974, 1981. 353p.

McMullin, Phillip W. *New York in 1800, an Index to the Federal Census Schedules of the State of New York, with Other Aids to Research*. Provo, UT: Gendex, 1971. 272p.

Steuart, Raeone Christensen. *New York 1800 Census Index*. Bountiful, UT: Heritage Quest, 2000. 611p.

_____. *United States 1800 Census Index*. Bountiful, UT: Heritage Quest, 2000. 4 vols. CD-ROM.

U.S. Federal Population Census Schedules, 1800. M32, Microfilm Reel Nos. 21-28.

1810

Eichholz, Alice, and James M. Rose. *Free Black Heads of Households in the New York State Federal Census, 1790-1830*. Gale Genealogy and Local History Series, No. 14. Detroit, MI: Gale Research, 1981. 301p.

Jackson, Ronald Vern. *New York Census Index, Online Edition*. Orem, UT: Ancestry.com, Inc., 1999. **http://www.ancestry.com**

_____, and Gary Ronald Teeples. *New York 1810 Census Index*. Bountiful, UT: Accelerated Indexing Systems, 1976, 1990. 364p.

U.S. Census Index Series, New England, New York, 1810. Orem, UT: Automated Archives, 1992. CD-ROM.

U.S. Federal Population Census Schedules, 1810. M252, Microfilm Reel Nos. 26-37.

1815

Jackson, Ronald Vern, and Gary Ronald Teeples. *New York 1815 Census Index*. North Salt Lake City, UT: Accelerated Indexing Systems International, 1984. 55, 11p.

1820

Eichholz, Alice, and James M. Rose. *Free Black Heads of Households in the New York State Federal Census, 1790-1830*. Gale Genealogy and Local History Series, No. 14. Detroit, MI: Gale Research, 1981. 301p.

Jackson, Ronald Vern. *New York Census Index, Online Edition*. Orem, UT: Ancestry.com, Inc., 1999. **http://www.ancestry.com**

_____, and Gary Ronald Teeples. *New York 1820 Census Index*. Bountiful, UT: Accelerated Indexing Systems, 1977. 537p.

U.S. Federal Population Census Schedules. 1820, M33, Microfilm Reel Nos. 62-79.

1830

Eichholz, Alice, and James M. Rose. *Free Black Heads of Households in the New York State Federal Census, 1790-1830*. Gale Genealogy and Local History Series, No. 14. Detroit, MI: Gale Research, 1981. 301p.

Census Index: U.S. Selected States/Counties, 1830. Family Archive CD 315. Novato, CA: Broderbund Software. CD-ROM.

Jackson, Ronald Vern. *New York Census Index, Online Edition*. Orem, UT: Ancestry.com, Inc., 1999. **http://www.ancestry.com**

_____, and Gary Ronald Teeples. *New York 1830 Census Index*. Bountiful, UT: Accelerated Indexing Systems, 1977. 773p.

_____. North Salt Lake City, UT: Accelerated Indexing Systems International, 1990. 773p.

U.S. Census Index, 1830-1839, New England, New York, Pennsylvania. Orem, UT: Automated Archives, 1992. 1 CD-ROM.

U.S. Federal Population Census Schedules. 1830, M19, Microfilm Reel Nos. 84-117.

1840

Census Index: U.S. Selected States/Counties, 1840. Family Archive CD 316. Novato, CA: Broderbund Software. CD-ROM.

Jackson, Ronald Vern. *New York Census Index, Online Edition*. Orem, UT: Ancestry.com, Inc., 1999. **http://www.ancestry.com**

_____, and Gary Ronald Teeples. *New York 1840 Census Index*. Salt Lake City, UT: Accelerated Indexing Systems, 1978, 1990. 1,032p.

Kelly, Arthur C. M. *New York Revolutionary War Pensioners in the 1840 Census*. Rhinebeck, NY: Kinship, 1995. 119p.

U.S. Census Index Series, New England, New York, 1840. Orem, UT: Automated Archives, 1992. CD-ROM.

U.S. Federal Population Census Schedules. 1840, M704, Microfilm Reel Nos. 263-353.

1850

Census Index: U.S. Selected States/Counties, 1850. Family Archive CD 317. Novato, CA: Broderbund Software. CD-ROM.

Jackson, Ronald Vern. *New York Census Index, Online Edition*. Orem, UT: Ancestry.com, Inc., 1999. **http://www.ancestry.com**

_____, and Gary Ronald Teeples. *New York 1850 Census Index*. Bountiful, UT: Accelerated Indexing Systems, 1978. 2 vols.

U.S. Census Index Series, New York, 1850. Orem, UT: Automated Archives, 1991. CD-ROM.

U.S. Federal Population Census Schedules. 1850, M432, Microfilm Reel Nos. 471-618.

1860

Jackson, Ronald Vern. *New York Census Index, Online Edition*. Orem, UT: Ancestry.com, Inc., 1999. **http://www.ancestry.com**

_____. *New York 1860, North, Federal Census Index*. West Jordan, UT: Genealogical Services, 1978, 1997. 873p.

_____. *New York 1860, South, Federal Census Index, Excludes Kings, New York and Queens Counties*. West Jordan, UT: Genealogical Services, 1988, 1997. 2 vols.

_____. *New York 1860, West, Federal Census Index*. West Jordan, UT: Genealogical Services, 1988, 1997.

U.S. Census Index Series, New York, 1860. Orem, UT: Automated Archives, 1991. CD-ROM.
U.S. Federal Population Census Schedules. 1860, M653, Microfilm Reel Nos. 717-885.

1870

Jackson, Ronald Vern. *New York Census Index, Online Edition.* Orem, UT: Ancestry.com, Inc., 1999.
http://www.ancestry.com
Silverman, Marlene. *Poles and Russians in the 1870 Census of New York City, Full Alphabetical Index for the Second Enumeration, with a Partial Index for the First Enumeration.* Washington, DC: Landsmen Press, 1993. 94, 74p.
_____. *A Polish Russian Name Index for the 1870 Census in New York City.* Washington, DC: Author, 1989. 6p.
Steuart, Raeone Christensen. *New York State 1870 Census Index.* Bountiful, UT: Heritage Quest, 1999. CD-ROM.
U.S. Federal Population Census Schedules. 1870, M593, Microfilm Reel Nos. 898-1120.

1880

Census Index: U.S. Selected States/Counties, 1880. Family Archive CD 320. Novato, CA: Broderbund Software. CD-ROM.
U.S. Federal Population Census Schedules. 1880, T9, Microfilm Reel Nos. 805-949.
U.S. Federal Population Census Schedules. 1880, Soundex. T765, 187 Microfilm Reels.

1890

Dilts, Bryan Lee. *1890 New York Census of Civil War Veterans or Their Widows.* Salt Lake City, UT: Index Pub., 1984. 451p.; 4 microfiche.
_____. 2nd ed. Bountiful, UT: Precision Indexing, 1993. 379p.
Jackson, Ronald Vern. *New York Census Index, Online Edition (Veterans Schedules; Naval Veterans Schedules).* Orem, UT: Ancestry.com, Inc., 1999.
http://www.ancestry.com
Steuart, Bradley. *New York 1890 Veterans Census Index.* Bountiful, UT: Heritage Quest, 1999. 379p.
U.S. Federal Population Census Schedules. 1890, M407, Microfilm Reel No. 3.
U.S. Federal Population Census Schedules. 1890, Index. M496, 2 Microfilm Reels.
U.S. Federal Population Census Schedules, Special Schedule, Enumerating Union Veterans and Widows of Union Veterans of the Civil War. 1890, M123, Microfilm Reel No. 46-57.

1900

U.S. Federal Population Census Schedules. 1900, T623, Microfilm Reel Nos. 1004-1179.
U.S. Federal Population Census Schedules. 1900, Soundex. T1062, 766 Microfilm Reels.

1910

U.S. Federal Population Census Schedules. 1910, T624, Microfilm Reel Nos. 920-1094. (No Soundex/Miracode Index was prepared by the Government for this State.)
Watkins, Susan Cotts. *After Ellis Island, Newcomers and Natives in the 1910 Census.* New York, NY: Russell Sage Foundation, 1994. 451p.

1920

U.S. Federal Population Census Schedules. 1920, T625, Microfilm Reel Nos. 1081-1281.
U.S. Federal Population Census Schedules. 1920, Soundex. M1578, 885 Microfilm Reels.

Albany County
1860

Davenport, David Paul. *The Matched Mortality and Population Schedules of the 1860 Census of Albany City and County, New York.* Rhinebeck, NY: Palatine Transcripts, 1987. 133p.

Bedford (Westchester County)
1790-1850
McLaughlin, Katherine Ross. *Index United States Census for Bedford, Westchester County, New York, 1790, 1810, 1820, 1830, 1840, 1850*. White Plains, NY: Author, 1964. 48p.

Bronx County
1925
Saray, Merton. *Bronx County, New York, 1925 Census Street Index*. Crystal Lake, IL: Author, 1994. 51p.

Brooklyn (Kings County)
1860
Jackson, Ronald Vern. *New York 1860, Kings and Queens Counties, Federal Census Index*. West Jordan, UT: Genealogical Services, 1987, 1997. 2 vols.
1870
Jackson, Ronald Vern. *Federal Index Census, 1870 New York Kings County, Includes City of Brooklyn*. West Jordan, UT: Genealogical Services, 1988, 1996. 588p.

Broome County
1825
Samuelsen, W. David. *Broome County, New York, State Census Index, 1825*. Salt Lake City, UT: Sampubco, 1996. 43p.

Cayuga County
1800, 1810
Wood, Robert V., Jr. *Cayuga County, New York State Federal Population Census Schedule Census Years, 1800 & 1810, Transcripts and Index*. Belmont, MA: Author, 1968. Unpgd.

Chautauqua County
1810
McCutcheon, Marie B. *Town of Ripley, New York State and Federal Census, 1810-1845*. Fredonia, NY: Chautauqua County Genealogical Society, 1994. 127p.
1825
Samuelson, W. David. *Chautauqua County, New York 1825 State Census Index*. Salt Lake City, UT: Sampubco, 1992. 36p.
1835
Samuelson, W. David. *Chautauqua County, New York 1835 State Census Index*. Salt Lake City, UT: Sampubco, 1992. 24p.
1845
McCutcheon, Marie B. *Town of Ripley, New York State and Federal Census, 1810-1845*. Fredonia, NY: Chautauqua County Genealogical Society, 1994. 127p.
1855
Anderson, Helen Traver. *Chautauqua County 1855 Census, Arkwright Township*. Jamestown, NY: Fenton Historical Center. 25p.
_____. *Chautauqua County 1855 Census, Busti Township*. Jamestown, NY: Fenton Historical Center, 1977. 42p.
_____. *Chautauqua County 1855 Census, Carroll Township*. Jamestown, NY: Fenton Historical Center. 33p.
_____. *Chautauqua County 1855 Census, Charlotte Township*. Jamestown, NY: Fenton Historical Center. 40p.
_____. *Chautauqua County 1855 Census, Chautauqua Township*. Jamestown, NY: Fenton Historical Center. 30p.

_____. *Chautauqua County 1855 Census, Cherry Creek Township.* Jamestown, NY: Fenton Historical Center. 29p.

_____. *Chautauqua County 1855 Census, Clymer Township.* Jamestown, NY: Fenton Historical Center. 29p.

_____. *Chautauqua County 1855 Census, Ellery Township.* Jamestown, NY: Fenton Historical Center. 43p.

_____. *Chautauqua County 1855 Census, Ellicott Township.* Jamestown, NY: Fenton Historical Center. pp. 62-92.

_____. *Chautauqua County 1855 Census, Ellington Township.* Jamestown, NY: Fenton Historical Center. 43p.

_____. *Chautauqua County 1855 Census, French Creek Township.* Jamestown, NY: Fenton Historical Center. 18p.

_____. *Chautauqua County 1855 Census, Gerry Township.* Jamestown, NY: Fenton Historical Center. 30p.

_____. *Chautauqua County 1855 Census, Hanover Township.* Jamestown, NY: Fenton Historical Center. 95p.

_____. *Chautauqua County 1855 Census, Harmony Township.* Jamestown, NY: Fenton Historical Center. 77p.

_____. *Chautauqua County 1855 Census, Kiantone Township.* Jamestown, NY: Fenton Historical Center, 1977. 12p.

_____. *Chautauqua County 1855 Census, Mina Township.* Jamestown, NY: Fenton Historical Center. 24p.

_____. *Chautauqua County 1855 Census, Poland Township.* Jamestown, NY: Fenton Historical Center. 30p.

_____. *Chautauqua County 1855 Census, Portland Township.* Jamestown, NY: Fenton Historical Center. 45p.

_____. *Chautauqua County 1855 Census, Ripley Township.* Jamestown, NY: Fenton Historical Center. 39p.

_____. *Chautauqua County 1855 Census, Sheridan Township.* Jamestown, NY: Fenton Historical Center. 37p.

_____. *Chautauqua County 1855 Census, Sherman Township.* Jamestown, NY: Fenton Historical Center. 30p.

_____. *Chautauqua County 1855 Census, Stockton Township.* Jamestown, NY: Fenton Historical Center. 38p.

_____. *Chautauqua County 1855 Census, Villenova Township.* Jamestown, NY: Fenton Historical Center. 34p.

_____. *Chautauqua County 1855 Census, Westfield Township.* Jamestown, NY: Fenton Historical Center. 67p.

Cortland County
1855
Index to New York State Population Census, 1855. Syracuse, NY: Cortland County Historical Society, 1980. Unpgd.

Delaware County
1790
Goerlich, Shirley Boyce. *Delaware County, New York Raw Materials from the Past, Including Boundary and Town Changes/Maps, 144th Regiment of Volunteers, 1790 Federal Census, Deaths and Marriages from Area Newspapers 1819-1900, an Index to Deaths & Marriages.* Bainbridge, NY: RSG Pub., 1994. Unpgd.
1850
Oman, Kitty R. Hilton. *The 1850 Census of Delaware County, New York.* Vancouver, WA: Author, 1988. 977p.
1875
New York State DAR. *Deaths in Delaware County, June 1, 1874 - June 1, 1875 from the 1875 Census.* Genealogical Records Committee Report, s2, v634. New York: New York DAR, Oneota Chapter, 1994.

Delaware County
1850
Oman, Kitty R. Hilton. *The 1850 Census of Delaware County, New York.* Vancouver, WA: Author, 1988. 977p.
1890
1890 Military Census, Delaware County, New York. Sauk Village, IL: Hanson Heritage Publications, 1985. 113p.

Denning (Ulster County)
1925
Van Wagenen, Carl. *1925 Census, Denning, Hardenburgh, Marbletown, Rochester, Shandaken and Woodstock, Ulster County, New York.* NY: Ulster County Genealogical Society, 1995. 162p.

Dutchess County
1810
Dutchess County Genealogical Society. *1810 Census with Index, Dutchess County, New York.* Rhinebeck, NY: Kinship, 1978, 1990. 181p.
1810 Census with Index, Dutchess County, New York. Poughkeepsie, NY: Dutchess County Genealogical Society, 1978. 177p.

Eastchester (Westchester County)
1790-1840
Ryan, Sheila. *Index, United States Census, Eastchester, Westchester County, New York, 1790, 1810, 1820, 1830, 1840.* White Plains, NY: Author, 1964. Unpgd.

Erie County
1850
U.S. Works Progress Admininistration. *Index of 1850 Census, Buffalo, Erie County, New York.* 820p.
Zintz, June Partridge. *Index to the 1850 Census of Black Rock, Erie County, New York, (Incorporated into the City of Buffalo in 1853).* Buffalo, NY: Western New York Genealogical Society, 1993. 175p.
1855
U.S. Works Progress Admininistration. *Index of 1855 Census, Buffalo, Erie County, New York.* 2 vols.
1860
Jackson, Ronald Vern. *New York 1860, Erie County, Federal Census Index.* West Jordan, UT: Genealogical Services, 1988, 1997. 639p.

Franklin County
1855
Brown, Carol W. *1855 New York State Census, Franklin County, New York.* Rochester, NY: Author, 1992. 14p.

Genesee County
1860
USGenWeb Census Project. New York, 1860 Genesee County. (Partial).
ftp://ftp.rootsweb.com/pub/census/ny/genesee/1870/

Greenburgh (Westchester County)
1790-1850
Ryan, Sheila. *Index, United States Census, Greenburgh, Westchester County, New York, 1790, 1810, 1820, 1830, 1840, 1850.* White Plains, NY: Author, 1964. Unpgd.

Hardenburgh (Ulster County)
1925
Van Wagenen, Carl. *1925 Census, Denning, Hardenburgh, Marbletown, Rochester, Shandaken and Woodstock, Ulster County, New York*. NY: Ulster County Genealogical Society, 1995. 162p.

Herkimer County
1800-1820
Wood, Ralph V. *Herkimer County, New York State, Federal Population Census Schedules 1800, 1810, 1820*. Cambridge, MA: Author, 1965.
1825
Samuelsen, W. David. *Herkimer County, New York 1825 State Census Index*. Salt Lake City, UT: Sampubco, 1996. 100p.
1835
Samuelsen, W. David. *Herkimer County, New York, 1835 State Census Index*. Salt Lake City, UT: Sampubco, 1994. 119p.
1845
Samuelsen, W. David. *Herkimer County, New York 1845 State Census Index*. Salt Lake City, UT: Sampubco, 1994. 27p.

Jefferson County
James, Patricia R. *Index to Early Records of Watertown, Jefferson County, New York*. Boise, ID: The Family Tree, 1988. 29p.
1810, 1820
Wood, Ralph V. *Jefferson and St. Lawrence Counties, New York State, 1810 and 1820 Federal Population Census Schedules*. Cambridge, MA: Author, 1963. 240p.
1865
Litchman, William M. *An Every-name Index for Agricultural Schedules, Industry Other than Agriculture Schedules, Marriages, Deaths, and Civil War Soldier Deaths in the 1865 New York State Census for Jefferson County*. Covington, KY: Kenton County Historical Society, 1996. 218p.
_____. *An Every-name Index of the 1865 New York State Census for Jefferson County*. Albuquerque, NM: Medley Publications, 1996. 10 vols.

Kent (Putnam County)
1850
Wheeler, Glendon E. *Extract and Alphabetical Index of the 1850 Federal Census M432-581, Town of Kent, Putnam County, New York*. Simi Valley, CA: Wheeler Historical Society, 1990. 90p.
1860
Wheeler, Glendon E. *Extract and Alphabetical Index of the 1860 Federal Census M653-842, Town of Kent, Putnam County, New York*. Moorpark, CA: Wheeler Historical Society, 1988. 21p.
1870
Wheeler, Glendon E. *Extract and Alphabetical Index of the 1870 Federal Census M593-1077, Town of Kent, Putnam County, New York*. Simi Valley, CA: Wheeler Historical Society, 1991. 111p.

Kings County
1810
USGenWeb Census Project. New York, 1810 Kings County.
ftp://ftp.rootsweb.com/pub/census/ny/kings/1810/
1860
Jackson, Ronald Vern. *New York 1860, Kings and Queens Counties, Federal Census Index*. West Jordan, UT: Genealogical Services, 1987, 1997. 2 vols.
1870
Jackson, Ronald Vern. *Federal Census Index, 1870 New York Kings County, Includes City of Brooklyn*. West Jordan, UT: Genealogical Services, 1988. 588p.

1925

Sarvay, Merton. *Kings County (Brooklyn) New York, 1925 Census, Street Index.* Crystal Lake, IL: Author, 1994. 97p.

Kingston (Ulster County)
1925

Van Wagenen, Carl. *1925 Census, Kingston, Ulster County, New York.* NY: Ulster County Genealogical Society, 1995. 350p.

Lewis County
1825

Samuelsen, W. David. *Lewis County, New York, State Census Index, 1825.* Salt Lake City, UT: Sampubco, 1996. 29p.

Long Island
1870

Jackson, Ronald Vern. *Long Island New York 1870 Federal Census Index.* North Salt Lake City, UT: Accelerated Indexing Systems International, 1989. 2 vols.

Steuart, Bradley W. *Long Island, NY 1870 Census Index.* Bountiful, UT: Precision Indexing, 1989. 2 vols.

_____. _____. Bountiful, UT: Precision Indexing, 1992. 17 microfiche.

Madison County
1855

Bracy, Isabel. *Index to the 1855 New York State Census of Madison County.* Syracuse, NY: Central New York Genealogical Society, 1977. Unpgd.

Marbletown (Ulster County)
1925

Van Wagenen, Carl. *1925 Census, Denning, Hardenburgh, Marbletown, Rochester, Shandaken and Woodstock, Ulster County, New York.* NY: Ulster County Genealogical Society, 1995. 162p.

Montgomery (Orange County)
1850

Weller, Ralph Harry. *The Census of 1850, Town of Montgomery, Orange County, New York.* Goshen, NY: Orange County Genealogical Society, 1992. 120p.

Montgomery County
1855

Davenport, David Paul. *The 1855 Census of Montgomery County, New York, an Index.* Rhinebeck, NY: Kinship, 1989. 314p.

New York City
1855-1925

Inskeep, Carolee R. *The Children's Aid Society of New York, an Index to the Federal, State, and Local Census Records of Its Lodging Houses, 1855-1925.* Baltimore, MD: Clearfield, Co., 1996. 150p.

_____. *The New York Foundling Hospital, an Index to the Federal, State, and Local Census Records, 1870-1925.* Baltimore, MD: Clearfield, Co., 1995. 339p.

1850

Jackson, Ronald Vern, and Gary Ronald Teeples. *New York City 1850 Census Index.* Bountiful, UT: Accelerated Indexing Systems, 1976. 382p.

1860

Jackson, Ronald Vern. *New York 1860, New York County, Federal Census Index*. West Jordan, UT: Genealogical Services, 1988, 1998. 2 vols.

1870

Census Index: New York City, 1870. Family Archive CD 287. Novato, CA: Broderbund Software. CD-ROM.

Silverman, Marlene. *Poles and Russians in the 1870 Census of New York City, Full Alphabetical Index for the Second Enumeration, with a Partial Index for the First Enumeration*. Washington, DC: Landsmen Press, 1993. 94, 74p.

Steuart, Raeone Christensen. *New York City, 1870 Census Index*. Bountiful, UT: Precision Indexing, 1997. 3 vols.

U.S. Census Index Series, New York City, 1870. Orem, UT: Automated Archives, 1994. CD-ROM.

1890

Jensen, Howard. *1890 New York City Police Census, Books 58-61. Online Database Edition*. Orem, UT: Ancestry.com, Inc., 1998.

http://www.ancestry.com

Oneida County

1800

Wood, Ralph V. *Oneida County, New York State, 1800 Federal Population Census Schedule*. Cambridge, MA: Author, 1962. 103p.

1810

Wood, Ralph V. *Oneida County, New York State Federal Population Census Schedule Census Year 1810, Transcript and Index*. Belmont, MA: Author, 1968. Unpgd.

1830

Gifford, John Dempster. *Index, 1830 Census Oneida County, New York, Town of Florence*. Springfield, MO: Author, 1978. 5p.

Onondaga County

1855-1892

Nostrant, Robert F. *New York State Census Index for Van Buren Town, Onondaga County, 1855, 1865, 1875 and 1892*. Baldwinsville, NY: Author, 1991. 112p.

Ontario County

1800

Wood, Ralph V. *Ontario County, New York State, 1800 Federal Population Census Schedule*. Cambridge, MA: Author, 1963. 59p.

1810

Wood, Ralph V. *Ontario County, New York State, 1810 Federal Population Census Schedule*. Cambridge, MA: Author, 1964. 162p.

Oswego County

1855

Rowlee, Byron. *Index to 1855 Manuscript Census of Oswego County*. Author, 1989. 473p.

_____. *Index to 1855 Population Census of Town of Volney*. Author. 48p.

Otsego County

1800

Wood, Ralph V. *Otsego County, New York State, 1800 Federal Population Census Schedule*. Cambridge, MA: Author, 1965. 186p.

Putnam County
1850
Wheeler, Glendon E. *Extract and Alphabetical Index of the 1850 Federal Census M432-581, Town of Kent, Putnam County, New York*. Simi Valley, CA: Wheeler Historical Society, 1990. 90p.
1860
Wheeler, Glendon E. *Extract and Alphabetical Index of the 1860 Federal Census M653-842, Town of Kent, Putnam County, New York*. Moorpark, CA: Wheeler Historical Society, 1988. 21p.
1870
Wheeler, Glendon E. *Extract and Alphabetical Index of the 1870 Federal Census M593-1077, Town of Kent, Putnam County, New York*. Simi Valley, CA: Wheeler Historical Society, 1991. 111p.

Queens County
1860
Jackson, Ronald Vern. *New York 1860, Kings and Queens Counties, Federal Census Index*. West Jordan, UT: Genealogical Services, 1987, 1997. 2 vols.
1925
Middleton, Mary Gene McCall. *Index of Towns and Villages in the 1925 New York State Census, Queens County*. South Orange, NJ: Author, 1990. 6p.

Richmond County
1800
USGenWeb Census Project. New York, 1800 Richmond County.
ftp://ftp.rootsweb.com/pub/census/ny/richmond/1800/
1820
USGenWeb Census Project. New York, 1820 Richmond County.
ftp://ftp.rootsweb.com/pub/census/ny/richmond/1820/

Ripley (Chautauqua County)
1810-1845
McCutcheon, Marie B. *Town of Ripley, New York State and Federal Census, 1810-1845*. Fredonia, NY: Chautauqua County Genealogical Society, 1994. 127p.

Rochester (Ulster County)
1925
Van Wagenen, Carl. *1925 Census, Denning, Hardenburgh, Marbletown, Rochester, Shandaken and Woodstock, Ulster County, New York*. NY: Ulster County Genealogical Society, 1995. 162p.

Rockland County
1910
Evans, Leon R. *Index, 1910 U.S. Federal Census, Rockland County, New York*. Katy, TX: Author, 1996. 2 vols.

Saint Lawrence County
1810
Wood, Ralph V. *Jefferson and St. Lawrence Counties, New York State, 1810 and 1820 Federal Population Census Schedules*. Cambridge, MA: Author, 1963. 240p.
1815
Jackson, Ronald Vern. *State Census Index, New York 1815, St. Lawrence County*. West Jordan, UT: Genealogical Services, 1990. Unpgd.
1820
Wood, Ralph V. *Jefferson and St. Lawrence Counties, New York State, 1810 and 1820 Federal Population Census Schedules*. Cambridge, MA: Author, 1963.

Saratoga County
1790
1790 Census Database, Saratoga County, New York.
http://ww.rootsweb.com/~nysarato/1790_int.htm

Saugerties (Ulster County)
1925
Van Wagenen, Carl. *1925 Census, Saugerties, Ulster County, New York.* NY: Ulster County Genealogical
Society, 1995. 124p.

Schenectady County
1855
Davenport, David Paul. *The 1855 Census of Schenectady County, New York, an Index.* Rhinebeck, NY:
Kinship, 1989. 228p.

Schoharie County
1855
Davenport, David Paul. *The 1855 Census of Schoharie County, New York, an Index.* Rhinebeck, NY: Kinship, 1988. 184p.

Seneca County
1810
Mayville, Elizabeth Caster. *Seneca County, New York, 1810 Federal Census Index. Heads of Household
Alphabetically Listed by Towns.* North Rose, NY: Author, 1985.
1850
Fischer, Carl W. *Index of the 1850 Census of Some Towns of Tompkins and Seneca Counties.* Bayside, NY:
Author, 1966. Unpgd.

Shandaken (Ulster County)
1925
Van Wagenen, Carl. *1925 Census, Denning, Hardenburgh, Marbletown, Rochester, Shandaken and Woodstock,
Ulster County, New York.* NY: Ulster County Genealogical Society, 1995. 162p.

Suffolk County
1776
Census of Suffolk County, New York, 1776. Lambertville, NJ: Hunterdon House, 1984. 56p.
1890
U.S. Federal Population Census Schedules. 1890, M407, Microfilm Reel No. 3.
U.S. Federal Population Census Schedules. 1890, Index. M496, 2 Microfilm Reels.

Syracuse (Onondaga County)
Lehaman, William C. *Revised Census Tract Street Index for Syracuse, New York.* Syracuse, NY: Author,
1936. Unpgd.

Tioga County
1925
Abstract of the 1825 New York State Census of Tioga County. Syracuse, NY: Central New York Genealogical
Society, 1996. 78p.

Tompkins County

1850

Fischer, Carl W. *Index of the 1850 Census of Some Towns of Tompkins and Seneca Counties*. Bayside, NY: Author, 1966. Unpgd.

Martin, Catherine Machan. *1850 Federal Census of Tompkins County, NY, Containing the Towns of Caroline, Danby, Dryden, Groton and Lansing*. Durand, MI: Author, 1986. 221p.

1860

Martin, Catherine Machan. *Index to 1860 Tompkins County, NY, Census*. Durand, MI: Author, 1985. 74p.

1870

Martin, Catherine Machan. *Index to 1870 Tompkins County, NY, Census*. Durand, MI: Author, 1986. 83p.

Ulster County

1925

Van Wagenen, Carl. *1925 Census, Denning, Hardenburgh, Marbletown, Rochester, Shandaken and Woodstock, Ulster County, New York*. NY: Ulster County Genealogical Society, 1995. 162p.

_____. *1925 Census, Kingston, Ulster County, New York*. NY: Ulster County Genealogical Society, 1995. 350p.

_____. *1925 Census, Saugerties, Ulster County, New York*. NY: Ulster County Genealogical Society, 1995. 124p.

Warren County

1850

McAlear, Robert. *1850 Population Census and 1850 Mortality Schedule, Warren County, New York*. Biography Press, 1976. 257p.

USGenWeb Census Project. New York, 1850 Warren County.

ftp://ftp.rootsweb.com/pub/census/ny/warren/1850/

1875

Lynch, Thomas J. *1875 Census Index, Warren County, New York*. Saratoga Springs, NY: Author, 1995. 57p.

Watertown (Jefferson County)

James, Patricia R. *Index to Early Records of Watertown, Jefferson County, New York*. Boise, ID: The Family Tree, 1988. 29p.

Westchester County

McLaughlin, Katherine Ross. *Index to Microfilms, U.S. Census, Westchester County, New York, 1800-1880*. Author, 1960. 13p.

1790

Fuller, Elizabeth Green. *Indexes to Westchester County Names in the Federal Censuses, 1790-1840*. Elmsford, NY: Westchester County Historical Society, 1994. 613p.

McLaughlin, Katherine Ross. *1790-1880 Census, White Plains, Westchester County, New York, Index*. Rev. ed. Author, 1964. Unpgd.

Ryan, Sheila. *Index, United States Census, Eastchester, Westchester County, New York, 1790, 1810, 1820, 1830, 1840*. White Plains, NY: Author, 1964. Unpgd.

_____. *Index, United States Census, Greenburgh, Westchester County, New York, 1790, 1810, 1820, 1830, 1840, 1850*. White Plains, NY: Author, 1964. Unpgd.

1800

Fuller, Elizabeth Green. *Indexes to Westchester County Names in the Federal Censuses, 1790-1840*. Elmsford, NY: Westchester County Historical Society, 1994. 613p.

McLaughlin, Katherine Ross. *1790-1880 Census, White Plains, Westchester County, New York, Index*. Rev. ed. Author, 1964. Unpgd.

1810

Fuller, Elizabeth Green. *Indexes to Westchester County Names in the Federal Censuses, 1790-1840*. Elmsford, NY: Westchester County Historical Society, 1994. 613p.

McLaughlin, Katherine Ross. *Index United States Census for Bedford, Westchester County, New York, 1790, 1810, 1820, 1830, 1840, 1850*. White Plains, NY: Author, 1964. 48p.

_____. *1790-1880 Census, White Plains, Westchester County, New York, Index*. Rev. ed. Author, 1964. Unpgd.

Ryan, Sheila. *Index, United States Census, Eastchester, Westchester County, New York, 1790, 1810, 1820, 1830, 1840*. White Plains, NY: Author, 1964. Unpgd.

_____. *Index, United States Census, Greenburgh, Westchester County, New York, 1790, 1810, 1820, 1830, 1840, 1850*. White Plains, NY: Author, 1964. Unpgd.

1820

Davis, Norman C. *Surname Index, 1800 Census, Westchester County, New York*. Port Chester, NY: Author, 1972. 6p.

Fuller, Elizabeth Green. *Indexes to Westchester County Names in the Federal Censuses, 1790-1840*. Elmsford, NY: Westchester County Historical Society, 1994. 613p.

McLaughlin, Katherine Ross. *Index United States Census for Bedford, Westchester County, New York, 1790, 1810, 1820, 1830, 1840, 1850*. White Plains, NY: Author, 1964. 48p.

_____. *1790-1880 Census, White Plains, Westchester County, New York, Index*. Rev. ed. Author, 1964. Unpgd.

Ryan, Sheila. *Index, United States Census, Eastchester, Westchester County, New York, 1790, 1810, 1820, 1830, 1840*. White Plains, NY: Author, 1964. Unpgd.

_____. *Index, United States Census, Greenburgh, Westchester County, New York, 1790, 1810, 1820, 1830, 1840, 1850*. White Plains, NY: Author, 1964. Unpgd.

1830, 1840

Fuller, Elizabeth Green. *Indexes to Westchester County Names in the Federal Censuses, 1790-1840*. Elmsford, NY: Westchester County Historical Society, 1994. 613p.

McLaughlin, Katherine Ross. *Index United States Census for Bedford, Westchester County, New York, 1790, 1810, 1820, 1830, 1840, 1850*. White Plains, NY: Author, 1964. 48p.

_____. *1790-1880 Census, White Plains, Westchester County, New York, Index*. Rev. ed. Author, 1964. Unpgd.

Ryan, Sheila. *Index, United States Census, Eastchester, Westchester County, New York, 1790, 1810, 1820, 1830, 1840*. White Plains, NY: Author, 1964. Unpgd.

_____. *Index, United States Census, Greenburgh, Westchester County, New York, 1790, 1810, 1820, 1830, 1840, 1850*. White Plains, NY: Author, 1964. Unpgd.

1850

Kent, David L., and John C. Baskin. *Westchester County, New York, the Index to That Half of Westchester County Omitted from the Accelerated Indexing Systems Index to the 1850 Federal Census of New York*. Austin, TX: Author, 1993. 85p.

McLaughlin, Katherine Ross. *1790-1880 Census, White Plains, Westchester County, New York, Index*. Rev. ed. Author, 1964. Unpgd.

Ryan, Sheila. *Index, United States Census, Greenburgh, Westchester County, New York, 1790, 1810, 1820, 1830, 1840, 1850*. White Plains, NY: Author, 1964. Unpgd.

1870

Jackson, Ronald Vern. *New York 1870 Westchester County Includes Yonkers and the Bronx before Annexation, Federal Census Index*. West Jordan, UT: Genealogical Services, 1998. 867p.

McLaughlin, Katherine Ross. *1790-1880 Census, White Plains, Westchester County, New York, Index*. Rev. ed. Author, 1964. Unpgd.

1890

U.S. Federal Population Census Schedules. 1890, M407, Microfilm Reel No. 3.

U.S. Federal Population Census Schedules. 1890, Index. M496, 2 Microfilm Reels.

Woodstock (Ulster County)
1925

Van Wagenen, Carl. *1925 Census, Denning, Hardenburgh, Marbletown, Rochester, Shandaken and Woodstock, Ulster County, New York*. NY: Ulster County Genealogical Society, 1995. 162p.

North Carolina

Henderson, Robert H. *Hendersons of Early North Carolina, a Beginning Survey of the People Using the Henderson Name from the North Carolina Census and Other Records*. Greer, SC: Author.

1790

Fulcher, Richard Carlton. *1770-1790 Census of the Cumberland Settlements, Davidson, Sumner and Tennessee Counties (In What Is Now Tennessee)*. Baltimore, MD: Genealogical Pub. Co., 1987. 253p.

Heinegg, Paul. *Free African Americans of North Carolina and Virginia Including the Family Histories of More than 80% of Those Counted as "All Other Free Persons" in the 1790 and 1800 Census*. Baltimore, MD: Genealogical Pub. Co., 1992. 462p.

_____. 2nd ed. Baltimore, MD: Genealogical Pub. Co., 1994. 699p.

_____. 3rd ed. Baltimore, MD: Genealogical Pub. Co., 1994. 825p.

Jackson, Ronald Vern. *North Carolina Census Index, Online Edition*. Orem, UT: Ancestry.com, Inc., 1999. **http://www.ancestry.com**

_____. *North Carolina 1790 Federal Census Index*. North Salt Lake, UT: Accelerated Indexing Systems International, 1990. 931p.

U.S. Bureau of the Census. *Heads of Families at the First Census of the United States Taken in the Year 1790, North Carolina*. Washington, DC: Government Printing Office, 1908. 227p.

_____. _____. Bountiful, UT: American Genealogical Lending Library, 1993. 292p.

_____. _____. North Salt Lake City, UT: Accelerated Indexing Systems International, 1990. 931p.

_____. _____. *Online Database Edition*. Orem, UT: Ancestry.com, Inc., 1999. **http://www.ancestry.com**

_____. *U.S. Federal Population Census Schedules*, 1790. T498, Microfilm Reel No. 2.

U.S. Federal Population Census Schedules, 1790. M637, Microfilm Reel No. 7.

1800

Bentley, Elizabeth Petty. *Index to the 1800 Census of North Carolina*. Baltimore, MD: Genealogical Pub. Co., 1977. 270p.

_____. _____. Baltimore, MD: Clearfield, 1995. 270p.

Heinegg, Paul. *Free African Americans of North Carolina and Virginia Including the Family Histories of More than 80% of Those Counted as "All Other Free Persons" in the 1790 and 1800 Census*. Baltimore, MD: Genealogical Pub. Co., 1992. 462p.

_____. 2nd ed. Baltimore, MD: Genealogical Pub. Co., 1994. 699p.

_____. 3rd ed. Baltimore, MD: Genealogical Pub. Co., 1994. 825p.

Jackson, Ronald Vern. *North Carolina Census Index, Online Edition*. Orem, UT: Ancestry.com, Inc., 1999. **http://www.ancestry.com**

_____, and Gary Ronald Teeples. *North Carolina 1800 Census Index*. Bountiful, UT: Accelerated Indexing Systems, 1974, 1981. 255p.

U.S. Federal Population Census Schedules, 1800. M32, Microfilm Reel Nos. 29-34.

1810

Bentley, Elizabeth Petty. *Index to the 1810 Census of North Carolina*. Baltimore, MD: Genealogical Pub. Co., 1978. 282p.

Jackson, Ronald Vern. *North Carolina Census Index, Online Edition*. Orem, UT: Ancestry.com, Inc., 1999. **http://www.ancestry.com**

_____, and Gary Ronald Teeples. *North Carolina 1810 Census Index*. Bountiful, UT: Accelerated Indexing Systems, 1976, 1981. 153p.

Smith, Dora Wilson. *North Carolina 1810 Census Index*. Thomson, IL: Heritage House, 1977. 356p.

U.S. Federal Population Census Schedules, 1810. M252, Microfilm Reel Nos. 38-43.

1820

Jackson, Ronald Vern. *North Carolina Census Index, Online Edition*. Orem, UT: Ancestry.com, Inc., 1999. **http://www.ancestry.com**

_____, and Gary Ronald Teeples. *North Carolina 1820 Census Index*. Bountiful, UT: Accelerated Indexing Systems, 1976. 162p.

Potter, Dorothy Williams. *Index to 1820 North Carolina Census, Supplemented from Tax Lists and other Sources*. Tullahoma, TN: Author, 1974. 509p.

_____. _____. Baltimore, MD: Genealogical Pub. Co., 1978. 509p.

U.S. Federal Population Census Schedules. 1820, M33, Microfilm Reel Nos. 80-85.

1830

Census Index: U.S. Selected States/Counties, 1830. Family Archive CD 315. Novato, CA: Broderbund Software. CD-ROM.

Jackson, Ronald Vern. *North Carolina Census Index, Online Edition*. Orem, UT: Ancestry.com, Inc., 1999. **http://www.ancestry.com**

_____, and Gary Ronald Teeples. *North Carolina 1830 Census Index*. Bountiful, UT: Accelerated Indexing Systems, 1976, 1981. 210p.

U.S. Federal Population Census Schedules. 1830, M19, Microfilm Reel Nos. 118-125.

1840

Census Index: U.S. Selected States/Counties, 1840. Family Archive CD 316. Novato, CA: Broderbund Software. CD-ROM.

Jackson, Ronald Vern. *North Carolina Census Index, Online Edition*. Orem, UT: Ancestry.com, Inc., 1999. **http://www.ancestry.com**

_____, and Gary Ronald Teeples. *North Carolina 1840 Census Index*. Bountiful, UT: Accelerated Indexing Systems, 1978. 225p.

Petty, Gerald McKinney. *Index of the 1840 Federal Census of North Carolina*. Columbus, OH: Author, 1974. 273p.

U.S. Federal Population Census Schedules. 1840, M704, Microfilm Reel Nos. 354-374.

1850

Almasy, Sandra L. *North Carolina Mortality Census, 1850, 1860, 1870, 1880*. Joliet, IL: Kensington Glen Pub., 1994. 13 vols.

Census Index: U.S. Selected States/Counties, 1850. Family Archive CD 317. Novato, CA: Broderbund Software. CD-ROM.

Census Microfilm Records: North Carolina, 1850. Family Archive CD 306. Novato, CA: Broderbund Software. CD-ROM.

Index of Individuals Born Outside the United States as Enumerated in the 1850 Census of North Carolina. Salt Lake City, UT: Research Department, The Genealogical Society of The Church of Jesus Christ of Latter-day Saints, 1972. 113p.

Jackson, Ronald Vern. *Mortality Schedules Index, Online Edition*. Orem, UT: Ancestry.com, Inc., 1999. **http://www.ancestry.com**

_____. *North Carolina Census Index, Online Edition*. Orem, UT: Ancestry.com, Inc., 1999. **http://www.ancestry.com**

_____, and Gary Ronald Teeples. *North Carolina 1850 Census Index*. Bountiful, UT: Accelerated Indexing Systems, 1976. 342p.

_____. *North Carolina 1850 Mortality Census Index*. Bountiful, UT: Accelerated Indexing Systems, 1989. 72p.

_____. *North Carolina 1850 Slave Schedule Census Index*. Salt Lake City, UT: Accelerated Indexing Systems International, 1988. Unpgd.

U.S. Census Index Series, Virginia, West Virginia, Maryland, North Carolina and the District of Columbia, 1850. Orem, UT: Automated Archives, 1991. CD-ROM.

U.S. Federal Population Census Schedules. 1850, M432, Microfilm Reel Nos. 619-649.

U.S. Federal Population Census Schedules. 1850, M432, Slave Schedules, Microfilm Reel Nos. 650-656.

1860

Almasy, Sandra L. *North Carolina Mortality Census, 1850, 1860, 1870, 1880.* Joliet, IL: Kensington Glen Pub., 1994. 13 vols.

Census Index: U.S. Selected States/Counties, 1860. Family Archive CD 318. Novato, CA: Broderbund Software. CD-ROM.

Jackson, Ronald Vern. *North Carolina Census Index, Online Edition.* Orem, UT: Ancestry.com, Inc., 1999. **http://www.ancestry.com**

_____, and Gary Ronald Teeples. *North Carolina 1860 Census Index.* North Salt Lake City, UT: Accelerated Indexing Systems, 1987. 2 vols.

_____. _____. West Jordan, UT: Genealogical Services, 1988, 1997.

_____. *North Carolina 1860 Federal Slave Schedule Census Index.* Salt Lake City, UT: Accelerated Indexing Systems International, 1990. 683p.

Robertson, Clara Hamlett. *Kansas Territorial Settlers of 1860 Who Were Born in Tennessee, Virginia, North Carolina and South Carolina.* Baltimore, MD: Genealogical Publishing Co., 1976. 187p.

U.S. Census Index, 1860, District of Columbia, Maryland, North Carolina, Virginia, West Virginia. Orem, UT: Automated Archives, 1992. CD-ROM.

U.S. Federal Population Census Schedules. 1860, M653, Microfilm Reel Nos. 886-919.

U.S. Federal Population Census Schedules. 1860, M653, Slave Schedules, Microfilm Reel Nos. 920-927.

1870

Almasy, Sandra L. *North Carolina Mortality Census, 1850, 1860, 1870, 1880.* Joliet, IL: Kensington Glen Pub., 1994. 13 vols.

Census Index: North Carolina/South Carolina, 1870. Family Archive CD 289. Novato, CA: Broderbund Software. CD-ROM.

Jackson, Ronald Vern. *North Carolina Census Index, Online Edition.* Orem, UT: Ancestry.com, Inc., 1999. **http://www.ancestry.com**

_____. *North Carolina 1870 Federal Census Index.* Salt Lake City, UT: Accelerated Indexing Systems, 1988. 2 vols.

Steuart, Bradley W. *North Carolina 1870 Census Index.* Bountiful, UT: Precision Indexing, 1989, 1999. 2 vols.; 22 microfiche.

_____. _____. Bountiful, UT: Heritage Quest, 1999. 2 vols.

Steuart, Raeone Christenson. *North and South Carolina 1870 Census Index Extracted from the Original U.S. Federal Census Schedules.* Series No. ACD-0029. Bountiful, UT: Heritage Quest, 1998. CD-ROM.

U.S. Federal Population Census Schedules. 1870, M593, Microfilm Reel Nos. 1121-1166.

1880

Almasy, Sandra L. *North Carolina Mortality Census, 1850, 1860, 1870, 1880.* Joliet, IL: Kensington Glen Pub., 1994. 13 vols.

U.S. Federal Population Census Schedules. 1880, T9, Microfilm Reel Nos. 950-988.

U.S. Federal Population Census Schedules. 1880, Soundex. T766, 79 Microfilm Reels.

1890

Almasy, Sandra L. *North Carolina 1890 Civil War Veterans Census, a Census of Veterans of the Union Armed Forces and Their Widows, Containing Also Information on Other U.S. Veterans and Many Confederate Veterans.* Middleton, WI: Kensington Glen Pub., 1990. 316p.

Jackson, Ronald Vern. *1890 North Carolina Census Index, Special Schedule of the Eleventh Census (1890) Enumerating Union Veterans and of Union Veterans of the Civil War.* North Salt Lake, UT: Accelerated Indexing Systems, 1984. 74p.

_____. *North Carolina Census Index, Online Edition (Veterans Schedules).* Orem, UT: Ancestry.com, Inc., 1999.

http://www.ancestry.com

_____. *North Carolina 1890*. North Salt Lake City, UT: Accelerated Indexing Systems International, 1984. 74p.

U.S. Federal Population Census Schedules. 1890, M407, Microfilm Reel No. 3.

U.S. Federal Population Census Schedules. 1890, Index. M496, 2 Microfilm Reels.

U.S. Federal Population Census Schedules, Special Schedule, Enumerating Union Veterans and Widows of Union Veterans of the Civil War. 1890, M123, Microfilm Reel No. 58.

Veterans' Schedules: U.S. Selected States, 1890. Family Archive CD 131. Novato, CA: Broderbund Software. CD-ROM.

1900

U.S. Federal Population Census Schedules. 1900, T623, Microfilm Reel Nos. 1180-1225.

U.S. Federal Population Census Schedules. 1900, Soundex. T1063, 168 Microfilm Reels.

1910

U.S. Federal Population Census Schedules. 1910, T624, Microfilm Reel Nos. 1095-1137.

U.S. Federal Population Census Schedules. 1910, Miracode Index, T1271, 178 Microfilm Reels.

1920

U.S. Federal Population Census Schedules. 1920, T625, Microfilm Reel Nos. 1282-1329.

U.S. Federal Population Census Schedules. 1920, Soundex. M1579, 166 Microfilm Reels.

Alamance County
1850

Chiarito, Marian Dodson. *Alamance County, North Carolina 1850 Census with Ancestors and Descendants of Selected Families*. Author, 1987. 236p.

Alexander County
1850

Staley, Linda McGalliard. *Alexander County, North Carolina 1850 Census*. Patterson, NC: Staley Pub. and Genealogical Research, 1987. 84p.

1860

Staley, Linda McGalliard. *Alexander County, North Carolina 1860 Census*. Patterson, NC: Staley Pub. and Genealogical Research, 1986. 97p.

1870

Miller, Evelina Davis. *1870 Census, Alexander County, North Carolina*. Hiddenite, NC: Author, 1994. 175p.

Anson County
1850

Garner, G. L. *Anson County, North Carolina, 1850 Federal Census*. Columbus, GA: Author, 1985. 122p.

Ashe County
1800

USGenWeb Census Project. North Carolina, 1800 Ashe County.
ftp://ftp.rootsweb.com/pub/census/nc/ashe/1800/

1810

Sebastian, Samuel, and Paul W. Gregory. *1810 Federal Census of Ashe County, North Carolina*. North Wilkesboro, NC: Wilkes Genealogical Society, 1975. 15p.

USGenWeb Census Project. North Carolina, 1810 Ashe County.
ftp://ftp.rootsweb.com/pub/census/nc/ashe/1810/

1850

Bare, Ina. *1850 Ashe County Census*. West Jefferson, NC: Ashe County Public Library. 83p.

Miller, Danny. *1850 Census, Ashe County, North Carolina*. Jefferson, NC: Ashe County Public Library, 1982. 99p.

1860

Miller, Danny. *1860 Census, Ashe County, North Carolina*. Jefferson, NC: Ashe County Public Library, 1986. 153p.

1880

Katzman, Mary Floy Schulz. *The 1880 Federal Census of Ashe County, North Carolina, Including the Mortality Schedule*. Framingham, MA: Author, 1992. 267p

Bertie County

1800

USGenWeb Census Project. North Carolina, 1810 Bertie County.

ftp://ftp.rootsweb.com/pub/census/nc/bertie/1810/

1860

Almasy, Sandra Lee. *Bertie County, North Carolina Census 1860, Population Schedule of the Eighth Census of the United States Free and Slave Inhabitants*. Middleton, WI: Kensington Glen Pub., 1996. 273p.

1880

Almasy, Sandra Lee. *Bertie County, North Carolina Census 1880, Population Schedule of the Tenth Census of the United States*. Middleton, WI: Kensington Glen Pub., 1996. 2 vols.

Bladen County

1820

1820 Census, Bladen County, North Carolina. 40p.

1830

Campbell, Wanda Suggs. *1830 Federal Census of Bladen County, North Carolina*. Elizabethtown, NC: Bladen County Bicentennial Commission, 1976. 31p.

1840

Population Schedule of the Sixth Census of the United States, 1840, Bladen County, North Carolina. Elizabethtown, NC: Bladen County Bicentennial Commission. 42p.

1850

Campbell, Wanda Suggs. *1850 Federal Census of Bladen County, North Carolina*. Elizabethtown, NC: Bladen County Bicentennial Commission, 1976. 124p.

Smith, Milton R. *Index to 1850 Federal Census of Bladen County, North Carolina*. Raleigh, NC: Author. Unpgd.

1860

Elam, Annie Merle W. *1860 Federal Census of Bladen County North Carolina*. Bladenboro, NC: Southeast Research. 185p.

Brunswick County

1800

Haskett, Delmas D. *Brunswick County, North Carolina 1800 Census*. Wilmington, NC: North Carolina Room, New Hanover County Public Library, 1989. Unpgd.

1810, 1820

Haskett, Delmas D. *Brunswick County, North Carolina, 1810 & 1820 Federal Censuses*. Wilmington, NC: Old New Hnover Genealogical Society, 1995. 28p.

1830

Haskett, Delmas D. *Brunswick County, North Carolina 1830 Federal Census*. Wilmington, NC: North Carolina Room, New Hanover County Public Library, 1989. 45p.

1840

Haskett, Delmas D. *Brunswick County, North Carolina 1840 Federal Census*. Wilmington, NC: North Carolina Room, New Hanover County Public Library, 1989. 46p.

1850

Thompson, Doris Lancaster. *1850 Federal Census of Brunswick County, North Carolina*. New Bern, NC: Dunn, 1976. 188p.

1860

Benton, Dorothy S. *1860 Federal Census, Brunswick County, North Carolina*. Whiteville, NC: Author, 1989. 202p.

Burke County

1800

USGenWeb Census Project. North Carolina, 1800 Burke County.
ftp://ftp.rootsweb.com/pub/census/nc/burke/1800/

1810

Pittman, Betsy Dodd. *Burke County, North Carolina, 1810 Federal Census*. Valdese, NC: Author, 1993. 84p.

1860

Swink, Daniel D., and Ted K. Tallent. *Federal Census and Mortality Schedule, Burke County, North Carolina, 1860*. Lawndale, NC: Author, 1983. 155p.

1870

Swink, Daniel D., and Ted K. Tallent. *1870 Federal Census and Mortality Schedule of Burke County, North Carolina*. Lawndale, NC: Author, 1987. 109p.

Cabarrus County

1850

Krimminger, Betty L., and James R. Wilson. *Seventh Census, Cabarrus County, North Carolina, 1850*. Chapel Hill, NC: Authors, 1985. 247p.

1860

Kratz, Steven C. *Cabaras County, North Carolina 1860 Census*. Salt Lake City, UT: Kratz Indexing, 1987. 34p.

Krimminger, Betty L., and James R. Wilson. *Eighth Census, Cabarrus County, North Carolina, 1860*. Chapel Hill, NC: Authors, 1987. 269p.

1870

Krimminger, Betty L., and James R. Wilson. *Ninth Census, Cabarrus County, North Carolina, 1870*. Chapel Hill, NC: Authors, 1990. 374p.

Caldwell County

1850

Staley, Linda M. *The 1850 Census of Caldwell County, North Carolina*. Lenoir, NC: Caldwell County Genealogical Society, 1984. 89p.

1860

Kratz, Steven C. *Caldwell County, North Carolina 1860 Census*. Salt Lake City, UT: Kratz Indexing, 1987. 26p.

Staley, Linda M. *The 1860 Census of Caldwell County, North Carolina*. Lenoir, NC: Caldwell County Genealogical Society, 1983. 116p.

1870

Hawkins, John O. *The 1870 Census of Caldwell County, North Carolina*. Lenoir, NC: Caldwell County Genealogical Society, 1983. 169p.

1900

Smith, David P. *1900 Census of Caldwell County, North Carolina*. Arden, NC: Author, 1992. 288p.

Carteret County

1880

Sanders, Rebecca W. *1880 Federal Census of Carteret County, North Carolina*. Author, 1978. 217p.

Caswell County
1850, 1860

Kendall, Katharine Kerr. *Caswell County, North Carolina Will Books, 1814-1843; Guardians' Accounts, 1819-1847, 1850 & 1860 Census Mortality Schedules, Powers of Attorney from Deed Books, 1777-1880*. Raleigh, NC: Author, 1983. 226p.

Williams, Mike K. *1850 Census of Caswell County, North Carolina*. Danville, VA: Author, 1997. 37p.

Catawba County
1850

Staley, Linda M. *Catawba County, North Carolina, 1850 Census*. Patterson, NC: Staley Pub. and Genealogical Research, 1987. 133p.

Cherokee County
1840

USGenWeb Census Project. North Carolina, 1840 Cherokee County.
ftp://ftp.rootsweb.com/pub/census/nc/cherokee/1840/

Cleveland County
1850

Ramey, Beatrix Blanton, Miles S. Philbeck, Jr., and Hedy Hughes Newton. *1850 Census, Cleveland County, North Carolina*. Spindale, NC: Genealogical Society of Old Tryon County, 1978. 211p.
1860
McEntire, Russell Hicks. *Federal Census, Cleveland County, North Carolina, 1860*. Rutherfordton, NC: Author, 1976. 255p.
1870
DePriest, Virginia Greene. *The 1870 Census of Cleveland County, North Carolina*. Shelby, NC: Author, 1979. 175p.
1880
DePriest, Virginia Greene. *The 1880 Census of Cleveland County, North Carolina*. Shelby, NC: Author, 1982. 226p.
1890
U.S. Federal Population Census Schedules. 1890, M407, Microfilm Reel No. 3.
U.S. Federal Population Census Schedules. 1890, Index. M496, 2 Microfilm Reels.
1900
DePriest, Virginia Greene. *The 1900 Census of Cleveland County, North Carolina*. Shelby, NC: Author, 1982. 695p.

Craven County
1850

Gwynn, Zae Hargett. *The 1850 Census of Craven County, North Carolina*. Kingsport, TN, 1961. 185p.
1860
Beauchamp, Eula Pearl. *1860 Census, Craven County, North Carolina*. New Bern, NC: Author, 1996. 119p.

Gwynn, Zae Hargett. *Surname Index of the 1860 Census of Craven County, North Carolina*. Author. 13p.
1870
Beauchamp, Eula Pearl. *1870 Census, Craven County, North Carolina*. New Bern, NC: Author. 437p.

Cumberland County
1850

Askea, Charles M., and Doris Anderson Askea. *North Carolina the 1850 Cumberland County, Census*. Kernersville, NC: Authors, 1987. 62p.

1860

Askea, Charles M., and Doris Anderson Askea. *1860 Cumberland County, North Carolina*. Kernersville, NC: Authors, 1983. 112p.

1870

Askea, Charles M., and Doris Anderson Askea. *North Carolina the 1870 Cumberland County, Census*. Kernersville, NC: Authors, 1985. 93p.

Currituck County

1860

Spencer, Jean Silvester. *Monograph of the 1860 Currituck County Census*. Moyock, NC: Spencer & Spencer, Ltd., 1986. 91p.

Darlington County

1850

1850 Census of Darlington County, South Carolina. Hemingway, SC: Three Rivers Historical Society, 1981. 158p.

Davidson County

1850

DiRaimo, Virginia E. *1850 Federal Census for Davidson County, North Carolina*. Kansas City, MO: Author, 1986. 133p.

1860

DiRaimo, Virginia E. *1860 Federal Census for Davidson County, North Carolina*. Kansas City, MO: Author, 1985. 147p.

1870

DiRaimo, Virginia E. *1870 Federal Census for Davidson County, North Carolina*. Kansas City, MO: Author, 1986. 207p.

1880

DiRaimo, Virginia E. *1880 Federal Census for Davidson County, North Carolina*. Kansas City, MO: Author, 1987. 239p.

Duplin County

1800

Register, Alvaretta Kenan. *The Second Census of the United States, 1800, Duplin County, North Carolina*. Norfolk, VA: Register, 1966. 30p.

1840

Haskett, Delmas D. *Duplin County, North Carolina, 1840 Federal Census*. Wilmington, NC: North Carolina Room, New Hanover County Public Library, 1991. 84p.

1860

Franks, Joyce Jones. *1860 Federal Census, Duplin County, North Carolina*. Rose Hill, NC: Duplin County Historical Society, 1994. 334p.

Edgecombe County

1830

Bradley, Stephen E., Jr. *The 1830 Federal Census, Edgecombe County, North Carolina*. South Boston, VA: Author, 1987. 129p.

1860

Bradley, Stephen E. *The 1860 Federal Census, Edgecombe County, North Carolina*. South Boston, VA: Author, 1989. 137p.

Forsyth County
1850
The 1850 Federal Census and Supplementary Schedules of Forsyth County, North Carolina. Winston-Salem, NC: Forsyth County Genealogical Society, 1984. 273p.
1860
The 1860 Federal Census and Supplementary Schedules of Forsyth County, North Carolina. Winston-Salem, NC: Forsyth County Genealogical Society, 1988. 330p.
1870
The 1870 Federal Census and Supplementary Schedules of Forsyth County, North Carolina. Winston-Salem, NC: Forsyth County Genealogical Society, 1988. 446p.

Franklin County
1830
Bradley, Stephen E., Jr. *the 1830 Federal Census, Franklin County, North Carolina.* South Boston, VA: Author, 1987. 89p.

Gaston County
1850
Goodnight, Libby Wyatt, Linda Adams Bell, Robert C. Carpenter. *The Complete 1850 Census of Gaston County, North Carolina.* Dallas, NC: Gaston County Historical Society, 1985. 199p.
1890
U.S. Federal Population Census Schedules. 1890, M407, Microfilm Reel No. 3.
U.S. Federal Population Census Schedules. 1890, Index. M496, 2 Microfilm Reels.

Gates County
1790-1840
Almasy, Sandra L. *Gates County, North Carolina 1790-1800-1810-1820-1830-1840 Census.* Rome, NY: Kensington Glen Pub., 1988. 170p.
1850, 1860
Almasy, Sandra L. *Gates County, North Carolina Census, 1850 & 1860.* Rome, NY: Kensington Glen Publishing, 1987. 194p.
1870
Almasy, Sandra L. *Gates County, North Carolina Census, 1870.* Rome, NY: Kensington Glen Publishing, 1989. 172p.
1880
Almasy, Sandra L. *Gates County, North Carolina Census, 1880.* Rome, NY: Kensington Glen Publishing, 1989. 199p.
1900
Powell, David. *1900 Gates County Census.* Greenville, NC: Author, 1994. 276p.

Graham County
1880
Aldridge, Bryan Keith. *1880 Graham County, North Carolina Census.* Marion, NC: Author, 1994. 71p.

Greene County
1800
Murphy, William L., Jr. *1800 Greene County, North Carolina Federal Census.* Raleigh, NC: Author, 1986. 32p.
1820
Murphy, William L., Jr. *1820 Greene County, North Carolina Federal Census.* Raleigh, NC: Author, 1986. 26p.

1830

Murphy, William L., Jr. *1830 Greene County, North Carolina Federal Census*. Raleigh, NC: Author, 1996. 60p.

1840

Murphy, William L., Jr. *1840 Greene County, North Carolina Federal Census*. Raleigh, NC: Author, 1996. 74p.

1850

Heiman, Kathryn. *Federal Population Schedules of the State of North Carolina Free Schedules of the 1850 Census of Greene County*. Anahuac, TX: Oak Island Research, 1977. 47p.

Kilpatrick, Mary Virginia. *1850 Census of Greene County, with Mortality Schedules, Compiled from Microfilmed Copies of the Census*. Raleigh, NC: Carolina Abstractors, 1987. 77p.

Murphy, William L., Jr. *1850 Greene County, North Carolina Federal Census*. Raleigh, NC: Author, 1984. 93p.

USGenWeb Census Project. North Carolina, 1850 Greene County.
ftp://ftp.rootsweb.com/pub/census/nc/greene/1850/

1860

Kilpatrick, Mary Virginia. *Greene County, North Carolina, 1860 Census Schedule*. Raleigh, NC: Carolina Abstractors, 1997. 138p.

Guilford County

1830

Jarrell, Lawrence E. *1830 Census, Guilford County, North Carolina*. Greensboro, NC: Guilford County Genealogical Society, 1997. 221p.

1840

_____. *1840 Census of Guilford County, North Carolina*. Greensboro, NC: Guilford County Genealogial Society, 1997. 227p.

1860

Browning, Mary A., and Dixie Matheny Normandy. *Guilford County, 1860, Annotated Abstract of the U.S. Population Schedule of 1860 for Guilford County, North Carolina*. Greensboro, NC: Guilford County Genealogical Society, 1991. 320p.

Halifax County

1810

Gammon, David Bryant. *1810 Federal Census, Halifax County, North Carolina*. Raleigh, NC: Author 1986. 53p.

1830

Bradley, Stephen E., Jr. *The 1830 Federal Census, Halifax County, North Carolina*. South Boston, VA: Author, 1987. 139p.

1840

Gammon, David Bryant. *1840 Federal Census, Halifax County, North Carolina*. Raleigh, NC: Author 1985. 74p.

1850

Gammon, David Bryant. *1850 Federal Census, Halifax County, North Carolina*. Raleigh, NC: Author 1981. 172p.

Harnett County

1860

Askea, Charles M., and Doris Anderson Askea. *The 1860 Harnett County, North Carolina Census*. Kernersville, NC: Authors, 1986. 49p.

1870

Askea, Charles M., and Doris Anderson Askea. *North Carolina the 1870 Harnett County Abstract Census*. Kernersville, NC: Authors, 1986. 54p.

1880

Askea, Charles M., and Doris Anderson Askea. *The 1880 Census, Third Census, Harnett County, North Carolina*. Kernersville, NC: Authors, 1987. 62p.

Haywood County
1850

Farlow, Betsy C. *Haywood County, North Carolina 1850 Federal Census*. Waynesville, NC: Haywood County Genealogical Society, 1998. 190p.

Medford, Robert Joseph. *The Families of Haywood and Jackson Counties, North Carolina Based on the 1850 Census Records*. Alexander, NC: WorldComm, 1996. 149p.

1870

Medford, Robert Joseph. *The Families of Haywood County, North Carolina Based on the 1870 Census Records*. Alexander, NC: WorldComm, 1995. 190p.

1880

Medford, Robert Joseph. *The Families of Haywood County, North Carolina Based on the 1880 Census Records*. Alexander, NC: WorldComm, 1995. 283p.

Henderson County
1840

Dorsey, Lois Tincher. *United States Census, 1840, Henderson County, North Carolina*. Hendersonville, NC: Genealogy Ltd., 1984. 46p.

1850

Dorsey, Lois Tincher. *United States Census, 1850, Henderson County, North Carolina*. Hendersonville, NC: Genealogy Ltd., 1983. 160p.

Hertford County
1850

Vann, J. A. *1850 Census of Hertford County, North Carolina, July – August 1850, Abstracts and Index*. Winton, NC: Albemarle Regional Library, 1984. 76p.

1870

Powell, David. *1870 Hertford County Census*. Greenville, NC: Liberty Shield Press, 1996. 229p.

1880

Powell, David. *1880 Hertford County Census*. Greenville, NC: Liberty Shield Press, 1995. 208p.

Hyde County
1850

Carawan, Seth D. *1850 Census of Hyde County, North Carolina, a Compilation of all Census Schedules Taken in the Year 1850*. Fairfield, NC: Hyde County Historical & Genealogical Society, 1996. 259p.

1900

Oakley, Crestena Anna Jennings. *The 1900 Census of Hyde County, North Carolina*. Fairfield, NC: Hyde County Historical & Genealogical Society. 299p.

1910

Oakley, Crestena Anna Jennings. *The 1910 Census of Hyde County, North Carolina*. Fairfield, NC: Hyde County Historical & Genealogical Society, 1990. 253p.

Jackson County
1850

Medford, Robert Joseph. *The Families of Haywood and Jackson Counties, North Carolina Based on the 1850 Census Records*. Alexander, NC: WorldComm, 1996. 149p.

1860

Felldin, Jeanne Robey. *1860 United States Census Index, the North Carolina Counties of Jackson and Nash*. Tomball, TX: Genealogical Publications, 1976. 10p.

Johnston County
1850

1850 Census of Johnston County, North Carolina, Population Schedule, Mortality Schedule, Slave Schedule. Smithfield, NC: Johnston County Genealogical Society, 1990. 106p.

Lincoln County
1790

DePriest, Virginia Greene. *The 1790 Federal Census, Morgan District, Lincoln County, Rutherford County*. Shelby, NC: Author, 1982. 78p.

1800

Dellinger, Paul H. *The 1800 Federal Census of Lincoln County, North Carolina*. Lincolnton, NC: Author, 1985. 94p.

1810

Dellinger, Paul H. *The 1810 Federal Census of Lincoln County, North Carolina*. Lincolnton, NC: Author, 1985. 112p.

1820

Dellinger, Paul H. *1820 Federal Census of Lincoln County, North Carolina Lincoln County West of the South Fork of the Catawba River, Page 1-33 [and] Lincoln County East of the South Fork of the Catawba River, Page 34-76*. Lincolnton, NC: Author, 1987. 99p.

1830

Dellinger, Paul H. *The 1830 Federal Census of Lincoln County, North Carolina*. Lincolnton, NC: Author, 1987. 135p.

1840

DePriest, Virginia Greene. *The 1840 Federal Census Lincoln County, North Carolina*. Shelby, NC: Author, 1983. 176p.

1850

Crow, Judson O. *1850 Census, Lincoln County, North Carolina*. Denver, NC: Author, 1983. 154p.

1860

Bishop, Brenda C. *1860 Census Transcription for Lincoln County, North Carolina*. Tallahassee, FL: Author, 1985. 47p.

Dellinger, Paul H. *The 1860 Census of Lincoln County, North Carolina*. Lincolnton, NC: Author, 1991. 147p.

1880

Dellinger, Paul H. *The 1880 Federal Census of Lincoln County, North Carolina*. Lincolnton, NC: Author, 1988. 303p.

McDowell County
1870

The 1870 Federal Census of McDowell County, North Carolina. Marion, NC: Jewell R. Randolph, 1997. 186p.

Macon County
1840

USGenWeb Census Project. North Carolina, 1840 Macon County.
ftp://ftp.rootsweb.com/pub/census/nc/macon/1840/

Madison County
1870

Williams, Sallyann J. *Index to 1870 Madison County, North Carolina, Federal Census, Extracted from Microfilm in 1988*. Whitehouse, TX: Author, 1988.

1890

Williams, Sally. *1890 Madison County, North Carolina Veterans Census*. Central Point, OR: Author, 1986. 26p.

Mecklenburg County
1850

Schmidt, Jennifer A. *1850 Census of Mecklenburg County, North Carolina (Including the Mortality and Slave Schedules)*. Charlotte, NC: Olde Mecklenburg Genealogical Society, 1994. 225p.

Mitchell County
1870

Gunter, Rhonda L. *1870 Federal Census, Mitchell County, North Carolina*. Spruce Pine, NC: Toe Valley Genealogical Society, 1991. 109p.

Montgomery County
1870

Graves, Lucas. *1870 Census, Montgomery County, North Carolina*. Asheboro, NC: Randolph County Genealogical Society, 1986. 90p.

Moore County
1860

Askea, Charles M., and Doris Anderson Askea. *North Carolina, the 1860 Moore County, North Carolina Census*. Kernersville, NC: Authors, 1987. 80p.

Nash County
1830

Nash County, North Carolina, 1830 Census. Savannah, MO: Andrew County Historical Society, 1980. 19p.

1850

Brantley, Flora. *North Carolina 1850 Nash County Census*. Raleigh, NC: Author, 1982. 143p.

1860

Felldin, Jeanne Robey. *1860 United States Census Index, the North Carolina Counties of Jackson and Nash*. Tomball, TX: Genealogical Publications, 1976. 10p.

Howell, Joan L. *Nash County, North Carolina Federal Census of 1860*. Lucama, NC: Generations Past, 1997. 246p.

1870

Howell, Joan L. *Nash County, North Carolina Federal Census of 1870 Population Schedule, Mortality Schedule, Agriculture Schedule, Products of Industry Schedule, Social Statistics Schedule*. Lucama, NC: Generations Past, 1997. 346p.

New Hanover County
1830

Haskett, Delmas D. *New Hanover County, North Carolina 1830 Census*. Wilmington, NC: North Carolina Room, New Hanover County Public Library, 1990. Unpgd.

1850

Jackson, Louise, Ellen Futch, and Mae B. Graves. *1850 Federal Census of New Hanover County, North Carolina*. Wilmington, NC: Author, 1982. 257p.

1860

Haskett, Delmas D., and Ann Hewlett Hutteman. *New Hanover County, North Carolina, 1860 Federal Census*. Wilmington, NC: North Carolina Room, New Hanover County Public Library, 1991. 401p.

1870

Haskett, Delmas D. *New Hanover County, North Carolina, 1870 Federal Census*. Wilmington, NC: Old New Hanover Genealogical Society, 1995. 3 vols.

Pasquotank County

1850

Sanders, Rebecca W. *1850 Federal Census, Pasquotank County, North Carolina*. Smithfield, NC: Sanders, 1979. 126p.

Polk County

1860

Padgett, Charles Barrett. *The 1860 Federal Census of Polk County, North Carolina*. Kings Mountain, NC: Author, 1984. 91p.

1870

Monteith, Frankie. *The 1870 Federal Census of Polk County, North Carolina*. Brevard, NC: Author, 1985. 77p.

1880

Monteith, Frankie. *The 1880 Federal Census of Polk County, North Carolina*. Brevard, NC: Author, 1987. 86, 6p.

Portsmouth Island

1790-1900

Cloud, Ellen Fulcher. *The Federal Census of Portsmouth Island, North Carolina, 1790-1900*. Ocracoke, NC: Live Oak Publications, 1995. Unpgd.

Randolph County

1790

USGenWeb Census Project. North Carolina, 1790 Randolph County.
ftp://ftp.rootsweb.com/pub/census/nc/randolph/1790/

1850

Simpson, Nancy Williams. *1850 Randolph County Census, North Carolina*. Wilkesboro, NC: Author, 1974. 152p.

1860

Simpson, Nancy Williams. *1860 Randolph County Census, North Carolina*. Wilkesboro, NC: Author. 162p.

1870

Grady, Daniel L. *1870 Federal Census, Randolph County, North Carolina*. Cincinnati, OH: Author, 1980. 166p.

1880

Grady, Daniel L. *1880 Federal Census, Randolph County, North Carolina*. Cincinnati, OH: Author. 179p.

1900

Grady, Evie Ruth Hill. *Blacks Living in Randolph County, North Carolina Federal Census, 1900*. Cincinnati, OH: Author, 1983. 68p.

Robeson County

1850

Harmon, Elaine Davis. *1850 Federal Census of Robeson County, North Carolina, Copied from Microfilm Roll #642 on File at the National Archives in Washington, D.C. and the Department of Archives and History in Raleigh, North Carolina*. Greenville, SC: Author, 1980. 182p.

USGenWeb Census Project. North Carolina, 1850 Robeson County.
ftp://ftp.rootsweb.com/pub/census/nc/robeson/1850/

Rockingham County

1850

The 1850 Federal Census of Rockingham County, North Carolina, Also Includes 1850 Mortality Schedule. Madison, NC: James Hunter Chapter, National Society, DAR, 1987. 150p.

1860

The 1860 Federal Census of Rockingham County, North Carolina. Madison, NC: James Hunter Chapter, DAR, 1988. 151p.

Rowan County
1850

Linn, Jo White. *1850 Census of Rowan County, North Carolina, a Genealogical Compilation of All Six Schedules.* Salisbury, NC: Author, 1992. 148p.

1860

1860 Census of Rowan County. Salisbury, NC: Genealogical Society of Rowan County, North Carolina, 1990. 127p.

1860 Census Surname Index, North Carolina, Rowan County. 57p.

1870

1870 Census of Rowan County. Salisbury, NC: Genealogical Society of Rowan County, 1989. 180p.

1870 Census of Rowan County, Providence Township. Salisbury, NC: Genealogical Society of Rowan County, 1988. 20p.

Rutherford County
1790

DePriest, Virginia Greene. *The 1790 Federal Census, Morgan District, Lincoln County, Rutherford County.* Shelby, NC: Author, 1982. 78p.

Koon, Sue Hill. *Rutherford County, North Carolina 1790 Census and 1782 Tax List.* Spindale, NC: Genealogical Society of Old Tryon County, 1974. 38p.

1830

Philbeck, Miles S. *1830 Census Rutherford County, North Carolina Free Schedules.* Forest City, NC: Genealogical Society of Old Tryon County, 1982. 64p.

1840

Jackson, Doris Hamrick. *1840 Federal Census, Rutherford County, North Carolina.* Shelby, NC: Author, 1983. 103p.

1850

Brooks, Roy. *1850 Census, Rutherford County, North Carolina.* Spindale, NC: Genealogical Society of Old Tryon County, 1976. 263p.

1870

Jackson, Doris Hamrick. *1870 Federal Census, Rutherford County, North Carolina.* Shelby, NC: Author, 1982. 345p.

Stanly County
1850

The 1850 Federal Census Stanly County, North Carolina. Albemarle, NC: Stanly County Genealogical Society, 1983. 78p.

USGenWeb Census Project. North Carolina, 1850 Stanly County.

ftp://ftp.rootsweb.com/pub/census/nc/stanly/1850/

1860

1860 Federal Census of Stanly County, North Carolina, Schedules 1-6. Albermarle, NC: Stanly County Genealogical Society, 1984. 103p.

1870

The 1870 Federal Census and Supplementary Schedules of Stanly County, North Carolina. Albemarle, NC: Stanly County Genealogical Society, 1993. 189p.

1880

Stanly County Genealogical Society. *The 1880 Federal Census and Supplementary Schedules of Stanly County, North Carolina.* Albemarle, NC: The Society, 1988. 262p.

1900

Horton, Brenda Honeycutt. *The 1900 Federal Census of Stanly County, North Carolina Population Schedule*. Mount Holly, NC: Author, 1996. Unpgd.

Stokes County
1800

USGenWeb Census Project. North Carolina, 1800 Stokes County.

ftp://ftp.rootsweb.com/pub/census/nc/stokes/1800/

1810

McBride, Cleo T., Al Blackman, Billy B. Medlin, and Faye Jarvis. *Stokes County, North Carolina, 1810 Federal Census*. Winston-Salem, NC: Forsyth County Genealogical Society, 1997. 111p.

USGenWeb Census Project. North Carolina, 1810 Stokes County.

ftp://ftp.rootsweb.com/pub/census/nc/stokes/1810/

USGenWeb Census Project. North Carolina, 1810 Stokes County. Manufacturers Census.

ftp://ftp.rootsweb.com/pub/census/nc/stokes/1810/

1830

USGenWeb Census Project. North Carolina, 1830 Stokes County.

ftp://ftp.rootsweb.com/pub/census/nc/stokes/1830/

1840

Stokes County, North Carolina, 1840 Federal Census. Winston-Salem, NC: Forsyth County Genealogical Society, 1988. 217p.

USGenWeb Census Project. North Carolina, 1840 Stokes County.

ftp://ftp.rootsweb.com/pub/census/nc/stokes/1840/

1850

The 1850 Federal Census and Supplementary Schedules of Stokes County, North Carolina. Winston-Salem, NC: Forsyth County Genealogical Society, 1985. 204p.

1850 Federal Census, Stokes County, North Carolina. Hope, AR: GAM Publications, 1976. 101p.

USGenWeb Census Project. North Carolina, 1850 Stokes County.

ftp://ftp.rootsweb.com/pub/census/nc/stokes/1850/

1860

The 1860 Federal Census of Stokes County, North Carolina, Also Includes 1860 Mortality Schedule with Index Which Includes the Head of Household and Any Person Within That Household with a Different Surname. Madison, NC: James Hunter Chapter, DAR, 1990. 130p.

USGenWeb Census Project. North Carolina, 1860 Stokes County. (Partial).

ftp://ftp.rootsweb.com/pub/census/nc/stokes/1860/

1870

The 1870 Federal Census of Stokes County, North Carolina, Including the 1870 Mortality Schedule. Madison, NC: James Hunter Chapter, DAR, 1993. 311p.

Surry County
1830

Snow, Carol Leonard. *1830 Census of Surry County, North Carolina*. Toast, NC: Author, 1994. 176p.

1840

Creed, Kathryn Susan, and Juanita B. Carpenter. *1840 Census of Surry County, North Carolina*. Mount Airy, NC: Authors, 1984. 205p.

1850

Snow, Carol Leonard. *1850 Census of Surry County, North Carolina*. Mount Airy, NC: Author, 1983. 270p.

1870

Snow, Carol Leonard. *1870 Population Schedule, Products of Industry Schedule and Mortality Schedule for Surry County, North Carolina*. Toast, NC: Author, 1991. 194p.

1880

Snow, Carol Leonard. *1880 Census of Surry County, North Carolina, Includes 1880 Population Schedule and 1880 Mortality Schedule*. Toast, NC: Author, 1992. 291p.

1900

Barrett, Lorna Wells. *Population Schedule of the Twelfth Census of the United States, 1900, Surry County, North Carolina*. Author. 569p.

Translyvania County

1870

Bishop, Brenda C. *1870 Census, North Carolina, Transcription for Transylvania County*. Tallahassee, FL: Author, 1985. 26p.

1880

Monteith, Frankie. *The 1880 Federal Census of Transylvania County, North Carolina*. Brevard, NC: Author, 1985. 96, 8p.

Tyrrell County

1850

Kelley, Teresa A. *1850 U.S. Census, Tyrrell County, North Carolina Enumerated 2 August-13 September 1850, Transcribed from Microcopy 435, Roll 646, National Archives, 1860 U.S. Census, Tyrrell County, North Carolina Enumerated 1 June-17 August 1860, Transcribed from Microcopy 653, Roll 915, National Archives*. Dale City, VA: Author, 1996. 228p.

Sheppard, Kay Midgett, and Sarah Midyett Hutcherson. *1850 Tyrell County, North Carolina Census*. Authors. 88p.

Union County

1850

1850 Census of Union County, South Carolina. Hemingway, SC: Three Rivers Historical Society, 1992. 205p.

Simpson, Nancy Williams. *1850 Union County Census, North Carolina*. Wilkesboro, NC: Author. 89p.

1860

Simpson, Nancy Williams. *1860 Union County Census, North Carolina*. Wilkesboro, NC: Author, 1982. 100p.

1870

Simpson, Nancy Williams. *1870 Union County Census, North Carolina*. Wilkesboro, NC: Author, 1983. 139p.

Wake County

1830, 1840

Wynne, Frances Holloway. *Wake County, North Carolina Census and Tax List Abstracts, 1830 and 1840*. Fairfax, VA: Author, 1985. 312p.

1850

USGenWeb Census Project. North Carolina, 1850 Wake County.
ftp://ftp.rootsweb.com/pub/census/nc/wake/1850/

Washington County

1860

Norman, Edwin A., and Sybble M. Smithwick. *1860 U.S. Census, Washington County, North Carolina*. Plymouth, NC: Washington County Genealogical Society, 1992. 94p.

Wayne County

1860

Howell, Frances Godwin. *North Carolina, Wayne County, 1860 Census*. Goldsboro, NC: Author, 1988. 264p.

Wilkes County
1810
Sebastian, Samuel. *1810 Census, Wilkes County, North Carolina*. North Wilkesboro, NC: Wilkes Genealogical Society. 23p.
1850
Cheek, Charles, and Mrs. J. W. Martindale. *1850 Census, Wilkes County, North Carolina*. North Wilkesboro, NC: Genealogical Society of the Original Wilkes County. 123p.
1860
Moore, R. Ivey, Samuel Sebastian, and Mrs. W. O. Absher. *1860 Census, Wilkes County, North Carolina*. North Wilkesboro, NC: Wilkes Genealogical Society. 153p.

Wilson County
1860
Howell, Frances Godwin. *Wilson County, North Carolina, Federal Census of 1860*. Goldsboro, NC: Wilson County Genealogial Society, 1993. 221p.

Yadkin County
1880
McCracken, Anne Whitaker. *1880 Federal Census of Yadkin County, North Carolina, with Maps, Comments, and Footnotes*. Marietta, GA: Chestnut Ridge Research, 1991. 230p.

Yancey County
1840
USGenWeb Census Project. North Carolina, 1840 Yancey County.
ftp://ftp.rootsweb.com/pub/census/nc/yancey/1840/
1860
Williams, Sally. *Index to the 1860 Yancey County, North Carolina Federal Census*. Medford, OR: Author, 1985. 16p.
1870
Williams, Sally. *Index to the 1870 Federal Cenus of Yancey County, North Carolina*. Central Point, OR: Author, 1983. 12p.
1880
Schultheis, Nancy. *1880 Yancey County Census, with Partial Marriage Information*. Alexander, NC: WorldComm, 1996. 279p.

North Dakota

1860
Census Index: U.S. Selected States/Counties, 1860. Family Archive CD 318. Novato, CA: Broderbund Software. CD-ROM.
Jackson, Ronald Vern. *Dakota Census Index, 1850 Pembina District*. Salt Lake City, UT: Accelerated Indexing Systems, 1982. 60, 16p.
_____. *Dakota 1860 Territorial Census Index*. Salt Lake City, UT: Accelerated Indexing Systems, 1980. 63p.
_____. *Mortality Schedules Index, Online Edition*. Orem, UT: Ancestry.com, Inc., 1999.
http://www.ancestry.com
U.S. Federal Population Census Schedules. 1860, M653, Microfilm Reel No. 94.

1870
Census Index: U.S. Selected States/Counties, 1870. Family Archive CD 319. Novato, CA: Broderbund Software. CD-ROM.

Guerrero, John. *Census Information Concerning Dakota and North Dakota Black Residents as Found in the United States Census Reports of 1870, 1880, 1885, 1900, 1910 and 1920.* Bismarck, ND: University of Mary Press, 1994. 231p.

Jackson, Ronald Vern. *North Dakota Census Index, Online Edition.* Orem, UT: Ancestry.com, Inc., 1999. **http://www.ancestry.com**

_____. *Dakota 1870 Territorial Census Index.* Salt Lake City, UT: Accelerated Indexing Systems, 1980, 1998. 179p.

_____. *Mortality Schedules Index, Online Edition.* Orem, UT: Ancestry.com, Inc., 1999. **http://www.ancestry.com**

_____. *U.S. Federal Census Index, North Dakota 1870, 1880, 1885 Mortality Schedules.* West Jordan, UT: Genealogical Services, 1984, 1998. 17p.

U.S. Federal Population Census Schedules. 1870, M593, Microfilm Reel No. 118.

1880

Census Index: U.S. Selected States/Counties, 1880. Family Archive CD 320. Novato, CA: Broderbund Software. CD-ROM.

Guerrero, John. *Census Information Concerning Dakota and North Dakota Black Residents as Found in the United States Census Reports of 1870, 1880, 1885, 1900, 1910 and 1920.* Bismarck, ND: University of Mary Press, 1994. 231p.

Jackson, Ronald Vern. *North Dakota Census Index, Online Edition.* Orem, UT: Ancestry.com, Inc., 1999. **http://www.ancestry.com**

_____. *Dakota 1880 Territorial Census Index.* Salt Lake City, UT: Accelerated Indexing Systems, 1980, 1996. 329p.

_____. *Mortality Schedules Index, Online Edition.* Orem, UT: Ancestry.com, Inc., 1999. **http://www.ancestry.com**

_____. *U.S. Federal Census Index, North Dakota 1870, 1880, 1885 Mortality Schedules.* West Jordan, UT: Genealogical Services, 1984, 1998. 17p.

1885

1885 Census Index, Dakota Territory. Bismark, ND: Bismarck Mandan Historical and Genealogical Society, 1995-1996. 7 vols.

Guerrero, John. *Census Information Concerning Dakota and North Dakota Black Residents as Found in the United States Census Reports of 1870, 1880, 1885, 1900, 1910 and 1920.* Bismarck, ND: University of Mary Press, 1994. 231p.

Jackson, Ronald Vern. *Dakota Territorial 1880 Mortality Schedule.* North Salt Lake City, UT: Accelerated Indexing Systems International, 1981, 1988. 44p.

_____. *North Dakota 1885 Census Index.* Salt Lake City, UT: Accelerated Indexing Systems International, 1976, 1982. 105p.

_____. *U.S. Federal Census Index, North Dakota 1870, 1880, 1885 Mortality Schedules.* West Jordan, UT: Genealogical Services, 1984, 1998. 17p.

1890

Helmer, Edith, Mary Ann Quiring, and Lily B. Zwolle. *1890 North Dakota Special Census, Enumerating Union Veterans and Widows of Union Veterans of the Civil War.* Lewistown, MT: Lewistown Genealogy Society, 1986. 49p.

Jackson, Ronald Vern. *1890 North Dakota Census Index Special Schedule of the Eleventh Census (1890) Enumerating Union Veterans and of Union Veterans of the Civil War.* North Salt Lake, UT: Accelerated Indexing Systems, 1986. 33p.

_____. *North Dakota Census Index, Online Edition.* Orem, UT: Ancestry.com, Inc., 1999. **http://www.ancestry.com**

U.S. Federal Population Census Schedules, Special Schedule, Enumerating Union Veterans and Widows of Union Veterans of the Civil War. 1890, M123, Microfilm Reel No. 59.

Veterans' Schedules: U.S. Selected States, 1890. Family Archive CD 131. Novato, CA: Broderbund Software. CD-ROM.

1900

Guerrero, John. *Census Information Concerning Dakota and North Dakota Black Residents as Found in the United States Census Reports of 1870, 1880, 1885, 1900, 1910 and 1920*. Bismarck, ND: University of Mary Press, 1994. 231p.

Ledoux, Albert H. *The French Canadian Families of the Plains and Upper Mountain States, Abstracts from the Federal Census of 1900*. Altoona, PA: Author, 1991. 2 vols.

U.S. Federal Population Census Schedules. 1900, T623, Microfilm Reel Nos. 1226-1234.

U.S. Federal Population Census Schedules. 1900, Soundex. T1064, 36 Microfilm Reels.

1910

Guerrero, John. *Census Information Concerning Dakota and North Dakota Black Residents as Found in the United States Census Reports of 1870, 1880, 1885, 1900, 1910 and 1920*. Bismarck, ND: University of Mary Press, 1994. 231p.

U.S. Federal Population Census Schedules. 1910, T624, Microfilm Reel Nos. 1138-1149. (No Soundex/ Miracode Index was prepared by the Government for this State).

1920

Guerrero, John. *Census Information Concerning Dakota and North Dakota Black Residents as Found in the United States Census Reports of 1870, 1880, 1885, 1900, 1910 and 1920*. Bismarck, ND: University of Mary Press, 1994. 231p.

U.S. Federal Population Census Schedules. 1920, T625, Microfilm Reel Nos. 1330-1343.

U.S. Federal Population Census Schedules. 1920, Soundex. M1580, 48 Microfilm Reels.

Barnes County
1885

Skjei, Jane. *The Dakota Territory 1885 Census, Barnes County Index*. Fargo, ND: North Dakota Institute for Regional Studies, North Dakota State University Libraries, 1994. 146p.

Benson County
1885

Index, Dakota Territory Index, Benson County. Bismarck, ND: Bismarck Mandan Historical and Genealogical Society, 1996. 26p.

Billings County
1885

Index, Dakota Territory 1885 Census, Billings County. Bismarck, ND: Bismarck Mandan Historical and Genealogical Society, 1996. 13p.

1900

Index of the 1900 Federal Census of Billings County, North Dakota. Horace, ND: Times Passages, 1998. 14p.

Burleigh County
1885

Index, Dakota Territory 1885 Census, Burleigh County. Bismarck, ND: Bismarck Mandan Historical and Genealogical Society, 1995. 128p.

Cass County
1885
Skjei, Jane, and Renee Well. *The Dakota Territory 1885 Census, Cass County Index*. Fargo, ND: North Dakota Institute for Regional Studies, North Dakota State University Libraries, 1991. 389p.

Dickey County
1885
Index, Dakota Territory Index, Dickey County. Bismarck, ND: Bismarck Mandan Historical and Genealogical Society, 1996. 58p.

Emmons County
1885
Index, Dakota Territory 1885 Census, Emmons County. Bismarck, ND: Bismarck Mandan Historical and Genealogical Society, 1995. 25p.
1900
Index of the 1900 Federal Census of Emmons County, North Dakota. Horace, ND: Times Passages, 1998. 60p.
Spurgin, Sandy Braun. *Emmons County, North Dakota, 1900 Census*. Decorah, IA: Anundsen, 1983. 331p.

Fargo
1885
Skjei, Jane, and Renee Well. *The Dakota Territory 1885 Census, Fargo Index*. Fargo, ND: North Dakota Institute for Regional Studies, North Dakota State University Libraries, 1991. 220p.

Griggs County
1885
Skjei, Jane. *The Dakota Territory, 1885 Census, Steele and Griggs Counties Index*. Fargo, ND: North Dakota Institute for Regional Studies, North Dakota State University Libraries, 1995. 136p.

Kidder County
1885
Index, Dakota Territory 1885 Census, Kidder County. Bismarck, ND: Bismarck Mandan Historical and Genealogical Society, 1995. 29p.

La Moure County
1885
Index, Dakota Territory Index, La Moure County. Bismarck, ND: Bismarck Mandan Historical and Genealogical Society, 1996. 35p.

Logan County
1885
Index, Dakota Territory 1885 Census, Logan County. Bismarck, ND: Bismarck Mandan Historical and Genealogical Society, 1996. 6p.
1900
Index of the 1900 Federal Census of Logan County, North Dakota. Horace, ND: Time Passages, 1998. 23p.

McLean County
1885
Index, Dakota Territory 1885 Census, McLean County. Bismarck, ND: Bismarck Mandan Historical and Genealogical Society, 1996. 16p.

McIntosh County
1910
Ketterling, LaRose. *1910 Federal Census, McIntosh County, North Dakota, Extraction*. Kansas City, MO: Kermit B. Karns, 1996. 303p.

Morton County
1885
Index, Dakota Territory 1885 Census, Morton County. Bismarck, ND: Bismarck Mandan Historical and Genealogical Society, 1996. 97p.

Nelson County
1885
Skjei, Jane. *The Dakota Territory, 1885 Census, Nelson and Ramsey Counties Index*. Fargo, ND: North Dakota Institute for Regional Studies, North Dakota State University Libraries, 1995. 157p.

Oliver County
1900
Index of the 1900 Federal Census of Oliver County, North Dakota. Horace, ND: Times Passages, 1998. 14p.

Ramsey County
1885
Skjei, Jane. *The Dakota Territory, 1885 Census, Nelson and Ramsey Counties Index*. Fargo, ND: North Dakota Institute for Regional Studies, North Dakota State University Libraries, 1995. 157p.

Richland County
1885
Skjei, Jane. *The Dakota Territory 1885 Census, Richland County Index*. Fargo, ND: North Dakota Institute for Regional Studies, North Dakota State University Libraries, 1993. 216p.

Rolette County
1885
Index, Dakota Territory Index, Rolette County. Bismarck, ND: Bismarck Mandan Historical and Genealogical Society, 1996. 36p.
1900
Quiring, Mary Ann, and Lily B. Zwolle. *1900 Federal Census and Index of Turtle Mountain Indian Reservation, Rolette County, North Dakota*. Authors, 1984. 278p.

Slope County
1920
USGenWeb Census Project. North Dakota, 1920 Slope County.
ftp://ftp.rootsweb.com/pub/census/nd/slope/1920/

Stark County
1885
Index, Dakota Territory Index, Stark County. Bismarck, ND: Bismarck Mandan Historical and Genealogical Society, 1996. 29p.

Steele County
1885
Skjei, Jane. *The Dakota Territory, 1885 Census, Steele and Griggs Counties Index*. Fargo, ND: North Dakota Institute for Regional Studies, North Dakota State University Libraries, 1995. 136p.

Stutsman County
1900
Barron, George L. *Index to 1900 U.S. Census for Stutsman County, North Dakota, Taken from T623 Roll Number 1232*. Jamestown, ND: Dickey Public Library, 1999. 217p.

Traill County
1885
Skjei, Jane. *The Dakota Territory, 1885 Census, Traill County Index*. Fargo, ND: North Dakota Institute for Regional Studies, North Dakota State University Libraries, 1992. 211p.

Ohio

1790
Jackson, Ronald Vern. *Ohio Census Index, Online Edition*. Orem, UT: Ancestry.com, Inc., 1999.
http://www.ancestry.com
_____. *First Census of the United States, 1790, Ohio North West Territorial Census Index*. North Salt Lake City, UT: Accelerated Indexing Systems, 1984. 79p.

1800
Jackson, Ronald Vern. *Ohio Census Index, Online Edition*. Orem, UT: Ancestry.com, Inc., 1999.
http://www.ancestry.com
_____. *Ohio 1800 Census Index*. North Salt Lake City, UT: Accelerated Indexing Systems International, 1986. 97p.

1820
1820 Federal Population Census, Ohio, Index. Columbus, OH: Ohio Library Foundation, 1964. 831p.
_____. Bountiful, UT: Precision Indexing, 1994, 1997. 585p.
Jackson, Ronald Vern. *Ohio Census Index, Online Edition*. Orem, UT: Ancestry.com, Inc., 1999.
http://www.ancestry.com
_____, and Gary Ronald Teeples. *Ohio 1820 Census Index*. Bountiful, UT: Accelerated Indexing Systems, 1977, 1997. 222p.
U.S. Federal Population Census Schedules. 1820, M33, Microfilm Reel Nos. 86-95.
Whisler, Jean Dougherty. *A Cross Reference for the Names Dougherty, Daugherty and Variant Spellings in the Index to the Federal Census for the Years 1820, 1830, 1840 for the State of Ohio*. Seattle, WA: Author, 1973. 35p.

1830
Census Index: U.S. Selected States/Counties, 1830. Family Archive CD 315. Novato, CA: Broderbund Software. CD-ROM.
1830-1839 U.S. Census Indexes, Mid-Atlantic, South, Mid-West. Orem, UT: Automated Archives, 1993. CD-ROM.
Jackson, Ronald Vern. *Ohio Census Index, Online Edition*. Orem, UT: Ancestry.com, Inc., 1999.
http://www.ancestry.com
_____, and Gary Ronald Teeples. *Ohio 1830 Census Index*. Bountiful, UT: Accelerated Indexing Systems, 1976. 400p.
Ohio Family Historians. *1830 Federal Population Census, Ohio, Index*. Columbus, OH: Ohio Library Foundation, 1964, 1976. 2 vols.
U.S. Federal Population Census Schedules. 1830, M19, Microfilm Reel Nos. 126-142.
Whisler, Jean Dougherty. *A Cross Reference for the Names Dougherty, Daugherty and Variant Spellings in the Index to the Federal Census for the Years 1820, 1830, 1840 for the State of Ohio*. Seattle, WA: Author, 1973. 35p.

1840

Census Index: U.S. Selected States/Counties, 1840. Family Archive CD 316. Novato, CA: Broderbund Software. CD-ROM.

Coffman, Mrs. M. F. *Census Records for Yoder Families, 1840, Pennsylvania and Ohio, from Microfilm at the National Archives.* Malvern, PA: Author, 1986. 18p.

_____. *Census Records for Yoder Family All Spellings, from Years 1790, 1800, 1810, 1820 and 1830, Pennsylvania. Taken from Printed Texts and Microfilm at the National Archives.* Malvern, PA: Author, 1985. 63p.

1840 United States Census Index, Mid-West, Great Lakes. Orem, UT: Automated Archives, 1994. CD-ROM.

Jackson, Ronald Vern. *Ohio Census Index, Online Edition.* Orem, UT: Ancestry.com, Inc., 1999. **http://www.ancestry.com**

_____, and Gary Ronald Teeples. *Ohio 1840 Census Index.* Bountiful, UT: Accelerated Indexing Systems, 1978, 1981. 600p.

U.S. Federal Population Census Schedules. 1840, M704, Microfilm Reel Nos. 375-434.

Whisler, Jean Dougherty. *A Cross Reference for the Names Dougherty, Daugherty and Variant Spellings in the Index to the Federal Census for the Years 1820, 1830, 1840 for the State of Ohio.* Seattle, WA: Author, 1973. 35p.

Wilkens, Cleo Goff, and F. Howard Wilkens. *Index to 1840 Federal Population Census of Ohio.* Ft. Wayne, IN: Author, 1969, 1975. Unpgd.

1850

Census Index: U.S. Selected States/Counties, 1850. Family Archive CD 317. Novato, CA: Broderbund Software. CD-ROM.

Corley, Betty J. *Index, Yeoman(s), Yeaman(s), Youman(s), U.S. Census Index of Ohio and Indiana, 1850, 1860, 1880, 1900, 1910.* Hyrum, UT: Author, 1989. 15p.

Jackson, Ronald Vern. *Mortality Schedules Index, Online Edition.* Orem, UT: Ancestry.com, Inc., 1999. **http://www.ancestry.com**

_____. *Ohio Census Index, Online Edition.* Orem, UT: Ancestry.com, Inc., 1999. **http://www.ancestry.com**

_____. *Ohio 1850 Census Index.* Bountiful, UT: Accelerated Indexing Systems, 1978. 2vols.

_____. *Ohio 1850 Mortality Census Index.* North Salt Lake City, UT: Accelerated Indexing Systems International, 1979. 326p.

Harshman, Lida Flynt. *Index to the 1850 Federal Population Census of Ohio.* Mineral Ridge, OH: Ohio Family Historians, 1972. 1,098p.

Ohioans in the California Census of 1850. Southern California Chapter, OGS, 1988. 88p.

U.S. Census Index Series, Indiana, Ohio, 1850. Orem, UT: Automated Archives, 1992. CD-ROM.

U.S. Federal Population Census Schedules. 1850, M432, Microfilm Reel Nos. 657-741.

1860

Corley, Betty J. *Index, Yeoman(s), Yeaman(s), Youman(s), U.S. Census Index of Ohio and Indiana, 1850, 1860, 1880, 1900, 1910.* Hyrum, UT: Author, 1989. 15p.

Harshman, Lida Flint. *Index to the 1860 Federal Population Census of Ohio.* Mineral Ridge, OH: Author, 1979. 2 vols.

Jackson, Ronald Vern. *Ohio Census Index, Online Edition.* Orem, UT: Ancestry.com, Inc., 1999. **http://www.ancestry.com**

_____, and Gary Ronald Teeples. *Ohio Northwest 1860 Federal Census Index.* North Salt Lake City, UT: Accelerated Indexing Systems International, 1990. 580p.

_____, and Gary Ronald Teeples. *Ohio South West 1860 Federal Census Index.* North Salt Lake City, UT: Accelerated Indexing Systems International, 1988. 782p.

U.S. Federal Population Census Schedules. 1860, M653, Microfilm Reel Nos. 928-1054.

1870

Jackson, Ronald Vern. *Ohio Census Index, Online Edition.* Orem, UT: Ancestry.com, Inc., 1999. **http://www.ancestry.com**

Steuart, Raeone Christensen. *Ohio 1870 Census Index*. Bountiful, UT: Heritage Quest, 1999. 6 vols. CD-ROM.
U.S. Federal Population Census Schedules. 1870, M593, Microfilm Reel Nos. 1167-1284.

1875
Darby, Earl Gilbert. *People Either Born in Ohio or Coming from Ohio to Kansas as Enumerated in the Riley County, Kansas, 1875 State Census*. Manhattan, KS: Author, 1970. 23p.

1880
Census Index: Ohio, 1880. Family Archive CD 20. Novato, CA: Broderbund Software. CD-ROM.
Census Index: U.S. Selected States/Counties, 1880. Family Archive CD 320. Novato, CA: Broderbund Software. CD-ROM.
Corley, Betty J. *Index, Yeoman(s), Yeaman(s), Youman(s), U.S. Census Index of Ohio and Indiana, 1850, 1860, 1880, 1900, 1910*. Hyrum, UT: Author, 1989. 15p.
Ohio 1880 Census Index. Bountiful, UT: Precision Indexing, 1991. 3 vols.
Darby, Earl Gilbert. *People Born in Ohio Who Were Enumerated in the 1880 Riley County, Kansas Census*. Manhattan, KS: Author, 1970. 35p.
Ohio Genealogical Society. *Ohio 1880 Census Index*. Bountiful, UT: Precision Indexing, 1991. 3 vols.
_____. *Ohio 1880 Census Index*. Orem, UT: Automated Archives, 1991. CD-ROM
U.S. Federal Population Census Schedules. 1880, T9, Microfilm Reel Nos. 989-1079.
U.S. Federal Population Census Schedules. 1880, Soundex. T767, 143 Microfilm Reels.

1890
Adams, Marilyn. *Index to Civil War Veterans and Widows in Southern Ohio, 1890, Federal Census, Vol. 1*. Columbus, OH: Franklin County Genealogical Society, 1986. 84p.
Jackson, Ronald Vern. *Ohio Census Index, Online Edition (Veterans Schedules)*. Orem, UT: Ancestry.com, Inc., 1999.
http://www.ancestry.com
U.S. Federal Population Census Schedules. 1890, M407, Microfilm Reel No. 3.
U.S. Federal Population Census Schedules. 1890, Index. M496, 2 Microfilm Reels.
U.S. Federal Population Census Schedules, Special Schedule, Enumerating Union Veterans and Widows of Union Veterans of the Civil War. 1890, M123, Microfilm Reel Nos. 60-75.

1900
Corley, Betty J. *Index, Yeoman(s), Yeaman(s), Youman(s), U.S. Census Index of Ohio and Indiana, 1850, 1860, 1880, 1900, 1910*. Hyrum, UT: Author, 1989. 15p.
U.S. Federal Population Census Schedules. 1900, T623, Microfilm Reel Nos. 1235-1334.
U.S. Federal Population Census Schedules. 1900, Soundex. T1065, 395 Microfilm Reels.

1910
Corley, Betty J. *Index, Yeoman(s), Yeaman(s), Youman(s), U.S. Census Index of Ohio and Indiana, 1850, 1860, 1880, 1900, 1910*. Hyrum, UT: Author, 1989. 15p.
U.S. Federal Population Census Schedules. 1910, T624, Microfilm Reel Nos. 1150-1241.
U.S. Federal Population Census Schedules. 1910, Miracode Index. T1272, 418 Microfilm Reels.

1920
U.S. Federal Population Census Schedules. 1920, T625, Microfilm Reel Nos. 1344-1450.
U.S. Federal Population Census Schedules. 1920, Soundex. M1581, 476 Microfilm Reels.

Adams County
1880
Slaughter, Raymond D. *Index 1880 Census of Adams County, Ohio*. Columbus, OH: Author, 1985. 22p.

1900
Slaughter, Raymond D. *Index 1900 Census of Adams County, Ohio*. Columbus, OH: Author, 1985. 24p.

Allen County
1830
Marbaugh, Elodee Nye. *The 1820 Federal Census of Darke & Mercer Counties, Ohio, the 1830 Federal Census of Mercer, Van Wert & Allen Counties, Ohio, the 1840 Federal Census of Van Wert County, Ohio*. Willshire, OH: Author, 1990. 156p.
1840
Leis, Maxine Gossett. *1840 Census, Allen County, Ohio*. Lima, OH: First Families of Allen County, Ohio, 1996. 40, 13p.

Ashland County
1880
Henney, Mary Jane Armstrong. *1880 Ashland County Census Index*. Mansfield, OH: OGS, Ashland County Chapter, 1986. 45p.

Ashtabula County
1820
Scott, Mildred Thompson. *1820 Census Index, Ashtabula County, Ohio*. Jefferson, OH: Ashtabula County Genealogical Society, 1979. 14p.
1870
Index of Names Contained in Census Returns of Ashtabula County, Ohio for 1870. Cleveland, OH: Western Reserve Historical Society, 1937. 2 vols.

Athens County
1820
Whiteman, Jane. *1820 Athens County, Ohio Census, Featuring an Every Name Index and Genealogical Research Notes*. Stuttgart, AR: Author, 1990. 57p.
1830
Schumacher, Beverly. *Index to the 1830 Census, Athens County, Ohio*. Athens, OH: Athens County Historical Society, 1983. 14p.
Whiteman, Jane. *1830 Athens County, Ohio Census, Featuring an Every Name Index and Genealogical Research Notes*. Stuttgart, AR: Author, 1990. 84p.
1840
Snyder, Altha. *Athens County, Ohio Index to the 1840 Federal Census*. Athens, OH: Athens County Historical Society & Museum; Athens County Genealogical Chapter, O.G.S., 1997. 32p.
1850
Whiteman, Jane. *1850 Athens County, Ohio Census, Begun July 15, 1850 by J.W. Bayard, Ass't. Marshal, Completed Oct. 17, 1850 by Lemuel Brown, Ass't. Marshal*. Dresden, AR: Author, 1978.; 1984. 227p.
_____. *Index to Wives' Maiden Names, 1850 Athens County, Ohio Census*. Oklahoma City, OK: Author, 1982. 41p.
1870
Schumacher, Beverly, and Marvin Fletcher. *Athens County, Ohio, Index to the 1870 Federal Census*. Athens, OH: Athens County Historical Society & Museum, 1984. 69p.
1880
Schumacher, Beverly, and Marvin Fletcher. *Athens County, Ohio, Index to the 1880 Federal Census*. Athens, OH: Athens County Historical Society & Museum, 1984. 85p.
1900
Davis, Mary Allen. *Athens County, Ohio, Index to the 1900 Federal Census*. Athens, OH: Athens County Historical Society & Museum, 1988. 95p.

1920

Athens County, Ohio, Index to the 1920 Federal Census. Athens, OH: Athens County Historical Society & Museum; Athens County Genealogical Chapter, O.G.S., 1997. 72p.

Auglaize County
1870

Werner, Betty Newland. *Index to 1870 U.S. Census, Auglaize County, Ohio*. LaPorte, IN: Author, 1987. 50p.

Belmont County
1890

Kilgallen, Marian Kowalski. *Index to Belmont County, Ohio 1890 Census of Veterans and Widows*. Boston, MA: Author, 1985. 25p.

1900

Johnson, Charles. *Index to 1900 Census, Belmont County, Ohio*. Unpgd.

Brown County
1820

The 1820 Head of Household Census Index of Brown County, Ohio. Georgetown, OH: Brown County Genealogical Society, 1989. 19p.

1870

Grady, Evie Ruth Hill. *Blacks Living in Brown County, Ohio, Federal Census, 1870*. Cincinnati, OH: Author, 1982. 38p.

1880

Grady, Evie Ruth Hill. *Negroes Living in Brown County, Ohio, 1880 Census, 1880*. Cincinnati, OH: Author, 1983. 44p.

1900

Grady, Evie Ruth Hill. *Negroes Living in Brown County, Ohio, 1900 Federal Census*. Cincinnati, OH: Author, 1983. 50p.

Butler County
1850

Gilbert, Audrey. *Butler County, Ohio 1850 Census*. Utica, KY: McDowell Publications, 1982. 278p.

1870

Grady, Evie Ruth Hill. *Blacks Living in Butler County, Ohio, Federal Census, 1870*. Cincinnati, OH: Author, 1982. 16p.

Shilt, Rose, and Audrey Gilbert. *1870 Butler County, Ohio Census*. Brookville, OH: Authors, 1997. 485p.

Carroll County
1880

Sell, Janet, and Shirley Anderson. *1880 Census Index, Carroll County, Ohio*. Carrollton, OH: Carroll County Genealogical Society, 1986. 46p.

Champaign County
1850

USGenWeb Census Project. Ohio, 1850 Champaign County.
ftp://ftp.rootsweb.com/pub/census/oh/champaign/1850/

Clark County
1820

Clark County, Ohio 1820 Census Index. Springfield, OH: Clark County Genealogical Society, 1995. 19p.

1870

Chaffee, Linda. *1870 Clark County, Ohio Census Index*. Beavercreek, OH: Author, 1998. 101p.

Clermont County
1820

Baer, Mabel Van Dyke. *Index Names of Heads of Families, Fourth Census, 1820 Clermont County, Ohio in the National Archives, Washington, DC*. Author, 1953. 46p.

1900

Grady, Evie Ruth Hill. *Blacks Living in Clermont County, Ohio, Federal Census, 1900*. Cincinnati, OH: Author, 1983. 80p.

Cleveland (Cuyahoga County)
1870

Jackson, Ronald Vern. *Cleveland, Ohio 1870 Federal Census Index*. Salt Lake City, UT: Accelerated Indexing Systems International, 1989. 624p.

Clinton County
1870, 1880

Williams, Josephine M. *Clinton County, Ohio, Index to the Census for the Years 1870, 1880, 1900, 1910*. Wilmington, OH: Clinton County Genealogical Society, 1990. 257p.

1890

U.S. Federal Population Census Schedules. 1890, M407, Microfilm Reel No. 3.

U.S. Federal Population Census Schedules. 1890, Index. M496, 2 Microfilm Reels.

1900

Slaughter, Raymond D. *Index, 1900 Census of Clinton County, Ohio*. Columbus, OH: Author, 1982. 32p.

Williams, Josephine M. *Clinton County, Ohio, Index to the Census for the Years 1870, 1880, 1900, 1910*. Wilmington, OH: Clinton County Genealogical Society, 1990. 257p.

1910

Williams, Josephine M. *Clinton County, Ohio, Index to the Census for the Years 1870, 1880, 1900, 1910*. Wilmington, OH: Clinton County Genealogical Society, 1990. 257p.

1920

1920 Census Index, Clinton County, Ohio. Wilmington, OH: Clinton County Genealogical Society, 1994. 91p.

Columbiana County
1820

Ross, Helen Pate. *Columbiana County, Ohio, 1820 Federal Census*. Sturtevant, WI: Author. 41p.

1850

USGenWeb Census Project. Ohio, 1850 Columbiana County.

ftp://ftp.rootsweb.com/pub/census/oh/columbiana/1850/

1860

Bell, Carol Willsey. *Index to 1860 Census, Columbiana County, Ohio, (Heads of Families)*. Youngstown, OH: Author, 1972. 55p.

1870

Bell, Carol Willsey. *Index to 1870 Census, Columbiana County, Ohio, (Heads of Families)*. Youngstown, OH: Author, 1980. 89p.

1880

Bell, Carol Willsey. *Columbiana County, Ohio, 1880 Census Index*. Youngstown, OH: Author, 1987. 39p.

Columbus (Franklin County)
1870

Jackson, Ronald Vern. *Columbus and Dayton, Ohio 1870 Federal Census Index*. Salt Lake City, UT: Accelerated Indexing Systems International, 1989. 576p.

Coshocton County
1830
1830 Census Index, Coshocton County, Ohio. Coshocton, OH: Coshocton County Chapter, Ohio Genealogical Society, 1985. 18p.
1870
Kinkade, Marjorie Cochran. *1870 Census Index, Coshocton County, Ohio*. Coshocton, OH: Coshocton County Genealogical Society, 1996. 211p.

Crawford County
1850
1850 Census of Crawford County, Ohio. Galion, OH: Crawford County Chapter, OGS, 1992. 532p.
1860
1860 Census of Crawford County, Ohio. Galion, OH: Crawford County Chapter, OGS. 407p.
1870
1870 Census of Crawford County, Ohio. Galion, OH: Crawford County Chapter, OGS, 1995. 435p.
1880
1880 Census of Crawford County, Ohio. Galion, OH: Crawford County Chapter, OGS. 421p.

Cuyahoga County
1870
Jackson, Ronald Vern. *Federal Census Index, Cuyahoga County, Ohio, 1870, with City of Cleveland*. West Jordan, UT: Genealogical Services, 1990, 1997. 623p.

Darke County
1820
Marbaugh, Elodee Nye. *The 1820 Federal Census of Darke & Mercer Counties, Ohio, the 1830 Federal Census of Mercer, Van Wert & Allen Counties, Ohio, the 1840 Federal Census of Van Wert County, Ohio*. Willshire, OH: Author, 1990. 156p.
1860
Shilt, Rose, and Audrey Gilbert. *1860 Darke County, Ohio Census*. Utica, KY: McDowell Publications, 1983. 241p.
1870
Shilt, Rose, and Audrey Gilbert. *1870 Darke County, Ohio Census*. Owensboro, KY: McDowell Publications, 1984. 393p.
1880
Shilt, Rose, and Audrey Gilbert. *1880 Darke County, Ohio Census*. Owensboro, KY: McDowell Publications, 1984. 385p.
1900
Shilt, Rose, and Audrey Gilbert. *1900 Darke County, Ohio Census*. Owensboro, KY: McDowell Publications, 1982. 425p.
1910
Shilt, Rose, and Audrey Gilbert. *1910 Darke County, Ohio Census*. Utica, KY: McDowell Publications, 1985. 441p.
1920
Shilt, Rose, and Audrey Gilbert. *1920 Darke County, Ohio Census*. Utica, KY: McDowell Publications, 1994. 460p.

Dayton (Montgomery County)
1860
Gilbert, Audrey. *1860 Census, Dayton, Ohio*. West Alexandria, OH: Author, 1992. 229p.
1870
Jackson, Ronald Vern. *Columbus and Dayton, Ohio 1870 Federal Census Index*. Salt Lake City, UT: Accelerated Indexing Systems International, 1989. 576p.

Delaware County
1870
Stilwell, Jenora. *Every Name Index to Federal Census for 1870, Delaware County, Ohio*. Delaware, OH: Delaware County Genealogical Society; Delaware County Historical Society, 1992. 2 vols.
1880
Cryder, Marilyn M., and George R. Cryder. *Index, "Heads of Family" from 1880 Census, Delaware County, Ohio*. Delaware, OH: Delaware County Historical Society; Delaware County Genealogical Society, 1983. 75p.
———. ———. Delaware, OH: Author, 1989. 122p.

Erie County
1870
Wunderley, Katharyn Huss. *1870 Entire Text of Introduction, U.S. Census Index for Erie County, Ohio*. Sandusky, OH: Erie County Chapter, OGS, 1991. 369p.

Fairfield County
1820
1820 Federal Population Census, Fairfield County, Ohio, Index. Columbus, OH: Ohio Library Foundation, 1964. Unpgd.
1870
Index to 1870 U.S. Census, Fairfield County, Ohio. Lancaster, OH: Fairfield County Chapter, OGS, 1982. 81p.
1880
Index to 1880 U.S. Census, Fairfield County, Ohio. Lancaster, OH: Fairfield County Chapter, OGS, 1984. 93p.
1900
Slaughter, Raymond D. *Index to the 1900 Census, Fairfield County, Ohio*. Columbus, OH: OGS, Fairfield County Chapter, 1982. 47p.
1910
Brown, Betty. *Index to the 1910 Census, Fairfield County, Ohio*. Lancaster, OH: Fairfield County Chapter, OGS, 1999. 120p.

Fayette County
1870
Fayette County, Ohio 1870 Census Index. Washington Court House, OH: Fayette County Genealogical Society, 1989. 57p.
Werner, Betty Newland. *Index to 1870 U.S. Census, Fayette County, Ohio*. LaPorte, IN: Author, 1987. 49p.

Fleming County
1880
Grady, Evie Ruth Hill. *Blacks Living in Fleming County, Ohio, Federal Census, 1880*. Cincinnati, OH: Author, 1983. 34p.
1900
Grady, Evie Ruth Hill. *Blacks Living in Fleming County, Ohio, Federal Census, 1900*. Cincinnati, OH: Author, 1983. 34p.

Franklin County
1830
Piton, Mary. *The 1830 U.S. Census of Franklin County, Ohio*. Columbus, OH: Franklin County Genealogical Society, 1984. 38p.

1870

Every Name Index to the 1870 Federal Population Census, Franklin County, Ohio. Columbus, OH: Franklin County Genealogical Society, 1999. 239p.

Jackson, Ronald Vern. *Federal Census Index Ohio 1870 Franklin & Montgomery Counties, with Cities of Columbus and Dayton.* West Jordan, UT: Genealogical Services, 1997. 567p.

1880

Yantis, Richard P., and Jane M. Yantis. *Blendon Township, Ohio 1880 Census and Genealogical Data, Including Westerville and Central College (Amalthea).* Columbus, OH: Franklin County Genealogical Society, 1987. 74p.

1910

Yantis, Richard P., and Jane M. Yantis. *Westerville, Ohio, 1910 Census and Genealogical Data.* Westerville, OH: Westerville Historical Society, 1985. 104p.

Fulton County
1850

Broglin, Jana Sloan. *Index to the 1850 Population and Agricultural Census, Fulton County, Ohio.* Fulton Chapter, OGS, 1993. 51p.

1860

Broglin, Jana Sloan. *Index to the 1860 Population Census, Fulton County, Ohio.* Fulton Chapter, OGS, 1994. 58p.

Geitgey, Mrs. Frances Harrsen. *Index to 1860 Federal Census of Fulton County, Ohio.* Culver City, CA: Author. 36p.

1870

Broglin, Jana Sloan. *Index to the 1870 Population and Agricultural Census, Fulton County, Ohio.* Fulton Chapter, OGS, 1993. 75p.

1880

Broglin, Jana Sloan. *Index to the 1880 Population and Agricultural Census, Fulton County, Ohio.* Decorah, IA: Anundsen, 1988. 97p.

1900

Broglin, Jana Sloan. *Index to the 1900 Population Census Fulton County, Ohio.* Fulton County, OH: Fulton County Chapter, OGS, 1996. 76p.

1920

Broglin, Jana Sloan. *Index to the 1920 Population Census Fulton County, Ohio.* Fulton County, OH: Fulton County Chapter, OGS, 1995. 101p.

Gallia County
1800-1820

Jones, Dennis R. *Gallia County, Ohio Residents, 1800-1825, Taken from Chattel Tax Lists, Land Tax Lists, Wolf Scalp Lists, 1800 & 1820 Census.* Baltimore, MD: Gateway Press, 1997. 291p.

1820

Pierce, Homer C. *1820 Census of Gallia County, Ohio.* Minerva, OH: Pierce Enterprises, 1976. 53p.

1830

Pierce, Homer C. *1830 Census of Gallia County, Ohio.* Minerva, OH: Pierce Enterprises, 1976. 80p.

1840

Pierce, Homer C. *1840 Census of Gallia County, Ohio.* Minerva, OH: Pierce Enterprises, 1976. 106p.

1870

Davis, Douglas V. *Index of Gallia County, Ohio 1870 Census.* Gallipolis, OH: OGS, Gallia County Chapter, 1987. 42p.

1880

Index of Gallia County, Ohio 1880 Census. Gallipolis, OH: OGS, Gallia County Chapter, 1989. 54p.

1900

Evans, Henrietta C., and Mary P. Wood. *Index of Gallia County, Ohio, 1900 Census.* Gallipolis, OH: Author, 1981. 40p.

Geauga County
1820

Ross, Helen Pate. *Geauga County, Ohio, 1820 Federal Census*. Sturtevant, WI: Author. 22p.

Greene County
1820

Ross, Helen Pate. *Green County, Ohio, 1820 Federal Census*. Sturtevant, WI: Author. 31p.

1830

USGenWeb Census Project. Ohio, 1830 Greene County.

ftp://ftp.rootsweb.com/pub/census/oh/greene/1830/

1870

Overton, Julie M. *Greene County, Ohio 1870 Census Index*. Xenia, OH: OGS, Greene County Chapter, 1991. 56p.

1880

Greene County, Ohio 1880 Census Index. Xenia, OH: OGS, Greene County Chapter, 1994. 78p.

1920

Index to the 1920 Census, Greene County, Ohio. Xenia, OH: Greene County Public Library, 1999. 3 vols.

Guernsey County
1820

Ross, Helen Pate. *Guernsey County, Ohio, 1820 Federal Census*. Sturtevant, WI: Author. 24p.

1850

Guernsey County, Ohio 1850 Federal Population Census, Roll No. 684. Cambridge, OH: Guernsey County Genealogical Society, OGS, 1991. 325p.

1880

1880 Census Index of Guernsey County, Ohio. Cambridge, OH: Guernsey County Genealogical Society, 1986. 84p.

Hamilton County
1870

Miller, Pamela, and Richard Rees. *1870 Census Index to Hamilton County, Ohio Including Cincinnati*. San Francisco, CA: Egeon Enterprises, 1988. 350p.

1890

U.S. Federal Population Census Schedules. 1890, M407, Microfilm Reel No. 3.

U.S. Federal Population Census Schedules. 1890, Index. M496, 2 Microfilm Reels.

Hancock County
1830, 1840

1830-1840 Census of Ohio, Hancock County. Findlay, OH: Hancock Chapter OGS. 48p.

1850

Hancock County, Ohio 1850 Census Index. Findlay, OH: Hancock County Chapter, OGS, 1988. 26p.

1860

Moorhead, Rex K. *Index to the 1860 Federal Population Census of Hancock County, Ohio*. Livonia, MI: Author, 1976, 1985. 35p.

1870

Moorhead, Rex K. *Index to the 1870 Federal Population Census of Hancock County, Ohio*. Livonia, MI: Author, 1976. 59p.

1880

1880 Federal Census Index, Hancock County, Ohio. Findlay, OH: Ohio Genealogical Society, Hancock County Chapter, 1993. 45p.

1900

1900 Federal Census Index, Hancock County, Ohio. Findlay, OH: Hancock County Chapter, OGS, 1993. 286p.

Hardin County
1870
Werner, Betty Newland. *Index to 1870 U.S. Census, Hardin County, Ohio*. LaPorte, IN: Author, 1986. 52p.
1880
Ramsey, Jerald. *Index to the 1880 Census of Hardin County, Ohio*. Decorah, IA: Anundsen Publishing, 1990. 73p.

Harrison County
1820
Schaar, Nancy Boothe. *Harrison County, Ohio, 1820 Census Index*. Sherrodsville, OH: Schaar Research Publications, 1996. 17p.
1830
Schaar, Nancy Boothe. *Harrison County, Ohio, 1830 Census Index*. Sherrodsville, OH: Schaar Research Services, 1996. 25p.
1840
Schaar, Nancy Boothe. *Harrison County, Ohio, 1840 Census Index*. Sherrodsville, OH: Schaar Research Services, 1998. 27p.

Highland County
1800
Breakfield, Genevieve. *Every Name Index 1800 Federal Census, Highland County, Ohio*. Hillsboro, OH: Southern Ohio Genealogical Society, 1999. 122p.
1850
1850 Census, Highland County, Ohio. Hillsboro, OH: Southern Ohio Genealogical Society, 1989. 218p.
1860
1860 Federal Census, Highland County, Ohio. Hillsboro, OH: Southern Ohio Genealogical Society, 1996. 254p.
1870
Breakfield, Genevieve. *1870 Census, Highland County, Ohio*. Hillsboro, OH: Southern Ohio Genealogical Society, 1995. 311p.
1880
Breakfield, Genevieve. *1880 Census, Highland County, Ohio*. Hillsboro, OH: Southern Ohio Genealogical Society, 1999. 122p.
1900
Breakfield, Genevieve. *Every Name Index, 1900 Federal Census, Highland County, Ohio*. Hillsboro, OH: Southern Ohio Genealogical Society, 1997. 125p.

Hocking County
1870
Index to 1870 Federal Census, Hocking County, Ohio. Logan, OH: Hocking County Chapter, OGS, 1991. 81p.
1880
Index to 1880 Federal Census, Hocking County, Ohio. Logan, OH: Hocking County Chapter, OGS, 1991. 108p.

Holmes County
1830
Holmes County, Ohio Revised Edition, 1830 Census Index with Chattel Tax Supplement. Millersburg, OH: Holmes County Genealogical Society Chapter, OGS, 1984. 13p.; 1991. 16p.
1880
1880 Holmes County Census Index. Millersburg, OH: Holmes County Public Library, 1991. 51p.

Hudson County
1850
Index to the 1850 Census of Hudson, Ohio. Hudson, OH: Hudson Genealogical Study Group, 1991. 26p.
1870
Caccamo, James F. *Index to the Federal Population Census of 1870 for Hudson, Ohio.* Hudson, OH: Hudson Library & Historical Society, 1982. 14p.
1880, 1890
Caccamo, James F. *Index to the Federal Population Census for Hudson, Ohio, 1880, to Which Has Been Appended the 1890 List of Civil War Veterans and Widows.* Hudson, OH: Hudson Library & Historical Society, 1983. 17p.

Huron County
1870
1870 Huron County, Ohio Federal Census Index. Norwalk, OH: Huron County Chapter, OGS, 1999. 213p.
Williams, Rebecca. *1870 Index of Bronson Township, Huron County Federal Census.* Author, 1990. 6p.
1880
1880 Census Index for Huron County, Ohio. Norwalk, OH: Huron County Chapter, OGS. 62p.

Jackson County
1870
Queen, Mary J. *1870 Census Index of Jackson County, Ohio.* Author, 1994. 31p.
Scott, Margaret. *1870 Jackson County, Ohio Census Index.* Columbus, OH: Author. 32p.

Jefferson County
1820
Ross, Helen Pate. *Jefferson County, Ohio, 1820 Federal Census.* Sturtevant, WI: Author. 45p.
1830
Harshman, Lida Flint. *Index 1830 Federal Census, Jefferson County, Ohio.* Mineral Ridge, OH: Author. 33p.
1870
Gill, Lance Douglas. *The 1870 Census Compilation of Steubenville and Jefferson County, Ohio.* Lordstown, OH: Author, 1987. 442p.
1890
The Eleventh Census of the United States Special Schedule Surviving Soldiers, Sailors, Marines, and Widows, etc., 1890 Veterans Census of Jefferson County, Ohio. Jefferson, OH: Jefferson County Genealogical Society, 1995, 1996. 140p.
1900
Roe, Richard. *An Every Name Index to the 1900 Census of Jefferson County, Ohio.* Steubenville, OH: Jefferson County Chapter, OGS, 1997. 423p.
1910
Roe, Richard. *Every Name Index to the 1910 Census of Jefferson County, Ohio.* Steubenville, OH: Jefferson County Chapter, OGS, 1998. 643p.
1920
Roe, Richard. *Index to Jefferson County, Ohio, 1920 Federal Census.* Steubenville, OH: Public Library of Steubenville & Jefferson County, 1998. 170p.

Knox County
1860
James, Peggie Seitz. *Knox County, Ohio, 1860 Federal Population Census Index (Heads of Families).* Munroe Falls, OH: Author, 1973. 66p.

Lake County
1840
Clark, Neva Sturgill. *State of Ohio Index 1840 Population Census for Lawrence and Lake Counties*. Welaka, FL: Author, 1976. 22p.

Lawrence County
1840
Clark, Neva Sturgill. *State of Ohio Index 1840 Population Census for Lawrence and Lake Counties*. Welaka, FL: Author, 1976. 22p.
1850
Coats, Wilma Stricklen. *1850 Census Lawrence County, Ohio*. Bicknell, IN: Author, 1985. 291p.
Lawrence County, Ohio, 1850 Federal Census. Springfield, MO: Catlett, 1985. 182p.
Schlaudt, Billee Hammond. *Surname Index, Lawrence County, Ohio, 1850 Census Record*. Houston, TX: Author. 25p.
1880
Shoemaker, Caryn R. *Lawrence County, Ohio, 1880 Census Index*. Minford, OH: Author, 1984. 97p.

Licking County
1820
Ross, Helen Pate. *Licking County, Ohio, 1820 Federal Census*. Sturtevant, WI: Author. 29p.
1830
Pheneger, Diane. *1830 Census, Hopewell Township, Licking County, Ohio*. Author, 1979. 6p.
1860
Barcus, Polly. *1860 Census of Licking County, Ohio*. Author. Unpgd.
1870
Index 1870 Federal Census Licking County, Ohio. Newark, OH: Licking County Genealogical Society, 1988. 113p.
1880
Pheneger, Diane. Index, *1880 Federal Census, Licking County, Ohio*. Newark, OH: Licking County Genealogical Society, 1982. 119p.

Logan County
1840
Moorer, James E. *1840 Census Index of Logan County, Ohio*. Bellefontaine, OH: Logan County Genealogical Society, 1995. Unpgd.
1870
Moorer, James E. *1870 Logan County, Ohio, Census*. Bellefontaine, OH: Logan County Genealogical Society, 1995. 244p.

Lorain County
1850
Index to the Census of 1850 for Lorain County, Ohio. Elyria, OH: Lorain County Historical Society, 1972. 51p.
1860
Index to the Census of 1860 for Lorain County, Ohio. Elyria, OH: Lorain County Historical Society, 1990. 102p.
1870
Index to the Census of 1870 for Lorain County, Ohio. Elyria, OH: Lorain County Chapter, OGS, 1989. 60p.
1880
Index to the Census of 1880 for Lorain County, Ohio. Elyria, OH: Lorain County Chapter, OGS, 1992. 71p.
1900
1900 Census Index of the Nine Southern Townships of Lorain County, Ohio. Wellington, OH: Wellington Genealogical Group, 1991. 71p.

Lucas County
1870
Read, Helen Hunt. *1870 Census Index to the City of Toledo in Lucas County, Ohio*. Toledo, OH: Author, 1990. 210p.

_____. *1870 Census Index to the Thirteen Townships of Lucas County Ohio, Including the City of Maumee, Excluding the City of Toledo*. Toledo, OH: Author, 1990. 174p.

Madison County
1870
Herman, Berthenia Davis. *1870 Census Index, Madison County, Ohio*. Author, 1993. 21p.

Mahoning County
1870
Nicolls, Barbara. *Mahoning County, Ohio 1870 Census Index*. New Castle, PA: Peace Makers, 1999. 279p.
1880
Simon, Margaret Miller. *Mahoning County, Ohio, 1880 Census Index*. Boardman, OH: Simon Homestead Book, 1993. 52p.

Marion County
1870
Marshall, Maxine. *1870 Census Index, Marion County, Ohio*. Marion, OH: Author, 1986. 43p.
1880
Index to the 1880 Census for Marion County, Ohio. Marion, OH: Marion Area Genealogy Society, 1983. 58p.

Medina County
1820
USGenWeb Census Project. Ohio, 1820 Medina County.
ftp://ftp.rootsweb.com/pub/census/oh/medina/1820/
1850
Vaughn, Helen, and Jesse Vaughn. *Medina County, Ohio, 1850 Federal Census Surname Index*. Medina, OH: Medina County Genealogical Society, 1988. 56p.

Meigs County
1820
Pierce, Homer C. *1820 Census of Meigs County, Ohio*. Minerva, OH: Pierce Enterprises, 1976. 52p.
USGenWeb Census Project. Ohio, 1820 Meigs County.
ftp://ftp.rootsweb.com/pub/census/oh/meigs/1820/
1830
Pierce, Homer C. *1830 Census of Meigs County, Ohio*. Minerva, OH: Pierce Enterprises, 1976. 72p.
1840
Pierce, Homer C. *1840 Census of Meigs County, Ohio*. Minerva, OH: Pierce Enterprises, 1976. 114p.
1870
Slaughter, Raymond D. *Surname Index, 1870 Census of Meigs County, Ohio*. Pomeroy, OH: Meigs County Pioneer and Historical Society, 1987, 1990. 30p.
1900
Slaughter, Raymond D. *Surname Index, 1900 Census of Meigs County, Ohio*. Pomeroy, OH: Meigs County Pioneer and Historical Society, 1990. 31p.

Mercer County
1830
Marbaugh, Elodee Nye. *The 1820 Federal Census of Darke & Mercer Counties, Ohio, the 1830 Federal Census of Mercer, Van Wert & Allen Counties, Ohio, the 1840 Federal Census of Van Wert County, Ohio*. Willshire, OH: Author, 1990. 156p.

1850

1850 Federal Census of Mercer County, Ohio Contains Name, Age, Occupation and Place of Birth for All Persons Enumerated in Mercer County in the Year 1850 Includes 1850 Mercer County Mortality Schedule. Celina, OH: Mercer County Chapter of the Ohio Genealogical Society, 1996. 127p.

1870

1870 Federal Census of Mercer County, Ohio. Celina, OH: Mercer County Chapter, OGS, 1995. 212p.

1880

1880 Census, Mercer County, Ohio. Celina, OH: OGS, Mercer County Chapter, 1985. 55p.

Miami County

1820

Ross, Helen Pate. *Miami County, Ohio, 1820 Federal Census*. Sturtevant, WI: Author. 22p.

1827

Boese, Virginia G. *1827 Quadrennial Enumeration of Adult White Males of Miami County, Ohio*. Troy, OH: Miami County Historical and Genealogical Society, 1996. 77p.

Monroe County

1820-1840

The Federal Census of Monroe County, Ohio, 1820, 1830, 1840. Woodsfield, OH: Monroe County Chapter, OGS, 1996. 125p.

Montgomery County

1820

Ross, Helen Pate. *Montgomery County, Ohio, 1820 Federal Census*. Sturtevant, WI: Author. 38p.

1850

Shilt, Rose, and Audrey Gilbert. *Montgomery County, Ohio 1850 Census*. Utica, KY: McDowell Publications, 1985. 343p.

1870

Every Name Index to the 1870 Federal Population Census, Franklin County, Ohio. Columbus, OH: Franklin County Genealogical Society, 1999. 239p.

Jackson, Ronald Vern. *Federal Census Index Ohio 1870 Franklin & Montgomery Counties, with Cities of Columbus and Dayton*. West Jordan, UT: Genealogical Services, 1997. 567p.

Shilt, Rose, and Audrey Gilbert. *Montgomery County, Ohio 1870 Census*. Utica, KY: McDowell Publications, 1986. 327p.

1880

Shilt, Rose, and Audrey Gilbert. *Montgomery County, Ohio 1880 Census*. Utica, KY: McDowell Publications, 1987. 388p.

Morgan County

1820, 1830

Morgan County, Ohio Census, 1820 & 1830. McConnelsville, OH: Morgan County Chapter, OGS, 1991. 182p.

1870

Census, 1870, Morgan County, Ohio. McConnelsville, OH: Morgan County Chapter of the OGS, 1993. 340p.

1880

Census, 1880 Morgan County, Ohio. McConnelsville, OH: Morgan County Chapter, OGS, 1995. 352p.

1900

Morgan County, Ohio, Index to the 1900 Population Census Schedules. McConnelsville, OH: Morgan County Chapter, OGS, 1986. 20p.

Slaughter, Raymond D. *Index, 1900 Census of Morgan County, Ohio*. Columbus, OH: Author, 1982. 20p.

1910

Census Index, 1910, Morgan County, Ohio. McConnelsville, OH: OGS, Morgan County Chapter, 1993. 126p.

Morrow County
1850

USGenWeb Census Project. Ohio, 1850 Morrow County.
ftp://ftp.rootsweb.com/pub/census/oh/morrow/1850/

Muskingum County
1820

Baker, Michael F. *The 1820 Federal Census for Muskingum County, Ohio.* South Zanesville, OH: Hargrove, 1988. 161p.

1870

Yinger, Hilda E., and Kenneth L. Yinger. *1870 Muskingum County, Ohio Census, Ninth Census of the United States.* Zanesville, OH: Authors, 1986. 116p.

Noble County
1850, 1860

Blake, Mrs. Lois. *Census Index, 1860 Noble County, Ohio and 1850 Index of Townships Taken to Form Noble County.* Caldwell, OH: Noble County Genealogical Society, 1986. 49, 43p.

1870, 1880

Blake, Mrs. Lois. *Census 1870 and 1880 Census Index of Noble County, Ohio.* Caldwell, OH: Noble County Genealogical Society, 1986. 55p.

Paulding County
1830-1860

Keck, Ray E. *Paulding County, Ohio, Census Index, 1830, 1840, 1850, 1860.* Paulding County, OH: Paulding County Chapter, OGS, 1996. Unpgd.

1870-1890

Keck, Ray E. *Paulding County, Ohio Census Index, 1870 & 1880, Special Census Index, 1890.* Paulding County, OH: Paulding County Chapter, OGS, 1996. Unpgd.

1900

Evett, Malcolm. *Paulding County, Ohio, 1900 Federal Census Index.* Paulding County, OH: Paulding County Chapter, OGS, 1993; 1997. Unpgd.

1910

Vitello, Pete, and Dee Vitello. *Paulding County, Ohio, 1910 Federal Census Index.* Paulding County, OH: Paulding County Chapter, OGS, 1998. 200p.

1920

Vitello, Pete, and Dee Vitello. *Paulding County, Ohio, 1920 Federal Census Index.* Paulding County, OH: Paulding County Chapter, OGS, 1997. 165p.

Perry County
1850

Census Perry County, Ohio 1850, Every Name, with Full Index. Junction City, OH: Ohio Genealogical Society, Perry County Chapter, 1998. 183p.

1870

Scott, Margaret. *1870 Perry County, Ohio, Census Index.* New Lexington, OH: Perry County Chapter, OGS, 1984. 33p.; 1989. 51p.

1900

Census Index 1900 Perry County, Ohio. Junction City, OH: Ohio Genealogical Society, Perry County Chapter, 1999. 225p.

Pickaway County

1870

Cochran, Freda M. *Jackson Township, Pickaway County, Ohio, 1870*. Circleville, OH: Author, 1989. 61p.

_____. *Muhlenberg Township, Pickaway County, Ohio, 1870*. Circleville, OH: Author, 1989. 116p.

_____. *Wayne Township, Pickaway County, Ohio, 1870*. Circleville, OH: Author, 1988. 28p.

Pike County

1870

Blaes, Karen S. *1870 Pike County Census, Alphabetized by Townships*. Author, 1987. 43p.

Scott, Ivan R., and Margaret Scott. *Census Index of Pike County, Ohio, 1870*. Columbus, OH: Authors, 1974. 38p.

Portage County

1850

Index of Names Contained in Census Returns of Portage County, Ohio for 1850. Cleveland, OH: Western Reserve Historical Society, 1933. 230p.

1870

1870 Portage County, Ohio Federal Population Census, an Every Name Index. Hudson, OH: Hudson Genealogical Study Group, 1999. 197p.

Preble County

1850

Shilt, Rose, and Anita Short. *The Federal Census, 1850 for Preble County, Ohio, Contains Names, Age, Occupation, and Place of Birth of Every Person Living In Preble County, the Year 1850*. Mansfield, OH: Ohio Genealogical Society, 1974. 195p.

1860

Gilbert, Audrey. *Preble County, Ohio 1860 Census*. Owensboro, KY: McDowell Publications, 1981. 269p.

1870

Gilbert, Audrey. *1870 Preble County, Ohio Census*. Owensboro, KY: McDowell Publications, 1982. 256p.

1880

Gilbert, Audrey. *Preble County, Ohio 1880 Census*. Owensboro, KY: McDowell Publications, 1983. 304p.

1900

Gilbert, Audrey. *Preble County, Ohio 1900 Census*. Owensboro, KY: McDowell Publications, 1980. 357p.

1910

Gilbert, Audrey. *Preble County, Ohio 1910 Census*. West Alexandria, OH: Author, 1984. 252p.

1920

Gilbert, Audrey. *Preble County, Ohio 1920 Census*. West Alexandria, OH: Author, 1993. 252p.

Putnam County

1890

Waterfield, Marjorie Featheringill. *1890 Special Veterans Census of Columbus Grove, Pleasant Township, Putnam County, Ohio, Plus 55 Photos of Civil War Veterans Taken about 1890 in or near Columbus Grove, Ohio*. Bowling Green, OH: Author, 1990. 46p.

Richland County

1870

Hidinger, Nancy Hill. *Richland County, Ohio Index to the 1870 Federal Population Census*. Mansfield, OH: Richland County Genealogical Society, 1995. 83p.

1880

Kinton, Maxine L. *1880 Federal Population Census, Richland County, Ohio Index*. Lexington, OH: Richland County Genealogical Society, 1986. 103p.

Rockbridge County

1860

Queen, Katherine J. *Index, 1860 Census of Rockbridge County, Virginia*. Columbus, OH: Author, 1986. 35p.

Ross County

1830

1830 Census of Ross County, Ohio. Chillicothe, OH: Ross County Genealogical Society, 1996. 161p.

1840

1840 Census of Ross County, Ohio. Chillicothe, OH: Ross County Genealogical Society, 1995. 221p.

1850

1850 Census of Ross County, Ohio. Chillicothe, OH: Ross County Genealogical Society, 1991. 2 vols.

1860

Cochran, Freda M. *Deerfield Township, Ross County, Ohio, 1860*. Circleville, OH: Author, 1988. Unpgd.

Sandusky County

1820

Ross, Helen Pate. *Sandusky and Union Counties, Ohio, 1820 Federal Census*. Sturtevant, WI: Author. 11p.

Smith, Kenneth B. *1820 and 1830 Sandusky County, Ohio Census Index*. Fremont, OH: Author. 14p.

1830

Smith, Kenneth B. *1820 and 1830 Sandusky County, Ohio Census Index*. Fremont, OH: Author. 14p.

1850

Smith, Kenneth B., and Sharon K. Hughes. *Sandusky County, Ohio U.S. Census Index 1850*. Fremont, OH: Sandusky County Kin Hunters, 1990. 329p.

1860

Luebke, Grace. *Index to the 1860 Federal Census of Sandusky County*. Elmore, OH: Author. Unpgd.

1870

Luebke, Grace. *Index to the 1870 Federal Census of Sandusky County*. Elmore, OH: Author. Unpgd.

Scioto County

1820

Crabtree, Rosemary. *Scioto County, Ohio 1820 Census*. Portsmouth, OH: Scioto County Chapter, OGS, 1988. 50p.

1830

1830 United States Census for Scioto County, Ohio. Portsmouth, OH: Scioto County Genealogical Society, 1996. 61p.

1870

1870 Scioto County, Ohio Federal Census Index. Portsmouth, OH: Scioto County Genealogy Society, 1979. 48p.

1880

Scott, Ivan R. *1880 Scioto County, Ohio Census Index*. Columbus, OH: Author, 1975. 73p.

Scott, Margaret. *1880 Scioto County, Ohio Census Index*. Columbus, OH: Author, 1985. 53p.

Seneca County

1830

Whiteside, Dora M. *Index to 1830 Seneca County, Ohio Census*. Tiffin, OH: Author, 1984. 37p.

1850

USGenWeb Census Project. Ohio, 1850 Seneca County. (Partial).

ftp://ftp.rootsweb.com/pub/census/oh/seneca/1850/

1870

Seneca County, Ohio 1870 Census, an Everyname Index. Tiffin, OH: Ohio Genealogical Society, Seneca County Chapter, 1999. 419p.

Shelby County
1870
Taglieber, Verna Geer. *1870 Shelby County, Ohio Census Index*. Sidney, OH: Shelby County Genealogical
    Society, 1992. 53p.
1910
Jensen, Gwyne Love. *Shelby County, Ohio, Index for the 1910 Census*. Middletown, OH: Author, 1989. 88p.

Stark County
1870
Jackson, Ronald Vern. *Federal Census Index Ohio 1870 Stark and Summit Counties, with Cities of Akron
    and Canton*. West Jordan, UT: Genealogical Services, 1997. 567p.
Wig, Clifford T., Dorothy H. Wig, and Thomas H. Wig. *1870 Census Index of Stark County, Ohio*. North
    Canton, OH: Stark County Chapter, OGS, 1988. 64p.
1880
Wig, Clifford T., Dorothy H. Wig, and Thomas H. Wig. *1880 Census Index of Stark County, Ohio*. North
    Canton, OH: Stark County Chapter, OGS, 1985. 69p.
_____. _____. *1880 Census Index of Stark County, Ohio*. North Canton, OH: Stark County Chapter, OGS,
    1985. 69p. 1988. 64p.
1890
*Special Schedules of the Eleventh Census of the United States, 1890, Schedules Enumerating Union Veterans
    and Widows of Union Veterans of the Civil War for Stark County, Ohio*. Stark County Chapter, OGS,
    1995. 90p.

Steubenville (Jefferson County)
1870
Gill, Lance Douglas. *The 1870 Census Compilation of Steubenville and Jefferson County, Ohio*. Lordstown,
    OH: Author, 1987. 442p.

Summit County
1870
Jackson, Ronald Vern. *Federal Census Index Ohio 1870 Stark and Summit Counties, with Cities of Akron
    and Canton*. West Jordan, UT: Genealogical Services, 1997. 567p.
1880
Summit County, Ohio 1880 Census Index. Akron, OH: Summit County Chapter, OGS, 1991. 90p.
1920
*Transcription and Index of 1920 Federal Population Census Summit County, Ohio for Hudson Village and
    Hudson Township*. Hudson, OH: Hudson Genealogical Study Group, 1994. 88p.

Trumbull County
1880
Ulam, Norman, and Mary Lou Keifer Ulam. *1880 Census Index of Trumbull County, Ohio*. Warren, OH:
    Trumbull County Chapter, OGS, 1991. 291p.

Tuscarawas County
1820
Libert, Ray. *1820 Census and Index, Tuscarawas County, Ohio*. New Philadelphia, OH: Tuscarawas County
    Genealogical Society, 1994. 41p. .
1830
Libert, Ray. *Index, 1830 Census, Tuscarawas County, Ohio*. New Philadelphia, OH: Tuscarawas
    County Genealogical Society, 1994. 117p.
1840
Libert, Ray. *1840 Census and Index, Tuscarawas County, Ohio*. New Philadelphia, OH: Tuscarawas County
    Genealogical Society, 1994. 192p.

1870

Libert, Ray. *1870 Census Index, Tuscarawas County, Ohio*. New Philadelphia, OH: Tuscarawas County Genealogical Society, 1993. 316p.

1880

1880 Census Index, Tuscarawas County, Ohio. New Philadelphia, OH: Tuscarawas County Genealogical Society, 1984. 69p.

Union County

1820

Ross, Helen Pate. *Sandusky and Union Counties, Ohio, 1820 Federal Census*. Sturtevant, WI: Author. 11p.

1870

Cochran, Freda M. *Union Township, Ross County, Ohio, 1870*. Circleville, OH: Author, 1988. 91p.

1870 Union County, Ohio, Census Index. Richwood, OH: Ancestrails Study Group, 1995. 106p.

Van Wert County

1830

Marbaugh, Elodee Nye. *The 1820 Federal Census of Darke & Mercer Counties, Ohio, the 1830 Federal Census of Mercer, Van Wert & Allen Counties, Ohio the 1840 Federal Census of Van Wert County, Ohio*. Willshire, OH: Author, 1990. 156p.

USGenWeb Census Project. Ohio, 1830 Van Wert County.

ftp://ftp.rootsweb.com/pub/census/oh/vanwert/1830/

1840

Marbaugh, Elodee Nye. *The 1820 Federal Census of Darke & Mercer Counties, Ohio, the 1830 Federal Census of Mercer, Van Wert & Allen Counties, Ohio the 1840 Federal Census of Van Wert County, Ohio*. Willshire, OH: Author, 1990. 156p.

1850

Marbaugh, Elodee Nye. *The 1850 Van Wert County, Ohio*. Willshire, OH: Author, 1985. 114p.

1860

Marbaugh, Elodee Nye. *The 1860 Van Wert County, Ohio*. Willshire, OH: Author. 246p.

1870

Marbaugh, Elodee Nye. *The 1870 Van Wert County, Ohio*. Willshire, OH: Author. 371p.

Vinton County

1880

Arledge, Tacy Ann. *Vinton County 1880 Index*. New Holland, OH: Author, 1983. 43p.

Washington County

1800

Jackson, Ronald Vern. *Ohio Census Index, Online Edition*. Orem, UT: Ancestry.com, Inc., 1999.

http://www.ancestry.com

Maxwell, Fay. *Index, 1800 Census, Washington County, Ohio When Northwest Territory. Index: Marriages 1791-1802, Both Males and Females Also Listed by Year; Other Vital Records*. Columbus, OH: Maxwell Publications, 1973. 21p.

1810

Jackson, Ronald Vern. *Ohio Census Index, Online Edition*. Orem, UT: Ancestry.com, Inc., 1999.

http://www.ancestry.com

1820

Sams, Catherine J. *1820 Washington County, Ohio Census*. Author, 1993. 51p.

1850

Cochran, Wes. *1850 Census of Washington County, Ohio*. Parkersburg, WV: Author, 1985. 371p.

1870

Cochran, Wes. *Washington County, Ohio, 1870 Census*. Parkersburg, WV: Author, 1988. 413p.

1880

Cochran, Wes. *Washington County, Ohio, 1880 Census*. Parkersburg, WV: Author, 1988. 547p.

Slaughter, Raymond D. *Index, 1880 Census of Washington County, Ohio*. Columbus, OH: Author, 1984. 47p.

1900

Cochran, Wes. *Washington County Ohio 1900 Census*. Parkersburg, WV: Author, 1996. 2 vols.

Slaughter, Raymond D. *Index, 1900 Census of Washington County, Ohio*. Columbus, OH: Author, 1982. 56p.

1910

Engle, Julia A. *1910 Census, Washington County, Ohio*. Author, 1998. 133p.

Wayne County

1820

Smith, Richard G. *The Federal Census of 1820, Wayne County, Ohio, Including Heads of Household*. Wooster, OH: Author. 71p.

Wipert, Bonnie, James L. Spink, and Elizabeth McCorkee. *Index to the 1820 Census of Wayne County, Ohio*. Wooster, OH: Authors, 1988. 19p.

1840

Wipert, Bonnie. *Index to the 1840 Census of Wayne County, Ohio*. Wooster, OH: Author, 1988. 51p.

1870

Vandersall, Lloyd K. *Index to Wayne County, Ohio, 1870 Census in Family Order*. Orrville, OH: Author, 1996. 64p.

1880

Smith, Richard G. *Census of 1880, Wayne County, Ohio*. Wooster, OH: Wayne County Historical Society, 1979. 323p.

1920

Vandersall, L. K. *Alphabetical Index to the Wayne County, Ohio, 1920 Census*. Orrville, OH: Author, 1998. 90p.

Williams County

1860

USGenWeb Census Project. Ohio, 1850 Williams County.

ftp://ftp.rootsweb.com/pub/census/oh/williams/1850/

1870

Gentit, Cynthia J. *Williams County, Ohio, 1870 Census and Index to Springfield Township*. Bryan, OH: Williams County Genealogical Society, Chapter OGS, 1997. 49p.

Hinkle, Cecelia Headley, and Mary Bowers Teeter. *Williams County, Ohio, 1870 Census, and Index to Northwest Township*. Bryan, OH: Williams County Genealogical Society, Chapter, OGS, 1998. 18p.

Lash, Pamela Pattison. *Williams County, Ohio 1870 Census and Index to Brady Township and the Village of West Unity*. Bryan, OH: Williams County Genealogical Society, Chapter, OGS, 1985. 26p.

_____. *Williams County, Ohio, 1870 Census and Index to Bridgewater Township*. Bryan, OH: Williams County Genealogical Society, Chapter OGS, 1987. 19p.

_____. *Williams County, Ohio, 1870 Census and Index to Center Township*. Bryan, OH: Williams County Genealogical Society, Chapter OGS. Unpgd.

_____. *Williams County, Ohio 1870 Census and Index to Florence Township*. Bryan, OH: Williams County Genealogical Society, Chapter OGS, 1988. 44p.

_____. *Williams County, Ohio, 1870 Census and Index to Jefferson Township*. Bryan, OH: Williams County Genealogical Society, Chapter OGS, 1987. 22p.

_____. *Williams County, Ohio, 1870 Census and Index to Madison Township and Village of Pioneer*. Bryan, OH: Williams County Genealogical Society, Chapter OGS, 1992. 18p.

_____. *Williams County, Ohio, 1870 Census and Index to Millcreek Township*. Bryan, OH: Williams County Genealogical Society, Chapter OGS, 1992. 13p.

Schad, Carol Sindel. *1870 St. Joseph Township, Williams County, Ohio Census*. Bryan, OH: Williams County Genealogical Society, 1997. 47p.

_____. *Williams County, Ohio, 1870 Census, and Index to Superior Township*. Bryan, OH: Williams County Genealogical Society, Chapter, OGS, 1998. 41p.

Teeter, Mary, and Ernestine Young. *Williams County Ohio, 1870 Census, Pulaski Township*. Bryan, OH: Williams County Genealogical Society, 1998. 41p.

Williams County, Ohio, 1870 Census, Springfield Township. Bryan, OH: Williams County Genealogical Society, Chapter, OGS, 1997. 55p.

1880

Schad, Carol Sindel. *Williams County Ohio, 1880 Census, St. Joseph Township*. Bryan, OH: Williams County Genealogical Society, 1998. 42p.

1900

Beck, Margaret L. *Index to 1900 Superior Township, Williams County, Ohio, Excluding Montpelier*. Churusbusco, IN: Author, 1984. 84p.

Wolfe County
1920

Bays, Carole. *1920 Wolfe County Census*. Dayton, OH: Author. 119p.

Wood County
1850

Index to 1850 U.S. Census of Wood County, Ohio. Bowling Green, OH: Wood County Chapter, OGS, 1988. 23p.

1860

Graham, James Q. *Project Heritage, Wood County, Ohio Index of the 1860 Federal Manuscript Census, Microfilm Edition*. Bowling Green, OH: Bowling Green State University, Center for Archival Collections, 1978. 441p.

1870

Index to 1870 U.S. Census of Wood County, Ohio. Bowling Green, OH: Wood County Chapter, OGS, 1985. 66p.; 1992. 51p.

1880

An Index to 1880 U.S. Census of Wood County, Ohio. Bowling Green, OH: Wood County Chapter, OGS, 1983. 105p.; 1988. 83p.

1900

Index to 1900 U.S. Census of Wood County, Ohio, Includes Heads of Households and All Other Surnames. Bowling Green, OH: Wood County Chapter, OGS, 1998. 140p.

1910

Index to 1910 U.S. Census of Wood County, Ohio, Includes Heads of Households and All Other Surnames. Bowling Green, OH: Wood County Chapter, OGS, 1998. 121p.

Wyandot County
1850

1850 Wyandot County, Ohio Federal Census Index, Microfilm Roll M432, Roll Number 741. Upper Sandusky, OH: OGS, Wyandot County Chapter, 1991. 33p.

1860

1860 Wyandot County, Ohio Federal Census Index, Microfilm Roll M653, Roll Number 1054. Upper Sandusky, OH: OGS, Wyandot County Chapter, 1991. 50p.

1870

1870 Wyandot County, Ohio Federal Census Index with 1870 Wyandot County Township Maps and Landowners (Microfilm Roll Number 1284). Upper Sandusky, OH: Wyandot County Chapter, OGS, 1988. 77p.

1880

Davis, Earl, Jr., and Jean Roszman Davis. *1880 Wyandot County Federal Census Index with List of Persons 60 Years or Older Extracted from the 1880 Census by the Daily Chief Newspaper.* Upper Sandusky, OH: Wyandot County Chapter, OGS, 1987. 69p.

1900

1900 Wyandot County, Ohio Federal Census Index, Microfilm Roll T623 Number 1334. Upper Sandusky, OH: Wyandot County Chapter, OGS, 1989. 93p.

1910

1910 Wyandot County, Ohio Federal Census Index. Upper Sandusky, OH: Wyandot County Chapter, OGS, 1989. 87p.

1920

1920 Wyandot County, Ohio Federal Census Index, Microfilm Roll T625, Roll Number 1449. Upper Sandusky, OH: Wyandot Tracers, 1993. 65p.

Oklahoma

Campbell's Abstract of Creek Freedman Census Cards and Index. Muskogee, OK: Phoenix Job Printing Co., 1915. 223p.

Expanded Index of the Peoria, Census Annuity Rolls and Administrations, 1874-1881, with Undated Material, Quapaw Agency, Indian Territory. Cullman, AL: Gregath Publishing. 32p.

Expanded Index of the Seneca, Census Annuity Rolls and List of Guardians and Administrators, December 30, 1873 - October 3, 1902, Quapaw Agency, Census. Cullman, AL: Gregath Publishing. 22p.

Koplowitz, Bradford S. *The Kaw Indian Census and Allotments.* Bowie, MD: Heritage Books, 1996. 91p.

1857

Census Roll of the Old Settler Party of Creeks, June 1857, Index to the Old Settlers Roll. Lawton, OK: Histree, 1981. 83p.

1860

Census Index: U.S. Selected States/Counties, 1860. Family Archive CD 318. Novato, CA: Broderbund Software. CD-ROM.

Jackson, Ronald Vern. *Oklahoma Census Index, Online Edition.* Orem, UT: Ancestry.com, Inc., 1999. **http://www.ancestry.com**

_____. *Oklahoma 1860 Census Index.* Bountiful, UT: Accelerated Indexing Systems, 1984. 215p.

_____. *U.S. Territorial Census Index Oklahoma, 1860 White Settlers in Indian Territory.* Rev. ed. West Jordan, UT: Genealogical Services, 1989, 1998. 67p.

Woods, Frances Jerome. *Indian Lands West of Arkansas (Oklahoma), Population Schedule of the United State Census of 1860.* Arrow Print Co., 1964. 72p.

1890

An Index to the 1890 United States Census of Union Veterans and Their Widows, in Oklahoma and Indian Territories (Including Old Greer County) and Soldiers Stationed at Military Installations in the Territories. Also, an Index to Records from the Oklahoma Union Soldiers' Home...and the Union Soldiers' Cemetery Record. Oklahoma City, OK: Oklahoma Genealogical Society, 1970. 53p.

Garrison, Linda Norman. *1890 Federal Census of the Oklahoma and Indian Territories Enumerating Union Veterans and Widows of Union Veterans of the Civil War.* Lawton, OK: Southwest Oklahoma Genealogical Society, 1991. 60p.

Jackson, Ronald Vern. *Oklahoma Census Index, Online Edition.* Orem, UT: Ancestry.com, Inc., 1999. **http://www.ancestry.com**

_____. *1890 Oklahoma Census Index, Special Schedule of the Eleventh Census, 1890, Enumerating Union Veterans and of Union Veterans of the Civil War.* North Salt Lake City, UT: Accelerated Indexing Systems, 1984. 37p.

Rex, Joyce A. *1890 Census of the Chickasaw Nation, Indian Territory*. Purcell, OK: McClain County Historical and Genealogical Society, 1992. 3 vols.

U.S. Federal Population Census Schedules, Special Schedule, Enumerating Union Veterans and Widows of Union Veterans of the Civil War. 1890, M123, Microfilm Reel No. 76.

Veterans' Schedules: U.S. Selected States, 1890. Family Archive CD 131. Novato, CA: Broderbund Software. CD-ROM.

Wagner, Rosalie. *Cherokee Nation, 1890 Census, Index of Persons Living under Permit in the Cooweescoowee and Delaware Districts*. Vinita, OK: Northeast Oklahoma Genealogical Society, 1986. 82p.

1895

Washburn, Faye Riddles. *1895 Comanche Tribe Census and Index (Microfilm Roll 211)*. Lawton, OK: Southwest Oklahoma Genealogical Society, 1992. 59p.

1900

U.S. Federal Population Census Schedules. 1900, T623, Microfilm Reel Nos. 1335-1344; 1843-1854.

U.S. Federal Population Census Schedules. 1900, Soundex. T1066, 43 Microfilm Reels; T1082, 42 Microfilm Reels.

Young, Gloryann Hankins. *1900 Census Index, Choctaw Nation Indian Territory, Oklahoma*. Wister, OK: Author, 1981. Unpgd.

1910

U.S. Federal Population Census Schedules. 1910, T624, Microfilm Reel Nos. 1242-1277.

U.S. Federal Population Census Schedules. 1910, Miracode Index. T1273, 143 Microfilm Reels.

1920

U.S. Federal Population Census Schedules. 1920, T625, Microfilm Reel Nos. 1451-1490.

U.S. Federal Population Census Schedules. 1920, Soundex. M1582, 155 Microfilm Reels.

Beaver County
1890

Sullivan, Vicki, and Mac R. Harris. *Index to the 1890 Oklahoma Territorial Census for the Counties of Kingfisher, Payne, and Beaver*. Oklahoma City, OK: Territorial Press, 1977. 154p.

Blue County
1885

Olsen, Monty. *1885 Choctaw Census Blue County*. Calera, OK: Bryan County Heritage Association, 1996. 87p.

Britton (Oklahoma County)
1900

Oklahoma DAR. *1900 Federal Census, Oklahoma Territory, Lincoln, Spring Creek and Britton Townships*. Genealogical Records Committee Report, s2, v106. Oklahoma DAR, 1995. 109p.

Broken Arrow (Tulsa County)
1904

Wise, Donald A. *First Census (1904) of Broken Arrow, Oklahoma*. Broken Arrow, OK: Broken Arrow Genealogical Society, 1994. 28p.

1910

Apsley, Marmie, Jack McGinty, Donald A. Wise, and Jerrie Townsend. *1910 Federal Census Schedules for the Town of Broken Arrow and the Adjoining Townships of Boles, Fry, Lynn Lane and Willow Springs*. Broken Arrow, OK: Broken Arrow Genealogical Society, 1993. 146p.

Craig County
1910

Lawson, Rowena. *1910 Indian Population, Oklahoma, Craig County*. Honolulu, HI: Author, 1983. 110p.

Edmond (Oklahoma County)
1860

Meggs, James, and Marjorie Meggs. *The 1890 Territorial Census of Oklahoma, Enumeration District No. 25 & 26, Townships 13 & 14, Edmond Area, Alphabetical*. Edmond, OK: Edmond Genealogical Society, 1995. Unpgd.

Kiamitia County
1885

Olsen, Monty. *1885 Choctaw Census Kiamitia County*. Calera, OK: Bryan County Heritage Association, 1996. 63p.

Kingfisher County
1890

Sullivan, Vicki, and Mac R. Harris. *Index to the 1890 Oklahoma Territorial Census for the Counties of Kingfisher, Payne, and Beaver*. Oklahoma City, OK: Territorial Press, 1977. 154p.

Lincoln (Jackson County)
1900

Oklahoma DAR. *1900 Federal Census, Oklahoma Territory, Lincoln, Spring Creek and Britton Townships*. Genealogical Records Committee Report, s2, v106. Oklahoma DAR, 1995. 109p.

McClain County
1890

Rex, Joyce A. *1890 Census of the Chickasaw Nation, Indian Territory*. Purcell, OK: McClain County Historical and Genealogical Society, 1992. 3 vols.

McCurtain County
1910

1910 U.S. Census McCurtain County, Oklahoma. Idabel, OK: McCurtain County Genealogical Society, 1989. 328p.

Mayes County
1910

Oklahoma DAR. *1910 Census, Mayes County, Oklahoma, Bryan Township*. Genealogical Records Committee Report, s2, v125. Oklahoma DAR, 1997. 24p.

Oklahoma DAR. *1910 Census, Mayes County, Oklahoma, Mazie Township*. Genealogical Records Committee Report, s2, v51. Oklahoma DAR, 1994. 53p.

Oklahoma DAR. *1910 Census, Mayes County, Oklahoma, River Township, White and Indian Schedules*. Genealogical Records Committee Report, s2, v125. Oklahoma DAR, 1997. 24p.

Oklahoma DAR. *1910 Census, Mayes County, Oklahoma, Saline Township*. Genealogical Records Committee Report, s2, v100. Oklahoma DAR, 1995. 34p.

Okmulgee County
1907

Doan, Patricia. *Index Original Census of Okmulgee, Oklahoma, 1907*. Okmulgee, OK: Okmulgee Public Library. 84p.

Payne County
1890

Sullivan, Vicki, and Mac R. Harris. *Index to the 1890 Oklahoma Territorial Census for the Counties of Kingfisher, Payne, and Beaver*. Oklahoma City, OK: Territorial Press, 1977. 154p.

Pontotoc County
1900

1900 Pontotoc County, Oklahoma Census. Ada, OK: Pontotoc County Historical and Genealogical Society, 1986. 186p.

1910

1910 Pontotoc County, Oklahoma Census. Ada, OK: Pontotoc County Historical and Genealogical Society, 1986. 288p.

1920

Glover, Jessie. *1920 Pontotoc County, Oklahoma Census Index, Roll #1479 and Roll #1480*. 58p.

Sequoyah County
1920

Oklahoma DAR. *1920 Sequoyah County, Oklahoma Census*. Genealogical Records Committee Report, s2, v110. Oklahoma DAR, 1996. 142p.;

_____. _____. s2, v111. Oklahoma DAR, 1996. 162p.

_____. _____. s2, v112. Oklahoma DAR, 1996. 159p.

_____. _____. s2, v113. Oklahoma DAR, 1996. 145p.

Spring Creek (Caddo County)
1900

Oklahoma DAR. *1900 Federal Census, Oklahoma Territory, Lincoln, Spring Creek and Britton Townships*. Genealogical Records Committee Report, s2, v106. Oklahoma DAR, 1995. 109p.

Tobucksy County
1896

Mason, Alma Burke. *1896 Tobucksy County, Choctaw Nation, Indian Territory*. McAlester, OK: Pittsburg County Genealogical and Historical Society. 16p.

Tulsa County
1910

Wise, Donald A. *1910 Federal Census Schedule for Tulsa County, Oklahoma*. Broken Arrow, Oklahoma: Re Tvkv'cke Press, 1991. Unpgd.

Woodward County
1900

Mooney, Frederick. *Woodward County, Oklahoma Census Index, 1900*. Amarillo, TX: Taproot Publications, 1986. 47p.

Oregon

Jackson, Ronald Vern. *Oregon Census Index, Online Edition*. Orem, UT: Ancestry.com, Inc., 1999.
http://www.ancestry.com

1840-1849

Jackson, Ronald Vern. *Oregon Census Index, Online Edition*. Orem, UT: Ancestry.com, Inc., 1999.
http://www.ancestry.com

_____. *Oregon Census Index 1840-1849*. North Salt Lake City, UT: Accelerated Indexing Systems International, 1980. Unpgd.

_____. *Oregon Census Index, 1844-1849*. West Jordan, UT: Genealogical Services, 1998. 79p.

1850

Census Index: U.S. Selected States/Counties, 1850. Family Archive CD 317. Novato, CA: Broderbund Software. CD-ROM.

Jackson, Ronald Vern. *Mortality Schedules Index, Online Edition*. Orem, UT: Ancestry.com, Inc., 1999.
http://www.ancestry.com

_____. *Oregon Census Index, Online Edition*. Orem, UT: Ancestry.com, Inc., 1999.
http://www.ancestry.com

_____, and Gary Ronald Teeples. *Oregon 1850 Territorial Census Index*. Bountiful, UT: Accelerated Indexing Systems, 1978. 83p.

Salisbury, Herbert J. *Pioneer Families of the Oregon Territory, 1850*. 2nd ed. Salem, OR: Oregon State Archives, Oregon State Library, 1961. 64p.

_____. *Online Database Edition*. Orem, UT: Ancestry.com, Inc., 1999.
http://www.ancestry.com

_____. *Washington Territorial Census Index, 1850 Census Extracted from the 1850 Oregon Census*. North Salt Lake, UT: Accelerated Indexing Systems International, 1982. 55p.

U.S. Federal Population Census Schedules. 1850, M432, Microfilm Reel No. 742.

1850-1859

Jackson, Ronald Vern. *Oregon Census Index, Online Edition*. Orem, UT: Ancestry.com, Inc., 1999.
http://www.ancestry.com

_____. *Oregon Census Index 1850-1859*. North Salt Lake City, UT: Accelerated Indexing Systems International, 1984. 92p.

1860

Dilts, Bryan Lee. *1860 Oregon Census Index, Heads of Households and Other Surnames in Households Index*. Salt Lake City, UT: Index Pub., 1985. 68p.

Haskin, Harley. *Oregon, 1880 Lake County Census*. Lebanon, OR: Author, 1978. 61p.

Jackson, Ronald Vern. *Mortality Schedules Index, Online Edition*. Orem, UT: Ancestry.com, Inc., 1999.
http://www.ancestry.com

_____. *Oregon Census Index, Online Edition*. Orem, UT: Ancestry.com, Inc., 1999.
http://www.ancestry.com

_____. *Oregon 1860 Federal Census Index*. West Jordan, UT: Genealogical Services, 1985, 1997. 257p.

Lacy, Ruby. *Oregon 1860 Census Index of Surnames*. Ashland, OR: Author, 1975. 50p.

Steuart, Raeone Christensen. *Oregon 1860 Census Index*. Bountiful, UT: Heritage Quest, 1999. 102p.

U.S. Federal Population Census Schedules. 1860, M653, Microfilm Reel Nos. 1,055-1,056.

1870

Dilts, Bryan Lee. *1870 Oregon Census Index, Heads of Households and Other Surnames in Households Index*. Salt Lake City, UT: Index Pub., 1985. 119p.

Jackson, Ronald Vern. *Federal Census Index, Oregon, 1870*. West Jordan, UT: Genealogical Services, 1985, 1996. 122p.

_____. *Mortality Schedules Index, Online Edition*. Orem, UT: Ancestry.com, Inc., 1999.
http://www.ancestry.com

_____. *Oregon Census Index, Online Edition*. Orem, UT: Ancestry.com, Inc., 1999.
http://www.ancestry.com

Steuart, Raeone Christensen. *Oregon 1870 Census Index*. Bountiful, UT: Heritage Quest, 1999. 215p.

U.S. Federal Population Census Schedules. 1870, M593, Microfilm Reel Nos. 1,285-1,288.

1880

Jackson, Ronald Vern. *Mortality Schedules Index, Online Edition.* Orem, UT: Ancestry.com, Inc., 1999.
http://www.ancestry.com

_____. *Oregon Census Index, Online Edition.* Orem, UT: Ancestry.com, Inc., 1999.
http://www.ancestry.com

_____. *Oregon 1880 Census Index.* North Salt Lake, UT: Accelerated Indexing Systems International, 1986. 219p.

U.S. Federal Population Census Schedules. 1880, T9, Microfilm Reel Nos. 1,080-1084.

U.S. Federal Population Census Schedules. 1880, Soundex. T768, 8 Microfilm Reels.

1890

Jackson, Ronald Vern. *Oregon Census Index, Online Edition.* Orem, UT: Ancestry.com, Inc., 1999.
http://www.ancestry.com

_____. *1890 Oregon Census Index, Special Schedule of the Eleventh Census (1890) Enumerating Union Veterans and of Union Veterans of the Civil War.* Salt Lake City, UT: Accelerated Indexing Systems, 1984, 1998. 87p.

Myers, Jane A. *Oregon State 1890 Special Federal Census of Union Veterans and Their Widows, Eleventh Census of the United States, 1890, Schedules Enumerating Union Veterans and Widows of Union Veterans of the Civil War, Oregon.* Cottage Grove, OR: Cottage Grove Genealogical Society, 1993. 460p.

U.S. Federal Population Census Schedules, Special Schedule, Enumerating Union Veterans and Widows of Union Veterans of the Civil War. 1890, M123, Microfilm Reel No. 77.

Veterans' Schedules: U.S. Selected States, 1890. Family Archive CD 131. Novato, CA: Broderbund Software. CD-ROM.

1900

U.S. Federal Population Census Schedules. 1900, T623, Microfilm Reel Nos. 1,345-1,353.

U.S. Federal Population Census Schedules. 1900, Soundex. T1067, 53 Microfilm Reels.

1910

U.S. Federal Population Census Schedules. 1910, T624, Microfilm Reel Nos. 1,278-1,291. (No Soundex/Miracode Index was prepared by the Government for this State.)

1920

U.S. Federal Population Census Schedules. 1920, T625, Microfilm Reel Nos. 1491-1506. (No Soundex/Miracode Index was prepared by the Government for this State.)

U.S. Federal Population Census Schedules. 1920, Soundex. M1583, 69 Microfilm Reels.

Astoria (Clatsop County)
1870, 1880

Penner, Liisa. *The Chinese in Astoria, Oregon, 1870-1880, a Look at Local Newspaper Articles, the Census, and Other Related Materials.* Astoria, OR: Author, 1990. 106p.

Champoeg County
1845

USGenWeb Census Project. Oregon, 1845 Champoeg County.
ftp://ftp.rootsweb.com/pub/census/or/champoeg/1845/

Clatsop County
1850

USGenWeb Census Project. Oregon, 1850 Clatsop County.
ftp://ftp.rootsweb.com/pub/census/or/clatsop/1850/

Coos County
1860
Dyal, Addie. *1860 Federal Census of Coos County, Oregon*. Salem, OR: Willamette Valley Genealogical Society, 1980. 14p.

Crook County
1900
Summers, Barbara. *Oregon 1900 Crook County Census with Index*. Bend, OR: Deschutes County Historical Society, 1988. 47p.
1910
Oregon 1910 Crook County Census with Index. Bend, OR: Deschutes County Historical Society, 1988. 109p.
1920
Summers, Barbara. *Oregon 1920 Crook County Census with Index*. Bend, OR: Genealogy Committee of Deschutes County Historical Society, 1995. 115p.

Curry County
1900
Felkel, Mildred, and Ruby Lacy. *Curry County, Oregon 1900 Census*. Medford, OR: Rogue Valley Genealogical Society, 1983. 45p.

Deschutes County
1920
Summers, Barbara. *Oregon 1920, Deschutes County Census with Index*. Bend, OR: Deschutes County Historical Society, 1995. 115p.

Jackson County
1853-1859
Lacy, Ruby, and Lida Childers. *Pioneer People of Jackson County*. Ashland, OR: Author, 1990. 301p.

Josephine County
1860
Haskin, Harley. *1860 Josephine County, Oregon, Census*. Lebanon, OR: End of Trail Researchers, 1974. 24p.
1880
Lacy, Ruby. *1880 Josephine County, Oregon Census*. Ashland, OR: Author, 1975. 57p.

Lane County
1900
Lane County, Oregon 1900 Census Index. Eugene, OR: Oregon Genealogical Society, 1984. 120p.
1905
Myers, Jane, Arlene Smith, and Betty Quimby. *1905 Military Census of Lane County, Oregon*. Cottage Grove, OR: Cottage Grove Genealogical Society, 1982. 258p.
1910
1910 Lane County, Oregon Census. Eugene, OR: Oregon Genealogical Society, 1992. 2 vols.

Lincoln County
1900
Lincoln County, Oregon 1900 Census Index. Eugene, OR: Oregon Genealogical Society, 1984. 19p.

Linn County
1850
Boyce, Lois M. *Linn County, Oregon Early 1850 Records*. Portland, OR: Boyce-Wheeler Publishing, 1983. 59p.

USGenWeb Census Project. Oregon, 1850 Linn County.
ftp://ftp.rootsweb.com/pub/census/or/linn/1850/
1900
Lincoln County, Oregon 1900 Census Index. Eugene, OR: Oregon Genealogical Society, 1984. 27p.
1905
Haskin, Harley. *1905 Oregon, State Military Enumeration of the Inhabitants of Linn County*. Lebanon, OR: Author, 1981. 418p.

Malheur County
1900
Malheur County, Oregon 1900 Census Index. Eugene, OR: Oregon Genealogical Society, 1984. 41p.
1910
Bartlett, Bonnie, Jan McKee, and Karen S. Olson. *1910 Malheur County, Oregon Census*. Eugene, OR: Oregon Genealogical Society, 1994. 159p.

Marion County
1880
Taylor, Carolyn. *1880 Marion County, Oregon Census Index*. Salem, OR: Author, 1980. 21p.

Poke County
1860
Haskin, Harley. *1860 Poke County, Oregon, Census*. Lebanon, OR: End of Trail Researchers, 1974. 48p.

Polk County
1856
Pompey, Sherman Lee. *Index to the 1856 State Census of Polk County, Oregon Territory*. Clovis, CA: Author. 9p.
1870
Branigar, Thomas. *Oregon, Polk County 1870 Census*. Salem, OR: Willamette Valley Genealogical Society, 1980. 89p.
1900
Taylor, Carolyn. *Index to Microfilm of the 1900 Polk County, Oregon Census*. Salem, OR: Author, 1986. 13p.

Tuality County
1845
USGenWeb Census Project. Oregon, 1845 Tuality County.
ftp://ftp.rootsweb.com/pub/census/or/tuality/1845/

Union County
1880
Taylor, Carolyn. *Oregon, Union County 1880 Census*. Salem, OR: Willamette Valley Genealogical Society, 1987. 123p.

Wasco County
1860-1880
Pryor, Estella. *Census Records 1860, 1870, 1880 of Hood River, Wasco County, Oregon*. Columbia Gorge Genealogical Society. 42p.

Yamhill County
1900
Kilgore, Ione Gaudette. *Yamhill County, Oregon 1900 Census*. McMinnville, OR: Yamhill County Genealogy Society, 1986.
1910
1910 Census Index Yamhill County, Oregon. McMinnville, OR: Yamhill County Genealogical Society, 1992. Unpgd.

Pennsylvania

1693
Craig, Peter Stebbins. *The 1693 Census of the Swedes on the Delaware Family Histories of the Swedish Lutheran Church Members Residing in Pennsylvania, Delaware, West New Jersey and Cecil County, Maryland, 1638-1693*. Studies in Swedish American Genealogy No. 3. Winter Park, FL: SAG Publications, 1993. 213p.

1790
Coffman, Mrs. M. F. *Census Records for Yoder Family All Spellings, from Years 1790, 1800, 1810, 1820 and 1830, Pennsylvania. Taken from Printed Texts and Microfilm at the National Archives*. Malvern, PA: Author, 1985. 63p.
_____. *Yoder Family Census Records for Pennsylvania, 1790 through 1840, Plus Index for 1850 Census*. Rev. 3rd ed. Malvern, PA: Author, 1991. 122p.
Jackson, Ronald Vern. *Pennsylvania Census Index, Online Edition*. Orem, UT: Ancestry.com, Inc., 1999.
http://www.ancestry.com
_____. *Pennsylvania 1790 Federal Census Index*. North Salt Lake, UT: Accelerated Indexing Systems International, 1990. 2 vols.
U.S. Bureau of the Census. *Heads of Families at the First Census of the United States Taken in the Year 1790, Pennsylvania*. Washington, DC: Government Printing Office, 1908. 227p.
_____. _____. Bountiful, UT: American Genealogical Lending Library, 1908, 1993. 426p.
_____. _____. *Online Database Edition*. Orem, UT: Ancestry.com, Inc., 1999.
http://www.ancestry.com
_____. *U.S. Federal Population Census Schedules*, 1790. T498, Microfilm Reel No. 2.
U.S. Federal Population Census Schedules, 1790. M637, Microfilm Reel Nos. 8-9.

1800
Coffman, Mrs. M. F. *Census Records for Yoder Family All Spellings, from Years 1790, 1800, 1810, 1820 and 1830, Pennsylvania. Taken from Printed Texts and Microfilm at the National Archives*. Malvern, PA: Author, 1985. 63p.
_____. *Yoder Family Census Records for Pennsylvania, 1790 through 1840, Plus Index for 1850 Census*. Rev. 3rd ed. Malvern, PA: Author, 1991. 122p.
Felldin, Jeanne Robey, and Gloria Kay Vandiver. *The 1800 Census of Pennsylvania*. Baltimore, MD: Genealogical Pub. Co., 1984, 1996. 453p.
Jackson, Ronald Vern. *Pennsylvania Census Index, Online Edition*. Orem, UT: Ancestry.com, Inc., 1999.
http://www.ancestry.com
_____, and Gary Ronald Teeples. *Pennsylvania 1800 Census Index*. Salt Lake City, UT: Accelerated Indexing Systems, 1972, 1977. 357p.
Stemmons, John D. *Pennsylvania in 1800; a Computerized Index to the 1800 Federal Population Schedules of the State of Pennsylvania, with Other Aids to Research*. Salt Lake City, UT: Author, 1972. 687p.
Steuart, Raeone Christensen. *Pennsylvania 1800 Census Index*. Bountiful, UT: Heritage Quest, 2000. 652p.
_____. *United States 1800 Census Index*. Bountiful, UT: Heritage Quest, 2000. 4 vols. CD-ROM.
U.S. Federal Population Census Schedules, 1800. M32, Microfilm Reel Nos. 35-44.

1810

Coffman, Mrs. M. F. *Census Records for Yoder Family All Spellings, from Years 1790, 1800, 1810, 1820 and 1830, Pennsylvania. Taken from Printed Texts and Microfilm at the National Archives.* Malvern, PA: Author, 1985. 63p.

_____. *Yoder Family Census Records for Pennsylvania, 1790 through 1840, Plus Index for 1850 Census.* Rev. 3rd ed. Malvern, PA: Author, 1991. 122p.

Jackson, Ronald Vern. *Pennsylvania Census Index, Online Edition.* Orem, UT: Ancestry.com, Inc., 1999. **http://www.ancestry.com**

_____, and Gary Ronald Teeples. *Pennsylvania 1810 Census Index.* Bountiful, UT: Accelerated Indexing Systems, 1976, 1981. 314p.

Ohio Family Historians. *Index to 1810 Census of Pennsylvania.* Columbus, OH: Ohio Library Foundation, 1966, 1980. 297p.

U.S. Federal Population Census Schedules, 1810. M252, Microfilm Reel Nos. 44-57.

1820

Coffman, Mrs. M. F. *Census Records for Yoder Family All Spellings, from Years 1790, 1800, 1810, 1820 and 1830, Pennsylvania. Taken from Printed Texts and Microfilm at the National Archives.* Malvern, PA: Author, 1985. 63p.

_____. *Yoder Family Census Records for Pennsylvania, 1790 through 1840, Plus Index for 1850 Census.* Rev. 3rd ed. Malvern, PA: Author, 1991. 122p.

Felldin, Jeanne Robey. *The 1820 Census of Pennsylvania.* Baltimore, MD: Genealogical Pub. Co., 1984. 453p.

Jackson, Ronald Vern. *Pennsylvania Census Index, Online Edition.* Orem, UT: Ancestry.com, Inc., 1999. **http://www.ancestry.com**

_____, and Gary Ronald Teeples. *Pennsylvania 1820 Census Index.* Bountiful, UT: Accelerated Indexing Systems, 1978. 406p.

U.S. Federal Population Census Schedules. 1820, M33, Microfilm Reel Nos. 1-3.

1830

Census Index: U.S. Selected States/Counties, 1830. Family Archive CD 315. Novato, CA: Broderbund Software. CD-ROM.

Coffman, Mrs. M. F. *Census Records for Yoder Family All Spellings, from Years 1790, 1800, 1810, 1820 and 1830, Pennsylvania. Taken from Printed Texts and Microfilm at the National Archives.* Malvern, PA: Author, 1985. 63p.

_____. *Yoder Family Census Records for Pennsylvania, 1790 through 1840, Plus Index for 1850 Census.* Rev. 3rd ed. Malvern, PA: Author, 1991. 122p.

Jackson, Ronald Vern. *Pennsylvania Census Index, Online Edition.* Orem, UT: Ancestry.com, Inc., 1999. **http://www.ancestry.com**

_____, and Gary Ronald Teeples. *Pennsylvania 1830 Census Index.* Bountiful, UT: Accelerated Indexing Systems, 1976. 531p.

U.S. Census Index, 1830-1839, New England, New York, Pennsylvania. Orem, UT: Automated Archives, 1992. CD-ROM.

U.S. Federal Population Census Schedules. 1830, M19, Microfilm Reel Nos. 143-166.

1840

Census Index: U.S. Selected States/Counties, 1840. Family Archive CD 316. Novato, CA: Broderbund Software. CD-ROM.

Coffman, Mrs. M. F. *Census Records for Yoder Families, 1840, Pennsylvania and Ohio, from Microfilm at the National Archives.* Malvern, PA: Author, 1986. 18p.

_____. *Yoder Family Census Records for Pennsylvania, 1790 through 1840, Plus Index for 1850 Census.* Rev. 3rd ed. Malvern, PA: Author, 1991. 122p.

Jackson, Ronald Vern. *Pennsylvania Census Index, Online Edition.* Orem, UT: Ancestry.com, Inc., 1999. **http://www.ancestry.com**

_____, and Gary Ronald Teeples. *Pennsylvania 1840 Census Index*. Bountiful, UT: Accelerated Indexing Systems, 1978, 1998. 746p.

U.S. Federal Population Census Schedules. 1840, M704, Microfilm Reel Nos. 435-503.

1850

Bentley, Elizabeth Petty. *Index to the 1850 Census of Pennsylvania*. Baltimore, MD: Genealogical Pub. Co., 1974, 1998. 522p.

Census Microfilm Records: Pennsylvania, 1850. Family Archive CD 305. Novato, CA: Broderbund Software. CD-ROM.

Corley, Betty J. *Index, Yeoman(s), Yeaman(s), Youman(s), U.S. Census Index Pennsylvania, 1850, 1860, 1880, 1900, 1910*. Hyrum, UT: Author, 1988. 5p.

Jackson, Ronald Vern. *Mortality Schedules Index, Online Edition*. Orem, UT: Ancestry.com, Inc., 1999. **http://www.ancestry.com**

_____. *Pennsylvania Census Index, Online Edition*. Orem, UT: Ancestry.com, Inc., 1999. **http://www.ancestry.com**

_____, and Gary Ronald Teeples. *Pennsylvania 1850 Census Index*. Bountiful, UT: Accelerated Indexing Systems, 1976, 1981. 2 vols.

_____. *U.S. Federal Census Index, Pennsylvania 1850 Mortality Schedules*. West Jordan, UT: Genealogical Services, 1982, 1998. 344p.

U.S. Census Index Series, Pennsylvania, Delaware and New Jersey, 1850. Orem, UT: Automated Archives, 1991. CD-ROM.

U.S. Federal Population Census Schedules. 1850, M432, Microfilm Reel Nos. 7434-840.

1860

Census Index: U.S. Selected States/Counties, 1860. Family Archive CD 318. Novato, CA: Broderbund Software. CD-ROM.

Corley, Betty J. *Index, Yeoman(s), Yeaman(s), Youman(s), U.S. Census Index Pennsylvania, 1850, 1860, 1880, 1900, 1910*. Hyrum, UT: Author, 1988. 5p.

Jackson, Ronald Vern. *Mortality Schedules Index, Online Edition*. Orem, UT: Ancestry.com, Inc., 1999. **http://www.ancestry.com**

_____. *Pennsylvania Census Index, Online Edition*. Orem, UT: Ancestry.com, Inc., 1999. **http://www.ancestry.com**

_____. *Pennsylvania 1860 Central*. Salt Lake City, UT: Accelerated Indexing Systems International, 1986. 661p.

_____. *Pennsylvania 1860 Central Federal Census Index, with Addendum Franklin County*. West Jordan, UT: Genealogical Services, 1986, 1997.

_____. *Pennsylvania 1860 East Federal Census Index, Excluding Philadelphia County*. West Jordan, UT: Genealogical Services, 1986, 1997.

_____. _____. North Salt Lake, UT: Accelerated Indexing Systems International, 1987. 1,097p.

_____. *Pennsylvania 1860 Mortality Schedules*. West Jordan, UT: Genealogical Services, 1982, 1998. 371p.

_____. *Pennsylvania 1860 West Federal Census Index, Excluding Allegheny and Butler Counties*. West Jordan, UT: Genealogical Services, 1986, 1997. 722p.

U.S. Census Index, 1860, Delaware, New Jersey and Pennsylvania. Orem, UT: Automated Archives, 1992. CD-ROM.

U.S. Federal Population Census Schedules. 1860, M653, Microfilm Reel Nos. 1,057-1,201.

1870

Census Index: Eastern Pennyslvania, 1870. Family Archive CD 286. Novato, CA: Broderbund Software. CD-ROM.

Census Index: Western Pennsylvania, 1870. Family Archive CD 285. Novato, CA: Broderbund Software. CD-ROM.

Delaware and New Jersey 1870 Census Index. ACD 0033. Bountiful, UT: Heritage Quest, 1998. CD-ROM.

Jackson, Ronald Vern. *Mortality Schedules Index, Online Edition*. Orem, UT: Ancestry.com, Inc., 1999. **http://www.ancestry.com**

_____. *Pennsylvania Census Index, Online Edition*. Orem, UT: Ancestry.com, Inc., 1999. **http://www.ancestry.com**

Steuart, Raeone Christensen. *Pennsylvania Central 1870 Census Index*. Bountiful, UT: Precision Indexing, 1997. 2 vols.

_____. *Pennsylvania East 1870 Census Index*. Bountiful, UT: Precision Indexing, 1994. 2 vols., 31 microfiche.

_____. *Pennsylvania 1870 Census Index*. Bountiful, UT: Heritage Quest, 1997. CD-ROM.

_____. *Pennsylvania West 1870 Census Index*. Bountiful, UT: Precision Indexing, 1994. 2 vols.; 26 microfiche.

U.S. Census Index Series, Pennsylvania East, 1870. Orem, UT: Automated Archives, 1994; 2000. CD-ROM.

U.S. Federal Population Census Schedules. 1870, M593, Microfilm Reel Nos. 1289-1470.

1880

Corley, Betty J. *Index, Yeoman(s), Yeaman(s), Youman(s), U.S. Census Index Pennsylvania, 1850, 1860, 1880, 1900, 1910*. Hyrum, UT: Author, 1988. 5p.

U.S. Federal Population Census Schedules. 1880, T9, Microfilm Reel Nos. 1085-1208.

U.S. Federal Population Census Schedules. 1880, Soundex. T769, 168 Microfilm Reels.

1890

Jackson, Ronald Vern. *Mortality Schedules Index, Online Edition*. Orem, UT: Ancestry.com, Inc., 1999. **http://www.ancestry.com**

_____. *Pennsylvania Census Index, Online Edition (Naval Veterans Schedules)*. Orem, UT: Ancestry.com, Inc., 1999. **http://www.ancestry.com**

U.S. Federal Population Census Schedules, Special Schedule, Enumerating Union Veterans and Widows of Union Veterans of the Civil War. 1890, M123, Microfilm Reel Nos. 78-91.

1900

Corley, Betty J. *Index, Yeoman(s), Yeaman(s), Youman(s), U.S. Census Index Pennsylvania, 1850, 1860, 1880, 1900, 1910*. Hyrum, UT: Author, 1988. 5p.

U.S. Federal Population Census Schedules. 1900, T623, Microfilm Reel Nos. 1354-1503.

U.S. Federal Population Census Schedules. 1900, Soundex. T1068, 590 Microfilm Reels.

1910

Corley, Betty J. *Index, Yeoman(s), Yeaman(s), Youman(s), U.S. Census Index Pennsylvania, 1850, 1860, 1880, 1900, 1910*. Hyrum, UT: Author, 1988. 5p.

U.S. Federal Population Census Schedules. 1910, T624, Microfilm Reel Nos. 1292-1435.

U.S. Federal Population Census Schedules. 1910, Miracode Index, T1274, 688 Microfilm Reels.

U.S. Federal Population Census Schedules. 1910, Separate Miracode Index for Philadelphia County, T1274, Microfilm Reel Nos. 529-688.

1920

U.S. Federal Population Census Schedules. 1920, T625, Microfilm Reel Nos. 1507-1669.

U.S. Federal Population Census Schedules. 1920, Soundex. M1584, 716 Microfilm Reels.

Adams County
1800

Lightner, William C. *An Alphabetical Listing of Heads of Households (With Age and Sex of All Members of Households) Included in the 1800 Federal Census of Adams County, Pennsylvania*. York, PA: South Central Pennsylvania Genealogical Society, 1982. 41p.

1860

Berg, Irene Roberta Williams. *1860 Census Index of Adams County, Pennsylvania*. Veradale, WA: Author. 60p.

Hankey, Joan R. *Index of 1860 Census, Gettysburg, Adams County, Pennsylvania*. Author, 1985. 33p.

1880

Hankey, Joan R. *Index of 1880 Census, Adams County, Pennsylvania*. Gettysburg, PA: Adams County Historical Society, 1996. 304p.

Allegheny County
1860

Jackson, Ronald Vern. *Pennsylvania 1860 Allegheny and Butler Counties, Census Index* . West Jordan, UT: Genealogical Services, 1986, 1997.

_____. *Pennsylvania 1860 Pittsburgh, (Allegheny and Butler Counties)*. Salt Lake City, UT: Accelerated Indexing Systems International, 1987. 809p.

1880

Heckla, Walter E. *1880 Census Union Township, Allegheny County, Pennsylvania Present Day Boro of Green Tree and Banksville of City of Pittsburgh*. Pittsburgh, PA: Western Pennsylvania Genealogical Society, 1989. 62p.

Bedford County
1800

USGenWeb Census Project. Pennsylvania, 1800 Bedford County.
ftp://ftp.rootsweb.com/pub/census/pa/bedford/1800/

1810

USGenWeb Census Project. Pennsylvania, 1810 Bedford County.
ftp://ftp.rootsweb.com/pub/census/pa/bedford/1810/

1820

USGenWeb Census Project. Pennsylvania, 1820 Bedford County.
ftp://ftp.rootsweb.com/pub/census/pa/bedford/1820/

1830

USGenWeb Census Project. Pennsylvania, 1830 Bedford County. (Partial).
ftp://ftp.rootsweb.com/pub/census/pa/bedford/1830/

Berks County
1779

Pennsylvania Septennial Census, Berks County, 1779. Reading, PA: Berks County Genealogical Society, 1989. 52p.

1850

Bentley, Elizabeth Petty. *Index to the 1850 Census of Pennsylvania, Berks County*. Baltimore, MD: Genealogical Pub., Co., 1976. 106p.

1860

Hesser, Gail H. *Index to the 1860 Census, Berks County, Pennsylvania*. Reading, PA: Author, 1984. 88p.

1870

Index to the 1870 Census, Berks County, Pennsylvania. Reading, PA: Berks County Genealogical Society, 1982. 187p.

Bradford County
1820

USGenWeb Census Project. Pennsylvania, 1820 Bradford County.
ftp://ftp.rootsweb.com/pub/census/pa/bradford/1820

Bucks County

1850

Bentley, Elizabeth Petty. *Index to the 1850 Census of Pennsylvania, Bucks County*. Baltimore, MD: Genealogical Pub., Co., 1976. 88p.

Flake, G. Raymond. *Index to the 1850 Census of Bucks County, Pennsylvania*. Chalfont, PA: Author. Unpgd.

1880

Brittingham, Janet R. *1880 Census Index of Bucks County, Pennsylvania*. Jamison, PA: Author, 1984. 172p.

1900

Myers, Thomas G. *1900 Census Index, Bucks County, Pennsylvania*. Holmdel, NJ: Author, 1993. Unpgd.

1910

Brittingham, Janet R. *1910 Census Index of Bucks County, Pennsylvania*. Jamison, PA: Author, 1984. 260p.

1920

Myers, Thomas G. *1920 Census Index, Bucks County, Pennsylvania*. Holmdel, NJ: Author, 1993. Unpgd.

Butler County

1800

Computer Index to Pennsylvania 1800 Census, Butler, Crawford and Mercer Counties. Salt Lake City, UT: Gen-Dex Worldwide, 1971. 34p.

Jackson, Ronald Vern. *Computer Index to Pennsylvania 1800 Census, Butler, Crawford and Mercer Counties*. Salt Lake City, UT: Gen-Dex Worldwide, 1971. 34p.

1860

Jackson, Ronald Vern. *Pennsylvania 1860 Allegheny and Butler Counties, Census Index* . West Jordan, UT: Genealogical Services, 1986, 1997.

_____. *Pennsylvania 1860 Pittsburgh, (Allegheny and Butler Counties)*. Salt Lake City, UT: Accelerated Indexing Systems International, 1987. 809p.

1870

Maxwell, Joan Zeigler. *Butler County, Pennsylvania, Everyname Index to the 1870 Federal Census*. Plano, TX: Author, 1983. 155p.

1880

1880 Census of Butler County, Ohio, Index. Middletown, OH: OGS, Butler County Chapter, 1987. Unpgd.

Cambria County

1810

USGenWeb Census Project. Pennsylvania, 1810 Cambria County.
ftp://ftp.rootsweb.com/pub/census/pa/cambria/1810/

1850

Strayer, Harold H. *1850 Census of Conemaugh Township, Cambria County, Pennsylvania, a Summary Transcript with Index*. Author, 1980.

1870

USGenWeb Census Project. Pennsylvania, 1870 Cambria County. (Partial).
ftp://ftp.rootsweb.com/pub/census/pa/cambria/1870/

Centre County

1800-1850

Lingle, Harry A. *Boggs Township Index of Decennial Census Records, 1820-1910*. Beech Creek, PA: Author, 1986. Unpgd.

_____. *Index to the Decennial Census Records for a Section of Bald Eagle Valley for the Years 1800 through 1910, Excepting 1890, Which Were Destroyed by Fire in Washington, DC*. Beech Creek, PA: Author. Unpgd.

1860

Hunter, Albert S. *Index to the 1860 Census of Centre County, Pennsylvania*. Author, 1983. 129p.

Lingle, Harry A. *Boggs Township Index of Decennial Census Records, 1820-1910*. Beech Creek, PA: Author, 1986. Unpgd.

_____. *Index to the Decennial Census Records for a Section of Bald Eagle Valley for the Years 1800 through 1910, Excepting 1890, Which Were Destroyed by Fire in Washington, DC*. Beech Creek, PA: Author. Unpgd.

1870-1910

Lingle, Harry A. *Boggs Township Index of Decennial Census Records, 1820-1910*. Beech Creek, PA: Author, 1986. Unpgd.

_____. *Index to the Decennial Census Records for a Section of Bald Eagle Valley for the Years 1800 through 1910, Excepting 1890, Which Were Destroyed by Fire in Washington, DC*. Beech Creek, PA: Author. Unpgd.

Chester County
1842

Jackson, Ronald Vern. *Chester County, Pennsylvania 1842 State Census Index*. Salt Lake City, UT: Accelerated Indexing Systems International, 1988. 55; 239p.

_____. *Pennsylvania Census Index, Online Edition*. Orem, UT: Ancestry.com, Inc., 1999.
http://www.ancestry.com
1857

Jackson, Ronald Vern. *Pennsylvania Census Index, Online Edition*. Orem, UT: Ancestry.com, Inc., 1999.
http://www.ancestry.com

_____. *Chester County, Pennsylvania 1857 State Census Index*. Salt Lake City, UT: Accelerated Indexing Systems International, 1989. 55; 214p.

Conemaugh (Cambria County)
1850

Strayer, Harold H. *1850 Census of Conemaugh Township, Cambria County, Pennsylvania, a Summary Transcript with Index*. Author, 1980, 1984. 33p.

Crawford County
1800

Computer Index to Pennsylvania 1800 Census, Butler, Crawford and Mercer Counties. Salt Lake City, UT: Gen-Dex Worldwide, 1971. 34p.

Jackson, Ronald Vern. *Computer Index to Pennsylvania 1800 Census, Butler, Crawford and Mercer Counties*. Salt Lake City, UT: Gen-Dex Worldwide, 1971. 34p.

Cumberland County
1800

Lightner, William C. *An Alphabetical Listing of Heads of Households (With Age and Sex of All Members of Households) Included in the 1800 Federal Census of Cumberland County, Pennsylvania*. York, PA: South Central Pennsylvania Genealogical Society, 1985. 69p.

Fayette County
1800

USGenWeb Census Project. Pennsylvania, 1800 Fayette County.
ftp://ftp.rootsweb.com/pub/census/pa/fayette/1800/

Franklin County
1860

Jackson, Ronald Vern. *Pennsylvania 1860 Central Federal Census Index, with Addendum Franklin County*. West Jordan, UT: Genealogical Services, 1986, 1997. Unpgd.

Fulton County
1850
1850 United States Census for Fulton County, Pennsylvania. McConnellsburg, PA: Fulton County Historical Society, 1988. 120p.

Schunk, John Frederick. *1850 U.S. Census, Fulton County, Pennsylvania.* Wichita, KS: S-K Publications, 1986. 389p.

1860
1860 United States Census for Fulton County, Pennsylvania. McConnellsburg, PA: Fulton County Historical Society, 1993. 124p.

1870
1870 United States Census for Fulton County, Pennsylvania. McConnellsburg, PA: Fulton County Historical Society, Inc., 1996. 124p.

Greene County
1820
Shultz, Mary E. *Greene County, Pennsylvania, 1820 Census.* Bowie, MD: Heritage Books, 1988. 90p.

Lancaster County
Hawbaker, Gary T., and Clyde L. Groff. *A New Index, Lancaster County, Pennsylvania, before the Federal Census.* Hershey, PA: Authors, 1981.

1800
Mallinson, James A. Jr., and Carla A. Mallinson. *A Cross-compilation of the 1798 US Direct Tax for Pennsylvania and the 1800 Federal Census for Pennsylvania, Lancaster County.* Salisbury, NC: 1987, 1988. 3 vols.

1850
Bentley, Elizabeth Petty. *Index to the 1850 Census of Pennsylvania, Lancaster County.* Baltimore, MD: Genealogical Pub., Co., 1975. 156p.

Collin, Bernadine T. *Index to U.S. Census, 1850 Montgomery County, Pennsylvania.* Norristown, PA: Historical Society of Montgomery County, 1975. Unpgd.

Frey, James Elwood. *Agricultural Schedules and Federal Census Schedules, 1850-1880, Brecknock Township, Lancaster County, Pennsylvania.* Morgantown, PA: Masthof Press, 1997. 138p.

1860
Frey, James Elwood. *Agricultural Schedules and Federal Census Schedules, 1850-1880, Brecknock Township, Lancaster County, Pennsylvania.* Morgantown, PA: Masthof Press, 1997. 138p.

1870
Frey, James Elwood. *Agricultural Schedules and Federal Census Schedules, 1850-1880, Brecknock Township, Lancaster County, Pennsylvania.* Morgantown, PA: Masthof Press, 1997. 138p.

Jackson, Ronald Vern. *Pennsylvania 1870 Lancaster County Federal Census Index.* Salt Lake City, UT: AGES, 1993. 731p.

1880
Frey, James Elwood. *Agricultural Schedules and Federal Census Schedules, 1850-1880, Brecknock Township, Lancaster County, Pennsylvania.* Morgantown, PA: Masthof Press, 1997. 138p.

Luzerne County
1850
Bentley, Elizabeth Petty. *Index to the 1850 Census of Pennsylvania, Luzerne and Wyoming Counties.* Baltimore, MD: Genealogical Pub. Co., 1974. 128p.

1870
Bleidner, Marjory Wylam. *Census Index, Luzerne County, Pennsylvania, 1870.* Marathon Shores, FL: Author, 1988. Unpgd.

_____. *Pennsylvania Census 1870, Luzerne County, Scranton.* Marathon Shores, FL: Author, 1988. Unpgd.

Jackson, Ronald Vern. *Pennsylvania 1870 Luzerne County Federal Census Index.* Salt Lake City, UT: AGES, 1993. 902p.

Lycoming County
1870
USGenWeb Census Project. Pennsylvania, 1870 Lycoming County.
ftp://ftp.rootsweb.com/pub/census/pa/lycoming/1870/

Mercer County
1800
Computer Index to Pennsylvania 1800 Census, Butler, Crawford and Mercer Counties. Salt Lake City, UT: Gen-Dex Worldwide, 1971. 34p.

Jackson, Ronald Vern. *Computer Index to Pennsylvania 1800 Census, Butler, Crawford and Mercer Counties.* Salt Lake City, UT: Gen-Dex Worldwide, 1971. 34p.

Mifflin County
1860
McClenahen, Dan. *Index for 1860 Mifflin County Census.* Author, 1983. Unpgd.

Monroe County
1850
Dittmer, Dorothy M. Bond, and Audrey M. Brazelton Maple. *1850 United States Census of Monroe County, Pennsylvania.* Akron, OH: Bond Research, 1986. 191p.

Northampton County
1790-1810
U.S. Works Progress Administration. *An Index of Names Appearing in the U.S. Census for Northampton County, Pennsylvania for the Years 1790, 1800, 1810.* Easton, PA: Easton Public Library, 1945. 236p.
1850
Bentley, Elizabeth Petty. *Index to the 1850 Census of Pennsylvania, Northampton County.* Baltimore, MD: Genealogical Pub. Co., 1974. 64p.

Perry County
1870
Long, Ron, and Elaine Long. *1870 Perry County, Pennsyslvania Census Index.* Ada, OK: Authors. Unpgd.

Philadelphia County
1850
Genealogical Society of Pennsylvania. *Heads of Families Index, 1850 Federal Census, County of Philadelphia.* Philadelphia, PA: Author, 1978. 2 vols.

Penrose, Maryly Barton. *Heads of Families Index, 1850 Federal Census, City of Philadelphia.* Franklin Park, NJ: Liberty Bell Associates, 1974. Unpgd.
1860
Jackson, Ronald Vern. *Pennsylvania 1860 Philadelphia.* Salt Lake City, UT: Accelerated Indexing Systems International, 1987. 806p.
1870
Steuart, Bradley W. *Philadelphia, Pennsylvania 1870 Census Index.* Bountiful, UT: Precision Indexing, 1989, 1999. 2 vols.; 21 microfiche.

Pittsburgh (Allegheny County)
1860
Jackson, Ronald Vern. *Pennsylvania 1860 Pittsburgh, (Allegheny and Butler Counties).* Salt Lake City, UT: Accelerated Indexing Systems International, 1987. 809p.

1870

Jackson, Ronald Vern. *Pittsburgh, Pennsylvania, 1870 Federal Census Index*. Salt Lake City, UT: Accelerated Indexing Systems International, 1990. 366p.

1880

Heckla, Walter E. *1880 Census Union Township, Allegheny County, Pennsylvania Present Day Boro of Green Tree and Banksville of City of Pittsburgh*. Pittsburgh, PA: Western Pennsylvania Genealogical Society, 1989. 62p.

Schuylkill County

1820

Dellock, Jean A. *Schuylkill County, Pennsylvania 1820 Census Index*. Frackville, PA: Author, 1994. 21p.

USGenWeb Census Project. Pennsylvania, 1820 Schuylkill County.

ftp://ftp.rootsweb.com/pub/census/pa/schuylkill/1820/

1830

USGenWeb Census Project. Pennsylvania, 1830 Schuylkill County.

ftp://ftp.rootsweb.com/pub/census/pa/schuylkill/1830/

1860

Bleidner, Marjory Wylam. *Census Index, 1860, Schuylkill County, Pennsylvania*. Marathon Shores, FL: Author, 1984. Unpgd.

Scranton (Lackawanna County)

1870

Bleidner, Marjory Wylam. *Pennsylvania Census 1870, Luzerne County, Scranton*. Marathon Shores, FL: Author, 1988. Unpgd.

Somerset County

1870

USGenWeb Census Project. Pennsylvania, 1870 Somerset County.

ftp://ftp.rootsweb.com/pub/census/pa/somerset/1870/

Sullivan County

1850

USGenWeb Census Project. Pennsylvania, 1850 Sullivan County.

ftp://ftp.rootsweb.com/pub/census/pa/sullivan/1850/

1860

USGenWeb Census Project. Pennsylvania, 1860 Sullivan County.

ftp://ftp.rootsweb.com/pub/census/pa/sullivan/1860/

1870

USGenWeb Census Project. Pennsylvania, 1870 Sullivan County.

ftp://ftp.rootsweb.com/pub/census/pa/sullivan/1870/

Tioga County

Watkins, Forrest W. *Tioga County, Pennsylvania, Records, Chatham Township Census*. Author, 1981. 303p.

1850

Ladd, Rhoda English. *Morris Township, Tioga County, Pennsylvania, Early History, Census, 1850, 1860, 1870, 1880, 1889, Newspaper Obituaries, Cemeteries*. Wellsboro, PA: Author, 1977. 295p.

1860-1880

Franke, Lola Wetherbee, and Mrs. A. William Ladd. *Early History of Delmar Township, Tioga County, Pennsylvania, Including Census Records of 1860, 1870, 1880*. Wellsboro, PA: Author, 1973. 180p.

Ladd, Rhoda English. *Morris Township, Tioga County, Pennsylvania, Early History, Census, 1850, 1860, 1870, 1880, 1889, Newspaper Obituaries, Cemeteries*. Wellsboro, PA: Author, 1977. 295p.

1889

Ladd, Rhoda English. *Morris Township, Tioga County, Pennsylvania, Early History, Census, 1850, 1860, 1870, 1880, 1889, Newspaper Obituaries, Cemeteries*. Wellsboro, PA: Author, 1977. 295p.

Union County
1850

Lontz, Mary Belle. *Union County, Pennsylvania, Census of 1850*. Milton, PA: Author, 1978. 249p.

Washington County
1790

Zinsser, Katherine K. *The 1783 Tax Lists and the 1790 Federal Census for Washington County, Pennsylvania*. Bowie, MD: Heritage Books, 1988. 131p.

Westmoreland County
1783

Westmoreland County, Pennsylvania, 1783 Census. Westminster, MD: Family Line Publications, 1990. 84p.

Wyoming County
1850

Bentley, Elizabeth Petty. *Index to the 1850 Census of Pennyslvania, Luzerne and Wyoming Counties*. Baltimore, MD: Genealogical Pub. Co., 1974. 128p.

York County
1800

Lightner, William C. *An Alphabetical Listing of Heads of Households (With Age and Sex of All Members of Households) Included in the 1800 Federal Census of York County, Pennsylvania*. York, PA: South Central Pennsylvania Genealogical Society, 1981. 2 vols.
1850
USGenWeb Census Project. Pennsylvania, 1850 York County.
ftp://ftp.rootsweb.com/pub/census/pa/york/1850/

Rhode Island

Conrad, Mark. *A Guide to Census Materials in the Rhode Island State Archives*. Providence, RI: Rhode Island State Archives, 1990. Unpgd.

1740-1743

Jackson, Ronald Vern. *Rhode Island Census Index, Online Edition*. Orem, UT: Ancestry.com, Inc., 1999.
http://www.ancestry.com

1747

Jackson, Ronald Vern. *Rhode Island Census Index, Online Edition*. Orem, UT: Ancestry.com, Inc., 1999.
http://www.ancestry.com
_____. *Rhode Island 1747*. North Salt Lake, UT: Accelerated Indexing Systems International, 1988. 49, 24p.

1774

Bartlett, John R. *Census of the Inhabitants of the Colony of Rhode Island and Providence Plantations, 1774*. Baltimore, MD: Genealogical Pub. Co., 1969. 238p.
_____. _____. Providence, RI: Knowles, Anthony & Co., State Printers, 1858.

_____. _____. *Online Database Edition*. Orem, UT: Ancestry.com, Inc., 1999.
http://www.ancestry.com
Brownell, Elijah Ellsworth. *Index of Rhode Island Census in 1774*. Author, 1954. 120p.

1777

Chamberlain, Mildred M. *The Rhode Island 1777 Military Census*. Baltimore, MD: Genealogical Publishing Co., 1985. 181p.
Jackson, Ronald Vern. *Rhode Island Census Index, Online Edition*. Orem, UT: Ancestry.com, Inc., 1999.
http://www.ancestry.com
_____. *Rhode Island 1777 State Census Index*. Salt Lake City, UT: Accelerated Indexing Systems, 1988. 166p.

1782

Holbrook, Jay Mack. *Rhode Island 1782 Census*. Oxford, MA: Holbrook Research Institute, 1979. 223p.
Jackson, Ronald Vern. *Rhode Island 1782*. North Salt Lake City, UT: Accelerated Indexing Systems International, 1988. 91p.

1790

Jackson, Ronald Vern. *Connecticut 1790, Rhode Island 1790 Federal Census Indexes*. North Salt Lake, UT: Accelerated Indexing Systems International, 1990. 709, 197p.
_____. *Rhode Island Census Index, Online Edition*. Orem, UT: Ancestry.com, Inc., 1999.
http://www.ancestry.com
U.S. Bureau of the Census. *Heads of Families at the First Census of the United States Taken in the Year 1790, Rhode Island*. Washington, DC: Government Printing Office, 1908. 71p.
_____. _____. *Online Database Edition*. Orem, UT: Ancestry.com, Inc., 1999.
http://www.ancestry.com
_____. _____. Bountiful, UT: American Genealogical Lending Library, 1993. 71p.
_____. _____. North Salt Lake City, UT: Accelerated Indexing Systems International, 1990. 71p.
_____. _____. *U.S. Federal Population Census Schedules*, 1790. T498, Microfilm Reel No. 3.
U.S. Federal Population Census Schedules, 1790. M637, Microfilm Reel No. 10.

1800

Jackson, Ronald Vern. *Rhode Island Census Index, Online Edition*. Orem, UT: Ancestry.com, Inc., 1999.
http://www.ancestry.com
_____. *Rhode Island 1800 Census*. Salt Lake City, UT: Accelerated Indexing Systems, 1972. 222p.
Rainwater, Margaret. *1800 South Carolina Census Index*. Houston, TX: Author, 1964. Unpgd.
Steuart, Raeone Christensen. *Rhode Island 1800 Census Index*. Bountiful, UT: Heritage Quest, 2000. 76p.
_____. *United States 1800 Census Index*. Bountiful, UT: Heritage Quest, 2000. 4 vols. CD-ROM.
U.S. Federal Population Census Schedules, 1800. M32, Microfilm Reel Nos. 45-46.
Volkel, Lowell M. *An Index to the 1800 Federal Census of Rhode Island*. Danville, IL: Author, 1970. 74p.

1810

Jackson, Ronald Vern. *Rhode Island Census Index, Online Edition*. Orem, UT: Ancestry.com, Inc., 1999.
http://www.ancestry.com
_____, and Gary Ronald Teeples. *Rhode Island 1810 Census Index*. Bountiful, UT: Accelerated Indexing Systems, 1976. 33p.
U.S. Census Index Series, New England, New York, 1810. Orem, UT: Automated Archives, 1992. CD-ROM.
U.S. Federal Population Census Schedules, 1810. M252, Microfilm Reel Nos. 58-59.

1820

Jackson, Ronald Vern. *Rhode Island Census Index, Online Edition*. Orem, UT: Ancestry.com, Inc., 1999.
http://www.ancestry.com

_____, and Gary Ronald Teeples. *Rhode Island 1820 Census Index*. Bountiful, UT: Accelerated Indexing
    Systems, 1976. 36p.
U.S. Federal Population Census Schedules. 1820, M33, Microfilm Reel Nos. 115-117.

1830

Census Index: U.S. Selected States/Counties, 1830. Family Archive CD 315. Novato, CA: Broderbund Soft-
    ware. CD-ROM.
Jackson, Ronald Vern. *Rhode Island Census Index, Online Edition*. Orem, UT: Ancestry.com, Inc., 1999.
http://www.ancestry.com
_____, and Gary Ronald Teeples. *Rhode Island 1830 Census Index*. Bountiful, UT: Accelerated Indexing
    Systems, 1977. 44p.
U.S. Census Index, 1830-1839, New England, New York, Pennsylvania. Orem, UT: Automated Archives,
    1992. 1 CD-ROM.
U.S. Federal Population Census Schedules. 1830, M19, Microfilm Reel Nos. 167-168.

1840

Census Index: U.S. Selected States/Counties, 1840. Family Archive CD 316. Novato, CA: Broderbund Soft-
    ware. CD-ROM.
Jackson, Ronald Vern. *Rhode Island Census Index, Online Edition*. Orem, UT: Ancestry.com, Inc., 1999.
http://www.ancestry.com
_____, and Gary Ronald Teeples. *Rhode Island 1840 Census Index*. Bountiful, UT: Accelerated Indexing
    Systems, 1976. 50p.
U.S. Census Index Series, New England, New York, 1840. Orem, UT: Automated Archives, 1992. CD-ROM.
U.S. Federal Population Census Schedules. 1840, M704, Microfilm Reel Nos. 504-506.

1850

Census Index: U.S. Selected States/Counties, 1850. Family Archive CD 317. Novato, CA: Broderbund Soft-
    ware. CD-ROM.
Census Microfilm Records: Connecticut and Rhode Island, 1850. Family Archive CD 308. Novato, CA:
    Broderbund Software. CD-ROM.
Jackson, Ronald Vern. *Rhode Island Census Index, Online Edition*. Orem, UT: Ancestry.com, Inc., 1999.
http://www.ancestry.com
_____, and Gary Ronald Teeples. *Rhode Island 1850 Census Index*.Bountiful, UT: Accelerated Indexing
    Systems, 1976. 125p.
U.S. Census Index Series, New England, 1850. Orem, UT: Automated Archives, 1991. CD-ROM.
U.S. Federal Population Census Schedules. 1850, M432, Microfilm Reel Nos. 841-847.

1860

Dilts, Bryan Lee. *1860 Rhode Island Census Index, Heads of Households and other Surnames in House-
    holds Index*. Salt Lake City, UT: Index Pub., 1985. 2 vols.
Jackson, Ronald Vern. *Rhode Island Census Index, Online Edition*. Orem, UT: Ancestry.com, Inc., 1999.
http://www.ancestry.com
_____. *Rhode Island 1860 Census Index*. Salt Lake City, UT: Accelerating Indexing Systems, 1985, 1994.
    61p.
_____. *Rhode Island 1860 Federal Census Mortality Index*. North Salt Lake City, UT: Accelerated Index-
    ing Systems International, 1990. 64p.
U.S. Federal Population Census Schedules. 1860, M653, Microfilm Reel Nos. 1202-1211.

1870

Dilts, Bryan Lee. *1870 Rhode Island Census Index, Heads of Households and other Surnames in House-
    holds Index*. Salt Lake City, UT: Index Pub., 1985. 272p.

Jackson, Ronald Vern. *Rhode Island Census Index, Online Edition*. Orem, UT: Ancestry.com, Inc., 1999.
http://www.ancestry.com
_____. *Rhode Island 1870*. North Salt Lake, UT: Accelerated Indexing Systems International, 1987. 1,131p.
_____. *Rhode Island 1870 Federal Census Mortality Index*. North Salt Lake City, UT: Accelerated Indexing Systems International, 1990. Unpgd.
Steuart, Raeone Christensen. *Rhode Island 1870 Census Index*. Bountiful, UT: Heritage Quest, 2000. 475p.
_____. *Connecticut and Rhode Island 1870 Census Index*. Bountiful, UT: Heritage Quest, 2000. CD-ROM.
U.S. Federal Population Census Schedules. 1870, M593, Microfilm Reel Nos. 1471-1512.

1880

U.S. Federal Population Census Schedules. 1880, T9, Microfilm Reel Nos. 1209-1216.
U.S. Federal Population Census Schedules. 1880, Soundex. T770, 11 Microfilm Reels.

1890

Jackson, Ronald Vern. *Rhode Island Census Index, Online Edition (Veterans Schedules)*. Orem, UT: Ancestry.com, Inc., 1999.
http://www.ancestry.com
_____. *Rhode Island 1890 Veterans Census Index*. Salt Lake City, UT: AGES, 1986. 164p.
U.S. Federal Population Census Schedules, Special Schedule, Enumerating Union Veterans and Widows of Union Veterans of the Civil War. 1890, M123, Microfilm Reel No. 92.
Veterans' Schedules: U.S. Selected States, 1890. Family Archive CD 131. Novato, CA: Broderbund Software. CD-ROM.

1900

U.S. Federal Population Census Schedules. 1900, T623, Microfilm Reel Nos. 1504-1513.
U.S. Federal Population Census Schedules. 1900, Soundex. T1069, 49 Microfilm Reels.

1910

U.S. Federal Population Census Schedules. 1910, T624, Microfilm Reel Nos. 1436-1445. (No Soundex/Miracode Index was prepared by the Government for this State.)

1920

U.S. Federal Population Census Schedules. 1920, T625, Microfilm Reel Nos. 1670-1681.
U.S. Federal Population Census Schedules. 1920, Soundex. M1585, 53 Microfilm Reels.

Newport County
1850

Rathbun, Robert Boehm. *1850 Federal Census, New Shoreham, Newport County, Rhode Island*. Bowling Green, KY: Author, 1994. 3 vols.

Providence County
1920

USGenWeb Census Project. Rhode Island, 1920 Providence County.
ftp://ftp.rootsweb.com/pub/census/ri/providence/1920/

South Carolina

Henderson, Robert H. *Hendersons of Early Georgia, a Beginning Survey of the People Using the Henderson Name from the South Carolina Census and Other Records*. Greer, SC: Author, 1997. Unpgd.
Jackson, Ronald Vern, Altha Polson, Shirley P. Zachrison. *Early South Carolina*. Bountiful, UT: Accelerated Indexing Systems.

1790

Jackson, Ronald Vern. *First Census of the United States, 1790, South Carolina.* Bountiful, UT: Accelerated Indexing Systems, 1978. 150p

_____. _____. Bountiful, UT: Accelerated Indexing Systems, 1990. 458p.

_____. _____. *South Carolina Census Index, Online Edition.* Orem, UT: Ancestry.com, Inc., 1999. **http://www.ancestry.com**

U.S. Bureau of the Census. *Heads of Families at the First Census of the United States Taken in the Year 1790, South Carolina.* Washington, DC: Government Printing Office, 1908. 227p.

_____. _____. *Online Database Edition.* Orem, UT: Ancestry.com, Inc., 1999. **http://www.ancestry.com**

_____. *U.S. Federal Population Census Schedules,* 1790. T498, Microfilm Reel No. 3.

U.S. Federal Population Census Schedules, 1790. M637, Microfilm Reel No. 11.

1800

Holcomb, Brent. *Index to the 1800 Census of South Carolina.* Baltimore, MD: Genealogical Pub. Co., 1980, 1997. 264p.

Jackson, Ronald Vern. *South Carolina Census Index, Online Edition.* Orem, UT: Ancestry.com, Inc., 1999. **http://www.ancestry.com**

Steuart, Raeone Christensen. *South Carolina 1800 Census Index.* Bountiful, UT: Heritage Quest, 2000. 223p.

_____. *United States 1800 Census Index.* Bountiful, UT: Heritage Quest, 2000. 4 vols. CD-ROM.

U.S. Federal Population Census Schedules, 1800. M32, Microfilm Reel Nos. 47-50.

1810

Holcomb, Brent. *Index to the 1800 Census of South Carolina.* Baltimore, MD: Genealogical Pub. Co., 1980.

Jackson, Ronald Vern. *South Carolina Census Index, Online Edition.* Orem, UT: Ancestry.com, Inc., 1999. **http://www.ancestry.com**

_____, and Gary Ronald Teeples. *South Carolina 1810 Census Index.* Bountiful, UT: Accelerated Indexing Systems, 1976. 97p.

U.S. Federal Population Census Schedules, 1810. M252, Microfilm Reel Nos. 60-62.

1820

Jackson, Ronald Vern. *South Carolina Census Index, Online Edition.* Orem, UT: Ancestry.com, Inc., 1999. **http://www.ancestry.com**

_____, and Gary Ronald Teeples. *South Carolina 1820 Census Index.* Bountiful, UT: Accelerated Indexing Systems, 1976. 156p.

Platt, Gwen. *South Carolina Index to the United States Census of 1820.* Tustin, CA: G.A.M. Publications, 1972. 426p.

U.S. Federal Population Census Schedules. 1820, M33, Microfilm Reel Nos. 118-121.

1830

Census Index: U.S. Selected States/Counties, 1830. Family Archive CD 315. Novato, CA: Broderbund Software. CD-ROM.

1830-1839 U.S. Census Indexes, Mid-Atlantic, South, Mid-West. Orem, UT: Automated Archives, 1993. CD-ROM.

Hazlewood, Jean Park. *Index, 1830 Census, South Carolina.* Fort Worth, TX: GenRePut, 1973. 433p.

Jackson, Ronald Vern. *South Carolina Census Index, Online Edition.* Orem, UT: Ancestry.com, Inc., 1999. **http://www.ancestry.com**

_____, and Gary Ronald Teeples. *South Carolina 1830 Census Index.* Bountiful, UT: Accelerated Indexing Systems, 1976. 115, 39p.

U.S. Federal Population Census Schedules. 1830, M19, Microfilm Reel Nos. 169-173.

1840

Census Index: U.S. Selected States/Counties, 1840. Family Archive CD 316. Novato, CA: Broderbund Software. CD-ROM.

Jackson, Ronald Vern. *South Carolina Census Index, Online Edition.* Orem, UT: Ancestry.com, Inc., 1999. **http://www.ancestry.com**

_____, and Gary Ronald Teeples. *South Carolina 1840 Census Index.* Bountiful, UT: Accelerated Indexing Systems, 1977, 1997. 119p.

U.S. Federal Population Census Schedules. 1840, M704, Microfilm Reel Nos. 507-516.

1850

Holcomb, Brent. *Index to the 1850 Mortality Schedule of South Carolina.* Easley, SC: Southern Historical Press, 1980. 48p.

Jackson, Ronald Vern. *Mortality Schedules Index, Online Edition.* Orem, UT: Ancestry.com, Inc., 1999. **http://www.ancestry.com**

_____. *South Carolina Census Index, Online Edition.* Orem, UT: Ancestry.com, Inc., 1999. **http://www.ancestry.com**

_____. *South Carolina 1850 Slave Schedule Census Index.* Salt Lake City, UT: Accelerated Indexing Systems International, 1988, 1996. 379p.

_____, and Gary Ronald Teeples. *South Carolina 1850 Census Index.* Bountiful, UT: Accelerated Indexing Systems, 1976, 1981. 174p.

_____. *South Carolina 1850 Mortality Census Index.* North Salt Lake City, UT: Accelerated Indexing Systems International, 1989. 35p.

U.S. Census Index Series, Alabama, Arkansas, Georgia, Florida, Louisiana, Mississippi, South Carolina, 1850. Orem, UT: Automated Archives, 1991. CD-ROM.

U.S. Federal Population Census Schedules. 1850, M432, Microfilm Reel Nos. 848-860.

U.S. Federal Population Census Schedules. 1850, M432, Slave Schedules, Microfilm Reel Nos. 861-868.

1860

Arnold, Jonnie Peeler. *Index to 1860 Federal Census of South Carolina.* Clarkesville, GA: Author, 1982. 256p.

_____. *Index to 1860 Mortality Schedule of South Carolina.* Clarkesville, GA: Author, 1982. 32p.

Census Index: U.S. Selected States/Counties, 1860. Family Archive CD 318. Novato, CA: Broderbund Software. CD-ROM.

Dilts, Bryan Lee. *1860 South Carolina Census Index, Heads of Household and Other Surnames in Household Index.* Salt Lake City, UT: Indexing Publishing, 1985; 1993. 2 vols.

Jackson, Ronald Vern. *Mortality Schedules Index, Online Edition.* Orem, UT: Ancestry.com, Inc., 1999. **http://www.ancestry.com**

_____. *South Carolina Census Index, Online Edition.* Orem, UT: Ancestry.com, Inc., 1999. **http://www.ancestry.com**

_____. *South Carolina 1860 Census Index.* Bountiful, UT: Accelerated Indexing Systems, 1988, 1998. 860p.

_____. *South Carolina 1860 Mortality Census Index.* North Salt Lake City, UT: Accelerated Indexing Systems International, 1989. 36p.

_____. *South Carolina 1860 Slave Schedule Census Index.* Salt Lake City, UT: Accelerated Indexing Systems International, 1990. 533p.

Steuart, Raeone Christensen. *South Carolina 1860 Census Index.* Bountiful, UT: Heritage Quest, 1999. 2 vols.

U.S. Census Index, 1860, Alabama, Arkansas, Florida, Louisiana, Mississippi, South Carolina. Orem, UT: Automated Archives, 1992. 1 CD-ROM.

U.S. Federal Population Census Schedules. 1860, M653, Microfilm Reel Nos. 1212-1228.

U.S. Federal Population Census Schedules. 1860, M653, Slave Schedules, Microfilm Reel Nos. 1229-1238.

1870

Census Index: North Carolina/South Carolina, 1870. Family Archive CD 289. Novato, CA: Broderbund Software. CD-ROM.

Jackson, Ronald Vern. *South Carolina 1870 Federal Census Index*. Salt Lake City, UT: Accelerated Indexing Systems International, 1990. 854p.

Steuart, Bradley W. *South Carolina 1870 Census Index*. Bountiful, UT: Precision Indexing, 1989, 1999. 2 vols.; 19 microfiche.

Steuart, Raeone Christensen. *North and South Carolina 1870 Census Index Extracted from the Original U.S. Federal Census Schedules*. Bountiful, UT: Heritage Quest, 1997. 2 vols.

_____. _____. Bountiful, UT: Heritage Quest, 1998. CD-ROM.

1880

U.S. Federal Population Census Schedules. 1880, T9, Microfilm Reel Nos. 1217-1243.
U.S. Federal Population Census Schedules. 1880, Soundex. T771, 56 Microfilm Reels.

1890

Jackson, Ronald Vern. *South Carolina Census Index, Online Edition*. Orem, UT: Ancestry.com, Inc., 1999. **http://www.ancestry.com**

_____. *1890 South Carolina Census Index, Special Schedule of the Eleventh Census (1890) Enumerating Union Veterans and of Union Veterans of the Civil War*. North Salt Lake, UT: Accelerated Indexing Systems, 1984, 1997. 58p.

U.S. Federal Population Census Schedules, Special Schedule, Enumerating Union Veterans and Widows of Union Veterans of the Civil War. 1890, M123, Microfilm Reel No. 93.

Veterans' Schedules: U.S. Selected States, 1890. Family Archive CD 131. Novato, CA: Broderbund Software. CD-ROM.

1900

U.S. Federal Population Census Schedules. 1900, T623, Microfilm Reel Nos. 1514-1545.
U.S. Federal Population Census Schedules. 1900, Soundex. T1070, 124 Microfilm Reels.

1910

U.S. Federal Population Census Schedules. 1910, T624, Microfilm Reel Nos. 1446-1474.
U.S. Federal Population Census Schedules. 1910, Soundex. T1275, 93 Microfilm Reels.

1920

U.S. Federal Population Census Schedules. 1920, T625, Microfilm Reel Nos. 1682-1713.
U.S. Federal Population Census Schedules. 1920, Soundex. M1586, 112 Microfilm Reels.

Abbeville County
1850

1850 U.S. Census, Abbeville County, South Carolina. Wichita, KS: S-K Publications, 1996. 600p.

Lawrence, Harold. *The 1850 Census of Abbeville District, South Carolina*. Tignall, GA: Boyd Publishing Co., 1981. 400p.

1860

Walker, Sonia L. *Abbeville County, South Carolina, a Compilation of Data from the 1860 Slave Schedule and a List of Free African Americans on the 1860 Census*. Abbeville, SC: Abbeville Books, 1997. 44p.

Anderson County

Alexander, Virginia Wood. *Pendleton District and Anderson County, South Carolina Wills, Estates, Inventories, Tax Returns, and Census Records*. Easley, SC: Southern Historical Press, 1980. 430p.

1830

Smith, T. L. *Index 1830 Census, Anderson County, South Carolina*. Fort Worth, TX: GenRePut Genealogical Research. 20p.

1850

1850 U.S. Census, Anderson County, South Carolina. Wichita, KS: S-K Publications, 1996. 600p.

Barnwell District

Jarrell, Lawrence E. *Early Barnwell, South Carolina Census*. High Point, NC: Alligator Creek Genealogy Publications, 1998. 53p.

1820

Jarrell, Lawrence E. *1820 Barnwell District, South Carolina Census*. High Point, NC: Alligator Creek Genealogy Publications, 1998. 53p.

1830

Index, 1830 Census, Barnwell County, South Carolina. Fort Worth, TX: GenRePut. 17p.

Beaufort County

Jarrell, Lawrence E. *Early Beaufort, South Carolina Census*. High Point, NC: Alligator Creek Genealogy Publications, 1998. 51p.

1850

Caldwell, Betsy McIntosh. *The 1850 Census of St. Luke's Parish, Beaufort County, South Carolina*. Bluffton, SC: Bluffton Historical Preservation Society, 1984. 62p.

Cherokee County
1910, 1920

Malone, Samuel Lorenzo. *Black Families in Cherokee County, South Carolina, as Taken from 1910-1920 Federal Census*. Rev. ed. Spartanburg, SC: Reprint Co., 1993. 93p.

Chesterfield County
1820

Thomas, Betty Wood. *1820 Census, Chesterfield County, South Carolina*. Pass Christian, MS: Willo Institute of Genealogy, 1967. 24p.

1850

Pigg, James C. *1850 Federal Agricultural Census for Chesterfield County, South Carolina*. Tega Cay, SC: Author, 1996. 99p.

_____. *Mortality Schedule 1850, 1860, 1870, 1880 Chesterfield County, South Carolina Federal Census*. Tega Cay, SC: Author, 1995. 22p.

1860-1880

Pigg, James C. *Mortality Schedule 1850, 1860, 1870, 1880 Chesterfield County, South Carolina Federal Census*. Tega Cay, SC: Author, 1995. 22p.

Colleton County
1830

Hazlewood, Fred L. *Index, 1830 Census, Colleton County, South Carolina*. Fort Worth, TX: GenRePut. 11p.

Darlington County
1850

Altman, Peggy B. *1850 Census of Darlington County, South Carolina*. Hemingway, SC: Three Rivers Historical Society, 1981. 158p.

Edgefield County
1860

McKinney, Margaret Vaughan. *Edgefield County, South Carolina, 1860 Census*. Augusta, GA: Augusta Genealogical Society. 447p.

Franklin County
1830
Bradley, Stephen E. *The 1830 Federal Census, Franklin County, North Carolina (Population Schedule)*. South Boston, VA: Author, 1987. 89p.

Georgetown County
Index 1830 Census, Georgetown County, South Carolina. Fort Worth, TX: GeRePut. 5p.

Greenville County
1850
1850 U.S. Census, Greenville County, South Carolina. Wichita, KS: S-K Publications, 1996. 600p.

Halifax County
1830
Bradley, Stephen E. *The 1830 Federal Census, Halifax County, North Carolina (Population Schedule)*. South Boston, VA: Author, 1987. 139p.

Horry County
1850
Woodard, Janet H. *Population Schedules of the Seventh Census of the United States, 1850, Roll 854, Horry County, South Carolina, Original Returns of the Assistant Marshals, White and Free Colored Population*. Charleston, SC: Author, 1980. 132p.
1860
Lewis, Catherince Heniford, and Ashley Patterson. *Index to the 1860 Census of Horry County, South Carolina*. Macon, GA: Waccamaw Records, 1989. 26p.
Lewis, Catherine Heniford. *1860 Census of Horry County, South Carolina*. Macon, GA: Waccamaw Records, 1996. 75p.

Kershaw County
1800
The Second Federal Census, 1800, South Carolina, Kershaw County. Camden, SC: Kershaw County Historical Society, 1970. 24p.
USGenWeb Census Project. South Carolina, 1800 Kershaw County.
ftp://ftp.rootsweb.com/pub/census/sc/kershaw/1800/
1830
Hazlewood, Fred L. *Index, 1830 Census, Kershaw County, South Carolina*. Fort Worth, TX, GenRePut. 9p.
1840
Draine, Tony, and John Skinner. *Kershaw District, South Carolina Census, 1840*. Columbia, SC: Congaree Publications, 1986. 47p.
1850
1850 Kershaw County, South Carolina, Census with Expanded Genealogical Information. Camden, SC: Catawba-Wateree Chapter, South Carolina Genealogical Society, 1997. 434p.

Laurens County
1800
Elliott, Irene Dillard. *Second Federal Census, 1800 Laurens County, South Carolina*. SC: University of South Carolina, 1959.
_____. _____. *Online Database Edition*. Orem, UT: Ancestry.com, Inc., 1999.
http://www.ancestry.com
1830
Smith, T. L. *Index 1830 Census, Laurens County, South Carolina*. Fort Worth, TX: GenRePut, 1973. 20p.

1850

Tucker, Donald J. *1850 Census, Laurens County, South Carolina.* No. Berwick, ME: Author, 1996. 47p.

Lexington County
1800

Holcomb, Brent. *1800 Lexington County Census.* Clinton, SC: Author, 1974. 16p.
1830

Hazlewood, Fred L. *Index, 1830 Census, Lexington County, South Carolina.* Fort Worth, TX: GenRePut. 9p.
1850

Lexington County, South Carolina, 1850 Census, with Genealogical Data on Many Families. Lexington, SC: Lexington County Genealogical Association, 1985. 376p.

Lexington County, South Carolina 1850 Census, with Genealogical Data on Most Families. 2nd ed. Lexington, SC: Lexington Genealogical Association, 1998. 446p.
1860

Trotter, Shirley F. Johnson. *1860 Census, Lexington County, South Carolina, with a Complete Index of Names Including the Mortality Schedule and the Slave Schedule.* Chapin, SC: Dutch Fork Chapter, South Carolina Genealogical Society, 1991. 262p.
1870

Trotter, Shirley F. Johnson. *1870 Census, Lexington County, South Carolina, with a Complete Name Index.* Chapin, SC: Dutch Fork Chapter, South Carolina Genealogical Society, 1989. 260, 79p.

Marion County
1850

Ward, Carolyn P. *1850 Census of Marion County, South Carolina.* Hemingway, SC: Author, 1978. 229p.

Marlboro County
1830

Hazlewood, Fred L. *Index, 1830 Census, Marlboro County, South Carolina.* Fort Worth, TX: GenRePut. 7p.

Newberry County
1790

Newberry County, South Carolina Census. Signal Mountain, TN: Mountain Press, 1999. 25p.
1810

Elliott, Mrs. R. D. *1810 Census, Newberry County, South Carolina.* Chattanooga, TN: Author. 8p.
1850

Wicker, Eleanor Clyburn. *Newberry County South Carolina 1850 Census with Genealogical Data on Many Families.* Newberry, SC: Newberry County Historical Society, 1985. 315p.
1870

Bundrick, Betty Mooney. *Newberry County, South Carolina 1870 Census with Mortality Schedules, Agriculture Schedules, Census Index.* Chapin, SC: Dutch Fork Chapter of the South Carolina Genealogical Society, 1990. 824p.

Orangeburg County

Jarrell, Lawrence E. *Early Orangeburg, South Carolina Census.* High Point, NC: Alligator Creek Genealogy Publications, 1998. 88p.
1820

Jarrell, Lawrence E. *1820 Orangeburg, South Carolina Census.* High Point, NC: Alligator Creek Genealogy Publications, 1998. 46p.
1830

Hazlewood, Fred L. *Index, 1830 Census, Orangeburg County, South Carolina.* Fort Worth, TX: GenRePut. 13p.

1850

Bronson, Patricia Packer. *An Index, U.S. Census 1850, Orangeburg District, South Carolina Schedule I*. Wye Mills, MD: Author, 1973. 81p.

Pendleton County
1810

Samuels, Nancy Timmons. *Pendleton District, South Carolina, 1810 Census*. Fort Worth, TX: Author, 1981. 73p.

Pickens County
1830

Sheriff, Anne, Tom Wilkinson, Lavinia Moore, and Jay Young. *Pickens District, South Carolina 1830 Census*. Central, SC: Faith Clayton Family Research Center, 1988. Unpgd.

1850

Bronson, Patricia Packer. *An Index U.S. Census, 1850, Pickens District, South Carolina, Schedule I*. Wye Mills, MD: Author, 1973. 124p.

Sheriff, G. Anne. *1850 Federal Slave Census of Pickens District, South Carolina, Eastern Division, Present-day Pickens County*. Central, SC: Author, 1991. 40p.

1860

Cheek, Linda Gale Smith. *Pickens District, South Carolina 1860 Census, 2nd and 5th Regiment, (Now Oconee and Pickens Counties)*. Easley, SC: Author, 1995. 466p.

Sheriff, G. Anne. *1860 Federal Slave Census of Pickens District, South Carolina, 5th Regiment, Present-day Pickens County*. Central, SC: Author, 1989. 38p.

Richland County
1830

Hazlewood, Fred L. *Index, 1830 Census, Richland County, South Carolina*. Fort Worth, TX: GenRePut. 10p.

Spartanburg County
1850

Gilbert, Horace Elbert, and Rodney Dusterhoft. *An Enhanced 1850 Census, Spartanburg District, South Carolina*. Spartanburg, SC: Pinckney District Chapter, South Carolina Genealogical Society, 1994. 367, 63p.

Sumter County
1850

Teel, Dorothy O. *1850 Census, Sumter District, South Carolina*. Hemingway, SC: Three Rivers Historical Society, 1983. 224p.

Union County
1850

Brock, Pettus. *1850 Federal Census, Union County, South Carolina*. Hickory Grove, SC: Broad River Basin Historical Society, 1992. 205p.

Williamsburg County
1810

USGenWeb Census Project. South Carolina, 1810 Williamsburg County.
ftp://ftp.rootsweb.com/pub/census/sc/williamsburg/1810/
1830

Index 1830 Census, Williamsburg County, South Carolina. Fort Worth, TX: GenRePut. 5p.

1850
USGenWeb Census Project. South Carolina, 1850 Williamsburg County.
ftp://ftp.rootsweb.com/pub/census/sc/williamsburg/1850/

York District
1850
Owens, Jo Roberts. *1850 Federal Census, York District, South Carolina.* York, SC: Author, 1987. 367p.

South Dakota

1860
Census Index: U.S. Selected States/Counties, 1860. Family Archive CD 318. Novato, CA: Broderbund Software. CD-ROM.
Jackson, Ronald Vern. *Dakota 1860 Territorial Census Index.* Salt Lake City, UT: Accelerated Indexing Systems, 1980. 150p.
_____. *Mortality Schedules Index, Online Edition.* Orem, UT: Ancestry.com, Inc., 1999.
http://www.ancestry.com
_____. *Dakota Territory 1860, This Index Includes Every Given Name on the Census Record.* North Salt Lake, UT: Accelerated Indexing Systems International, 1980. Unpgd.
U.S. Federal Population Census Schedules. 1860, M653, Microfilm Reel No. 94.

1870
Census Index: U.S. Selected States/Counties, 1870. Family Archive CD 319. Novato, CA: Broderbund Software. CD-ROM.
Guerrero, John. *Census Information Concerning Dakota and North Dakota Black Residents as Found in the United States Census Reports of 1870, 1880, 1885, 1900, 1910 and 1920.* Bismarck, ND: University of Mary Press, 1994. 231p.
Jackson, Ronald Vern. *South Dakota Census Index, Online Edition.* Orem, UT: Ancestry.com, Inc., 1999.
http://www.ancestry.com
_____. *Dakota 1870 Territorial Census Index.* Salt Lake City, UT: Accelerated Indexing Systems, 1980, 1998. 60; 179p.
_____. *Mortality Schedules Index, Online Edition.* Orem, UT: Ancestry.com, Inc., 1999.
http://www.ancestry.com
U.S. Federal Population Census Schedules. 1870, M593, Microfilm Reel No. 118.

1880
Census Index: U.S. Selected States/Counties, 1880. Family Archive CD 320. Novato, CA: Broderbund Software. CD-ROM.
Guerrero, John. *Census Information Concerning Dakota and North Dakota Black Residents as Found in the United States Census Reports of 1870, 1880, 1885, 1900, 1910 and 1920.* Bismarck, ND: University of Mary Press, 1994. 231p.
Jackson, Ronald Vern. *South Dakota Census Index, Online Edition.* Orem, UT: Ancestry.com, Inc., 1999.
http://www.ancestry.com
_____. *Dakota 1880 Territorial Census Index.* Salt Lake City, UT: Accelerated Indexing Systems, 1980. 329p.
_____. *Dakota Territorial Census Index.* Salt Lake City, UT: Accelerated Indexing Systems, 1980. 25p.
_____. *Dakota Territorial 1880 Mortality Schedule.* North Salt Lake City, UT: Accelerated Indexing Systems International, 1988. 44p.
_____. *Mortality Schedules Index, Online Edition.* Orem, UT: Ancestry.com, Inc., 1999.
http://www.ancestry.com

1885

Guerrero, John. *Census Information Concerning Dakota and North Dakota Black Residents as Found in the United States Census Reports of 1870, 1880, 1885, 1900, 1910 and 1920.* Bismarck, ND: University of Mary Press, 1994. 231p.

1885 Census Index, Dakota Territory. Bismarck, ND: Bismarck Mandan Historical and Genealogical Society, 1995-1996. 7 vols.

Jackson, Ronald Vern. *Mortality Schedules Index, Online Edition.* Orem, UT: Ancestry.com, Inc., 1999. **http://www.ancestry.com**

_____. *South Dakota Census Index, Online Edition.* Orem, UT: Ancestry.com, Inc., 1999. **http://www.ancestry.com**

_____. *South Dakota 1885 Census Index.* Bountiful, UT: Accelerated Indexing Systems, 1981. 296p.

1890

Jackson, Ronald Vern. *1890 South Dakoka Census Index Special Schedule of the Eleventh Census (1890) Enumerating Union Veterans and of Union Veterans of the Civil War.* North Salt Lake City, UT: Accelerated Indexing Systems, 1985, 1998. 115p.

_____. *South Dakota Census Index, Online Edition.* Orem, UT: Ancestry.com, Inc., 1999. **http://www.ancestry.com**

U.S. Federal Population Census Schedules. 1890, M407, Microfilm Reel No. 3.

U.S. Federal Population Census Schedules. 1890, Index. M496, 2 Microfilm Reels.

U.S. Federal Population Census Schedules, Special Schedule, Enumerating Union Veterans and Widows of Union Veterans of the Civil War. 1890, M123, Microfilm Reel No. 94.

Veterans' Schedules: U.S. Selected States, 1890. Family Archive CD 131. Novato, CA: Broderbund Software. CD-ROM.

1900

Ledoux, Albert H. *The French Canadian Families of the Plains and Upper Mountain States, Abstracts from the Federal Census of 1900.* Altoona, PA: Author, 1991. 2 vols.

U.S. Federal Population Census Schedules. 1900, T623, Microfilm Reel Nos. 1545-1556.

U.S. Federal Population Census Schedules. 1900, Soundex. T1071, 44 Microfilm Reels.

1910

U.S. Federal Population Census Schedules. 1910, T624, Microfilm Reel Nos. 1475-1489. (No Soundex/Miracode Index was prepared by the Government for this State.)

1920

U.S. Federal Population Census Schedules. 1920, T625, Microfilm Reel Nos. 1714-1727.

U.S. Federal Population Census Schedules. 1920, Soundex. M1587, 48 Microfilm Reels.

Ellis County
1890

U.S. Federal Population Census Schedules. 1890, M407, Microfilm Reel No. 3.

U.S. Federal Population Census Schedules. 1890, Index. M496, 2 Microfilm Reels.

Hood County
1890

U.S. Federal Population Census Schedules. 1890, M407, Microfilm Reel No. 3.

U.S. Federal Population Census Schedules. 1890, Index. M496, 2 Microfilm Reels.

Hutchinson County
1880

Seibert, Ronald Jay. *Hutchinson County, South Dakota 1880 Census.* Lakewood, OH: Author, 1980. 125p.

Kaufman County
1890
U.S. Federal Population Census Schedules. 1890, M407, Microfilm Reel No. 3.
U.S. Federal Population Census Schedules. 1890, Index. M496, 2 Microfilm Reels.

Lawrence County
1880
Harrison, Joan. *The 1880 Federal Census of Ft. Meade, Lawrence County, Dakota Territory, South Dakota,
Copied from National Archives Microfilm, Series T9, Roll 113*. Rapid City, SD: Rapid City Society for
Genealogical Research, 1986. 23p.

Rusk County
1890
U.S. Federal Population Census Schedules. 1890, M407, Microfilm Reel No. 3.
U.S. Federal Population Census Schedules. 1890, Index. M496, 2 Microfilm Reels.

Trinity County
1890
U.S. Federal Population Census Schedules. 1890, M407, Microfilm Reel No. 3.
U.S. Federal Population Census Schedules. 1890, Index. M496, 2 Microfilm Reels.

Union County
1890
U.S. Federal Population Census Schedules. 1890, M407, Microfilm Reel No. 3.
U.S. Federal Population Census Schedules. 1890, Index. M496, 2 Microfilm Reels.

Tennessee

Jackson, Ronald Vern. *Tennessee Early Census Index*. Salt Lake City, UT: AGES, 1980. Unpgd.

1790
Fulcher, Richard Carlton. *1770-1790 Census of the Cumberland Settlements, Davidson, Sumner and Ten-
nessee Counties (In What Is Now Tennessee)*. Baltimore, MD: Genealogical Pub. Co., 1987. 253p.
U.S. Federal Population Census Schedules, 1790. M637. Records did not survive for this state.

1810
Jackson, Ronald Vern. *Tennessee Census Index, Online Edition*. Orem, UT: Ancestry.com, Inc., 1999.
http://www.ancestry.com
_____. *Tennessee 1810*. North Salt Lake City, UT: Accelerated Indexing Systems International, 1985. 36p.
U.S. Federal Population Census Schedules, 1810. M252, Microfilm Reel No. 63.

1820
Bentley, Elizabeth Petty. *Index to the 1820 Census of Tennessee*. Baltimore, MD: Clearfield, 1981, 1996.
287p.
Jackson, Ronald Vern. *Tennessee 1820 Census*. Bountiful, UT: Accelerated Indexing Systems, 1974. 597p.
U.S. Federal Population Census Schedules. 1820, M33, Microfilm Reel Nos. 122-125.

1830
Census Index: U.S. Selected States/Counties, 1830. Family Archive CD 315. Novato, CA: Broderbund Software. CD-ROM.

1830-1839 U.S. Census Indexes, Mid-Atlantic, South, Mid-West. Orem, UT: Automated Archives, 1993. CD-ROM.

Jackson, Ronald Vern. *Tennessee Census Index, Online Edition.* Orem, UT: Ancestry.com, Inc., 1999. **http://www.ancestry.com**

_____, and Gary Ronald Teeples. *Tennessee 1830 Census Index.* Bountiful, UT: Accelerated Indexing Systems, 1976. 213p.

Sistler, Byron. *1830 Census East Tennessee.* Nashville, TN: Author, 1995. 276p.

U.S. Federal Population Census Schedules. 1830, M19, Microfilm Reel Nos. 174-182.

1840

Census Index: U.S. Selected States/Counties, 1840. Family Archive CD 316. Novato, CA: Broderbund Software. CD-ROM.

Jackson, Ronald Vern. *Tennessee Census Index, Online Edition.* Orem, UT: Ancestry.com, Inc., 1999. **http://www.ancestry.com**

_____, and Gary Ronald Teeples. *Tennessee 1840 Census Index.* Bountiful, UT: Accelerated Indexing Systems, 1976. 260p.

Sistler, Byron. *1840 Census, Tennessee.* Nashville, TN: Author, 1986. 597p.

U.S. Federal Population Census Schedules. 1840, M704, Microfilm Reel Nos. 517-537.

1850

Corley, Betty J. *Index, Yeoman(s), Yeaman(s), Youman(s), U.S. Census Index, 1850, 1860, 1880, Alabama, Florida, Kentucky, Louisiana, Maryland, Mississippi, Tennessee, Texas, Virginia, Includes Various Other Spellings.* Hyrum, UT: Author, 1988. 5p.

Jackson, Ronald Vern. *Federal Census Index, Tennessee 1850 Slave Schedules Index.* West Jordan, UT: Genealogical Services, 1989, 1997. Unpgd.

_____. *Mortality Schedules Index, Online Edition.* Orem, UT: Ancestry.com, Inc., 1999. **http://www.ancestry.com**

_____. *Tennessee Census Index, Online Edition.* Orem, UT: Ancestry.com, Inc., 1999. **http://www.ancestry.com**

_____, and Gary Ronald Teeples. *Tennessee 1850 Census Index.* Salt Lake City, UT: Accelerated Indexing Systems, 1977, 1981. 452p.

_____. *Tennessee 1850 Mortality Census Index.* North Salt Lake City, UT: Accelerated Indexing Systems International, 1979. 109p.

Sistler, Byron, and Barbara Sistler. *1850 Census, Tennessee.* Evanston, IL: Sistler & Associates, 1974-1976. 8 vols.

_____. *1850 Census, Tennessee, Index to the Surname Armstrong, Armston.* Evanston, IL: Sistler & Associates, 1972. 6p.

_____. *1850 Census, Tennessee, Index to the Surname Austin, Austen, Auston.* Evanston, IL: Sistler & Associates, 1972. 5p.

_____. *1850 Census, Tennessee, Index to the Surname Boyd, Boid, Boyed.* Evanston, IL: Sistler & Associates, 1972. 7p.

_____. *1850 Census, Tennessee, Index to the Surname Burton.* Evanston, IL: Sistler & Associates, 1972. 6p.

_____. *1850 Census, Tennessee, Index to the Surname Cannon.* Evanston, IL: Sistler & Associates, 1972. 4p.

_____. *1850 Census, Tennessee, Index to the Surname Carter.* Evanston, IL: Sistler & Associates, 1972. 16p.

_____. *1850 Census, Tennessee, Index to the Surname Davis.* Evanston, IL: Sistler & Associates, 1972. 29p.

_____. *1850 Census, Tennessee, Index to the Surname Evans.* Evanston, IL: Sistler & Associates, 1972. 9p.

_____. *1850 Census, Tennessee, Index to the Surname Hodge.* Evanston, IL: Sistler & Associates, 1972. 8p.

_____. *1850 Census, Tennessee, Index to the Surname Murphy.* Evanston, IL: Sistler & Associates, 1972. 5p.

U.S. Census Index Series, Kentucky and Tennessee, 1850. Orem, UT: Automated Archives, 1991. CD-ROM.

U.S. Federal Population Census Schedules. 1850, M432, Microfilm Reel Nos. 869-901.

U.S. Federal Population Census Schedules. 1850, M432, Slave Schedules, Microfilm Reel Nos. 902-907.

1860

Census Index: U.S. Selected States/Counties, 1860. Family Archive CD 318. Novato, CA: Broderbund Software. CD-ROM.

Corley, Betty J. *Index, Yeoman(s), Yeaman(s), Youman(s), U.S. Census Index, 1850, 1860, 1880, Alabama, Florida, Kentucky, Louisiana, Maryland, Mississippi, Tennessee, Texas, Virginia, Includes Various Other Spellings*. Hyrum, UT: Author, 1988. 5p.

Jackson, Ronald Vern. *Federal Census Index, Tennessee 1860 Slave Schedules*. West Jordan, UT: Genealogical Services, 1990, 1997. 675p.

_____. *Mortality Schedules Index, Online Edition*. Orem, UT: Ancestry.com, Inc., 1999.
http://www.ancestry.com

_____. *Tennessee Census Index, Online Edition*. Orem, UT: Ancestry.com, Inc., 1999.
http://www.ancestry.com

_____, and Gary Ronald Teeples. *Tennessee 1860 Census Index*. North Salt Lake City, UT: Accelerated Indexing Systems, 1981. 4 vols.

Robertson, Clara Hamlett. *Kansas Territorial Settlers of 1860 Who Were Born in Tennessee, Virginia, North Carolina and South Carolina*. Baltimore, MD: Genealogical Publishing Co., 1976. 187p.

U.S. Federal Population Census Schedules. 1860, M653, Microfilm Reel Nos. 1239-1280.

U.S. Federal Population Census Schedules. 1860, M653, Slave Schedules, Microfilm Reel Nos. 1281-1286.

1870

Sistler, Byron, and Barbara Sistler. *1870 Census, Tennessee*. Nashville, TN: Author, 1985. 2 vols.

Steuart, Raeone Christensen. *Tennessee 1870 Census Index*. Bountiful, UT: Heritage Quest, 1998. 3 vols. 1999. CD-ROM.

U.S. Federal Population Census Schedules. 1870, M593, Microfilm Reel Nos. 1513-1572.

1880

Corley, Betty J. *Index, Yeoman(s), Yeaman(s), Youman(s), U.S. Census Index, 1850, 1860, 1880, Alabama, Florida, Kentucky, Louisiana, Maryland, Mississippi, Tennessee, Texas, Virginia, Includes Various Other Spellings*. Hyrum, UT: Author, 1988. 5p.

Sistler, Barbara, and Samuel Sistler. *Index to the 1880 Census of East Tennessee*. Nashville, TN: Byron Sistler and Associates, 1997. 334p.

U.S. Federal Population Census Schedules. 1880, T9, Microfilm Reel Nos. 1244-1287.

U.S. Federal Population Census Schedules. 1880, Soundex. T772, 86 Microfilm Reels.

1890

Jackson, Ronald Vern. *Federal Census Index, Tennessee, 1890 Union Veterans Schedules*. West Jordan, UT: Genealogical Services, 1989; 1997. 376p.

_____. *Tennessee Census Index, Online Edition*. Orem, UT: Ancestry.com, Inc., 1999.
http://www.ancestry.com

U.S. Federal Population Census Schedules, Special Schedule, Enumerating Union Veterans and Widows of Union Veterans of the Civil War. 1890, M123, Microfilm Reel Nos. 95-98.

Veterans' Schedules: U.S. Selected States, 1890. Family Archive CD 131. Novato, CA: Broderbund Software. CD-ROM.

1891

Reed, Sue S. *Enumeration of Male Inhabitants of Twenty-one Years of Age and Upward, Citizens of Tennessee, January 1, 1891, as Provided for by an Act of General Assembly of Tennessee, Passed January 15, 1891, and Approved January 22, 1891*. Houston, TX: Author, 1989-1992. 16 vols.

1900

U.S. Federal Population Census Schedules. 1900, T623, Microfilm Reel Nos. 1557-1606.
U.S. Federal Population Census Schedules. 1900, Soundex. T1072, 187 Microfilm Reels.

1910

Reynolds, Clarence Lee. *Reynolds, Runnells, and Other Spellings, 1910 U.S. Census, Tennessee.* Lynchburg, OH: Author, 1985. 35p.
U.S. Federal Population Census Schedules. 1910, T624, Microfilm Reel Nos. 1490-1526.
U.S. Federal Population Census Schedules. 1910, Soundex. T1276, 142 Microfilm Reels.
U.S. Federal Population Census Schedules. 1910, Separate Soundex for Cities of Chattanooga, Knoxville, Memphis and Nashville, T1276, Microfilm Reel Nos. 112-142.

1920

U.S. Federal Population Census Schedules. 1920, T625, Microfilm Reel Nos. 1728-1771.
U.S. Federal Population Census Schedules. 1920, Soundex. M1588, 162 Microfilm Reels.

Anderson County
1850
Gammell, Paula. *1850 United States Census, Anderson County, Tennessee.* Oak Ridge, TN: Author, 1984. 91p.
1870
Hutton, Edith Wilson, and Imogene Hall Thacker. *Transcription, Federal Census Schedule, Anderson County, Tennessee, 1870, Indexed.* Knoxville, TN: Author, 1984. 96p.
1880
Sistler, Byron, and Barbara Sistler. *1880 Census, Tennessee, Transcription for Anderson County.* Evanston, IL: Sistler & Associates, 1978. 51p.
1920
Kelley, Wanda Daugherty. *Population Schedule of the United States Census of 1920 for Anderson County, Tennessee.* Author. 458p.

Bedford County
1850
Porch, Deane. *Bedford County, Tennessee, 1850 Census.* Franklin, TN: Lynch, 1969. 49p.
1880
Sistler, Byron, and Barbara Sistler. *1880 Census, Tennessee, Transcription for Bedford County.* Evanston, IL: Sistler & Associates, 1978. 124p.

Benton County
1840
Smith, Jonathan Kennon. *An Abstract of the 1840 United States Census for Benton County, Tennessee.* Memphis, TN: Author, 1977. 106p.
1850
Brown, John C., and Catheryn C. Brown. *The 1850 U.S. Census of Benton County, Tennessee.* Eva. TN: Author, 1978. 153p.
1880
Brown, John C., and Catheryn C. Brown. *The 1880 U.S. Census of Benton County, Tennessee.* Eva. TN: Author, 1978. 217p.

Bledsoe County
1830
Douthat, James L. *1830 Census, Sequatchie Valley, Marion, Bledsoe Counties.* Signal Mountain, TN: Mountain Press, 1986. 15p.

1840

Douthat, James L. *1840 Census, Sequatchie Valley, Marion, Bledsoe Counties*. Signal Mountain, TN: Author, 1982. 25p.

1850

USGenWeb Census Project. Tennessee, 1850 Bledsoe County.

ftp://ftp.rootsweb.com/pub/census/tn/bledsoe/1850/

1870

Kirkeminde, Patricia Barclay. *1870 Census of Bledsoe County, Tennessee*. Crossville, TN: Author, 1980. 39p.

1880

Sistler, Byron, and Barbara Sistler. *1880 Census, Tennessee, Transcription for Bledsoe County*. Evanston, IL: Sistler & Associates, 1978. 30p.

Blount County
1840

Templin, David H., and Cherel Bolin Henderson. *1840 Population Schedule of the United States Census, Blount County, Tennessee*. Maryville, TN: Authors, 1981. 58p.

1860

Templin, David H., and Cherel Bolin Henderson. *Population Schedule of the United States Census of 1860 for Blount County, Tennessee*. Maryville, TN: Author, 1982. 258p.

1870

Brown, Kenneth A., and Mary Ruth H. Brown. *United States Census of 1870 for Blount County, Tennessee*. Maryville, TN: Printers, Inc., 1983. 332p.

1880

Sistler, Byron, and Barbara Sistler. *1880 Census, Tennessee, Transcription for Blount County*. Evanston, IL: Sistler & Associates, 1978. 150p.

Bradley County
1850

Bradley County, Tennessee, 1850 Federal Census; Including Personal Information, Names, Age, Sex of Individual Family Members, Vocations, Value of Real Estate, Place of Birth by State or Country. 1850 Mortality Schedule. 1850 Federal Census (In Numerical Order by Residence) Statistics: Population Agricultural Production, Vocations, a Complete Alphabetical Index of Individual Names. Cleveland, TN: Author, 1973. 350p.

1870

Bradley County Tennessee 1870 Census Index. Cleveland, TN: Cleveland Public Library, 1987. 73p.

1880

Sistler, Byron, and Barbara Sistler. *1880 Census, Tennessee, Transcription for Bradley County*. Evanston, IL: Sistler & Associates, 1979. 59p.

1900

Bradley County, Tennessee, 1900 Census Index. Cleveland, TN: Cleveland Public Library, 1989. 91p.

Campbell County
1860

Hutton, Edith Wilson, and Imogene Hall Thacker. *Transcription, Federal Census Schedule, Campbell County, Tennessee, 1860, Indexed Federal Mortality Schedule, Campbell County, Tennessee, 1860 List of Slave Owners, Campbell County, Tennessee*. Knoxville, TN: Author, 1982. 157p.

1870

Hutton, Edith Wilson, and Imogene Hall Thacker. *Transcription, Federal Census Schedule, Campbell County, Tennessee 1870, Indexed*. Authors, 1983.

1880

Sistler, Byron, and Barbara Sistler. *1880 Census, Tennessee, Transcription for Campbell County*. Evanston, IL: Sistler & Associates, 1978. 92p.

1900

Cox, Connie White. *Transcription, Federal Census Schedule, Campbell County, Tennessee, 1900, Indexed.* Knoxville, TN: Author, 1984. 385p.

Cannon County
1850

Porch, Deane. *Cannon County, Tennessee.* Franklin, TN: Mrs. Clyde Lynch, 1974. 185p.

Carroll County
1850

The Seventh Census of the United States, 1850, Carroll County, Tennessee. McKenzie, TN: Carroll County Historical Society, 1979. 318p.

1860

Brown, John C., and Catheryn C. Brown. *The Eighth Census of the United States, 1860, Carroll County, Tennessee.* McKenzie, TN: Carroll County Historical Society, 1979. 271p.

Carter County
1830

USGenWeb Census Project. Tennessee, 1830 Carter County.
ftp://ftp.rootsweb.com/pub/census/tn/carter/1830/

1840

USGenWeb Census Project. Tennessee, 1840 Carter County.
ftp://ftp.rootsweb.com/pub/census/tn/carter/1840/

1850

Stout, Jerry Ann Kinnear. *1850 U.S. Federal Census of Carter County, Tennessee with Additional Information from Marriage Records.* Wichita, KS: Author, 1997. 115p.

1860

Stout, Jerry Ann Kinnear. *1860 U.S. Federal Census of Carter County, Tennessee, with Marriage Information from Carter County and Johnson County, Tennessee Marriage Records.* Author, 1996. 115p.

1870

Bishop, Brenda C. *1870 Census, Tennessee, Transcription for Carter County.* Elizabethtown, TN: Author, 1983. 56p.

1880

Sistler, Byron, and Barbara Sistler. *1880 Census, Tennessee, Transcription for Carter County.* Evanston, IL: Sistler & Associates, 1978. 48p.

Chattanooga (Hamilton County)
1910

U.S. Federal Population Census Schedules. 1910, Separate Soundex for Cities of Chattanooga, Knoxville, Memphis and Nashville, T1276, Microfilm Reel Nos. 112-142.

Cheatham County
1860

Dalton, Robert E., and Lynette Hamilton Dalton. *Cheatham County, Tennessee, Census of 1860.* Memphis, TN: Dalton and Dalton, 1986.

1880

Sistler, Byron, and Barbara Sistler. *1880 Census, Tennessee, Transcription for Cheatham County.* Evanston, IL: Sistler & Associates, 1978. 41p.

1920

Cheatham County, Tennessee Census Index, Online Edition. Orem, UT: Ancestry.com, Inc., 1999.
http://www.ancestry.com

Clay County

1920

Young, Denise. *1920 Census of Clay County, Tennessee. Online Database Edition*. Orem, UT: Ancestry.com, Inc., 1999.

http://www.ancestry.com

Cocke County

1840

Templin, David H., and Cherel Bolin Henderson. *1840 Population Schedule of the United States Census, Cocke County, Tennessee*. Maryville, TN: Authors, 1981. 37p.

1860

Templin, David H., and Cherel Bolin Henderson. *Population Schedule of the United States Census of 1860 for Cocke County, Tennessee*. Maryville, TN: Authors, 1983. 198p.

1880

Sistler, Byron. *1880 Census, Cocke County, Tennessee*. Nashville, TN: Byron Sistler & Associates, 1996. 106p.

Coffee County

1850

Porch, Deane. *Coffee County, Tennessee, 1850 Census*. Franklin, TN: Mrs. Clyde Lynch, 1969. 167p.

1860

Bridgewater, Betty Anderson. *1860 Federal Census of Coffee County, Tennessee*. Manchester, TN: Coffee County Historical Society, 1980. 170p.

Cumberland County

1860

Kirkeminde, Patricia Barclay. *1860 Census of Cumberland County, Tennessee*. Crossville, TN: Author, 1982. 25p.

1870

Kirkeminde, Patricia Barclay. *1870 Census of Cumberland County, Tennessee*. Crossville, TN: Author, 1980. 30p.

Davidson County

1850

Porch, Deane. *Davidson County, Tennessee, 1850 Census*. Fort Worth, TX: American Reference Publishers, 1969. 419p.

DeKalb County

1840

Parsley, Jorene Washer. *DeKalb County 1840, Eleven Districts, Population 5868*. Smithfield, TN: Author, 1985. 52p.

1850

Parsley, Jorene Washer. *Population Schedule of the United States Census of 1850 (Seventh Census) for DeKalb County, Tennessee*. Smithfield, TN: Author, 1988. 103p.

1860

Parsley, Jorene Washer. *Population Schedule of the United States Census of 1860 (Eighth Census) for DeKalb County, Tennessee*. Smithfield, TN: Author, 1979. 199p.

1870

Parsley, Jorene Washer. *Population Schedule of the United States Census of 1870 (Ninth Census) for DeKalb County, Tennessee*. Smithfield, TN: Author, 1985. 234p.

1880

Parsley, Jorene Washer. *Population Schedule of the United States Census of 1880 (Tenth Census) for DeKalb County, Tennessee*. Smithfield, TN: Author. 250p.

1900

Parsley, Jorene Washer. *Population Schedule of the United States Census of 1900 for DeKalb County, Tennessee.* Smithfield, TN: Author, 1988. 233p.

Dickson County
1860

Baker, Georgia L. *1860 Census for Dickson County, Tennessee with Index.* Nashville, TN: Richland Press, 1999. 223p.

Dyer County
1850

USGenWeb Census Project. Tennessee, 1850 Dyer County.
ftp://ftp.rootsweb.com/pub/census/tn/dyer/1850/
1860

Felldin, Jeanne Robey, and Charlotte Magee Tucker. *1860 United States Census Surname Index, the Tennessee Counties of Dyer, Fayette, and Tipton.* Tomball, TX: Genealogical Publications, 1976. 24p.

Fayette County
1860

Felldin, Jeanne Robey, and Charlotte Magee Tucker. *1860 United States Census Surname Index, the Tennessee Counties of Dyer, Fayette, and Tipton.* Tomball, TX: Genealogical Publications, 1976. 24p.

Fentress County
1830, 1840

Hatfield, Wanda June. *Early Records, Fentress County, Tennessee, 1830, 1840, 1850 Census.* Signal Mountain, TN: Mountain Press, 1988. 123p.
1850

1850 Fentress County Census. Huntsville, TN: Scott County Historical Society, 1985. 56p.

Hatfield, Wanda June. *Early Records, Fentress County, Tennessee, 1830, 1840, 1850 Census.* Signal Mountain, TN: Mountain Press, 1988. 123p.
1860

1860 Fentress County Census. Huntsville, TN: Scott County Historical Society, 1985. 128p.
1880

Hatfield, Wanda June. *Fentress County, Tennessee, United States Census, 1880.* Signal Mountain, TN: Mountain Press, 1986. 80p.
1910

Hatfield, Wanda June. *1910 Federal Census of Fentress County, Tennessee.* Signal Mountain, TN: Mountain Press, 1989. 112p.

Franklin County
1840

Phillips, Judy Henley. *Franklin County, Tennessee in the Year 1840, Featuring the 1840 Census with Abstracts of the 1840 Court Minutes and Deeds.* Tullahoma, TN: Author, 1985. 142p.

Swenson, Helen Smothers. *Franklin County, Tennessee 1860 Census, with Head of Household Marriages.* Round Rock, TX: Author, 1981. 214p.
1870

Phillips, Judy Henley. *1870 Franklin County, Tennessee Census.* Tullahoma, TN: Author, 1986. 258p.
1900

Powers, Mary Osweiler. *1900 Franklin County, Tennessee Census, Index Only.* Signal Mountain, TN: Mountain Press, 1990. 37p.

Giles County

1840

McCann, M. Janell. *Giles County, Tennessee, 1840 Federal Census*. Ft. Worth, TX: Author, 1989. 40p.

1860

White, Edward Jackson, and Clara M. Parker. *Giles County Census, 1860*. Ethridge, TN: Authors, 1987. 299p.

Grainger County

1860

Carpter, Mrs. V. K. *Eighth Census of the United States, 1860, Grainger County, Tennessee, Free Population Schedules*. Fort Smith, AR: Century Enterprises of Ft. Smith, 1975. 119p.

Grundy County

1850-1880

Sherrill, Charles A. *Grundy County Tennessee Special Census Records, 1850-1880, Agricultural Schedules, Slave Population Schedules, Mortality Schedules Products of Industry Schedules*. Mt. Juliet, TN: Author, 1996. 147p.

Hamilton County

1860

Douthat, James L. *1860 Hamilton County, Tennessee*. Signal Mountain, TN: Author, 1989. 85p.

1880

Sistler, Byron. *1880 Census, Hamilton County, Tennessee*. Nashville, TN: Byron Sistler & Associates, 1996. 236p.

Hancock County

1860

USGenWeb Census Project. Tennessee, 1860 Hancock County.
ftp://ftp.rootsweb.com/pub/census/tn/hancock/1860/

1880

Sistler, Byron. *1880 Census, Hancock County, Tennessee*. Nashville, TN: Byron Sistler & Associates, 1996. 63p.

Hardin County

1833

Brown, Albert. *The 1833 Census of Males 21 & Over, Hardin County, Tennessee*. Bethel Springs, TN: Author, 1994. 21p.

1850

USGenWeb Census Project. Tennessee, 1850 Hardin County.
ftp://ftp.rootsweb.com/pub/census/tn/hardin/1850/

Hawkins County

1830-1850

Lawson, Rowena. *Hawkins County, Tennessee, 1830-1850 Censuses*. Bowie, MD: Heritage Books, 1987. 205p.

1880

Sistler, Byron. *1880 Census, Hawkins County, Tennessee*. Nashville, TN: Byron Sistler & Associates, 1996. 146p.

Henderson County

1870

Green, Exie Johnson. *Ninth Census of the United States, 1870, Henderson County, Tennessee*. Hope, AR: Author, 1984. 183p.

Henry County
1850
Gossum, Mary Louise, and Don Simmons. *Henry County, Tennessee, Census of 1850.* Melber, KY: Simmons Historical Publications, 1994. 242p.
1880
McNutt, Gwyn Bellamy. *1880 Census Index, Henry County, Tennessee.* Paris, TN: Author, 1989. 58p.
1900
McNutt, Gwyn Bellamy. *1900 Census Index, Henry County, Tennessee.* Paris, TN: Author, 1989. 60p.

Hickman County
1860
Hickman County, Tennessee United States Census, 1860. Centerville, TN: Thomas Stewart Easley Chapter No. 1814, United Daughters of the Confederacy, 1982. 230p.
1910
Tatum, Rubye and Bruce Tatum. *1910 Census, Hickman County, Tennessee.* Lyles, TN: Authors, 1984. 504p.

Houston County
1850
Finley, Nina. *1850 Census of Houston County Area.* Erin, TN: Friends of the Library, Houston County Public Library, 1996. 58p.
1860
Finley, Nina. *1860 Census of Houston County Area.* Erin, TN: Friends of the Library, Houston County Public Library, 1996. 63p.
1880
Finley, Nina. *1880 Agricultural Census of Houston County Area.* Erin, TN: Friends of the Library, Houston County Public Library, 1996. 49p.
_____. *1880 Census of Houston County Area.* Erin, TN: Friends of the Library, Houston County Public Library, 1996. 48p.
1900
Finley, Nina. *1900 Census of Houston County Area.* Erin, TN: Friends of the Library, Houston County Public Library, 1996. 61p.

Humphreys County
1860
Johnson, Susy A. *1860 Census, Humphreys County, Tennessee.* Rosell, IL: Author, 1976. 213p.
1870
Clifton, Betty Faries. *1870 Census of Humphreys County, Tennessee.* Taylorsville, CA: Author, 1979. 217p.
1880
Fischer, Marjorie Hood, and Ruth Blake Burns. *1880 Census, Humphreys County, Tennessee.* Vista, CA: RAM Press, 1987. 247p.

Jackson County
1840
Lee, Ramona Hudson. *Jackson County, Tennessee, 1840 U.S. Census, Includes Special Index to Pensioners for Revolutionary or Military Services and Surname Index.* Mountain Home, AR: Author, 1984. 89p.
1860
McComb, Joyce Bradley. *Jackson County, Tennessee, 1860 Federal Census, USA.* Lexington, SC: Author, 1992. 206p.
1920
Young, Denise. *Jackson County, Tennessee 1920 Census.* Online Database Edition. Orem, UT: Ancestry.com, Inc., 1999.
http://www.ancestry.com

James County
1880
James County, Tennessee 1880 Census Index. Cleveland, TN: Cleveland Public Library, 1989. 291p.

Jefferson County
1830
USGenWeb Census Project. Tennessee, 1830 Jefferson County.
ftp://ftp.rootsweb.com/pub/census/tn/jefferson/1830/
1840
Templin, David H., and Cherel Bolin Henderson. *1840 Population Schedule of the United States Census, Jefferson County, Tennessee*. Maryville, TN: Authors, 1981. 65p.
1850
Underwood, Burl. *Population Schedule of the United States Census of 1850 for Jefferson County, Tennessee*. Knoxville, TN: Author, 1977. 231p.

Johnson County
1860
Wilson, Walter W. *Johnson County, Tennessee, 1860 Census*. Los Alamos, NM: Author, 1979. 140p.
1880
Gentry, Thomas W., and Bettye G. Morley. *Johnson County, Tennessee, 1880 Census*. Johnson City, TN: Postal Instant Press, 1982. 192p.
1900
Gentry, Thomas W., and Bettye G. Morley. *Johnson County, Tennessee, 1900 Census*. Johnson City, TN: Postal Instant Press, 1984. 199p.

Knox County
1880
Sistler, Byron. *1880 Census, Knox County, Tennessee*. Nashville, TN: Byron Sistler & Associates, 1996. 322p.
1910
U.S. Federal Population Census Schedules. 1910, Separate Soundex for Cities of Chattanooga, Knoxville, Memphis and Nashville, T1276, Microfilm Reel Nos. 112-142.

Lauderdale County
1840, 1850
Davis, Bettie B. *Lauderdale County, Tennessee 1840 Census, 1850 Census, and 1850 Mortality Schedule*. Memphis, TN: Author, 1983. 65p.

Lawrence County
1850
Carter, Marymaud Killen, and Joan Coffey Hudgins. *1850 Census, Lawrence County, Tennessee (Including Some Other Early Records)*. Lawrence, TN: Authors, 1973. 164p.
1870
Carpenter, Viola H., and Marymaud Killen Carter. *Lawrence County, Tennessee 1870 Census*. Columbia, TN: P-Vine Press, 1977. 214p.
1880
Carpenter, Viola H., and Marymaud Killen Carter. *Lawrence County, Tennessee 1880 Census*. Columbia, TN: P-Vine Press, 1982. 305p.

Lincoln County
1820
Waller, Jane Warren. *Lincoln County, Tennessee 1820 Census*. Batavia, IL: Lincoln County Tennessee Pioneers, 1973. 94p.

Loudon County
1910

Smallen, Tammy L. *1910 Loudon County, Tennessee Census*. Loudon, TN: Author, 1995. 396p.

McMinn County
1880

Sistler, Byron. *1880 Census McMinn County, Tennessee*. Nashville, TN: Author, 1995. 104p.

McNairy County
1840

Brown, Albert. *Pensioners List, 1835, 1840, 1883, McNairy County, Tennessee*. Bethel Springs, TN: Author, 1993. 15p.

1850

Porch, Deane. *McNairy County, Tennessee, 1850 Census*. Franklin, TN: Lynch, 1975. 252p.

1860

Brown, Albert. *The 1860 Census and Index McNairy County, Tennessee*. Bethel Springs, TN: Author, 1990. 299p.

1870

Brown, Albert. *Index to the 1870 Census, McNairy County, Tennessee*. Bethel Springs, TN: Author, 1994. Unpgd.

1880

Brown, Albert. *The 1880 Census and Index McNairy County, Tennessee*. Bethel Springs, TN: Author, 1992. 286p.

1900

Brown, Albert. *1900 Census and Index McNairy County, Tennessee*. Bethel Springs, TN: Author, 1994. Unpgd.

1910

Brown, Albert. *1910 Census & Index McNairy County, Tennessee*. Bethel Springs, TN: Author, 1994. Unpgd.

Macon County
1850

Porch, Deane. *Macon County, Tennessee, 1850 Census*. Franklin, TN: Lynch, 1975. 137p.

1870, 1880

Macon County, Tennessee, 1870 and 1880 Census. Lafayette, TN: Macon County Historical Society, 1995. 207; 282p.

1900

Crumpton, Barbara. *1900 Census, Macon County, Tennessee*. Duncan, OK: Creative Copies, 1988. 367p.

Madison County
1870

Wiggins, Joy Darlene. *Madison County, Tennessee, 1870 Census*. Jackson, TN: Author, 1992. 101p.

Marion County
1830

Douthat, James L. *1830 Census, Sequatchie Valley, Marion, Bledsoe Counties*. Signal Mountain, TN: Mountain Press, 1986. 15p.

1840

Douthat, James L. *1840 Census, Sequatchie Valley, Marion, Bledsoe Counties*. Signal Mountain, TN: Author, 1982. 25p.

1850

Douthat, James L. *1850 Marion County, Tennessee*. Signal Mountain, TN: Author, 1982. 60p.

USGenWeb Census Project. Tennessee, 1850 Marion County.
ftp://ftp.rootsweb.com/pub/census/tn/marion/1850/
1880
Sistler, Byron. *1880 Census Marion County, Tennessee.* Nashville, TN: Author, 1995. 85p.

Marshall County
1850
Porch, Deane. *Marshall County, Tennessee, 1850 Census.* Nashville, TN: Author, 1967. 283p.

Maury County
1850
Porch, Deane. *1850 Census, Maury County, Tennessee.* Nashville, TN: Author, 1966. 403p.
1860
Thurman, Sandra Wilson. *Maury County, Tennessee, 1860 Census.* Columbia, TN: P-Vine Press, 1981. 265p
1870
McKennon, Sara Tom. *Maury County, Tennessee 1870 Census.* Columbia, TN: P-Vine Press, 1984. 501p.
1880
Sistler, Byron, and Barbara Sistler. *1880 Census, Tennessee, Transcription for Maury County.* Evanston, IL: Sistler & Associates, 1979. 202p.

Meigs County
1840
Broyles, Bettye J., and William R. Snell. *1840 United States Census, Meigs County, Tennessee.* Cleveland, TN: Bradley County Historical Society, 1983. 20p.

Memphis (Shelby County)
1910
U.S. Federal Population Census Schedules. 1910, Separate Soundex for Cities of Chattanooga, Knoxville, Memphis and Nashville, T1276, Microfilm Reel Nos. 112-142.

Monroe County
1880
McConkey, Lynn. *1880 Monroe County Census.* Vonore, TN: Vonore Historical Society, 1995. 251p.

Moore County
1880
Phillips, Judy Henley. *1880 Moore County, Tennessee Census.* Tullahoma, TN: Author, 1986. 110p.

Morgan County
1850
Cross, Lee M. *Morgan County, Tennessee, 1850 Census.* Bowie, MD: Heritage Books, 1985. 75p.
Porch, Deane. *Morgan County, Tennessee, 1850 Census.* Franklin, TN: Lynch, 1973. 78p.
1880
Sistler, Byron. *1880 Census, Morgan County, Tennessee.* Nashville, TN: Byron Sistler & Associates, 1996. 44p.

Nashville (Davidson County)
1910
U.S. Federal Population Census Schedules. 1910, Separate Soundex for Cities of Chattanooga, Knoxville, Memphis and Nashville, T1276, Microfilm Reel Nos. 112-142.

Obion County
1850
Porch, Deane. *Obion County, Tennessee, 1850 Census*. Franklin, TN: Lynch, 1973. 156p.

Overton County
1850
USGenWeb Census Project. Tennessee, 1850 Overton County.
ftp://ftp.rootsweb.com/pub/census/tn/overton/1850/
1920
Young, Denise. *Fourteenth Census of the United States, Overton County, Tennessee*. Washington, DC: Government Printing Office, 1920. *Online Database Edition*. Orem, UT: Ancestry.com, Inc., 1999.
http://www.ancestry.com

Perry County
1860
Malone, Royleta Clopton. *1860 Perry County, Tennessee, Census, Including Slave Schedule and Mortality Schedule, with Full Name Index*. Salt Lake City, UT: Author, 1988. 71p.
1900
Bridges, Alec F. *1900 Federal Census, Perry County, Tennessee*. Columbia, TN: Author, 1996. Unpgd.

Polk County
1840
Snell, William R. *1840 Federal Census, Polk County, Tennessee*. Cleveland, TN: Bradley County Historical Society, 1982. 25p.

Putnam County
1900
Clark, Fred L., and Azilee Wilkerson. *The United States Twelfth Census of Putnam County, Tennessee, 1900*. Quebeck, TN: Author, 1994. 407p.

Rhea County
1850
Hutcherson, Willis Reed, and Pollyanna Creekmore. *1850 Rhea County, Tennessee*. Signal Mountain, TN: Author, 1983. 92p.
1910
Tallent, Seth. *Index to the 1910 Census, Rhea County, Tennessee*. Author, 1990. 114p.

Roane County
1830, 1840
Bailey, Robert L. *Roane County, Tennessee, 1830 & 1840 Censuses and 1830 & 1840 Tax Lists*. Roane County, TN: Roane County Genealogical Society, 1995. 175p.
1850
1850 Census of Roane County, Tennessee. Roane County Genealogical Society, 1997. 331p.
1870
Roane County, Tennessee Census of 1870. Kingston, TN: Roane County Genealogical Society, 1986. 2 vols.
1900
Pierce, Patsy, and Marilyn McCluen. *1900 Census, Roane County, Tennessee*. Rockwood, TN: Authors, 1988. 576p.

Robertson County
1850
Porch, Deane. *Robertson County, Tennessee, 1850 Census*. Nashville, TN: Author, 1968. 272p.

Rutherford County
1850
Porch, Deane. *1850 Census of Rutherford County, Tennessee*. Nashville, TN: Author, 1967. 403p.

Sequatchie County
1860
Douthat, James L. *1860 Sequatchie County, Tennessee*. Signal Mountain, TN: Author, 1983. 45p.
1870
Hobbs, Norma Dennis, and Sara Agee Goins. *United States Census, Sequatchie County, Tennessee, 1870*. 38p.

Sevier County
1830
McMahon, Blanche C., and Pollyana Creekmore. *Sevier County, Tennessee, Population Schedule of the United States Census of 1830 (Fifth Census) for Sevier County, Tennessee*. Knoxville, TN: Author, 1956. 49p.
1840
Templin, David. *1840 Population Schedule of the United States Census, Sevier County, Tennessee*. Maryville, TN: Author. pp. 156-189.
1850
USGenWeb Census Project. Tennessee, 1850 Sevier County.
ftp://ftp.rootsweb.com/pub/census/tn/sevier/1850/
1880
Sistler, Byron. *1880 Census, Sevier County, Tennessee*. Nashville, TN: Byron Sistler & Associates, 1996. 101p.

Shelby County
1891
Reed, Sue S. *Shelby County, Tennessee, Enumeration of Male Inhabitants of Twenty-one Years of Age and Upward, Citizens of Tennessee, January 1, 1891, as Provided for by an Act of General Assembly of Tennessee, Passed January 15, 1891, and Approved January 22, 1891*. Houston, TX: Author, 1989. 790p.

Smith County
1850
McKinney, Mrs. Robert Q. *1850 Census, Smith County, Tennessee and Index*. Author, 1976. 79p.
1910
Partlow, Thomas E. *Smith County, Tennessee, Census of 1910*. Lebanon, TN: Author, 1995. 417p.
1920
Partlow, Thomas E. *Smith County, Tennessee, Census of 1920*. Lebanon, TN: Author, 1995. 387p.

Sullivan County
1850
Hunt, Sheila Steele. *1850 Sullivan County, Tennessee Census*. Kingsport, TN: Author, 1997. 257p.
1860
Hunt, Sheila Steele. *1860 Sullivan County, Tennessee Census*. Kingsport, TN: Author, 1997. 301p.

1870

1870 U.S. Federal Census, Sullivan County, Tennessee. Bristol, VA: Holston Territory Genealogical Society, 1994. 292p.

Sumner County
1850

Porch, Deane. *Sumner County, Tennessee, 1850 Census.* Franklin, TN: Lynch, 1972. 341p.

1870

1870 U.S. Census, Sumner County, Tennessee. Gallatin, TN: Sumner County Archives, 1995. 230p.

Tipton County
1860

Felldin, Jeanne Robey, and Charlotte Magee Tucker. *1860 United States Census Surname Index, the Tennessee Counties of Dyer, Fayette, and Tipton.* Tomball, TX: Genealogical Publications, 1976. 6p.

Tyrell County
1850

Sheppard, Kay Midgett, and Sarah Midyett Hutcherson. *1850 Tyrell County, North Carolina Census.* Authors. 88p.

Unicoi County
1880

Padgett, Hilda Britt. *1880 Census Unicoi County, Tennessee.* Erwin, TN: Author, 1995. 43p.

Sistler, Byron. *1880 Census, Unicoi County, Tennessee.* Nashville, TN: Byron Sistler & Associates, 1996. 27p.

1900

Padgett, Hilda Britt. *1900 Census Unicoi County, Tennessee.* Erwin, TN: Author, 1995. 56p.

1910

Padgett, Hilda Britt. *1910 Census Unicoi County, Tennessee.* Erwin, TN: Author, 1995. 66p.

1920

Padgett, Hilda Britt. *1920 Census, Unicoi County, Tennessee.* Erwin, TN: Author, 1996. 118p.

Union County
1880

Sistler, Byron. *1880 Census, Union County, Tennessee.* Nashville, TN: Byron Sistler & Associates, 1996. 69p.

1900

Holloway, Evelyn, and Sonja Collins. *Transcription, Federal Census Schedule, Union County, Tennessee 1900, Indexed.* Corryton, TN: Authors, 1985. 278p.

1910

Collins, Sonja Jo Smith. *Transcription, Federal Census Schedule, Union County, Tennessee 1910, Indexed.* Corryton, TN: Author, 1985. 231p.

1920

Carter, Martha Jean Atkins. *Union County, Tennessee 1920 Federal Census.* Knoxville, TN: Author, 1997. 213p.

Van Buren County
1860

Rhinehart, Margret. *United States Census, Van Buren County, Tennessee, 1860.* Spencer, TN: Van Buren County Historical Society, 1982. 36p.

1870

Rhinehart, Margret. *United States Census, Van Buren County, Tennessee, 1870*. Spencer, TN: Van Buren County Historical Society, 1982. 44p.

1880

Rhinehart, Margret. *United States Census, Van Buren County, Tennessee, 1880*. Spencer, TN: Van Buren County Historical Society, 1983. 89p.

1900

Rhinehart, Margret. *United States Census, Van Buren County, Tennessee, 1900*. Spencer, TN: Van Buren County Historical Society, 1983. 109p.

1910

Rhinehart, Margret. *United States Census, Van Buren County, Tennessee, 1910*. Spencer, TN: Van Buren County Historical Society, 1984. 114p.

Warren County

1830

Gant, Wanda Muncey. *Warren County, Tennessee 1830 Census Information Updated 1996*. McMinnville, TN: Author, 1996. 62p.

_____. *Warren County, Tennessee, Research Information and 1830 Census, with Index*. McMinnville, TN: Author, 1994. 58p.

1840

Bridgewater, Betty Anderson. *1840 Federal Census of Warren County, Tennessee, Together with Three Early Warren County Documents*. McMinnville, TN: Eliza Lyon Mitchell Chapter, The Questers, 1985. 44p.

1870

Hillis, Robert A. C., Jr. *1870 Warren County, Tennessee*. Signal Mountain, TN: Mountain Press, 1988.

1880

Hillis, Robert A. C., Jr. *1880 Warren County, Tennessee*. Signal Mountain, TN: Mountain Press, 1988. 164p.

1900

Hillis, Robert A. C., Jr. *1900 Warren County, Tennessee*. Signal Mountain, TN: Mountain Press, 1988.

1910

Hillis, Robert A. C., Jr. *1910 Warren County, Tennessee*. Signal Mountain, TN: Mountain Press, 1988.

Washington County

1830

Streleski, Nelda Skilbeck. *Washington County, Tennessee 1830 Federal Census*. Decatur, IL: Decatur Genealogical Society, 1968. 25p.

Weakley County

1850

Porch, Deane. *Weakley County, Tennessee, 1850 Census*. Fort Worth, TX: Miran Pub., 1973. 265p.

1880

1880 Census of Weakley County, Tennessee. Martin, TN: Weakley County Genealogical Society, 1987. 2 vols.

Williamson County

1840

Lynch, Louise Gillespie. *Williamson County, Tennessee, 1840 Census*. Franklin, TN: Author 1980. 61p.

Wilson County

1880

Partlow, T. E. *Wilson County, Tennessee, Federal Census of 1880, Districts 1-13 Index*. Lebanon, TN: Author. 2 vols.

_____. *Wilson County, Tennessee, Federal Census of 1880, Districts 14-25 Index*. Lebanon, TN: Author. 2 vols.

1900

Partlow, T. E. *Wilson County, Tennessee, Federal Census of 1900, Districts 1-25 Index*. Lebanon, TN: Author. 2 vols.

Texas

De Leon, Arnoldo. *Tejanos and the Numbers Game, a Socio-historical Interpretation from the Federal Censuses, 1850-1900*. Albuquerque, NM: University of New Mexico Press, 1989. 119p.

1820-1829

Jackson, Ronald Vern. *Texas 1820-29*. Salt Lake City, UT: Accelerated Indexing Systems International, 1982. 65p.

Mullins, Marion Day. *Index to First Census of Texas, 1829-1836*. Fort Worth, TX: Fort Worth Genealogical Society, 1958. 25p.

1830

Census Index: U.S. Selected States/Counties, 1830. Family Archive CD 315. Novato, CA: Broderbund Software. CD-ROM.

White, Gifford E. *1830 Citizens of Texas*. Austin, TX: Eakin Press, 1983. 282p.

1830-1839

Jackson, Ronald Vern. *Texas 1830-39*. Salt Lake City, UT: Accelerated Indexing Systems International, 1981. 91p.

Mullins, Marion Day. *Index to First Census of Texas, 1829-1836*. Fort Worth, TX: Fort Worth Genealogical Society, 1958. 25p.

1840

Census Index: U.S. Selected States/Counties, 1840. Family Archive CD 316. Novato, CA: Broderbund Software. CD-ROM.

1850

Census Index: U.S. Selected States/Counties, 1850. Family Archive CD 317. Novato, CA: Broderbund Software. CD-ROM.

Corley, Betty J. *Index, Yeoman(s), Yeaman(s), Youman(s), U.S. Census Index, 1850, 1860, 1880, Alabama, Florida, Kentucky, Louisiana, Maryland, Mississippi, Tennessee, Texas, Virginia, Includes Various Other Spellings*. Hyrum, UT: Author, 1988. 5p.

Ervin, Morton L. *Index to Ervin/Irvin, etc. Surnames in the Texas Censuses, 1850 to 1920*. Albuquerque, NM: Ervin Pub., 1998. 238p.

Jackson, Ronald Vern. *Mortality Schedules Index, Online Edition*. Orem, UT: Ancestry.com, Inc., 1999.
http://www.ancestry.com

_____. *Texas Census Index, Online Edition*. Orem, UT: Ancestry.com, Inc., 1999.
http://www.ancestry.com

_____, and Gary Ronald Teeples. *Texas 1850 Census Index*. Bountiful, UT: Accelerated Indexing Systems, 1976. 108p.

_____. *Texas 1850 Slave Schedules Index*. North Salt Lake City, UT: Accelerated Indexing Systems International, 1988. 153p.

Jennings, H. Marvin. *Jennings in Texas, Census Index, 1850 and Soundex, 1880-1900*. Waco, TX: Author, 1982. 133p.

U.S. Federal Population Census Schedules. 1850, M432, Microfilm Reel Nos. 908-916.

U.S. Federal Population Census Schedules. 1850, M432, Slave Schedules, Microfilm Reel Nos. 917-918.

Usry, John M. *1850 Central Texas Census Index*. Waco, TX: Central Texas Genealogical Society, 1985. 100p.

1860

Census Index: U.S. Selected States/Counties, 1860. Family Archive CD 318. Novato, CA: Broderbund Software. CD-ROM.

Corley, Betty J. *Index, Yeoman(s), Yeaman(s), Youman(s), U.S. Census Index, 1850, 1860, 1880, Alabama, Florida, Kentucky, Louisiana, Maryland, Mississippi, Tennessee, Texas, Virginia, Includes Various Other Spellings*. Hyrum, UT: Author, 1988. 5p.

Ervin, Morton L. *Index to Ervin/Irvin, etc. Surnames in the Texas Censuses, 1850 to 1920*. Albuquerque, NM: Ervin Pub., 1998. 238p.

Jackson, Ronald Vern. *Mortality Schedules Index, Online Edition*. Orem, UT: Ancestry.com, Inc., 1999. **http://www.ancestry.com**

_____. *Texas Census Index, Online Edition*. Orem, UT: Ancestry.com, Inc., 1999. **http://www.ancestry.com**

_____. *Texas 1860 U.S. Federal Census Index*. West Jordan, UT: Genealogical Services, 1985, 1997. 465p.

_____. *Texas 1860 Slave Schedule*. North Salt Lake City, UT: Accelerated Indexing Systems International, 1990. 428p.

The State of Texas Federal Population Schedules; Seventh Census of the United States, 1850. Huntsville, AR: Century Enterprises, 1969. 5 vols.

U.S. Census Index Series, Texas. 1860, 1870, 1880, 1890. Orem, UT: Automated Archives, 1992. CD-ROM.

U.S. Federal Population Census Schedules. 1860, M653, Microfilm Reel Nos. 1287-1308.

U.S. Federal Population Census Schedules. 1860, M653, Slave Schedules, Microfilm Reel Nos. 1309-1312.

1870

Census Index: U.S. Selected States/Counties, 1870. Family Archive CD 319. Novato, CA: Broderbund Software. CD-ROM.

Ervin, Morton L. *Index to Ervin/Irvin, etc. Surnames in the Texas Censuses, 1850 to 1920*. Albuquerque, NM: Ervin Pub., 1998. 238p.

Jackson, Ronald Vern. *Mortality Schedules Index, Online Edition*. Orem, UT: Ancestry.com, Inc., 1999. **http://www.ancestry.com**

_____. *Texas Census Index, Online Edition*. Orem, UT: Ancestry.com, Inc., 1999. **http://www.ancestry.com**

_____. *Texas 1870 Census Index*. North Salt Lake City, UT: Accelerated Indexing Systems International, 1987, 1996. 2 vols.

U.S. Census Index Series, Texas. 1860, 1870, 1880, 1890. Orem, UT: Automated Archives, 1992. CD-ROM.

U.S. Federal Population Census Schedules. 1870, M593, Microfilm Reel Nos. 1573-1609.

1880

Census Index: U.S. Selected States/Counties, 1880. Family Archive CD 320. Novato, CA: Broderbund Software. CD-ROM.

Corley, Betty J. *Index, Yeoman(s), Yeaman(s), Youman(s), U.S. Census Index, 1850, 1860, 1880, Alabama, Florida, Kentucky, Louisiana, Maryland, Mississippi, Tennessee, Texas, Virginia, Includes Various Other Spellings*. Hyrum, UT: Author, 1988. 5p.

1880 Census of 13 County West Texas Area. San Angelo, TX: Wilma Roberts. 90p.

Ervin, Morton L. *Index to Ervin/Irvin, etc. Surnames in the Texas Censuses, 1850 to 1920*. Albuquerque, NM: Ervin Pub., 1998. 238p.

Jackson, Ronald Vern. *Mortality Schedules Index, Online Edition*. Orem, UT: Ancestry.com, Inc., 1999. **http://www.ancestry.com**

_____. *Texas Census Index, Online Edition*. Orem, UT: Ancestry.com, Inc., 1999. **http://www.ancestry.com**

_____. *Texas 1880 Federal Census Index*. Salt Lake City, UT: Accelerated Indexing Systems, 1989, 1996. 2 vols.

Jennings, H. Marvin. *Jennings in Texas, Census Index, 1850 and Soundex, 1880-1900*. Waco, TX: Author, 1982. 133p.

Terry, Robert M. *The 1880 Soundex for Texas Terry Families, Including Terry Marriages to 1920*. Enid, OK: Terry Family Historian, 1984. 55p.

U.S. Census Index Series, Texas. 1860, 1870, 1880, 1890. Orem, UT: Automated Archives, 1992. CD-ROM.

U.S. Federal Population Census Schedules. 1880, T9, Microfilm Reel Nos. 1288-1334.

U.S. Federal Population Census Schedules. 1880, Soundex. T773, 77 Microfilm Reels.

1890

Dilts, Bryan Lee. *1890 Texas Census Index of Civil War Veterans or Their Widows*. Salt Lake City, UT: Index Pub., 1984. 69p.; 1 microfiche.

_____. 2nd ed.; 1992. 74p.; 1996. 67p.

Jackson, Ronald Vern. *Texas Census Index, Online Edition (Veterans Schedules)*. Orem, UT: Ancestry.com, Inc., 1999.

http://www.ancestry.com

Partin, SheRita Kae Vaughn. *Texas Departed, an Index of the 1890 Mortality Schedules of Texas*. Nacogdoches, TX: Partin Publications, 1996. 2 vols.

U.S. Census Index Series, Texas. 1860, 1870, 1880, 1890. Orem, UT: Automated Archives, 1992. CD-ROM.

U.S. Federal Population Census Schedules, Special Schedule, Enumerating Union Veterans and Widows of Union Veterans of the Civil War. 1890, M123, Microfilm Reel Nos. 99-102.

Veterans' Schedules: U.S. Selected States, 1890. Family Archive CD 131. Novato, CA: Broderbund Software. CD-ROM.

Yanks and Some Rebs in Texas, 1890. Nacogdoches, TX: Ericson Books, 1991. 443p.

1900

Ervin, Morton L. *Index to Ervin/Irvin, etc. Surnames in the Texas Censuses, 1850 to 1920*. Albuquerque, NM: Ervin Pub., 1998. 238p.

U.S. Federal Population Census Schedules. 1900, T623, Microfilm Reel Nos. 1607-1681.

U.S. Federal Population Census Schedules. 1900, Soundex. T1073, 286 Microfilm Reels.

1910

Ervin, Morton L. *Index to Ervin/Irvin, etc. Surnames in the Texas Censuses, 1850 to 1920*. Albuquerque, NM: Ervin Pub., 1998. 238p.

Jennings, H. Marvin. *Jennings in Texas, Census Index, 1850 and Soundex, 1880-1900*. Waco, TX: Author, 1982. 133p.

U.S. Federal Population Census Schedules. 1910, T624, Microfilm Reel Nos. 1527-1611.

U.S. Federal Population Census Schedules. 1910, Soundex. T1277, 262 Microfilm Reels.

1920

Ervin, Morton L. *Index to Ervin/Irvin, etc. Surnames in the Texas Censuses, 1850 to 1920*. Albuquerque, NM: Ervin Pub., 1998. 238p.

U.S. Federal Population Census Schedules. 1920, T625, Microfilm Reel Nos. 1772-1860.

U.S. Federal Population Census Schedules. 1920, Soundex. M1589, 373 Microfilm Reels.

Anderson County
1870

1870 Census, Anderson County, Texas. Palestine, TX: Anderson County Genealogical Society, 1973, 1993. 86p.

1890

1890 Tax Records, Anderson County, Texas and Including the 1890 Marriage Records and the 1890 Census of Union Veterans of the Civil War. Tyler, TX: East Texas Genealogical Society, 1995. 173p.

Angelina County
1850

Krisch, Lucille, and Helen Smothers Swenson. *1850 Census and First Taxpayers of Angelina County, Texas.* St. Louis, MO: Ingmire, 1981. 21p.

Townsend, Joann Burnside. *1850 Angelina County, Texas, Federal Census, Annotated.* Lufkin, TX: Lufkin Genealogical and Historical Society, 1996. 57p.

Bandera County
1860

Kight, L. L. *1860 Bandera County, Texas, Federal Census.* Arlington, TX: G.T.T. Publishing, 1996. 17p.

Bell County
1870

Index to the 1870 Federal Census of Bell County, Texas. Temple, TX: Temple Genealogical Society, 1986. 157p.

Bosque County
1860

Felldin, Jeanne Robey, and Charlotte Magee Tucker. *The 1860 United States Census Surname Index, the Texas Counties of Bosque, Bowie, Brazoria, Brazos, Brown, Burnet, Calhoun and Comanche.* Tomball, TX: Genealogical Publications, 1976. 24p.

Bowie County
1850

Cheatham, Belzora. *Slaves and Slave Owners of Bowie County, Texas, in 1850, 1850 Bowie County Slave Census with Information from the 1850 Free Census.* Chicago, IL: Author, 1996. 95p.

The 1850 Federal Census of Bowie County, Texas, with Surname Index. Texarkana, TX: Texarkana Genealogical Society, 1981. 29p.

1860

Bowie County, Texas 1860 Federal Census. Texarkana, TX: Texarkana U.S.A. Genealogical Society. 38p.

Felldin, Jeanne Robey, and Charlotte Magee Tucker. *The 1860 United States Census Surname Index, the Texas Counties of Bosque, Bowie, Brazoria, Brazos, Brown, Burnet, Calhoun and Comanche.* Tomball, TX: Genealogical Publications, 1976. 24p.

1870

The 1870 Federal Census of Bowie County, Texas, with Surname Index. Texarkana, TX: Texarkana Genealogical Society, 1982. 58p.

1880

Bowie County, Texas 1880 Federal Census. Texarkana, TX: Texarkana U.S.A. Genealogical Society. 1984. 254p.

Brazoria County
1860

Burkholder, Nanetta Key. *The 1860 Census of Brazoria County, Texas.* Brazosport, TX: Brazosport Genealogical Society, 1978. 30p.

Felldin, Jeanne Robey, and Charlotte Magee Tucker. *The 1860 United States Census Surname Index, the Texas Counties of Bosque, Bowie, Brazoria, Brazos, Brown, Burnet, Calhoun and Comanche.* Tomball, TX: Genealogical Publications, 1976. 24p.

1870

Burris, Gary W. *Index to the Ninth United States Census of Brazoria County, Texas*. Author, 1988. 148p.

1900

1900 U.S. Census, Brazoria County, Texas Index. Alvin, TX; Alvin Museum Society, 1982. 147p.

Brazos County

1850

Collie Cooper, Mary, and Allie Whitley. *Brazos County, Texas, 1860 Census, Also 1842 Brazos County Tax Rolls and Surname Index, 1850 Brazos County Census*. Bryan, TX: Author, 1983. 59p.

USGenWeb Census Project. Texas, 1850 Brazos County.

ftp://ftp.rootsweb.com/pub/census/tx/brazos/1850/

1860

Felldin, Jeanne Robey, and Charlotte Magee Tucker. *The 1860 United States Census Surname Index, the Texas Counties of Bosque, Bowie, Brazoria, Brazos, Brown, Burnet, Calhoun and Comanche*. Tomball, TX: Genealogical Publications, 1976. 24p.

1870

Collie Cooper, Mary. *Brazos County, Texas 1870 Census*. Bryan, TX: Author, 1987. 242p.

Brown County

1860

Felldin, Jeanne Robey, and Charlotte Magee Tucker. *The 1860 United States Census Surname Index, the Texas Counties of Bosque, Bowie, Brazoria, Brazos, Brown, Burnet, Calhoun and Comanche*. Tomball, TX: Genealogical Publications, 1976. 24p.

USGenWeb Census Project. Texas, 1860 Brown County.

ftp://ftp.rootsweb.com/pub/census/tx/brown/1860/

Burleson County

1850

USGenWeb Census Project. Texas, 1850 Burleson County.

ftp://ftp.rootsweb.com/pub/census/tx/burleson/1850/

Burnet County

1860

Felldin, Jeanne Robey, and Charlotte Magee Tucker. *The 1860 United States Census Surname Index, the Texas Counties of Bosque, Bowie, Brazoria, Brazos, Brown, Burnet, Calhoun and Comanche*. Tomball, TX: Genealogical Publications, 1976. 24p.

Caldwell County

1860

Brice, Donaly E. *1860 Census of Caldwell County, Texas*. Luling, TX: Genealogical and Historical Society of Caldwell County, 1993. 118p.

1870

Brice, Donaly E. *1870 Census of Caldwell County, Texas*. Luling, TX: Genealogical and Historical Society of Caldwell County, 1984. 190p.

1880

Moody, Mary C. *Every Name Index to the 1880 Caldwell County, Texas Federal Census*.Arlington, TX: Blackstone Pub. Co., 1996. 108p.

1890

Moody, Mary C. *1890 Caldwell County, Texas Census, Uniquely Reconstructed and Annotated*. Arlington, TX: Blackstone Pub. Co., 1995. 271p.

Calhoun County
1850

McCown, Leonard Joe. *Calhoun County, Texas Seventh Census of the United States, 1850; Free Inhabitants, Slave Inhabitants, Persons Who Died, Productions of Agriculture, Social Statistics, A. W. Hicks, Assistant Marshal.* Irving, TX: Author, 1978. 64p.

1860

Felldin, Jeanne Robey, and Charlotte Magee Tucker. *The 1860 United States Census Surname Index, the Texas Counties of Bosque, Bowie, Brazoria, Brazos, Brown, Burnet, Calhoun and Comanche.* Tomball, TX: Genealogical Publications, 1976. 24p.

McCown, Leonard Joe. *Calhoun County, Texas Eighth Census of the United States, 1860; Free Inhabitants, Slave Inhabitants, Persons Who Died, Productions of Agriculture, Products of Industry, Social Statistics, C.C. Hoerton, Assistant Marshal.* Irving, TX: Author, 1978. 118p.

1870

McCown, Leonard Joe. *Calhoun County, Texas Ninth Census of the United States, 1870; Inhabitants, Persons Who Died, Productions of Agriculture, Products of Industry, Social Statistics, Sylvanus Sandford, Assistant Marshal.* Irving, TX: Author, 1978. 184p.

1880

McCown, Leonard Joe. *Calhoun County, Texas Tenth Census of the United States, 1880; Inhabitants, Productions of Agriculture, Persons Who Died [Mortality] ; Supplemental Schedules Idiots, Blind, Pauper and Indigent Inhabitants, Henry M. Constable, Enumerator.* Irving, TX: Author, 1978. 138p.

Cass County
1860

USGenWeb Census Project. Texas, 1860 Cass County.
ftp://ftp.rootsweb.com/pub/census/tx/cass/1860/

1880

Moody, Mary C. *Every Name Index to 1880 Cass County, Texas, Federal Census.* Arlington, TX: Blackstone Pub. Co., 1995. 152p.

1890

Cass County, Texas, Records of 1890. Atlanta, TX: Cass County Genealogical Society, 1990. 201p.

Moody, Mary C. *1890 Cass County, Texas Census Uniquely Reconstructed and Annotated.* Arlington, TX: Blackstone Pub., 1994. 276p.

Chambers County
1900

Clark, Kendon L. *Index to the 1900 Census of Chambers County, Texas.* Author. Unpgd.

Cherokee County
1850

USGenWeb Census Project. Texas, 1850 Cherokee County.
ftp://ftp.rootsweb.com/pub/census/tx/cherokee/1850

1870

Crawford, Helen Wooddell. *1870 Federal Census of Cherokee County, Texas.* Author, 1983. 154p.

1880

Bueckner, Flossie Dement. *Surname Index, 1880, Cherokee County, Texas.* Cypress, TX: Author, 1980. 13p.

Clay County
1860

USGenWeb Census Project. Texas, 1860 Clay County.
ftp://ftp.rootsweb.com/pub/census/tx/clay/1860/

Cochran County
1900
USGenWeb Census Project. Texas, 1900 Cochran County.
ftp://ftp.rootsweb.com/pub/census/tx/cochran/1900/
1910
USGenWeb Census Project. Texas, 1910 Cochran County.
ftp://ftp.rootsweb.com/pub/census/tx/cochran/1910
1920
USGenWeb Census Project. Texas, 1920 Cochran County.
ftp://ftp.rootsweb.com/pub/census/tx/cochran/1920/

Coleman County
1870
USGenWeb Census Project. Texas, 1870 Coleman County.
ftp://ftp.rootsweb.com/pub/census/tx/coleman/1870/

Collin County
1850
Collin County, Texas, 1850 Census and Mortality Schedule. Richardson, TX: Bland, 1979. 42p.
1860
Bland, Jeanette Bickley. *Collin County, Texas 1860 Census.* Spring Hill Press, 1980. 129p.

Colorado County
1850
USGenWeb Census Project. Texas, 1850 Colorado County.
ftp://ftp.rootsweb.com/pub/census/tx/colorado/1850/

Comanche County
1860
Felldin, Jeanne Robey, and Charlotte Magee Tucker. *The 1860 United States Census Surname Index, the Texas Counties of Bosque, Bowie, Brazoria, Brazos, Brown, Burnet, Calhoun and Comanche.* Tomball, TX: Genealogical Publications, 1976. 24p.

Hudson, Weldon I., and Shirley Brittain Cawyer. *Comanche County, Texas Census Records, 1860 and 1870 Federal Census, with Index to the 1880 Heads of Households and the Special 1890 Census of Union Veterans and Widows, also the 1860 Slave List and 1867 Voter's Registration.* Fort Worth, TX: Author, 1981. 91p.

1870
Hudson, Weldon I., and Shirley Brittain Cawyer. *Comanche County, Texas Census Records, 1860 and 1870 Federal Census, with Index to the 1880 Heads of Households and the Special 1890 Census of Union Veterans and Widows, also the 1860 Slave List and 1867 Voter's Registration.* Fort Worth, TX: Author, 1981. 91p.

Coryell County
1880
USGenWeb Census Project. Texas, 1880 Coryell County.
ftp://ftp.rootsweb.com/pub/census/tx/coryell/1880/

Dallas County
1860
1860 Census, Dallas County, Texas. Mesquite, TX: Mesquite Historical and Genealogical Society. 144p.

1890

1890 Tax Rolls of Dallas County, Texas, Index to the Assessment of Property in Dallas County, Texas Owned by Residents and Rendered for Taxation by the Owners or Agent Thereof for the Year 1890. Duncanville, TX: Duncanville Genealogical Society, 1997. 110p.

Dawson County
1910

Index to the Dawson County, Texas 1910 Census, an Every-name Index Including Ages and States of Birth. Lamesa, TX: Lamesa Area Genealogical Society, 1991. 32p.

Deaf Smith County
1900

USGenWeb Census Project. Texas, 1900 Deaf Smith County.
ftp://ftp.rootsweb.com/pub/census/tx/deafsmith/1900/

Denton County
1860

Coyle, Thomas E. *Denton County, Texas, 1860 Census with Index.* Lewisville, TX: Coyle Data Co., 1991. 151p.

1870

Tate, Mary M. *Records of Denton County, Texas, 1870, United States Ninth Federal Census, 1 June 1870 through 31 December 1870 Including Mortality Schedule, Agriculture Schedule List of Taxpayers for 1870 and Surname Index.* Denton, TX: Author, 1989. 126p.

1880

White, Diana Pearson. *Household Index, Federal Census of 1880, Denton County, Texas, with Non-resident Tax Assessment Rolls.* Denton, TX: Author, 1988. 69p.

Dickens County
1900

Shirley, M. *1900 Census Index, Dickens County.* Abilene, TX: Author, 1985. 24p.

Ellis County
1850

1850 and 1860 Federal Census of Ellis County, Texas. Waxahachie, TX: Ellis County Genealogical Society, 1985. 131p.

USGenWeb Census Project. Texas, 1850 Ellis County. (Partial).
ftp://ftp.rootsweb.com/pub/census/tx/ellis/1850/

1860

1850 and 1860 Federal Census of Ellis County, Texas. Waxahachie, TX: Ellis County Genealogical Society, 1985. 131p.

1880

1880 Census, Ellis County, Texas. Waxahachie, TX: Ellis County Genealogical Society, 1990. 547p.

Fairfield (Freestone County)
1860

Butler, Steven R. *Historical & Genealogical Handbook of Freestone County, Texas, Including 1860 Federal Census & Mortality Schedule, 1885 Map of Fairfield, Texas.* Rev. ed. Richardson, TX: Author, 1997. 116p.

Fannin County
1850

Ingmire, Frances Terry. *Fannin County, Texas 1850 Census and Consorts.* St. Louis, MO: Author, 1981. 84p.

USGenWeb Census Project. Texas, 1850 Fannin County.
ftp://ftp.rootsweb.com/pub/census/tx/fannin/1850/
1860
Newhouse, Patricia Armstrong. *Federal Population Census, 1860, Fannin County, Texas.* Honey Grove, TX: Newhouse Publications, 1980. 113p.
1870
Ingmire, Frances Terry. *Fannin County, Texas 1870 Census.* St. Louis, MO: Author, 1986. 189p.

Fort Bend County
1850
USGenWeb Census Project. Texas, 1850 Ft Bend County.
ftp://ftp.rootsweb.com/pub/census/tx/fortbend/1850/

Franklin County
1880
Hazlewood, Jean Park. *Index 1880 Census Franklin County, Texas.* Fort Worth, TX:Gen Re Put, 1975. 58p.
Mercer, Gerald A. *1880 Federal Census of Franklin County, Texas.* 1976. 115p.

Freestone County
1860
Butler, Steven R. *Historical & Genealogical Handbook of Freestone County, Texas, Including 1860 Federal Census & Mortality Schedule, 1885 Map of Fairfield, Texas.* Rev. ed. Richardson, TX: Author, 1997. 116p.

Frio County
1880
USGenWeb Census Project. Texas, 1880 Frio County.
ftp://ftp.rootsweb.com/pub/census/tx/frio/1880/

Goliad County
1850
USGenWeb Census Project. Texas, 1850 Goliad County.
ftp://ftp.rootsweb.com/pub/census/tx/goliad/1850/

Gregg County
1900
Griffith, Carolyn. *1900 Gregg County, Texas Census. Online Database Edition.* Orem, UT: Ancestry.com, Inc., 1999.
http://www.ancestry.com
1910
Griffith, Carolyn. *1910 Gregg County, Texas Census. Online Database Edition.* Orem, UT: Ancestry.com, Inc., 1999.
http://www.ancestry.com
Wilkins, John W. *Kinfolk and Neighbors in Justice Precincts 4, 5, and 6 Based on 1910 United States Census.* Gladewater, TX: Author, 1983. 63p.

Hall County
1880
USGenWeb Census Project. Texas, 1880 Hall County.
ftp://ftp.rootsweb.com/pub/census/tx/hall/1880/

Hamilton County
1880

Moody, Mary C. *Every Name Index to the 1880 Hamilton County, Texas Federal Census*. Arlington, TX: Blackstone, 1997. 60p.

1890

Moody, Mary C. *1890 Hamilton County, Texas Census, Uniquely Reconstructed and Annotated*. Arlington, TX: Blackstone Pub. Co., 1996.172p.

Harris County
1870

The 1870 Census of Harris County, Texas with Index. Houston, TX: Houston Genealogical Forum, 1992. 242p.

1880

Ruff, Nancy Blakeley. *Harrison County, Texas, Caucasian Residents in 1880*. Baltimore, MD: Gateway Press, 1987. 375p.

Hays County
1850

USGenWeb Census Project. Texas, 1850 Hays County.
ftp://ftp.rootsweb.com/pub/census/tx/hays/1850/

Henderson County
1850

Corder, Mrs.Claude. *1850-1860 Census of Henderson County, Texas, Including Slave Schedule and 1846 Tax List*. Athens, TX: Henderson County Historical Society, 1984. 242p.

USGenWeb Census Project. Texas, 1850 Henderson County.
ftp://ftp.rootsweb.com/pub/census/tx/henderson/1850/
1860

Corder, Mrs. Claude. *1850-1860 Census of Henderson County, Texas, Including Slave Schedule and 1846 Tax List*. Athens, TX: Henderson County Historical Society, 1984. 242p.

1880

Henderson County, Texas Tenth Federal Population Census, 1880. Mabank, TX: Root Seekers Genealogy Society, 1997. 235p.

Hidalgo County
1870

Stinson, Virginia Gilkey. *Index to 1870 Census, Hidalgo County, Texas*. Author, 1976. 15p.

Hockley County
1900

USGenWeb Census Project. Texas, 1900 Hockley County.
ftp://ftp.rootsweb.com/pub/census/tx/hockley/1900/
1910

USGenWeb Census Project. Texas, 1910 Hockley County.
ftp://ftp.rootsweb.com/pub/census/tx/hockley/1910/
1920

USGenWeb Census Project. Texas, 1920 Hockley County.
ftp://ftp.rootsweb.com/pub/census/tx/hockley/1920/

Hood County
1880

Woods, Frances Jerome, and Doris Lewis. *Hood County, Texas; United States Census of 1880 and Marriage Records, 1875-1885*. Austin, TX: Printing Craft, 1964. 141p.

Hopkins County
1860
Davis, Frat Edward. *1860 Census of Hopkins County, State of Texas, Free Inhabitants in the County of Hopkins, State of Texas Enumerated in the Year 1860*. Sulphur Springs, TX: Hopkins County Genealogical Society, 1984. 144p.
1870
Davis, Frat Edward. *1870 Census of Hopkins County*. Sulphur Springs, TX: Hopkins County Genealogical Society, 1985. 280p.
1910
Payne, Linda. *1910 Census, Hopkins County, Texas*. Sulphur Springs, TX: Hopkins County Genealogical Society, 1996. 2 vols.

Houston County
1880
Jackson, Mary B. *Houston County, Texas 1880 Federal Census T9-1312 Vol. 18 218-594*. Author, 1985. 2 vols.
1900
Davis, Kathryn Hooper. *1900 Census, Houston County, Texas*. Nacogdoches, TX: Ericson Books, 1995. 386p.

Hunt County
1850
Ingmire, Mrs. Frances Terry. *1850 Census Hunt County, Texas, Seventh Census of the United States*. St. Louis, MO: Author, 1981. 22p.

Story, Loraine Dodson. *Early Records of Hunt County, Texas, (1850 Census, 1850 Mortality Schedule, 1850 Slave Schedule, 93 Marriages, 1847-1851)*. Farmersville, TX: Search-N-Print, 1979. 42p.
1860
Ingmire, Mrs. Frances Terry. *1860 Census Hunt County, Texas, Seventh Census of the United States*. St. Louis, MO: Author, 1981. 34p.

Story, Loraine Dodson. *1860 Census of Hunt County, Texas (Includes the 1860 Mortality and Slave Schedules)*. Farmersville, TX: Search-N-Print, 1979. 144p.
1870
Ingmire, Mrs. Frances Terry. *1870 Census Hunt County, Texas, Seventh Census of the United States*. St. Louis, MO: Author, 1979. 149p.

Hutchinson County
1900-1920
Morrison, Cleo McGraw. *Census Index, Hutchinson County, Texas, 1900, 1910 and 1920*. Hutchinson County, TX: Author, 1996. 59p.

Jack County
1870
Ingmire, Frances Terry. *Population Schedules of the Ninth Census of the United States, 1870 Roll 1593, Texas, Volume 11, Jack County*. St. Louis, MO: Author, 1980. 22p.

Jackson County
1860
Ingmire, Frances Terry. *1860 U.S. Census Population Schedule of Jackson County, Texas*. St. Louis, MO: Author, 1981. 147p.
1870
Ingmire, Frances Terry. *National Archives Microfilm Publications, Microcopy No. 593, Population Schedules of the Ninth Census of the United States, 1870, Roll 1593, Texas Volume 11, Jackson County*. St. Louis, MO: Author, 1981. 63p.

1880

Hazlewood, Jean Park. *Index 1880 Census Jackson County, Texas.* Fort Worth, TX: GenRePut, 1974. 69p.

Jasper County
1860

Folsom, Jimmy G. *1860 Population Census, Jasper County, Texas.* Jasper, TX: Author, 1986. 59p.

1880

Hazlewood, Jean Park. *Index 1880 Census Jasper County, Texas.* Fort Worth, TX: GenRePut, 1974. 69p.

1900

Truett, Versie Graham. *1900 Census of Jasper County, Texas.* Zavalla, TX: Author, 1992. 176p.

1920

Truett, Versie Graham. *1920 Census of Jasper County, Texas.* Zavalla, TX: Author, 1994. 361p.

Jefferson County
1850

Ingmire, Frances Terry, and Helen Smothers Swenson. *Jefferson County, Texas 1850 Census and Consorts.* St. Louis, MO: Author, 1981. 67p.

1870

Ingmire, Frances Terry. *1870 U.S. Census of Jefferson County, Texas.* St. Louis, MO: Author, 1980. 53p.

Johnson County
1860

Basham, L. Malcolm. *1860 Johnson County, Texas, Federal Census, Including a Statistical Profile of Residents.* Dallas, TX: Author, 1995. 162p.

Kaufman County
1860

Index, 1860 Federal Census for Kaufman County, Texas. Kaufman County Genealogical Society, 1988. 76p.

Kerr County
1860-1880

Powell, Maxine Smith, and Sidney Dean Smith. *1860, 1870, 1880 Federal Censuses of Kerry County, Texas.* Fredericksburg, TX: Kerrville Genealogical Society, 1997. 120p.

1910

USGenWeb Census Project. Texas, 1910 Kerr County.
ftp://ftp.rootsweb.com/pub/census/tx/kerr/1910/

1920

USGenWeb Census Project. Texas, 1920 Kerr County.
ftp://ftp.rootsweb.com/pub/census/tx/kerr/1920/

Kerry County
1860-1880

Powell, Maxine Smith, and Sidney Dean Smith. *1860, 1870, 1880 Federal Censuses of Kerry County, Texas.* Fredericksburg, TX: Kerrville Genealogical Society, 1997. 120p.

Lamar County
1860

Lane, Mary Stinson Claunch, and Elizabeth Blevins Booth. *1860 Federal Census of Lamar County, Texas.* Fort Worth, TX: Author, 1978. 125p.

1870

Lane, Mary Stinson Claunch. *1870 Lamar County, Texas Federal Census.* Paris, TX: Author, 1993. 303p.

Leon County
1850, 1860
Leon County, Texas, Census, 1850-1860. Centerville, TX: Leon County Genealogical Society, 1983. 79p.
1880
Leon County, Texas, 1880 Census, 1890 Tax Roll. Centerville, TX: Leon County Genealogical Society, 1985. 274p.

Leon County, Texas, 1880 Census, Supplement Additions and Corrections. Centerville, TX: Leon County Genealogical Society, 1986. 122p.

Moody, Mary C. *Every Name Index to the 1880 Leon County, Texas Federal Census.* Arlington, TX: Blackstone Pub., 1999. 73p.

Liberty County
1860
1860 Census, Liberty County, Texas. Liberty, TX: Liberty County Historical Survey Committee. 71p.
1870
1870 Census, Liberty County, Texas. Liberty, TX: Liberty County Historical Survey Committee. 148p.
1880
Calhoon, Joyce, and Sandra Pickett. *Census of 1880, Liberty County, Texas.* Liberty, TX: Liberty County Historical Commission, 1979. 129p.

Limestone County
1860
Sharp, Walterine Hollingsworth, and Sandra Haney Tedford. *1860 Census of Limestone County, Texas.* Farmersville, TX: Search-N-Print, 1984. 96p.
1870
Strickland, David Neil. *Household 1870 Surname Census.* Mexia, TX: Limestone Genealogy Association, 1988. 53p.
1880
Moody, Mary C. *Every Name Index to 1880 Limestone County, Texas, Federal Census.* Arlington, TX: Blackstone Pub. Co., 1989. 147p.
1890
Moody, Mary C. *1890 Limestone County, Texas Census Uniquely Reconstructed and Annotated.* Arlington, TX: Blackstone Pub., 1988. 272p.

Lubbock County
1880
USGenWeb Census Project. Texas, 1880 Lubbock County.
ftp://ftp.rootsweb.com/pub/census/tx/lubbock/1880/
1900
USGenWeb Census Project. Texas, 1900 Lubbock County.
ftp://ftp.rootsweb.com/pub/census/tx/lubbock/1900/

McLennan County
1870
Usry, John M. *Index to 1870 U.S. Census McLennan County, Texas.* Waco, TX: Central Texas Genealogical Society, 1976. 60p.
1910
Usry, John M. *1910 McLennan County Census Index.* Waco, TX: Central Texas Genealogical Society, 1984. 772p.

Madison County
1860
Stevens, Audrey. *1860 Census of Madison County, Texas*. Madisonville, TX: Madison County Genealogical Society, 1990. 46p.

Mason County
1900
Capps, Joyce. *Mason County Census for 1900*. Fredonia, TX: Author, 1982. 172p.

Matagorda County
1860
Brown, Shirley Ledwig. *1860 Census, Matagorda County, Texas*. Bay City, TX: Matagorda County Genealogical Society, 1981. 76p.
1870
Brown, Shirley Ledwig. *1870 Census, Matagorda County, Texas*. Bay City, TX: Matagorda County Genealogical Society, 1982. 112p.
1880
Felldin, Jeanne Robey, and Charlotte Magee Tucker. *1880 United States Census Surname Index, the Texas Counties of Matagorda, Menard and Milam*. Tomball, TX: Genealogical Publications, 1976. 20p.

Medina County
1850
USGenWeb Census Project. Texas, 1850 Medina County.
ftp://ftp.rootsweb.com/pub/census/tx/medina/1850

Menard County
1880
Felldin, Jeanne Robey, and Charlotte Magee Tucker. *1880 United States Census Surname Index, the Texas Counties of Matagorda, Menard and Milam*. Tomball, TX: Genealogical Publications, 1976. 20p.

Milam County
1880
Felldin, Jeanne Robey, and Charlotte Magee Tucker. *1880 United States Census Surname Index, the Texas Counties of Matagorda, Menard and Milam*. Tomball, TX: Genealogical Publications, 1976. 20p.

Montgomery County
1870
Montgomery County, Texas, 1870 Census. Conroe, TX: Montgomery County Genealogical Society, 1983. 79p.
1880
1880 Census of the United States, Montgomery County, Texas. Conroe, TX: Montgomery County Genealogical & Historical Society, 1984. 246p.
Moody, Mary C. *Every Name Index to 1880 Montgomery County, Texas, Federal Census*. Arlington, TX: Blackstone Pub. Co., 1994. 79p.
1890
Moody, Mary C. *1890 Montgomery County, Texas Census Uniquely Reconstructed and Annotated*. Arlington, TX: Blackstone Pub., 1993. 202p.
1900
1900 Montgomery County, Texas Census Index. Conroe, TX: Montgomery County Genealogical and Historical Society, 1985. 110p.

1910

1910 Montgomery County, Texas Census Index. Conroe, TX: Montgomery County Genealogical and Historical Society, 1986. 95p.

Nacogdoches County
1860

Ericson, Carolyn Reeves. *The People of Nacogdoches County in 1860 an Edited Census.* Author, 1978. 136p.

1870

Ericson, Carolyn Reeves. *The People of Nacogdoches County in 1870 an Edited Census.* Author, 1977. 210p.

1880

Hazlewood, Jean Park. *Index 1880 Census, Nacogdoches County, Texas.* Fort Worth, TX: GenRePut, 1974. 127p.

1910

Davis, Kathryn Hooper. *1910 Census, Nacogdoches County, Texas.* Nacogdoches, TX: Ericson Books, 1994. 418p.

1920

Davis, Kathryn Hooper. *1920 Census, Nacogdoches County, Texas.* Nacogdoches, TX: Ericson Books, 1998. 456p.

Navarro County
1870

Claunch, Alta Hillman. *1870 Federal Census of Navarro County, Texas.* Dublin, TX: Author, 1995. 136p.

Newton County
1870, 1880

Claunch, Alta Hillman. *1870 and 1880 Federal Census of Newton County, Texas.* Dublin, TX: Author, 1995. 150p.

1910

Davis, Kathryn Hooper. *1910 Census, Newton County, Texas.* Nacogdoches, TX: Ericson Books, 1991. 202p.

Nueces County
1850

USGenWeb Census Project. Texas, 1850 Nueces County.
ftp://ftp.rootsweb.com/pub/census/tx/nueces/1850/
1860

USGenWeb Census Project. Texas, 1860 Nueces County.
ftp://ftp.rootsweb.com/pub/census/tx/nueces/1860/

Panola County
1850

USGenWeb Census Project. Texas, 1850 Panola County.
ftp://ftp.rootsweb.com/pub/census/tx/panola/1850/
USGenWeb Census Project. Texas, 1850 Panola County. (Mortality Schedule).
ftp://ftp.rootsweb.com/pub/census/tx/panola/1850/1850occ.txt
USGenWeb Census Project. Texas, 1850 Panola County. Slave Schedule.
ftp://ftp.rootsweb.com/pub/census/tx/panola/1850/
1860

USGenWeb Census Project. Texas, 1860 Panola County.
ftp://ftp.rootsweb.com/pub/census/tx/panola/1860/

Parker County
1910
Doss, Donnell. *Index to the Census, 1910 Parker County, Texas*. Weatherford, TX: Author. 27p.

Pecos County
1880
Adams, Martin O., Florence H. Cummings, and Marsha Lea Daggett. *Population Schedule of the Pecos County, Texas, 10th Federal Census of 1880, Transcribed from National Archives Microfilm Publications, Microcopy No. T-9, Roll 1323, with a Concise History of the County, Map, Acknowledgments, Census Interpretation, Tabulation, Summarization and Index*. Fort Stockton, TX: Sierra Madera, 1980. 112p.

Polk County
1850
USGenWeb Census Project. Texas, 1850 Polk County.
ftp://ftp.rootsweb.com/pub/census/tx/polk/1850/
1860
Harper, Mary M. *1860 Census Polk County, Texas*. Titusville, FL: Author, 1984. 110p.
1870
Harper, Mary M. *1870 Census Polk County, Texas*. Titusville, FL: Author, 1986. 209p.

Presidio County
1870
Cummings, Florence H. *Population Schedule of the Presidio County, Texas, 9th Federal Census of 1870, Transcribed from National Archives Microfilm Publications, Microcopy No. 593, Roll 1601, with a Concise History of the Vast Area Encompassed Therein, Acknowledgments, Searching Aids, Tabulations of Each Page*. Fort Stockton, TX: Sierra Madera, 1979. 159p.

Red River County
1860
Davis, Kathryn Hooper. *Red River County, Texas, 1860 Census*. Nacogdoches, TX: Ericson Books, 1998. 99p.

Lane, Mary Stinson Claunch, and Elizabeth Blevins Booth. *1860 Federal Census of Red River County, Texas*. Fort Worth, TX: Author, 1978. 110p.

Refugio County
1850
USGenWeb Census Project. Texas, 1850 Refugio County.
ftp://ftp.rootsweb.com/pub/census/tx/refugio/1850/
1870
Swenson, Helen Smothers. *1870 U.S. Census Population Schedule of Refugio County, Texas*. St. Louis, MO: Ingmire, 1980. 76p.

Rockwell County
1880
Sharp, Walterine Hollingsworth, and Sandra Haney Tedford. *1880 Census of Rockwell County, Texas*. Farmersville, TX: Search-N-Print, 1982. 109p.

Robertson County
1860
Collie Cooper, Mary. *Robertson County, Texas, 1860 Census*. Bryan, TX: Collie-Cooper Enterprises, 1985. 69p.

Rusk County
1850
USGenWeb Census Project. Texas, 1850 Rusk County.
ftp://ftp.rootsweb.com/pub/census/tx/rusk/1850/
USGenWeb Census Project. Texas, 1850 Rusk County. Slave Schedule.
ftp://ftp.rootsweb.com/pub/census/tx/rusk/1850/

1860
Dunn, Mary Franklin Deason. *Rusk County, Texas, 1860 Census*. Henderson, TX: Author, 1982. 262p.

Sabine County
1835
Schluter, Helen Gomer. *1835 Sabine District, Texas Census*. Fort Worth, TX: Author, 1983. 56p.
1850
Schluter, Helen Gomer, and Blanche Finely Toole. *1850 Sabine County, Texas Census with Added Family Information and Corrections and Some Civil War Records*. Westminster, CO: Author, 1979. 51p.
USGenWeb Census Project. Texas, 1850 Sabine County.
ftp://ftp.rootsweb.com/pub/census/tx/sabine/1850/
1860
Schluter, Helen Gomer, and Blanche Finely Toole. *1860 Sabine County, Texas Census with Added Family Information and Corrections and Some Civil War Records*. Fort Worth, TX: Author, 1983. 84p.
1870
Toole, Blanche Finley. *1870 Census, Sabine County*. Nacogdoches, TX: Ericson Books, 1983. 90p.
1880
Toole, Blanche Finley. *1880 Census, Sabine County*. Nacogdoches, TX: Ericson Books, 1983. 115p.

San Augustine County
1850
USGenWeb Census Project. Texas, 1850 San Augustine County.
ftp://ftp.rootsweb.com/pub/census/tx/sanaugustine/1850/

San Patricio County
1850
USGenWeb Census Project. Texas, 1850 San Patricio County.
ftp://ftp.rootsweb.com/pub/census/tx/sanpatricio/1850/

San Saba County
1860
1860 Texas Census, San Saba County. San Saba County Historical Survey Committee. 11p.
1870, 1880
1870 and the 1880 Census of San Saba County, Texas. San Saba County Historical Survey Committee. 132p.

Shelby County
1870
Davis, Kathryn Hooper. *1870 Census, Shelby County, Texas*. Nacogdoches, TX: Ericson Books, 1989. 122p.
1910
Davis, Kathryn Hooper. *1910 Census, Shelby County, Texas*. Nacogdoches, TX: Ericson Books, 1990. 461p.
1920
Davis, Kathryn Hooper. *1920 Census, Shelby County, Texas*. Nacogdoches, TX Ericson Books, 1997. 434p.

Smith County
1850

Burks, Loyd. *1850 & 1860 Federal Censuses, Smith County, Texas*. Tyler, TX: East Texas Genealogical Society, 1984. 245p.

USGenWeb Census Project. Texas, 1850 Smith County.

ftp://ftp.rootsweb.com/pub/census/tx/smith/1850/

1860

Burks, Loyd. *1850 & 1860 Federal Censuses, Smith County, Texas*. Tyler, TX: East Texas Genealogical Society, 1984. 245p.

USGenWeb Census Project. Texas, 1860 Smith County.

ftp://ftp.rootsweb.com/pub/census/tx/smith/1860/

1870

Pollan, Howard O. *1870 Federal Census, Smith County, Texas*. Tyler, TX: East Texas Genealogical Society, 1978. 308p.

Stephens County
1870

USGenWeb Census Project. Texas, 1870 Stephens County.

ftp://ftp.rootsweb.com/pub/census/tx/stephens/1870/

Sutton County
1920

Index to 1920 Sutton County, Texas, Federal Census. Sonora, TX: Historical Research Associates, 1994. 33p.

Travis County
1880

Moody, Mary C. *Every Name Index to the 1880 Travis County, Texas Federal Census*. Arlington, TX: Blackstone Pub. Co., 1990. 235p.

1890

Moody, Mary C. *1890 Travis County, Texas Census, Uniquely Reconstructed and Annotated*. Arlington, TX: Blackstone Pub. Co., 1991. 2 vols.

Van Zandt County
1850

USGenWeb Census Project. Texas, 1850 Van Zandt County.

ftp://ftp.rootsweb.com/pub/census/tx/vanzandt/1850/

1880

1880 Census of Van Zandt County, Texas. Canton, TX: Van Zandt County Genealogical Society, 1994. 316p.

1890

Creasey, Sibyl. *1890 in Van Zandt County, County Records, School Records, Special 1890 Federal Census, Biographies, Newspaper Extracts*. Canton, TX: Van Zandt County Genealogical Society, 1997. 337p.

1900

Index to the 1900 Van Zandt County Federal Census. Canton, TX: Van Zandt County Genealogical Society. 64p.

Walker County
1870

Stewart, Lucy Alice Bruce. *1870 Census of the United States of America, Walker County, Texas*. Huntsville, TX: Walker County Genealogical Society, 1979. 158p.

1880

Moody, Mary C. *Every Name Index to the 1880 Walker County, Texas Federal Census*. Arlington, TX: Blackstone Pub. Co., 1993. 90p.

1890

Moody, Mary C. *1890 Walker County, Texas Census, Uniquely Reconstructed and Annotated*. Arlington, TX: Blackstone Pub. Co., 1992. 202p.

Washington County
1850

USGenWeb Census Project. Texas, 1850 Washington County.
ftp://ftp.rootsweb.com/pub/census/tx/washington/1850/

Wheeler County
1880

Mooney, Fredrick W. *Wheeler County, Texas Marriage Book I, and, 1880 Census of Wheeler County*. Amarillo, TX: TapRoots Research and Publications, 1993. 54p.

Williamson County
1870

1870 Census, Williamson County, Texas. Round Rock, TX: Williamson County Genealogical Society, 1988. 122p.

1880

Emry, Linda. *1880 Federal Census, Williamson County, Texas*. Round Rock, TX: Williamson County Genealogical Society, 1991. 290p.

Wise County
1860

Gonzalez, Catherine Troxell. *1860 Wise County, Texas Census Index*. Rhome, TX: Author. 12p.
USGenWeb Census Project. Texas, 1860 Wise County.
ftp://ftp.rootsweb.com/pub/census/tx/wise/1860/
1880

Gonzalez, Catherine Troxell. *1880 Wise County, Texas Census Index*. Rhome, TX: Author. 46p.
1900
Index to the 1900 Federal Census for Wise County, Texas. 76p.

Wood County
1880

Reed, Sharon. *Wood County, Texas, 1880 Census Index*. Mineola, TX: Northeast Texas Genealogical Society, 1977. 61p.

Utah

1850

Burns, Annie Walker. *First Families of Utah, as Taken from the 1850 Census of Utah*. Washington, DC: Author, 1949. 115p.
Jackson, Ronald Vern. *Utah Census Index, Online Edition*. Orem, UT: Ancestry.com, Inc., 1999.
http://www.ancestry.com
_____, and Gary Ronald Teeples. *Utah 1850 Census Index*. Bountiful, UT: Accelerated Indexing Systems, 1978. 55, 28p.
U.S. Federal Population Census Schedules. 1850, M432, Microfilm Reel No. 919.

1856

Dilts, Bryan Lee. *1856 Utah Census Index, an Every Name Index.* Salt Lake City, UT: Index Pub., 1983. 292p.; 3 fiche.

Jackson, Ronald Vern. *Mortality Schedules Index, Online Edition.* Orem, UT: Ancestry.com, Inc., 1999. **http://www.ancestry.com**

_____. *Utah Census Index, Online Edition.* Orem, UT: Ancestry.com, Inc., 1999. **http://www.ancestry.com**

_____. *Utah 1856 Territorial Census Index.* Salt Lake City, UT: Accelerated Indexing Systems, 1983. 953p.

1860

Census Index: U.S. Selected States/Counties, 1860. Family Archive CD 318. Novato, CA: Broderbund Software. CD-ROM.

Jackson, Ronald Vern. *Mortality Schedules Index, Online Edition.* Orem, UT: Ancestry.com, Inc., 1999. **http://www.ancestry.com**

_____. *Utah Census Index, Online Edition.* Orem, UT: Ancestry.com, Inc., 1999. **http://www.ancestry.com**

_____. *Utah 1860 Territorial Census Index.* Salt Lake City, UT: Accelerated Indexing Systems, 1979. 576p.

U.S. Federal Population Census Schedules. 1860, M653, Microfilm Reel Nos. 1313-1314.

1870

Jackson, Ronald Vern. *Mortality Schedules Index, Online Edition.* Orem, UT: Ancestry.com, Inc., 1999. **http://www.ancestry.com**

_____. *Utah Census Index, Online Edition.* Orem, UT: Ancestry.com, Inc., 1999. **http://www.ancestry.com**

_____. *Utah 1870.* North Salt Lake City, UT: Accelerated Indexing Systems International, 1987. 273p.

U.S. Federal Population Census Schedules. 1870, M593, Microfilm Reel Nos. 1610-1613.

1880

Jackson, Ronald Vern. *Mortality Schedules Index, Online Edition.* Orem, UT: Ancestry.com, Inc., 1999. **http://www.ancestry.com**

_____. *Utah Census Index, Online Edition.* Orem, UT: Ancestry.com, Inc., 1999. **http://www.ancestry.com**

_____. *Utah 1880 Federal Census Index.* Salt Lake City, UT: Accelerated Indexing Systems International, 1989. 380p.

_____, and Wilma Winmill, Shirley P. Zachrison. *Utah 1880 Mortality Schedule.* Bountiful, UT: Accelerated Indexing Systems, 1981. 47p.

U.S. Federal Population Census Schedules. 1880, T9, Microfilm Reel Nos. 1335-1339.

U.S. Federal Population Census Schedules. 1880, Soundex. T774, 15 Microfilm Reels.

1890

Jackson, Ronald Vern. *Utah Census Index, Online Edition.* Orem, UT: Ancestry.com, Inc., 1999. **http://www.ancestry.com**

_____. *1890 Utah Census Index, Special Schedule of the Eleventh Census (1890) Enumerating Union Veterans and of Union Veterans of the Civil War.* Salt Lake City, UT: Accelerated Indexing Systems, 1983. 55; 15p.

U.S. Federal Population Census Schedules, Special Schedule, Enumerating Union Veterans and Widows of Union Veterans of the Civil War. 1890, M123, Microfilm Reel No. 103.

Veterans' Schedules: U.S. Selected States, 1890. Family Archive CD 131. Novato, CA: Broderbund Software. CD-ROM.

1900

U.S. Federal Population Census Schedules. 1900, T623, Microfilm Reel Nos. 1682-1688.
U.S. Federal Population Census Schedules. 1900, Soundex. T1074, 29 Microfilm Reels.

1910

U.S. Federal Population Census Schedules. 1910, T624, Microfilm Reel Nos. 1602-1611. (No Soundex/
Miracode Index was prepared by the Government for this State.)

1920

U.S. Federal Population Census Schedules. 1920, T625, Microfilm Reel Nos. 1861-1869.
U.S. Federal Population Census Schedules. 1920, Soundex. M1590, 33 Microfilm Reels.

Beaver County
1900

Owen, Clint. *Beaver County, Utah 1900 Federal Census Schedules. Online Database Edition*. Orem, UT:
Ancestry, Inc., 1999.
http://www.ancestry.com

Iron County
1910

Owen, Clint.*1910 Federal Census, Iron County, Utah. Online Database Edition*. Orem, UT: Ancestry, Inc.,
1999.
http://www.ancestry.com

Vermont

Bunker, Paul Delmont. *The Bunkers of Vermont, Being Copies of All Records Contained in the Vermont
Censuses of 1790-1850 Inclusive Which Refer to Members of the Bunker Family. Taken from the Origi-
nal Records of the Census Bureau, Washington, DC*. Washington, DC: Author, 1932. 16p.
Jackson, Ronald Vern, Altha Polson, and Shirley P. Zachrison. *Early Vermont*. Bountiful, UT: Accelerated
Indexing Systems, 1980. Unpgd.

1771

Holbrook, Jay Mack. *Vermont 1771 Census*. Oxford, MA: Holbrook Research Institute, 1982. 102p.

1790

Jackson, Ronald Vern. *New Hampshire 1790, Vermont 1790 Federal Census Indexes*. North Salt Lake City,
UT: Accelerated Indexing Systems International, 1990. 252p.
_____. *Vermont Census Index, Online Edition*. Orem, UT: Ancestry.com, Inc., 1999.
http://www.ancestry.com
U.S. Bureau of the Census. *Heads of Families at the First Census of the United States taken in the Year 1790,
Vermont*. Washington, DC: Government Printing Office, 1908. 95p.
_____. _____. Bountiful, UT: Accelerated Indexing Systems, 1978. 95p.
_____. _____. *Online Database Edition*. Orem, UT: Ancestry.com, Inc., 1999.
http://www.ancestry.com
_____. *U.S. Federal Population Census Schedules*, 1790. T498, Microfilm Reel No. 3.
U.S. Federal Population Census Schedules, 1790. M637, Microfilm Reel No. 12.

1800

Heads of Families at the Second Census of the United States Taken in the Year 1800, Vermont. Montpelier,
VT: Vermont Historical Society, 1938. 233p.

Jackson, Ronald Vern. *Vermont 1800 Census Index*. Bountiful, UT: Accelerated Indexing Systems, 1976. 324p.

Steuart, Raeone Christensen. *Vermont 1800 Census Index*. Bountiful, UT: Heritage Quest, 2000. 161p.

_____. *United States 1800 Census Index*. Bountiful, UT: Heritage Quest, 2000. 4 vols. CD-ROM.

U.S. Federal Population Census Schedules, 1800. M32, Microfilm Reel Nos. 51-52.

1810

Jackson, Ronald Vern. *Vermont Census Index, Online Edition*. Orem, UT: Ancestry.com, Inc., 1999. **http://www.ancestry.com**

_____, and Gary Ronald Teeples. *Vermont 1810 Census Index*. Bountiful, UT: Accelerated Indexing Systems, 1976, 1994. 83p.

U.S. Census Index Series, New England, New York, 1810. Orem, UT: Automated Archives, 1992. CD-ROM.

U.S. Federal Population Census Schedules, 1810. M252, Microfilm Reel Nos. 64-65.

1820

Jackson, Ronald Vern. *Vermont Census Index, Online Edition*. Orem, UT: Ancestry.com, Inc., 1999. **http://www.ancestry.com**

_____, Gary Ronald Teeples, and David Schaefermeyer. *Vermont 1820 Census Index*. Bountiful, UT: Accelerated Indexing Systems, 1978. 94p.

U.S. Federal Population Census Schedules. 1820, M33, Microfilm Reel Nos. 126-128.

1830

Census Index: U.S. Selected States/Counties, 1830. Family Archive CD 315. Novato, CA: Broderbund Software. CD-ROM.

Jackson, Ronald Vern. *Vermont Census Index, Online Edition*. Orem, UT: Ancestry.com, Inc., 1999. **http://www.ancestry.com**

_____, and Gary Ronald Teeples. *Vermont 1830 Census Index*. Bountiful, UT: Accelerated Indexing Systems, 1977. 120p.

U.S. Census Index, 1830-1839, New England, New York, Pennsylvania. Orem, UT: Automated Archives, 1992. 1 CD-ROM.

U.S. Federal Population Census Schedules. 1830, M19, Microfilm Reel Nos. 183-188.

1840

Census Index: U.S. Selected States/Counties, 1840. Family Archive CD 316. Novato, CA: Broderbund Software. CD-ROM.

Jackson, Ronald Vern. *Vermont Census Index, Online Edition*. Orem, UT: Ancestry.com, Inc., 1999. **http://www.ancestry.com**

_____, and Gary Ronald Teeples. *Vermont 1840 Census Index*. Bountiful, UT: Accelerated Indexing Systems, 1978. 132p.

U.S. Census Index Series, New England, New York, 1840. Orem, UT: Automated Archives, 1992. CD-ROM.

U.S. Federal Population Census Schedules. 1840, M704, Microfilm Reel Nos. 538-548.

1850

Census Index: U.S. Selected States/Counties, 1850. Family Archive CD 317. Novato, CA: Broderbund Software. CD-ROM.

Jackson, Ronald Vern. *Mortality Schedules Index, Online Edition*. Orem, UT: Ancestry.com, Inc., 1999. **http://www.ancestry.com**

_____. *Vermont Census Index, Online Edition*. Orem, UT: Ancestry.com, Inc., 1999. **http://www.ancestry.com**

_____, and Gary Ronald Teeples. *Vermont 1850 Census Index*. Bountiful, UT: Accelerated Indexing Systems, 1978. 252p.

U.S. Census Index Series, New England, 1850. Orem, UT: Automated Archives, 1991. CD-ROM.

U.S. Federal Population Census Schedules. 1850, M432, Microfilm Reel Nos. 920-931.

1860

Census Index: U.S. Selected States/Counties, 1860. Family Archive CD 318. Novato, CA: Broderbund Software. CD-ROM.

Jackson, Ronald Vern. *Federal Census Index, Vermont 1860*. West Jordan, UT: Genealogical Services, 1987, 1997. 398p.

_____, *Mortality Schedules Index, Online Edition*. Orem, UT: Ancestry.com, Inc., 1999.
http://www.ancestry.com

_____. *Vermont Census Index, Online Edition*. Orem, UT: Ancestry.com, Inc., 1999.
http://www.ancestry.com

_____. *Vermont 1860 Census Index*. North Salt Lake City, UT: Accelerated Indexing Systems, 1986, 1997. 398p.

U.S. Census Index, 1860, Vermont. Orem, UT: Automated Archives, 1994. CD-ROM.

U.S. Federal Population Census Schedules. 1860, M653, Microfilm Reel Nos. 1315-1329.

1870

Jackson, Ronald Vern. *Mortality Schedules Index, Online Edition*. Orem, UT: Ancestry.com, Inc., 1999.
http://www.ancestry.com

_____. *U.S. Federal Census Index Vermont 1870 Mortality Schedules*. West Jordan, UT: Genealogical Services. 62p.

Steuart, Raeone Christensen. *Vermont 1870 Census Index*. Bountiful, UT: Heritage Quest, 2000. 712p.

_____. *Maine, New Hampshire and Vermont 1870 Census Index*. Bountiful, UT: Heritage Quest, 2000. CD-ROM.

U.S. Federal Population Census Schedules. 1870, M593, Microfilm Reel Nos. 1614-1682.

1880

U.S. Federal Population Census Schedules. 1880, T9, Microfilm Reel Nos. 1340-1350.
U.S. Federal Population Census Schedules. 1880, Soundex. T775, 15 Microfilm Reels.

1890

Dilts, Bryan Lee. *1890 Virginia Census Index of Civil War Veterans or their Widows*. Bountiful, UT: Precision Index, 1986. 32p.

Jackson, Ronald Vern. *Vermont 1890 Federal Census Index of Veterans*. Salt Lake City, UT: Accelerated Indexing Systems International, 1976. 156p.

U.S. Federal Population Census Schedules, Special Schedule, Enumerating Union Veterans and Widows of Union Veterans of the Civil War. 1890, M123, Microfilm Reel No. 105.

Veterans' Schedules: U.S. Selected States, 1890. Family Archive CD 131. Novato, CA: Broderbund Software. CD-ROM.

1900

U.S. Federal Population Census Schedules. 1900, T623, Microfilm Reel Nos. 1689-1696.
U.S. Federal Population Census Schedules. 1900, Soundex. T1075, 41 Microfilm Reels.

1910

U.S. Federal Population Census Schedules. 1910, T624, Microfilm Reel Nos. 1612-1618. (No Soundex/Miracode Index was prepared by the Government for this State.)

1920

U.S. Federal Population Census Schedules. 1920, T625, Microfilm Reel Nos. 1870-1876.
U.S. Federal Population Census Schedules. 1920, Soundex. M1591, 32 Microfilm Reels.

Bennington County
1810

Brownell, Elijah Ellsworth. *Bennington County, Vermont, Genealogical Gleanings*. Philadelphia, PA: Author, 1941. 213p.

Rutland County
1810

Brownell, Elijah Ellsworth. *Rutland County, Vermont, Genealogical Gleanings*. Philadelphia, PA: Author, 1942. 323p.

Virginia

1760

Virginia in 1760, a Reconstructed Census. Miami Beach, FL: T.L.C. Genealogy, 1996. 375p.

1782, 1783

Workman, Velma Ballard. *First Federal Census, 1782-83, Virginia Territory*. Canton, MI: Author, 1985. 215p.

1787

Schreiner Yantis, Netti, and Florence Speakman. *The 1787 Census of Virginia, an Accounting of the Name of Every White Male Tithable over 21 Years*. Springfield, VA: Genealogical Books in Print, 1987. 3 vols.

1790

Heinegg, Paul. *Free African Americans of North Carolina and Virginia Including the Family Histories of More than 80% of Those Counted as "All Other Free Persons" in the 1790 and 1800 Census*. Baltimore, MD: Genealogical Pub. Co., 1992. 462p.

_____. 2nd ed. Baltimore, MD: Genealogical Pub. Co., 1994. 699p.

_____. 3rd ed. Baltimore, MD: Genealogical Pub. Co., 1994. 825p.

Rutherford, Dolores Crumrine. *The Page Family in Virginia Census, 1790 to 1850*. Carmichael, CA: Author, 1998. 207p.

U.S. Bureau of the Census. *Heads of Families at the First Census of the United States Taken in the Year 1790, Virginia*. Washington, DC: Government Printing Office, 1908. 227p.

_____. _____. Online Database Edition. Orem, UT: Ancestry.com, Inc., 1999.
http://www.ancestry.com

_____. _____. Bountiful, UT: American Genealogical Lending Library, 1993. 189p.

_____. *U.S. Federal Population Census Schedules*. T498, Microfilm Reel No. 3.

1800

Heinegg, Paul. *Free African Americans of North Carolina and Virginia Including the Family Histories of More than 80% of Those Counted as "All Other Free Persons" in the 1790 and 1800 Census*. Baltimore, MD: Genealogical Pub. Co., 1992. 462p.

_____. 2nd ed. Baltimore, MD: Genealogical Pub. Co., 1994. 699p.

_____. 3rd ed. Baltimore, MD: Genealogical Pub. Co., 1994. 825p.

Rutherford, Dolores Crumrine. *The Page Family in Virginia Census, 1790 to 1850*. Carmichael, CA: Author, 1998. 207p.

1810

Bentley, Elizabeth Petty. *Index to the 1810 Census of Virginia*. Baltimore, MD: Genealogical Pub. Co., 1980. 366p.

Crickard, Madeline W. *Index to the 1810 Virginia Census, Heads of Families Listed in the Third Census of the United States.* Parson, WV: McClain Print Co., 1971. 293p.

Jackson, Ronald Vern. *Virginia Census Index, Online Edition.* Orem, UT: Ancestry.com, Inc., 1999. **http://www.ancestry.com**

_____, and Gary Ronald Teeples. *Virginia 1810 Census Index.* Bountiful, UT: Accelerated Indexing Systems, 1978. 355p.

Rutherford, Dolores Crumrine. *The Page Family in Virginia Census, 1790 to 1850.* Carmichael, CA: Author, 1998. 207p.

U.S. Federal Population Census Schedules, 1810. M252, Microfilm Reel Nos. 66-71.

1820

Felldin, Jeanne Robey, and Charlotte Magee Tucker. *The 1820 Census of Virginia.* Baltimore, MD: Genealogical Pub. Co., 1976. 486p.

Jackson, Ronald Vern. *Virginia Census Index, Online Edition.* Orem, UT: Ancestry.com, Inc., 1999. **http://www.ancestry.com**

_____, and Gary Ronald Teeples. *Virginia 1820 Census Index.* Bountiful, UT: Accelerated Indexing Systems, 1976. 267p.

Rutherford, Dolores Crumrine. *The Page Family in Virginia Census, 1790 to 1850.* Carmichael, CA: Author, 1998. 207p.

U.S. Federal Population Census Schedules. 1820, M33, Microfilm Reel Nos. 129-142.

1830

Census Index: U.S. Selected States/Counties, 1830. Family Archive CD 315. Novato, CA: Broderbund Software. CD-ROM.

1830-1839 U.S. Census Indexes, Mid-Atlantic, South, Mid-West. Orem, UT: Automated Archives, 1993. CD-ROM.

Jackson, Ronald Vern. *Virginia Census Index, Online Edition.* Orem, UT: Ancestry.com, Inc., 1999. **http://www.ancestry.com**

_____, and Gary Ronald Teeples. *Virginia 1830 Census Index.* Bountiful, UT: Accelerated Indexing Systems, 1976. 309p.

Rutherford, Dolores Crumrine. *The Page Family in Virginia Census, 1790 to 1850.* Carmichael, CA: Author, 1998. 207p.

U.S. Federal Population Census Schedules. 1830, M19, Microfilm Reel Nos. 189-201.

1840

Census Index: U.S. Selected States/Counties, 1840. Family Archive CD 316. Novato, CA: Broderbund Software. CD-ROM.

Jackson, Ronald Vern. *Virginia Census Index, Online Edition.* Orem, UT: Ancestry.com, Inc., 1999. **http://www.ancestry.com**

_____, and Gary Ronald Teeples. *Virginia 1840 Census Index.* Bountiful, UT: Accelerated Indexing Systems, 1978. 337p.

Rutherford, Dolores Crumrine. *The Page Family in Virginia Census, 1790 to 1850.* Carmichael, CA: Author, 1998. 207p.

U.S. Federal Population Census Schedules. 1840, M704, Microfilm Reel Nos. 549-579.

1850

Census Index: U.S. Selected States/Counties, 1850. Family Archive CD 317. Novato, CA: Broderbund Software. CD-ROM.

Corley, Betty J. *Index, Yeoman(s), Yeaman(s), Youman(s), U.S. Census Index, 1850, 1860, 1880, Alabama, Florida, Kentucky, Louisiana, Maryland, Mississippi, Tennessee, Texas, Virginia, Includes Various Other Spellings.* Hyrum, UT: Author, 1988. 5p.

Census Microfilm Records: Virginia, 1850. Family Archive CD 309. Novato, CA: Broderbund Software. CD-ROM.

Jackson, Ronald Vern. *Mortality Schedules Index, Online Edition.* Orem, UT: Ancestry.com, Inc., 1999. **http://www.ancestry.com**

———. *U.S. Federal Census Index Virginia, 1850 Mortality Schedules.* West Jordan, UT: Genealogical Services, 1987, 1998. 25p.

———. *U.S. Federal Census Index, Virginia, 1850 Slave Schedules.* West Jordan, UT: Genealogical Services. Unpgd.

———. *Virginia Census Index, Online Edition.* Orem, UT: Ancestry.com, Inc., 1999. **http://www.ancestry.com**

———. *Virginia 1850 Slave Schedule Census Index.* Salt Lake City, UT: Accelerated Indexing Systems International, 1988. Unpgd.

———, and Gary Ronald Teeples. *Virginia 1850 Census Index.* Bountiful, UT: Accelerated Indexing Systems, 1976. 628p.

Rutherford, Dolores Crumrine. *The Page Family in Virginia Census, 1790 to 1850.* Carmichael, CA: Author, 1998. 207p.

Sorensen, Willa Thomas. *1850 Virginia Smiths.* Goodyear, AR: Author. 94p.

U.S. Census Index Series, Virginia, West Virginia, Maryland, North Carolina and the District of Columbia, 1850. Orem, UT: Automated Archives, 1991. CD-ROM.

U.S. Federal Population Census Schedules. 1850, M432, Microfilm Reel Nos. 932-982.

U.S. Federal Population Census Schedules. 1850, M432, Slave Schedules, Microfilm Reel Nos. 983-993.

1860

Census Index: U.S. Selected States/Counties, 1860. Family Archive CD 318. Novato, CA: Broderbund Software. CD-ROM.

Corley, Betty J. *Index, Yeoman(s), Yeaman(s), Youman(s), U.S. Census Index, 1850, 1860, 1880, Alabama, Florida, Kentucky, Louisiana, Maryland, Mississippi, Tennessee, Texas, Virginia, Includes Various Other Spellings.* Hyrum, UT: Author, 1988. 5p.

Jackson, Ronald Vern. *Virginia Census Index, Online Edition.* Orem, UT: Ancestry.com, Inc., 1999. **http://www.ancestry.com**

———. *Virginia 1860 Federal Census Index.* North Salt Lake City, UT: AGES, 1988. 894p.

Robertsson, Clara Hamlett. *Kansas Territorial Settlers of 1860 Who Were Born in Tennessee, Virginia, North Carolina and South Carolina.* Baltimore, MD: Genealogical Publishing Co., 1976. 187p.

U.S. Census Index, 1860, District of Columbia, Maryland, North Carolina, Virginia, West Virginia. Orem, UT: Automated Archives, 1992. CD-ROM.

U.S. Federal Population Census Schedules. 1860, M653, Microfilm Reel Nos. 1330-1385.

U.S. Federal Population Census Schedules. 1860, M653, Slave Schedules, Microfilm Reel Nos. 1,386-1,397.

1870

Census Index: U.S. Selected States/Counties, 1870. Family Archive CD 319. Novato, CA: Broderbund Software. CD-ROM.

Census Index Virginia and West Virginia, 1870. Family Archive CD 290. Novato, CA: Broderbund, 1997. CD-ROM.

Jackson, Ronald Vern. *Virginia Census Index, Online Edition.* Orem, UT: Ancestry.com, Inc., 1999. **http://www.ancestry.com**

———. *Virginia 1870 Federal Census Index, Excluding Richmond and Henrico Counties.* North Salt Lake City, UT: Accelerated Indexing Systems International, 1991. 3 vols.

Steuart, Raeone Christensen. *Virginia 1870 Census Index.* Bountiful, UT: Heritage Quest, 1999. 4 vols.

———. *Virginia and West Virginia 1870 Census Index.* Bountiful, UT: Heritage Quest, 1990. CD-ROM.

1880

Corley, Betty J. *Index, Yeoman(s), Yeaman(s), Youman(s), U.S. Census Index, 1850, 1860, 1880, Alabama, Florida, Kentucky, Louisiana, Maryland, Mississippi, Tennessee, Texas, Virginia, Includes Various Other Spellings.* Hyrum, UT: Author, 1988. 5p.

U.S. Federal Population Census Schedules. 1880, T9, Microfilm Reel Nos. 1351-1395.
U.S. Federal Population Census Schedules. 1880, Soundex. T776, 82 Microfilm Reels.

1890

Dilts, Bryan Lee. *1890 Virginia Census Index of Civil War Veterans or Their Widows.* Salt Lake City, UT: Indexing Publishing, 1986. 32p.

Jackson, Ronald Vern. *Virginia Census Index, Online Edition (Veterans Schedules; Naval Veterans Schedules).* Orem, UT: Ancestry.com, Inc., 1999.
http://www.ancestry.com

_____. *Virginia 1890 Census Index.* Salt Lake City, UT: AGES, 1976. 109p.

U.S. Federal Population Census Schedules, Special Schedule, Enumerating Union Veterans and Widows of Union Veterans of the Civil War. 1890, M123, Microfilm Reel No. 106-107.

Veterans' Schedules: U.S. Selected States, 1890. Family Archive CD 131. Novato, CA: Broderbund Software. CD-ROM.

Weaver, Jeffrey C. *The 1890 Union Veterans Census for Southwest Virginia Counties.* Clintwood, VA: Mullins Printing, 1992. 20p.

1900

U.S. Federal Population Census Schedules. 1900, T623, Microfilm Reel Nos. 1697-1740.
U.S. Federal Population Census Schedules. 1900, Soundex. T1076, 164 Microfilm Reels.

1910

U.S. Federal Population Census Schedules. 1910, T624, Microfilm Reel Nos. 1619-1652.
U.S. Federal Population Census Schedules. 1910, Miracode Index. T1278, 1283 Microfilm Reels.

1920

U.S. Federal Population Census Schedules. 1920, T625, Microfilm Reel Nos. 1877-1919.
U.S. Federal Population Census Schedules. 1920, Soundex. M1592, 168 Microfilm Reels.

Accomack County
1800

Jackson, Ronald Vern. *Virginia Census Index, Online Edition.* Orem, UT: Ancestry.com, Inc., 1999.
http://www.ancestry.com

_____, and Gary Ronald Teeples. *Virginia 1800 Accomack County Census Index.* Bountiful, UT: Accelerated Indexing Systems, 1976. 13p.

1850

Koger, Celestine G. *1850 Slave Inhabitants Schedule of Accomack County, Virginia.* Bowie, MD: Heritage Books, 1995. 250p.

Scherzinger, Patricia. *Accomack County, Virginia 1850 Census.* Bowie, MD: Heritage Books, 1988. 128p.

Albemarle County
1850, 1860

Fischer, Myra Smith. *Index for 1850 and 1860 U.S. Census of Albemarle County, Virginia.* Memphis, TN: Author, 1961. 2 vols.

Alexandria County
1850

Tallichet, Marjorie D. *Alexandria, Virginia, City and County, 1850 Census.* Bowie, MD: Heritage Books, 1986. 104p.

Alleghany County
1830, 1840

Childs, Helen V. *Alleghany County, Virginia, Census for the Years 1830, 1840, 1850*. Charleston, WV: Hamilton, 1979. 68p.

1850

Childs, Helen V. *Alleghany County, Virginia, Census for the Years 1830, 1840, 1850*. Charleston, WV: Hamilton, 1979. 68p.

USGenWeb Census Project. Virginia, 1850 Alleghany County.
ftp://ftp.rootsweb.com/pub/census/va/alleghany/1850/

Amherst County
1850

USGenWeb Census Project. Virginia, 1850 Amherst County.
ftp://ftp.rootsweb.com/pub/census/va/amherst/1850/
1880

Johnson, Mary M. *Index to the 1880 Census of Amherst County, Virginia*. Author, 1993. 98p.
1900

Averett, Lewis Hobgood. *Index to the 1900 Census of Amherst County, Virginia*. Author, 1992. 80p.

Appomattox County
1850

Farrar, Stuart McDearmon. *1850 Census of Appomattox County, Virginia*. Pamplin, VA: Author, 1975. 115p.
1860

Farrar, Stuart McDearmon. *1860 Census of Appomattox County, Virginia*. Pamplin, VA: Author, 1984. 115p.
1880

Averett, Lewis Hobgood. *Index to the 1880 Census of Appomattox County, Virginia*. Author, 1992. 55p.
1900

Averett, Lewis Hobgood. *Index to the 1900 Census of Appomattox County, Virginia*. Author, 1993. 43p.

Augusta County
1850

USGenWeb Census Project. Virginia, 1850 Augusta County.
ftp://ftp.rootsweb.com/pub/census/va/augusta/1850/
Weaver, Dorothy Lee. *Augusta County 1850 Census*. Athens, GA: Iberian Pub. Co., 1991. 584p.

Bedford County
1850

USGenWeb Census Project. Virginia, 1850 Bedford County.
ftp://ftp.rootsweb.com/pub/census/va/bedford/1850/
1880

Averett, Lewis Hobgood. *Index to the 1880 Census of Bedford County, Virginia*. Author, 1992. 167p.
1900

Averett, Lewis Hobgood. *Index to the 1900 Census of Bedford County, Virginia*. Author, 1992. 134p.

Bland County
1870

Shannon, Mary Paul Beaudrias. *1870 Bland County, Virginia Census Index*. Pearisbury, VA: Author, 1980. 10p.

Boone County
1850

USGenWeb Census Project. Virginia, 1850 Boone County.
ftp://ftp.rootsweb.com/pub/census/va/boone/1850/

Botetourt County
1850
USGenWeb Census Project. Virginia, 1850 Botetourt County.
ftp://ftp.rootsweb.com/pub/census/va/botetourt/1850/
1860
USGenWeb Census Project. Virginia, 1860 Botetourt County. (Partial).
ftp://ftp.rootsweb.com/pub/census/va/botetourt/1860/

Brooke County
1810
USGenWeb Census Project. Virginia, 1810 Brooke County.
ftp://ftp.rootsweb.com/pub/census/va/brooke/1810/

Brunswick County
1850
Simmons, Don. *Brunswick County, Virginia. Census of 1850.* Melber, KY: Simmons Historical Publications, 1989. 97p.

USGenWeb Census Project. Virginia, 1850 Brunswick County.
ftp://ftp.rootsweb.com/pub/census/va/brunswick/1850/

Buchanan County
1860
Atkins, Oscar Thomas. *Buchanan County, Virginia Families, 1860, Taken in Part from the Federal Census of Buchanan County, Virginia for 1860.* Williamson, WV: Author, 1997. 61p.

Stewart, Jesse, and Leah Stewart. *1860 Census, Buchanan County, Virginia.* Grundy, VA: Authors, 1984. 62p.

Weaver, Jeffrey C. *The 1860 Agriculture Census of Buchanan County, Virginia.* Clintwood, VA: Mullins Printing, 1992. Unpgd.
1870
Mitchell, Maxine P. *Index to the Buchanan County Census 1870.* Author, 1983. 12p.

Stewart, Jesse, and Leah Stewart. *1870 Federal Census, Buchanan County, Virginia.* Grundy, VA: Authors, 1985. 104p.
1880
Stewart, Jesse, and Leah Stewart. *1880 Federal Census, Buchanan County, Virginia.* Grundy, VA: Authors, 1984. 137p.
1900
Stewart, Jesse, and Leah Stewart. *1900 Federal Census, Buchanan County, Virginia.* Grundy, VA: Authors, 1984. 218p.
1910
Stewart, Jesse, and Leah Stewart. *1910 Federal Census, Buchanan County, Virginia.* Grundy, VA: Authors, 1984. 281p.

Buckingham County
1810-1840
Hull, Janice J. R. *Index to the United States Census for Buckingham County, Virginia.* Westminster, MD: Family Line Publications, 1996. 2 vols.
1850
Hull, Janice J. R. *Index to the United States Census for Buckingham County, Virginia.* Westminster, MD: Family Line Publications, 1996. 2 vols.

Weisiger, Benjamin B., III. *Buckingham County, Virginia 1850 United States Census.* Richmond, VA: Author, 1984. 151p.
1860
Hull, Janice J. R. *Index to the United States Census for Buckingham County, Virginia.* Westminster, MD: Family Line Publications, 1996. 2 vols.

Kidd, James Randolph, Jr. *Buckingham County, Virginia, 1860 Federal Census, Buckingham County Records*. Athens, GA: Iberian Pub. Co., 1994. 169p.

1870

Hull, Janice J. R. *Index to the United States Census for Buckingham County, Virginia*. Westminster, MD: Family Line Publications, 1996. 2 vols.

Cabell County
1860

1860 Cabell County, Virginia Census Index. Charleston, WV: West Virginia Archives & History Division, 1981. 19p.

Caroline County
1850

Sprouse, Mark Anderson. *Caroline County, Virginia Federal Census of 1850*. Athens, GA: Iberian Publishing Co., 1997. 182p.

Carroll County
1850

Alderman, John P. *1850 Census, Annotated, Carroll County, Virginia*. Hillsville, VA: Author, 1979. 134p.

1860

Dean, Camilla Browder. *Carroll County, Virginia 1860 Census*. Mount Airy, NC: Author, 1997. 177p.

1870

Dean, Camilla Browder. *Carroll County, Virginia 1870 Census*. Mount Airy, NC: Author, 1997. 236p.

Charlotte County
1850

Evans, June Banks. *Census of 1850, Charlotte County, Virginia*. New Orleans, LA: Bryn Ffyliaid Publications, 1989. 132p.

Nance, Joanne Lovelace. *Charlotte County, Virginia, 1850 Population Census and Mortality Schedule, with Statistical Analyses*. Charlottesville, VA: N.W. Lapin Press, 1989. 126p.

USGenWeb Census Project. Virginia, 1850 Charlottte County.

ftp://ftp.rootsweb.com/pub/census/va/charlotte/1850

1870

USGenWeb Census Project. Virginia, 1870 Charlotte County.

ftp://ftp.rootsweb.com/pub/census/va/charlotte/1870/

Chesterfield County
1850

Weisiger, Benjamin B., III. *Chesterfield County, Virginia 1850 United States Census*. Richmond, VA: Author, 1988. 204p.

Clay County
1850

Bobbitt, John W. *Families in 1850 of Clay, Nicholas, and Webster Counties, West Virginia*. Washington, DC: Author, 1980. 77p.

Craig County
1870

Dunlap, Wilma Walker. *1870 Census, Craig County, Virginia*. St. Louis, MO: Tree Art Publishers, 1977. 61p.

1880

Dunlap, Wilma Walker. *1880 Census, Craig County, Virginia*. St. Louis, MO: Tree Art Publishers, 1983. 85p.

Culpeper County
1820

Hodge, Robert Allen. *An Index for the 1820 Federal Census for Culpeper County, Virginia*. Fredericksburg, VA: Author, 1973. 19p.

Cumberland County
1850

Wolf, Carolyn Zogg. *The 1850 Federal Census of Cumberland County, Virginia*. Woodsfield, OH: Author, 1987. 66p.

Dickenson County
1900

Vanover, Joan Short, Barbara (Kendrick) Vanover, and Gregory Lynn Vanover. *Dickenson County, Virginia 1900 Census*. Pound, VA: Authors, 1984. 175p.

Essex County
1850

Wright, Sue. *Essex County, Virginia, 1850 U.S. Census*. Arkadelphia, AR: Poplar Grove Press, 1995. 95p.
1860

Wright, Sue. *Essex County, Virginia, 1860 U.S. Census*. Arkadelphia, AR: Poplar Grove Press, 1995. 107p.

Fairfax County
1820

McMillion, Lynn C., and Jane K. Wall. *Fairfax County, Virginia 1820 Federal Population Census and Census of Manufactures*. Vienna, VA: Author, 1976. 54p.

Floyd County
1860

Weaver, Jeffrey C. *The 1860 Floyd County, Virginia Census*. Clintwood, VA: Mullins, 1993. 128p.
1890

Moore, Marjorie Fluor. *1890 Census Floyd County, Virginia*. Santa Ana, CA: Author, 1990. 164p.

Franklin County
1850

USGenWeb Census Project. Virginia, 1850 Franklin County.
ftp://ftp.rootsweb.com/pub/census/va/franklin/1850/
Robuck, Karen Mann. *Franklin County, Virginia 1850 and 1860 Censuses*. Baltimore, MD: Gateway, 1990. 402p.
1860

Robuck, Karen Mann. *Franklin County, Virginia 1850 and 1860 Censuses*. Baltimore, MD: Gateway, 1990. 402p.

Fredericksburg County
1820

Hodge, Robert Allen. *An Index for the 1820 Federal Census for Fredericksburg County, Virginia*. Fredericksburg, VA: Author, 1973. 5p.

1830

Hodge, Robert Allen. *An Index for the 1830 Federal Census for Fredericksburg, Virginia.* Fredericksburg, VA: Author, 1973. 5p.

Giles County
1850

Stewart, Jesse, and Leah Stewart. *1850 Federal Census, Giles County, Virginia.* Grundy, VA: Author. 68p.

1860

Davis, Charley L. *Giles County, Virginia, 1860 Census Annotated Family Histories, Births, Marriages, Deaths.* Oakton, VA: Author, 1991. 328p.

Shannon, Mary Paul Beaudrias. *1860 Giles County, Virginia Census Index.* Pearisbury, VA: Author, 1980. 12p.

1870

Shannon, Mary Paul Beaudrias. *1870 Giles County, Virginia Census Index.* Pearisbury, VA: Author, 1982. 9p.

Gloucester County
1870

Rilee, Cyrus Fleming. *The 1870 Census of the 10,132 Inhabitants of Gloucester County, Virginia.* Albuquerque, NM: Author, 1997. 271p.

1880

Rilee, Cyrus Fleming. *The 1880 Census of the 11,825 Inhabitants of Gloucester County, Virginia.* Albuquerque, NM: Author, 1997. 271p.

Goochland County
1860

Egeland, Marie. *Goochland County, Virginia the 1860 Census and Mortality Schedule.* Manassas, VA: Author, 1984. 72p.

Grayson County
1850

Weaver, Jeffrey C. *The 1850 Grayson County Virginia Agricultural Schedule, Federal Census.* Arlington, VA: Author, 1992. 45p.

1870

Weaver, Jeffrey C. *The 1870 Federal Census of Grayson County, Virginia.* Clintwood, VA: Mullins. 454p.

Halifax County
1785

Adamson, Martin. *1785 Halifax County, Virginia Heads of Families.*
http://www.genealogy.org/~ajmorris/misc/val785hf.htm

Henrico County
1850

Richmond City and Henrico County, Virginia, 1850 United States Census. Richmond, VA: Virginia Genealogical Society, 1977. 500p.

1870

Jackson, Ronald Vern. *Richmond, Virginia 1870 Including Henrico County, Virginia Federal Census Index.* Salt Lake City, UT: Accelerated Indexing Systems International, 1981. 321p.

Henry County
1790-1840

Vestal Miller, Anne. *Six Decades Index, 1790, 1800 1810, 1820, 1830, 1840, of Henry County, Virginia.* Author, 1988. 72p.

1850

Vestal Miller, Anne. *1850 Federal Census of Henry County, Virginia*. Sterling, VA: Old Mill Printers, 1991. 112p.

Isle of Wight
1850-1880

Almasy, Sandra Lee. *Mortality Census 1850-1880, Isle of Wight, Nansemond and Southampton Counties, Virginia*. Rome, NY: Kensington Glen Pub., 1988. 112p.

James City County
1840

Evans, June Banks. *Census of 1840, James City County, Virginia*. New Orleans, LA: Bryn Ffyliaid Publications, 1988. 16p.

Lee County
1850

Daughters of the American Revolution. Virginia. Lovelady Chapter, Pennington Gap. *The Seventh Population Census of the United States for Lee County, Virginia, 1850*. Searcy, AR: Presley Research, 1977. 255p.

1870

Treadway, Mark Douglas. *Lee County, Virginia, 1870 Census*. Monroe, MI: Author, 1995. 131p.

Lincoln County
1790

DePriest, Virginia Greene. *The 1790 Federal Census, Morgan District, Lincoln County, Rutherford County, Virginia*. Shelby, NC: Author, 1982. 78p.

Loudon County
1900

Loudoun County, Virginia Census Index 1900. Leesburg, VA: Thomas Balch Library, 1996. 137p.

1910

Loudoun County, Virginia Census Index 1910. Leesburg, VA: Thomas Balch Library, 1996. 117p.

Louisa County
Pre-1790

Davis, Rosalie Edith. *Louisa County, Virginia, Tithables and Census, 1743-1785*. Manchester, MO: Heritage Trails, 1981. 198p.

Lunenburg County
1810

Evans, June Banks. *Census of 1810, Lunenburg County, Virginia*. New Orleans, LA: Bryn Ffyliaid Publications, 1990. 43p.

1820

Evans, June Banks. *Census of 1820, Lunenburg County, Virginia*. New Orleans, LA: Bryn Ffyliaid Publications, 1990. 35p.

1830

Evans, June Banks. *Census of 1830, Lunenburg County, Virginia*. New Orleans, LA: Bryn Ffyliaid Publications, 1990. 45p.

1840

Evans, June Banks. *Census of 1840, Lunenburg County, Virginia*. New Orleans, LA: Bryn Ffyliaid Publications, 1990. 41p.

1850

Jones, Susan D. *Lunenburg County, Virginia 1850 Census*. Owensboro, KY: Cook-McDowell Publications, 1981. 105p.

Steltzner, Mildred W. *Index 1850 Federal Census United States, Lunenburg County, Virginia*. 50p.

1860

Evans, June Banks. *Census of 1860, Lunenburg County, Virginia*. New Orleans, LA: Bryn Ffyliaid Publications, 1990. 130p.

Lynchburg County
1910

Averett, Lewis Hobgood. *Index to the 1910 Census of Lynchburg, Virginia*. Author, 1993. 190p.

Mathews County
1810-1840

Bradley, Stephen E., Jr. *Mathews County, Virginia Censuses 1810, 1820, 1830, 1840*. Keysville, VA: Author. 93p.

Mecklenburg County
1820

Simmons, Don. *Mecklenburg County, Virginia, Census of 1820*. 1976. 37p.

1840

Simmons, Don. *Mecklenburg County, Virginia, Census of 1840*. 1975. 36p.

1850

Simmons, Don. *Mecklenburg County, Virginia, Census of 1850*. 1976. 178p.

USGenWeb Census Project. Virginia, 1850 Mecklenburg County.

ftp://ftp.rootsweb.com/pub/census/va/mecklenburg/1850/

1870

USGenWeb Census Project. Virginia, 1870 Mecklenburg County.

ftp://ftp.rootsweb.com/pub/census/va/mecklenburg/1870/

Middlesex County
1810

USGenWeb Census Project. Virginia, 1810 Middlesex County.

ftp://ftp.rootsweb.com/pub/census/va/middlesex/1810/

1850

Felldin, Jeanne Robey, and Charlotte Magee Tucker. *1850 Census of Middlesex County, Virginia, with an Added Surname Index*. Tomball, TX: Genealogical Publications, 1978. 52p.

Wright, Sue. *Middlesex County, Virginia, 1850 U.S. Census*. Arkadelphia, AR: Poplar Grove Press, 1995. 56p.

1860

Wright, Sue. *Middlesex County, Virginia, 1860 U.S. Census*. Arkadelphia, AR: Poplar Grove Press, 1995. 58p.

1880

Traylor, Catherine Moore. *Marriage Records, 1853-1904, Middlesex County, Virginia, Federal Census, 1880, Middlesex County, Virginia*. Bowie, MD: Heritage Books, 1998. 352p.

Montgomery County
1810

Lent, Robertalee, and June B. Barekman. *Montgomery County, Virginia 1810 Census Schedule and Index*. Post Falls, ID: Genealogical Reference Builders, 1966. Unpgd.

1850

Burton, Charles T. *Montgomery County, Virginia, 1850 Census*. Troutville, VA: Author. 68p.

Morgan County
1850
USGenWeb Census Project. Virginia, 1850 Morgan County.
ftp://ftp.rootsweb.com/pub/census/va/morgan/1850/

Nansemond County
1850, 1860
Almasy, Sandra Lee. *Mortality Census 1850-1880, Isle of Wight, Nansemond and Southampton Counties, Virginia.* Rome, NY: Kensington Glen Pub., 1988. 112p.
1870
Almasy, Sandra Lee. *Mortality Census 1850-1880, Isle of Wight, Nansemond and Southampton Counties, Virginia.* Rome, NY: Kensington Glen Pub., 1988. 112p.
_____. *Nansemond County, Virginia Census 1870.* Joliet, IL: Kensington Glen Pub., 1993. 278p.
1880
Almasy, Sandra Lee. *Mortality Census 1850-1880, Isle of Wight, Nansemond and Southampton Counties, Virginia.* Rome, NY: Kensington Glen Pub., 1988. 112p.

Nelson County
1880
Averett, Lewis Hobgood. *Index to the 1880 Census of Nelson County, Virginia.* Author, 1993. 89p.
1900
Averett, Lewis Hobgood. *Index to the 1900 Census of Nelson County, Virginia.* Author, 1993. 74p.

New Kent County
1840
Evans, June Banks. *Census of 1840, New Kent County, Virginia.* New Orleans, LA: Bryn Ffyliaid Publications, 1989. 28p.

Nicholas County
1850
Bobbitt, John W. *Families in 1850 of Clay, Nicholas, and Webster Counties, West Virginia.* Washington, DC: Author, 1980. 77p.

Norfolk County
1850
Sanders, Rebecca Willis. *1850 Federal Census, Norfolk County, Virginia.* Smithfield, NC: Author, 1979. 487p.
1900
Berent, Irwin M. *The East European Jewish Immigrant in America a Compilation of the 1900 Norfolk Census.* Norfolk, VA: Jewish Genealogical Club of Tidewater, 1982. 28p.

Nottoway County
1850
Matheny, E. R. *1850 Census of Nottoway County, Virginia.* Richmond, VA: Author, 1967. 94p.
1860
Weaver, Jeffrey C. *The 1860 Federal Census for Nottoway County, Virginia.* Clintwood, VA: Mullins Print, 1993. 43p.

Page County
1850
Vestal Miller, Anne, and Howard G. Miller. *1850 Federal Census of Page County, Virginia.* Sterling, VA: Old Mill Printers, 1991. 130p.

Patrick County
1850
Roberson, Rhonda S. *1850 Census of Patrick County, Virginia*. Clintwood, VA: Author. 209p.
1870
Kirkman, Eunice B. *1870 Census of Patrick County, Virginia*. Stuart, VA: Author, 1995. 242p.

Pendleton County
1810
Harter, Mary E. McCollam. *Pendleton County, Virginia Marriage Bonds 1791-1853, Complete 1810 Census*. Key West, FL: Author, 1979. 98p.

Pittsylvania County
1850
Alphabetical Index to the Population Census of Pittsylvania County, Virginia, 1850. Danville, VA: Genealogical Services, 1979. 286p.
1880
Halstead, Claude, and Marily Lowe Halstead. *1880 Census Index of Pittsylvania County and Danville, Virginia*. Danville, VA: VA-NC Piedmont Genealogical Society, 1983. 100p.

Prince George County
1810-1840
Bradley, Stephen E., Jr. *Prince George County, Virginia Censuses 1810, 1820, 1830, 1840*. Keysville, VA: Author, 1991. 93p.

Prince William County
1810
Peters, Joan W. *Prince William County Census, Free Negro Families 1810, 1840-1860*. Broad Run, VA: Albemarle Research, 1996. Unpgd.
Turner, Ronald Ray. *Prince William County, Virginia, 1810 Census, Alphabetically Arranged*. Manassas, VA: Author, 1996. 35p.
1840-1860
Peters, Joan W. *Prince William County Census, Free Negro Families 1810, 1840-1860*. Broad Run, VA: Albemarle Research, 1996. Unpgd.
1880
Turner, Ronald Ray. *Prince William County, Virginia, 1880 Census, Alphabetically Arranged*. Manassas, VA: Author, 1996. 245p.
1900
Turner, Ronald Ray. *Prince William County, Virginia, 1900, Alphabetically Arranged*. Manassas, VA: Author, 1997. 303p.
1920
Turner, Ronald Ray. *Prince William County, Virginia, 1920, Alphabetically Arranged*. Manassas, VA: Author, 1997. 325p.

Princess Anne County
1850
Sanders, Rebecca Willis. *1850 Federal Census, Princess Anne County, Virginia*. Smithfield, NC: Author, 1978. 96p.

Pulaski County
1840, 1850
Douthat, James L. *Early Pulaski County, Virginia Settlers, 1840-1850 Census*. Signal Mountain, TN: Author, 1985. 41p.

1860

Weaver, Jeffrey C. *1860 Census, Pulaski County, Virginia*. Clintwood, VA: Mullins Printing, 1992. 77p.

Richmond County
1850

Hammack, Russell, and Gertrude Hammack. *1850 Census of Richmond County, Virginia*. Warsaw, VA: Rappahannock Community College, 1993. 138p.

Richmond City and Henrico County, Virginia, 1850 United States Census. Richmond, VA: Virginia Genealogical Society, 1977. 500p.

USGenWeb Census Project. Virginia, 1850 Richmond County.
ftp://ftp.rootsweb.com/pub/census/va/richmond/1850/
1870

Jackson, Ronald Vern. *Richmond, Virginia 1870 Including Henrico County, Virginia Federal Census Index*. Salt Lake City, UT: Accelerated Indexing Systems International, 1981. 321p.

Rockbridge County
1860

Queen, Katherine J. *Index, 1860 Census of Rockbridge County, Virginia*. Columbus, OH: Author, 1986. 35p.

Rockingham County
1880

Ritchie, Patricia Turner. *Index to the 1880 Census for Rockingham County, Virginia*. Athens, GA: Iberian Pub. Co., 1990. 97p.

_____. 1992. 173p.

Russell County
1840

USGenWeb Census Project. Virginia, 1840 Russell County.
ftp://ftp.rootsweb.com/pub/census/va/russell/1840/
1850

Roberson, Rhonda S. *1850 Census of Russell County, Virginia*. Clintwood, VA: Author. 186p.

Scott County
1850

Ball, Bonnie Sage, and Samuel B. Shumate. *Scott County, Virginia, U.S. Census, 1850*. Berryville, VA: Virginia Book Co., 1963. 182p.
1870

Perry, Zandra Addington. *1870 Scott County, Virginia Census*. Ermine, KY: Author, 1990. 295p.

Shenandoah Oounty
1860

Vann, Marvin J. *Shenandoah County, Virginia, a Study of the 1860 Census with Supplemental Data*. Bowie, MD: Heritage Books, 1993.
1870

Vann, Marvin J. *Shenandoah County, Virginia, a Study of the 1870 Census*. Bowie, MD: Heritage Books, 1994. 609p.

Southampton County
1850

Almasy, Sandra Lee. *Mortality Census 1850-1880, Isle of Wight, Nansemond and Southampton Counties, Virginia*. Rome, NY: Kensington Glen Pub., 1988. 112p.

USGenWeb Census Project. Virginia, 1850 Southampton County.
ftp://ftp.rootsweb.com/pub/census/va/southampton/1850/
1860-1880
Almasy, Sandra Lee. *Mortality Census 1850-1880, Isle of Wight, Nansemond and Southampton Counties, Virginia.* Rome, NY: Kensington Glen Pub., 1988. 112p.

Smyth County
1850
USGenWeb Census Project. Virginia, 1850 Smyth County.
ftp://ftp.rootsweb.com/pub/census/va/smyth/1850/

Sussex County
1840
Evans, June Banks. *Census of 1840, Sussex County, Virginia.* New Orleans, LA: Bryn Ffyliaid Publications, 1990. 44p.

Tazewell County
1820
Carpenter, Elizabeth M. *1820 Census of Tazewell County, Virginia.* Norton, VA: Author. 14p.
1850
Cassell, R. Vaughn. *1850 Census of Tazewell County, Virginia, Free Schedule, Slave Schedule, Mortality Schedule, Industry Schedule.* Wytheville, VA: Author, 1986. 99p.
1860
McIntosh, Francis W., and Elise Greenup Jourdan. *1860 Federal Census, Tazewell County, Virginia.* Corona, CA: Author, 1990. 171p.

Tyler County
1850
USGenWeb Census Project. Virginia, 1850 Tyler County.
ftp://ftp.rootsweb.com/pub/census/va/tyler/1850/

Warwick County
1840
Evans, June Banks. *Census of 1840, Warwick County, Virginia.* New Orleans, LA: Bryn Ffyliaid Publications, 1988. 8p.
1850
Matheny, E. R. *1850 Census of Warwick County, Virginia.* Richmond, VA: Author, 1966. 26p.

Weaver County
1860
Weaver, Jeffrey C. *The 1860 Agricultural Census of Wise County, Virginia.* Arlington, VA: Author, 1992. 43p.

Webster County
1850
Bobbitt, John W. *Families in 1850 of Clay, Nicholas, and Webster Counties, West Virginia.* Washington, DC: Author, 1980. 77p.

Wise County
1870
Stewart, Jesse, and Leah Stewart. *1870 U.S. Census, Wise County, Virginia.* Grundy, VA: Authors, 1986. 56p.

Wyoming County
1860
Evans, June Banks. *Census of 1860, Wyoming County, Virginia*. New Orleans, LA: Bryn Ffyliaid Publications, 1981. 54p.

Wythe County
1810-1850
Douthat, James L. *Early Wythe Settlers, Wythe County, Virginia, 1810-1850 Census*. Signal Mountain, TN: Author, 1984. 149p.
1860
Douthat, James L. *1860 Wythe County, Virginia, Census*. Signal Mountain, TN: Author, 1986. 77p.
1870
Smith, Timothy D. *Wythe County, Virginia 1870 Census Index with Supplementary Lists and Tables*. Wytheville, VA: Kegley Library, Wytheville Community College, 1985. 60p.
1880
Douthat, James L. *1880 Wythe County, Virginia, Census*. Signal Mountain, TN: Author, 1981. 140p.

York County
1830
Evans, June Banks. *Census of 1830 York County, Virginia*. New Orleans, LA: Bryn Ffyliaid Publications, 1989. 34p.
1840
Evans, June Banks. *Census of 1840 York County, Virginia*. New Orleans, LA: Bryn Ffyliaid Publications, 1989. 23p.

Washington

1850
Jackson, Ronald Vern. *Federal Census Index, Washington Mortality Schedules, 1850, 1860, 1870, 1880*. West Jordan, UT: Genealogical Services, 1997. 4 vols.
_____. *Mortality Schedules Index, Online Edition*. Orem, UT: Ancestry.com, Inc., 1999.
http://www.ancestry.com
_____. *Washington Census Index, Online Edition*. Orem, UT: Ancestry.com, Inc., 1999.
http://www.ancestry.com
_____. *Washington Territorial Census Index, 1850 Census Extracted from the 1850 Oregon Census*. North Salt Lake City, UT: Accelerated Indexing Systems International, 1982. 55p.

1857
Jackson, Ronald Vern. *Washington Census Index, Online Edition*. Orem, UT: Ancestry.com, Inc., 1999.
http://www.ancestry.com
_____. *Washington Territorial Census Index, 1857, 1860 and 1861 State Censuses*. Bountiful, UT: Accelerated Indexing Systems, 1982. 42p.

1860
Census Index: U.S. Selected States/Counties, 1860. Family Archive CD 318. Novato, CA: Broderbund Software. CD-ROM.
Jackson, Ronald Vern. *Federal Census Index, Washington Mortality Schedules, 1850, 1860, 1870, 1880*. West Jordan, UT: Genealogical Services, 1997. 4 vols.
_____. *Mortality Schedules Index, Online Edition*. Orem, UT: Ancestry.com, Inc., 1999.
http://www.ancestry.com

_____. *Washington Census Index, Online Edition*. Orem, UT: Ancestry.com, Inc., 1999.
http://www.ancestry.com

_____. *Washington 1860 Territorial Census Index*. Salt Lake City, UT: Accelerated Indexing Systems, 1979. 149p.

_____. *Washington Territorial Census Index, 1857, 1860 and 1861 State Censuses*. Bountiful, UT: Accelerated Indexing Systems, 1982. 42p.

Savage, Nellie P., and William H. Blue. *Washington Pioneers from the State of Maine, 1860-1870*. Seattle, WA: Seattle Genealogical Society, 1989. 85p.

Stucki, J. U. *Index to the First Federal Census, Territory of Washington*. Huntsville, AR: Century Enterprises, Genealogical Services, 1972. 61p.

U.S. Federal Population Census Schedules. 1860, M653, Microfilm Reel No. 1,398.

1861

Jackson, Ronald Vern. *Washington Census Index, Online Edition*. Orem, UT: Ancestry.com, Inc., 1999.
http://www.ancestry.com

_____. *Washington Territorial Census Index, 1857, 1860 and 1861 State Censuses*. Bountiful, UT: Accelerated Indexing Systems, 1982. 42p.

1870

Census Index: U.S. Selected States/Counties, 1870. Family Archive CD 319. Novato, CA: Broderbund Software. CD-ROM.

Jackson, Ronald Vern. *Federal Census Index, Washington Mortality Schedules, 1850, 1860, 1870, 1880*. West Jordan, UT: Genealogical Services, 1997. 4 vols.

_____. *Mortality Schedules Index, Online Edition*. Orem, UT: Ancestry.com, Inc., 1999.
http://www.ancestry.com

_____. *Washington Census Index, Online Edition*. Orem, UT: Ancestry.com, Inc., 1999.
http://www.ancestry.com

_____. *Washington 1870 Territorial Census Index*. Salt Lake City, UT: Accelerated Indexing Systems, 1979. 300p.

Savage, Nellie P., and William H. Blue. *Washington Pioneers from the State of Maine, 1860-1870*. Seattle, WA: Seattle Genealogical Society, 1989. 85p.

U.S. Federal Population Census Schedules. 1870, M593, Microfilm Reel No. 1683.

1880

Census Index: U.S. Selected States/Counties, 1880. Family Archive CD 320. Novato, CA: Broderbund Software. CD-ROM.

Jackson, Ronald Vern. *Federal Census Index, Washington Mortality Schedules, 1850, 1860, 1870, 1880*. West Jordan, UT: Genealogical Services, 1997. 4 vols.

_____. *Mortality Schedules Index, Online Edition*. Orem, UT: Ancestry.com, Inc., 1999.
http://www.ancestry.com

_____. *Washington Census Index, Online Edition*. Orem, UT: Ancestry.com, Inc., 1999.
http://www.ancestry.com

_____. *Washington 1880 Census Index*. Bountiful, UT: Accelerated Indexing Systems, 1980. 182p.

U.S. Federal Population Census Schedules. 1880, T9, Microfilm Reel Nos. 1396-1398.

U.S. Federal Population Census Schedules. 1880, Soundex. T777, 4 Microfilm Reels.

1890

Jackson, Ronald Vern. *Washington Census Index, Online Edition*. Orem, UT: Ancestry.com, Inc., 1999.
http://www.ancestry.com

_____. *1890 Washington Census Index, Special Schedule of the Eleventh Census (1890) Enumerating Union Veterans and of Union Veterans of the Civil War*. Salt Lake City, UT: Accelerated Indexing Systems, 1985. 56; 89p.

U.S. Federal Population Census Schedules, Special Schedule, Enumerating Union Veterans and Widows of Union Veterans of the Civil War. 1890, M123, Microfilm Reel No. 108.

Veterans' Schedules: U.S. Selected States, 1890. Family Archive CD 131. Novato, CA: Broderbund Software. CD-ROM.

1900

U.S. Federal Population Census Schedules. 1900, T623, Microfilm Reel Nos. 1741-1754.

U.S. Federal Population Census Schedules. 1900, Soundex. T1077, 70 Microfilm Reels.

1910

1910 Federal Census with Index. Yakima, WA: Yakima Valley Genealogical Society, 1984. 2 vols.

U.S. Federal Population Census Schedules. 1910, T624, Microfilm Reel Nos. 1653-1675. (No Soundex/Miracode Index was prepared by the Government for this State.)

1920

U.S. Federal Population Census Schedules. 1920, T625, Microfilm Reel Nos. 1920-1946.

U.S. Federal Population Census Schedules. 1920, Soundex. M1593, 118 Microfilm Reels.

Benton County

Lines, Jack M. *Yakima County Territorial Census, 1871-1883-1885-1887 Including Benton County, Formed in 1905 Including 1871-1883 for Kittitas & Chelan Counties (Kittitas County Formed in 1883, Chelan in 1899).* Yakima, WA: Yakima Valley Genealogical Society, 1983. 199p.

Chelan County

Lines, Jack M. *Yakima County Territorial Census, 1871-1883-1885-1887 Including Benton County, Formed in 1905 Including 1871-1883 for Kittitas & Chelan Counties (Kittitas County Formed in 1883, Chelan in 1899).* Yakima, WA: Yakima Valley Genealogical Society, 1983. 199p.

Clallam County
1860

USGenWeb Census Project. Washington, 1860 Clallam County.
ftp://ftp.rootsweb.com/pub/census/wa/clallam/1860/

Island County
1860

USGenWeb Census Project. Washington, 1860 Island County.
ftp://ftp.rootsweb.com/pub/census/wa/island/1860/

Kittitas County

Lines, Jack M. *Yakima County Territorial Census, 1871-1883-1885-1887 Including Benton County, Formed in 1905 Including 1871-1883 for Kittitas & Chelan Counties (Kittitas County Formed in 1883, Chelan in 1899).* Yakima, WA: Yakima Valley Genealogical Society, 1983. 199p.

1885-1889

Kittitas County 1885-1887-1889 Washington Territorial Censuses. Yakima, WA: Yakima Valley Genealogical Society, 1982. 295p.

Seattle (King County)

Hayner, Norman Sylvester, and June V. Strother. *Street Index to the Census Tracts of Seattle.* Seattle, WA: Works Progress Administration, University of Washington, 1939. pp. 169-297.

1910

Miller, Thomas F. *West Seattle, Federal Census and Index of 1910*. Anaheim, CA: Author, 1998. 268p.

Thurston County
1910

Index to the 1910 Federal Census of Thurston County, Washington. Olympia, WA: Olympia Genealogical Society, 1997. 155p.

Wahkiakim County
1854-1892

Huerd, Evelyn Morris. *Wahkiakum County, Census, 1854, 1857, 1860, 1870, 1880, 1885, 1887, 1892*. Longview, WA: Lower Columbia Genealogical Society, 1994. 227p.

Walla Walla County
1880

Index to the 1880 Federal Census of Walla Walla County, Washington Territory. Richland, WA: Tri-City Genealogical Society, 1980. 74p.

Roberts, Evelyn Rice. *Index to the 1880 Federal Census of Walla Walla County, Washington Territory*. Pasco, WA: Tri-City Genealogical Society, 1969. 78p.

Whitman County
1880

Ballowe, Patricia Jewell. *Index to the 1880 Census of Whitman County, Washington Territory*. Pasco, WA: Tri-City Genealogical Society, 1970. 77p.

Yakima County
1871

Lines, Jack M. *Yakima County Territorial Census, 1871-1883-1885-1887 Including Benton County, Formed in 1905 Including 1871-1883 for Kittitas & Chelan Counties (Kittitas County Formed in 1883, Chelan in 1899)*. Yakima, WA: Yakima Valley Genealogical Society, 1983. 199p.

1880

Roberts, Evelyn Rice. *Index to the 1880 Federal Census of Yakima County, Washington Territory*. Pasco, WA: Tri-City Genealogical Society, 1971. 30p.

1883-1887

Lines, Jack M. *Yakima County Territorial Census, 1871-1883-1885-1887 Including Benton County, Formed in 1905 Including 1871-1883 for Kittitas & Chelan Counties (Kittitas County Formed in 1883, Chelan in 1899)*. Yakima, WA: Yakima Valley Genealogical Society, 1983. 199p.

West Virginia

1850

Census Index: U.S. Selected States/Counties, 1850. Family Archive CD 317. Novato, CA: Broderbund Software. CD-ROM.

Jackson, Ronald Vern. *Mortality Schedules Index, Online Edition*. Orem, UT: Ancestry.com, Inc., 1999.
http://www.ancestry.com

Pearlman, Agnes Branch. *(West) Virginia's Southern Counties, 1850 Census Surname Index*. Santa Ana, CA: Author, 1976. 4 vols.

U.S. Census Index Series, Virginia, West Virginia, Maryland, North Carolina and the District of Columbia, 1850. Orem, UT: Automated Archives, 1991. CD-ROM.

Pearlman, Agnes Branch. *(West) Virginia's Southern Counties 1850 Census Surname Index*. Santa Ana, CA: Author, 1976. 83p.

1860

Census Index: U.S. Selected States/Counties, 1860. Family Archive CD 318. Novato, CA: Broderbund Software. CD-ROM.

Jackson, Ronald Vern. *Mortality Schedules Index, Online Edition*. Orem, UT: Ancestry.com, Inc., 1999. **http://www.ancestry.com**

_____. *Mortality Schedule, West Virginia 1860*. Bountiful, UT: Accelerated Indexing Systems, 1979. 44p.

_____. *West Virginia Census Index, Online Edition*. Orem, UT: Ancestry.com, Inc., 1999. **http://www.ancestry.com**

_____. *West Virginia 1860 Federal Census Index*. West Jordan, UT: Genealogical Services, 1988, 1997. 889p.

U.S. Census Index, 1860, District of Columbia, Maryland, North Carolina, Virginia, West Virginia. Orem, UT: Automated Archives, 1992. CD-ROM.

1870

Census Index: U.S. Selected States/Counties, 1870. Family Archive CD 319. Novato, CA: Broderbund Software. CD-ROM.

Census Index: Virginia, West Virginia, 1870. Family Archive CD 290. Novato, CA: Broderbund Software, 1997. CD-ROM.

Jackson, Ronald Vern. *Mortality Schedules Index, Online Edition*. Orem, UT: Ancestry.com, Inc., 1999. **http://www.ancestry.com**

_____. *Mortality Schedule, West Virginia 1870*. Bountiful, UT: Accelerated Indexing Systems, 1979. 38p.

_____. *West Virginia Census Index, Online Edition*. Orem, UT: Ancestry.com, Inc., 1999. **http://www.ancestry.com**

_____. *West Virginia 1870 Federal Census Index*. Salt Lake City, UT: Accelerated Indexing Systems, 1988. 425p.

Steuart, Raeone Christensen. *Virginia and West Virginia 1870 Census Index Extracted from the Original U.S. Federal Census Schedules*. Bountiful, UT: Heritage Quest, 1998. CD-ROM.

_____. *West Virginia 1870 Census Index*. Bountiful, UT: Precision Indexing, 1990. 1,096p.

U.S. Federal Population Census Schedules. 1870, M593, Microfilm Reel Nos. 1684-1702.

1880

Jackson, Ronald Vern. *Mortality Schedules Index, Online Edition*. Orem, UT: Ancestry.com, Inc., 1999. **http://www.ancestry.com**

_____. *West Virginia 1860 Mortality Schedule Census Index*. Salt Lake City, UT: Accelerated Indexing Systems International, 1979. 44p.

Marsh, William A. *1880 Census of West Virginia, Compiled Alphabetically by Counties*. Parsons, WV: McClain Print, 1979-1992. 13 vols.

_____. *1880 Census of West Virginia, Index*. Baltimore, MD: Gateway Press, Inc., 1993. 1,200p.

U.S. Federal Population Census Schedules. 1880, T9, Microfilm Reel Nos. 1399-1416.

U.S. Federal Population Census Schedules. 1880, Soundex. T778, 32 Microfilm Reels.

1890

Dilts, Bryan Lee. *1890 West Virginia Census Index of Civil War Veterans or Their Widows*. Salt Lake City, UT: Indexing Publishing, 1986. 63p.

Jackson, Ronald Vern. *West Virginia Census Index, Online Edition (Veterans Schedules)*. Orem, UT: Ancestry.com, Inc., 1999. **http://www.ancestry.com**

_____. *West Virginia 1890 Veterans*. North Salt Lake City, UT: Accelerated Indexing Systems International, 1986. 220p.

U.S. Federal Population Census Schedules, Special Schedule, Enumerating Union Veterans and Widows of Union Veterans of the Civil War. 1890, M123, Microfilm Reel Nos. 109-110.

Veterans' Schedules: U.S. Selected States, 1890. Family Archive CD 131. Novato, CA: Broderbund Software. CD-ROM.

1900

U.S. Federal Population Census Schedules. 1900, T623, Microfilm Reel Nos. 1755-1776.

U.S. Federal Population Census Schedules. 1900, Soundex. T1078, 92 Microfilm Reels.

1910

U.S. Federal Population Census Schedules. 1910, T624, Microfilm Reel Nos. 1676-1699.

U.S. Federal Population Census Schedules. 1910, Miracode Index. T1279, 108 Microfilm Reels.

1920

U.S. Federal Population Census Schedules. 1920, T625, Microfilm Reel Nos. 1947-1974.

U.S. Federal Population Census Schedules. 1920, Soundex. M1594, 109 Microfilm Reels.

Barbour County
1850

Cochran, Wes *1850 Census of Barbour County, (West) Virginia*. Parkersburg, WV: Author, 1985. 111p.

Tetrick, Willis Guy. *Census Returns of Barbour and Taylor Counties, West Virginia for 1850*. Clarksburg, WV: Clarksburg Pub. Co., 1932. 391p.

1860

Cochran, Wes. *1860 Census of Barbour County, West Virginia*. Parkersburg, WV: Author, 1986. 111p.

1870

Challender, Marian Waters. *1870 Barbour County, West Virginia Census*. Squires Family Researchers, 1985. 138p.

Challender, Marian Waters, Charles Gilchrist, and Joy Gilchrist. *1870 Barbour County, West Virginia Census*. Lafayette, OH: Author, 1985. 138p.

Berkeley County

Morrow, Dale Walton, and Deborah Jensen Morrow. *Berkeley County, Virginia, Now West Virginia, Complete Census, 1870*. Authors, 1983. 15p.

Boone County
1860

Olafson, Sigfus. *1860 Census of Boone County, West Virginia*. Madison, WV: Author, 1979. 142p.

1880

Turner, David Anderson. *The Families of Boone County, West Virginia, the 1880 Census, Annotated*. Authors, 1981. 144p.

1900

Turner, David Anderson. *The Families of Boone County, West Virginia, the 1900 Census, Annotated*. Authors, 1985. 215p.

Braxton County
1850

Cochran, Wes. *1850 Census of Braxton County, West Virginia*. Parkersbury, WV: Author. 1986. 52p.

1860

Cochran, Wes. *1860 Census of Braxton County, West Virginia*. Parkersbury, WV: Author. 1986. 61p.

1870

Cochran, Wes. *1870 Census of Braxton County, West Virginia*. Parkersbury, WV: Author. 1986. 80p.

1900

Cochran, Wes. *1900 Census of Braxton County, West Virginia*. Parkersbury, WV: Author. 1995. 2 vols.

Cabell County
1810-1850

Eldridge, Carrie. *Cabell County Census Locator, Who, Where, What, 1850, 1840, 1830, 1820, 1810, Cabell County, Virginia/West Virginia*. Chesapeake, OH: Author, 1992. 260p.

1860

Hippert, Ernestine. *1860 Cabell County, West Virginia Census, Annotated*. Huntington, WV: KYOWVA Genealogical Society, 1993. 256p.

Schlaudt, Billee Hammond. *Index, 1860 Cabell County, West Virginia Census*. Houston, TX: Author, 1994. 79p.

Calhoun County
1900

Cochran, Wes. *Calhoun County, West Virginia 1900 Census*. Parkersburg, WV: Author, 1994. 250p.

Doddridge County
1850

Cochran, Wes. *1850 Census of Doddridge County, (West) Virginia*. Parkersburg, WV: Author, 1985. 36p.

Fayette County
1840

Harper, Bonnie Blake. *The 1840 United States Census of Fayette County, West Virginia, Index*. Cincinnati, OH: Author, 1985. 23p.

1850

Aicher, Inez M. *1850 Census of Fayette County, Virginia, Now West Virginia*. Lansing, WV: Author, 1986. 96p.

1860

Aicher, Inez M. *1860 Census of Fayette County, Virginia, Now West Virginia*. Lansing, WV: Author. 143p.

Gilmer County
1860

Cochran, Wes. *1860 Census, Gilmer County, West Virginia*. Parkersburg, WV: Author. 49p.

1870

Cocran, Wes. *1870 Census of Gilmer County, West Virginia*. Parkersburg, WV: Author, 1985. 56p.

Grant County
1910

Ross, Clara Mae Alt. *Thirteenth Census of the United States, 1910 Population, Grant County, West Virginia*. Ozark, MO: Dogwood Printing, 1992. 199p.

Hampshire County
1782-1850

Michael, Glen E. *Hampshire County, Virginia, (Now West Virginia), 1782-1850, Heads of Families and Index to the United States Census*. Winchester, VA: Author, 1976. 114p.

1850

Tetrick, W. Guy. *Census Returns of Harrison County (West) Virginia for 1850, Copied from the Original Federal Census Records in the Census Bureau, Washington, DC*. Clarksburg, WV: Clarksburg Pub. Co., 1930. 318p.

1860

Oates, Daniel P. *The 1860 Federal Census of Hampshire County, Virginia Present Day Hampshire and Mineral County, West Virginia (With Maiden Names Added)*. Cullman, AL: Greegath Pub. Co., 1990. 329p.

Hancock County
1850

Olash, Freida Barnhart. *1850 Census, Hancock County, Virginia-West Virginia*. Apollo, PA: Closson Press, 1983. 116p.

Hardy County
1840

Felldin, Jeanne Robey, and Charlotte Magee Tucker. *The 1840 United States Census Index, the (West) Virginia Counties of Hardy and Harrison*. Tomball, TX: Genealogical Publications, 1976. 27p.

Harrison County
1840

Felldin, Jeanne Robey, and Charlotte Magee Tucker. *The 1840 United States Census Index, the (West) Virginia Counties of Hardy and Harrison*. Tomball, TX: Genealogical Publications, 1976. 27p.

Jackson County
1860

Hite, Delmer R. *1860 Census of Jackson County, West Virginia*. Ripley, WV: Jackson County Historical Society of West Virginia, 1982. 335p.

1900

Miihlbach, Carolyn Thomas. *Families of Grant District, Jackson County, West Virginia, in 1900 Census Data and Genealogical Information*. Ravenswood, WV: Author, 1985. 208p.

Slaughter, Raymond D. *Index 1900 Census of Jackson County, West Virginia*. Columbus, OH: Author, 1982. 17p.

Kanawha County
1850

1850 Kanawha, Virginia Census. Elkview, WV: West Virginia's Genealogy Society, 1983. 237p.

1860

Turner, David A., and Sigfus Olafson. *Kanawha County, West Virginia Census*. South Charleston, WV: Kanawha Valley Genealogical Society, Inc., 1983.

Lewis County
1850

Cochran, Wes. *1850 Census of Lewis County, West Virginia*. Parkersburg, WV: Author, 1983. 121p.

Tetrick, W. Guy. *Census Returns of Lewis County (West) Virginia for 1850, Copied from the Original Federal Census Records in the Census Bureau, Washington, DC*. Clarksburg, WV: Clarksburg Pub. Co., 1930. 287p.

Logan County
1830

Schreiner Yantis, Netti. *1830 Census of Logan County, Virginia (Now West Virginia)*. Springfield, VA: 1970. 10p.

1840

Pearlman, Agnes Branch. *1840 Census and Index for Logan County, Virginia (Later West Virginia)*. Santa Ana, CA: Eco-View, 1976. 16p.

Marion County
1860

Felldin, Jeanne Robey, and Charlotte Magee Tucker. *1860 United States Census, Marion County, (West) Virginia Surname Index*. Tomball, TX: Genealogical Publications, 1976. 10p.

Marshall County
1840

Estlack, Helen Jane, and Elizabeth E. Mullett. *Marshall County, West Virginia, 1840 Census*. New Martinsville, WV: Wetzel County Genealogical Society, 1991. 36p.

Stout, Linda Goddard. *The 1840 Census of Marshall County, Virginia, Now West Virginia*. Proctor, WV: Tri-County Researcher, 1991. 94p.

1900

Cochran, Wes. *Marshall County, West Virginia 1900 Census*. Parkersburg, WV: Author, 1998. 48p.

Mason County
1860

Cochran, Wes. *Mason County, West Virginia 1860 Census*. Parkersburg, WV: Author, 1997. 112p.

1900

Slaughter, Raymond D. *Index 1900 Census of Mason County, West Virginia*. Columbus, OH: Author, 1982. 22p.

1910

Cochran, Wes. *Mason County, West Virginia 1910 Census, Arbuckle District*. Parkersburg, WV: Author, 1997. 60p.

Mineral County
1860

Oates, Daniel P. *The 1860 Federal Census of Hampshire County, Virginia Present Day Hampshire and Mineral County, West Virginia (With Maiden Names Added)*. Cullman, AL: Greegath Pub. Co., 1990. 329p.

Monongalia County
1860

Cochran, Wes. *1860 Census, Monongalia County, West Virginia*. Parkersburg, WV: Author, 1987. 160p.

Monroe County
1850

Felldin, Jeanne Robey, and Charlotte Magee Tucker. *The 1850 United States Census, Monroe County (West) Virginia, Surname Index*. Tomball, TX: Genealogical Publications, 1976. 7p.

1870

West Virginia DAR. *Index to 1860 Monroe County, Virginia, Census*. Genealogical Records Committee Report, s2, v22. WV: West Virginia DAR, 1997. 110p.

Morgan County
1860

Morgan County West Virginia 1860 Census. Berkeley Springs, WV: Morgan County Historical and Genealogical Society, 1993. 97p.

1870

Morgan County West Virginia 1870 Census. Berkeley Springs, WV: Morgan County Historical and Genealogical Society, 1992. 117p.

Nicholas County
1820-1840

Bryant, Neva Jane Stout. *1820-1840 Census of Nicholas County, (West) Virginia*. Daleville, VA: Author, 1996. 40p.

1850

Bryant, Neva Jane Stout. *1850 Census of Nicholas County, (West) Virginia*. Daleville, VA: Author, 1996. 97p.

Ohio County
1810

McGhee, Lucy Kate. *Ohio County, West Virginia, 1810 United States Census of Ohio County, Virginia*. Washington, DC: Author, 1964. 47, 25p

1840

Mullett, Elizabeth Estlack, and Helen J. Estlack. *Ohio County, West Virginia, 1840 Census*. New Martinsville, WV: Wetzel County Genealogical Society, 1991. 70p.

Pendleton County
1860

Cochran, Wes. *Pendleton County, West Virginia 1860 Census*. Parkersburg, WV: Author. 73p.

1870

Cochran, Wes. *Pendleton County, West Virginia 1870 Census*. Parkersburg, WV: Author. 1993. 79p.

Pleasants County
1860

Cochran, Wes, Martha Metz, and Linda Camp. *1860 Census of Pleasants County, West Virginia*. Parkersburg, WV: Author, 1982. 39p.

Preston County
1850

Cochran, Wes. *1850 Census of Preston County, (West) Virginia*. Parkersburg, WV: Author, 1985. 148p.

Putnam County
1880

Slaughter, Raymond D. *Index, 1880 Census of Putnam County, West Virginia*. Columbus, OH: Author, 1988. 18p.

1900

Slaughter, Raymond D. *Index 1900 Census of Putnam County, West Virginia*. Columbus, OH: Author, 1982. 16p.

Raleigh County
1870

Turner, Ronald R. *Raleigh County, West Virginia, 1870 Census Annotated*. Fairview Park, OH: Author, 1986. 85p.

Randolph County
1850

Cochran, Wes. *1850 Census of Randolph County, West Virginia*. Parkersburg, WV: Author, 1985. 64p.

Roane County
1870

Cochran, Wes. *Roane County, West Virginia 1870 Census*. Parkersburg, WV: Author. 1992. Unpgd.

1880

Comuzie, Janet. *Roane County, West Virginia, 1880 Census*. Elkview, WV: West Virginia Genealogy Soc., 1984. 263p.

1900

Cochran, Wes. *Roane County, West Virginia 1900 Census*. Parkersburg, WV: Author. 1992. 2 vols.

Taylor County
1850

Tetrick, Willis Guy. *Census Returns of Barbour and Taylor Counties, West Virginia for 1850*. Clarksburg, WV: Clarksburg Pub. Co., 1932. 391p.

1890

Taylor County, West Virginia, Special Schedule of the Eleventh Census (1890) Enumerating Union Veterans and Widows of Union Veterans of the Civil War. Grafton, WV: Melba Pender Zinn, 1989. 33p.

Tucker County
1860

Cochran, Wes. *Tucker County, West Virginia 1860 Census*. Parkersburg, WV: Author. 1993. 19p.

Tyler County
1820-1840

Estlack, Helen Jane, and Elizabeth Estlack Mullett. *Tyler County, West Virginia, 1820, 1830, 1840 Census*. New Martinsville, WV: Wetzel County Genealogical Society, 1991. 57p.

1850

Wright, Hilda Hays. *The 1850 Census of Tyler County (West) Virginia*. Middlebourne, WV: Tyler County Heritage & Historical Society, 1989. 66p.

1890

Hill, Ken. *Wetzel and Tyler Counties, West Virginia, 1890 Census of Union Veterans and Widows*. New Martinsville, WV: Wetzel County Genealogical Society, 1981. 72p.

Upshur County
1870

Cochran, Wes. *Upshur County, West Virginia 1870 Census*. Parkersburg, VV: Author, 1987. 101p.

1900

Wolfe, Lemoyne Wentz, and Karon King. *1900 Census of Upshur County West Virginia*. Fort Union, VA: Wedgewood Publishing, 1996. 204p.

Wayne County
1820

Pettit, Sheri K. *1870 Wayne County, West Virginia, Census*. Huntington, WV: Author, 1997. 194p.

1860

1860 Wayne County, Virginia Census Index. Charleston, WV: West Virginia Department of Culture and History, 1981. 14p.

Wetzel County
1860

Hassig, Carol. *The 1860 Census of Wetzel County, Virginia, Now West Virginia*. New Martinsville, WV: Wetzel County Genealogical Society, 1982. 103p.

1880

1880 Census of Wetzel County, West Virginia. New Martinsville, WV: Wetzel County Genealogical Society, 1986. 171p.

1890

Hill, Ken. *Wetzel and Tyler Counties, West Virginia, 1890 Census of Union Veterans and Widows*. New Martinsville, WV: Wetzel County Genealogical Society, 1981. 72p.

1900

Center District, Wetzel County, West Virginia, 1900 Census. New Martinsville, WV: Wetzel County Genealogical Society, 1982. 60p.

Grant District, Wetzel County, West Virginia, 1900 Census. New Martinsville, WV: Wetzel County Genealogical Society, 1982. 147p.

Green District, Wetzel County, West Virginia, 1900 Census. New Martinsville, WV: Wetzel County Genealogical Society, 1982. 99p.

Magnolia District, Wetzel County, West Virginia, 1900 Census. New Martinsville, WV: Wetzel County Genealogical Society, 1982. 92p.

Proctor District, Wetzel County, West Virginia 1900 Census. New Martinsville, WV: Wetzel County Genealogical Society, 1982. 69p.

Wirt County
1860
Cochran, Wes. *1860 Census of Wirt County, West Virginia*. Parkersburg, WV: Author, 1979. 50p.
1870
Cochran, Wes. *1870 Census of Wirt County, West Virginia*. Parkersburg, WV: Author, 1980. 68p.

Wood County
1840
Cochran, Wes. *1840 Census of Wood County*. Parkersburg, WV: Author, 1985. 19p.
1860
Metz, Martha, Linda Camp, and Wes Cochran. *1860 Census of Wood County, West Virginia*. Parkersburg, WV: Cochran, 1978. 154p.
1899
Cochran, Wes. *Wood County, West Virginia 1900 Census*. Parkersburg, WV: Author. 1995. 59p.
1920
Cochran, Wes. *Wood County, West Virginia 1920 Census Lubeck and Tygart Districts*. Parkersburg, WV: Author. 1993. 94p.

Wyoming County
Pearlman, Agnes Branch. *Genealogical Index and Gazetteer for Bowman's Reference Book of Wyoming County History, with Corrections and Additions to Census Section*. Santa Ana, CA: Eco-View, 1976. Unpgd.
1850
Mullins, Billie Hill. *Wyoming County, West Virginia, 1850 Federal Census*. Logan, WV: Author, 1997. 44p.
_____, and Jeff Weaver. *Wyoming County, West Virginia, 1850-1860*. Clintwood, VA: Mullins Printing, 1989, 1997. 44p.
Schunk, John Frederick. *1850 U.S. Census, Wyoming County, West Virginia*. Wichita, KS: S-K Publications, 1986. 75p.
1860
Evans, June Banks. *Census of 1860, Wyoming County, Virginia*. New Orleans, LA: Bryn Ffyliaid Publications, 1981. 54p.
Mullins, Betty, and Jeff Weaver. *Wyoming County, West Virginia, 1850-1860*. Clintwood, VA: Mullins Printing, 1989. Unpgd.
1870
Richardson, James E. *1870 Wyoming County, West Virginia Census*. Charleston, WV: Author, 1991. 107p.
1890
Williams, Sally Seaman. *1890 Wyoming County, West Virginia Veterans Census*. Whitehouse, TX: Author, 1986. 10p.
1900
Williams, Sally Seaman. *1900 Wyoming County, West Virginia Veterans Census*. Medford, OR: Traveling Seminar, 1986. 3 vols.

Wisconsin

Hanson, Andrew, and Lisa Busby. *Census Tract Atlas of Wisconsin.* Madison, WI:Applied Population Laboratory, Dept. of Rural Sociology, College of Agricultural and Life Sciences, University of Wisconsin-Madison/Extension, 1993. 182p.

1820
Jackson, Ronald Vern. *Wisconsin Census Index, Online Edition.* Orem, UT: Ancestry.com, Inc., 1999. **http://www.ancestry.com**
_____. *Wisconsin 1820 Federal Census Index.* Salt Lake City, UT: Accelerated Indexing Systems International, 1989. 64p.

1830
Census Index: U.S. Selected States/Counties, 1830. Family Archive CD 315. Novato, CA: Broderbund Software. CD-ROM.
1830-1839 U.S. Census Indexes, Mid-Atlantic, South, Mid-West. Orem, UT: Automated Archives, 1993. CD-ROM.
Jackson, Ronald Vern. *Wisconsin Census Index, Online Edition.* Orem, UT: Ancestry.com, Inc., 1999. **http://www.ancestry.com**
_____. *Wisconsin 1830 Federal Census Index.* Salt Lake City, UT: Accelerated Indexing Systems International, 1989. 66p.

1836
Jackson, Ronald Vern. *Wisconsin Census Index, Online Edition.* Orem, UT: Ancestry.com, Inc., 1999. **http://www.ancestry.com**
_____, and Gary Ronald Teeples. *Wisconsin 1836 Census Index.* Bountiful, UT: Accelerated Indexing Systems International, 1976. 24p.

1837
Jackson, Ronald Vern. *Wisconsin Census Index, Online Edition.* Orem, UT: Ancestry.com, Inc., 1999. **http://www.ancestry.com**
_____. *Wisconsin 1837 Census Index.* Salt Lake City, UT: Accelerated Indexing Systems International, 1984, 76p.

1838
Jackson, Ronald Vern. *Wisconsin Census Index, Online Edition.* Orem, UT: Ancestry.com, Inc., 1999. **http://www.ancestry.com**
_____. *Wisconsin 1838 Census Index.* Bountiful, UT: Accelerated Indexing Systems, 1984. 79p.

1840
Census Index: U.S. Selected States/Counties, 1840. Family Archive CD 316. Novato, CA: Broderbund Software. CD-ROM.
1840 United States Census Index, Mid-West, Great Lakes. Orem, UT: Automated Archives, 1994. CD-ROM.
Jackson, Ronald Vern. *Wisconsin Census Index, Online Edition.* Orem, UT: Ancestry.com, Inc., 1999. **http://www.ancestry.com**
_____, and Gary Ronald Teeples. *Wisconsin 1840 Census Index.* Bountiful, UT: Accelerated Indexing Systems International, 1978. 96p.
U.S. Federal Population Census Schedules. 1840, M704, Microfilm Reel No. 580.

1842

Jackson, Ronald Vern. *Wisconsin Census Index, Online Edition*. Orem, UT: Ancestry.com, Inc., 1999. **http://www.ancestry.com**

_____. *Wisconsin 1842 Census Index*. Bountiful, UT: Accelerated Indexing Systems, 1984. 110p.

1846

Jackson, Ronald Vern. *Wisconsin Census Index, Online Edition*. Orem, UT: Ancestry.com, Inc., 1999. **http://www.ancestry.com**

_____. *Wisconsin 1846*. North Salt Lake City, UT: Accelerated Indexing Systems International, 1978. 480p.

1850

Census Index: U.S. Selected States/Counties, 1850. Family Archive CD 317. Novato, CA: Broderbund Software. CD-ROM.

Corley, Betty J. *Index, Yeoman(s), Yeaman(s), Youman(s), U.S. Census Index, Minnesota, Wisconsin, Michigan, 1850, 1860, 1880 Includes Various Other Spellings*. Hyrum, UT: Author, 1988. 6p.

Jackson, Ronald Vern. *Mortality Schedules Index, Online Edition*. Orem, UT: Ancestry.com, Inc., 1999. **http://www.ancestry.com**

_____. *Wisconsin Census Index, Online Edition*. Orem, UT: Ancestry.com, Inc., 1999. **http://www.ancestry.com**

_____. *Wisconsin 1850 Mortality*. North Salt Lake City, UT: Accelerated Indexing Systems International, 1987. 36p.

_____, and Gary Ronald Teeples. *Wisconsin 1850 Census Index*. Bountiful, UT: Accelerated Indexing Systems International, 1978. 231p.

U.S. Census Index Series, Iowa, Illinois, Michigan, Missouri, Minnesota, Wisconsin, 1850. Orem, UT: Automated Archives, 1992. CD-ROM.

U.S. Federal Population Census Schedules. 1850, M432, Microfilm Reel Nos. 994-1009.

1855

1855 Wisconsin State Census Index. Rhinelander, WI: Northwoods Genealogy Society, 1990. 9 vols.

Jackson, Ronald Vern. *Wisconsin Census Index, Online Edition*. Orem, UT: Ancestry.com, Inc., 1999. **http://www.ancestry.com**

_____. *Wisconsin 1855 Census Index*. Bountiful, UT: Accelerated Indexing Systems, 1984. 417p.

1860

Census Index: U.S. Selected States/Counties, 1860. Family Archive CD 318. Novato, CA: Broderbund Software. CD-ROM.

Corley, Betty J. *Index, Yeoman(s), Yeaman(s), Youman(s), U.S. Census Index, Minnesota, Wisconsin, Michigan, 1850, 1860, 1880 Includes Various Other Spellings*. Hyrum, UT: Author, 1988. 6p.

Jackson, Ronald Vern. *Wisconsin Census Index, Online Edition*. Orem, UT: Ancestry.com, Inc., 1999. **http://www.ancestry.com**

_____. *Wisconsin 1860 Federal Census Index*. West Jordan, UT: Genealogical Services, 1989, 1997. 2 vols.

U.S. Census Index, 1860, Wisconsin. Orem, UT: Automated Archives, 1994. CD-ROM.

U.S. Federal Population Census Schedules. 1860, M653, Microfilm Reel Nos. 1399-1438.

1865

Noonan, Barry Christopher. *1865 Wisconsin State Census, the Six Surviving Counties, Dunn, Green, Jackson, Kewaunee, Ozaukee, Sheboygan*. Madison, WI: Author, 1993. 353p.

1870

Census Index: U.S. Selected States/Counties, 1870. Family Archive CD 319. Novato, CA: Broderbund Software. CD-ROM.

Steuart, Raeone Christensen. *Wisconsin 1870 Census Index.* Bountiful, UT: Heritage Quest, 2000. CD-ROM.

U.S. Federal Population Census Schedules. 1870, M593, Microfilm Reel Nos. 1703-1747.

1880

Corley, Betty J. *Index, Yeoman(s), Yeaman(s), Youman(s), U.S. Census Index, Minnesota, Wisconsin, Michigan, 1850, 1860, 1880 Includes Various Other Spellings.* Hyrum, UT: Author, 1988. 6p.

U.S. Federal Population Census Schedules. 1880, T9, Microfilm Reel Nos. 1417-1453.

U.S. Federal Population Census Schedules. 1880, Soundex. T779, 51 Microfilm Reels.

1885

Wisconsin. Secretary of State. *Tabular Statements of the Census Enumeration, and the Agricultural, Mineral and Manufacturing Interests of the State ... Also Alphabetical List of the Soldiers and Sailors of the Late War Residing in the State June 20, 1885.* Madison, WI: Madison Democrat Printing Co., 1886. 791, 387p.

1890

Jackson, Ronald Vern. *Wisconsin Census Index, Online Edition (Veterans Schedules).* Orem, UT: Ancestry.com, Inc., 1999.

http://www.ancestry.com

_____. *1890 Wisconsin Veterans Census Index.* Salt Lake City, UT: Accelerated Indexing Systems, 1988. 485p.

_____. *Wisconsin 1890 Federal Census Index.* Salt Lake City, UT: Accelerated Indexing Systems International, 1988. 495p.

U.S. Federal Population Census Schedules, Special Schedule, Enumerating Union Veterans and Widows of Union Veterans of the Civil War. 1890, M123, Microfilm Reel Nos. 111-116.

Veterans' Schedules: U.S. Selected States, 1890. Family Archive CD 131. Novato, CA: Broderbund Software. CD-ROM.

1895

Wisconsin Census Enumeration, 1895, Names of Ex-soldiers and Sailors Residing in Wisconsin, June 20, 1895. Madison, WI: Democrat Printing Co., 1896. 363p.

1900

U.S. Federal Population Census Schedules. 1900, T623, Microfilm Reel Nos. 1777-1825.

U.S. Federal Population Census Schedules. 1900, Soundex. T1079, 188 Microfilm Reels.

1910

U.S. Federal Population Census Schedules. 1910, T624, Microfilm Reel Nos. 1700-1744. (No Soundex/Miracode Index was prepared by the Government for this State.)

1920

U.S. Federal Population Census Schedules. 1920, T625, Microfilm Reel Nos. 1975-2024.

U.S. Federal Population Census Schedules. 1920, Soundex. M1595, 196 Microfilm Reels.

Brown County
1860

USGenWeb Census Project. Wisconsin, 1860 Brown County.

ftp://ftp.rootsweb.com/pub/census/wi/brown/1860/

Dane County
1910
Index to the 1910 Federal Population Census of Dane County, Wisconsin. Madison, WI: Wisconsin State Genealogical Society, 1993. 161p.

Dodge County
1840
Pompey, Sherman Lee. *Index to the 1840 Census of Dodge, Fond Du Lac, Manitowac, Marquette, Portage, Sauk, Sheboygan and Winnebago Counties, Wisconsin Territory.* Clovis, CA: Author, 1970. Unpgd.

Door County
1910
1910 Federal Census Door County, Wisconsin, Alphabetical Index and as Enumerated. Sturgeon Bay, WI: Peninsula Genealogical Society, 1994. 181p.

Dunn County
1865
Noonan, Barry Christopher. *1865 Wisconsin State Census, the Six Surviving Counties, Dunn, Green, Jackson, Kewaunee, Ozaukee, Sheboygan.* Madison, WI: Author, 1993. 353p.

Florence County
1910
Pasowicz, Joseph, Jr., and Joan Pasowicz. *Florence County, Wisconsin 1910 Federal Census, Commonwealth & Long Lake Townships.* Fence, WI: Genealogical Data Services, 1985. 151p.

_____. *Florence County, Wisconsin 1910 Federal Census, Florence Township.* Fence, WI: Genealogical Data Services, 1985. 400p.

_____. *Florence County, Wisconsin 1910 Federal Census, Homestead Township.* Fence, WI: Genealogical Data Services, 1985. 187p.

Fond Du Lac County
1838
Rentmeister, Jean R. *1846 Territorial Census of Wisconsin for Winnebago County; 1838 & 1842 Territorial Census of Wisconsin for Fond du Lac County; 1842 Territorial Census of Wisconsin for Winnebago County.* Fond du Lac, WI: Author, 1979. 12p.
1840
Pompey, Sherman Lee. *Index to the 1840 Census of Dodge, Fond Du Lac, Manitowac, Marquette, Portage, Sauk, Sheboygan and Winnebago Counties, Wisconsin Territory.* Clovis, CA: Author, 1970. Unpgd.
1842
Rentmeister, Jean R. *1846 Territorial Census of Wisconsin for Winnebago County; 1838 & 1842 Territorial Census of Wisconsin for Fond du Lac County; 1842 Territorial Census of Wisconsin for Winnebago County.* Fond du Lac, WI: Author, 1979. 12p.

Grant County
1850
Jentz, Helen. *1850 Grant County Census Index.* Author, 1994. 15p.
1870
Matl, Fran H. *Comprehensive Name Index to 1870 U.S. Census, Grant County, Wisconsin.* Author, 1994. 203p.

Green County
1865
Noonan, Barry Christopher. *1865 Wisconsin State Census, the Six Surviving Counties, Dunn, Green, Jackson, Kewaunee, Ozaukee, Sheboygan.* Madison, WI: Author, 1993. 353p.

Iron County
1910

Penrose, Russell K. *An Abstract of the 1910 Census of the United States for Iron County, Wisconsin*. Seguin, TX: Author, 1997. 170p.

Jackson County
1865

Noonan, Barry Christopher. *1865 Wisconsin State Census, the Six Surviving Counties, Dunn, Green, Jackson, Kewaunee, Ozaukee, Sheboygan*. Madison, WI: Author, 1993. 353p.

Kewaunee County
1865

Noonan, Barry Christopher. *1865 Wisconsin State Census, the Six Surviving Counties, Dunn, Green, Jackson, Kewaunee, Ozaukee, Sheboygan*. Madison, WI: Author, 1993. 353p.

Lafayette County
1880

Matl, Fran H., and Glenn J. Matl. *Index to 1880 United States for Lafayette County, Wisconsin*. Shullsburg, WI: Authors, 1985. 62p.

1885

Matl, Fran H., and Glenn J. Matl. *1885 Wisconsin State Census for Lafayette County*. Shullsburg, WI: Authors, 1994. 104p.

1910

Matl, Fran H., and Glenn J. Matl. *1910 U.S. Census Index for Lafayette County, Wisconsin*. Shullsburg, WI: Authors. 386p.

Lincoln County
1890

USGenWeb Census Project. Wisconsin, 1890 Lincoln County.
ftp://ftp.rootsweb.com/pub/census/wi/lincoln/1890/

Madison
1910

1910 Census Index, Madison, Wisconsin and Town of Madison. Madison, WI: Wisconsin State Genealogical Society, 1991. 86p.

Manitowac County
1840

Pompey, Sherman Lee. *Index to the 1840 Census of Dodge, Fond Du Lac, Manitowac, Marquette, Portage, Sauk, Sheboygan and Winnebago Counties, Wisconsin Territory*. Clovis, CA: Author, 1970. Unpgd.

Marquette County
1840

Pompey, Sherman Lee. *Index to the 1840 Census of Dodge, Fond Du Lac, Manitowac, Marquette, Portage, Sauk, Sheboygan and Winnebago Counties, Wisconsin Territory*. Clovis, CA: Author, 1970. Unpgd.

Milwaukee County
1846, 1847

Milwaukee County, Wisconsin Censuses of 1846 & 1847. Miami Beach, FL: T.LC. Genealogy, 1991. 104p.

1860

Jackson, Ronald Vern. *Milwaukee and Winnebago County, Wisconsin 1860 Federal Census Index*. Salt Lake City, UT: Accelerated Indexing Systems International, 1989. 395p.

_____. *Wisconsin 1860 Milwaukee and Winnebago Counties, Federal Census Index*. West Jordan, UT: Genealogical Services, 1991, 1997.

1880

Turney, Bessie Rauchfuss. *Village of Bay View, Wisconsin Census of 1880*. Milwaukee, WI: Milwaukee County Genealogical Society, 1992. 30, 64p.

Oconto County
1880

USGenWeb Census Project. Wisconsin, 1880 Oconto County. (Partial).
ftp://ftp.rootsweb.com/pub/census/wi/oconto/1880/

Ozaukee County
1865

Noonan, Barry Christopher. *1865 Wisconsin State Census, the Six Surviving Counties, Dunn, Green, Jackson, Kewaunee, Ozaukee, Sheboygan*. Madison, WI: Author, 1993. 353p.

Portage County
1840

Pompey, Sherman Lee. *Index to the 1840 Census of Dodge, Fond Du Lac, Manitowac, Marquette, Portage, Sauk, Sheboygan and Winnebago Counties, Wisconsin Territory*. Clovis, CA: Author, 1970. Unpgd.

1850

Portage County, Wisconsin, 1850 Federal Census with Index and Mortality Schedule. Stevens Point, WI: Stevens Point Area Genealogical Society, 1980. 24p.

USGenWeb Census Project. Wisconsin, 1850 Portage County.
ftp://ftp.rootsweb.com/pub/census/wi/portage/1850/

1900

Portage County, Wisconsin, 1850 Federal Census with Index and Mortality Schedule. Stevens Point, WI: Stevens Point Genealogical Society. 33p.

USGenWeb Census Project. Wisconsin, 1900 Portage County.
ftp://ftp.rootsweb.com/pub/census/wi/portage/1900/

Richland County
1870

Leget, Jean. *Wisconsin 1870 Census in the County of Richland, Wisconsin*. Brewer, WI: Brewer Public Library, 1986. 277p.

River Falls
1910

An Alphabetized and Annotated Version of the 1900 Census and the 1910 Census of River Falls, Wisconsin. River Falls, WI: Pierce County Historical Association, 1996. 74p.

St. Croix County
1850

Miller, Willis Harry, and Harold Weatherhead. *1850 Census for St. Croix County, Wisconsin with a Historical Sketch*. Hudson, WI: St. Croix County Historical Society, 1950. 33p.

Sauk County
1840

Pompey, Sherman Lee. *Index to the 1840 Census of Dodge, Fond Du Lac, Manitowac, Marquette, Portage, Sauk, Sheboygan and Winnebago Counties, Wisconsin Territory*. Clovis, CA: Author, 1970. Unpgd.

Sheboygan County
1840
Pompey, Sherman Lee. *Index to the 1840 Census of Dodge, Fond Du Lac, Manitowac, Marquette, Portage, Sauk, Sheboygan and Winnebago Counties, Wisconsin Territory*. Clovis, CA: Author, 1970. Unpgd.
1865
Noonan, Barry Christopher. *1865 Wisconsin State Census, the Six Surviving Counties, Dunn, Green, Jackson, Kewaunee, Ozaukee, Sheboygan*. Madison, WI: Author, 1993. 353p.

Winnebago County
1840
Pompey, Sherman Lee. *Index to the 1840 Census of Dodge, Fond Du Lac, Manitowac, Marquette, Portage, Sauk, Sheboygan and Winnebago Counties, Wisconsin Territory*. Clovis, CA: Author, 1970. Unpgd.
1842, 1846
Rentmeister, Jean R. *1846 Territorial Census of Wisconsin for Winnebago County; 1838 & 1842 Territorial Census of Wisconsin for Fond du Lac County; 1842 Territorial Census of Wisconsin for Winnebago County*. Fond du Lac, WI: Author, 1979. 12p.
1860
Jackson, Ronald Vern. *Milwaukee and Winnebago County, Wisconsin 1860 Federal Census Index*. Salt Lake City, UT: Accelerated Indexing Systems International, 1989. 395p.

_____. *Wisconsin 1860 Milwaukee and Winnebago Counties, Federal Census Index*. West Jordan, UT: Genealogical Services, 1991, 1997. 395p.

Wyoming

1860
Census Index: U.S. Selected States/Counties, 1860. Family Archive CD 318. Novato, CA: Broderbund Software. CD-ROM.

Jackson, Ronald Vern. *Wyoming Census Index, Online Edition*. Orem, UT: Ancestry.com, Inc., 1999.
http://www.ancestry.com

_____, and Gary Ronald Teeples. *Wyoming 1860 Census Index*. North Salt Lake City, UT: Accelerated Indexing Systems International, 1983. 55, 9p.

_____, Scott Rosenkilde, and W. David Samuelson. *Wyoming 1860 Territorial Census Index*. Bountiful, UT: Accelerated Indexing Systems, 1984. 30, 5p.

1870
Census Index: U.S. Selected States/Counties, 1870. Family Archive CD 319. Novato, CA: Broderbund Software. CD-ROM.

Howard, Mrs. John. *The 1870 and 1880 Wyoming Mortality Schedules*. Fort Wayne, IN: Allen County Public Library, 1983. 17p.

Jackson, Ronald Vern. *Mortality Schedules Index, Online Edition*. Orem, UT: Ancestry.com, Inc., 1999.
http://www.ancestry.com

_____. *Wyoming Census Index, Online Edition*. Orem, UT: Ancestry.com, Inc., 1999.
http://www.ancestry.com

_____, and Gary Ronald Teeples. *Wyoming 1870 Territorial Census Index*. Bountiful, UT: Accelerated Indexing Systems, 1978. 56, 73p.

U.S. Federal Population Census Schedules. 1870, M593, Microfilm Reel No. 1748.

1880
Census Index: U.S. Selected States/Counties, 1880. Family Archive CD 320. Novato, CA: Broderbund Software. CD-ROM.

Howard, Mrs. John. *The 1870 and 1880 Wyoming Mortality Schedules*. Fort Wayne, IN: Allen County Public Library, 1983. 17p.

Jackson, Ronald Vern. *Mortality Schedules Index, Online Edition*. Orem, UT: Ancestry.com, Inc., 1999.
http://www.ancestry.com
_____. *Wyoming Census Index, Online Edition*. Orem, UT: Ancestry.com, Inc., 1999.
http://www.ancestry.com
_____, and Gary Ronald Teeples. *Wyoming 1880 Census Index*. Bountiful, UT: Accelerated Indexing Systems, 1980. 266p.
U.S. Federal Population Census Schedules. 1880, T9, Microfilm Reel No. 1454.
U.S. Federal Population Census Schedules. 1880, Soundex. T780, 1 Microfilm Reel.

1890
Jackson, Ronald Vern. *1890 Wyoming Census Index*. Salt Lake City, UT: Accelerated Indexing Systems, 1983. 19p.
_____. *1890 Wyoming Census Index, Special Schedule of the 11th Census Enumerating Union Veterans and Widows of Union Veterans of the Civil War*. Salt Lake City, UT: Accelerated Indexing Systems, 1983. 58, 19p.
_____. *Wyoming Census Index, Online Edition*. Orem, UT: Ancestry.com, Inc., 1999.
http://www.ancestry.com
U.S. Federal Population Census Schedules, Special Schedule, Enumerating Union Veterans and Widows of Union Veterans of the Civil War. 1890, M123, Microfilm Reel No. 117.
Veterans' Schedules: U.S. Selected States, 1890. Family Archive CD 131. Novato, CA: Broderbund Software. CD-ROM.

1900
U.S. Federal Population Census Schedules. 1900, T623, Microfilm Reel Nos. 1826-1827.
U.S. Federal Population Census Schedules. 1900, Soundex. T1080, 14 Microfilm Reels.

1910
Dilts, Bryan Lee. *1910 Wyoming Census Index, Heads of Households and other Surnames in Households Index*. Salt Lake City, UT: Index Publications, 1985. 245p.
_____. 2nd ed. Bountiful, UT: Precision Indexing, 1992. 245p.
Jackson, Ronald Vern. *Wyoming Census Index, Online Edition*. Orem, UT: Ancestry.com, Inc., 1999.
http://www.ancestry.com
U.S. Federal Population Census Schedules. 1910, T624, Microfilm Reel Nos. 1745-1747. (No Soundex/Miracode Index was prepared by the Government for this State.)

1920
U.S. Federal Population Census Schedules. 1920, T625, Microfilm Reel Nos. 2025-2029.
U.S. Federal Population Census Schedules. 1920, Soundex. M1596, 17 Microfilm Reels.

Carbon County
1870
USGenWeb Census Project. Wyoming, 1870 Carbon County.
ftp://ftp.rootsweb.com/pub/census/wy/carbon/1870/

Laramie County
1870
USGenWeb Census Project. Wyoming, 1870 Laramie County.
ftp://ftp.rootsweb.com/pub/census/wy/laramie/1870/

Sweetwater County
1920
USGenWeb Census Project. Wyoming, 1920 Sweetwater County.
ftp://ftp.rootsweb.com/pub/census/wy/sweetwater/1920/

GENERAL TOPICS

African Americans
General
1870

African Americans in the 1870 Census. Family Archive CD 165. Novato, CA: Broderbund Software. CD-ROM.

Alabama
1850

Jackson, Ronald Vern, and Gary Ronald Teeples. *Alabama 1850 Slave Schedule Census Index.* Salt Lake City, UT: Accelerated Indexing Systems International, 1988. 160p.

U.S. Federal Population Census Schedules. 1850, M432, Slave Schedules, Microfilm Reel Nos. 17-24.

USGenWeb Census Project. Alabama. 1850 Washington County. Slave Schedule.

ftp://ftp.rootsweb.com/pub/census/al/washington/1850/

1860

Jackson, Ronald Vern. *Alabama 1860 Slave Schedule.* North Salt Lake City, UT: Accelerated Indexing Systems, 1990. 645p.

Senn, Susie K. *The 1860 Federal Slave Schedule for Pike County, Alabama.* Brundige, AL: Author, 1995. 53p.

U.S. Federal Population Census Schedules. 1860, M653, Slave Schedules, Microfilm Reel Nos. 27-36.

Arkansas
1850

Jackson, Ronald Vern, and Gary Ronald Teeples. *Arkansas 1850 Slave Schedule Census Index.* Salt Lake City, UT: Accelerated Indexing Systems International, 1988. 55; 112p.

U.S. Federal Population Census Schedules. 1850, M432, Slave Schedules, Microfilm Reel No. 32.

Wade, Ophelia Richardson. *Mississippi County, Arkansas Vital Records, Land Entry Book 1826-1889, Index to Wills 1862-1925, Post Office History 1836-1974; Complete 1840 Federal Census, 1850-1860 Slave Schedules, 1850-1860-1870 Mortality Records.* Bragg City, MO: Author, 1974. 87p.

1860

Jackson, Ronald Vern. *Arkansas 1860 Slave Schedule.* North Salt Lake City, UT: Accelerated Indexing Systems International, 1991. 237p.

U.S. Federal Population Census Schedules. 1860, M653, Slave Schedules, Microfilm Reel Nos. 53-54.

Wade, Ophelia Richardson. *Mississippi County, Arkansas Vital Records, Land Entry Book 1826-1889, Index to Wills 1862-1925, Post Office History 1836-1974; Complete 1840 Federal Census, 1850-1860 Slave Schedules, 1850-1860-1870 Mortality Records*. Bragg City, MO: Author, 1974. 87p.

1870
Wade, Ophelia Richardson. *Mississippi County, Arkansas Vital Records, Land Entry Book 1826-1889, Index to Wills 1862-1925, Post Office History 1836-1974; Complete 1840 Federal Census, 1850-1860 Slave Schedules, 1850-1860-1870 Mortality Records*. Bragg City, MO: Author, 1974. 87p.

California
African Americans in Los Angeles and Los Angeles Township, Extracts from United States Censuses. Los Angeles, CA: California African American Genealogical Society, 1995. Unpgd.

Delaware
1850
Jackson, Ronald Vern. *Delaware 1850, 1860 Slave Schedules*. North Salt Lake City, UT: Accelerated Indexing Systems International, 1986. 59, 18p.

U.S. Federal Population Census Schedules. 1850, M432, Slave Schedules, Microfilm Reel No. 55.

1860
Jackson, Ronald Vern. *Delaware 1850, 1860 Slave Schedules*. North Salt Lake City, UT: Accelerated Indexing Systems International, 1986. 59, 18p.

U.S. Federal Population Census Schedules. 1860, M653, Slave Schedules, Microfilm Reel No. 100.

District of Columbia
1850
Jackson, Ronald Vern. *District of Columbia 1850 Slave Schedule*. North Salt Lake City, UT: Accelerated Indexing Systems International, 1988. 52, 26p.

U.S. Federal Population Census Schedules. 1850, M432, Slave Schedules, Microfilm Reel No. 57.

1860
U.S. Federal Population Census Schedules. 1860, M653, Slave Schedules, Microfilm Reel No. 105.

Florida
1850
Jackson, Ronald Vern, and Gary Ronald Teeples. *Florida 1850 Slave Schedule Census Index*. Salt Lake City, UT: Accelerated Indexing Systems International, 1988. 68p.

U.S. Federal Population Census Schedules. 1850, M432, Slave Schedules, Microfilm Reel No. 60.

1860
Jackson, Ronald Vern, and Gary Ronald Teeples. *Florida 1860 Slave Schedule Census Index*. Salt Lake City, UT: Accelerated Indexing Systems International, 1990. 55, 106p.

U.S. Federal Population Census Schedules. 1860, M653, Slave Schedules, Microfilm Reel No. 110.

Alachua County
1840
USGenWeb Census Project. Florida, 1840 Alachua County. Slave Schedule.
ftp://ftp.rootsweb.com/pub/census/fl/alachua/1840/
1850
USGenWeb Census Project. Florida, 1850 Alachua County. Slave Schedule.
ftp://ftp.rootsweb.com/pub/census/fl/alachua/1850/

Benton County
1850
USGenWeb Census Project. Florida, 1850 Benton County. Slave Schedule.
ftp://ftp.rootsweb.com/pub/census/fl/benton/1850/

Dade County
1850
USGenWeb Census Project. Florida, 1850 Dade County. Slave Schedule.
ftp://ftp.rootsweb.com/pub/census/fl/dade/1850/

Duval County
1850
USGenWeb Census Project. Florida, 1850 Duval County. Slave Schedule.
ftp://ftp.rootsweb.com/pub/census/fl/duval/1850/

Franklin County
1850
USGenWeb Census Project. Florida, 1850 Franklin County. Slave Schedule.
ftp://ftp.rootsweb.com/pub/census/fl/franklin/1850/

Hillsborough County
1850
USGenWeb Census Project. Florida, 1850 Hillsborough County. Slave Schedule.
ftp://ftp.rootsweb.com/pub/census/fl/hillsborough/1850/

Holmes County
1850
USGenWeb Census Project. Florida, 1850 Holmes County. Slave Schedule.
ftp://ftp.rootsweb.com/pub/census/fl/holmes/1850/

Levy County
1850
USGenWeb Census Project. Florida, 1850 Levy County. Slave Schedule.
ftp://ftp.rootsweb.com/pub/census/fl/levy/1850/

Marion County
1850
USGenWeb Census Project. Florida, 1850 Marion County. Slave Schedule.
ftp://ftp.rootsweb.com/pub/census/fl/marion/1850/

Rusk County
1850
USGenWeb Census Project. Florida, 1850 Rusk County. Slave Schedule.
ftp://ftp.rootsweb.com/pub/census/fl/rusk/1850/

Saint Lucie County
1850
USGenWeb Census Project. Florida, 1850 St. Lucie Slave Schedule.
ftp://ftp.rootsweb.com/pub/census/fl/stlucie/1850/

Georgia
1850
Hageness, MariLee Beatty. *Slaveowner Census, 1850, Henry County, Georgia.* Anniston, AL: MLH Research, 1995. 8p.

Jackson, Ronald Vern. *Georgia 1850 Slave Schedule Census Index*. Salt Lake City, UT: Accelerated Indexing Systems International, 1988. Unpgd.

U.S. Federal Population Census Schedules. 1850, M432, Slave Schedules, Microfilm Reel Nos. 88-96.

1860

Clayton County, Georgia, 1860 Census Including Slave and Mortality Census. Jonesboro, GA: Ancestors Unlimited, 1985. 84p.

Holloman, Ann Brown Clark. *Hart County, Georgia 1860 Census, Including Slave Schedule and Mortality Schedule*. Albany, GA: Author, 1961. Unpgd.

Jackson, Ronald Vern. *Georgia 1860 Slave Schedule Census Index*. North Salt Lake City, UT: Accelerated Indexing Systems International, 1990. 787p.

U.S. Federal Population Census Schedules. 1860, M653, Slave Schedules, Microfilm Reel Nos. 142-153.

1870

Clayton County, Georgia, 1870 Census Including Slave and Mortality Census. Jonesboro, GA: Ancestors Unlimited, 1987. 105p.

Kentucky
1840

Norris, William V. *1840 U.S. Census, Clark County, Kentucky, (From U.S. Census Microfilm), and Index, with Slave Summary*. Jacksonville, FL: Author, 1983. 40p.

1850

Jackson, Ronald Vern. *Kentucky 1850 Slave Schedule Census Index*. North Salt Lake City, UT: Accelerated Indexing Systems International, 1990. 665p.

U.S. Federal Population Census Schedules. 1850, M432, Slave Schedules, Microfilm Reel Nos. 223-228.

1860

U.S. Federal Population Census Schedules. 1860, M653, Slave Schedules, Microfilm Reel Nos. 401-406.

1870

Grady, Evie Ruth Hill. *Blacks Living in Mason County, Kentucky, Federal Census, 1870*. Cincinnati, OH: Author, 1983. 33p.

1880

Grady, Evie Ruth Hill. *Blacks Living in Fleming County, Kentucky, Federal Census, 1880*. Cincinnati, OH: Author, 1983. 34p.

_____. *1880 Mason County, Kentucky Federal Census, Black Inhabitants*. Cincinnati, OH: Author, 1984. 87p.

1900

Grady, Evie Ruth Hill. *Blacks Living in Fleming County, Kentucky, Federal Census, 1900*. Cincinnati, OH: Author, 1983. 34p.

_____. *1900 Mason County, Kentucky Federal Census, Black Inhabitants*. Cincinnati, OH: Author, 1984. 83p.

Harris, Theodore H.H. *Afro-American Residents of Kenton County, Kentucky, the 1900 Kenton County, Kentucky Census*. Covington, KY: Author, 1991. 17p.

Louisiana
1810, 1820

Roux, Vincent M. *Louisiana's Households of Free People of Color Residing Outside of Orleans Parish & the City of New Orleans in 1810 & 1820*. San Francisco, CA: Author, 195. 72p.

1830

Head, Wanda Volentine. *Claiborne Parish, Louisiana 1830, 1840 and 1850 Censuses with 1850 Mortality Schedule and Slave Holders*. Shreveport, LA: J&W Enterprises, 1996. 165p.

1840

Dill, Harry F. *Some Slaveholders and Their Slaves, Union Parish, Louisiana, 1839-1865*. Bowie, MD: Heritage Books, 1997. 195p.

Head, Wanda Volentine. *Claiborne Parish, Louisiana 1830, 1840 and 1850 Censuses with 1850 Mortality Schedule and Slave Holders.* Shreveport, LA: J&W Enterprises, 1996. 165p.

1850

Dill, Harry F. *Some Slaveholders and Their Slaves, Union Parish, Louisiana, 1839-1865.* Bowie, MD: Heritage Books, 1997. 195p.

Head, Wanda Volentine. *Claiborne Parish, Louisiana 1830, 1840 and 1850 Censuses with 1850 Mortality Schedule and Slave Holders.* Shreveport, LA: J&W Enterprises, 1996. 165p.

Kerns, Gloria Lambert and Claude B. Slaton. *Livingston Parish, Louisiana Mortality and Slave Schedules 1850, 1860, 1870, 1880.* Baker, LA: Folk Finders. 30p.

U.S. Federal Population Census Schedules. 1850, M432, Slave Schedules, Microfilm Reel Nos. 242-247.

1860

Jackson, Ronald Vern. *Louisiana 1860 Slave Schedules Index.* Salt Lake City, UT: Accelerated Indexing Systems International, 1988. 431p.

Kerns, Gloria Lambert, and Claude B. Slaton. *Livingston Parish, Louisiana Mortality and Slave Schedules 1850, 1860, 1870, 1880.* Baker, LA: Folk Finders. 30p.

U.S. Federal Population Census Schedules. 1860, M653, Slave Schedules, Microfilm Reel Nos. 427-431.

1865

Dill, Harry F. *Some Slaveholders and Their Slaves, Union Parish, Louisiana, 1839-1865.* Bowie, MD: Heritage Books, 1997. 195p.

1870

Dill, Harry F. *African American Inhabitants of Rapides Parish, Louisiana, 1 June - 4 September 1870.* Bowie, MD: Heritage Books, 1998. 373p.

Jackson, Ronald Vern. *Louisiana 1850 Slave Schedule Census Index.* Salt Lake City, UT: Accelerated Indexing Systems International, 1988. 405p.

Kerns, Gloria Lambert, and Claude B. Slaton. *Livingston Parish, Louisiana Mortality and Slave Schedules 1850, 1860, 1870, 1880.* Baker, LA: Folk Finders. 30p.

1880

Kerns, Gloria Lambert, and Claude B. Slaton. *Livingston Parish, Louisiana Mortality and Slave Schedules 1850, 1860, 1870, 1880.* Baker, LA: Folk Finders. 30p.

Maryland
1832

Hynson, Jerry M. *Free African Americans of Maryland 1832, Including Allegany, Anne Arundel, Calvert, Caroline, Cecil, Charles, Dorchester, Frederick, Kent, Montgomery, Queen Ann's, and St. Mary's Counties.* Westminster, MD: Family Line Publications, 1998. 161p.

1850

U.S. Federal Population Census Schedules. 1850, M432, Slave Schedules, Microfilm Reel Nos. 300-302.

1860

U.S. Federal Population Census Schedules. 1860, M653, Slave Schedules, Microfilm Reel Nos. 484-485.

Mississippi
1850

Jackson, Ronald Vern. *Mississippi 1850 Slave Schedules Index.* Salt Lake City, UT: Accelerated Indexing Systems, 1988. 465p.

U.S. Federal Population Census Schedules. 1850, M432, Slave Schedules, Microfilm Reel Nos. 383-390.

1860

Jackson, Ronald Vern. *Mississippi 1860 Slave Schedule.* North Salt Lake City, UT: Accelerated Indexing Systems International, 1990. 528p.

Morse, Bonnie. *Newton County, Mississippi 1860 Census and Slave Schedule.* Mobile, AL: Author, 1984. 257p.

U.S. Federal Population Census Schedules. 1860, M653, Slave Schedules, Microfilm Reel Nos. 595-604.

Missouri
1850

Bishop, Bernadine LaRose, and Dorothy Amburgy Griffith. *1850 Census, Sainte Genevieve County, Missouri, Population Schedule, Mortality Schedule, Slave Schedule*. St. Louis, MO: St. Louis Genealogical Society, 1991. 62p.

Jackson, Ronald Vern. *Missouri 1850 Slave Schedules, Federal Census Index.* West Jordan, UT: Genealogical Services, 1988; 1996. 388p.

U.S. Federal Population Census Schedules. 1850, M432, Slave Schedules, Microfilm Reel Nos. 422-424.

USGenWeb Census Project. Missouri, 1850 Holt County Slave Schedule.

ftp://ftp.rootsweb.com/pub/census/mo/holt/1850/slav.txt

USGenWeb Census Project. Missouri, 1850 Schuyler County. Slave Schedule.

ftp://ftp.rootsweb.com/pub/census/mo/schuyler/1850/slave.txt

1860

U.S. Federal Population Census Schedules. 1860, M653, Slave Schedules, Microfilm Reel Nos. 661-664.

1880

Haymon, Serena Abbess. *Amite County, Mississippi 1880 United States Census, Black Families*. Greenwell Springs, LA: Author, 1994. 364p.

1886

Shumway, Bob, Sarah Shumway, and Serena Abbess Haymong. *1886 Natchez, Adams County, Mississippi Census Black Families*. Pride, LA: F & M Enterprises, 1994. 262p.

New Jersey
1850

Jackson, Ronald Vern. *New Jersey 1850 Slave Schedule Census*. Salt Lake City, UT: Accelerated Indexing Systems International, 1988. Unpgd.

U.S. Federal Population Census Schedules. 1850, M432, Slave Schedules, Microfilm Reel No. 466.

New York
1790-1830

Eichholz, Alice and James M. Rose. *Free Black Heads of Households in the New York State Federal Census, 1790-1830*. Gale Genealogy and Local History Series, No. 14. Detroit, MI: Gale Research, 1981. 301p.

North Carolina
1790, 1800

Heinegg, Paul. *Free African Americans of North Carolina and Virginia Including the Family Histories of More than 80% of Those Counted as "All Other Free Persons" in the 1790 and 1800 Census*. Baltimore, MD: Genealogical Pub. Co., 1992. 462p.

_____. 2nd ed. Baltimore, MD: Genealogical Pub. Co., 1994. 699p.

_____. 3rd ed. Baltimore, MD: Genealogical Pub. Co., 1994. 825p.

1850

1850 Census of Johnston County, North Carolina, Population Schedule, Mortality Schedule, Slave Schedule. Smithfield, NC: Johnston County Genealogical Society, 1990. 106p.

Jackson, Ronald Vern. *North Carolina 1850 Slave Schedule Census Index*. Salt Lake City, UT: Accelerated Indexing Systems International, 1988. Unpgd.

U.S. Federal Population Census Schedules. 1850, M432, Slave Schedules, Microfilm Reel Nos. 650-656.

1860

Almasy, Sandra Lee. *Bertie County, North Carolina Census 1860, Population Schedule of the Eighth Census of the United States Free and Slave Inhabitants*. Middleton, WI: Kensington Glen Pub., 1996. 273p.

Jackson, Ronald Vern. *North Carolina 1860 Federal Slave Schedule Census Index*. Salt Lake City, UT: Accelerated Indexing Systems International, 1990. 683p.

U.S. Federal Population Census Schedules. 1860, M653, Slave Schedules, Microfilm Reel Nos. 920-927.

1900

Grady, Evie Ruth Hill. *Blacks Living in Randolph County, North Carolina Federal Census, 1900*. Cincinnati, OH: Author, 1983. 68p.

North Dakota
1870-1920

Guerrero, John. *Census Information Concerning Dakota and North Dakota Black Residents as Found in the United States Census Reports of 1870, 1880, 1885, 1900, 1910 and 1920*. Bismarck, ND: University of Mary Press, 1994. 231p.

Ohio
1870

Grady, Evie Ruth Hill. *Blacks Living in Brown County, Ohio, Federal Census, 1870*. Cincinnati, OH: Author, 1982. 38p.

_____. *Blacks Living in Butler County, Ohio, Federal Census, 1870*. Cincinnati, OH: Author, 1982. 16p.

1800

Grady, Evie Ruth Hill. *Blacks Living in Fleming County, Ohio, Federal Census, 1880*. Cincinnati, OH: Author, 1983. 34p.

_____. *Negroes Living in Brown County, Ohio, 1880 Census, 1880*. Cincinnati, OH: Author, 1983. 44p.

1900

Grady, Evie Ruth Hill. *Blacks Living in Clermont County, Ohio, Federal Census, 1900*. Cincinnati, OH: Author, 1983. 80p.

_____. *Blacks Living in Fleming County, Ohio, Federal Census, 1900*. Cincinnati, OH: Author, 1983. 34p.

_____. *Negroes Living in Brown County, Ohio, 1900 Federal Census*. Cincinnati, OH: Author, 1983. 50p.

South Carolina
1850

Jackson, Ronald Vern. *South Carolina 1850 Slave Schedule Census Index*. Salt Lake City, UT: Accelerated Indexing Systems International, 1988. 379p.

Sheriff, G. Anne. *1850 Federal Slave Census of Pickens District, South Carolina, Eastern Division, Present-day Pickens County*. Central, SC: Author, 1991. 40p.

U.S. Federal Population Census Schedules. 1850, M432, Slave Schedules, Microfilm Reel Nos. 861-868.

1860

Jackson, Ronald Vern. *South Carolina 1860 Slave Schedule Census Index*. Salt Lake City, UT: Accelerated Indexing Systems International, 1990. 533p.

Sheriff, G. Anne. *1860 Federal Slave Census of Pickens District, South Carolina, 5th Regiment, Present-day Pickens County*. Central, SC: Author, 1989. 38p.

Trotter, Shirley F. Johnson. *1860 Census, Lexington County, South Carolina, with a Complete Index of Names Including the Mortality Schedule and the Slave Schedule*. Chapin, SC: Dutch Fork Chapter, South Carolina Genealogical Society, 1991. 262p.

U.S. Federal Population Census Schedules. 1860, M653, Slave Schedules, Microfilm Reel Nos. 1229-1238.

Walker, Sonia L. *Abbeville County, South Carolina, a Compilation of Data from the 1860 Slave Schedule and a List of Free African Americans on the 1860 Census*. Abbeville, SC: Abbeville Books, 1997. 44p.

1910, 1920

Malone, Samuel Lorenzo. *Black Families in Cherokee County, South Carolina, as Taken from 1910-1920 Federal Census*. Rev. ed. Spartanburg, SC: Reprint Co., 1993. 93p.

South Dakota
1870-1920

Guerrero, John. *Census Information Concerning Dakota and North Dakota Black Residents as Found in the United States Census Reports of 1870, 1880, 1885, 1900, 1910 and 1920*. Bismarck, ND: University of Mary Press, 1994. 231p.

Tennessee
1850

Jackson, Ronald Vern. *Federal Census Index, Tennessee 1850 Slave Schedules Index*. West Jordan, UT: Genealogical Services, 1989, 1997. Unpgd.

Sherrill, Charles A. *Grundy County Tennessee Special Census Records, 1850-1880, Agricultural Schedules, Slave Population Schedules, Mortality Schedules Products of Industry Schedules*. Mt. Juliet, TN: Author, 1996. 147p.

U.S. Federal Population Census Schedules. 1850, M432, Slave Schedules, Microfilm Reel Nos. 902-907.

1860

Hutton, Edith Wilson, and Imogene Hall Thacker. *Transcription, Federal Census Schedule, Campbell County, Tennessee, 1860, Indexed Federal Mortality Schedule, Campbell County, Tennessee, 1860 List of Slave Owners, Campbell County, Tennessee*. Knoxville, TN: Author, 1982. 157p.

Jackson, Ronald Vern. *Federal Census Index, Tennessee 1860 Slave Schedules*. West Jordan, UT: Genealogical Services, 1990, 1997. 675p.

Malone, Royleta Clopton. *1860 Perry County, Tennessee, Census, Including Slave Schedule and Mortality Schedule, with Full Name Index*. Salt Lake City, UT: Author, 1988. 71p.

Sherrill, Charles A. *Grundy County Tennessee Special Census Records, 1850-1880, Agricultural Schedules, Slave Population Schedules, Mortality Schedules Products of Industry Schedules*. Mt. Juliet, TN: Author, 1996. 147p.

U.S. Federal Population Census Schedules. 1860, M653, Slave Schedules, Microfilm Reel Nos.1281-1286.

1870, 1880

Sherrill, Charles A. *Grundy County Tennessee Special Census Records, 1850-1880, Agricultural Schedules, Slave Population Schedules, Mortality Schedules Products of Industry Schedules*. Mt. Juliet, TN: Author, 1996. 147p.

Texas
1850

Cheatham, Belzora. *Slaves and Slave Owners of Bowie County, Texas, in 1850, 1850 Bowie County Slave Census with Information from the 1850 Free Census*. Chicago, IL: Author, 1996. 95p.

Corder, Mrs. Claude. *1850-1860 Census of Henderson County, Texas, Including Slave Schedule and 1846 Tax List*. Athens, TX: Henderson County Historical Society, 1984. 242p.

Jackson, Ronald Vern. *Texas 1850 Slave Schedules Index*. North Salt Lake City, UT: Accelerated Indexing Systems International, 1988. 153p.

Story, Loraine Dodson. *Early Records of Hunt County, Texas, (1850 Census, 1850 Mortality Schedule, 1850 Slave Schedule, 93 Marriages, 1847-1851)*. Farmersville, TX: Search-N-Print, 1979. 42p.

U.S. Federal Population Census Schedules. 1850, M432, Slave Schedules, Microfilm Reel Nos. 917-918.

USGenWeb Census Project. Texas, 1850 Rusk County. Slave Schedule.

ftp://ftp.rootsweb.com/pub/census/tx/rusk/1850/

1860

Corder, Mrs. Claude. *1850-1860 Census of Henderson County, Texas, Including Slave Schedule and 1846 Tax List*. Athens, TX: Henderson County Historical Society, 1984. 242p.

Hudson, Weldon I., and Shirley Brittain Cawyer. *Comanche County, Texas Census Records, 1860 and 1870 Federal Census, with Index to the 1880 Heads of Households and the Special 1890 Census of Union Veterans and Widows, also the 1860 Slave List and 1867 Voter's Registration*. Fort Worth, TX: Author, 1981. Unpgd.

Jackson, Ronald Vern. *Texas 1860 Slave Schedule*. North Salt Lake City, UT: Accelerated Indexing Systems International, 1990. 428p.

McCown, Leonard Joe. *Calhoun County, Texas Eighth Census of the United States, 1860; Free Inhabitants, Slave Inhabitants, Persons Who Died, Productions of Agriculture, Products of Industry, Social Statistics, C.C. Hoerton, Assistant Marshall*. Irving, TX: Author, 1978. 118p.

Story, Loraine Dodson. *1860 Census of Hunt County, Texas (Includes the 1860 Mortality and Slave Schedules)*. Farmersville, TX: Search-N-Print, 1979. 144p.

U.S. Federal Population Census Schedules. 1860, M653, Slave Schedules, Microfilm Reel Nos. 1309-1312.

Virginia

1790, 1800

Heinegg, Paul. *Free African Americans of North Carolina and Virginia Including the Family Histories of More than 80% of Those Counted as "All Other Free Persons" in the 1790 and 1800 Census.* Baltimore, MD: Genealogical Pub. Co., 1992. 462p.

_____. 2nd ed. Baltimore, MD: Genealogical Pub. Co., 1994. 699p.

_____. 3rd ed. Baltimore, MD: Genealogical Pub. Co., 1994. 825p.

1810, 1840

Peters, Joan W. *Prince William County Census, Free Negro Families 1810, 1840-1860.* Broad Run, VA: Albemarle Research, 1996. Unpgd.

1850

Jackson, Ronald Vern. *U.S. Federal Census Index, Virginia, 1850 Slave Schedules.* West Jordan, UT: Genealogical Services. Unpgd.

_____. *Virginia 1850 Slave Schedule Census Index.* Salt Lake City, UT: Accelerated Indexing Systems International, 1988. Unpgd.

Peters, Joan W. *Prince William County Census, Free Negro Families 1810, 1840-1860.* Broad Run, VA: Albemarle Research, 1996. Unpgd.

U.S. Federal Population Census Schedules. 1850, M432, Slave Schedules, Microfilm Reel Nos. 983-993.

1860

Peters, Joan W. *Prince William County Census, Free Negro Families 1810, 1840-1860.* Broad Run, VA: Albemarle Research, 1996. Unpgd.

U.S. Federal Population Census Schedules. 1860, M653, Slave Schedules, Microfilm Reel Nos. 1386-1397.

Chinese Americans

1870, 1880

Penner, Liisa. *The Chinese in Astoria, Oregon, 1870-1880, a Look at Local Newspaper Articles, the Census, and Other Related Materials.* Astoria, OR: Author, 1990. 106p.

Dutch Americans

1880

Swierenga, Robert P. *Dutch in Chicago and Cook County, 1880 Federal Census, an Alphabetical Index.* Kent, Ohio: Author, 1992. Unpgd.

_____. *Dutch in Indiana 1880 Federal Census, an Alphabetical Index.* Kent, OH: Author, 1994. 81p.

1900

Swierenga, Robert P. *Dutch in Indiana 1900 Federal Census, an Alphabetical Index.* Kent, OH: Author, 1994. 92p.

Franco-Americans

1850-1880

Ledoux, Albert H. *The French Canadian Families of Kankakee and Iroquois Counties, Illinois, Abstracts from the Federal Census 1850 through 1880.* Johnston, PA: Author, 1990. 2 vols.

1880

Ledoux, Albert H. *The Franco-Americans of Connecticut, 1880.* Altoona, PA: Author, 1977. 257p.

1900

Ledoux, Albert H. *The French Canadian Families of the Plains and Upper Mountain States, Abstracts from the Federal Census of 1900.* Altoona, PA: Author, 1991. 2 vols.

Immigration

1850

Index of Individuals Born Outside the United States as Enumerated in the 1850 Census of North Carolina. Salt Lake City, UT: Research Department, The Genealogical Society of The Church of Jesus Christ of Latter-day Saints, 1972. 113p.

Irish Americans
1850

Kendall, Margaret M. G. *Irish in the 1850 Mason County, Kentucky Federal Census*. Maysville, KY: Mason County Museum, 1980. 30p.

Italian Americans
1910

Sandel, Mary E., and Edward Sandel. *Italian Immigrants in the 1910 U.S. Census of Tangipahoa Parish, Louisiana*. Roseland, LA: Tabor-Lucas Publications, 1993. 158p.

Vitelli, Tom. *Vitelli, Vitali Soundex Database to all U.S. Censuses*. Online Database Edition. Orem, UT: Ancestry.com, Inc., 1998.

http://www.ancestry.com

Jewish Americans
1900

Berent, Irwin M. *The East European Jewish Immigrant in America a Compilation of the 1900 Norfolk Census*. Norfolk, VA: Jewish Genealogical Club of Tidewater, 1982. 28p.

Mexican Americans
1850-1900

De Leon, Arnoldo. *Tejanos and the Numbers Game, a Socio-historical Interpretation from the Federal Censuses, 1850-1900*. Albuquerque, NM: University of New Mexico Press, 1989. 119p.

Military
General
1793

Norton, James S. *New Jersey in 1793, an Abstract and Index to the 1793 Militia Census of the State of New Jersey*. Salt Lake City, UT: Author, 1973. 515p.

1900

U.S. Federal Population Census Schedules. 1900, Military & Naval Bases. T1081, Microfilm Reel Nos. 1838-1842.

U.S. Federal Population Census Schedules. 1900, Military & Naval Bases, Soundex. T1081, 32 Microfilm Reels.

1905

Myers, Jane, Arlene Smith, and Betty Quimby. *1905 Military Census of Lane County, Oregon*. Cottage Grove, OR: Cottage Grove Genealogical Society, 1982.

1910

U.S. Federal Population Census Schedules. 1910, Military & Naval Bases, T624, Microfilm Reel No. 1,784.

1920

U.S. Federal Population Census Schedules. 1920, Overseas Military & Naval Bases; U.S. Consular Service, T625, Microfilm Reel Nos. 2,040-2,041.

U.S. Federal Population Census Schedules. 1920, Soundex, Overseas Military & Naval Bases; U.S. Consular Service. T1600, 18 Microfilm Reels.

U.S. Federal Population Census Schedules. 1920, Canal Zone; Civilian, Military and Naval Personnel, T625, Microfilm Reel No. 2,042.

U.S. Federal Population Census Schedules. 1920, Soundex, Canal Zone; Civilian, Military and Naval Personnel, T1600, 2 Microfilm Reels.

Military—Revolutionary War
General
1840

A Census of Pensioners for Revolutionary or Military Services, with Their Names, Ages and Places of Residence under the Act for Taking the Sixth Census, Bound with a General Index Prepared by the Genealogical Society of Utah of The Church of Jesus Christ of Latter-day Saints. Baltimore, MD: Genealogical Publishing, Co., 1996. 577p.

Genealogical Society of Utah of The Church of Jesus Christ of Latter-day Saints. *A General Index to a Census of Pensioners for Revolutionary or Military Service, 1840.* Baltimore, MD: Genealogical Publishing, Co., 1965. 382p.

Kentucky
1840

Minix, Sharroll K. *1840 Special Federal Census of Kentucky Pensioners of Revolutionary or Military Service.* Salyersville, KY: Magoffin County Historical Society, 1983. 28p.

Norris, William V. *1840 U.S. Census, Clark County, Kentucky, (From U.S. Census Microfilm), and Index, with Slave Summary.* Jacksonville, FL: Author, 1983. 40p.

New Jersey
1840, 1850

Tanco, Barbrae Owens. *The 1850 Census Together with Index, Atlantic, Burlington, and Bergen Counties, New Jersey Including the 1840 List of Revolutionary and Military Pensioners Residing in Those Counties.* Fort Worth, TX: Millican Press, 1973. 1,029p.

_____. *The 1850 Census Together with Index, Gloucester, Hunterdon and Hudson Counties, New Jersey, Including the 1840 List of Revolutionary and Military Pensioners Residing in Those Counties.* Fort Worth, TX: Millican Press, 1974. 1,009p.

_____. *The 1850 Census Together with Index, New Jersey, Including the 1840 List of Revolutionary and Military Pensioners.* Ft. Worth, TX: Millican Press, 1973.

New York
1840

Kelly, Arthur C. M. *New York Revolutionary War Pensioners in the 1840 Census.* Rhinebeck, NY: Kinship, 1995. 119p.

Tennessee
1840

Lee, Ramona Hudson. *Jackson County, Tennessee, 1840 U.S. Census, Includes Special Index to Pensioners for Revolutionary or Military Services and Surname Index.* Mountain Home, AR: Author, 1984. 89p.

Military—Civil War
General
1890

Jackson, Ronald Vern. *1890 US Vessels and Navy Census Index, Special Schedule of the Eleventh Census (1890) Enumerating Union Veterans and of Union Veterans of the Civil War.* Salt Lake City, UT: Accelerated Indexing Systems, 1983. 41p.

Veterans' Schedules: U.S. Selected States, 1890. Family Archive CD 131. Novato, CA: Broderbund Software. CD-ROM.

Alabama
1890
Veterans' Schedules: U.S. Selected States, 1890. Family Archive CD 131. Novato, CA: Broderbund Software. CD-ROM.

1907
Hageness, MariLee Beatty. *1907 Confederate Soldiers Census, Baldwin County, Alabama.* Author, 1995. 8p.

_____. *1907 Confederate Soldiers Census, Bibb County, Alabama.* Author, 1995. 13p.

_____. *1907 Confederate Soldiers Census, Cleburne County, Alabama.* Author, 1994.

_____. *1907 Confederate Soldiers Census, Colbert County, Alabama.* Author, 1995. 10p.

_____. *1907 Confederate Soldiers Census, DeKalb County, Alabama.* Author, 1995. 12p.

_____. *1907 Confederate Soldiers Census, Etowah County, Alabama.* Author, 1995. 12p.

_____. *1907 Confederate Soldiers Census, Henry County, Alabama.* Author, 1995. 20p.

_____. *1907 Confederate Soldiers Census, Marengo County, Alabama.* Author, 1995. 17p.

_____. *1907 Confederate Soldiers Census, Perry County, Alabama.* Author, 1995. 13p.

_____. *1907 Confederate Soldiers Census, Tallapoosa County, Alabama.* Author, 1994. 21p.

Johnson, Dorothy Scott. *1907 Confederate Census, Limestone, Morgan & Madison Counties, Alabama.* Huntsville, AL: Johnson Historical Publications, 1981. 65p.

Jones, Homer T. *Census of Confederate Veterans Residing in Southeast Alabama in 1907.* Carollton, MS: Pioneer Publishing, 1998. 261p.

Master Index to 1907 Census of Alabama Confederate Soldiers, Indexed and Compiled from Alabama State Archives Microfilm. Cullman, AL: Gregath Pub. Co. 100p.

Arkansas
1911
McLane, Bobbie Jones. *An Index to the Three Volumes, Arkansas 1911 Census of Confederate Veterans.* Hot Springs, AR: Author, 1988. 245p.

District of Columbia
1890
Jackson, Ronald Vern. *1890 District of Columbia Census Index, Special Schedule of the Eleventh Census (1890) Enumerating Union Veterans and of Union Veterans of the Civil War, this Index Includes Every Name Listed on the Census Record.* North Salt Lake City, UT: Accelerated Indexing Systems, 1983. 44p.

Veterans' Schedules: U.S. Selected States, 1890. Family Archive CD 131. Novato, CA: Broderbund Software. CD-ROM.

Georgia
1870
Griffith, Jessie June Brandon. *1870 Census and Mortality Schedules of Chattooga County, Georgia, Plus Confederate Soldier Information, Where They Enlisted, Fought and Where They Died.* Fort Oglethorp, GA: Price. 102p.

Illinois
1860
Macon County, Illinois Military Census, Militia Roll. Decatur, IL: Decatur Genealogical Society, 1991. 170p.

1862, 1863
Military Census of Sangamon County, Illinois, in Pursuance of General Orders No. 99, of the War Department, and Instructions of the Adjutant General of the State of Illinois, 1862 and 1863. Springfield, IL: Sangamon County Genealogical Society, 1992. 196p.

1890

Veterans' Schedules: U.S. Selected States, 1890. Family Archive CD 131. Novato, CA: Broderbund Software. CD-ROM.

Kansas
1885

VanDyne, Robert A. *Kansas Settlers of the Grand Army of the Republic, 1885.* Salina, KS: Smoky Valley Genealogical Society and Library, 1992. 82p.

Kentucky
1890

Cunagin, Judy Murray. *1900 Perry County, Kentucky Census, with Heads of Household Index, Special 1890 Census for Perry County, Kentucky, Enumerating Soldiers, Sailors or Widows.* Indianapolis, IN: Author, 1986. 247p.

Dilts, Bryan Lee. *1890 Kentucky Census Index of Civil War Veterans or Their Widows.* Salt Lake City, UT: Index Pub. Co., 1984. 135p.

1890 Special Census, Surviving Union Veterans and Widows of the Civil War in Magoffin County, Kentucky. Salyersville, KY: Magoffin County Historical Society, 1982. 13p.

Jackson, Ronald Vern. *1890 Kentucky Census Index, Special Schedule of the Eleventh Census (1890) Enumerating Union Veterans and of Union Veterans of the Civil War.* Salt Lake City, UT: Accelerated Indexing Systems, 1984. 2 vols.

Veterans' Schedules: U.S. Selected States, 1890. Family Archive CD 131. Novato, CA: Broderbund Software. CD-ROM.

Louisiana
1870

Sandel, Elias Wesley, and Mary E. Sandel. *Early Tangipahoa Parish, Including the 1870 (1st) Census, Confederate Soldiers, Towns, Old Families, Voters, Pensioners, Parish Officials, Excerpts from Old Newspapers, the First Schools.* Author, 1984. 359p.

1890

Dilts, Bryan Lee. *1890 Louisiana Census Index of Civil War Veterans or Their Widows.* Salt Lake City, UT: Index Pub., 1984. 211p.

Jackson, Ronald Vern. *1890 Louisiana Census Index, Special Schedule of the Eleventh Census (1890) Enumerating Union Veterans and of Union Veterans of the Civil War.* Salt Lake City, UT: Accelerated Indexing Systems, 1984. 126p.

Veterans' Schedules: U.S. Selected States, 1890. Family Archive CD 131. Novato, CA: Broderbund Software. CD-ROM.

1911

Burns, Loretta Elliott. *1911 Louisiana Census, Confederate Veterans or Widows.* Pasadena, TX: C&L Printing, 1995. 98p.

Jenks, Houston C. *1911 Louisiana Census, Confederate Veterans or Widows.* Baton Rouge, LA: Author, 1989.

Maine
1890

Dilts, Bryan Lee. *1890 Maine Census Index of Civil War Veterans or Their Widows.* Salt Lake City, UT: Index Pub., 1984. 156p.

Jackson, Ronald Vern. *Federal Census Index, Maine 1890, Union Veterans.* West Jordan, UT: Genealogical Services, 1996. 441p.

Veterans' Schedules: U.S. Selected States, 1890. Family Archive CD 131. Novato, CA: Broderbund Software. CD-ROM.

Maryland
1890

Dilts, Bryan Lee. *1890 Maryland Census Index of Civil War Veterans or Their Widows*. Salt Lake City, UT: Index Pub., 1984. 69p.

Powell, Jody. *Eastern Shore of Maryland, 1890 Census of Civil War Veterans*. Roanoke, TX: Author, 1993. 112p.

Veterans' Schedules: U.S. Selected States, 1890. Family Archive CD 131. Novato, CA: Broderbund Software. CD-ROM.

Massachusetts
1890

Dilts, Bryan Lee. *1890 Massachusetts Census Index of Civil War Veterans or Their Widows*. Salt Lake City, UT: Index Pub., 1985. 222p.

Steuart, Raeone Christensen. *Massachusetts 1890 Veterans Census Index*. Bountiful, UT: Heritage Quest, 1999. 280p.

Veterans' Schedules: U.S. Selected States, 1890. Family Archive CD 131. Novato, CA: Broderbund Software. CD-ROM.

Michigan
1890

Dilts, Bryan Lee. *1890 Michigan Census Index of Civil War Veterans or Their Widows*. Salt Lake City, UT: Index Publications, 1985. 2 microfiche.

Index to the United States Census of Kalamazoo County, Michigan, 1860, 1870, 1880 and the Veterans Rolls for 1890. Kalamazoo, MI: Kalamazoo Valley Genealogical Society and the Kalamazoo Public Library, 1986. 216p.

Marrs, Donna M. *1890 Federal Census Index to Schedules Enumerating Union Veterans and Widows of Union Veterans of the Civil War, Otsego County, Michigan*. Gaylord, MI: Gaylord Fact Finders Genealogical Society, 1995. 5p.

Miller, Sharon L. *1890 United States Census Schedule Enumerating Union Veterans and Widows of Union Veterans of the Civil War in Muskegon County, Michigan*. Muskegon, MI: Author, 1984. 40p.

Steuart, Raeone Christensen. *Michigan 1890 Veterans Census Index*. Bountiful, UT: Heritage Quest, 1999. 321p.

Veterans' Schedules: U.S. Selected States, 1890. Family Archive CD 131. Novato, CA: Broderbund Software. CD-ROM.

Minnesota

Dilts, Bryan Lee. *1890 Minnesota Census Index of Civil War Veterans or Their Widows*. Salt Lake City, UT: Index Publications, 1985. 96p.

Steuart, Raeone Christensen. *Minnesota 1890 Veterans Census Index*. Bountiful, UT: Heritage Quest, 1999. 141p.

Mississippi

Dilts, Bryan Lee. *1890 Mississippi Census Index of Civil War Veterans or Their Widows*. Salt Lake City, UT: Index Publications, 1985.

Loftiss, Betty Arnold. *Tate County, Mississippi Confederate Soldiers Pension Records with Their Census Genealogy Records*. Coldwater, MS, 1994. 186p.

Steuart, Raeone Christensen. *Mississippi 1890 Veterans Census Index*. Bountiful, UT: Heritage Quest, 1999. 45p.

Veterans' Schedules: U.S. Selected States, 1890. Family Archive CD 131. Novato, CA: Broderbund Software. CD-ROM.

Missouri
1885
VanDyne, Robert A. *Kansas Settlers of the Grand Army of the Republic, 1885*. Salina, KS: Smoky Valley Genealogical Society and Library, 1992. 82p.

1890
DeGood, Harold. *An Index, Civil War Veterans and Widows, 1890 Census*. Columbia, MO: Missouri State Genealogical Association, 1994. 3 vols.

Dilts, Bryan Lee. *1890 Missouri Census Index of Civil War Veterans or Their Widows*. Salt Lake City, UT: Index Publications, 1985.

_____. 2nd ed. Bountiful, UT:Precision Indexing, 1993. 304p.

Graham, Margery M. *Harrison County, Missouri 1890 Special Census Schedule*. MO: Author, 1990. 86p.

Mayfield, J. Hoyle. *1890 Special Census of Union Veterans and Widows, Also 1850, 1860, 1870, 1880 Mortality Schedules of Texas County, Missouri*. Houston, TX: Texas County, Missouri Genealogical & Historical Society, 1996. 60p.

Special Schedule of the Eleventh Census (1890) Enumerating Union Veterans and Widows of Union Veterans of the Civil War, Andrew County, Missouri; Mortality Schedule, Andrew County, Missouri, 1850, 1860, 1870, 1880. Savannah, MO: Andrew County Historical Society. 36p.

Montana
1890
Jackson, Ronald Vern. *1890 Montana Census Index, Special Schedule of the Eleventh Census (1890) Enumerating Union Veterans and of Union Veterans of the Civil War*. Salt Lake City, UT: Accelerated Indexing Systems, 1984. 46p.

Veterans' Schedules: U.S. Selected States, 1890. Family Archive CD 131. Novato, CA: Broderbund Software. CD-ROM.

Nebraska
1890
Veterans' Schedules: U.S. Selected States, 1890. Family Archive CD 131. Novato, CA: Broderbund Software. CD-ROM.

Nevada
1890
Jackson, Ronald Vern. *1890 Nevada Census Index, Special Schedule of the Eleventh Census, 1890, Enumerating Union Veterans and of Union Veterans of the Civil War*. Salt Lake City, UT: Accelerated Indexing Systems International, 1983. 62p.

Veterans' Schedules: U.S. Selected States, 1890. Family Archive CD 131. Novato, CA: Broderbund Software. CD-ROM.

New Hampshire
1890
Jackson, Ronald Vern. *1890 New Hampshire Census Index, Special Schedule of the Eleventh Census, 1890, Enumerating Union Veterans and of Union Veterans of the Civil War*. Salt Lake City, UT: Accelerated Indexing Systems International, 1985. 169p.

Veterans' Schedules: U.S. Selected States, 1890. Family Archive CD 131. Novato, CA: Broderbund Software. CD-ROM.

New Jersey
1890
Veterans' Schedules: U.S. Selected States, 1890. Family Archive CD 131. Novato, CA: Broderbund Software. CD-ROM.

New Mexico
1890

Veterans' Schedules: U.S. Selected States, 1890. Family Archive CD 131. Novato, CA: Broderbund Software. CD-ROM.

New York
1865

Litchman, William M. *An Every-name Index for Agricultural Schedules, Industry Other than Agriculture Schedules, Marriages, Deaths, and Civil War Soldier Deaths in the 1865 New York State Census for Jefferson County.* Covington, KY: Kenton County Historical Society, 1996. Unpgd.

1890

Dilts, Bryan Lee. *1890 New York Census of Civil War Veterans or Their Widows.* Salt Lake City, UT: Index Pub., 1984. 451p.

1890 Military Census, Delaware County, New York. Sauk Village, IL: Hanson Heritage Publications, 1985. 113p.

North Carolina
1890

Almasy, Sandra L. *North Carolina 1890 Civil War Veterans Census, a Census of Veterans of the Union Armed Forces and Their Widows, Containing Also Information on Other U.S. Veterans and Many Confederate Veterans.* Middleton, WI: Kensington Glen Pub., 1990. 316p.

Jackson, Ronald Vern. *1890 North Carolina Census Index, Special Schedule of the Eleventh Census (1890) Enumerating Union Veterans and of Union Veterans of the Civil War.* North Salt Lake City, UT: Accelerated Indexing Systems, 1984. 74p.

Veterans' Schedules: U.S. Selected States, 1890. Family Archive CD 131. Novato, CA: Broderbund Software. CD-ROM.

Williams, Sally. *1890 Madison County, North Carolina Veterans Census.* Central Point, OR: Author, 1986. 26p.

North Dakota
1890

Helmer, Edith, Mary Ann Quiring, and Lily B. Zwolle. *1890 North Dakota Special Census, Enumerating Union Veterans and Widows of Union Veterans of the Civil War.* Lewistown, MT: Lewistown Genealogy Society, 1986. 49p.

Jackson, Ronald Vern. *1890 North Dakoka Census Index Special Schedule of the Eleventh Census (1890) Enumerating Union Veterans and of Union Veterans of the Civil War.* North Salt Lake City, UT: Accelerated Indexing Systems, 1986. 33p.

Veterans' Schedules: U.S. Selected States, 1890. Family Archive CD 131. Novato, CA: Broderbund Software. CD-ROM.

Ohio
1890

Adams, Marilyn. *Index to Civil War Veterans and Widows in Southern Ohio, 1890, Federal Census, Vol. 1.* Columbus, OH: Franklin County Genealogical Society, 1986. 84p.

Caccamo, James F. *Index to the Federal Population Census for Hudson, Ohio, 1880, to Which Has Been Appended the 1890 List of Civil War Veterans and Widows.* Hudson, OH: Hudson Library & Historical Society, 1983. 17p.

The Eleventh Census of the United States Special Schedule Surviving Soldiers, Sailors, Marines, and Widows, etc., 1890 Veterans Census of Jefferson County, Ohio. Jefferson, OH: Jefferson County Genealogical Society, 1996. 140p.

Special Schedules of the Eleventh Census of the United States, 1890, Schedules Enumerating

Union Veterans and Widows of Union Veterans of the Civil War for Stark County, Ohio. Stark County Chapter, OGS, 1995. 90p.

Waterfield, Marjorie Featheringill. *1890 Special Veterans Census of Columbus Grove, Pleasant Township, Putnam County, Ohio, plus 55 Photos of Civil War Veterans Taken about 1890 in or near Columbus Grove, Ohio.* Bowling Green, OH: Author, 1990. 46p.

Oklahoma
1890

Garrison, Linda Norman. *1890 Federal Census of the Oklahoma and Indian Territories Enumerating Union Veterans and Widows of Union Veterans of the Civil War.* Lawton, OK: Southwest Oklahoma Genealogical Society, 1991. 60p.

An Index to the 1890 United States Census of Union Veterans and Their Widows, in Oklahoma and Indian Territories (Including Old Greer County) and Soldiers Stationed at Military Installations in the Territories. Also, an Index to Records from the Oklahoma Union Soldiers' Home...and the Union Soldiers' Cemetery Record. Oklahoma City, OK: Oklahoma Genealogical Society, 1970. 53p.

Veterans' Schedules: U.S. Selected States, 1890. Family Archive CD 131. Novato, CA: Broderbund Software. CD-ROM.

Oregon
1890

Jackson, Ronald Vern. *1890 Oregon Census Index, Special Schedule of the Eleventh Census (1890) Enumerating Union Veterans and of Union Veterans of the Civil War.* Salt Lake City, UT: Accelerated Indexing Systems, 1984. 55; 87p.

Myers, Jane A. *Oregon State 1890 Special Federal Census of Union Veterans and Their Widows Eleventh Census of the United States, 1890, Schedules Enumerating Union Veterans and Widows of Union Veterans of the Civil War, Oregon.* Cottage Grove, OR: Cottage Grove Genealogical Society, 1993. 460p.

Veterans' Schedules: U.S. Selected States, 1890. Family Archive CD 131. Novato, CA: Broderbund Software. CD-ROM.

1905

Myers, Jane A., Arlene Smith, and Betty Quimby. *1905 Military Census of Lane County, Oregon.* Cottage Grove, OR: Cottage Grove Genealogical Society, 1982. 258p.

Rhode Island
1890

Veterans' Schedules: U.S. Selected States, 1890. Family Archive CD 131. Novato, CA: Broderbund Software. CD-ROM.

South Carolina
1890

Jackson, Ronald Vern. *1890 South Carolina Census Index, Special Schedule of the Eleventh Census (1890) Enumerating Union Veterans and of Union Veterans of the Civil War.* North Salt Lake City, UT: Accelerated Indexing Systems, 1984. 58p.

Veterans' Schedules: U.S. Selected States, 1890. Family Archive CD 131. Novato, CA: Broderbund Software. CD-ROM.

South Dakota
1890

Jackson, Ronald Vern. *1890 South Dakoka Census Index Special Schedule of the Eleventh Census (1890) Enumerating Union Veterans and of Union Veterans of the Civil War.* North Salt Lake City, UT: Accelerated Indexing Systems, 1985. 115p.

Veterans' Schedules: U.S. Selected States, 1890. Family Archive CD 131. Novato, CA: Broderbund Software. CD-ROM.

Tennessee
1890

Jackson, Ronald Vern. *Federal Census Index, Tennessee, 1890 Union Veterans Schedules*. West Jordan, UT: Genealogical Services, 1989; 1997. 376p.

Veterans' Schedules: U.S. Selected States, 1890. Family Archive CD 131. Novato, CA: Broderbund Software. CD-ROM.

Texas
1890

Dilts, Bryan Lee. *1890 Texas Census Index of Civil War Veterans or Their Widows*. Salt Lake City, UT: Index Pub., 1984. 69p.

1890 Tax Records, Anderson County, Texas and Including the 1890 Marriage Records and the 1890 Census of Union Veterans of the Civil War. Tyler, TX: East Texas Genealogical Society, 1995. 173p.

Hudson, Weldon I., and Shirley Brittain Cawyer. *Comanche County, Texas Census Records, 1860 and 1870 Federal Census, with Index to the 1880 Heads of Households and the Special 1890 Census of Union Veterans and Widows, also the 1860 Slave List and 1867 Voter's Registration*. Fort Worth, TX: Author, 1981.

Veterans' Schedules: U.S. Selected States, 1890. Family Archive CD 131. Novato, CA: Broderbund Software. CD-ROM.

Yanks and Some Rebs in Texas, 1890. Nacogdoches, TX: Ericson Books, 1991. 443p.

Utah
1890

Jackson, Ronald Vern. *1890 Utah Census Index, Special Schedule of the Eleventh Census (1890) Enumerating Union Veterans and of Union Veterans of the Civil War*. Salt Lake City, UT: Accelerated Indexing Systems, 1983. 55; 15p.

Veterans' Schedules: U.S. Selected States, 1890. Family Archive CD 131. Novato, CA: Broderbund Software. CD-ROM.

Vermont
1890

Veterans' Schedules: U.S. Selected States, 1890. Family Archive CD 131. Novato, CA: Broderbund Software. CD-ROM.

Virginia
1890

Dilts, Bryan Lee. *1890 Virginia Census Index of Civil War Veterans or Their Widows*. Salt Lake City, UT: Indexing Publishing, 1986. 32p.

Veterans' Schedules: U.S. Selected States, 1890. Family Archive CD 131. Novato, CA: Broderbund Software. CD-ROM.

Weaver, Jeffrey C. *The 1890 Union Veterans Census for Southwest Virginia Counties*. Clintwood, VA: Mullins Printing, 1992. 20p.

Washington
1890

Jackson, Ronald Vern. *1890 Washington Census Index, Special Schedule of the Eleventh Census (1890) Enumerating Union Veterans and of Union Veterans of the Civil War*. Salt Lake City, UT: Accelerated Indexing Systems, 1985. 89p.

Veterans' Schedules: U.S. Selected States, 1890. Family Archive CD 131. Novato, CA: Broderbund Software. CD-ROM.

West Virginia
1890

Dilts, Bryan Lee. *1890 West Virginia Census Index of Civil War Veterans or Their Widows*. Salt Lake City, UT: Indexing Publishing, 1986. 63p.

Hill, Ken. *Wetzel and Tyler Counties, West Virginia, 1890 Census of Union Veterans and Widows*. New Martinsville, WV: Wetzel County Genealogical Society, 1981. 72p.

Jackson, Ronald Vern. *West Virginia 1890 Veterans*. North Salt Lake City, UT: Accelerated Indexing Systems International, 1986. 220p.

Taylor County, West Virginia, Special Schedule of the Eleventh Census Enumerating Union Veterans and Widows of Union Veterans of the Civil War. Grafton, WV: Melba Pender Zinn, 1989. 33p.

Veterans' Schedules: U.S. Selected States, 1890. Family Archive CD 131. Novato, CA: Broderbund Software. CD-ROM.

Williams, Sally Seaman. *1890 Wyoming County, West Virginia Veterans Census*. Whitehouse, TX: Author, 1986. 10p.

Wisconsin
1885

Secretary of State. *Tabular Statements of the Census Enumeration, and the Agricultural, Mineral and Manufacturing Interests of the State...Also Alphabetical List of the Soldiers and Sailors of the Late War Residing in the State June 20, 1885*. Madison, WI: Madison Democrat Printing Co., 1886. 791, 387p.

1890

Jackson, Ronald Vern. *1890 Wisconsin Veterans Census Index*. Salt Lake City, UT: Accelerated Indexing Systems, 1988. 485p.

Veterans' Schedules: U.S. Selected States, 1890. Family Archive CD 131. Novato, CA: Broderbund Software. CD-ROM.

1895

Wisconsin Census Enumeration, 1895, Names of Ex-soldiers and Sailors Residing in Wisconsin, June 20, 1895. Madison, WI: Democrat Printing Co., 1896. 363p.

Wyoming
1890

Jackson, Ronald Vern. *1890 Wyoming Census Index, Special Schedule of the 11th Census Enumerating Union Veterans and Widows of Union Veterans of the Civil War*. Salt Lake City, UT: Accelerated Indexing Systems, 1983. 58, 19p.

U.S. Federal Population Census Schedules, Special Schedule, Enumerating Union Veterans and Widows of Union Veterans of the Civil War. 1890, M123, 118 Microfilm Reels.

Veterans' Schedules: U.S. Selected States, 1890. Family Archive CD 131. Novato, CA: Broderbund Software. CD-ROM.

Native Americans
General
1932

Bowen, Jeff. *1932 Hopi and Navajo Native American Census, with Birth and Death Rolls*. Hixson, TN: Bowen Genealogy, Native American Research and Publications, 1997. Unpgd.

Arkansas
1860

Federal Population Schedule of the United States Census, 1860. Indian Lands West of Arkansas. Tulsa, OK: Oklahoma Yesterday Publications. 79p.

USGenWeb Census Project. AR, 1860 Indian Lands.

ftp://ftp.rootsweb.com/pub/census/ar/indianlands/1860/

Woods, Frances Jerome. *Indian Lands West of Arkansas (Oklahoma), Population Schedule of the United State Census of 1860.* Arrow Print Co., 1964. 72p.

Bannock
1894
Teter, Thomas Benton. *1894 Census of the Bannock and Shoshone Indians of Fort Hall, Idaho.* Author. 30p.

California
1900
Thornburg, Nancy C. *Twelfth Census of the United States, Schedule No. 1, Population, 1900, Alpine County, California, Including Special Inquiries Relating to Indians.* Markleeville, CA: Alpine County Museum, 1994. 150p.
1905, 1906
Kelsey, C. E. *Census of Non-reservation California Indians, 1905-1906.* Berkeley, CA: Archaeological Research Facility, Dept. of Anthropology, 1971. 118p.
1910
Thornburg, Nancy C. *Thirteenth Census of the United States, 1910, Population, Alpine County, California, Including Special Inquiries Relating to Indians.* Markleeville, CA: Alpine County Museum, 1990. 125p.
Watson, Larry. S. *California Special Indian Census, 1910.* Yuma, AZ: Histree, 1993. 211p.

Cherokee
1835
Baker, Imogene. *Cherokee Indians Index, Micro-copy #T496, Roll #1, Census Roll of Cherokee Indians East of the Mississippi and Index to Roll, 1835.* Ellington, MO: Reynolds County Genealogical & Historical Society, 1986. 21p.
Felldin, Jeanne Robey, and Charlotte Magee Tucker. *Index to the 1835 Census of the Cherokee Indians East of the Mississippi River, Excerpted from National Archives Microfilm Publication No. T-496.* Tomball, TX: Genelogical Publications, 1976. 15p.
Parrish, Donna. *Census Index of Forsyth County, Georgia, 1834-1900.* Cumming, GA: Author, 1981. 155p.
1851
Crumpton, Barbara. *1851 Chapman Roll of the Eastern Cherokee.* Duncan, OK: Creative Copies, 1986. 78p.
Hines, Richard. *Index to the 1851 Cherokee Old Settler Roll.* Mobile, AL: Sena Exchange, 1995. 35p.
1890
Wagner, Rosalie. *Cherokee Nation, 1890 Census, Index of Persons Living under Permit in the Cooweescoowee and Delaware Districts.* Vinita, OK: Northeast Oklahoma Genealogical Society, 1986. 82p.
1895
U.S. Bureau of Indian Affairs. *Old Settle Cherokee Census Roll, 1895 and Index to Payment Roll, 1896.* Washington, DC: National Archives and Records Service, 1966. 2 microfilm.
1900
Parrish, Donna. *Census Index of Forsyth County, Georgia, 1834-1900.* Cumming, GA: Author, 1981. 155p.

Chickasaw
1890
Rex, Joyce A. *1890 Census of the Chickasaw Nation, Indian Territory.* Purcell, OK: McClain County Historical and Genealogical Society, 1992. 3 vols.
Wiltshire, Betty Couch. *Choctaw and Chickasaw Early Census Records.* Carrollton, MS: Pioneer Pub., 1997. 174p.

Choctaw
LeMaster, Arlene. *Indian Records, Choctaw Nation, Indian Territory, Final Rolls.* Poteau, OK: Family Heritage Resources, 1990.

Strickland, Ben, and Jean Strickland. *Records of Choctaw Trading Post, St. Stephens, Mississippi Territory*. Moss Point, MS: Authors, 1984.

Wiltshire, Betty Couch. *Choctaw and Chickasaw Early Census Records*. Carrollton, MS: Pioneer Pub., 1997. 174p.

1885

Olsen, Monty. *1885 Choctaw Census Blue County*. Calera, OK: Bryan County Heritage Association, 1996. 87p.

_____. *1885 Choctaw Census Kiamitia County*. Calera, OK: Bryan County Heritage Association, 1996. 63p.

1896

Mason, Alma Burke. *1896 Tobucksy County, Choctaw Nation, Indian Territory*. McAlester, OK: Pittsburg County Genealogical and Historical Society. 16p.

1900

Young, Gloryann Hankins. *1900 Census Index, Choctaw Nation Indian Territory, Oklahoma*. Wister, OK: Author, 1981.

Colorado

Echo Hawk, Roger C. *Indentured Spirits: A Census of Human Remains and Inventory of Associated Funerary Objects at the Colorado Historical Society*. Denver, CO: Society, 1997. 584p.

Comanche

1895

Washburn, Faye Riddles. *1895 Comanche Tribe Census and Index (Microfilm Roll 211)*. Lawton, OK: Southwest Oklahoma Genealogical Society, 1992. 59p.

1917

Garrison, Linda Norman. *1917 Census of the Comanche Indian Tribe of the Kiowa Agency, Anadarko, Oklahoma*. Author, 1990. 71p.

Creek

Campbell, John Bert. *Campbell's Abstract of Creek Freedman Census Cards and Index*. Muskogee, OK: Phoenix Job Printing, 1915. 223p.

_____. *Campbell's Abstract of Creek Indian Census Cards and Index*. Muskogee, OK: Phoenix Job Printing, 1915. 430p.

1832 Census of the Creek Nation, East. Mobile, AL: South Eastern Native American Exchange, 1996. 198p.

Felldin, Jeanne Robey, and Charlotte Magee Tucker. *1832 Census of Creek Indians*. Tomball, TX: Genealogical Publications, 1978. Unpgd.

Watson, Larry S. *Census Roll of the Old Settler Party of Creeks, June, 1857, Index to the Old Settlers Roll*. Lawton, OK: Histree, 1981. 83p.

_____. *Creek Census 1832, Abbott & Parsons Roll*. Yuma, AZ: Histree, 1987. 223p.

Kiowa

1917

Garrison, Linda Norman. *1917 Census of the Comanche Indian Tribe of the Kiowa Agency, Anadarko, Oklahoma*. Author, 1990. 71p.

Michigan

1860-1920

Native American, Federal Census Indexes with Special Lists, Mason County and Oceana County, Michigan, 1860-1920. Unpgd.

North Dakota
1900
Quiring, Mary Ann, and Lily B. Zwolle. *1900 Federal Census and Index of Turtle Mountain Indian Reservation, Rolette County, North Dakota.* Authors, 1984. 278p.

Oklahoma
Campbell's Abstract of Creek Freedman Census Cards and Index. Muskogee, OK: Phoenix Job Printing Co., 1915. 223p.

Koplowitz, Bradford S. *The Kaw Indian Census and Allotments.* Bowie, MD: Heritage Books, 1996. 91p.
1860
Woods, Frances Jerome. *Indian Lands West of Arkansas (Oklahoma), Population Schedule of the United State Census of 1860.* Arrow Print Co., 1964. 72p.
1873-1902
Expanded Index of the Seneca, Census Annuity Rolls and List of Guardians and Administrators, December 30, 1873 – October 3, 1902, Quapaw Agency, Census. Cullman, AL: Gregath Publishing. 22p.
1874-1881
Expanded Index of the Peoria, Census Annuity Rolls and Administrations, 1874-1881, with Undated Material, Quapaw Agency, Indian Territory. Cullman, AL: Gregath Publishing. 32p.
1890
Wagner, Rosalie. *Cherokee Nation, 1890 Census, Index of Persons Living under Permit in the Cooweescoowee and Delaware Districts.* Vinita, OK: Northeast Oklahoma Genealogical Society, 1986. Unpgd.
1910
Lawson, Rowena. *1910 Indian Population, Oklahoma, Craig County.* Honolulu, HI: Author, 1983. 110p.

Shawnee
1885-1858
Dunbar, Bobbie. *Kansas Territory Census, 1855-1858; Shawnee Indians 1857 Census and Land Records of the Shawnees.* Richland, MO: Author, 1992. 93p.

Shoshone
1894
Teter, Thomas Benton. *1894 Census of the Bannock and Shoshone Indians of Fort Hall, Idaho.* Author. 30p.

Utes
Robinson, Doreen. *Census Records for Southern Utes of Navajo Springs, Colorado. Online Database Edition.* Orem, UT: Ancestry.com, Inc., 1998.
http://www.ancestry.com

Polish Americans
1870
Silverman, Marlene. *Poles and Russians in the 1870 Census of New York City, Full Alphabetical Index for the Second Enumeration, with a Partial Index for the First Enumeration.* Washington, DC: Landsmen Press, 1993. 94, 74p.

_____. *A Polish Russian Name Index for the 1870 Census in New York City.* Washington, DC: Author, 1989. 6p.
1910
Hollowak, Thomas L. *Polish Heads of Household in Maryland, an Index to the 1910 Census.* Westminster, MD: Family Line Publications, 1990.

Russian Americans

1870

Silverman, Marlene. *Poles and Russians in the 1870 Census of New York City, Full Alphabetical Index for the Second Enumeration, with a Partial Index for the First Enumeration.* Washington, DC: Landsmen Press, 1993. 94, 74p.

Swedish Americans

1693

Craig, Peter Stebbins. *The 1693 Census of the Swedes on the Delaware Family Histories of the Swedish Lutheran Church Members Residing in Pennsylvania, Delaware, West New Jersey and Cecil County, Maryland, 1863-1693.* Studies in Swedish American Genealogy No. 3. Winter Park, FL: SAG Publications, 1993. 213p.